Pets Welcome™

NATIONAL: SECOND EDITION

The Best and Most Informative Guide to Hotels, Motels, Inns & Resorts that Welcome You and Your Pet

By Nadine Guarrera and Hugo N. Gerstl

Associate Editors: Colleen M. Olis, Herb Chelner, Lorraine Gerstl, River Gurtin, Elaine MacDonald, Erle T. MacDonald, Howard Morton, Kristi Padley, Brad Smith

FOUR PAWS PRESS

Library of Congress Cataloguing-in-Publication Data

Pets Welcome™ National: Second Edition

The Best and Most Informative Guide to Hotels, Motels, Inns & Resorts that Welcome You and Your Pet

Guarrera, Nadine (1974-)
Gerstl, Hugo N. (1941-)
ISBN 0-971008-90-6
CIP 2001 132176
$19.95 Soft Cover
Includes index

Cover design by Smith Bowen Communications, Inc., Monterey, CA
www.smithbowen.com

Interior by Cimarron Design, www.cimarrondesign.com

Copyright 2001 by FOUR PAWS PRESS, LLC

Published by Four Paws Press, LLC
2600 Garden Road, Suite 224
Monterey, CA 93940

www.fourpawspress.com

Printed in the United States of America by Banta Book Group

Published May 2001

20 18 16 14 12 10 9 8 7 6 5 4 3 2 1

FOUR PAWS PRESS

Contents

Abbreviations Used in this Book

AAA	American Automobile Association
ABA	American Breeders Association
AKC	American Kennel Club
AARP	American Association of Retired Persons

Introduction
FROM THE PUBLISHER

Welcome to the first of the "New Generation" Pets Welcome™ books! As a small company, there was nothing that could be done without a coordinated effort of everyone on our staff. But mostly, it's thanks to you, our loyal readers, that this book is here in its present format. We have received your letters, suggestions, phone calls, plaudits and brickbats—and we have responded. You said:

- **Give us less artist drawings, more places, and more hard information.** We've responded. There are nearly three times as many lodgings as there were in the first *Pets Welcome™ National Edition*—over one thousand places that will make you and your pet feel at home, wherever you travel in this great land of ours. Artist renditions, while pretty, don't necessarily give you the information you need. You'll find this edition packed with useful information and facts about the area as well as the lodging.

- **Give us a book that's easy to carry on the trip.** We've done that. We've reduced the dimensions of the book from 6×9" to a very cartable 5×8" format. The book has expanded from 480 pages to 608 pages, but it's lighter than the first book because we've used lighter-weight, fully opaque paper.

- **Give us something meaningful for "us."** We've not only scoured the country for many more lodgings, but we've asked—often successfully—that the lodgings extend discounts to Pets Welcome™ readers. That does not mean that a lodging gets a higher rating because it gives a Pets Welcome™ discount. You'll find that nearly one out of every three places listed in this book has graciously agreed to give Pets Welcome™ readers a discount, generally averaging around 10% off of rack rates, some more, some less. And we've searched the country for meaningful products and services when you and your pet are on the road.

We've discovered **1-800 HELP 4 PETS,** a remarkable service that will insure that your pet is safe and can be located anywhere, any time. 1-800 HELP 4 PETS has agreed to give a special offer to readers of the Pets Welcome™ series.

Those wonderful folks at **CREATIVE PET PRODUCTS** in Minnetrista, Minnesota have just the thing for your pet—whether or not you're on the road. Whether it's their Bow-Ow! or Me-Ow! first aid kit, or their comprehensive Pet Travel Pack that contains everything you need to make your pet's vacation as much fun as yours, we certainly endorse and recommend their fine family of products to you.

We dedicate this edition to you and to that wonderful pet of yours—dog, cat, bird, horse, even more unusual pets—without whom there'd be no need for this book.

About the Pets Welcome™ Series

Our story began in 1996 when our predecessor, a small cookbook-guidebook publisher was looking for a new series of interesting books. As we were brainstorming one morning, we came upon a common denominator: All of us had pets or had grown up with pets. All of us felt we were betraying a member of the family when we had to leave a beloved pet at home. We felt, erroneously, that places which accepted pets were...well...doggy. The few guides that were around were dog-specific, or they were little more than lists culled from another book or from the internet. Hints about traveling with your pet were minimal, guesswork or nonexistent.

We started with one book, *Pets Welcome™: California*. While the entries were good ones, and while we provided a rating system (3, 4 or 5 paws), the book itself wasn't really complete. That often happens first time out. But as our predecessor expanded, we learned from our mistakes. Each book was better than the last.

Today, Pets Welcome™ covers the entire United States. Our goal remains the same as it was at the beginning: to make it possible for you to travel with your pet and to provide a meaningful, happy experience for each of you.

Updates

Four Paws Press thoroughly updates each guidebook as often as possible. Between editions, we urge you to contact us at our website, **www.fourpawspress.com.** You may rest assured of one thing: *we will respond to you.*

Research and Ratings

Our researchers try to gather sufficient practical information to enable you to make informed choices and to ensure that you and your pet have the happiest travel experience possible. They also research areas of interest to your pet in different regions of our great country. They don't stay in every hotel, motel, B&B or lodge recommended in this book. However, our editorial staff consists of seasoned travelers who are able to cut through the promotional materials, photographs and word descriptions and get a "feel" for a given lodging. Once a candidate for listing has been pre-screened, we seek information, including the names of pet-friendly references. In some instances, we will telephone and speak with employees of the establishment under consideration. On occasion, we may visit and spot check accommodations to check standards and prices, but the most important feedback comes from you, our readers. Sometimes members of our staff work under cover. Other times they're quite open. But one thing has been—and always will be—a constant:

> *No one at Four Paws Press ever accepts freebies, gifts, money, discounts, or anything else in exchange for a positive write-up. And none of our Pets Welcome™ guidebooks contain any advertising for any accommodation listed in this or any of our Pets Welcome™ books.*

What the Ratings Mean

At the heart of this book are our ratings of each establishment. Any rating system is highly subjective and is a "snapshot" or series of snapshots of a given lodging at a given time. Sometimes you may not agree with our ratings, or you will find that a lodging has changed from the time you were last there. Our ratings are based on a number of factors, including appearance of the accommodations, cleanliness, amenities for humans and pets, price, pet friendly attitude, and nearby attractions designed to give your pet as wonderful a holiday as you. As in our earlier editions, we use the "paw" system. Lodgings are rated 2, 3, 4 or 5 Paws.

2 Paws Clean, comfortable establishment with better than average amenities for humans and pets.

3 Paws Significant first-class amenities and accommodations. Charming atmosphere.

4 Paws Luxury class accommodations, extra touches, fine furnishings, significant quality.

5 Paws Truly one-of-a-kind, world class lodging that is almost a vacation destination in itself.

Pets Welcome™ Hints for Traveling With Your Pet

If you are planning a trip and you share your life with a pet, you have a few decisions to make before you set off. The following are some tips to help you plan a safer and smoother trip for both you and your pet.

Should You Take Your Pet?

Some pets are not suited for travel because of temperament, illness or physical impairment. If you have any doubts about whether it is appropriate for your pet to travel, talk to your veterinarian. If you decide your pet should not travel with you, consider the alternatives: have a responsible friend or relative look after your pet, board your pet at a kennel or hire a sitter to visit, feed and exercise your pet.

If a friend or relative is going to take care of your pet, ask if that person can take your pet into his or her home. Animals can get lonely when left at home alone. Be sure your pet is comfortable with his or her temporary caretaker and any pets that person has.

If you choose to board your pet, get references and inspect the kennel. Your veterinarian or local shelter can help you select a facility. If you are hiring a sitter, interview the candidates and check their references. (A pet sitter may be preferable if your pet is timid or elderly and needs the comfort of familiar surroundings during your absence.)

Whatever option you choose, remember that your pet should be up to date on all vaccinations and in sound health. Whoever is caring for your pet should know the telephone number(s) at which you can be reached, the name and telephone number of your veterinarian, and your pet's medical or dietary needs. Be sure that your pet is comfortable with the person you have chosen to take care of him or her.

Bringing Your Pet

1 Bring your pet's own food, dishes, grooming supplies, bedding, waste removal supplies, leash, collar with I.D. tags, a first-aid kit and a bottle of water from home. These will make your pet more comfortable, decrease the chances of an upset stomach from a strange brand of food and help prepare you for emergencies. Maintain the normal feeding and walking schedules as much as possible. Be sure to bring old bath towels or paper towels in case of an accident and plastic bags in which to dispose of your pet's waste. It is a good idea to bring a picture of your pet for identification purposes in case you and your pet become separated. Creative Pet Products' "Pet Passport" is a most worthwhile document to take with you.

2 Bring your pet's vaccination records with you when traveling within the state, and a health certificate when traveling out of state. If you plan on boarding your pet at any time during your vacation, call the kennel to reserve his or her space, to see what they require you to bring and to find out if they require a health certificate.

Although pets may travel freely throughout the United States as long as they have proper documentation, Hawaii requires a 120-day quarantine for all dogs and cats. Hawaii's quarantine regulations vary by species, so check prior to travel.

If you and your pet are traveling from the United States to Canada, you must carry a certificate issued by a veterinarian that clearly identifies the animal and certifies that the dog or cat has been vaccinated against rabies during the preceding 36 month period. Different Canadian provinces may have different requirements. Be sure to contact the government of the province you plan to visit.

If you and your pet are traveling to Mexico, you must carry a health certificate prepared by your veterinarian within two weeks of the day you cross the border. The certificate must include a description of your pet, the lot number of the rabies vaccine used, indication of distemper vaccination and a veterinarian's statement that the animal is free from infectious or contagious disease. This certificate must be stamped by an office of the U.S. Department of Agriculture (USDA). The fee for the stamp is $4.

3 Tape the address of where you are staying on the back of your pet's I.D. tag, or add a laminated card or new I.D. tag to your pet's collar, or add a second collar with a friend's or family member's phone number. It is always a good idea to have a second contact person on your pet's collar in case of a natural disaster so that someone out of your area can be contacted if you and your pet become separated.

4 Do not leave your pets unattended in the hotel room. The surroundings are new and unfamiliar to your animal, which may cause him or her to become upset and destroy property he or she normally would not, or to bark excessively and disturb your neighbors. You will also run the risk of your pet escaping. If a maid should open the door to clean your room, the pet may see that as a chance to escape to find you, or they may attack the maid out of fear.

5 Train your pet to accept being in a carrier. This will come in handy if you ever need to travel by plane. Make sure the carrier has enough room for your pet to stand up comfortably and to turn around inside. Be sure to trim your pet's nails so they don't get caught in the carrier's door or ventilation holes. It is wise to acclimate your pet to the carrier in the months or weeks preceding your trip. Permit your pet to explore the carrier. Place your pet's food dish inside the carrier and confine him or her to the carrier for brief periods.

Pet carriers may be purchased from pet-supply stores or bought directly from domestic airlines. Select a carrier that has enough room to permit your animal to sit and lie down, but is not large enough to allow your pet to be tossed about during travel. You can make the carrier more comfortable by lining the interior with shredded newspaper or a towel.

To introduce your pet to car travel in the carrier, confine him or her in the carrier and take short drives around the neighborhood. If properly introduced to car travel, most dogs and cats will quickly adjust to and even enjoy car trips.

Carriers come in handy in hotel rooms, too. If your pet is already used to being in a carrier, he or she will not object if you leave him/her in one long enough to go out to breakfast.

Never take your pet with you if you will have to leave him/her in the car. If it is 85°F outside, within minutes the inside of the car can reach over 160°F, even with the windows cracked, causing heat stroke and possibly death. According to The Humane Society of the United States, the signs of heat stress are: heavy panting, glazed eyes, a rapid pulse, unsteadiness, a staggering gait, vomiting or a deep red or purple tongue. If heat stoke does occur, the pet must be cooled by dousing it with water and applying ice packs to its head and neck. He/she should then be taken to a veterinarian immediately.

6 **When your pet is confined to a crate, the best way to provide water** is to freeze it in the cup that hooks onto the door of the crate. That way your pet will get needed moisture without the water splashing all over the crate. Freezing water in your pet's regular water bowl also works well for car trips.

7 **Be sure to put your pet's favorite toys and bedding in the crate.** Label the crate with "LIVE ANIMAL" and "THIS END UP," plus the address and telephone number of your destination, as well as your home address and telephone number and the number of someone to contact in case of an emergency.

8 **When traveling by plane be sure to book the most direct flights possible.** The less your pet has to be transferred from plane to plane, the less chance of you being separated. This is also very important when traveling in hot or cold weather. You don't want your pet to have to wait in the cargo hold of a plane or be exposed to bad weather any longer than necessary. Check with the airlines for the type of crate they require and any additional requirements. They are very strict about the size and type of crate you may carry on board.

If your pet is a cat or a small dog, take him or her on board with you. Be sure to contact airlines to find out the specific requirements for this option. If you pursue this option, you have two choices: airlines will accept either hard-sided carriers or soft-sided carriers, which may be more comfortable for your pet. Only certain brands of soft-sided carriers are acceptable to certain airlines, so call your airline to find out what carrier to use.

If your pet must travel in the cargo hold, you can increase the chances of a safe flight for your pet by following these tips:

- Use direct flights. You will avoid the mistakes that occur during airline transfers and possible delays in getting your pet off the plane.

- Always travel on the same flight as your pet. Ask the airline if you can watch your pet being loaded into and unloaded from the cargo hold.

- Do not ship pug-nosed dogs and cats (such as Pekingese, Chow Chows and Persians) in the cargo hold. These breeds have short nasal passages that leave them vulnerable to oxygen deprivation and heat stroke in cargo holds.

- If traveling during the summer or winter months, choose flights that will accommodate the temperature extremes: early morning or late evening flights are better in the summer; afternoon flights are better in the winter.

- Fit your pet with two pieces of identification—a permanent I.D. tag with your name, home address and telephone number, and a temporary travel I.D. with the address and telephone number where you or a contact person can be reached, or, better yet, a **1-800-HELP-4-PETS I.D.**

  Affix a travel label to the carrier, stating your name, permanent address and telephone number, and final destination. The label should clearly state where you or a contact person can be reached as soon as the flight arrives.

- Your pet should not be given tranquilizers unless they are prescribed by your veterinarian. Make sure your veterinarian understands that this prescription is for air travel.

- Do not feed your pet for four to six hours prior to air travel.

- Try not to fly with your pet during busy travel times such as holidays and summer. Your pet is more likely to undergo rough handling during hectic travel periods.

- Carry a current photo of your pet, or, better yet, a CREATIVE PET PRODUCTS "Pet Passport" with you. If your pet is lost during the trip, a photograph will make it easier for airline employees to search effectively.

• When you arrive at your destination, open the carrier as soon as you are in a safe place and examine your pet. If anything seems wrong, take your pet to a veterinarian immediately. Get the results of the examination in writing, including the date and time.

Do not hesitate to complain if you witness the mishandling of an animal—either yours or someone else's—at any airport.

9 **Do not feed your pet before traveling.** Small amounts of water can be given before the trip. If possible, put ice cubes in the water tray attached to the inside of your pet's kennel. A full water bowl will only spill and cause discomfort. This reduces the risk of an upset stomach or an accident in his crate or your car. When traveling by car, remember that your pet needs rest stops as often as you do. It is a good idea for everyone to stretch their legs from time to time. If your pet is unfamiliar with car travel, then get him/her accustomed to the car gradually. Start a few weeks before your trip with short trips around town and extend the trips a little each time. Then he/she will become accustomed to the car before your trip and it will be more pleasant for all involved.

10 **Before any trip, have your veterinarian examine your pet to ensure that he or she is in good health.** A veterinary examination is a requisite for obtaining the legal documents required for many forms of travel.

In addition to the examination, your veterinarian should provide necessary vaccinations such as rabies, distemper, infectious hepatitis and leptospirosis. If your pet is already up to date on these, obtain written proof.

Do not give your pet any drug not prescribed or given to you by your veterinarian.

11 **Dogs who enjoy car travel need not be confined** to a carrier if your car has a restraining harness (available at pet-supply stores) or if you are accompanied by a passenger who can restrain the dog. Because most cats are not as comfortable traveling in cars, for their own safety as well as yours, it is best to keep them in a carrier.

Dogs and cats should always be kept safely inside the car. Pets who are allowed to stick their heads out the window can be injured by particles of debris or become ill from having cold air forced into their lungs. Never transport a pet in the back of an open pickup truck.

Stop frequently to allow your pet to exercise and eliminate. Never permit your pet to leave the car without a collar, I.D. tag and leash.

Never leave your pet unattended in a parked car. On warm days, the temperature in your car can rise to 160°F in a matter of minutes, even with the windows opened slightly. Furthermore, an animal left alone in a car is an open invitation to pet thieves.

12 **Traveling by Train:** Amtrak currently does not accept pets for transport unless they are assistance dogs. Many trains in European countries allow pets. Generally, it is the passengers' responsibility to feed and exercise their pets at station stops.

13 **Traveling by Ship:** With the exception of assistance dogs, only a few cruise lines accept pets—normally only on ocean crossings and frequently confined to kennels. Some lines permit pets in private cabins. Contact cruise lines in advance to find out their policies and which of their ships have kennel facilities. If you must use the ship's kennel, make sure it is protected from the elements. Follow the general guidelines suggested for other modes of travel when planning a ship voyage.

14 **If Your Pet Is Lost:** Whenever you travel with your pet, there is a chance that you and your pet will become separated. It only takes a moment for an animal to stray and become lost. If your pet is missing, immediately canvass the area. Should your pet not be located within a few hours, take the following actions:

- If you have subscribed to 1-800 HELP 4 PETS, call them as soon as you notice your pet missing and follow the instructions they give you to help them locate your pet.

- Contact the animal control departments and humane societies within a sixty-mile radius of where your pet strayed. Check with them each day.

- Post signs at intersections and in storefronts throughout the area.

- Provide a description and a photograph of your missing pet to the police, letter carriers or delivery people.

Do Your Part to Make Your Pet a Welcome Guest

Many hotels, restaurants and individuals will give your pet special consideration during your travels. It is important for you to do your part to ensure that dogs and cats will continue to be welcomed as traveling companions. Obey local animal-control ordinances, keep your animal under restraint, be thoughtful and courteous to other travelers and have a good trip!

Pets Welcome™ Hints for *Two-legged* Travelers

Although we realize that this book is primarily aimed at traveling pets, we feel it would be remiss if we did not include what we feel are important travel hints for those two-legged travelers who accompany their four-legged friends.

Packing

- Always carry important travel documents, medication, jewelry, currency and anything else of substantial value in your carry-on luggage.

- Always make sure you carry proof of medical insurance, driver's license, motorists' insurance identity card, portable alarm clock, and AARP, AAA, or other membership cards needed to get you the best deals.

- Pack lightly! A good hint is to pack half of what you think you will need, then cut that amount in half. Bring only what you think you will need, pack tightly to maximize your space. If possible, two carry-ons should be plenty, no matter how long you'll be away.

- Pack toiletries in plastic bottles and store them in a separate plastic bag in case of leakage.

- Check seasonal weather conditions for the area you'll be visiting. Include necessities like an umbrella, jacket, etc.

- If you'll be traveling overseas, pack an electric adapter kit for small appliances. Make sure you have the proper adapter for the countries you'll be visiting.

- Make certain you label each piece of your luggage with your name and address.

Airline Travel

- Proper identification—with a photo of yourself—is a must.

- Check in at least one hour prior to domestic flights and two hours prior to international flights. This is particularly important when traveling with your pet.

- When checking luggage, give yourself extra time for processing. Most airlines have limitations on the number or size of bags than can be checked.

- On longer flights, pack reading material, special medication or dietary needs, and a warm jacket or sweater to make yourself more comfortable.

- As soon as you are seated in the plane, set your watch forward or back to the time zone at your intended place of arrival.

- Get terminal, flight, and gate information when meeting family or friends at the airport.

- Advise the airline of any special dietary needs well in advance of your flight—preferably when booking your flight.

Car Rental Tips

- Have your current driver's license and insurance card ready to present before renting any vehicle.

- Call in advance for rental reservations, a list of additional locations where the car may be returned, and hours of operation for all rental locations where you might be.

- When you make reservations, find out what special rates are available for such memberships as AAA, AARP, corporate, military, etc. Compare each rate—some are better than others.

- Check weekly rates, weekend rates, anything that will get you the lowest cost. Don't hesitate to compare the rates of different rental companies to make sure you get the absolute lowest rate available for the size or type of vehicle you want.

- Find out if your credit card covers such things as insurance, collision damage waiver, etc.

- If there is any damage to the vehicle, take photographs for your own records before you drive the car out of the rental car lot. If there is any damage to the vehicle caused while it is in your possession, take photographs for your own records.

- When returning your vehicle, allow adequate time for an inspection and resolution of any extra billing charges, discrepancies, questions, or disputes.

Hotels, Motels, and Other Accommodations

- When you make reservations, find out what special rates are available for such memberships as AAA, AARP, corporate, military, etc. Compare each rate—some are better than others. Check weekly rates, weekend rates, anything that will get you the lowest cost.

- Hotels may offer seasonal discounts or promotions. Contact the hotel concerned or your travel agent to find out about any special discounts for which you might qualify.

- When making reservations, be sure to indicate your room preferences, such as non-smoking, double bed, etc., and let the lodgings know you'll be coming with your pet.

- If you are not satisfied with your room on check-in, contact the front desk to request a room change or extra amenities to make your stay more comfortable.

- Ask the front desk for sightseeing tips, dining reservations, or help getting tickets to special events.

- Ask about shuttle service to and from major airports.

- Make sure that people at home will know key points along your route, when you'll be there, and how to contact you in an emergency—*and have a wonderful trip!*

What Is Meant by "Types of Lodging" in this Pets Welcome™ Guide

Hotel:
Low- or high-rise establishments with a full range of services, as well as on-premises food and/or beverage outlets or restaurants, shops, conference facilities, and recreation facilities. May have a concierge service to help you make reservations for restaurants, entertainment venues, etc.

Motel:
Less formal than a hotel. Usually low-rise (1-4 stories), with fewer services than a hotel. May or may not have restaurants (usually adjacent), limited public areas, limited recreational facilities.

Resort:
A full service establishment, which may be a vacation destination in and of itself. Usually on quite ample grounds with substantial recreational facilities, food and beverage outlets, ranging from informal to formal, an extensive range of recreational and entertainment facilities, concierge services, and self-contained programs.

Bed & Breakfast (B&B):
Quite limited service. Generally a smaller, owner-operated establishment, which emphasizes the "personal touch." May be historical, quirky, usually long on charm, shorter on absolute privacy. A continental or full, hot breakfast is included in the room rate.

Condominium or Apartment:
Apartment-style units with limited services. Limited housekeeping services, but more room for your money. May include kitchen facilities, dishes in suite, and a homey feel.

Motor Inn or Motor Lodge:
More services than a motel, but less services than a hotel. Usually a single or multi-story place that offers on-premises food and/or beverage service, meeting and banquet facilities, and some recreational facilities.

Cottage or Cabin:
Limited service. Individual housing units that offer one or more separate sleeping areas, a living room, and cooking facilities. May be quite rustic, generally very informal.

Suites:
(May be in hotel, motel, motor inn, etc.) One or more bedrooms and a living room/sitting area, closed off by a wall. May or may not have a partition bedroom door.

Guest Ranch:
Usually a ranch on a large spread offering unique activities, such as riding horses and camping. Generally informal.

RV Park:
Space where you can hook up your recreational vehicle or motor home. Very, very informal.

Pets Welcome™
Highly Recommends:

Creative Pet Products, Inc.

Don Knutson has created unique and highly useful products for pets. You won't find pet food here, but you will find such things as a **Pet Passport** (with all relevant and important information about your pet); the **Bow-Ow!** or **Me-Ow! Pet First Aid Kit**; and the **Travel Pet** kit for every pet—cleverly housed in a "suitcase" the size of a purse. The Travel Pet features absolutely everything you need to make your pet's trip as much fun as yours!

Creative Pet Products, Inc.
4090 County Road 44, Suite B
Minnetrista, MN 55364

Telephone: (952) 474-0614
FAX: (952) 474-0680
E-mail: D. Knutson@att.net

1-800-HELP-4-PETS

A basic I.D. tag with your home telephone number and address doesn't work when you're not there to answer the call. The **1-800-HELP-4-PETS 24-hour I.D. tag** works nationwide. If your pet is lost while traveling with you, call 1-800-HELP-4-PETS and they'll put you in touch with the person who found him/her. 1-800-HELP-4-PETS also provides emergency veterinarian referral anywhere in the U.S. if your pet is injured or becomes ill while traveling. 1-800-HELP-4-PETS has a special offer for readers of the Pets Welcome™ series.

1-800-HELP-4-PETS
8721 Santa Monica Blvd., PMB 710
Los Angeles, CA 90069-8722

Telephone: (800) 435-7473
FAX: (213) 637-9311
Website: www.help4pets.com
E-mail: mail@help4pets.com

Map of the United States

CANADA

MAINE

INNESOTA

Lake
Superior

Duluth

VERMONT ★Augusta
Montpelier ★ NEW
HAMPSHIRE
Concord Boston

St. Paul Eau Claire
nneapolis

Lake
Huron

Lake
Ontario NEW YORK
Albany ★ MASSACHUSETTS
Rochester ★Providence
Hartford★ RHODE ISLAND

WISCONSIN MICHIGAN
Milwaukee★ Lansing
Madison★

Lake Michigan

Lake
Erie Buffalo

CONNECTICUT

IOWA
Cedar Rapids
Chicago Ann Arbor Detroit
Cleveland PENNSYLVANIA New York
NEW JERSEY

naha Des Moines Harrisburg ★Trenton
★Philadelphia

in ILLINOIS INDIANA OHIO Pittsburgh Wilmington
MARYLAND★Dover
Indianapolis ★Columbus DELAWARE
ka Kansas City Springfield Dayton Washington D. C.★ Annapolis
St. Louis Cincinnati WEST VIRGINIA
Jefferson City Louisville ★Charleston
★Frankfort ★Richmond
Ohio R. KENTUCKY VIRGINIA Norfolk

MISSOURI

Greensboro Raleigh

★Fayetteville Knoxville
Nashville NORTH CAROLINA Atlantic Ocean
ansas R. Memphis TENNESSEE Charlotte

Little Rock ★Columbia Wilmington
ARKANSAS Birmingham ★Atlanta SOUTH CAROLINA
Macon Charleston

MISSISSIPPI Montgomery
Shreveport Jackson★ GEORGIA Savannah
LOUISIANA ALABAMA

Mobile
Baton Rouge★ Biloxi Tallahassee Jacksonville
ston New Orleans

Galveston Orlando

Tampa

FLORIDA

Gulf of Mexico Fort Myers West Palm Beach
Miami

Key West

ALABAMA

Nicknames: Heart of Dixie, Camellia State

Population: 4,369,862

Area: 52,237 square miles

Climate: Long, hot summers, mild winters, abundant rainfall.

Capital: Montgomery

Entered Union: December 14, 1819

Motto: We dare defend our rights.

Song: Alabama

Flower: Camellia

Tree: Southern Longleaf Pine

Bird: Yellowhammer

Famous Alabamans: Hank Aaron, Tallulah Bankhead, Hugo Black, George Washington Carver, Nat King Cole, W.C. Handy, Helen Keller, Coretta Scott King, Joe Louis, Willie Mays, Jesse Owens.

History: The Creek, Choctaw, Cherokee, Alabama and Chickasaw peoples inhabited Alabama when the Europeans arrived. The first Europeans, Spanish explorers, arrived in the early 1500s. In 1702, the French settled Mobile Bay, but in 1763 France ceded the territory to England. The Spanish then seized Mobile Bay and it remained Spanish until U.S. troops took over in 1813. In 1814, General Andrew Jackson removed the Creeks and resettled them to Oklahoma. The state seceded from the Union in 1861. Montgomery was the first capital. Alabama was readmitted in 1868.

AUBURN, ALABAMA (Pop. 33,800)

Auburn University Hotel & Dixon Conference Center

241 South College Street
Auburn, AL 36830
800-228-2876 • 334-821-8200
www.auhcc.com
auhotel@auburn.edu

Type of Lodging: Hotel

Room Rates: $74–$149. AAA, AARP and *10% Pets Welcome*™ discounts.

Pet Charges & Deposits: None.

Pet Policy: None. All Pets Welcome.

Amenities: Cable TV, pool.

Pet Amenities: List of nearby veterinarians maintained. Exercise area. Chewacla State Park, Duck Samford Park and Kiesel Park nearby.

Rated: 4 Paws — 248 rooms and 5 suites.

It may seem like going back to school, but university lodgings were never like this. The charming old architecture is gracefully augmented by modern additions. The quaint, friendly college town of Auburn has a plethora of historical sites and entertainment. The Horizon Restaurant is a standout. Most important, there is no limit on pets, and no extra charges, with lots of space to run and play in nearby parks.

Tutwiler Wyndham International

Park Place at 21st Street North
Birmingham, AL 35203
800-WYNDHAM • 205-322-2100
www.wyndham.com

Type of Lodging: Hotel
Room Rates: $129–$178. AAA and AARP discounts.
Pet Charges & Deposits: $25 per stay.
Pet Policy: Sorry, no cats. No pets over 25 lbs.
Amenities: Cable TV, refrigerators, safes.
Pet Amenities: List of nearby veterinarians maintained. Exercise area. Linn Park is adjacent to hotel. Oak Mountain State Park is located 12 miles south of town.
Rated: 4 Paws — 147 rooms and 52 suites.

With the discovery of coal, iron ore and limestone in the late 19th century, Birmingham grew into the South's largest industrial center. Today, it is the largest and most cosmopolitan city in Alabama. Guests may stroll into the past at the Arlington Antebellum Home and Gardens. Or visit the Birmingham Civil Rights Institute to see first-hand the hard lessons learned through past struggles. The designated historical district is the hottest place in town. The Alabama Sports Hall of Fame commemorates Jesse Owens, Joe Namath, Hank Aaron, Joe Louis and other famous Alabama athletes. Your pet will love Oak Mountain, Alabama's largest state park, located 12 miles south of town.

Key West Inn

10535 State Highway 168
Boaz, AL 35957
800-833-0555 • 256-593-0800
www.keywestinn.net/boaz.html

Type of Lodging: Inn
Room Rates: $43–$64, including continental breakfast. AAA, AARP and **10% Pets Welcome™** discounts.
Pet Charges & Deposits: $5 per day.
Pet Policy: Designated rooms only.
Amenities: Cable TV, refrigerators, microwaves.
Pet Amenities: None.
Rated: 2 Paws — 41 rooms.

Part of the South's newest value priced inns, which bill themselves as "Amazingly Affordable…Surprisingly Stylish," Key West Inn is located just across the street from the "shoppers' paradise"—over 130 factory outlets. Free local calls, free discount shopping coupons and in-room coffee are some of the amenities designed to make you and your pet more comfortable. There is a large selection of restaurants nearby.

Shoney's Inn

946 Lake Mitchell Road
Clanton, AL 35045
800-222-2222 • 205-280-0306
www.shoneysinn.com

Type of Lodging: Inn

Room Rates: $41–$62, including full breakfast and Shoney's Restaurant Discount Coupon. AAA, AARP, Seniors and Group discounts.

Pet Charges & Deposits: $20 refundable deposit.

Pet Policy: Reasonable weight limit. Pets must not be left unattended.

Amenities: Cable TV, pool, safe.

Pet Amenities: List of nearby veterinarians maintained. Exercise area.

Rated: 2 Paws — 74 rooms.

Located 45 miles north of Montgomery and 45 miles south of Birmingham, Clanton is near the Tri Lakes region (Lay, Mitchell and Jordan Lakes), Confederate Park and the Heaton Pecan Farm. Shoney's Inn features special boat and truck parking with electrical hookups and a dump station, free local calls, complimentary coffee and newspaper in the lobby. There are non-smoking and handicap facilities available and kids stay free in their parents' room. Try to stop by during peach season (Mid-May through September) and share in the succulent fruit.

Best Western Fairwinds Inn

1917 Commerce Avenue Northwest
Cullman, AL 35055
888-559-0549 • 256-737-5009

Type of Lodging: Motel

Room Rates: $55–$80, including continental breakfast. AAA and AARP discounts.

Pet Charges & Deposits: $5 per day.

Pet Policy: No pets over 50 lbs. Designated rooms only.

Amenities: Cable TV, refrigerators, microwaves, pools

Pet Amenities: List of nearby veterinarians maintained. Dog runs. Exercise area. Park nearby.

Rated: 3 Paws — 50 rooms.

John Cullman, a German immigrant, hoped to establish a self-sustaining colony of his countrymen when he bought a tract of land in 1872. Starting out with only five German families, the project was so successful that it became the county seat only six years later. The Clarkson Covered Bridge, seven miles west, is one of the state's largest such bridges. The Ave Maria Grotto is especially noteworthy: Brother Joseph, a Benedictine monk, spent over 50 years decorating the grotto with over 100 miniatures of famous churches, buildings and shrines from many parts of the world.

Ramada Inn

Highway 82 and Riverside Drive
Eufaula, AL 36027
334-687-2021

Type of Lodging: Hotel

Room Rates: $50–$56. AAA and AARP discounts.

Pet Charges & Deposits: None

Pet Policy: No pets over 15 lbs.

Amenities: Cable TV, safes.

Pet Amenities: Lakepoint State Park is located on North Highway 431.

Rated: 2 Paws — 96 rooms. 1999 Gold Key Award Winner.

Eufaula National Wildlife Refuge, an 11,184-acre refuge on the Chattahoochee River, provides a feeding and resting habitat for more than 280 species of birds. You can enjoy fishing, boating and water skiing on Lake Eufaula and then wander through the scores of antebellum homes built in the Greek Revival, Italianate and Victorian styles.

Bon Secour Lodge

16730 Oyster Bay Place
Gulf Shores, AL 36542
334-968-7814
www.bonsecourlodge.com
riverrat@gulftel.com

Type of Lodging: Guest Ranch & Cottages

Cottage Rates: $60–$85.

Pet Charges & Deposits: $10 per stay.

Pet Policy: Sorry, no cats. Manager's prior approval required.

Amenities: Cable TV, complete kitchens, guest laundry, grills, boat launch and slips, covered dock, fishing guide.

Pet Amenities: List of nearby veterinarians maintained. Exercise area. Alabama Gulf State Park, Gulf Shores Beach, Bon Secour National Wildlife Refuge, Weeks Bay Estuarine Research Reserve all nearby. Dog walking available. River access for swimming.

Rated: 2 Paws — 7 cottages.

The Bon Secour Lodge encourages guests to bring their "lounging around" clothes, fishing pole, a good book, boats and *Pets Welcome™*. Gulf Shores is Mobile Bay's Pleasure Island with beaches, excellent fishing and scenic golf courses. The Bon Secour National Wildlife Reserve boasts 6,500 acres with everything from dunes to woodlands. The nature and hiking trails are open daily.

Mentone Springs Hotel Bed & Breakfast

6114 Highway 117
Mentone, AL 35984
800-404-0100 • 256-634-4040

Type of Lodging: B&B

Room Rates: $54–$79, including full breakfast.

Pet Charges & Deposits: None.

Pet Policy: Sorry, no cats. Manager's prior approval required. Pets must not be left unattended.

Amenities: None.

Pet Amenities: List of nearby veterinarians maintained. Desoto Park nearby.

Rated: 3 Paws — 10 rooms and 1 suite. Listed on the National Register of Historic Places

Owners Claudia and Dave Wasson proudly say, "The hotel is our home…We welcome you in!" This beautiful Queen Anne Victorian has an amazing history. Originally constructed in 1884, by 1916 it had 81 rooms, a nine-hole golf course, tennis courts and other attractions. The hotel flourished through the Roaring '20s, then went into decline, finally being sold in 1946 to cover debts. Today, this proud lady is being lovingly restored. Just as in 1884, all ground-floor rooms have a shared bath while the upstairs rooms have private baths. The hotel is located in the center of Mentone and breakfasts are cooked to order. Within an hour you can be at the Tennessee Aquarium, the Southern Belle, Weiss Lake (the Crappie Capital of the World), the Boaz Outlet Center and Chickamauga Military Park.

La Quinta Inn Mobile

816 South Beltline Highway
Mobile, AL 36609
800-531-5900 • 334-343-4051
www.laquinta.com
lq0804gm@laquinta.com

Type of Lodging: Hotel

Room Rates: $59–$89, including continental breakfast. AAA and AARP discounts.

Pet Charges & Deposits: None.

Pet Policy: No pets over 20 lbs. Pets must not be left unattended.

Amenities: Cable TV, pool, coffeemakers, guest laundry, free local calls, dataports.

Pet Amenities: List of nearby veterinarians maintained.

Rated: 3 Paws — 120 rooms and 2 suites.

Alabama's only seaport, Mobile is on the west side of the Mobile River. Mobile's Mardi Gras, although smaller in size than New Orleans', is supposedly the original pre-Lenten carnival. First observed in 1703 and suspended during the Civil War, the festivities have been held continuously since 1866. Mobile is most beautiful during the azalea season (March through April). The Mobile Museum of Art and Mobile's historic districts are well worth seeing.

Shoney's Inn

5472-A Inn Road
Mobile, AL 36619
800-222-2222 • 334-660-1520
www.shoneysinn.com

Type of Lodging: Hotel

Room Rates: $44–$59, including continental breakfast. AAA, AARP, AKC and ABA discounts.

Pet Charges & Deposits: $25 refundable deposit.

Pet Policy: Designated rooms only.

Amenities: Cable TV, safes, pools.

Pet Amenities: List of nearby veterinarians maintained.

Rated: 2 Paws — 118 rooms and 13 suites.

Shoney's Inn is 15 minutes away from Bellingrath Gardens and a scant ten minutes to the downtown Historic District. Mobile Bay and the U.S.S. Alabama are nearby. Kids stay free in their parents' room and Shoney's Restaurant is adjacent to the hotel.

Coliseum Inn

1550 Federal Drive
Montgomery, AL 36107
800-876-6835 • 334-265-0586

Type of Lodging: Motel

Room Rates: $37–$43, including continental breakfast. AARP discount.

Pet Charges & Deposits: $3 per day. $3 nonrefundable deposit.

Pet Policy: Pets must be in carriers.

Amenities: Cable TV.

Pet Amenities: None.

Rated: 2 Paws — 40 rooms.

Founded in 1817, Montgomery became the capital of Alabama in 1846 and the first capital of the Confederacy in 1861. In the mid-1950s, Rosa Parks was arrested for not giving up her bus seat to a white man. For 381 days, Martin Luther King led a boycott of city buses until the Supreme Court ordered their desegregation. Montgomery sprawls across seven hills overlooking the Alabama River. Today, it is one of the largest livestock markets and dairy centers in the Southeast. The Alabama Shakespeare Festival runs from mid-November to mid-September and is noteworthy. The First White House of the Confederacy, the Alabama State Capitol and Old Alabama Town are certainly worth seeing, as is the Scott & Zelda Fitzgerald Museum, where the couple lived from 1931 to 1932 (Zelda was born in Montgomery and spent most of her life there).

Grace Hall Bed & Breakfast Inn

506 Lauderdale Street
Selma, AL 36701
334-875-5744
www.selmaalabama.com/gracehal.htm
adman@wwisp.com

Type of Lodging: B&B

Room Rates: $69–$125, including full breakfast and tour of the mansion.

Pet Charges & Deposits: $10 per stay.

Pet Policy: Inquire about weight limitations. Designated rooms only. Manager's prior approval required.

Amenities: Cable TV.

Pet Amenities: Dog bones and treats provided for the four-legged guests. List of nearby veterinarians maintained. Exercise area. Bloch Park is located on Dallas Avenue.

Rated: 3 Paws — 6 rooms.

Step out of the present and into the gracious past the moment you take your first look at Grace Hall. Built in 1857, this antebellum mansion mixes elements of older neoclassicism with newer Victorian trends with stunning results. Guestrooms open onto a courtyard. In Selma, the five blocks of Water Avenue that survived the Civil War constitute one of the few remaining antebellum riverfront business districts in the South. Selma is, of course, synonymous with the Civil Rights Movement and the battles of the mid-1960s. Today, this arsenal of the Confederacy quietly celebrates its graceful past.

ALASKA

Nickname: The Last Frontier

Population: 619,500

Area: 615,230

Climate: SE, SW and Central regions: moist and mild; far north: extremely dry. Extended summer days, winter nights throughout.

Capital: Juneau

Entered Union: January 3, 1959

Motto: North to the future.

Song: Alaska's Flag

Flower: Forget-Me-Not

Tree: Sitka Spruce

Bird: Willow Ptarmigan

Famous Alaskans: Tom Bodett, Susan Butcher, Ernest Gruening, Jefferson "Soapy" Smith.

History: Early inhabitants of the state were the Tlingit-Halda. The Aleut and Inuit (Eskimo), who arrived about 4,000 years ago from Siberia, lived in coastal areas. Vitus Bering, a Dane working for Russia, arrived in 1741. A Russian settlement was established on Kodiak Island in 1784. The Russian-American Company controlled the region by 1799. Secretary of State William Seward bought Alaska from Russia for $7.2 million in 1867, a bargain some called "Seward's Folly." Gold was discovered in the Klondike in 1896, starting the famed Alaska Gold Rush. Alaska became a U.S. territory in 1912 and was admitted to the Union in 1959.

Hillside on Gambell Motel & RV Park

2150 Gambell Street
Anchorage, AK 99503
800-478-6008 • 907-258-6006
www.hillside-alaska.com
info@hillside-alaska.com

Type of Lodging: Motel and RV Park
Room Rates: $51–$129.
Pet Charges & Deposits: $5 per day.
Call for deposit information.
Pet Policy: None. All Pets Welcome.
Amenities: Cable TV, refrigerators, microwaves.
Pet Amenities: List of nearby veterinarians maintained. City parks and Chester Creek Walking Trail nearby.
Rated: 3 Paws — 26 rooms and 1 suite.

Hillside on Gambell Motel & RV Park provides orderly, comfortable and affordable accommodations, whether you choose to arrive in your recreational vehicle or trailer, or prefer to stay in the motel. Anchorage, Alaska's largest city, is home to more than half of the state's residents. Situated on a high bluff between the two branches of the Cook Inlet, it lies as far west as the Hawaiian Islands and as far north as Helsinki, Finland. In 1964, one of the strongest earthquakes in history destroyed much of downtown Anchorage, which was swiftly rebuilt. The dramatic beauty of the nearby mountains, inlets and glaciers offers an easily accessible sample of Alaska's natural splendors. Must-see Anchorage attractions include the Alaska Native Heritage Center and the Anchorage Museum of History and Art.

TRI Bed & Breakfast of Glacier Bay

P.O. Box 214
Gustavus, AK 99826
907-697-2425
www.glacierbaylodging.com
trigbay@pluto.he.net

Type of Lodging: B&B
Cottage Rates: $85–$99, including full or continental breakfast.
Pet Charges & Deposits: None.
Pet Policy: Designated rooms only. Manager's prior approval required.
Amenities: Refrigerators, microwaves, BBQ, bikes.
Pet Amenities: List of nearby veterinarians maintained. Exercise area. Glacier Bay National Park is located 3 miles away.
Rated: 3 Paws — 3 cottages.

Thomas & Rhio Imboden—TRI—your hosts, are a piece of Alaska history in and of themselves. Since 1973, Thomas has backpacked and kayaked through the Western United States. Thomas and Rhio have lived in Gustavus since 1990 and are year-round residents. The first three years were without electricity, with their only modern conveniences a hand water pump and gasoline lights. Today, each of the cottages is separate from the others, with privacy insured by first growth forest on the seven-acre homestead. Glacier Bay National Park is one of the most scenic spots in Alaska. Within the park, you'll find 15,320-foot Mount Fairweather, some of the world's most impressive tidewater glaciers and Glacier Bay itself, 65 miles long and 2½ to ten miles wide. A ten-mile road connects the park headquarters with Gustavus, where charter vessels and air and boat service to Juneau are available.

Fort Seward Lodge

39 Modbay Road
Haines, AK 99827
800-478-7772 • 907-766-2009
www.ftsewardlodge.com
ftsewardlodge@wytbear.com

Type of Lodging: Motel
Room Rates: $50–$95. Military and Seniors discounts.
Pet Charges & Deposits: $5 per day. $50 refundable deposit.
Pet Policy: None. All Pets Welcome.
Amenities: Cable TV, restaurant, lounge, ocean views, kitchenettes.
Pet Amenities: None.
Rated: 3 Paws — 10 rooms.

Built in the early 1900s, the historic building in which the Lodge is found formerly housed the fort's Post Exchange and was an important part of Fort William H. Seward, the regimental headquarters for all of Alaska. The original building included a soda fountain, gym, movie house, library and a two-lane bowling alley. Today, it affords restful rooms within walking distance of downtown Haines. Haines lies in a spectacular setting on the Chilkat Peninsula between the waters of the Inside Passage and the Chilkat River. One of the largest groups of bald eagles in the world gathers on the 48,000-acre Chilkat Bald Eagle Preserve from late October through December each year. Chilkat Native American Dances take place at the Chilkat Center for the Arts, Sunday through Thursday, May through September.

Driftwood Inn & RV Park

135 West Bunnell Avenue
Homer, AK 99603
800-478-8019 • 907-235-8019
www.thedriftwoodinn.com
driftinn@xyz.net

Type of Lodging: Inn
Room Rates: $64–$74.
Pet Charges & Deposits: None.
Pet Policy: Designated rooms only.
Amenities: None.
Pet Amenities: List of nearby veterinarians maintained. Exercise area. Bishop's Beach nearby.
Rated: 3 Paws — 20 rooms and 1 suite.

Driftwood Inn & RV Park is a home away from home in a quiet, peaceful setting overlooking beautiful Kachemak Bay, with its mountains, glaciers and coves. The Inn affords super spotless rooms, cozy double beds, some with single bunk beds above. There's a television in all rooms and both private and shared baths. Kachemak Bay, a 30-mile arm of the lower Cook Inlet, provides a usually ice-free harbor. The city is linked by daily air service with Anchorage. Skyline Drive, accessible from West and East Hill Roads, follows the rim of the plateau behind the town and offers access to ski slopes and views of the Bay.

Kenai Peninsula Condos

Box 3416
Soldotna, AK 99669
800-362-1383 • 907-262-1383
www.alaska-kenai-peninsula.com
kpcondos@alaska.com

Type of Lodging: Guest Ranch & Condos

Condo Rates: $89–$150. AAA, AARP, AKC, ABA and *10% Pets Welcome™* discounts.

Pet Charges & Deposits: $3 per day.

Pet Policy: Designated rooms only. Manager's prior approval required. Cats must have cages.

Amenities: Cable TV, fully equipped kitchens.

Pet Amenities: List of nearby veterinarians maintained. There is an excellent veterinary hospital 200 yards from the property. Exercise area. Numerous forested areas on and near property including Kenai National Wildlife Refuge, Soldotna City Park, Alaska State Park and Kenai City Park.

Rated: 3 Paws — 8 condos.

Why stay in a motel when you can rent a large condominium for comparable rates? Kenai Peninsula Condos affords large, two-bedroom units that comfortably sleep six. Free laundry, free coffee, full kitchens with freezer (to store the fish you caught), microwaves, picnic tables, BBQs—all this and a great location in a quiet area five minutes from the Kenai River. The Kenai River claims to be the world record holder for the size of its salmon, rainbow trout and halibut. Soldotna's postwar development was assured when the U.S. Government opened the area up for homesteading by WWII veterans. Located on the Kenai Peninsula at the junction of Sterling and Kenai Spur Highways, the area is rich with opportunities for year-round recreation.

Gate Creek Cabins

Mile 10.5 Petersville Road
P.O. Box 13390
Trapper Creek, AK 99683
907-733-1393
www.gatecreekcabins.com

Type of Lodging: Cabins

Cabin Rate: $45.

Pet Charges & Deposits: $10 per stay.

Pet Policy: Sorry, no cats. Manager's prior approval required. Pets must not be left unattended.

Amenities: Cable TV, fully equipped kitchens, sauna.

Pet Amenities: List of nearby veterinarians maintained. Exercise area of 8 acres of open land. Denali National Park Area nearby.

Rated: 3 Paws — 5 cabins on 8 acres with 2 ponds.

The Gate Creek Cabins are located on historic Petersville Road at the South Gateway to Denali National Park area. The cabins are built to be cozy, modern, yet authentic and have easy access to all the recreational activities for which Alaska is so famous. Each log cabin is completely self-contained with full kitchens and bathrooms. Your pet will love exploring the 8-acre property with its two ponds.

Westmark Valdez

100 Fidalgo Drive
P.O. Box 468
Valdez, AK 99686
800-544-0970 • 907-835-4391
www.westmarkhotels.com
wmvaldez@alaska.net

Type of Lodging: Hotel

Room Rates: $89–$129. AAA, AARP and *10% Pets Welcome™* discounts.

Pet Charges & Deposits: None.

Pet Policy: Designated rooms only.

Amenities: Cable TV.

Pet Amenities: List of nearby veterinarians maintained. Nearby trails: Mineral Creek, Shoup Glacier and Goat Trail.

Rated: 3 Paws — 86 rooms.

The Westmark Valdez offers a variety of rooms: some compact, some spacious, some modern, others with slightly older appointments. The hotel also houses the Captain's Table Restaurant and the Wheelhouse Lounge. Surrounded by mountain peaks that pierce the clouds, Valdez is called the "Switzerland of Alaska" because snowcapped mountains ring it. It's the northernmost ice-free port in the United States. Nearby glaciers in Prince William Sound include Blackstone, Mears, Shoup and Columbia. The city of Valdez is the terminal for the Alaska pipeline. Worthington Glacier, 30 miles east on Richardson Highway, is Alaska's most accessible glacier.

ARIZONA

Nicknames: Grand Canyon State, Copper State

Population: 4,778,332

Area: 114,006 square miles

Climate: Clear, hot, and dry in the southern regions and northern plateau; high central areas have heavy winter snows.

Capital: Phoenix

Entered Union: Feb. 14, 1912

Motto: *Ditat Deus* (God enriches).

Song: Arizona

Flower: Saguaro Cactus Blossom

Tree: Paloverde

Bird: Cactus Wren

Famous Arizonans: Cochise, Geronimo, Barry Goldwater, Zane Grey, John McCain, Frank Lloyd Wright.

 History: Anasazi, Mogollon and Hohokam civilizations inhabited the area from 300 B.C. to 1300 A.D. The Pueblo peoples—Navajo, Zuni and Apache—arrived during the 15th century. Marcos de Niza, a Franciscan, and Estevanico, a former black slave, explored the area in 1539. Francisco Kiino, a Jesuit missionary, established missions between 1692-1711. Tubac, a Spanish fort, became the first European settlement in 1752. Spain ceded Arizona to Mexico in 1821. The U.S. took over in 1848 after the Mexican War. The area below the Gila River was obtained from Mexico in the Gadsden Purchase in 1863. Geronimo surrendered in 1886, ending the Apache wars.

San Jose Lodge

1002 Naco Highway
Bisbee, AZ 85603
520-432-5761
www.sanjoselodge.com
sanjoselodge@cs.com

Type of Lodging: Motel

Room Rates: $60–$95. AAA discount.

Pet Charges & Deposits: $10 per day.

Pet Policy: Sorry, no cats. Designated rooms only. Pets must be on leashes.

Amenities: Cable TV, refrigerators, microwaves, pool, restaurant.

Pet Amenities: List of nearby veterinarians maintained. Exercise area.

Rated: 2 Paws — 37 rooms and 6 suites.

The San Jose Lodge is located ten minutes away from historic Old Bisbee. While there, you can take an exciting ride through the Queen Mine, visit the Mining Museum or stroll down the main street to Brewery Gulch. Tombstone—remember the Gunfight at the OK Corral?—is 25 miles north of Bisbee, while the Mexican border is minutes away. It's a 20-minute drive to cross the border at Agua Prieta, Sonora, Mexico for shopping. There are several small lakes for the fisherman, all within a two-hour radius of the property.

Best Western Bullhead City Inn

1126 Highway 95
Bullhead City, AZ 86429
800-634-4463 • 520-754-3000

Type of Lodging: Motel

Room Rates: $39–$99, including continental breakfast. AAA, AARP and *10% Pets Welcome*™ discounts.

Pet Charges & Deposits: $5 per stay. $25 refundable deposit.

Pet Policy: None. All Pets Welcome.

Amenities: Cable TV, refrigerators, microwaves.

Pet Amenities: Exercise area.

Rated: 3 Paws — 89 rooms.

Located in the heart of sun and fun on the Colorado River, the Best Western Bullhead City Inn is close to all water activities, watercraft rental, an 18-hole championship golf course and outlet mall shopping. It's only a few miles from Laughlin and the Nevada casinos. Go a few miles more and you'll come to the beautiful Lake Mohave. There's plenty of large vehicle and RV parking, a restaurant adjacent to the property and a very Pets Welcome atmosphere.

Sunridge Hotel & Conference Center

839 Landon Drive
Bullhead City, AZ 86429
800-977-4242 • 520-754-4700
www.rentor.com/hotels/sunridge.htm
sunridge@ispchannel.com

Type of Lodging: Hotel

Room Rates: $39–$125, including continental breakfast. AAA and AARP discounts.

Pet Charges & Deposits: $100 refundable deposit.

Pet Policy: Designated rooms only.

Amenities: Cable TV, pool, Jacuzzi, refrigerators, microwaves.

Pet Amenities: List of nearby veterinarians maintained. Exercise area.

Rated: 3 Paws — 148 rooms and 4 suites.

Laughlin, Nevada and river gambling are minutes away. Oatman, an authentic western ghost town is less than an hour away. Lake Havasu City is one hour's drive south to the city known for its English Village and the world-famous London Bridge (sorry, you're thinking of Tower Bridge—it's not the one in the pictures). A wonderful destination.

Comfort Inn

340 North Industrial Drive
Camp Verde, AZ 86322
800-228-5750 • 520-567-9000
www.comfortinn.com
comfortinn@sedona.net

Type of Lodging: Hotel

Room Rates: $44–$89, including continental breakfast. AAA and AARP discounts.

Pet Charges & Deposits: $15 per stay.

Pet Policy: Designated rooms only.

Amenities: Cable TV, pool.

Pet Amenities: None.

Rated: 2 Paws — 85 rooms.

Comfort Inn is located in the heart of Arizona, 90 miles north of Phoenix and 56 miles south of Flagstaff and the stunning Red Rock country immortalized in Arizona Highways. At an altitude of 3,133 feet, the climate is ideal, with mild weather year around. The historic mining town of Jerome is a scant 20 miles away, as is the Verde Canyon Railway. Montezuma's Castle, the Red Rocks of Sedona, Fort Verde State Park and Tuzigoot National Monument are all less than 18 miles away. The Comfort Inn has bus parking, a wine and cheese reception, game nights, dataports, free newspaper and free local calls. This is the Great Southwest at its very best.

Microtel Inn & Suites

504 Industrial Drive
Camp Verde, AZ 86322
800-771-7171 • 520-567-3700
www.microtelinnaz.com
stay@microtelinnaz.com

Type of Lodging: Motel
Room Rates: $44–$94, including continental breakfast. AAA, AARP and *10%* **Pets Welcome™** discounts.
Pet Charges & Deposits: $10 per day.
Pet Policy: Designated rooms only.
Amenities: Cable TV, refrigerators, microwaves, pool, hot tubs, guest laundry.
Pet Amenities: List of nearby veterinarians maintained. Dog runs. Exercise area. Fort Verde State Park and Butler Park are minutes away.
Rated: 3 Paws — 38 rooms and 25 suites.

Experience the Arizona you always see in the magazines or read about in travel guides: Sedona, the incredibly gorgeous Oak Creek Canyon, the Verde Canyon Train, Cliff Castle Casino—take the train into Arizona's other "grand canyon" for an unforgettable experience. The Verde Canyon, accessible only by rail, features flora and fauna, lush riparian habitat, crimson cliffs, Native American ruins, a 680-foot tunnel and more. Microtel focuses on value and you won't be disappointed here. Chiropractic approved mattresses, free local calls, dataports, free cable television and free guest laundry are all welcomed amenities.

Arizona Mountain Inn

4200 Lake Mary Road
Flagstaff, AZ 86001
800-239-5236 • 520-774-8959
www.arizonamountaininn.com
arizonamountaininn@msn.com

Type of Lodging: B&B & Cabins
Room Rates: $80–$390, including continental breakfast in the B&B suites only.
Pet Charges & Deposits: $5 per day. $50 refundable deposit.
Pet Policy: Sorry, no cats. Designated cabins only. Limit two pets per cabin.
Amenities: Cable TV, fully equipped kitchens, hot tubs, playground.
Pet Amenities: List of nearby veterinarians maintained. Exercise area. Surrounded on three sides by the Coconino National Forest with lots of trails.
Rated: 3 Paws — 17 cabins and 3 B&B suites on 13 acres.

This lovely Tudor-style inn and cabins are tucked away on 13 acres of secluded Ponderosa pines bordered by the Coconino National Forest. There are breathtaking views of the San Francisco Peaks. The Inn has cabins ranging from a cozy one-bedroom cabin to a Hogan-style cabin large enough to accommodate 16 people. All cabins include a wood-burning fireplace, fully equipped kitchen, outdoor BBQ grill and much more. Kids can play at the full-size playground with slide, merry-go-round, swing set and even a miniature cabin. The city of Flagstaff, home of Northern Arizona University, is a mile away. Travel 99 miles farther up the road, you come to the Grand Canyon.

InnSuites Hotel

1008 East Route 66
Flagstaff, AZ 86001
800-898-9124 • 520-774-7356
www.innsuites.com
insuitefl@aol.com

Type of Lodging: Hotel

Suite Rates: $59–$109, including continental breakfast, evening social hour and Manager's Wednesday BBQ. AAA, AARP and *10% Pets Welcome™* discounts.

Pet Charges & Deposits: $25 per day. $25 refundable deposit.

Pet Policy: Designated rooms only. Manager's prior approval required.

Amenities: Cable TV, microwaves, refrigerators, pool, hot tubs, fitness center, guest laundry.

Pet Amenities: Doggy bag available. List of nearby veterinarians maintained. Park nearby.

Rated: 2 Paws — 126 suites.

InnSuites Hotel is nestled among the pine-covered hillsides of the Arizona Mountain Country, gateway to the Grand Canyon. The picturesque community is a year-round recreation mecca. Start with a scenic skyride to the summit of Mount Humphreys (great skiing in winter!) with its unforgettable panoramic view. Visit ancient cliff dwellings in Walnut Canyon, the Sunset Crater or Lowell Observatory, where the planet Pluto was discovered. InnSuites Hotel features free local calls, free limited faxes and copies, free morning paper and free cable television. There's P.J.'s Breakfast Café adjacent to the property.

Residence Inn By Marriott

3440 North Country Club Drive
Flagstaff, AZ 86004
800-331-3131 • 520-526-5555
www.ri-destinations.com
sales@ri-destinations.com

Type of Lodging: Hotel

Suite Rates: $89–$199, including hot breakfast buffet and weekday Hospitality hour. AAA and AARP discounts.

Pet Charges & Deposits: $10 per day. $100 flat fee for extended stay.

Pet Policy: Designated rooms only.

Amenities: Cable TV, fully equipped kitchens, pool, Jacuzzi, Sportcourt®.

Pet Amenities: List of nearby veterinarians maintained. Exercise area. Bark Park is 5 miles away and Buffalo Park is 3 miles away. Urban trail outside of hotel.

Rated: 3 Paws — 102 suites.

Residence Inn provides the quality you've come to expect from the Marriott chain. It's 1½ hours from the Grand Canyon, 20 minutes from Native American ancient ruins and is near the Hopi and Navajo Native American reservations. This residential-style hotel offers the genuine comforts of home: spacious suites with separate living areas and fully equipped kitchens. Pleasant extras include a daily complimentary newspaper and breakfast buffet. The property is located in a quiet residential neighborhood with views of the mountains backed by forest. There's golfing right across the street. "Flag" has an easy climate making summer days pleasant and with just enough snow to provide a great skiing experience.

Super 8 Motel

3725 North Kasper
Flagstaff, AZ 86004
888-324-9131 • 520-526-0818
www.super8.com
2918@hotel.cendant.com

Type of Lodging: Motel
Room Rates: $35–$89, including continental breakfast. AAA and AARP discounts.
Pet Charges & Deposits: None.
Pet Policy: None. All Pets Welcome.
Amenities: Cable TV.
Pet Amenities: There is a family of feral cats that live next door that guests may pet and watch hotel staff feed nightly. List of nearby veterinarians maintained. Dog runs. Exercise area. Bushmaster Park is ½ mile away.
Rated: 4 Paws — 90 rooms.

Cleanliness and value are hallmarks of the Super 8 chain and the Flagstaff, Arizona property is no exception. Free coffee and donuts for guests, reasonable rates and large rooms make this motel a fine choice. Flagstaff's historic Museum Club Saloon is within walking distance. Within an easy day's drive of Sedona and the Oak Creek Canyon, the Meteor Crater, Walnut Canyon National Monument, the San Francisco Peaks, the inactive volcano of Sunset Crater, the Wupatki Native American Ruins and, of course, the Grand Canyon.

Rancho Sonora Inn & RV Park

9198 North Highway 79
Florence, AZ 85232
520-868-8000
rancho@c2i2.com

Type of Lodging: Inn
Room Rates: $54–$150, including continental breakfast.
Pet Charges & Deposits: $10 per day.
Pet Policy: Designated rooms only. Manager's prior approval required.
Amenities: Refrigerators, microwaves, pool, spas.
Pet Amenities: List of nearby veterinarians maintained. Exercise area. Lots of room to walk your pet.
Rated: 2 Paws — 6 rooms and 3 suites.

The original spirit of this 1930s adobe guest ranch has been preserved and enhanced with the addition of modern amenities. Unique rooms with private baths open onto the walled, mission-like courtyard. The RV Park is adjacent with concrete pads, telephone access and full hookups. Off the beaten path, yet only an hour's drive to Tucson or Phoenix, Rancho Sonora Inn & RV Park can be found amidst towering saguaro cactus, abundant vegetation and wildlife of the Sonoran desert. The Inn is located five miles south of historic Florence on Highway 79.

Lake of the Woods Resort

P.O. Box 777
Lakeside, AZ 85929
520-368-5353
www.privatelake.com
information@l-o-w.com

Type of Lodging: Resort
Room Rates: $58–$294.
Pet Charges & Deposits: None.
Pet Policy: None. All Pets Welcome.
Amenities: Cable TV, refrigerators, microwaves, Jacuzzi, spas.
Pet Amenities: List of nearby veterinarians maintained. Exercise area. Woodland Park and Mogollon Rim Overlook nearby.
Rated: 4 Paws — 30 cabins. Rated "Best of the Best" two years running by Market Surveys of America.

Lake of the Woods Resort is a beautiful lakefront resort located in the White Mountains. They offer you and your pet a private lake, large expanse of open forest and many other amenities. Guests have their choice of either rustic log cottages or modern cabins.

Arizona Golf Resort & Conference Center

420 South Power Road
Mesa, AZ 85206
800-528-8282 • 480-832-3202
www.azgolfresort.com
azgolf@earthlink.com

Type of Lodging: Hotel & Golf Resort
Room Rates: $69–$179, including continental breakfast. AAA and AARP discounts.
Pet Charges & Deposit: None.
Pet Policy: Pets must not be left unattended.
Amenities: Cable TV, refrigerators, microwaves, safes, pool, whirlpool, Jacuzzi, fitness center, tennis and basketball courts, complimentary bicycles, volleyball, croquet, 3 restaurants.
Pet Amenities: List of nearby veterinarians maintained. Exercise area. Jefferson Park is located on Broadway and 71st Street.
Rated: 4 Paws — 187 rooms and suites.

This place has absolutely everything you need for a first class vacation—why go anywhere else? The "why" is because you're 30 minutes from Scottsdale, 30 miles from Phoenix Sky Harbor Airport and 30 minutes from the fabled Superstition Mountains and Lost Dutchman's Mine. Arizona Golf Resort contains a championship golf course nestled on a beautiful 150-acre resort oasis, surrounded by tropical palms, flowers and the convenience of shopping, restaurants and theaters just moments away. And Pets are Welcome!

Motel In The Pines

80 West Pinewood Road
P.O. Box 18171
Munds Park, AZ 86017
800-574-5080

Type of Lodging: Motel

Room Rates: $35–$85, including morning coffee. AAA, AARP, AKC, ABA, Seniors, Government, Military and *10% Pets Welcome*™ discounts.

Pet Charges & Deposits: $3 per day. $30 refundable deposit.

Pet Policy: Designated rooms only. Manager's prior approval required. Pets must not be left unattended.

Amenities: Cable TV, refrigerators, microwaves, fireplaces.

Pet Amenities: List of nearby veterinarians maintained. Exercise area. Coconino National Forest nearby.

Rated: 2 Paws — 22 rooms and 4 suites

Experience the magnificence of Northern Arizona, two hours easy drive from Phoenix, 20 minutes south of Flagstaff. The two-story motel is located in shady pines. The Pinewood Country Club Golf Course is less than half of a mile away. Want some extra-special Arizona beauty? Highway 179 to Sedona and Oak Creek Canyon is minutes away.

Inn of Payson

801 North Beeline Highway
Payson, AZ 85541
800-247-9477 • 520-474-3241
www.innofpayson.com

Type of Lodging: Hotel

Room Rates: $49–$149, including continental breakfast. AAA and AARP discounts.

Pet Charges & Deposits: $10 per day.

Pet Policy: Designated rooms only. Manager's prior approval required.

Amenities: Cable TV, refrigerators, microwaves, safes, pool, whirlpool.

Pet Amenities: List of nearby veterinarians maintained. Exercise area. Rumsey Park is located ½ mile away.

Rated: 3 Paws — 99 rooms and 1 suite.

It's been known as Green Valley, Long Valley, Big Valley and Union City. First settled by miners seeking wealth, Payson was, alas, a bust. But cattle and lumber provided riches. Today, surrounded by the lakes and dense woodlands of the Tonto National Forest and the nearby Mogollon Rim, the area has become a wilderness getaway for visitors. The Inn of Payson, located up in Arizona's sparkling, cool Mogollon Rim country, nestled among majestic mountains and surrounded by ponderosa pines, is a sanctuary from everyday tedium and a short cut to the wild forests of eastern Arizona.

Embassy Suites Hotel – Biltmore

2630 East Camelback Road
Phoenix, AZ 85016
800 EMBASSY • 602-955-3992
www.embassysuites.com
esbiltmoresales@worldnet.att.net

Type of Lodging: Hotel

Suite Rates: $99–$249, including full breakfast. AAA and AARP discounts.

Pet Charges & Deposits: $25 per stay.

Pet Policy: Sorry, no cats. No pets over 25 lbs. Designated rooms only.

Amenities: Cable TV, refrigerators, microwaves, safes, pool, Jacuzzi, restaurant.

Pet Amenities: List of nearby veterinarians maintained. Dreamy Draw Park is located at 51st and Northern; Squaw Peak Park is located on Lincoln and 22nd Street; and Granada Park is located on Lincoln and 20th Street.

Rated: 3 Paws — 232 suites.

The Embassy Suites Phoenix – Biltmore is nestled in Phoenix's most prestigious residential area. The Biltmore area is a major core of business, shopping, dining and nightlife and is only ten minutes away from Sky Harbor Airport. There are conference and meeting facilities for as many as 350 people and those legendary Embassy Suites breakfasts. The Omaha Steakhouse is the property's in-house restaurant. There's a heated outdoor pool, whirlpool and fitness center. The hotel provides easy access to golf, Biltmore Fashion Park and Scottsdale. You and your pet won't be bored here.

Holiday Inn Express Hotel & Suites – Chandler

15221 South 50th Street
Phoenix, AZ 85044
800-HOLIDAY • 480-785-8500
www.phoenixpackages.com

Type of Lodging: Hotel

Room Rates: $49–$169, including continental breakfast. AAA, AARP, AKC and *20% Pets Welcome™* discounts.

Pet Charges & Deposits: $5 per day.

Pet Policy: No pets over 100 lbs.

Amenities: Cable TV, refrigerators, microwaves, pool, whirlpool, spas, waterfall, guest laundry, fitness room.

Pet Amenities: List of nearby veterinarians maintained. South Mountain Park is located on Baseline Road and 48th Street.

Rated: 3 Paws — 100 rooms and 25 suites. Ranked #1 Holiday Inn Express in Arizona.

Kids stay free, warm cookies on arrival and television with VCR are only a few of the many welcome amenities offered at this Holiday Inn Express. Just down the block, visit Club Disney or take a jaunt around the ice rink at Polar Ice. Try your luck at Arizona's largest casino, Gila River Casino, only two miles from the hotel. An extra secret: The T-Bone Steakhouse, located on south 19th Avenue in the foothills south of and above Phoenix, has been a favorite of our company president for more than 35 years! Colossal steaks, reasonable prices, a priceless view—by the way, do not wear a tie when you go there, unless you can spare it.

Lexington Hotel

100 West Clarendon
Phoenix, AZ 85023
877-253-9749 • 602-279-9811
www.phxihc.com

Type of Lodging: Hotel

Room Rates: $60–$129. AAA, AARP
and *10% Pets Welcome™* discounts.

Pet Charges & Deposits: $100 refundable deposit.

Pet Policy: None. All Pets Welcome.

Amenities: Cable TV, refrigerators,
microwaves, pool, whirlpool, restaurant.

Pet Amenities: List of nearby veterinarians maintained. Exercise area.

Rated: 3 Paws — 180 rooms.

You could hardly be more centrally located in Phoenix than the Lexington Hotel. Just west of Central Avenue, ³/₁₀ of a mile south of Indian School Road, the hotel has indoor corridors, a heated pool and a restaurant. Don't miss the nearby Heard Museum of native cultures and art, one of the finest Native American museums in the country. The Desert Botanical Gardens, a highlight of any visit to Phoenix, covers more than 145 acres in Papago Park and is devoted exclusively to arid land plants of the world. March through May is the height of the wildflower blooming season and you shouldn't miss this glorious time in the Valley of the Sun.

Premier Inn

10402 North Black Canyon Highway
Phoenix, AZ 85051
800-786-6835 • 602-943-2371

Type of Lodging: Motel

Room Rates: $40–$85, including continental breakfast. AAA and AARP discounts.

Pet Charges & Deposits: None.

Pet Policy: Sorry, no puppies.
Designated rooms only. Manager's prior approval required.

Amenities: Cable TV, refrigerators,
microwaves, pool, hot tubs, jogging trail.

Pet Amenities: List of nearby veterinarians maintained. Dog runs. Exercise area. City park nearby.

Rated: 2 Paws — 253 rooms.

More than 20 original and reconstructed buildings spread over a wide area recreate life in Arizona, as it was in the '80s—the 1880s. Costumed living-history interpreters re-enact life in territorial Arizona. Melodramas are staged in the Opera House. All this takes place at the Pioneer Arizona Living History off Interstate 17 at Exit 225 (Pioneer Road), near the pet-friendly Premier Inn. The two-story Inn has two pools, one of them heated. The motel is within walking distance of many restaurants, movie theaters and the Southwest's second largest mall.

Super 8 Motel

1105 East Sheldon Street
Prescott, AZ 86301
800-800-8000 • 520-776-1282
www.innworks.com

Type of Lodging: Motel
Room Rates: $45–$75, including continental breakfast. AAA and AARP discounts.
Pet Charges & Deposits: $10 per stay.
Pet Policy: Sorry, no cats. Designated rooms only. Manager's prior approval required.
Amenities: Cable TV, safes, pool, one free 8-minute long distance call each night.
Pet Amenities: Exercise area. Prescott National Forest surrounds the city.
Rated: 2 Paws — 70 rooms.

Prescott has a golden history—in fact, when the miners prospecting for gold hit pay dirt in 1863, the cash-poor Union designated Arizona as a U.S. territory. President Abraham Lincoln chose an area just north of Prescott as the first seat of government because the gold fields were nearby. In 1867, the capital was moved to Tucson; the capital returned to Prescott ten years later, but in 1889 it moved permanently to Phoenix. Surrounded by pine forests instead of desert, most buildings were wooden structures rather than the adobe of the Sonoran desert. There are plenty of mountains around Prescott, the Prescott National Forest encircles the city, and there are plenty of opportunities to camp, ride horseback, hike, fish and picnic.

Days Inn of Prescott Valley

7875 East Highway 69
Prescott Valley, AZ 86314
800-329-7466 • 520-772-8600

Type of Lodging: Motel
Room Rates: $59–$85, including continental breakfast. AAA, AARP and *10% Pets Welcome™* discounts.
Pet Charges & Deposits: $50 refundable deposit.
Pet Policy: None. All Pets Welcome.
Amenities: Cable TV, pool, hot tubs.
Pet Amenities: List of nearby veterinarians maintained. Mountain Valley Park is located off Robert Road.
Rated: 3 Paws — 56 rooms and 3 suites. Award-Winning Motel.

Days Inn has ample RV and bus parking, 24-hour coffee and tea service and a meeting room for up to 50 people. It's only eight miles to Prescott's historic "Whiskey Row," where old-timers used to "belly up to the bar" at 40 saloons within the city—one by one. Jerome, Arizona's liveliest ghost town is 30 miles away and Sedona is less than an hour away. There's a family fun park and Young's Family Farm in the immediate area and if golf is your passion, you're in luck here: there are several public golf courses nearby.

Days Inn

520 East Highway 70
Safford, AZ 85546
800-DAYS INN • 520-428-5000

Type of Lodging: Hotel

Room Rates: $65–$120, including continental breakfast. AAA and AARP discounts.

Pet Charges & Deposits: $20 per stay. $20 refundable deposit.

Pet Policy: None. All Pets Welcome.

Amenities: Cable TV, refrigerators, microwaves, pool, spa, restaurants, lounge, guest laundry.

Pet Amenities: List of nearby veterinarians maintained. Exercise area. Safford City Park is located on the block of 10th and 11th Streets and West Highway 70.

Rated: 3 Paws — 41 rooms and 2 suites.

Safford, founded in 1874 by farmers whose previous holdings had been washed away by the Gila River, was the first American settlement in the Gila Valley. It's 36 miles from the valley to the top of 10,720-foot Mount Graham. If you're driving there, you'll traverse five of the seven ecological zones in Western North America. The region south of Safford has hot mineral baths and rockhound areas that allow you to seek and gather agates, chalcedony roses and fire agates. Days Inn is a convenient, lovely accommodation that allows you to take advantage of all these things. The property has two restaurants and a cocktail lounge, guest laundry, voicemail, dataports, an outdoor pool and spa.

Ramada Inn Spa Resort

420 East Highway 70
Safford, AZ 85546
877-RAMADA-8 • 520-428-3200
www.ramadainn-sparesort.com
ramadainn@uswestmail.net

Type of Lodging: Hotel

Room Rates: $80–$150, including continental breakfast. AAA and AARP discounts.

Pet Charges & Deposits: $20 per stay. $20 refundable deposit.

Amenities: Cable TV, refrigerators, microwaves, safes, pool, whirlpool, pizza parlor, lounge.

Pet Amenities: List of nearby veterinarians maintained. Exercise area. Safford City Park is located on the block between 10th and 11th Streets and West Highway 70.

Rated: 4 Paws — 96 rooms and 6 suites. 1998–1999 Ramada Inn of the Year. Two-Time Gold Key Award Winner.

Ramada Inn Spa Resort is within walking distance to a driving range and putting green. There's a four-plex theater and family dining close by. Ramada boasts a 20-person hydrotherapy pool, cedar-lined his and hers saunas, a shuffleboard court, horseshoe pit, five-hole putting green and 2,100 square feet of banquet and meeting space, with top-of-the-line electronic and video equipment to help make any conference or presentation a big success.

Hampton Inn – Old Town

4415 North Civic Center Plaza
Scottsdale, AZ 85251
800-HAMPTON • 480-941-9400
www.amdest.com/az/scottsdale/hi/
  hampton.html

Type of Lodging: Hotel
Room Rates: $39–$155, including continental breakfast. AAA, AARP, ABA discounts.
Pet Charges & Deposits: $50 per stay (50% discount on charge when mentioning Pets Welcome).
Pet Policy: None. All Pets Welcome.
Amenities: Cable TV, safes, pool.
Pet Amenities: Dog biscuits at check-in. List of nearby veterinarians maintained. Exercise area. Indian School Park is located at 4289 North Hayden Road. Chaparral Park is located at 5401 North Hayden and has dog runs.
Rated: 4 Paws – 113 rooms and 13 suites.

Hampton Inn is in the very heart of Scottsdale, located 4 blocks from Fashion Square Mall and ¼ mile to the Fifth Avenue shops and Old Town Scottsdale. The amenities are virtually limitless: free newspaper, free local and long-distance access calls, free cable television, coffeemakers, irons and ironing boards and guest laundry. Aside from the fact that Scottsdale is surrounded by Phoenix, it has its own plethora of attractions: the San Francisco Giants Spring Training Camp, Arizona State University, Sun Devil Stadium, Phoenix Zoo and Desert Botanical Gardens. There are many resort and public golf courses within a 30-minute drive and numerous casinos within a five-mile radius. What a vacation paradise!

Homestead Village Guest Studios

3560 North Marshall Way
Scottsdale, AZ 85251
480-994-0297
www.stayhsd.com

Type of Lodging: Hotel
Suite Rates: $39–$91.
Pet Charges & Deposits: $75 per stay.
Pet Policy: None. All Pets Welcome.
Amenities: Cable TV, fully equipped kitchens, guest laundry.
Pet Amenities: None.
Rated: 4 Paws – 121 suites.

Designed for extended stay travelers, each studio room features a kitchen—something you won't find in a typical hotel. Not only do you find a kitchen with full-size refrigerator, microwave, stovetop, cooking and dining utensils, you'll also find a workspace with dataports, voicemail, free local calls and long distance access, an iron and ironing board, guest laundry and fitness club access. The hotel is a short block off Scottsdale Road. Scottsdale is the "Not-So-Wild" West— where everything is "dude-friendly." The whole of the Valley of the Sun is at your disposal—and, of course, your pet's disposal as well.

InnSuites Hotel

7707 East McDowell Road
Scottsdale, AZ 85257
800-238-8851• 480-941-1202
www.innsuites.com
Scottsdale@innsuites.com

Type of Lodging: Hotel

Suite Rates: $49–$99, including breakfast buffet, evening social hour and Wednesday Night Manager's BBQ. AAA, AARP and *10% Pets Welcome™* discounts.

Pet Charges & Deposits: $50 refundable deposit.

Pet Policy: No pets over 50 lbs. Designated rooms only.

Amenities: Cable TV, refrigerators, microwaves, pool, whirlpool, fitness center.

Pet Amenities: Eldorado Park is located at 77th Street and McDowell Road.

Rated: 2 Paws — 121 suites.

InnSuites Hotel is nestled in the heart of Scottsdale, overlooking quiet, picturesque Eldorado Park. Adjacent to the Coronado and Continental Golf Courses, InnSuites offers guests free airport shuttle to and from Phoenix Sky Harbor Airport (six minutes from the Hotel). Free local calls, free morning paper, cable television and free bicycles for rides in Eldorado Park are added bonuses. P.J.'s Café is open for breakfast, lunch and dinner. There's a fitness center on the property—and it's minutes to anywhere in the Valley of the Sun.

Ramada Valley Ho Resort

6850 Main Street
Scottsdale, AZ 85251
800-321-4952 • 480-945-6321
www.scottsdalevalleyho.com
ramada@getnet.com

Type of Lodging: Inn

Room Rates: $59–$129. AAA and AARP discounts.

Pet Charges & Deposits: $25 nonrefundable deposit.

Pet Policy: Limit one pet per room.

Amenities: Cable TV, refrigerators, pool, Jacuzzi, restaurant.

Pet Amenities: List of nearby veterinarians maintained. Exercise area including 14 acres for walking your pet.

Rated: 3 Paws — 251 rooms and 50 suites.

Ramada Valley Ho Resort is located in the heart of Old Town Scottsdale, near some of the finest dining, shopping and golfing in the state. There's a complimentary airport shuttle. Each room and suite offers a king-sized or two double beds and cable television. All rooms have private balconies or patios. Summerfield's Restaurant and Lounge features delicious American food in a relaxed, Southwestern atmosphere—it's conveniently located adjacent to the main lobby.

Best Western Inn of Sedona

1200 West Highway 89A
Sedona, AZ 86336
800-292-6344 • 520-282-3072
www.innofsedona.com
innofsedona@sedona.net

Type of Lodging: Motel

Room Rates: $100–$135, including continental breakfast. AAA, AARP and *10% Pets Welcome™* discounts.

Pet Charges & Deposits: $10 per stay.

Pet Policy: Designated rooms only. Manager's prior approval required.

Amenities: Cable TV, refrigerators, pool, Jacuzzi.

Pet Amenities: List of nearby veterinarians maintained. Exercise area.

Rated: 3 Paws — 110 rooms.

The Inn of Sedona is a strikingly attractive three-story Southwestern-style building, in the shadow of the stunning Red Rock country. The view as you drive into the parking lot is a "must see to be believed." Activities in the area vary from hot air balloon rides to helicopter rides to horseback rides to exploring ancient Native American ruins. The Grand Canyon is within an easy day's drive. Then there are the gift shops, exclusive art galleries, hiking, biking, jeep tours, fishing, golfing…all in one of the most beautiful areas in the world.

Oak Creek Terrace Resort

4548 North Highway 89A
Sedona, AZ 86336
800-224-2229 • 520-282-3562
www.oakcreekterrace.com
octresor@sedona.net

Type of Lodging: Motel & Resort

Room Rates: $72–$165. AAA and AARP discounts.

Pet Charges & Deposits: $25 nonrefundable deposit.

Pet Policy: Sorry, no cats. No pets over 25 lbs. Designated rooms only. Pets must be on leash.

Amenities: Cable TV, refrigerators, microwaves, Jacuzzis, fireplaces, VCRs.

Pet Amenities: List of nearby veterinarians maintained.

Rated: 2 Paws — 11 rooms and 6 suites.

Oak Creek Terrace Resort is located five miles north of Sedona in the exquisite Oak Creek Canyon. The Resort features on-site Jeep rentals and nearby activities are limitless: Native American ruins, horseback riding, golf, fishing, biking, train rides, hiking. The Resort has in-room Jacuzzis and fireplaces. Relax by the creek in double hammocks and swings—or bring your fishing pole because the creek is well stocked with trout. A marvelous holiday venue for you and your pet.

Sedona Super 8 Motel

2545 West Highway 89A
Sedona, AZ 86336
800-858-7245 • 520-282-1533
www.sedonasuper8.com
super8@sedona.net

Type of Lodging: Motel

Room Rates: $55–$99. AAA discount.

Pet Charges & Deposits: Call for refundable deposit.

Pet Policy: No pets over 15 lbs. Designated rooms only.

Amenities: Pool, restaurant.

Pet Amenities: List of nearby veterinarians maintained. Exercise area. Park nearby.

Rated: 2 Paws — 66 rooms. Pride of Super 8 Property Award Winner.

Situated in the heart of one of the world's true beauty spots, Super 8 has private spa rooms, a restaurant and conference rooms. Tennis, hiking, fishing, sightseeing, over 40 art galleries, shopping, dining (fast food to gourmet) and an 18-hole championship golf course are minutes away. Backcountry Jeep tours and Legends of Sedona Ranch horseback rides are highlights of this remarkable, ever-changing area.

Best Western Mission Inn

3460 East Fry Boulevard
Sierra Vista, AZ 85635
877-937-8386 • 520-458-8500

Type of Lodging: Motel

Room Rates: $65–$85, including continental breakfast. AAA, AARP, Military, Government, Corporate and **10% Pets Welcome™** discounts.

Pet Charges & Deposits: If pets are not declared at check-in, $10 per day charge will be added.

Pet Policy: No pets over 50 lbs. Cats allowed only if in carriers. Limit one pet per room. Manager's prior approval required.

Amenities: Cable TV, refrigerators, microwaves, pool, guest laundry.

Pet Amenities: Exercise area. Veterans Park is across the street.

Rated: 3 Paws — 40 rooms.

Best Western Mission Inn is in historic Cochise County, near Fort Huachuca, one of the largest employers in the southwest. The Kartchner Caverns, Tombstone, Bisbee, the Coronado National Monument and Bird Watchers Paradise are all nearby. Nogales, Mexico is an hour southwest. Mission Inn has airy rooms with double vanities. Amenities include kids stay free in their parents' room, dataports and guest laundry. This is Apache country, the Old West as it really was, but with the modern feel of the Best Western chain.

Super 8 Motel

100 Fab Avenue
Sierra Vista, AZ 85635
800-800-8000 • 520-459-5380
www.innworks.com

Type of Lodging: Motel

Room Rates: $45–$65, including continental breakfast. AAA and AARP discounts.

Pet Charges & Deposits: $10 per stay.

Pet Policy: Sorry, no cats. Manager's prior approval required.

Amenities: Cable TV, refrigerators, safes, pool, one free 8-minute long distance call each night.

Pet Amenities: Exercise area.

Rated: 2 Paws — 52 rooms.

Sierra Vista, at an elevation of 4,600 feet, is close to the historic past of giant Fort Huachuca. Nestled on the eastern slopes of the Huachuca Mountains, the city overlooks the San Pedro River Valley. The Coronado National Memorial, San Pedro Riparian Conservation area and Ramsey Canyon Preserve attract nature lovers year-round. Super 8 is located just off the main entrance to Fort Huachuca. The two-story motel has reasonable prices and is a fine starting point from which to explore the wonders of nature.

Windemere Hotel & Conference Center

2047 South Highway 92
Sierra Vista, AZ 85635
800-825-4656 • 520-459-5900
www.windemere-hotel.com
reservations@windemere-hotel.com

Type of Lodging: Hotel

Room Rates: $73–$86, including full breakfast buffet. AAA, AARP, Corporate, Military and *10% Pets Welcome™* discounts.

Pet Charges & Deposits: $50 refundable deposit.

Pet Policy: None. All Pets Welcome.

Amenities: Cable TV, refrigerators, microwaves, honor bars, safes, pool, whirlpool, hot tubs, coffeemakers, irons and ironing boards, hairdryers.

Pet Amenities: List of nearby veterinarians, Exercise area. Kartchner Caverns State Park is located off Highway 90 in Benson and Coronado National Memorial Park is nearby.

Rated: 4 Paws — 149 rooms and 3 suites.

The Windemere Hotel offers spacious guestrooms, either with mountain views or with views of the inviting pool. All rooms feature voicemail, electronic door locks and beautiful amenities. There's a large convention center with multiple meeting rooms. The Windemere is host to Schooners' Restaurant and Oyster Club, Sierra Vista's most notable fine dining and seafood restaurant—and its only oyster bar. Fort Huachuca, a National Historic Landmark, is home to the U.S. Army Intelligence Center and School. The Old West, from Tombstone to Bisbee, the Kartchner Caverns, Ramsey Canyon and old Mexico are within easy striking distance.

Super 8 Motel

75 East Commercial Street
P.O. Box 1920
St. Johns, AZ 85936-1920
800-800-8000 • 520-337-2990

Type of Lodging: Motel

Room Rates: $36–$44, including toast bar, coffee and tea. AAA, AARP and *10% Pets Welcome*™ discounts.

Pet Charges & Deposits: $25 refundable deposit.

Pet Policy: None. All Pets Welcome.

Amenities: Cable TV, refrigerators, microwaves.

Pet Amenities: City park is only 5 blocks away.

Rated: 2 Paws — 31 rooms.

The Petrified Forest is 40 miles away and the Painted Desert is 30 miles distant. The Apache County Historical Society Museum displays pioneer artifacts, mammoth bones, Native American artifacts, antique guns and slot machines. Lyman Lake State Park, ten miles south, is an area of rolling grassland that's home to a small buffalo herd. The lake boasts water skiing in summer months and since St. Johns is 5,650 feet above sea level, you might want to bring a coat or jacket, even during the summer months. Rooms at the Super 8 are generously proportioned and pleasant. It's less than an hour to the Sunrise Ski Area.

Quality Inn & Suites

16741 North Greasewood Street
Surprise, AZ 85374
800-228-5151 • 623-583-3500
www.qualityinn.com/hotel/AZ118

Type of Lodging: Hotel

Room Rates: $59–$109, including continental breakfast. AAA, AARP, AKC and *10% Pets Welcome*™ discounts.

Pet Charges & Deposits: $5 per day.

Pet Policy: No pets over 25 lbs. Designated rooms only. Manager's prior approval required.

Amenities: Cable TV, refrigerators, microwaves, safes, pool, spa, fitness room.

Pet Amenities: None.

Rated: 3 Paws — 69 rooms and suites.

Quality Inn's location could hardly be better for your Phoenix-Sun City vacation. It's 45 minutes to downtown Phoenix or Sky Harbor Airport, ten minutes to the Sun City Sundome, 15 minutes to Arrowhead Mall or the Peoria Sportsplex. The Inn is convenient to Sun City, Sun City West, Luke Air Force Base and features complimentary in-room coffee, guest laundry and a small meeting room. The attractive three-story building has interior corridors for security and safety.

Silver Creek Inn

825 North Main Street
P.O. Box 980
Taylor, AZ 85939
888-246-5440 • 520-536-2600
sci@cybertrails.com

Type of Lodging: Motel
Room Rates: $46–$76, including continental breakfast. AAA, AARP and *10% Pets Welcome*™ discounts.
Pet Charges & Deposits: $10 per stay. $10 nonrefundable deposit.
Pet Policy: No pets over 25 lbs. Manager's prior approval required.
Amenities: Cable TV, refrigerators, microwaves, Jacuzzi, spa, fitness room.
Pet Amenities: None.
Rated: 2 Paws — 42 rooms

During the summer of 1878, hardy Mormon pioneers settled on the Stinson Ranch. In that same year, Taylor and Snowflake (actually named after Erastas Snow and William J. Flake) became town sites. Today, the two towns—sister communities—share many joint social activities, including the July 24th Pioneer Days Celebration with BBQs, a family rodeo, a parade and softball tournaments. Taylor and Snowflake are located in an area of unusual contrasts—high, barren deserts to the north and great mountain ranges to the south. The Petrified Forest National Park encompasses the Petrified Forest, Painted Desert and Navajo Native American Reservation. To the south and west, hike and explore the natural beauty of the White Mountains, Sitgreaves National Forest and the spectacular Mogollon Rim. There's plenty of fishing during the summer and ample skiing during the winter.

Ghost Ranch Lodge

801 West Miracle Mile
Tucson, AZ 85705
800-456-7565 • 520-791-7565
www.ghostlodge.com
ghstranch@aol.com

Type of Lodging: Motel
Room Rates: $42–$98, including continental breakfast. AAA, AARP and *10% Pets Welcome*™ discounts.
Pet Charges & Deposits: None.
Pet Policy: None. All Pets Welcome.
Amenities: Cable TV, pool, whirlpool.
Pet Amenities: List of nearby veterinarians maintained. Dog runs. Exercise area. Jacobs Park is located at Fairview and Prince Roads.
Rated: 4 Paws — 70 rooms and 13 suites.

Old West meets Southwestern tomorrow. The Ghost Ranch Lodge is a long-established, centrally located one-story facility with eight acres of attractively landscaped grounds and a cactus garden. Most rooms surround the garden. Old Tucson Studios is a Wild West frontier outpost playland, while Biosphere 2 Center and Kitt Peak National Observatory are renowned innovative institutions. Mission San Xavier del Bac, nine miles south, the "White Dove of the Desert," is a magnificent, snow white example of Spanish mission architecture, which was built in the years between 1783 and 1797. Old Mexico, Nogales, is a little more than an hour away.

The Golf Villas at Oro Valley

10950 North La Cañada
Tucson, AZ 85737
888-388-0098 • 520-498-0098
www.thegolfvillas.com

Type of Lodging: Guest Ranch & Condominium Resort

Suite Rates: $99–$499, including welcome basket. AAA, AARP and *10% Pets Welcome*™ discounts.

Pet Charges & Deposits: Call for refundable deposit.

Pet Policy: No pets over 50 lbs.

Amenities: Cable TV, refrigerators, microwaves, pool, whirlpool, Jacuzzi, spa, country club privileges.

Pet Amenities: List of nearby veterinarians maintained. Exercise area. Saguaro National Park; Catalina State Park and Tohono Chul Park nearby.

Rated: 4 Paws — 89 suites.

The Golf Villas at Oro Valley is Arizona's only AAA Four-Diamond rated condominium resort. Here you'll find all the luxuries and amenities of a world-class resort with the added convenience of spacious condominium-style villas. Championship golf courses are so close at hand: Tucson National, home of the PGA Tour Tucson Open and The Raven at Sabino Springs. Desert Jeep tours, horseback riding, hot air ballooning, bird watching—it's all here, in the city that averages more than 350 days of sunshine each year, with daytime temperatures averaging 70 degrees. The area's low humidity and clear skies make for truly breathtaking sunsets and spectacular star-filled nights.

Holiday Inn City Center

181 West Broadway
Tucson, AZ 85701
800-448-8276 • 520-624-8711
www.holidayinntucson.com
hitucson1@aol.com

Type of Lodging: Hotel

Room Rates: $59–$250. AAA, AARP and *10% Pets Welcome*™ discounts.

Pet Charges & Deposits: $50 refundable deposit.

Pet Policy: None. All Pets Welcome.

Amenities: Cable TV, refrigerators, microwaves, pool.

Pet Amenities: List of nearby veterinarians maintained. Exercise area. Saguaro National Park nearby.

Rated: 3 Paws — 300 rooms and 9 suites.

The Holiday Inn is a spectacular 12-story high-rise lodging, as centrally located as you can get—with incredible city views to boot. Less than ten miles from Tucson International Airport, it's adjacent to the Tucson Convention Center complex, within the Historic and Arts Districts and across from the Federal and State government buildings. The University of Arizona campus is ten minutes away. The hotel's Coyote Café serves breakfast, lunch and dinner. All of the wonders of Tucson are at your fingertips.

Loews Ventana Canyon Resort

7000 North Resort Drive
Tucson, AZ 85750
800-234-5117 • 520-299-2020
www.loewshotels.com
loews@azstarnet.com

Type of Lodging: Resort

Room Rates: $110–$345. AAA, AARP, AKC and ABA discounts.

Pet Charges & Deposits: None.

Pet Policy: Designated rooms only.

Amenities: Cable TV, honor bar, safes, pool, Jacuzzi, robes.

Pet Amenities: Placemat, pet treats, food and water bowl provided for the four-legged guests. List of nearby veterinarians maintained. Exercise area. Udall Park is located at Tanque Verde and Sabino Canyon. Sabino Canyon Recreation Area nearby. On-site hiking and nature trails.

Rated: 5 Paws — 371 rooms and 27 suites.

The Loews Ventana Canyon Resort is superbly situated at the foot of the Catalina Mountains. There are two heated pools, saunas, steam rooms, whirlpools and a playground. For a fee, you can play the 18-hole golf course, play on eight lighted tennis courts or enjoy a relaxing massage. The three- and four-story structures blend in perfectly with the naturally beautiful area. Loews is located 13 miles northeast of downtown Tucson.

Rodeway Inn

1365 West Grant Road
Tucson, AZ 85745
800-228-2000 • 520-622-7791
www.zmchotel.com

Type of Lodging: Motel

Room Rates: $49–$109, including continental breakfast. AAA and AARP discounts.

Pet Charges & Deposits: $10 per stay.

Pet Policy: None. All Pets Welcome.

Amenities: Cable TV, refrigerators, pool, whirlpool, lounge, fitness room.

Pet Amenities: Exercise area. Jacobs Park is located at Fairview and Prince Roads.

Rated: 3 Paws — 146 rooms

Rodeway Inn is convenient to the University of Arizona, Sonora Desert Museum, Old Tucson, Biosphere 2 and Santa Cruz River Walk. In less than 20 minutes, you can stand in the same spot where your favorite Western movie star stood—see a reenactment of an Old West shoot-out at Old Tucson. Enjoy fascinating native plants and wildlife as you tour the world-famous Sonoran Desert Museum. Experience the excitement of nearby casinos or watch the horses run at Rillito Park.

Mountain Side Inn

642 East Route 66
Williams, AZ 86046
800-462-9381 • 520-635-4431
www.mtsideinn.com
mtside@bmol.com

Type of Lodging: Inn

Room Rates: $49–$86. AAA and AARP discounts.

Pet Charges & Deposits: $10 per day.

Pet Policy: Sorry, no cats. Designated rooms only.

Amenities: Cable TV, safes, pool, whirlpool, restaurant, lounge.

Pet Amenities: Exercise area. Bill Williams Monument Park is located on Railroad Avenue.

Rated: 3 Paws — 95 rooms and 1 suite.

Williams was named after Bill Williams, an early mountain man who guided trappers through the wilderness. Today, it's a small resort town at the base of Bill Williams Mountain (downhill and cross-country skiing), at an elevation of 6,752 feet above sea level. It's at the beginning of the major entrance to Grand Canyon National Park. Your pet will love the surrounding Kaibab National Forest. Mountain Side Inn boasts Miss Kitty's Western Steakhouse, with free live entertainment and dancing nightly. Outdoor family activities and games complete the picture of a wonderful vacation destination.

Holiday Inn Express

816 Transcon Lane
Winslow, AZ 86047
520-289-2960
holliney@winslow-az.net

Type of Lodging: Hotel

Room Rates: $60–$85, including full complimentary breakfast. AAA, AARP and *10% Pets Welcome™* discounts.

Pet Charges & Deposits: $20 refundable deposit for large dogs only.

Pet Policy: Designated rooms for large dogs only.

Amenities: Cable TV, refrigerators, microwaves, pool, whirlpool.

Pet Amenities: List of nearby veterinarians maintained. Dog runs. Exercise area. Winslow City Park is only ½ mile away. Standing on a Corner Park is only 2 miles away.

Rated: 3 Paws — 53 rooms and 4 suites

Just 22 miles west of Winslow, you'll come to Meteor Crater, one of nature's most spectacular sites. The vast crater, 550 feet deep, nearly one mile across and 2.4 miles in circumference, was formed nearly 50,000 years ago when a meteorite, estimated to have been 150 feet across and weighing several hundred thousand tons, slammed into the rocky plain. Because the terrain is very similar to that of the moon, NASA once trained Apollo astronauts here. The Homolovi Ruins State Park, three miles east of Winslow, is situated on 4,000 acres containing more than 300 archeological sites, including pueblo ruins and petroglyphs. Winslow is a railroad center as well as an important shipping and trading locale.

Best Western Coronado

233 Fourth Avenue
Yuma, AZ 85364
877-234-5567 • 520-783-4453
www.bwcoronado.com
ypeach@bwcoronado.com

Type of Lodging: Hotel

Room Rates: $60–$90, including full breakfast. AAA and AARP discounts.

Pet Charges & Deposits: None.

Pet Policy: No pets over 15 lbs. Designated rooms only.

Amenities: Cable TV, refrigerators, microwaves, safes, pool, Jacuzzis, dataports.

Pet Amenities: List of nearby veterinarians maintained. Exercise area. Colorado River Park nearby.

Rated: 3 Paws — 86 rooms and 20 suites.

This long-established lodging has a variety of accommodations, from cozy to large. All rooms are nicely furnished. The Yuma Landing Restaurant, "Good Food at a Price That's Nice," is next door. Located two blocks from the historic district, you can visit Yuma Crossing State Historical Park, where the U.S. Army Quartermaster Depot stored and distributed supplies from 1864 through 1883, or Yuma Territorial Prison State Historic Park. The Colorado River, and California, is a stone's throw away.

Best Western InnSuites Hotel

1450 Castle Dome Avenue
Yuma, AZ 85364
800-922-2034 • 520-783-8341
http://insuites.com
isyuma@attmail.com

Type of Lodging: Hotel

Suite Rates: $74–$144, including full breakfast, evening social hour and Wednesday Night Manager's BBQ. AAA, AARP, Corporate and Government discounts.

Pet Charges & Deposits: $25 refundable deposit.

Pet Policy: Manager's prior approval required.

Amenities: Cable TV, refrigerators, safes, pool, Jacuzzi, tennis courts, business center.

Pet Amenities: List of nearby veterinarians maintained. Dog runs. Exercise area. Parks nearby.

Rated: 3 Paws — 166 suites.

Best Western InnSuites Hotel, "your suite choice," features a complimentary breakfast buffet, fax and copy service, unlimited local calls, two lighted tennis courts and P.J.'s Poolside Café. Close to Yuma Territorial Prison Historic Park, the Century House Museum, Quechan Native America Museum, Fort Yuma and the Yuma Art Center, this is surely one of the most comfortable and inviting lodgings in the area. Old Mexico's a mere 23 miles away.

Holiday Inn Express

3181 South Fourth Avenue
Yuma, AZ 85364
877-800-6689 • 520-344-1420

Type of Lodging: Motel

Room Rates: $89–$99, including continental breakfast and Manager's Cocktail Party. AAA, AARP and *10% Pets Welcome™* discounts.

Pet Charges & Deposits: None.

Pet Policy: No pets over 75 lbs.

Amenities: Cable TV, refrigerators, microwaves, safes, pool, Jacuzzi.

Pet Amenities: List of nearby veterinarians maintained. Exercise area. Local Park is across the street from the motel.

Rated: 3 Paws — 120 rooms.

Holiday Inn Express is conveniently located on the Interstate 8 Business Loop. Bathrooms have a full bath with tub and shower. There's a telephone with dataport capability next to every bed. Travelers may take advantage of fax service, free local calls and small meeting capabilities. San Luis, Mexico is only 23 miles away. Enjoy boating and fishing on the Colorado River. There are beautifully manicured golf courses and the famous California Sand Dunes nearby.

Shilo Inn Conference Hotel

1550 South Castle Dome Road
Yuma, AZ 85365
800-222-2244 • 520-782-9511
www.shiloinns.com
yuma@shiloinns.com

Type of Lodging: Hotel

Room Rates: $91–$255, including full breakfast buffet. AAA and AARP discounts.

Pet Charges & Deposits: $10 per day. $50 refundable deposit.

Pet Policy: No pets over 25 lbs. Designated rooms only. Manager's prior approval required.

Amenities: Cable TV, refrigerators, microwaves, fitness room, steam room, guest laundry.

Pet Amenities: Pet beds and treats provided. List of nearby veterinarians maintained. Exercise area.

Rated: 3 Paws — 134 rooms and 15 suites.

Situated in the heart of the "American Sahara," seven minutes from Algodones, Mexico, Shilo Inn Conference Hotel offers graceful southwestern furnishings in a beautiful, four-story hotel on landscaped grounds. Start your day off with a complimentary newspaper and a full breakfast buffet. Yuma enjoys a sunny, dry climate, with winter temperatures in the 70s and sunshine 93% of the time. Martinez Lake, the "Water Wonderland in the Desert," affords excellent fishing, boating and water skiing. It's located 35 miles north on Highway 95. Lemons, oranges, tangelos, grapefruit, mandarins, tangerines, limes and dates have been grown for many years in this area. Some orchards have shops on the grounds where you can buy produce almost as soon as it is picked.

ARKANSAS

Nicknames: The Natural State; Razorback State

Population: 2,551,373

Area: 53,182 square miles

Climate: Long, hot summers, mild winters, generally abundant rainfall.

Capital: Little Rock

Entered Union: June 15, 1836

Motto: *Regnat Populus* (The People Rule).

Song: Arkansas

Flower: Apple Blossom

Tree: Pine

Bird: Mockingbird

Famous Arkansans: Glen Campbell, Johnny Cash, Bill Clinton, Dizzy Dean, James W. Fulbright, John Grisham, Douglas MacArthur, Scottie Pippen.

 History: Quapaw, Caddo, Osage, Cherokee and Choctaw peoples lived in the area at the time of the first European contact. It was part of the Louisiana Purchase in 1803. In 1819, it became a territory. Arkansas seceded only after the Civil War had begun. More than 10,000 Arkansans fought on the Union side. Arkansas made history during the early days of the Civil Rights movement, when Little Rock's schools were integrated over the objection of then Governor Orval Faubus. It was dramatically thrust into the spotlight in 1992, when native William Jefferson "Bill" Clinton became U.S. President.

Ramada Inn

16732 Interstate 30, Exit 117
Benton, AR 72015
501-776-1900
www.ramada.com

Type of Lodging: Motel

Room Rates: $49–$149, including free coffee. AAA, AARP and *10% Pets Welcome*™ discounts.

Pet Charges & Deposits: $6 per day.

Pet Policy: No pets over 20 lbs. Designated rooms only.

Amenities: Cable TV, refrigerators, microwaves, pool.

Pet Amenities: List of nearby veterinarians maintained. Exercise area. Tyndall Park nearby.

Rated: 3 Paws — 104 rooms and 2 suites.

Located in a suburb of Little Rock, approximately equidistant from the center of Arkansas' largest city, Hot Springs National Park and the Ouachita Mountains, Benton is close to the center of the state. The staff is pleased to welcome you and your pet to "the Natural State."

Alpen Dorf Motel

6554 Highway 62
Eureka Springs, AR 72632
800-771-9876 • 501-253-9475
www.eureka-usa.com/alpendorf
alpdorf@nwaft.com

Type of Lodging: Motel

Room Rates: $27–$120, including continental breakfast. AARP discount.

Pet Charges & Deposits: $5 per day.

Pet Policy: Designated rooms only.

Amenities: Cable TV, refrigerators, microwaves, pool, Jacuzzis, playground, picnic area.

Pet Amenities: List of nearby veterinarians maintained. Lake Leatherwood and Harmon Park nearby.

Rated: 3 Paws — 26 rooms and 4 suites.

Family owned and operated, the Alpen Dorf Motel is a tranquil hideaway, where you can listen to the sounds of nature in comfortably furnished accommodations in a quiet country setting, yet still be close to the center of Eureka Springs' excitement. The Motel is one mile east of The Great Passion Play. Most rooms look onto the peaceful Ozark Mountains. The Honeymoon Suite features a Roman marble Jacuzzi tub for two. Nearby is the New Holy Land Tour, a 50-acre tract that recreates the features of the region where Christ lived.

Best Western Inn Of The Ozarks

Highway 62 West
P.O. Box 431
Eureka Springs, AR 72632
800-552-3785 • 501-253-9768
www.eureka-usa.com/bestinn
bestinn@ipa.net

Type of Lodging: Resort

Room Rates: $49–$99. AAA and AARP discounts.

Pet Charges & Deposits: None.

Pet Policy: Pets must not be left unattended in room.

Amenities: Cable TV, pool, whirlpool, restaurant.

Pet Amenities: List of nearby veterinarians maintained. Exercise area.

Rated: 3 Paws — 118 rooms and 4 suites.

Singles, couples, families, tour groups, conventions—Inn of the Ozarks rolls out the red carpet for everyone. The employees have been with the Inn for years—they anticipate and take care of your every need. The resort features Myrtie Mae's Restaurant as well as the Forest Manor Dining Room. Tennis, miniature golf, a large family game room shuffleboard and, of course, room for your pet to roam with you.

Carriage Inn at Busch Mountain

20856 Highway 62 West
Eureka Springs, AR 72631
800-255-8828 • 501-253-8828
www.thecarriageinn.com
carriage@ipa.net

Type of Lodging: B&B

Suite Rates: $100–$129, including full breakfast. *10% Pets Welcome™* discount.

Pet Charges & Deposits: None.

Pet Policy: Sorry, no cats. Small pets only. Manager's prior approval required.

Amenities: Refrigerators, microwaves, Jacuzzi, antiques.

Pet Amenities: List of nearby veterinarians maintained. Exercise area. Beaver Lake Park and White River Park nearby.

Rated: 3 Paws — 3 suites.

Nestled among the hills and valleys of the Ozark Mountains, the Carriage Inn, with its vaulted ceilings, gracefully exposed beams and other fascinating architectural features, has three secluded, tasteful guest suites. This unique lodging was an actual working carriage house in the early 1900s. Each suite is furnished with antiques. There are porch swings for you to relax in while you enjoy the mountain scenery. Chilled wine awaits your arrival. For guests looking to cook on their own, the inn provides a microwave, refrigerator and coffeemaker with an assortment of delicious coffees, teas and hot chocolate. Enjoy the attractions in nearby Eureka Springs. You can even visit an historic Civil War battlefield 11 miles away.

Eureka Sunset Bed & Breakfast

10 Dogwood Ridge
Eureka Springs, AR 72632
888-253-9565 • 501-253-9565
www.eureka-usa.com/sunset
esunset@ipa.net

Type of Lodging: B&B

Suite Rates: $95–$125, including full breakfast.

Pet Charges & Deposits: Call for refundable deposit.

Pet Policy: No pets over 50 lbs.

Amenities: Cable TV, refrigerators, microwaves, Jacuzzi.

Pet Amenities: List of nearby veterinarians maintained. Exercise area. Six wooded acres for walking pets. Lake Leatherwood City Park is located 2 miles west on Highway 62.

Rated: 3 Paws — 2 suites.

Fulfill your fantasy in the mystical, magical kingdom of Eureka Springs. Enjoy solitude amid tall, whispering pines, oaks and dogwoods on acres of pristine natural beauty. Hike to a spring frequented by whitetail deer and elusive wild turkeys. There are two entirely different suites: The Picket Suite with its lofty vaulted ceiling and skylight has a balcony soaring over treetops and a wooded ravine below. Annie's Song is a charming ground-level suite with all the amenities. Both suites have queen beds, luxurious linens and comfy robes. There are wood-burning stone fireplaces and mirrored Jacuzzis for two with separate showers. Candlelight and soft fragrances delight the senses.

Lazee Daze Log Cabin Resort

5432 Highway 23 South
Eureka Springs, AR 72632
800-760-7413 • 501-253-7026
www.logcabinresort.com
lazedaze@ipa.net

Type of Lodging: Resort

Cabin Rates: $110–$245.

Pet Charges & Deposits: $50 deposit of which $30 is refundable.

Pet Policy: Sorry, no cats. Manager's prior approval required. Pets must not be left unattended.

Amenities: Fully equipped kitchens, Jacuzzi, hot tubs, spas, fireplaces, BBQs.

Pet Amenities: List of nearby veterinarians maintained. Withrow Springs State Park on Highway 23.

Rated: 2 Paws — 6 cabins on 63 wooded acres.

The cabins are of log construction, romantically rustic and located on 63 wooded acres. Some of them have intricate, hand-carved woodwork and wood-burning fireplaces. The cabins are located among the peaceful quiet and the magnificent vistas of the Ozark Mountains. There are numerous hiking trails in the area. The Last Precinct Police Museum depicts the history of the police officer, beginning with crime fighting in the Wild West and progressing to the present. Numerous Victorian mansions abound in the area.

Roadrunner Inn

3034 Mundell Road
Eureka Springs, AR 72631
888-253-8166 • 501-253-8166
www.eureka-springs-usa.com/
 roadrunner
roadrunner@ipa.net

Type of Lodging: Motel
Room Rates: $29–$47. AARP discount.
Pet Charges & Deposits: None.
Pet Policy: Sorry, no cats. Designated rooms only. Manager's prior approval required. Pets must not be left unattended.
Amenities: Kitchenettes.
Pet Amenities: List of nearby veterinarians maintained. Exercise area. Starkey Park is located a mile away on Mundell Road.
Rated: 3 Paws — 12 rooms.

The Roadrunner is located on a peninsula surrounded by beautiful Beaver Lake, atop a ridge some 300 feet above lake level. This provides spectacular views from each guestroom. Twenty minutes by country road from Eureka Springs, the Roadrunner's location is very secluded and quiet, away from traffic and noise. The motel is situated on a State of Arkansas and National Wildlife Federation Certified Backyard Wildlife Habitat. You can see more than a dozen species of birds as well as deer, armadillo and an occasional fox or raccoon at the Inn's feeding stations.

Best Western of Hope

Interstate 30 and Highway 278
P.O. Box 6611
Hope, AR 71802
800-429-4494 • 870-777-9222

Type of Lodging: Motel
Room Rates: $50–$65, including continental breakfast. AAA, AARP and *10% Pets Welcome*™ discounts.
Pet Charges & Deposits: None.
Pet Policy: None. All Pets Welcome.
Amenities: Refrigerators, microwaves, safes, pool.
Pet Amenities: List of nearby veterinarians maintained. Exercise area. Hope City Park is located on Park Drive.
Rated: 4 Paws — 74 rooms.

Hope is the birthplace of President Bill Clinton, who immortalized it in 1992 when he said, "I still believe in a place called Hope." There's a refrigerator in every room at Best Western and a Western Sizzlin' Restaurant with spacious facilities accommodating up to 250 people. Hope, known as the "Home of the World's Largest Watermelons," celebrates its Watermelon Festival each August.

Box Hound Marina, RV Park & Resort

1313 Tri Lakes Drive
Horseshoe Bend, AR 72512
888-829-5440 • 870-670-4496

Type of Lodging: Cabins

Cabin Rates: $40–$65. $240–$390 per week.

RV Rates: $14–$20 per night. $85 per week. $300 per month.

Pet Charges & Deposits: None.

Pet Policy: None. All Pets Welcome. Horses welcome.

Amenities: Refrigerators, microwaves.

Pet Amenities: List of nearby veterinarians maintained. Exercise area. Ozark National Forest nearby.

Rated: 4 Paws — 4 cabins and 6 RV hookups.

Kick back and find out what the term "rustic" means. Located on beautiful Crown Lake, this is a fisherman's paradise: trophy bass, state-record saugeye, slab crappie, clear water catfish. There are two 18-hole golf courses. The nearby White and Spring Rivers offer some of the best trout fishing in the Ozarks. Enjoy an outdoor cookout with picnic tables and BBQ grills provided.

Hidden Bay Resort

15 County Road 120
Oakland, AR 72661
870-431-8121
www.hiddenbayresort.net
hiddenbayresort@superiorinter.net

Type of Lodging: Resort

Cabin Rates: $45.

Pet Charges & Deposits: $5 per day.

Pet Policy: None. All Pets Welcome.

Amenities: Refrigerators, microwaves, pool.

Pet Amenities: List of nearby veterinarians maintained. Exercise area.

Rated: 3 Paws — 6 cabins on beautiful Bull Shoals Lake.

This fishing and family resort is located in the midst of the Ozark Mountains. Each cabin has two bedrooms with kitchenettes. The resort's park-like grounds offer a swimming pool, covered picnic pavilion with BBQ, freezer, refrigerator, picnic table, chairs and a campfire pit. There are virtually no mosquitoes, but you will see an abundance of wildlife—it's not unusual to see a deer or wild turkey on or around the resort. It's also a bird watcher's paradise with the Bald Eagle returning in the fall. Bull Shoals Lake has more than 49,000 acres of clear water, 1,050 miles of shoreline and it's well known for largemouth, small mouth, Kentucky and white bass, crappie, catfish, bluegill, walleye, rainbow trout and striper.

Baymont Inn & Suites

5102 North Stateline Avenue
Texarkana, AR 71854
800-301-0200 • 870-773-1000
www.baymontinns.com

Type of Lodging: Inn

Room Rates: $49–$104, including continental breakfast. AAA, AARP, AKC, ABA and *10% Pets Welcome™* discounts.

Pet Charges & Deposits: None.

Pet Policy: No pets over 50 lbs.

Amenities: Cable TV, pool, irons and ironing boards, hairdryers, coffeemakers.

Pet Amenities: One of the host hotels for the annual Dog Show each June. List of nearby veterinarians maintained. Exercise area. Spring Lake Park is located on 43rd and Park Avenue.

Rated: 3 Paws — 88 rooms and 15 suites.

The Arkansas-Texas state line runs approximately through the center of the dual town. Residents on both sides of the border enjoy the Perot Theater, a restored 1924 facility that presents a variety of Broadway-type shows. Special business classrooms in the Baymont are equipped with speakerphones, ergonomic chairs, special task lighting and convenient modem jacks. There's a golf course one block from the property. Historic downtown Texarkana is four miles away. Within a 20-mile drive, you can enjoy Wright Patman Lake or visit the Red River Arsenal.

Best Western Inn

1053 Highway 49 West
West Helena, AR 72390
800-884-8632 • 870-572-2592

Type of Lodging: Motel

Room Rates: $60–$80, including deluxe continental breakfast. AAA and AARP discounts.

Pet Charges & Deposits: None.

Pet Policy: Small pets only. Designated rooms only. Manager's prior approval required.

Amenities: Cable TV, refrigerators, microwaves, pool, Jacuzzi.

Pet Amenities: List of nearby veterinarians maintained. Exercise area.

Rated: 3 Paws — 44 rooms and 20 suites.

The Isle of Capri casinos, the Lady Luck and Country Casino, are four miles away on Bypass Highway. It's 35 miles to the Tunica casinos. West Helena, in the far eastern part of Arkansas, near the Mississippi State line and the Mighty Mississippi River abuts its sister city, Helena, where early laws set the speed limit as a trot or a pace and prohibited the firing of guns within the town limits except for just cause. There was plenty of firing on July 4, 1863, when Confederate troops unsuccessfully tried to wrest the town from occupying Union forces. Helena was the hometown of country singer Harold Jenkins, who became more successful when he called himself Conway Twitty. The King Biscuit Blues Festival takes place in October.

CALIFORNIA

Nicknames: Golden State
Population: 33,145,121
Area: 158,869 square miles
Climate: Moderate temperatures and rainfall along the coast; extremes in the interior.
Capital: Sacramento
Entered Union: Sept. 9, 1850
Motto: Eureka (I Have Found It).
Song: I Love You, California
Flower: Golden Poppy

Tree: California Redwood
Bird: California Valley Quail
Famous Californians: Luther Burbank, Tom Hanks, William Randolph Hearst, Marilyn Monroe, John Muir, Richard Nixon, Ronald Reagan, Sally Ride, John Steinbeck, Tiger Woods.

History: Early inhabitants included more than 100 Native American tribes. The first settlement was the Spanish mission at San Diego in 1769, the first in a string founded by Junipero Serra. In 1846, U.S. settlers fomented the Bear Flag Revolt in protest against Mexican rule. U.S. forces occupied California. Mexico ceded the area to the United States in 1848. That same year, gold was discovered, sparking the most famous Gold Rush in history. When the Owens River project brought plentiful water from Northern to Southern California, a small pueblo, Los Angeles emerged as the second largest city in the U.S.

ANDERSON, CALIFORNIA (Pop. 8,300)

Anderson Valley Inn

2861 McMurry Drive
Anderson, CA 96007
800-324-6732 • 530-365-2566

Type of Lodging: Motel
Room Rates: $46–$96, including continental breakfast. AAA and AARP discounts.
Pet Charges & Deposits: $5 per day.
Pet Policy: None. All Pets Welcome.
Amenities: Cable TV, refrigerators, microwaves.
Pet Amenities: Dog runs.
Rated: 3 Paws — 62 rooms.

Anderson Valley Inn is centrally located, close to the Interstate 5, Central Anderson Exit. Rooms are quiet, clean and affordable. There's plenty of outdoor recreation for you and your pet. Shasta and Whiskeytown Lakes are nearby. Lassen Volcanic National Park is an easy day trip and Anderson River Park affords 325 acres on the Sacramento River.

Lake Oroville Bed & Breakfast

240 Sunday Drive
Berry Creek, CA 95916
800-455-5253 • 530-589-0700
www.lakeoroville.com/lakeoroville
lakeinn@cncnet.com

Type of Lodging: B&B

Room Rates: $105–$145, including full breakfast. AAA, Humane Society, Doris Day and *50% off 2nd Night Pets Welcome*™ discounts.

Pet Charges & Deposits: $10 per day.

Pet Policy: Manager's prior approval required.

Amenities: Cable TV, refrigerators, microwaves, game room, reading room.

Pet Amenities: Pet sitting available. List of nearby veterinarians maintained. Exercise area. Large number of parks in the area.

Rated: 3 Paws — 6 rooms on 40 acres.

Blending the comfort and quiet of yesteryear with the luxury and convenience of today, Lake Oroville Bed & Breakfast is a romantic, gracious place. Five of the six beautifully appointed rooms have whirlpool tubs and the property has forty acres filled with native trees, wildflowers, butterflies, rabbits and deer. Lake Oroville is little more than an hour north of Sacramento, California's lively capital city. When in the capital, make sure to visit Old Sacramento for a fun time steeped in history.

Alpine Village Suites Lodge

546 Pine Knot Avenue
P.O. Box 1713
Big Bear Lake, CA 92315
800-2 BIG BEAR • 909-866-5460
www.alpinevillagesuites.com
alpine@pineknot.com

Type of Lodging: Motel, Condos & Cabins

Room Rates: $98–$398. AAA, AARP, AKC, ABA and *10% Pets Welcome*™ discounts.

Pet Charges & Deposits: $100 refundable deposit.

Pet Policy: No pets over 50 lbs.

Amenities: Fully equipped kitchens, Jacuzzi.

Pet Amenities: Dog treats available. List of nearby veterinarians maintained. Exercise area. Park on Big Bear Boulevard and Pine Knot Avenue.

Rated: 2 Paws — 10 rooms and 6 cabins.

Alpine Village Suites provides suites with fireplaces, full kitchens and pleasing amenities in the high country above Southern California's "Inland Empire." It's hard to believe you're higher than any place east of the Mississippi. Yet it's only 30 miles to the "Big Cities" of San Bernardino and Riverside. Camping, picnicking, mountain biking and other outdoor activities abound year-round. The Lodge is 100 yards from Big Bear Lake and 1½ miles from the ski slopes in the village.

Golden Bear Cottages

39367 Big Bear Boulevard
Big Bear Lake, CA 92315
909-866-2010
www.goldenbear.net
gbc@bigbearlake.com

Type of Lodging: Cottages

Cottage Rates: $69–$279. AAA, AARP and *10% Pets Welcome*™ discounts.

Pet Charges & Deposits: $10 per day.

Pet Policy: None. All Pets Welcome.

Amenities: Cable TV, refrigerators, microwaves, pool, whirlpool, Jacuzzi, spas.

Pet Amenities: List of nearby veterinarians maintained. Exercise area. Big Bear Parks and Recreation, Swim Beach and Pine Knot Landing nearby.

Rated: 3 Paws — 27 cottages.

Established in 1924, the Golden Bear Cottages are nestled among majestic pines on nearly three scenic acres in the Big Bear Lake area. There's a beautiful heated pool and spa, sand lot volleyball, ping-pong, horseshoes, basketball, shuffleboard and a play area for younger kids. This all-season resort is located just 1½ blocks from Big Bear Lake, 1½ miles from Big Bear's quaint village shops and minutes away from Big Bear's ski resorts, Big Bear Mountain and Snow Summit.

Timberline Lodge

39921 Big Bear Boulevard
P.O. Box 1955
Big Bear Lake, CA 92315
800-830-4111 • 909-866-4141
www.thetimberlinelodge.com

Type of Lodging: Lodge & Guest Ranch

Room Rates: $71–$240. AAA discount.

Pet Charges & Deposits: $10 per day.

Pet Policy: Designated rooms only.

Amenities: Cable TV, pool.

Pet Amenities: List of nearby veterinarians maintained. Exercise area includes 3 acres with lots of room for pets to enjoy.

Rated: 3 Paws — 15 cabins on 3 acres.

Relax and enjoy the family atmosphere you'll find at the Timberline Lodge. Individual cabins afford fireplaces, daily cleaning service, full kitchens and complete housekeeping needs, with linen, bedding, microwaves and coffeemakers. Timberline Lodge is close to Big Bear and the ski slopes, fine dining, fishing, boating, hiking and horseback riding. The Lodge is located on three acres that you and your pet can enjoy together.

Holiday Inn Express

600 West Donlon Street
Blythe, CA 92225
760-921-2300
www.hiexpress.com/blytheca

Type of Lodging: Motel

Room Rates: $79–$119, including continental breakfast. AAA and AARP discounts.

Pet Charges & Deposits: $10 per day.

Pet Policy: No pets over 40 lbs.

Amenities: Cable TV, refrigerators, microwaves, pool, whirlpool, guest laundry, irons & ironing boards, hairdryers, coffeemakers, free local calls.

Pet Amenities: Dog runs. Miller Park is located on Lovekin Boulevard and 14th Street.

Rated: 2 Paws — 66 rooms and 2 suites.

Holiday Inn Express offers inviting, immaculate and spacious rooms. Kids stay free with their parents and local calls are free. Blythe is right in the middle of the California desert, one mile from the Colorado River, which marks California's eastern frontier. Colorado River is a sportsman's paradise with every kind of water sport you can imagine. It gets a bit warm in the summer, but all rooms at Holiday Inn Express are air-conditioned.

Woodfin Suites

3100 East Imperial Highway
Brea, CA 92821
800-WOODFIN • 714-579-3200
www.woodfinsuitehotels.com

Type of Lodging: Hotel

Suite Rates: $89–$169, including full breakfast and social hour. AAA, AARP and *15% Pets Welcome*™ discounts.

Pet Charges & Deposits: $5 per day. $150 refundable deposit.

Pet Policy: None. All Pets Welcome.

Amenities: Cable TV, refrigerators, microwaves, safes, pool, Jacuzzi, VCRs, stoves, free cookies at night.

Pet Amenities: List of nearby veterinarians maintained. Exercise area. Craig Park is located at Imperial Highway and State College.

Rated: 3 Paws — 88 suites.

Woodfin Suites, an all-suite hotel, is perfect for families. It's bright, cheery, upscale and wonderfully situated within an easy drive of everything that makes up the Los Angeles experience. It's worth whispering that Brea is even closer to the Orange County experience—translation DISNEYLAND—the mouse magnet to the entire area. Of course, if you insist on strolling down Hollywood Boulevard, seeing Southern California's legendary beaches, or hobnobbing with the ultra-rich and ultra-beautiful in Beverly Hills, Bel Air and the like, who are we to stop you?

Best Western Ruby Inn

333 Main Street (U.S. Highway 395)
Bridgeport, CA 93517
800-WESTERN • 760-932-7241
www.bestwestern.com/rubyinn

Type of Lodging: Motel
Room Rates: $70–$160. AAA and AARP discounts.
Pet Charges & Deposits: None.
Pet Policy: Designated rooms only. Pets must not be left unattended.
Amenities: Cable TV, refrigerators, hairdryers, irons and ironing boards, BBQ, Jacuzzi, spa.
Pet Amenities: List of nearby veterinarians maintained. Exercise area.
Rated: 3 Paws — 30 rooms.

Best Western Ruby Inn sports newly remodeled rooms with direct dial phones. Tiny Bridgeport could not be further from the world's perception of California. It's not near a city of any size, it's not glitzy and it's not in the desert. However, it is in mountain country, 42 miles from the eastern entrance to Yosemite National Park. It's 20 miles to Bodie Ghost Town State Historical Park; and the Mono Lake Tufa Reserve and glorious fall colors make this a wonderful, truly "off the beaten path" destination in the Golden State.

Red Roof Inn

777 Airport Boulevard
Burlingame, CA 94010
800-RED ROOF • 650-342-7772
www.redroof.com
i0228b@redroof.com

Type of Lodging: Motel
Room Rates: $90–$160. AAA discount.
Pet Charges & Deposits: None.
Pet Policy: No pets over 25 lbs.
Amenities: Pool, restaurant.
Pet Amenities: Exercise area.
Rated: 2 Paws — 213 rooms.

Red Roof Inn offers bright, cheery, newly remodeled rooms, a 24-hour restaurant and a heated outdoor pool. It's five minutes from San Francisco International Airport, 20 minutes from downtown San Francisco and 45 minutes north of San Jose and the Silicon Valley. San Francisco seems, with justification, to be every American's favorite city and it is a magical place indeed. Little Cable Cars really do climb halfway to the stars, Chinatown is inimitable and the venues of North Beach will embrace your memories for years to come.

Calimesa Inn Motel

1205 Calimesa Boulevard
Calimesa, CA 91310
909-795-2536

Type of Lodging: Motel
Room Rates: $48–$63, including continental breakfast. AAA discount.
Pet Charges & Deposits: $6 per day.
Pet Policy: No pets over 40 lbs. Designated rooms only. Manager's prior approval required.
Amenities: Refrigerators, pool, spas.
Pet Amenities: None.
Rated: 2 Paws — 36 rooms.

Calimesa Inn Motel affords you and your pet sparkling, cozy rooms at a very affordable price in the Yucaipa-Calimesa desert area. Calimesa, on Interstate 10 east of San Bernardino, celebrates a street market each week. The Chumash Native American casino is nearby, as is the entire Palm Springs-Palm Desert area.

Calipatria Inn & Suites

700 North Sorensen Avenue
Calipatria, CA 92233
800-830-1113 • 760-348-7348

Type of Lodging: Motel
Room Rates: $55–$130, including continental breakfast. AAA, AARP and *10% Pets Welcome™* discounts.
Pet Charges & Deposits: None.
Pet Policy: None. All Pets Welcome.
Amenities: Cable TV, refrigerators, microwaves, pool, whirlpool, Jacuzzi, spas.
Pet Amenities: Old sheets provided for bedding and pet cleanup. List of nearby veterinarians maintained. Dog runs. Exercise area. Salton Sea Recreation Area nearby.
Rated: 4 Paws — 34 rooms and 6 suites.

The beautiful Calipatria Inn & Suites gives you a feeling of airiness with modern desert architecture. Rooms are immaculate, bright and thoroughly inviting. Calipatria, on Highway 111, is located in California's southeastern desert, near the east shore of the Salton Sea, a 35 × 15-mile body of water created by the floodwaters from the Colorado River in 1905. It's one of the world's largest inland bodies of water, but only 20 feet deep. The climate of the desert terrain around the Sea is hot and dry. There are many opportunities to engage in water sports and bird watching in the vicinity.

Inns of America

751 Raintree Drive
Carlsbad, CA 92009
800-826-0778 • 760-931-1185
www.innsofamerica.com
carlsbad@innsofamerica

Type of Lodging: Hotel
Room Rates: $59–$80, including continental breakfast. Call for group rates during dog shows. AAA, AARP, AKC and ABA discounts.
Pet Charges & Deposits: $10 per day.
Pet Policy: None. All Pets Welcome.
Amenities: Cable TV, refrigerators, microwaves, pool.
Pet Amenities: List of nearby veterinarians maintained. Pet area. Dog beach is 15 minutes away.
Rated: 3 Paws — 125 rooms.

Inns of America is housed in a beautiful three-story structure only one block from the beach. Rooms are spacious, fresh and inviting. There's a heated pool and local calls are free. San Diego, California's second largest city, is 40 minutes south, but the immediate vicinity has its own plethora of attractions. The inn is minutes away from some of Southern California's most beautiful beaches and to Legoland California, a 128-acre gallery of structures made from multicolored plastic LEGOS. The "animals" in Safari Park are made of LEGOS. If you want to see real animals in a reasonably native habitat, the San Diego Wild Animal Park is not to be missed.

Casa de Carmel

Monte Verde & Ocean Avenue
P.O. Box 2747
Carmel, CA 93921
800-262-1262 • 831-624-7738
www.casadecarmel.com
innkeeper@casadecarmel.com

Type of Lodging: Inn
Room Rates: $115–$135, including continental breakfast. AARP discount.
Pet Charges & Deposits: $20 per day or $30 per day for two pets.
Pet Policy: Pets must not be left unattended
Amenities: Cable TV, refrigerators, microwaves, coffeemakers.
Pet Amenities: List of nearby veterinarians maintained. Carmel Beach nearby—world's best beach for pets.
Rated: 3 Paws — 135 rooms and 7 suites.

Casa de Carmel is a romantic inn, virtually in the center of town. Asking the editorial staff of Pets Welcome™ to be objective about the Monterey Peninsula is like asking someone to be objective about the person he or she loves most in the world. It's our home base. Stroll up and down Carmel's "main drag," Ocean Avenue and mingle with the tourists and the locals. It's a friendly place and wandering the art galleries and restaurants of the byways is as much fun for those who live and work here, as for the myriad visitors who frequent the Peninsula each year.

Lincoln Green Inn

Carmelo between 15th & 16th Streets
P.O. Box 2747
Carmel, CA 93921
800-262-1262 • 831-624-7738
www.vagabondshouseinn.com
innkeeper@vagabondshouseinn.com

Type of Lodging: Cottages

Cottage Rates: $185–$225. AARP discount.

Pet Charges & Deposits: $20 per day or $30 per day for two pets

Pet Policy: Pets must not be left unattended.

Amenities: Cable TV, refrigerators, microwaves, coffeemakers.

Pet Amenities: List of nearby veterinarians maintained. Carmel Beach nearby – world's best beach for pets.

Rated: 3 Paws – 4 cottages.

Lincoln Green Inn is a series of wonderful little cottages in a residential area of Carmel about a mile south of Ocean Avenue, the main drag. It's within easy walking distance of Clint Eastwood's Mission Ranch and the stunning Carmel Mission (Mission San Carlos de Borromeo), headquarters of Padre Junipero Serra, who founded most of California's missions in the 18th century. A visit to the Mission is like stepping back in time and place—namely, to Spain in the 1700s. It's a captivating venue, one of just many in this remarkable area of California.

Vagabond's House Inn

Fourth & Dolores Streets
P.O. Box 2747
Carmel, CA 03021
800-262-1262 • 831-624-7738
www.vagabondshouseinn.com
innkeeper@vagabondshouseinn.com

Type of Lodging: B&B

Room Rates: $115–$195, including continental breakfast. AARP discount.

Pet Charges & Deposits: $20 per day or $30 per day for two pets

Pet Policy: Pets must not be left unattended.

Amenities: Cable TV, refrigerators, coffeemakers.

Pet Amenities: List of nearby veterinarians maintained. Carmel Beach nearby – world's best beach for pets.

Rated: 3 Paws – 13 rooms.

Vagabond's House is a wonderful bed & breakfast, with all the charm that makes Carmel such a world destination. You're remarkably close to the 17-Mile Drive through Pebble Beach, said to rival the most beautiful areas of the world and home of the most famous golf courses in the world—Pebble Beach, Spyglass Hill, Monterey Peninsula Country Club, Cypress Point and Poppy Hills. The destination resorts of the Pebble Beach Lodge and the Inn at Spanish Bay are only a short drive away.

Quail Lodge Resort & Golf Club

8205 Valley Greens Drive
Carmel, CA 93923
888-828-8787 • 831-624-2888
www.quail-lodge-resort.com
qul@peninsula.com

Type of Lodging: Resort

Room Rates: $245–$410, including continental breakfast and fitness walk.

Pet Charges & Deposits: $100 per stay.

Pet Policy: Sorry, no cats.

Amenities: Cable TV, honor bar, pool, whirlpool, hot tubs, spas, fitness room, restaurant.

Pet Amenities: Bed, dishes, treats and pet menu available. Pet sitters available. List of nearby veterinarians maintained. Dog runs. Exercise area. Carmel Beach nearby—world's best beach for pets.

Rated: 5 Paws — 84 rooms and 16 suites.

Quail Lodge is not technically in Carmel-by-the-Sea. It's a few miles out Carmel Valley Road and it's a world-renowned destination resort in its own right. In one of the Golden State's most beautiful areas, Point Lobos State Reserve is a standout. Spend several hours here walking through glorious forests to the edge of the Pacific. Stop in at the Whaler's Cabin, or gasp with surprised delight as you watch frolicking sea otters or harbor seals in the ocean a hundred feet below. Then, increase your appreciation of the spectacular by driving south on Highway One, 26 miles to Big Sur, one of the most stunningly beautiful and dramatic spots on Earth that easily rivals the Amalfi Drive. Have lunch at Nepenthe or Ventana, Dietjens or Rocky Point—your choices are almost limitless.

Sunset House Bed & Breakfast

*Second House Southeast of Ocean
Avenue on Camino Real*
P.O. Box 1925
Carmel, CA 93921
831-624-4890
www.sunset-carmel.com
sunsetbb@redshift.com

Type of Lodging: B&B

Room Rates: $190–$230, including expanded breakfast. AAA and **mid-week Pets Welcome™** discounts.

Pet Charges & Deposits: $20 per day.

Pet Policy: Sorry, no cats. No pets over 150 lbs. Designated rooms only.

Amenities: Cable TV, refrigerators, Jacuzzi, fireplaces.

Pet Amenities: List of nearby veterinarians maintained. Dog runs. Exercise area. City parks, beaches and trails nearby.

Rated: 3 Paws — 4 rooms.

Sunset House Bed & Breakfast has four charming, "Carmel cozy" rooms and serves an expanded breakfast to boot. You can't go to Carmel without going down to "the" beach—a mile-long strand of sugar sand where you'll find nearly as many dogs as people. To the north, Pebble Beach; to the south, Carmel Point curves along until you get to the next cove, Stewart's Beach, and gaze at Point Lobos across a small bay. Did you know that the Monterey Peninsula boasts over 300 restaurants, many of them among the finest in the country?

Wayside Inn

Corner of 7th & Mission Streets
P.O. Box 101
Carmel, CA 93921
800-433-4732 • 831-624-5336
www.innsbythesea.com
reserve@innsbythesea.com

Type of Lodging: Inn

Room Rates: $109–$269, including continental breakfast. AAA, AARP and **10–40% Pets Welcome™** discounts.

Pet Charges & Deposits: Credit card imprint deposit.

Pet Policy: Designated rooms only. Pets must not be left unattended.

Amenities: Cable TV, refrigerators, coffeemakers.

Pet Amenities: List of nearby veterinarians maintained. Exercise area. Carmel Beach, Garland Regional Park, Mission Trail Park, Point Lobos State Reserve. Point Sur Historic Park, Andrew Molera State Park and other state parks nearby.

Rated: 3 Paws — 18 rooms and 4 suites.

Wayside Inn's airy rooms and suites, many with full kitchens and wood burning fireplaces, are designed to accommodate your entire family, pets included. Complimentary continental breakfast and newspaper are delivered to your door every day. You're just a short stroll to Carmel's shops, restaurants and galleries. You're also just over the hill from Monterey, where you can walk the "Path of History," with historic old adobes, many with original 18th and 19th century furnishings, surrounded by beautifully maintained gardens.

La Quinta Inn

150 Bonita Road
Chula Vista, CA 91910
800-531-5900 • 619-691-1211
www.laquinta.com

Type of Lodging: Motel

Room Rates: $79–$155, including continental breakfast. AAA and AARP discounts.

Pet Charges & Deposits: None.

Pet Policy: No pets over 50 lbs.

Amenities: Cable TV, refrigerators, microwaves, pool.

Pet Amenities: List of nearby veterinarians maintained. Exercise area. Sweetwater Municipal Park nearby.

Rated: 3 Paws — 140 rooms and 2 suites.

Chula Vista's La Quinta Inn is housed in striking, mission-style structures. Guestrooms feature fresh décor, rich wood furniture, large desks, bright bathrooms, coffeemakers and alarm clock radios. Chula Vista is a scant seven miles from the U.S.-Mexico border and you can travel to another country in less than ten minutes—make sure you buy auto insurance for the trip before you do! California's second most populous city, San Diego has the best climate in the United States and a worthy array of indoor and outdoor entertainments. World-renowned San Diego Zoo, Sea World, the San Diego Wild Animal Park, Seaport Village and Old Town are just a few of literally hundreds of reasons to make this an ideal vacation destination.

Days Inn Corning

3475 Highway 99 West (South Avenue
Exit / Interstate 5)
Corning, CA 96021
800-245-3655 • 530-824-2000

Type of Lodging: Motel

Room Rates: $35–$70, including continental breakfast. AAA, AARP, Costco, Entertainment Card, Military, Government and *10% Pets Welcome*™ discounts.

Pet Charges & Deposits: $5 per day. Call for deposit information.

Pet Policy: Designated rooms only.

Amenities: Cable TV, refrigerators, microwaves, pool.

Pet Amenities: Pet bowls and treats available. List of nearby veterinarians maintained. Exercise area. Woodson State Park nearby.

Rated: 3 Paws — 62 rooms and 2 suites.

Days Inn is a clean, cost-conscious and pet-friendly establishment, located two hours north of Sacramento and one hour south of Redding. You're an easy drive away from Lassen Volcanic National Park, which covers 106,000 acres where the Cascades join the Sierra Nevada mountain range. In addition to Lassen Peak and Cinder Cone, the park contains two shield volcanoes, Prospect Peak and Mount Harkness, both topped with cinder cones, with trails leading to their summits. Throughout the park you'll find smaller volcanoes, lava flows, fumaroles, boiling springs, boiling lakes and mud pots. It's a geologic wonderland, well worth a side trip.

Best Value Inn

440 Highway 101 North
Crescent City, CA 95531
707-464-4141
www.bestvalueinn.com

Type of Lodging: Inn
Room Rates: $41–$75. AAA and AARP discounts.
Pet Charges & Deposits: $5 per day.
Pet Policy: Sorry, no cats or pit bulls. No pets over 50 lbs. Designated rooms only. Manager's prior approval required.
Amenities: Cable TV, Jacuzzi, sauna, microfridges.
Pet Amenities: List of nearby veterinarians maintained. Exercise area. Redwoods National Park nearby.
Rated: 2 Paws — 58 rooms and 3 suites.

Best Value Inn represents fine value, dollar for dollar, coast to coast. The Crescent City branch of this chain is loaded with thoughtful amenities. Crescent City was founded in 1853 as a gold mining supply center. Lake Earl Wildlife Area, five miles north of the city, contains 5,000 acres of wildlife habitat and makes for wonderful walks. The Battery Point Lighthouse is a working 1856 lighthouse with museum, nautical artifacts, antique clocks, photographs of shipwrecks and lighthouses.

Cedar Lake Motel

4201 Dunsmuir Avenue
Dunsmuir, CA 96025
530-235-4332
www.cedarlodgedunsmuir.com

Type of Lodging: Motel
Room Rates: $45–$125. AAA, AARP and **5% *Pets Welcome*™** discounts.
Pet Charges & Deposits: $5 per day.
Pet Policy: Sorry, no cats. No pets over 100 lbs. Designated rooms only. Manager's prior approval required. Pets must be on leash at all times.
Amenities: Cable TV, coffeemakers.
Pet Amenities: List of nearby veterinarians maintained. Sacramento River is 2 blocks away. Castle Crags State Park is 6 miles south; city park is a mile away; and national forest is 2 miles away from the motel.
Rated: 2 Paws — 10 rooms and 5 suites.

Cedar Lake Motel provides roomy yet affordable lodgings in Dunsmuir, one of the closest towns to spectacular Mount Shasta. Castle Crags State Park has granite crags towering more than 4,000 feet over the nearby Sacramento River. To the west are the Trinity Alps, while half-day's trip to the east, you'll arrive at Lava Beds National Monument, a 46,500-acre area characterized by cinder cones, deep chasms and more than 300 lava tube caves, some of which contain permanent ice. Free-use flashlights are available at the Visitor Center.

Railroad Park Resort

100 Railroad Park Road
Dunsmuir, CA 96024
530-235-4440
www.rrpark.com

Type of Lodging: Motel
Room Rates: $45–$95.
Pet Charges & Deposits: $10 per day.
Pet Policy: None. All Pets Welcome.
Amenities: Cable TV, refrigerators, microwaves, pool, spas.
Pet Amenities: List of nearby veterinarians maintained. Exercise area. Lodging's own grounds are park-like with a natural setting in its own private canyon with acres of dog area next to the creek. There is a pond in which your pet may swim.
Rated: 4 Paws — 27 rooms.

This is a unique motel. Many of the rooms are in restored railroad cabooses! It's an eclectic, fun place to stay. Dunsmuir is located seven miles south of Mount Shasta, in the beautiful Sacramento River Canyon, just off the Interstate 5. Dunsmuir is an old railroad town. The Sacramento River and the surrounding area are loaded with outdoor activities such as fishing, camping, hiking and skiing.

Brunners Inn & Suites

215 North Imperial Avenue
El Centro, CA 92243
800-453-8581 • 760-352-6431

Type of Lodging: Inn
Room Rates: $65–$85, including full breakfast. AAA discount.
Pet Charges & Deposits: None.
Pet Policy: Cats only. Sorry, no other pets.
Amenities: Cable TV, VCRs, refrigerators, microwaves, pool, Jacuzzi.
Pet Amenities: List of nearby veterinarians maintained. Exercise area. Buckler Park is located on 6th and Audrey.
Rated: 3 Paws — 65 rooms and 20 suites.

Brunners is a wonderful budget choice for accommodations. Spacious king- and queen-sized bedrooms, in-room coffee service, a swimming pool and spa are only a few of the many appreciated amenities. El Centro is situated in one of the world's richest farming areas. Irrigation transformed a barren desert, much of it below sea level (El Centro itself is 45 feet below sea level) into an incredible jigsaw puzzle of verdant fields. The Navy's Blue Angels do their winter training at the nearby Naval Air Facility.

Sunrise Inn & Suites

129 Fourth Street
Eureka, CA 95501
800-909-9751 • 707-993-9751

Type of Lodging: Motel
Room Rates: $35–$65, including continental breakfast. AAA and AARP discounts.
Pet Charges & Deposits: $4 per day.
Pet Policy: Manager's prior approval required.
Amenities: Cable TV, refrigerators, microwaves, Jacuzzi.
Pet Amenities: Sequoia Park nearby.
Rated: 2 Paws — 20 rooms and 5 suites.

Sunrise Inn & Suites offers relaxing rooms at value conscious prices. Eureka is the chief port between the San Francisco Bay and the Columbia River. It's a lumbering, industrial and commercial city on Humboldt Bay. The wealth of the city is apparent in its renovated 19th century Old Town, replete with Victorian mansions, specialty shops, art galleries and the like. At the Blue Ox Millworks, visitors can learn about boat building and late 19th century woodworking in an authentic Victorian millwork shop. Humboldt Bay Harbor Cruise allows you to ride a 1910 ferry on a 75-minute cruise around the bay.

Best Western Franciscan Inn

1635 South Mission Road
Fallbrook, CA 92028
800-527-1234 • 760-728-6174
www.bestwestern.com/franciscaninn

Type of Lodging: Inn
Room Rates: $70–$90, including continental breakfast. AARP discount.
Pet Charges & Deposits: $10 per stay. Credit card imprint required as deposit.
Pet Policy: No pets over 25 lbs. Designated rooms only. Manager's prior approval required.
Amenities: Cable TV, refrigerators, microwaves, safes, pool, whirlpool.
Pet Amenities: None.
Rated: 2 Paws — 50 rooms.

Best Western Franciscan Inn offers the high quality accommodations and amenities typical of this outstanding chain. Fallbrook is convenient to Southern California's Inland Empire, a year-round vacationland stretching from Los Angeles in the northwest to San Diego in the south, then inland to Poway and north to San Bernardino. While in the area, sample everything from San Diego's Coronado Island to the inland Lawrence Welk Family Resort, from Orange County's Knott's Berry Farm to Lake Arrowhead, 6,000 feet above San Bernardino in the high mountains.

Tenaya Lodge at Yosemite

1122 Highway 41
Fish Camp, CA 93623
800-635-5807 • 559-683-6555
www.tenayalodge.com

Type of Lodging: Guest Ranch & Resort Hotel

Room Rates: $99–$279. AAA and AARP discounts.

Pet Charges & Deposits: $50 nonrefundable deposit.

Pet Policy: Designated rooms only.

Amenities: Cable TV, honor bar, safes, pools, hot tubs, spa.

Pet Amenities: Exercise area. Yosemite National Park is 2 miles north on Highway 41 where leashes are required and pets are not allowed on marked trails.

Rated: 3 Paws — 244 rooms and 20 suites.

Yosemite's natural splendor has inspired the photographs of Ansel Adams and the writings of John Muir as well as captivated millions of visitors. Just two miles from the national park's south entrance, you will find the Tenaya Lodge. Surrounded by acres of Sierra National Forest, this smoke-free resort invites guests to escape the hustle and bustle of the outside world. Spend the day exploring the natural wonders of the area with your pet, before escaping to the spa to relieve stress with a relaxing massage. The Guest Experience Center will arrange outings from mountain biking to a ride on a steam-driven logging train.

Seabird Lodge

191 South Street
Fort Bragg, CA 95437
800-345-0022 • 707-964-4731
www.seabirdlodge.com

Type of Lodging: Motel

Room Rates: $60–$100. AAA, AARP and *10% Pets Welcome™* discounts.

Pet Charges & Deposits: $8 per day.

Pet Policy: No pets over 30 lbs. Designated rooms only. Limit two pets per room.

Amenities: Cable TV, refrigerators, coffeemakers, pool, whirlpool.

Pet Amenities: List of nearby veterinarians maintained. Large exercise area. Russian Gulch State Park, Jughandle State Reserve and other parks nearby.

Rated: 2 Paws — 65 rooms. The Lodge is owned and operated by pet owners and lovers.

Seabird Lodge is a wonderful choice if you're traveling on northern California's spectacular Mendocino coast. Each guestroom has warm oak and rattan furnishings, an oversized bed, cable television, refrigerator and coffeemaker. Fort Bragg was established in 1857 to oversee the Mendocino Native American Reservation. The fort was abandoned and subsequently became a major lumber and port town. The Skunk Train, which carries you in 1925 and 1935 vintage cars, travels from Fort Bragg through Willits to Northspur, passing through redwood groves and tunnels and over the Noyo River.

Travelodge

3093 North Parkway Drive
Fresno, CA 93722
800-276-7745 • 559-276-7745
www.travelodge.com
tlongreen@aol.com

Type of Lodging: Motel
Room Rates: $39–$69, including continental breakfast. AAA discount.
Pet Charges & Deposits: $5 per day. $50 refundable deposit.
Pet Policy: Designated rooms only.
Amenities: Cable TV, refrigerators, microwaves, pool, Jacuzzi.
Pet Amenities: Dog runs. Exercise area.
Rated: 2 Paws — 115 rooms.

Travelodge provides cost-conscious, dependable and neat accommodations in Fresno, one of inland California's largest cities. Although it's in the center of the San Joaquin Valley, an agricultural area in which over a million acres are under irrigation, it's a surprisingly sophisticated, up-to-date and livable city. Guided tours of the Kearney Mansion Museum in Kearney Park show many original furnishings and wall coverings. Blossom Trail is 63 miles long and encompasses vineyards, orchards and historical points of interest.

Travelodge – Highway 41

3876 North Blackstone Avenue
Fresno, CA 93726
559-229-9840
www.travelodge.com

Type of Lodging: Motel
Room Rates: $50–$70, including continental breakfast. AAA, AARP, AKC, ABA and *20% Pets Welcome*™ discounts.
Pet Charges & Deposits: $5 per day.
Pet Policy: Small pets only.
Amenities: Cable TV, refrigerators, microwaves, pool.
Pet Amenities: List of nearby veterinarians maintained. Dog runs. Manchester Park is a few blocks away and Woodward Park is located on Friant Road.
Rated: 2 Paws — 38 rooms and 3 suites.

Sister to the previous Travelodge, this Travelodge likewise provides neat and budget-sensitive lodgings that will help you and your pet to enjoy your sojourn in Fresno. The Fresno Metropolitan Museum of Art, History & Science features an impressive Asian art collection, while Wild Water Adventures offers over 20 water rides and amusements, including water slides, flumes, a wave pool and a kid's play area.

Best Western Humboldt House Inn

701 Redwood Drive
Garberville, CA 95542
800-528-1234 • 707-923-2771
www.bestwestern.com/humboldthouseinn

Type of Lodging: Motel
Room Rates: $72–$97, including continental breakfast. AAA and AARP discounts.
Pet Charges & Deposits: None.
Pet Policy: Designated rooms only.
Amenities: Cable TV, refrigerators, pool, Jacuzzi.
Pet Amenities: List of nearby veterinarians maintained. Tooby Park is located 1½ miles away and Humboldt Redwoods State Park is 6 miles away.
Rated: 3 Paws — 76 rooms and suites.

Best Western Humboldt House Inn, a delightful, three-story inn, contains air-conditioned guestrooms and suites, most with private patios and view balconies. You'll rest in soundproof rooms, swim in a heated pool and relax in a soothing Jacuzzi. The inn is situated at the south entrance to the spectacular Avenue of the Giants and California Redwoods State Park, 65 miles south of Eureka, 200 miles north of San Francisco. Here are the world's tallest trees. Over 100 miles of unspoiled beaches, more than 30 national, state and county parks and all kinds of festivals, museums and historic sites.

Holiday Inn Santa Barbara-Goleta

5650 Calle Real
Goleta, CA 93117
805-964-6241
msolon@bristolhotels.com

Type of Lodging: Hotel
Room Rates: $90–$160. AAA and AARP discounts.
Pet Charges & Deposits: $25 per stay.
Pet Policy: None. All Pets Welcome.
Amenities: Cable TV, pool.
Pet Amenities: List of nearby veterinarians maintained. Dog runs. Exercise area.
Rated: 3 Paws — 160 rooms.

Holiday Inn, clean, comfortable and moderately priced for the spectacular Santa Barbara area, is a fine choice when you're in Southern California's most charming city. The Queen of all Missions is a symbol of Santa Barbara. Not to be outdone, the elegant and impressive County Courthouse at 1100 Anacapa Street was built in 1929 and is a marvelous example of Spanish-Moor-style architecture. The Santa Barbara Museum of Art and the University of California are noteworthy sights, as is the marvelous waterfront.

Alta Sierra Village Inn

11858 Tammy Way
Grass Valley, CA 95949
800-992-5300 • 530-273-9102

Type of Lodging: Motel
Room Rates: $59–$179, including full breakfast.
Pet Charges & Deposits: $10 per stay
Pet Policy: Designated rooms only. Manager's prior approval required. Leash law enforced. Pets must not be left unattended.
Amenities: Cable TV.
Pet Amenities: List of nearby veterinarians maintained. Exercise area. Empire Park is 6 miles away.
Rated: 2 Paws — 14 rooms and 2 suites.

Alta Sierra Village Inn is tucked away in the beautifully wooded Sierra foothills, just an hour from Sacramento, two hours from San Francisco, Tahoe and Reno. Most rooms have private decks overlooking Gold Lake and the 18th fairway of the Alta Sierra Country Club. Each split-level room is furnished with a king- or queen-sized bed, or two double beds, color television and complimentary coffee. Grass Valley's Gold Rush days still linger. The Empire Mine is one of the oldest, largest and richest mines in California. You can pan for gold along the many rivers. The area abounds in old Victorian houses and the nostalgia of the 1880s manifests itself in the many antique shops throughout the area. Historic buildings in Grass Valley and nearby Nevada City have been restored to their original splendor.

Golden Chain Motel

13363 Highway 49
Grass Valley, CA 95949
530-273-7279

Type of Lodging: Motel
Room Rates: $48–$98, including continental breakfast.
Pet Charges & Deposits: $10 per day.
Pet Policy: No pets over 20 lbs.
Amenities: Cable TV, pool, picnic area.
Pet Amenities: Dog runs. Exercise area includes 4 acres.
Rated: 2 Paws — 21 rooms.

The Golden Chain Motel provides pleasant accommodations on tree-shaded grounds. Air conditioning, direct dial phones, a heated pool, picnic and BBQ area, and a covered bridge are welcome amenities. Grass Valley is in Gold Rush Country and while there you should not miss Columbia State Historic Park, which covers 12 square blocks in the old business district. It's been restored to its Gold Rush days appearance, with a schoolhouse, bank, newspaper building, barbershop, saloons, the Wells Fargo Express Company building, the Fallon Hotel, City Hotel, Masonic Temple and an old-time apothecary. It's a fabulous living history park.

Groveland Hotel

18767 Main Street
P.O. Box 289
Groveland, CA 95321
800-273-3314
www.groveland.com

Type of Lodging: Inn
Room Rates: $135–$210, including wine social in evening. AAA and *10% Pets Welcome™* discounts.
Pet Charges & Deposits: None.
Pet Policy: Manager's prior approval required.
Amenities: Cable TV, whirlpool, restaurant.
Pet Amenities: List of nearby veterinarians maintained. Yosemite National Park nearby. National Park leash laws in effect. Certain trails are not available to pets.
Rated: 3 Paws — 14 rooms and 3 suites. Voted among the Top 10 Inns in Country Inns magazine.

The Groveland Hotel is worth a visit, even if you don't have the good fortune to stay here. It's housed in a restored 1849 adobe (prestatehood!) and a 1914 Queen Anne hotel. It's modeled after the Larkin House, the first American mansion. In its formative years, the town was successively known as Savage's Diggings and Garrotte, before it achieved its much more pleasant name. There are several whitewater river trips in the area and it's one of the closest towns to the western entrance to spectacular Yosemite National Park.

Gualala Country Inn

47955 Center Street
P.O. Box 697
Gualala, CA 95445
800-564-4466 • 707-884-4343
www.gualala.com
countryinn@gualala.com

Type of Lodging: Inn
Room Rates: $92–$165, including continental breakfast. AAA, AARP and *seasonal Pets Welcome™* discounts.
Pet Charges & Deposits: $10 per stay.
Pet Policy: Pets must not be left unattended, are not allowed in the lobby and must be on a leash.
Amenities: Cable TV.
Pet Amenities: None.
Rated: 2 Paws — 20 rooms.

The Gualala Country Inn, situated on the Mendocino coastline, just across the Gualala River from the world-renowned Sea Ranch, overlooks the Pacific Ocean, the Gualala River and the beach. Accommodations have either an ocean and/or river views. Some guestrooms and the cozy parlor have views of crashing waves and a long sandy beach. The inn offers an excellent vantage point to watch the fall and spring migration of the California Gray Whales. Gualala is located halfway between Bodega Bay and Mendocino on California's exquisite, romantic North Coast, above San Francisco.

Surf Motel at Gualala

39170 South Highway 1
P.O. Box 695
Gualala, CA 95445
800-451-SURF • 707-884-3571
www.gualala.com
surfmotel@gualala.com

Type of Lodging: Motel
Room Rates: $92–$179. AAA, AARP and *seasonal Pets Welcome*™ discounts.
Pet Charges & Deposits: $10 per stay.
Pet Policy: None. All Pets Welcome.
Amenities: Cable TV, refrigerators, microwaves.
Pet Amenities: None.
Rated: 3 Paws — 20 rooms.

Watch the crashing surf, the whales, breathtaking sunsets and fall asleep to the sounds of the sea at the Surf Motel in Gualala. All rooms include cable television, two-line speakerphones with dataports, wake-up calls, refrigerator, microwave and electronic door locks for security. Gualala is one of those magic getaway places where you stroll the dramatic beach, read a good book while overlooking the Pacific Ocean or wander about the forested countryside north of San Francisco Bay. It's a romantic dreamland.

Sorensen's Resort

14255 Highway 88
Hope Valley, CA 96120
800-423-9949 • 530-694-2203
www.sorensensresort.com

Type of Lodging: Inn
Cabin Rates: $80–$450.
Pet Charges & Deposits: None.
Pet Policy: Designated cabins only.
Amenities: Fully equipped kitchens.
Pet Amenities: List of nearby veterinarians maintained. Exercise area.
Rated: 3 Paws — 33 cabins.

Sorensen's Resort is made up of rustic cabins in a sparsely populated area perfectly suited for such accommodations. Hope Valley is convenient to lovely Alpine Lake, as well as to Calaveras Big Trees State Park, a 6,073-acre park that contains some of the finest specimens of Sierra redwoods. Snowshoeing and cross-country skiing are popular winter activities in the area.

Fireside Inn

54540 North Circle Drive
Idyllwild, CA 92549
877-797-3473 • 909-659-2966
www.thefireside-inn.com
tfi@thefireside-inn

Type of Lodging: Inn
Room Rates: $60–$110. AAA, AARP and *10% Pets Welcome*™ discounts.
Pet Charges & Deposits: None.
Pet Policy: None. All Pets Welcome.
Amenities: Cable TV, fully equipped kitchens, fireplaces.
Pet Amenities: List of nearby veterinarians maintained. Idyllwild County Park nearby.
Rated: 4 Paws — 8 cottages.

Fireside Inn, located three blocks from most shops and restaurants in Idyllwild, is a real European hideaway. It affords single-story, smoke-free duplex cottages and a separate, private cottage surrounded by natural landscape and the San Jacinto Mountains. Idyllwild, one of California's most popular all-season resorts, rests at an elevation of 5,400 feet above sea level, 110 miles from Los Angeles, 117 miles from San Diego, 54 miles from Palm Springs and 58 miles from Riverside. There are plenty of hiking trails, rock climbing venues and camping opportunities in the area.

Best Western Date Tree Hotel

81-909 Indio Boulevard
Indio, CA 92201
800-292-5599 • 760-347-3421
www.datetree.com

Type of Lodging: Hotel
Room Rates: $59–$129, including continental breakfast. AAA, AARP and *10% Pets Welcome*™ discounts.
Pet Charges & Deposits: $50 refundable deposit.
Pet Policy: Designated rooms only.
Amenities: Cable TV, refrigerators, microwaves, pool, whirlpool.
Pet Amenities: List of nearby veterinarians maintained. Dog runs.
Rated: 3 Paws — 111 rooms and 8 suites.

Beautifully appointed Best Western Date Tree Hotel is an oasis in the highly irrigated desert community of Indio, America's largest producer of dates. Free local calls, kids stay free in their parents' room, an outdoor heated Olympic-sized pool and a large spa are delightful, upscale amenities. The Coachella Valley Museum and Cultural Center displays Native American artifacts, old farm and household equipment, changing art exhibits and a blacksmith shop.

Quality Inn

43505 Monroe Street
Indio, CA 92201
800-228-5151 • 760-347-4044
www.qualityinnindio.com

Type of Lodging: Motel
Room Rates: $49–$149, including continental breakfast. *10% Pets Welcome™* discount.
Pet Charges & Deposits: None.
Pet Policy: None. All Pets Welcome.
Amenities: Cable TV, refrigerators, microwaves, pool, whirlpool.
Pet Amenities: List of nearby veterinarians maintained. Dog runs. Indio Municipal Park is located ½ mile south on Monroe Street.
Rated: 4 Paws — 62 rooms.

Striking, snow-white Quality Inn provides exquisite, beautifully laid-out accommodations in the desert agricultural community of Indio. Among the things to do in this area (only 30 miles from Palm Springs) are hot air ballooning, horseback riding, the Palm Springs Aerial Tramway, Joshua Tree National Monument and a host of golf and tennis facilities.

Super 8 Motel

81753 Highway 111
Indio, CA 92201
760-342-0264

Type of Lodging: Motel
Room Rates: $46–$99. AAA, AARP, VIP, Corporate, Government, Seniors and *10% Pets Welcome™* discounts.
Pet Charges & Deposits: $20 per stay.
Pet Policy: Designated rooms only.
Amenities: Cable TV, refrigerators, pool.
Pet Amenities: List of nearby veterinarians maintained. Exercise area is a large, open lot adjacent to the motel.
Rated: 2 Paws — 70 rooms.

Super 8 Motel is known for its immaculate and spotless rooms at a budget conscious price. The Indio branch of this fine chain is located next to a movie theater, in the immediate area of several restaurants and a major supermarket. It's 20 miles to casinos on the nearby Morongo Native American Reservation. In Indio, the General Patton Memorial Museum contains memorabilia from World War II and other eras of American military history and includes displays of tanks and artillery.

Best Western Inn

33410 Powers Drive
P.O. Box 539
Kettleman City, CA 93239
800-381-1116 • 559-386-0804

Type of Lodging: Motel
Room Rates: $65–$100, including continental breakfast. AAA, AARP and *Pets Welcome*™ discounts.
Pet Charges & Deposits: $2 per day.
Pet Policy: No pets over 50 lbs. Designated rooms only.
Amenities: Satellite TV, refrigerators, microwaves, safe, pool, Jacuzzi, coffeemakers.
Pet Amenities: Pet treats at front desk. A small park is located 1½ miles north.
Rated: 3 Paws — 56 rooms.

Best Western Inn is housed in a striking facility with equally attractive rooms and amenities. Its location is on the road to anywhere in California: two hours to the coast, two hours to the Sequoias, halfway between Los Angeles and San Francisco. Bakersfield, conveniently close to Kettleman City, near the southern end of the San Joaquin Valley, is an important shipping and marketing center for oil, natural gas and farm products. The California Living Museum contains a cross-section of California wildlife and native plants, some of which are endangered. Forty miles north of Bakersfield is Colonel Allenworth State Historic Park, the only California town founded, financed and governed by African-Americans. It offers a visitor center, furnished historic buildings, a picnic area and a campground.

Residence Inn La Jolla

8901 Gilman Drive
La Jolla, CA 92037
800-331-3131 • 858-587-1770
www.residenceinn.com/lajca

Type of Lodging: Hotel
Suite Rates: $169–$219, including breakfast buffet and weekday Hospitality Hour. AAA, AARP and AKC discounts.
Pet Charges & Deposits: $10 per day. $75 nonrefundable deposit.
Pet Policy: Designated rooms only.
Amenities: Cable TV, fully equipped kitchen, pool, Jacuzzi.
Pet Amenities: Pet treats and doggie dishes. List of pet-friendly places at the front desk. Dog runs. Gilman Park nearby.
Rated: 3 Paws — 216 suites.

The Residence Inn by Marriott provides first-class suites, including fully equipped kitchens and large living areas, most with wood-burning fireplaces. La Jolla is one of San Diego's premier communities. Sea World, the University of California and the beaches are minutes away. On any given day, in any given season, you can catch major league sports, whether it's baseball's San Diego Padres or football's San Diego Chargers. The Scripps Institution of Oceanography is an excellent aquarium.

Casa Laguna Bed and Breakfast Inn

2510 South Coast Highway
Laguna Beach, CA 92651
800-233-0449 • 949-494-2996
www.casalaguna.com
info@casalaguna.com

Type of Lodging: B&B

Room Rates: $95–$295, including extended continental breakfast and daily wine & cheese hour. AAA and AARP discounts.

Pet Charges & Deposits: $10 per day.

Pet Policy: None. All Pets Welcome.

Amenities: Cable TV, refrigerators, microwaves, pool, Jacuzzi.

Pet Amenities: Exercise area. Victoria Beach and Laguna Canyon Park nearby.

Rated: 3 Paws — 15 rooms and 6 suites. Voted "Best B&B" in Orange County by Orange County Register last 4 years in a row.

Terraced on a hillside amid tropical gardens and flower-splashed patios, the Casa Laguna Inn exudes an ambiance of bygone days, when Laguna Beach was developing its reputation as an artists' colony and hideaway for Hollywood film stars. The mission-style architecture features guestrooms and suites that are decorated in a mixture of antique, collectables and contemporary furnishings. The many beautiful garden areas include the aviary patio, beneath a family of Queen palms, the bougainvillea-splashed courtyard and the ocean-view pool deck with its banana and avocado trees. Two beaches are located across from the Casa. This property is very popular with pet owners, as there are several walkways and other areas to exercise your pet.

Oxford Inn & Suites

1651 West Avenue K
Lancaster, CA 93534
800-522-3050 • 661-949-3423
www.oxfordsuites.com
oxfordinn@gnet.com

Type of Lodging: Inn

Room Rates: $99–$129, including deluxe continental breakfast. AAA and AARP discounts.

Pet Charges & Deposits: $15 per stay.

Pet Policy: No pets over 20 lbs.

Amenities: Cable TV, refrigerators, microwaves, pool, Jacuzzi.

Pet Amenities: List of nearby veterinarians maintained. Exercise area. Lancaster Park nearby.

Rated: 2 Paws — 103 rooms and 67 suites.

Oxford Inn & Suites provides modern, moderately priced upscale lodging in the Antelope Valley, just north of the Los Angeles basin. The high desert city, established in 1884 along the Southern Pacific Railroad Line, grew through farming and mining activities, then expanded geometrically with the development of Muroc Bombing and Gunnery Range, which later became Edwards Air Force Base. Lancaster's population grew even faster during the 1980s, when it became a bedroom community for Los Angeles. The Lancaster Performing Arts Center presents musicals, dance, drama and children's events from September through May. Hot air balloon rides over the Antelope Valley are a popular and exciting tourist activity.

Dow Villa Motel

310 South Main Street
P.O. Box 955
Lone Pine, CA 93545
800-824-9317 • 760-876-5521
www.dowvillamotel.com
dowvilla@gnet.com

Type of Lodging: Motel
Room Rates: $58–$115. AAA, AARP
and *10% Pets Welcome*™ discounts.
Pet Charges & Deposits: Credit card
imprint required as deposit.
Pet Policy: Designated rooms only.
Amenities: Cable TV, VCRs, refrigerators, microwaves, pool, whirlpool, Jacuzzi, hairdryers.
Pet Amenities: List of nearby veterinarians maintained. Parks nearby.
Rated: 3 Paws — 42 rooms.

The Dow Villa Motel provides generous and impressive rooms with king- and queen-sized beds, free local calls, a large heated pool and a rejuvenating outdoor spa. Lone Pine is set in the heart of the beautiful eastern Sierras. It's the gateway to both Mount Whitney (14,496 feet), the highest point in the contiguous United States and to Death Valley National Park (282 feet below sea level), the lowest point in the Western Hemisphere. The Alabama Hills, granite boulders near Lone Pine, were used as a backdrop for over 300 movies, most of them Westerns. Stand in the footsteps of John Wayne, Humphrey Bogart, Gene Autry, Roy Rogers and Clint Eastwood, where they filmed such classics as "Tycoon," "High Sierra," "Boots and Saddles," and "Joe Kidd."

Liberty Inn

22683 Avenue 18½
Madera, CA 93637
559-675-8697

Type of Lodging: Motel
Room Rates: $50–$66, including continental breakfast. AAA and AARP discounts.
Pet Charges & Deposits: $5 per day. $25 refundable deposit.
Pet Policy: Designated rooms only.
Amenities: Cable TV, microwaves, refrigerators, pool, Jacuzzi, hot tubs, spas.
Pet Amenities: Madera Central Park is located off Cleveland Avenue.
Rated: 2 Paws — 35 rooms and 5 suites.

Liberty Inn is a well-priced lodging in the Madera area with generous accommodations. There's ample parking, indoor swimming pool, indoor spa and sauna and restaurants nearby. Madera is 15 minutes north of Fresno. It's convenient to Sequoia and Kings Canyon National Parks, a landscape studded with the world's largest trees, the giant sequoias, many of which are more than 200 feet high and have trunks more than 30 feet in diameter. Only trails penetrate the wilderness of both parks, meaning that the beauties of the High Sierra backcountry are available only to hikers.

Sierra Nevada Rodeway Inn

164 Old Mammoth Road
P.O. Box 918
Mammoth Lakes, CA 93546
800-824-5132 • 760-934-2515
www.mammothsnri.com
mammothsnri@qnet.com

Type of Lodging: Hotel

Room Rates: $59–$399. AAA and AARP discounts.

Pet Charges & Deposits: $25 refundable deposit. *Pet deposit waived on presentation of Pets Welcome™ book.*

Pet Policy: Designated rooms only.

Amenities: Cable TV, refrigerators, microwaves, pool, spa.

Pet Amenities: List of nearby veterinarians maintained. Inyo National Forest surrounds the town. A city park is located 2 blocks away.

Rated: 2 Paws — 133 rooms and 23 suites.

Sierra Nevada Rodeway Inn affords tastefully appointed rooms in a mountain lodge theme. Standard rooms have two queen-sized beds, private bath, phone and cable television. Located along scenic Highway 395, Mammoth is known as one of the world's finest ski resorts. During the summer months, you'll find fabulous trout fishing, hiking, golf and mountain biking, as well as fascinating sightseeing. Devil's Postpile, Rainbow Falls, Hot Creek, Mono Lake, Bodie Ghost Town and Yosemite National Park are just minutes away from Mammoth.

Miners Inn Motel

5181 Highway 49 North
P.O. Box 2248
Mariposa, CA 95338
888-646-2244 • 209-742-7777
www.yosemite-rooms.com
minersinn@yosemite-rooms.com

Type of Lodging: Motel

Room Rates: $59–$149. AAA and AARP discounts.

Pet Charges & Deposits: $5 per day.

Pet Policy: None. All Pets Welcome.

Amenities: Cable TV, pool, hot tubs.

Pet Amenities: List of nearby veterinarians maintained. Mariposa County Park is located a mile away. Yosemite National Park is 30 miles away where leashes are required and pets are not allowed on marked trails.

Rated: 3 Paws — 76 rooms and 2 suites.

Miner's Inn Motel is a well-priced, convenient and comfortable place on the doorstep of Yosemite National Park. The California State Mining and Mineral Museum and the Mariposa Museum and History Center provide attractive, comprehensive displays of minerals, gold, diamonds and other gems that reflect the wealth found in Mariposa's mines. The Yosemite Valley, 30 miles away, is justifiably world famous—it is one of the most stunningly beautiful landscapes on Earth. El Capitan, Half Dome and other scenes are immortalized in Ansel Adams' timeless photographs.

Stanford Inn By The Sea

Coast Highway 1 at Comptche-Ukiah Road
P.O. Box 487
Mendocino, CA 95460
800-331-8884 • 707-937-5615
www.stanfordinn.com
info@stanfordinn.com

Type of Lodging: Resort

Room Rates: $242–$365, including full breakfast. AAA and *10% Pets Welcome*™ discounts.

Pet Charges & Deposits: $25 per stay for first pet, $12.50 for second pet.

Pet Policy: Manager's prior approval required. Pets must not be left unattended.

Amenities: Cable TV, refrigerators, microwaves, pool, Jacuzzi, hot tubs, spas, fitness room.

Pet Amenities: Dog bones, dishes and furniture covers provided at check-in. List of nearby veterinarians maintained. Exercise area. Headlands State Park is adjacent to the Inn. Russian Gulch State Park is 4 miles north on Highway 1. Big River Beach, just across the river, is an excellent place for dogs.

Rated: 5 Paws — 31 rooms.

The Stanford Inn By The Sea is truly a one-of-a-kind place, justifiably earning the highest rating we give. The Stanford Inn embodies the very best of the rugged Mendocino Coast. Rather than an inn with gardens, the Stanford Inn is a small, working, certified organic garden and farm with an inn. Rooms and suites are paneled with pine and redwood and decorated with antiques, work from local artists and indoor plants. All have wood-burning fireplaces with queen- or king-sized beds. One- or two-bedroom suites provide a separate living room with a wood-burning fireplace. Everywhere, there are views of the dramatic Mendocino Coast. Lovely, relaxing strolls, nature at its best, here is paradise.

Bay Park Hotel

1425 Munras Avenue
Monterey, CA 93940
800-338-3564 • 831-649-1020
www.bayparkhotel.com
baypark@montereybay.com

Type of Lodging: Hotel
Room Rates: $79–$229. AAA discount.
Pet Charges & Deposits: $10 per day
Pet Policy: No pets over 50 lbs. Designated rooms only. Pet sheets to put on the furniture.
Amenities: Cable TV, refrigerators, pool, hot tubs.
Pet Amenities: List of nearby veterinarians maintained. Don Dahvee Park is located on Munras Avenue and Soledad Drive.
Rated: 3 Paws — 80 rooms.

The staff welcomes you and your pet to Monterey's Bay Park Hotel, which is not only strategically located at the base of the hill between Monterey and Carmel, but which also provides large and well-furnished rooms. The Monterey Peninsula is not only known as the golf capital of the world, but it has a plethora of attractions. Attractive Fisherman's Wharf with its shops and restaurants (Domenico's is a special favorite) is nearby.

The Beach Resort

2600 Sand Dunes Drive
Monterey, CA 93940
800-242-8627 • 831-394-3321
www.montereybeachresort.com
information@montereybeachresort.com

Type of Lodging: Hotel
Room Rates: $119–$289. AAA and AARP discounts.
Pet Charges & Deposits: $30 per stay.
Pet Policy: No pets over 50 lbs. Designated rooms only. Pets must be on leash while on property
Amenities: Cable TV, refrigerators, pool, Jacuzzi, restaurant, bar, fitness room, business center.
Pet Amenities: Treats, special furniture covers, key card ID and outdoor pet watering area available. List of nearby veterinarians maintained. Dog runs. Exercise area. Monterey State Beach is a few feet away.
Rated: 3 Paws — 196 rooms.

Attractive upscale accommodations and the only truly beachfront location on the Peninsula make The Beach Resort a welcoming place indeed. You can't really see Monterey unless you've visited the world-famous Monterey Bay Aquarium—the largest and most impressive oceanarium in the Western Hemisphere. It doesn't hurt that the Aquarium is located right on Cannery Row—in an old cannery, in fact. Two standout restaurants in the area, Paradiso and The Whaling Station Inn, are the creation of internationally renowned television chef John Pisto, a native of the Peninsula. This is the only hotel located directly on the beach. In fact, it sits between two state parks.

Victorian Inn

487 Foam Street
Monterey, CA 93940
800-232-4141 • 831-373-5700
www.victorianinn.com
reservations@innsofmonterey.com

Type of Lodging: Inn

Room Rates: $159–$389, including continental breakfast and afternoon wine & cheese hour. AAA and AARP discounts.

Pet Charges & Deposits: $100 deposit of which $75 is refundable.

Pet Policy: Designated rooms only.

Amenities: Cable TV, refrigerators, honor bar, Jacuzzi, fireplaces.

Pet Amenities: Pooch package includes dog bowl, dog cookies and bottled water. Oceanside Recreation Trail is located 2 blocks away.

Rated: 3 Paws — 66 rooms and 2 suites.

Victorian Inn is a wonderful choice of accommodations when you're visiting the fabled Monterey Peninsula. It's convenient to just about everyplace you'll want to visit, from the nearby Path Of History and Allen Knight Maritime Museum, to Pacific Grove, "Butterfly Town, U.S.A.," where the Monarch butterflies come to spend their winter. If you're fortunate enough to be here in the early spring, you might be lucky enough to catch the annual migration of gray whales from Alaska to Baja California.

Best Western El Rancho

2460 North Main Street
Morro Bay, CA 93442
800-628-3500 • 805-772-2212
www.bestwesterncalifornia.com

Type of Lodging: Motel

Room Rates: $49–$149. AAA and AARP discounts.

Pet Charges & Deposits: $10 per stay.

Pet Policy: None. All Pets Welcome.

Amenities: Cable TV, refrigerators, microwaves, pool.

Pet Amenities: List of nearby veterinarians maintained. Beach is only ¼ mile away.

Rated: 3 Paws — 27 rooms.

Best Western El Rancho is a pet-friendly and well-appointed lodging in a particularly noteworthy area of the central California coast. There's a restaurant, a heated pool, in-room coffee and direct dial telephones. The area is named for Morro Rock, a huge, cone-shaped monolith that juts 578 feet out of the Pacific Ocean. Thirty minutes away is "must see" Hearst Castle, sitting astride La Cuesta Encantada (The Enchanted Hill). Construction started in 1919 and continued until 1947, when ill health forced William Randolph Hearst to abandon the project. Today, it consists of 165 rooms, including the 115-room main house and three guesthouses. The main residence is a huge Mediterranean Revival-style building where Hearst's art collection and antiques are displayed. Pools, fountains and statuary grace the landscaped gardens, which overlook San Simeon and the Pacific Ocean.

Swiss Holiday Lodge

2400 South Mount Shasta Boulevard
Mount Shasta, CA 96067
530-926-3446

Type of Lodging: Motel

Room Rates: $30–$100, including continental breakfast. AAA, AARP and *10% Pets Welcome*™ discounts.

Pet Charges & Deposits: $5 per day.

Pet Policy: Small pets only. Designated rooms only.

Amenities: Cable TV, refrigerators, microwaves, pool, whirlpool, Jacuzzi.

Pet Amenities: List of nearby veterinarians maintained. Dog runs. Exercise area. Mount Shasta City Park nearby.

Rated: 2 Paws — 20 rooms and 1 suite.

Swiss Holiday Lodge rests in the quiet shadows of towering Mount Shasta. The motel enjoys sweeping vistas in every direction. Rooms are equipped with individual climate controls, cable television and complimentary coffee and tea. Mount Shasta is the northern gateway to Whiskeytown-Shasta-Trinity Recreation Area, the Shasta-Trinity National Forest and nearby Lake Siskiyou. Both cross-country and downhill skiing facilities are located a mere eight miles away.

Blue Iguana Inn

11794 North Ventura Avenue
Ojai, CA 93023
805-646-5277
www.blueiguanainn.com
blueiguanaresv@aol.com

Type of Lodging: Inn

Room Rates: $95–$189, including continental breakfast on weekends only. AAA and *10% Pets Welcome*™ discounts.

Pet Charges & Deposits: $20 per day.

Pet Policy: Sorry, no cats. No pets over 35 lbs.

Amenities: Cable TV, refrigerators, microwaves, honor bar, pool, Jacuzzi.

Pet Amenities: List of nearby veterinarians maintained. Exercise area. Libbey City Park is located on Ojai Avenue between Signal and Montgomery Streets. Los Padres National Forest nearby.

Rated: 3 Paws — 4 rooms and 7 suites.

The Blue Iguana Inn is an enchanting experience. The Spanish-European-style complex surrounds a central courtyard and Sunset Magazine, Travel & Leisure Magazine, HGTV's "Vacation Living," and Elmer Dills' Vacation Getaways have recommended the lodging. Ojai, a short distance from romantic Santa Barbara, sits in a valley surrounded by high mountains. It's a popular artist colony and retreat, which prides itself on presenting community theater productions and works of prominent California artists. While in the area, be sure to visit the charming Danish community of Solvang, which has captivated the hearts of millions over the years.

Travelodge

580 Oro Dam Boulevard
Oroville, CA 95965
800-578-7878 • 530-533-7070

Type of Lodging: Motel

Room Rates: $55–$155, including continental breakfast. AAA and AARP discounts.

Pet Charges & Deposits: Call for deposit information.

Pet Policy: Designated rooms only. Pets must be kept on leash.

Amenities: Cable TV, refrigerators, microwaves, pool.

Pet Amenities: List of nearby veterinarians maintained. Dog runs. Exercise area. Playtown U.S.A. Park is located 4 blocks away.

Rated: 2 Paws — 70 rooms and 1 suite.

With a heated outdoor pool, newly remodeled rooms and many fine amenities, Travelodge is a fine choice in the Oroville area. Quite close to Sacramento, Oroville nevertheless maintains its allure as a tourist destination in its own right. Oroville Dam is the tallest earthen dam in the world and Feather Falls is the sixth-highest waterfall in the nation. Beautiful Lake Oroville has 167 miles of shoreline. You might want to check out the 1863 Chinese Temple and Garden, the Pioneer Museum, Cherokee Museum, Ehmann Home and the Oregon City Museum.

Desert Patch Inn

73758 Shadow Mountain Drive
Palm Desert, CA 92260
800-350-9758 • 760-346-9161
www.desertpatch.com
desertpatch@earthlink.net

Type of Lodging: B&B

Room Rates: $59–$104, including continental breakfast.

Pet Charges & Deposits: Credit card imprint required as deposit.

Pet Policy: Designated rooms only. Manager's prior approval required. Pets must be on leash.

Amenities: Cable TV, refrigerators, microwaves, pool, whirlpool.

Pet Amenities: Dog runs. Exercise area. Palm Desert Civic Park is located at San Pablo and Fred Waring Drive.

Rated: 2 Paws — 11 rooms and 3 suites.

You'll find it hard to believe you're in the middle of the desert when you look out the window from anywhere on Desert Patch Inn's charming property. It's green everywhere you look, with lush gardens and palm trees surrounding your every step. There's a heated swimming pool and hot spa. A short walk away, you'll find El Paseo Drive, the "Rodeo Drive" (Beverly Hills) of the desert, a renowned shopping area with restaurants, art galleries and boutiques. Spend your days exploring the nearby mountain wilderness on a Jeep safari, hiking legendary Native American canyons, prowling the Living Desert Reserve Wildlife and Botanical Gardens, rising above the desert in a hot air balloon, or just relaxing poolside with a good book and all the sun you'll ever need.

Inn at Deep Canyon

74470 Abronia Trail
Palm Desert, CA 92260
800-253-0004 • 760-346-8061
www.inn-adc.com
innkeeper@inn-adc.com

Type of Lodging: Inn
Room Rates: $59–$209, including continental breakfast. AAA, AARP and **20%** **Pets Welcome™** discounts.
Pet Charges & Deposits: None.
Pet Policy: No pets over 70 lbs. Designated rooms only.
Amenities: Cable TV, refrigerators, pool, Jacuzzi, coffeemakers, kitchenettes.
Pet Amenities: List of nearby veterinarians maintained. Exercise area. Palm Desert Civic Park is located at San Pablo & Fred Waring Drive.
Rated: 3 Paws — 30 rooms and 2 suites.

The Inn at Deep Canyon affords spacious rooms and suites. Most rooms overlook a palm-shaded garden, swimming pool and hydrotherapy spa. Palm Desert claims to be the upscale sister city to Palm Springs. They're both among Southern California's most fashionable and ritzy winter resorts, with almost 350 days of sunshine each year and an average daily temperature of 75°F. The idyllic setting had been the location of many Hollywood productions, as well as the home of a large segment of the entertainment community. Nationally known golf tournaments are held on several of the area's 93 golf courses.

Crowne Plaza Cabaña Palo Alto

4290 El Camino Real
Palo Alto, CA 94306
800-2 CROWNE • 650-857-0787
www.crowneplazacabana.com

Type of Lodging: Hotel
Room Rates: $195–$205. AAA and AARP discounts.
Pet Charges & Deposits: $25 per stay. $100 deposit.
Pet Policy: No pets over 25 lbs. Designated rooms only.
Amenities: Cable TV, refrigerators, pool, hot tubs.
Pet Amenities: Pets Welcome Package includes bowl, treats and pooper scooper. List of nearby veterinarians maintained. Exercise area. Mitchell Park is located off East Charleston and Old Middlefield.
Rated: 3 Paws — 174 rooms and 20 suites.

Crowne Plaza Cabaña is a decidedly upscale, first-class Palo Alto tradition. Originally owned and developed by Doris Day, one of the most pet-friendly human beings on the planet, it was awarded the Mobil Five-Star rating in 1963. Mention the words Palo Alto and the words Stanford University immediately come to mind—that great institution is 2½ miles from the hotel. Stanford Shopping Center and downtown Palo Alto are also only 2½ miles away. Paramount's Great America is ten miles away, as is San Jose, key to the Silicon Valley.

Oxford Suites

651 Five Cities Drive
Pismo Beach, CA 93449
800-982-7848 • 805-773-3773
www.oxfordsuites.com
oxfordsuitespismo@worldnet.att.net

Type of Lodging: Hotel

Suite Rates: $79–$139, including full breakfast and evening reception. AAA, AARP and *Pets Welcome*™ discounts.

Pet Charges & Deposits: $5 per day with a $10 minimum. $100 or credit card refundable deposit.

Pet Policy: No pets over 50 lbs. Designated rooms only. Pets must not be left unattended.

Amenities: Cable TV, refrigerators, microwaves, pool, guest laundry, whirlpool.

Pet Amenities: List of nearby veterinarians maintained. Exercise area. Pismo Beach State Park nearby.

Rated: 3 Paws — 133 suites.

Oxford Suites' tastefully appointed suites are designed to provide comfort and convenience away from home. Hotel services include guest laundry, valet service, safe deposit boxes, fax and copy services, a convenience shop with food, beverage, gifts and video movie rental. Pismo Beach is the classic California beach town, a land of sea breezes, sandy beaches and spectacular sunsets. Fish off the 1,200-foot pier, kayak off the shoreline, rent a four-wheel drive vehicle to explore the endless sand dunes or ride horseback on the beach.

Hilton Pleasanton at The Club

7050 Johnson Drive
Pleasanton, CA 94588
800-445-8667 • 925-463-8000
www.pleasantonhilton.com

Type of Lodging: Hotel

Room Rates: $89–$279. AAA discount

Pet Charges & Deposits: $10 per day

Pet Policy: None. All Pets Welcome.

Amenities: Cable TV, irons and ironing boards, pool, whirlpool, hot tubs, spa, health club, restaurant, lounge.

Pet Amenities: Exercise area.

Rated: 3 Paws — 294 rooms and 4 suites.

You'll find everything that makes a world-class hotel at the Hilton Pleasanton at the Club. Each of the luxurious guestrooms features a work desk, three dual-phones with voicemail and dataports, terry cloth robes and complimentary newspaper delivered daily. Car rental services, valet parking and a gift shop are a few added amenities. Pleasanton is at the gateway to San Francisco Bay and all East Bay communities. It's 17 miles from Oakland, 33 miles from San Francisco International Airport and there's transportation available to the hotel. The Alameda County Fairgrounds has one of the oldest racetracks in America: Spanish Don Augustin Bernal built it in 1858.

Poway Country Inn

13845 Poway Road
Poway, CA 92064
800-648-6320 • 858-748-6320
www.pinnaclehotelsusa.com
pci@pinnaclehotelsusa.com

Type of Lodging: Hotel
Room Rates: $62–$99, including continental breakfast. AAA and AARP discounts.
Pet Charges & Deposits: None.
Pet Policy: No pets over 25 lbs. Designated rooms only. Manager's prior approval required.
Amenities: Cable TV, refrigerators, microwaves, pool, Jacuzzi, coffeemakers, irons and ironing boards, hairdryers.
Pet Amenities: List of nearby veterinarians maintained. Dog runs. Poway Park is located on Middland Road.
Rated: 3 Paws — 43 rooms.

Poway Country Inn offers charming country décor in a two-story structure with exterior corridors. Free local calls and a complimentary continental breakfast are welcome amenities. In nearby San Diego, the Maritime Museum encompasses three historic vessels: the 1863 tall ship Star Of India, the 1889 ferry Berkeley and the 1904 steam yacht Medea. Closer to Poway, San Diego's Wild Animal Park embraces 2,000 acres, housing 3,200 animals, which are able to roam over expanses of land that simulate Africa, Asia and Australia.

Days Inn & Suites

5 John Sutter Street
Red Bluff, CA 96080
800-DAYS INN • 530-527-6130
www.daysinn.com

Type of Lodging: Inn
Room Rates: $42–$100, including continental breakfast. AAA, AARP, AKC and *10% Pets Welcome™* discounts.
Pet Charges & Deposits: $5 per day.
Pet Policy: Designated rooms only.
Amenities: Cable TV, refrigerators, microwaves, pool, hairdryers, alarm clock radios, dataports, free local calls.
Pet Amenities: List of nearby veterinarians maintained. Dog runs. City parks nearby.
Rated: 2 Paws — 47 rooms.

If you are looking for pleasing Northern California hospitality, plan to stay at Days Inn in Red Bluff. Clean rooms, a courteous staff, free local calls and free continental breakfast ensure that your stay is relaxing. William B. Ide Adobe State Historic Park, an 1850 adobe, serves as a memorial to the founder and president of the short-lived Bear Flag Republic. California was actually an independent country for 24 days, until the outbreak of the Mexican-American War and the occupation of the area by U.S. troops. Red Bluff is also convenient to the Sacramento River, Mount Lassen and Mount Shasta.

Redcrest Resort

26459 Avenue of the Giants
Redcrest, CA 95569
707-722-4208

Type of Lodging: Cottages

Cottage Rates: $50–$100. AAA discount.

Pet Charges & Deposits: $5 per day.

Pet Policy: None. All Pets Welcome.

Amenities: Whirlpool, hot tubs, refrigerators, playground, BBQs, campfire area, guest laundry.

Pet Amenities: List of nearby veterinarians maintained. Exercise area. Humboldt Redwoods State Park nearby.

Rated: 2 Paws – 10 cottages.

Redcrest Resort was featured on Huell Howser's California Gold & Road Trip Travel Show (PBS TV) and in AAA Westways magazine. The Resort is located on the Avenue of the Giants, which winds through Humboldt Redwoods State Park. Redcrest, between Garberville and Eureka, is on the Avenue of the Giants, a 33-mile road that challenges the senses, not your driving. The route is flat, with gentle curves that hug the banks of the Eel River as it winds through massive redwood trees. Eureka, with more Victorian houses per capita than any city in California, is less than 30 miles away.

Oxford Suites

1967 Hilltop Drive
Redding, CA 96002
800-762-0133 • 530-221-0100
www.oxfordsuites.com

Type of Lodging: Hotel

Suite Rates: $69–$89, including full breakfast. AAA, AARP, Business and *Pets Welcome™* discounts.

Pet Charges & Deposits: $15 per stay.

Pet Policy: No pets over 20 lbs.

Amenities: Cable TV, refrigerators, microwaves, safes, pool, Jacuzzi.

Pet Amenities: Exercise area.

Rated: 3 Paws – 139 suites.

Conveniently located just off Interstate 5 and only minutes west of downtown Redding, Oxford Suites offers tastefully appointed suites, designed to provide comfort and convenience in an impressive three-story structure. Hotel services include guest laundry, valet service and a convenience shop. When in Redding, be sure to visit Redding State Historic Park, formerly a Gold Rush Mining town, now a very lively Gold Rush relic. Shasta Dam, reputedly the world's highest center-overflow spillway and Lake Shasta, a glorious place for boating, house boating and all kinds of water sports, are nearby and notable.

Edgewater Inn

1977 West Manning Avenue
Reedley, CA 93654
800-479-5855 • 559-637-7777

Type of Lodging: Motel

Room Rates: $53–$79, including continental breakfast. AAA, AARP and *10% Pets Welcome™* discounts.

Pet Charges & Deposits: $7 per day.

Pet Policy: Sorry, no cats. Designated rooms only. Manager's prior approval required. Pets must not be left unattended.

Amenities: Refrigerators, pool, Jacuzzi.

Pet Amenities: List of nearby veterinarians maintained. Kings Canyon National Park nearby. Kings River is 100 feet away.

Rated: 3 Paws — 46 rooms and 2 suites.

Edgewater Inn offers large, comfortable rooms in a two-story structure with exterior corridors. It's a little more than an hour from Sequoia and Kings Canyon National Parks, 2½ hours to Yosemite and a scant 30 minutes to Pine Flat Lake. Reedley, "The World's Fruit Basket," is located on the Blossom Trail, 12 miles from major freeways where you can make connections not only to the National Parks, but to the scenic back country with some of California's most beautiful lakes.

El Bonita Motel

195 Main Street
St. Helena, CA 94574
800-541-3284 • 707-963-3216
www.elbonita.com
elbonita1@aol.com

Type of Lodging: Motel

Room Rates: $89–$279, including continental breakfast.

Pet Charges & Deposits: $5 per day.

Pet Policy: None. All Pets Welcome.

Amenities: Refrigerators, microwaves, pool, whirlpool, hot tubs, sauna.

Pet Amenities: List of nearby veterinarians maintained. Exercise area. City and county parks nearby.

Rated: 3 Paws — 41 rooms and 5 suites.

Located in the heart of the Napa Valley, the El Bonita Motel is a St. Helena tradition that has earned itself a reputation for providing guests with an immaculate place to stay surrounded by a warm and friendly atmosphere. St. Helena is as centrally located as you can get in California's romantic Wine Country. Within a few miles, you will find scores of the most famous wineries in the world, many offering tours and wine tastings. In nearby Calistoga, treat yourself to decadent luxury by enjoying a mud bath, followed by a relaxing body massage.

Campton Place Hotel

340 Stockton Street
San Francisco, CA 94108
800-235-4300 • 415-781-5555
www.camptonplace.com
reserve@campton.com

Type of Lodging: Hotel
Room Rates: $325–$2,000. AAA discount.
Pet Charges & Deposits: $35 per day.
Pet Policy: None. All Pets Welcome.
Amenities: Cable TV, honor bar, safes, acclaimed restaurant.
Pet Amenities: Union Square nearby.
Rated: 5 Paws — 101 rooms and 9 suites.

Just steps from San Francisco's Union Square and a step up from most hotels is one of the truly luxurious hotels in the world—Campton Place. The accommodations at the Campton Place Hotel frequent the list of the "Readers Choice Awards" of Condé Nast Traveler magazine, which has ranked it "One of the top 25 U.S. hotels." The small niceties of a European inn combined with the polished precision of a grand hotel—concierge, newspaper delivery, thick robes and valet parking. As long as you're in America's favorite city, enjoy Chinatown, North Beach, the Wharf, the Golden Gate Bridge, Golden Gate Park, Haight-Ashbury, the theater district...

Laurel Inn

444 Presidio Avenue
San Francisco, CA 94115
800-552-8735 • 415-567-8467
www.thelaurelinn.com

Type of Lodging: Inn
Room Rates: $145–$169, including continental breakfast. AAA discount.
Pet Charges & Deposits: None.
Pet Policy: Pets may not be left unattended.
Amenities: Cable TV, refrigerators, microwaves.
Pet Amenities: List of nearby veterinarians maintained. Parks nearby: Presidio of San Francisco, Presidio and Pacific; Alta Plaza, Clay and Scott Streets.
Rated: 3 Paws — 49 rooms.

The Laurel Inn gives you casual elegance in the atmospheric Pacific Heights area of "the City." You'll appreciate the care given to the smallest details. The Laurel Inn is surrounded by delightful shops, cafes and nearby parks. It's convenient to Union Square, the Financial District and San Francisco's popular sights and attractions. San Francisco has so many attractions; it's hard to know where to start. Golden Gate Park houses the Steinhart Aquarium and wonderful Japanese Tea Gardens. There's Chinatown ("Grant Avenue, San Francisco, California U.S.A."), Little Italy and a host of ethic neighborhoods to discover, each more fascinating than the one before.

Pan Pacific Hotel

500 Post Street
San Francisco, CA 94102
800-533-6465 • 415-771-8600
www.panpac.com
guest@sfo.pan-pacific.com

Type of Lodging: Hotel
Room Rates: $310–$2,800. AAA and AARP discounts.
Pet Charges & Deposits: $75 per stay.
Pet Policy: No pets over 25 lbs. Designated rooms only.
Amenities: Cable TV, refrigerators, safes, fitness center, business center.
Pet Amenities: Treats available. List of nearby veterinarians maintained. Union Square is just steps away.
Rated: 4 Paws — 329 rooms and 35 suites.

The Pan Pacific Hotel, centrally located in America's favorite city, provides world-class accommodations. San Francisco's Exploratorium contains more than 650 interactive exhibits. Almost every tourist takes the boat trip to Alcatraz Island, home of the notorious prison that figures in so many legends of the 1930s and '40s. It's worth it! Drive over the Golden Gate Bridge to Sausalito, or the Bay Bridge to Oakland and Berkeley—anywhere you go, you're sure to be fascinated.

Best Western Royal Oak Hotel

214 Madonna Road
San Luis Obispo, CA 93405
800-545-4410 • 805-544-4410
www.pacificplazahotels.com
info@royaloakhotel.com

Type of Lodging: Hotel
Room Rates: $69–$130, including continental breakfast. AAA and AARP discounts.
Pet Charges & Deposits: $10 per stay.
Pet Policy: No pets over 75 lbs.
Amenities: Cable TV, pool, hot tubs.
Pet Amenities: Laguna Park is adjacent to the hotel.
Rated: 3 Paws — 99 rooms.

Best Western Royal Oak Hotel is a wonderful place to stay where calls are free, as is the delicious continental breakfast. San Luis Obispo is convenient to beaches, hot springs, horseback riding, hiking trails, wineries, the Hearst Castle complex, arts and crafts fairs and numerous antique shops. The Apple Farm features a working reproduction of a 19th century millhouse on San Luis Creek. Visitors can watch a 14-foot water wheel that powers a gristmill, cider press and ice cream maker through a series of gears and pulleys.

Heritage Inn Bed & Breakfast

978 Olive Street
San Luis Obispo, CA 93405
805-544-7440

Type of Lodging: B&B
Room Rates: $85–$150, including full breakfast.
Pet Charges & Deposits: $35 per stay.
Pet Policy: Sorry, no cats. Manager's prior approval required. Pets allowed Sunday through Thursday only.
Amenities: None.
Pet Amenities: Cat in residence. List of nearby veterinarians maintained. Exercise area. Montaña de Oro, Los Osos, Laguna Parks nearby on Madonna Road
Rated: 2 Paws — 7 rooms.

Experience the romance of a turn-of-the-century inn while your hostess pampers you with home-style hospitality. Be forewarned, there is a terminally spoiled cat in residence. Mission San Luis Obispo de Tolosa, "the Prince of Missions," built in 1772, is now a parish church. In order to repel flaming arrows from unfriendly natives, the mission was built with a tile roof instead of a thatch roof. A museum contains various artifacts of the Chumash Native Americans.

Sands Suites & Motel

1930 Monterey Street
San Luis Obispo, CA 93401
800- 441-4657• 805-544-0500
www.sandssuites.com

Type of Lodging: Motel

Room Rates: $59–$169, including continental breakfast. AAA and AARP discounts.

Pet Charges & Deposits: $10 per stay.

Pet Policy: None. All Pets Welcome.

Amenities: Cable TV, VCRs, refrigerators, microwaves, honor bar, safes, pool.

Pet Amenities: List of nearby veterinarians maintained. Cuesta County Park is located on Loomis Street. Santa Rosa Park is located at Santa Rosa & Murray Streets.

Rated: 3 Paws – 55 rooms and 15 suites.

Sands Suites & Motel is proud to present clean and cheery rooms, as well as a very pet-friendly staff. It's conveniently close to Cal Poly University, the Old Mission and historic downtown. The on-premises deli and general store has just about everything you'll need. Start your weekend early with a BBQ dinner at the outdoor Farmers Market and Street Fair. The San Luis Obispo Children's Museum lets children learn through more than 25 interactive exhibits.

Best Western Big America

1725 North Broadway
Santa Maria, CA 93454
800-423-3213 • 805-922-5200
www.bigamerica.com
info@bigamerica.com

Type of Lodging: Hotel

Room Rates: $69–$109, including continental breakfast. AAA, AARP and *10% Pets Welcome™* discounts.

Pet Charges & Deposits: None.

Pet Policy: No pets over 30 lbs.

Amenities: Cable TV, refrigerators, microwaves, safes, pool, Jacuzzi, restaurant.

Pet Amenities: List of nearby veterinarians maintained. Exercise area. Preisker Park is located on Broadway & Preisker. Waller Park is located on Broadway and Waller Lane.

Rated: 3 Paws – 106 rooms and 16 suites.

Best Western Big America is up to the high, first-class standards you'd expect of a Best Western property: fresh guestrooms with upscale amenities. Santa Maria is close to Vandenberg Air Force Base, the West Coast space launch facility. The Santa Maria Museum of Flight displays the Fleet Model 2, the Stinson V77 Reliant and an extensive collection of model airplanes, from the Wright Brothers pioneering effort to the Stealth Bomber.

Holiday Inn Express

28976 West Plaza Drive
Santa Nella, CA 95322
800-428-3687 • 209-826-8282
www.hiexpress.com/santanellaca

Type of Lodging: Motel

Room Rates: $60–$85, including continental breakfast. AAA, AARP and *10% Pets Welcome™* discounts.

Pet Charges & Deposits: None.

Pet Policy: Designated rooms only.

Amenities: Refrigerators, pool, whirlpool, spas.

Pet Amenities: List of nearby veterinarians maintained. Exercise area. San Luis State Park nearby.

Rated: 3 Paws — 100 rooms.

Holiday Inn Express is an impressive lodging, with a landscaped courtyard and guestrooms, all designed with soothing colors for the ultimate in relaxation. Santa Nella is on Interstate 5, on the way to just about anywhere in California. If you want an absolute, unsung treat, known only to a very few (hundred thousand) California "locals," go to nearby Los Baños and ask where to find the Woolgrowers Restaurant—it's not easy to find and it looks like an absolute dump from the outside. When you first enter, it still doesn't look like anything special. But once in the main dining room, you'll be treated to a reasonably priced (cash only) family-style meal that you'll never forget.

Herrington's Sierra Pines Resort

104 Main Street
Sierra City, CA 96125
800- 682-9848 • 530-862-1151

Type of Lodging: Resort

Room Rates: $49–$90. AAA, AARP, AKC, ABA and *10% Pets Welcome™* discounts.

Pet Charges & Deposits: None.

Pet Policy: None. All Pets Welcome.

Amenities: None.

Pet Amenities: List of nearby veterinarians maintained. Exercise area. Tahoe National Forest nearby.

Rated: 4 Paws — 21 rooms on 50 acres of river frontage in the forest.

Nestled at the base of the Sierra Buttes, Sierra Pines Resort is located in historic Sierra City. Founded in 1850 and once a booming mine town, today it's a popular tourist area. The motel accommodations are wood-paneled with cable television, covered decks overlooking the river and king-sized or double beds. Within a radius of nine miles, there are more than 20 sparkling mountain lakes, providing a spectacular setting for summer fishing, boating, hiking and sightseeing. During the winter, cross-country skiing and snowmobiling are just minutes away. Tahoe's North Shore is within an hour's drive.

Alder Inn

1072 Ski Run Boulevard
South Lake Tahoe, CA 96150
800-544-0056 • 530-544-4485

Type of Lodging: Motel

Room Rates: $65–$136, including continental breakfast. AAA, AARP and *10% Pets Welcome™* discounts.

Pet Charges & Deposits: $10 per day.

Pet Policy: Cats must be declawed. Manager's prior approval required. Pets must not be left unattended.

Amenities: Cable TV, refrigerators, pool, whirlpool, hot tubs, complimentary shuttles.

Pet Amenities: Pet sitters available but they must be reserved as they are very much in demand. List of nearby veterinarians maintained. Dog runs. Exercise area. El Dorado National Forest and Tahoe National Forest surround the Inn.

Rated: 2 Paws — 24 rooms.

Alder Inn provides moderately priced, attractive and spacious accommodations in one of California's, and the nation's, premier year-round vacation destination. Lake Tahoe holds enough water to cover the entire state of California to a depth of 14 feet; its water is 97% pure—the same as distilled water. It is 22 miles long, 12 miles wide and rests at an altitude of 6,229 feet above sea level. World famous ski venues, such as Squaw Valley (1960 Winter Olympics) and Heavenly Valley compete for the tourist dollar with a host of Nevada gaming casinos and world-class entertainments. Oh yes, Lake Tahoe straddles the California-Nevada border.

Tahoe Keys Resort/Lake Tahoe Reservation Bureau

599 Tahoe Keys Resort
South Lake Tahoe, CA 96150
800-698-2463 • 530-544-5397
www.tahoevacationguide.com
info@tahoevacationguide.com

Type of Lodging: Vacation rentals

Room Rates: $99–$1,100. AAA, AARP and *10% Pets Welcome™* discounts.

Pet Charges & Deposits: $25 per stay. $100 refundable deposit.

Pet Policy: Designated rentals only. Manager's prior approval required.

Amenities: Amenities vary from property to property.

Pet Amenities: List of nearby veterinarians maintained. Various parks and outdoor recreation areas nearby.

Rated: 3 Paws — 220 vacation rentals.

Whether it's a cabin, a condo, a home, whether you want mountainside or lake views, Tahoe Keys Resort/Lake Tahoe Reservation Bureau can provide it for you in every price range. Lake Tahoe is justifiably famous the world over as a perfect vacation spot. In winter, there are 15 fabulous ski resorts within an hour's drive of one another. In summer, you have blue skies, incredible mountain and lake vistas. And throughout the year, you have magnificent, opulent casinos with entertaining shows and exciting games of chance.

Sierra Lodge

43175 Sierra Drive
Three Rivers, CA 93271
800-367-8879 • 559-561-3681
http://sierralodge.theworks.com

Type of Lodging: Motel

Room Rates: $42–$175, including continental breakfast. AAA and AARP discounts.

Pet Charges & Deposits: $5 per day. $20 refundable deposit.

Pet Policy: Designated rooms only. Manager's prior approval required.

Amenities: Cable TV, refrigerators, microwaves, pool.

Pet Amenities: List of nearby veterinarians maintained. Sequoia and Kings Canyon National Parks are 3½ miles away.

Rated: 2 Paws — 17 rooms and 5 suites.

Sierra Lodge is located near the gates to Sequoia and Kings Canyon National Park. Enjoy comfort when you choose a room with a wood-burning fireplace, kitchenette, refrigerator and private deck. Three Rivers is a Sierra Foothill gem, nestled among 3,000-foot peaks, splashed by three snow-fed streams and bathed in California's citrus zone climate. Mineral King offers backpackers an unsurpassed experience: a peaceful mountain retreat in the incredible backcountry wilderness.

Inn at Truckee

11506 Deerfield Drive
Truckee, CA 96160
888-773-6888 • 530-587-8888
www.innattruckee.com

Type of Lodging: Motel

Room Rates: $69–$140, including continental breakfast. AAA and AARP discounts.

Pet Charges & Deposits: $15 per stay.

Pet Policy: None. All Pets Welcome.

Amenities: Cable TV, hot tubs, sauna.

Pet Amenities: List of nearby veterinarians maintained. Donner Memorial State Park, Donner Lake, Lake Tahoe, numerous national forest areas and reservoirs nearby.

Rated: 3 Paws — 43 rooms.

The Inn at Truckee is an attractive, three-story structure with interior corridors leading to clean and cozy rooms. Truckee, just minutes from Squaw Valley and the north shore of Lake Tahoe, was a lawless 19th century lumber and railroad town. Today, it's a robust, touristy 19th century replica, with "Western" storefronts on its main shopping street, an old railroad depot and an active railroad track running through the center of town. Donner Lake and numerous ski areas are nearby. The Donner Memorial Park commemorates the ill-fated Donner expedition of 1846-47 when 89 persons were trapped in the High Sierra, without food. By the time 47 members of the party were rescued, some had resorted to cannibalism to stay alive.

Summerfield Suites by Wyndham

1000 Westmount Drive
West Hollywood, CA 90069
800-833-4353 • 310-657-7400
www.wyndham.com

Type of Lodging: Hotel

Suite Rates: $139–$189, including full breakfast. *50% Pets Welcome™* discount.

Pet Charges & Deposits: $10 per day. $75–$150 nonrefundable cleaning charge.

Pet Policy: No pets over 75 lbs. Cats must be declawed.

Amenities: Cable TV, refrigerators, microwaves, safes, pool, Jacuzzi, sauna, guest laundry.

Pet Amenities: West Hollywood Park is located on San Vicente & Melrose.

Rated: 3 Paws — 110 suites.

Summerfield Suites, with spacious Junior, Executive and One-bedroom suites, affords luxurious accommodations away from home, whether you're here for business or a vacation. West Hollywood is so close to everything in L.A. Stroll down fabled Rodeo Drive in Beverly Hills, spot the stars in the sidewalk on Hollywood Boulevard, take a drive through Bel Air and view the homes of world-famous stars. You're minutes away from the Sunset Strip. Or drive to Mulholland Drive and view it all—the Valley and the Basin. This is the L.A. experience! The lodging is located in a residential area so many people regularly walk their dogs in the area. Fido might make a new friend.

Granzella's Inn

391 Sixth Street
Williams, CA 95987
800-643-8614 • 530-473-3310

Type of Lodging: Inn

Room Rates: $65–$95, including continental breakfast. AAA and AARP discounts.

Pet Charges & Deposits: $10 per stay.

Pet Policy: Limit two pets per room.

Amenities: Cable TV, pool, hot tubs, refrigerators, microwaves.

Pet Amenities: None.

Rated: 3 Paws — 34 rooms and 9 suites.

Granzella's furnishes spick 'n' span accommodations in a pleasant, two-story structure. Williams is perfectly situated off Interstate 5, between Sacramento and Redding. The Sacramento Valley Museum, in the Williams High School building, has exhibits depicting life in the Sacramento Valley from the mid-1800s to the 1930s. There's an apothecary, a doll museum, a millinery, dress shop and an old-fashioned general store.

Holiday Inn

21101 Ventura Boulevard
Woodland Hills, CA 91364
800-HOLIDAY • 818-883-6110
www.holiday-inn.com/woodlandhills

Type of Lodging: Hotel
Room Rates: $99–$169, including continental breakfast. AAA and AARP discounts.
Pet Charges & Deposits: $25 per week.
Pet Policy: Small pets only. Designated rooms only.
Amenities: Cable TV, refrigerators, pool, restaurant, fitness room, coffeemakers.
Pet Amenities: Exercise area. Serrania Park is located approximately a mile away on 20865 Wells Drive.
Rated: 3 Paws — 124 rooms.

Comfort, convenience and value in Southern California are hallmarks of the Holiday Inn. Rooms are spotlessly maintained. Woodland Hills is in the very heart of Los Angeles' fabled San Fernando Valley and the Holiday Inn is right "on the boulevard." An interesting scenic side trip: instead of driving the freeways into Los Angeles, take your time and drive through Malibu Canyon to the beach. Then drive the Pacific Coast Highway south to Santa Monica, an eclectic community adjacent to even quirkier Venice. Now, that's the way to see L.A.!

Redwoods In Yosemite

P.O. Box 2085
Yosemite National Park, CA 95389
209-375-6666
www.redwoodsinyosemite.com
info@redwoodsinyoesmite.com

Type of Lodging: Vacation Homes
House Rates: $90–$600. AAA discount.
Pet Charges & Deposits: $10 per day.
Pet Policy: Designated rooms only.
Amenities: Amenities vary from property to property.
Pet Amenities: List of nearby veterinarians maintained. Inside Yosemite National Park. National Park leash laws in effect. Certain trails are not available to pets.
Rated: 3 Paws — 130 fully furnished houses.

You will surely enjoy all the comforts of home at the Redwoods in Yosemite. Nestled among the trees, you can select a rustic log cabin or a spacious mountain vacation home. Relax by a crackling fire in the rock fireplace and stargaze at a night sky so dark you can see the Milky Way. Yosemite is one of the world's tourist destination areas and with justifiable reason. The Redwoods are near Wawona, the southwest entry to the Park. Badger Pass is an excellent choice for skiing in the winter and you're surprisingly close to Yosemite Valley. What you won't believe is that it's even more beautiful than the Ansel Adams photographs!

Days Inn Yuba City

700 North Palora Avenue
Yuba City, CA 95991
800-DAYS INN • 530-674-1711
www.daysinn.com

Type of Lodging: Inn

Room Rates: $45–$64, including continental breakfast. AAA, AARP and AKC discounts.

Pet Charges & Deposits: $7 per day. Credit card refundable deposit required.

Pet Policy: None. All Pets Welcome.

Amenities: Refrigerators, microwaves, pool.

Pet Amenities: City park nearby.

Rated: 2 Paws — 50 rooms.

Days Inn Yuba City affords bright, comfortable rooms, a large outdoor heated pool and a kids stay free policy that gives you a welcomed feeling. Yuba City Mall is half a mile away. Beale Air Force Base is five miles from the lodging. It's 45 miles to Sacramento, California's state capital. While there, be sure to visit the State Capitol, as impressive for its grounds and exhibits as it is for its stature among Capitol buildings.

COLORADO

Nickname: Centennial State

Population: 4,056,133

Area: 104,100 square miles

Climate: Low relative humidity, abundant sunshine, wide daily, seasonal temperature ranges, alpine conditions in high mountains.

Capital: Denver

Entered Union: August 1, 1876

Motto: *Nil Sine Numine* (Nothing Without Providence).

Song: Where the Columbines Grow

Flower: Rocky Mountain Columbine

Tree: Colorado Blue Spruce

Bird: Lark Bunting

Famous Coloradans: Tim Allen, Molly Brown, Scott Carpenter, Jack Dempsey, Douglas Fairbanks, Lowell Thomas.

 History: Approximately 2,000 years ago, early civilization centered around Mesa Verde. Later, Ute, Pueblo, Arapahoe and Cheyenne peoples lived in the area. The U.S. acquired eastern Colorado in the Louisiana Purchase in 1803. After the Mexican War, 1846-48, U.S. immigrants settled in the east, former Mexicans in the south. Gold was discovered in 1858. A population boom followed. Displaced Native Americans protested, resulting in the Sand Creek Massacre (1864) where more than 200 Cheyenne and Arapahoe were killed. All Native Americans were later moved to the Oklahoma Territory. For a wonderful look at the Colorado that was, consider reading (or re-reading) James Michener's *Centennial.*

Hotel Aspen

110 West Main Street
Aspen, CO 81611
800-527-7369 • 970-925-3441
www.hotelaspen.com
hotlaspn@rof.net

Type of Lodging: Hotel

Room Rates: $89–$269, including continental breakfast. AAA and AARP discounts.

Pet Charges & Deposits: $10 per day.

Pet Policy: Designated rooms only.

Amenities: Cable TV, refrigerators, microwaves, safes, pool, Jacuzzi, coffeemakers, hairdryers, irons and ironing boards.

Pet Amenities: List of nearby veterinarians maintained. Exercise area. Paepke Park is across the street and White River National Forest is only 5 blocks away.

Rated: 3 Paws — 45 rooms.

Billing itself as "a contemporary classic," Hotel Aspen's claim may not be far off the mark. Rooms are large and beautifully appointed, featuring king- or queen-sized beds, wet bars and refrigerators. It is only four blocks from the center of town. Aspen's story is a replay of "The Unsinkable Molly Brown." An 1,840-pound, 93% pure silver nugget was displayed at the Columbian Exposition of 1893. Scarcely a few months later, supply exceeded demand and, in the Panic of 1893, Colorado's economy, and Aspen's lifeline, collapsed. Things remained stagnant until the late 1930s, when Aspen's first ski area was built. The rest is history. The little city in the Roaring Fork Valley has become one of America's premier, if not *the* premier, ski resort.

Boulder Mountain Lodge

91 Four Mile Canyon Drive
Boulder, CO 80302
800-458-0882 • 303-444-0882
www.bouldermountainlodge.com
bldmtnlodge@aol.com

Type of Lodging: Motel

Room Rates: $53–$123.

Pet Charges & Deposits: $50 refundable deposit.

Pet Policy: Designated rooms only.

Amenities: Refrigerators, microwaves, pool, hot tubs.

Pet Amenities: List of nearby veterinarians maintained. Betaso Preserve is located directly behind the motel and consists of 600 acres of pristine beauty.

Rated: 2 Paws — 22 rooms and 5 suites.

Wouldn't you rather be in the mountains, surrounded by tall trees, wildflowers and majestic rock formations, visited by deer, entertained by high-country birds and relaxed by the sounds of a quiet stream? It's hard to believe that Boulder Mountain Lodge is five minutes from downtown Boulder, on Four Mile Creek. The location, between a creek and hillside in the pines, is secluded and peaceful. There are campsites as well as rooms, kitchenette units and suites. Family-owned and operated, you'll find all the modern amenities and yet you're truly away from it all. The combination of climate, scenery and the University of Colorado make Boulder one of the loveliest cities in the nation.

Pearl Street Inn

1820 Pearl Street
Boulder, CO 80302
888-810-1302 • 303-444-5584
www.pearlstreetinn.com

Type of Lodging: B&B
Room Rates: $119–$179, including full breakfast.
Pet Charges & Deposits: $10 per stay.
Pet Policy: Manager's prior approval required.
Amenities: Courtyard.
Pet Amenities: None.
Rated: 3 Paws — 7 rooms and 1 suite.

Built as a private residence in 1898, the Pearl Street Inn is an elegant bed and breakfast with a sense of privacy and serenity. Overlooking the garden courtyard, each room has a cathedral ceiling, wood-burning fireplace, private bath, exquisite antiques and fresh flowers. Guests are greeted in the morning with friendly smiles and an abundant gourmet breakfast. Pearl Street Inn is within walking distance of Boulder's finest shops, galleries and restaurants on historic Pearl Street Mall. A brief car ride can take you to any one of Boulder's parks, trails or forested areas for hours of peaceful exploration.

Residence Inn by Marriott

3030 Center Green Drive
Boulder, CO 80301
800-331-3131 • 303-449-5545

Type of Lodging: Hotel
Suite Rates: $119–$189, including continental breakfast and evening Hospitality Hour. AAA and AARP discounts.
Pet Charges & Deposits: $5–$8 per day. $50 nonrefundable deposit.
Pet Policy: None. All Pets Welcome.
Amenities: Fully equipped kitchens, pool, Jacuzzi, guest laundry.
Pet Amenities: None.
Rated: 3 Paws — 128 suites.

When looking for a home away from home, a short business trip or an extended family vacation, the Residence Inn by Marriott is a natural choice. Here guests will find spacious suites with separate living and sleeping areas. Some include inviting fireplaces, where you can relax with a good book or a glass of wine. The fully equipped kitchens are perfect for preparing your own meals or for a quick, late-night snack. All rooms include in-room movies, work desks with lamps, voicemail and dataports on phones. Located two miles from downtown Boulder, it is a short drive to Rocky Mountain National Park, Coors Brewing Company and the Eldora Ski Resort.

Chipita Lodge Bed & Breakfast

9090 Chipita Park Road
Chipita Park, CO 80809
877-CHIPITA • 719-684-8454
www.chipitalodge.com
chipitainn@aol.com

Type of Lodging: B&B

Room Rates: $98–$150, including continental breakfast.

Pet Charges & Deposits: $50 refundable deposit.

Pet Policy: Designated rooms only. Manager's prior approval required.

Amenities: Cable TV, refrigerators, microwaves, hot tubs.

Pet Amenities: List of nearby veterinarians maintained. Dog runs. Exercise area. Garden of the Gods Park, Pikes Peak Park and Barr Camp Park nearby.

Rated: 2 Paws — 4 rooms.

Located at the base of Pike's Peak, Chipita Lodge was built in 1927 of native logs and stone. Four unique, rustic, romantic rooms await your pleasure. Eight miles west of Colorado Springs, Chipita Lodge once served as a general store, post office, community center and land development office. Situated on a hill overlooking Chipita Lake, the lodge has been carefully restored and converted into a bed and breakfast. Area attractions include the Pike's Peak Cog Railway, Garden of the Gods, the U.S. Air Force Academy, Cave of the Winds and hiking and biking trails.

Radisson Inn & Suites Colorado Springs Airport

1645 North Newport Road
Colorado Springs, CO 80916
800-333-3333 • 719-597-7000
www.radisson.com
radissoncos@hotmail.com

Type of Lodging: Hotel

Room Rates: $69–$139, including full breakfast. AAA, AARP and *10% Pets Welcome*™ discounts.

Pet Charges & Deposits: $100 refundable deposit.

Pet Policy: No pets over 50 lbs.

Amenities: Cable TV, coffeemakers, hairdryers, irons and ironing boards, dataports, pool, hot tubs, restaurant.

Pet Amenities: List of nearby veterinarians maintained. Exercise area. Palmer Park, the largest city park, is 4 miles away. Neighborhood park is located a mile west of property.

Rated: 3 Paws — 135 rooms and 65 suites. Eight-time Presidential Award Winner.

Welcome to beautiful Colorado Springs. The Radisson is conveniently located just minutes from Colorado Springs Airport, ten minutes from downtown and easily accessible to all major attractions. Standard in-room amenities include a wet bar, coffeemaker, work desk, dataports, two-line telephones, hairdryer, iron and ironing board and a comfortable sitting area. Start your day with a steaming cup of coffee, a complimentary newspaper and a full buffet breakfast. BC's, the hotel's restaurant, has a panoramic view of Pike's Peak and the Front Range. The Garden of the Gods, Pike's Peak and all of Colorado Springs' major attractions await you.

Anasazi Motor Inn

640 South Broadway
Cortez, CO 81321
800-972-6232 • 970-565-3773

Type of Lodging: Motel

Room Rates: $51–$71, including coffee. AAA, AARP discounts.

Pet Charges & Deposits: $50 refundable deposit.

Pet Policy: Pets must not be left unattended.

Amenities: Refrigerators, pool, hot tubs, volleyball pit, walking path, restaurant.

Pet Amenities: List of nearby veterinarians maintained. Dog runs. Exercise area. Mesa Verde Park nearby.

Rated: 2 Paws — 86 rooms.

The Anasazi Motor Inn, located in the heart of the ancient Anasazi Empire (the largest archaeological site in the country) is a full service motel. To the north is unsurpassed mountain scenery. To the southwest, you'll find the Ute and Navajo Reservations and unique desert landscapes. To the east, Mesa Verde National Park is a short drive. One of the closest places you'll find to the Four Corners area, where you can place one hand (or foot) in Colorado, another in Utah and your other extremities in New Mexico and Arizona.

Econo Lodge Cortez

2020 East Main Street
Cortez, CO 81321
800-553-2666 • 970-565-3474

Type of Lodging: Motel

Room Rates: $36–$139, including continental breakfast. AAA, AARP, AKC, ABA, Rental Car, Corporate, VIP and *10% Pets Welcome™* discounts.

Pet Charges & Deposits: $20 refundable deposit.

Pet Policy: Designated rooms only.

Amenities: Cable TV, refrigerators, microwaves, safes, pool, hot tubs.

Pet Amenities: List of nearby veterinarians maintained. Exercise area. Mesa Verde National Park is 8 miles away. Cortez Civic Park is located ½ mile from the property on Main Street and Mildred Road.

Rated: 2 Paws — 68 rooms and **2** suites. Gold Medal Winner.

Econo Lodge's rooms have recently been renovated. There is lots of dining and shopping within walking distance. Biking and hiking trails are nearby. Mesa Verde National Park, some of the most fascinating Native American ruins you'll ever see, is minutes away. Ute Mountain Casino is 12 miles away, boating and fishing are eight miles and golf is 2½ miles from the motel. Four Corners is within hailing distance.

Holiday Inn Express

2121 East Main Street
Cortez, CO 81321
800-626-5652 • 970-565-6000
www.coloradoholiday.com
holiday@fone.net

Type of Lodging: Hotel
Room Rates: $78–$109, including continental breakfast. AAA, AARP, AKC, ABA and *10% Pets Welcome*™ discounts.
Pet Charges & Deposits: None.
Pet Policy: Designated rooms only.
Amenities: Cable TV, safes, pool, Jacuzzi, lounge, fitness center.

Pet Amenities: The Durango Kennel Club stays at the hotel every year. List of nearby veterinarians maintained. Great walking area behind the hotel. Several city parks are about 1½ miles down the road.
Rated: 3 Paws — 92 rooms and 8 suites.

Holiday Inn Express is located next to the Cortez Conference Center and Koko's Friendly Pub. Start your day with a deluxe complimentary continental breakfast. There's an indoor pool, sauna, hot tub, weight room, airport shuttle and tour assistance service. Gaming and casino entertainment is 15 minutes away, with golf and tennis practically across the street. Holiday Inn Express is a great entry point for the San Juan Skyway, often called "America's Most Beautiful Drive."

Tomahawk Lodge

728 South Broadway
Cortez, CO 81321
800-643-7705 • 970-565-8521

Type of Lodging: Motel
Room Rates: $45–$75, including coffee and tea in the office. AAA, AARP, AKC, ABA and *10% Pets Welcome*™ discounts.
Pet Charges & Deposits: $25 refundable deposit.
Pet Policy: Sorry, no cats. Designated rooms only. Manager's prior approval required. Pets must not be left unattended.
Amenities: Cable TV, pool.
Pet Amenities: List of nearby veterinarians maintained. Cortez Civic Park is located on Main Street and Mildred Road. Paque de Vida is located at Mildred Road and Montezuma.
Rated: 2 Paws — 38 rooms.

A one-story lodging, Tomahawk Lodge allows you to make free local calls. Native American dances are performed in the City Park at 7:30 p.m., Monday through Saturday, Memorial Day weekend through Labor Day. The Four Corners monument, 35 miles away, is the only place in the country where four states meet. A concrete monument bearing each state's seal marks the juncture of Arizona, Colorado, New Mexico and Utah. The Ute, Hopi and Navajo sell their wares near the site.

Black Nugget Motel

2855 West Victory Way
Craig, CO 81625-4001
970-824-8161
blacknuggetmotel@yahoo.com

Type of Lodging: Motel

Room Rates: $34–$55, including continental breakfast. AAA, AARP, Commercial and Government discounts.

Pet Charges & Deposits: $4 per day.

Pet Policy: Designated rooms only. Manager's prior approval required.

Amenities: Cable TV, refrigerators, microwaves.

Pet Amenities: List of nearby veterinarians maintained. Dog runs. Exercise area. City park nearby.

Rated: 2 Paws — 20 rooms.

The Black Nugget Motel is located on U.S. Highway 40 at the heart of the meandering canyons of the Yampa and Green Rivers. The motel is situated on top of a hill, above the noise, with a panoramic view of the beautiful Yampa Valley. It's located 40 minutes from the ski areas in Steamboat Springs. Denver elk, antelopes, deer and eagles are plentiful in the surrounding mountains. The Museum of Northwest Colorado contains Native American artifacts, rock collections and items pertaining to local history.

Hawthorn Suites Denver Tech Center

5001 South Ulster Street
Denver, CO 80237
303-804-9900
www.hawthorn.com
dtchhawthorn@aol.com

Type of Lodging: Hotel

Suite Rates: $89–$149, including full breakfast and weekday Manager's Reception. AAA, AARP and *10% Pets Welcome*™ discounts.

Pet Charges & Deposits: $125 nonrefundable deposit.

Pet Policy: No pets over 25 lbs. Designated rooms only. Manager's prior approval required.

Amenities: Cable TV, fully equipped kitchens, safes, pool, Jacuzzi, fireplaces.

Pet Amenities: Welcome Basket available. List of nearby veterinarians maintained. City parks nearby.

Rated: 3 Paws — 123 suites.

Hawthorn Suites is a homey all-suite hotel. So that it can be ready and waiting for you upon arrivalake sure to mention that you would like to reserve your special Pets Welcome Basket. This surprisingly charming hotel is located in the heart of Denver's Technology Center with easy access to Mile High Stadium, Downtown Denver and Coors Field.

❖ ❖ ❖ ❖ ❖

Hotel Monaco Denver

1717 Champa Street @ 17th
Denver, CO 80202
800-397-5380 • 303-296-1717
www.monaco-denver.com
reservations@monaco-denver.com

Type of Lodging: Hotel
Room Rates: $125–$1,800, including wine hour and morning coffee. AAA and AARP discounts.
Pet Charges & Deposits: None.
Pet Policy: None. All Pets Welcome.
Amenities: Honor bar, spas, fax machines, CD players.
Pet Amenities: Live goldfish upon request. Dog biscuits and walking service available. List of nearby veterinarians. Dog runs. Exercise area. City Park nearby.
Rated: 5 Paws — 189 rooms and 32 suites.

Downtown Denver's 5-Paw Hotel Monaco Denver is a blast into the past—pure, elemental escape into a time of steamer trunks, exotic ports of call, private telegrams. Despite its long-ago, faraway feel, it's smack dab in the middle of Denver's central business district: one block to the mile-long Sixteenth Street Pedestrian Mall, just a few blocks to the Denver Performing Arts Center. This ultra-sophisticated, high-style luxury hotel is located in the completely renovated historic 1917 Railway Exchange Building and the 1937 Art Moderne Title Building. This place is so unique, you could easily spend your whole vacation here. Guestrooms and suites continue the fantasy. Royal blue chairs with gold stars, black-and-white striped ottomans and glass-fronted armoires with silk draperies contribute to some of the sensual out-of-this-world environments—even though they have all of the modern conveniences.

But in case you can't bring your pet, this extremely pet-friendly property offers travelers a temporary pet—a complimentary goldfish. A companion goldfish may be requested when making a reservation or at check-in and is delivered to the guest's room for their stay. The trained hotel staff administers goldfish care and feeding.

Loews Giorgio Hotel

4150 East Mississippi Avenue
Denver, CO 80246
800-345-9172 • 303-782-9300
www.loewshotels.com

Type of Lodging: Hotel

Room Rates: $89–$299, including continental breakfast on weekends only. AAA, AARP and *10% Pets Welcome*™ discounts.

Pet Charges & Deposits: None.

Pet Policy: Designated rooms only.

Amenities: Cable TV, refrigerators, microwaves, safes, hairdryers.

Pet Amenities: Loews has a marvelous "Loews Loves Pets" Program that is unique and exceptional. List of nearby and on-call veterinarians and "pet-friendly" restaurants. There's a complimentary pet walking service and a listing of pet walkers, pet sitters and groomers in the area. Exercise area. Washington Park is located at Mississippi and Franklin.

Rated: 5 Paws — 183 rooms and 19 suites.

The Loews Giorgio Hotel rates a Pets Welcome™ Notable 5-Paw Award because of the wonderful array of pet services offered. There are "Bark Breakfasts," with "Ask The Vet" stations and pet grooming stations. The attractions of Denver are many and varied—it's a tremendous place to be—and at Loews Giorgio Hotel it's a truly pet-friendly place to vacation. Loews has a marvelous "Loews Loves Pets" Program that is unique and exceptional. The welcome amenities include a welcome letter from the General Manager's hotel pet; a separate sheet that explains services available for your pet; a map highlighting areas to walk your pet and attractions for your pet; a logo pet mat, a logo bowl for water; a bag of pet treats and a pet toy. Loews provides a pet room service menu, along with some prepared foods on the regular Room Service menu (i.e. fillet for dogs, salmon for cats) and a "Do Not Disturb" sign that indicates that there is a pet in the room with "WOOF" on one side and "MEOW" on the other. Loews provides several dog and cat beds in different sizes, leashes and collars in different sizes, litter box, litter and pooper scooper.

Days Inn Durango

1700 County Road 203
Durango, CO 81301
800-338-1116 • 970-259-1430
daysinndurango@frontier.net

Type of Lodging: Hotel
Room Rates: $60–$100, including continental breakfast. AAA and AARP discounts.
Pet Charges & Deposits: None.
Pet Policy: Pets must not be left unattended.
Amenities: Cable TV, safes, pool, Jacuzzis, fitness room.
Pet Amenities: Exercise area. Mesa Verde National Park is 40 miles west.
Rated: 2 Paws — 95 rooms.

Nestled in the beautiful Animas River Valley, Days Inn offers breathtaking mountain and valley views. The lodging has an indoor pool, two giant Jacuzzis, saunas, a fitness room, massage therapy, a ski area and downtown shuttle from mid-December through late March. Durango is a natural gateway to one of the most scenic areas of the state. Because they are geologically younger than other Colorado ranges, the San Juans present a more jagged, precipitous and dramatic appearance. The largest and best preserved Anasazi Native American cliff dwellings in the Southwest are in Mesa Verde National Park.

Doubletree Hotel Durango

501 Camino Del Rio
Durango, CO 81301
970-259-6580
www.doubletree.com
gm@rldu.doubletree.com

Type of Lodging: Hotel
Room Rates: $69–$375, including Doubletree Chocolate Chip Cookies. AAA, AARP and *5% Pets Welcome*™ discounts.
Pet Charges & Deposits: $10 per day
Pet Policy: None. All Pets Welcome.
Amenities: Cable TV, pool, hot tubs, spas, saunas.
Pet Amenities: List of nearby veterinarians maintained. Exercise area. River walk directly behind the hotel. Santa Rita and Mesa Verde National Parks nearby.
Rated: 3 Paws — 157 rooms and 2 suites.

The Doubletree Hotel provides complimentary airport transportation. Enjoy river views and grilled entrees at the Edgewater Grille. The Lounge overlooks the river and the Patio Café (open in summer) allows you to take advantage of the sun on the riverside patio. Visit the Durango and Silverton Narrow Gauge Railroad, Mesa Verde National Park and Aztec Ruins National Monument. Walk to shopping and other activities in historic downtown Durango.

Quality Inn & Suites

455 South Camino Del Rio
Durango, CO 81303-7997
888-259-7903 • 970-259-7900

Type of Lodging: Hotel

Room Rates: $59–$149, including continental breakfast. AAA, AARP, AKC and *10% Pets Welcome™* discounts.

Pet Charges & Deposits: $50 refundable deposit for cash customers only.

Pet Policy: Designated rooms only. Manager's prior approval required.

Amenities: Cable TV, refrigerators, microwaves, pool, whirlpool, hot tubs.

Pet Amenities: List of nearby veterinarians maintained. Exercise area. Park nearby.

Rated: 3 Paws — 98 rooms and 24 suites.

Quality Inn & Suites features the fine accommodations you've come to expect throughout the chain. Contemporary furnishings and interior corridors are housed in a three-story lodging area. While in Durango there's a fine choice of evening activities: Bar D Chuckwagon features chuckwagon suppers and a stage show highlighting songs and stories in an atmosphere reminiscent of the Old West. The Diamond Circle Melodrama offers late 19th century melodrama and vaudeville shows.

Central Motel

201 West Platte Avenue
Fort Morgan, CO 80701
970-867-2401

Type of Lodging: Motel

Room Rates: $43–$80, including coffee and hot chocolate. AAA and AARP discounts.

Pet Charges & Deposits: $5 per stay.

Pet Policy: Designated rooms only. Manager's prior approval required.

Amenities: Cable TV, refrigerators, microwaves.

Pet Amenities: List of nearby veterinarians maintained. Exercise area. Riverside Nature Park is located at South Platte River and Interstate 76.

Rated: 2 Paws — 13 rooms and 6 suites.

The Central Motel has well-lighted rooms, varying in size. The one-story structure has exterior corridors and a designated smoking area. Early check-in and late checkout are special amenities. The present city of Fort Morgan emerged from a military post established on the South Platte River to protect travelers. Later, it became a station on the Overland Trail from the Missouri River to Denver. Fort Morgan was the childhood home of 1940s era bandleader Glenn Miller. The Fort Morgan Museum features exhibits delineating the area's history, including a 1920s soda fountain and a collection of Native American artifacts. This is the kind of community immortalized in James Michener's *Centennial.*

Snowshoe Motel

521 Main Street
P.O. Box 400
Frisco, CO 80443
800-445-8658 • 970-668-3444
www.snowshoemotel.com
snowshoe@springnet.com

Type of Lodging: Motel

Room Rates: $45–$105, including continental breakfast. AAA and AARP discounts.

Pet Charges & Deposits: $10 per stay. $10 refundable deposit.

Pet Policy: No pets over 70 lbs. Designated rooms only.

Amenities: Cable TV, refrigerators, microwaves, whirlpool, sauna, kitchenettes.

Pet Amenities: Walter Byron Park nearby.

Rated: 2 Paws — 36 rooms and 2 suites.

The Snowshoe Motel is located in the heart of Summit County, close to major ski resorts: Breckenridge, Keystone, Copper Mountain and Arapahoe Basin. The Motel offers freshly remodeled rooms, cable television, free local calls and complimentary coffee each morning in the front lobby. Several rooms with kitchenettes are available. There's a two-bedroom suite complete with kitchen and jetted tub. The site of Frisco was a favorite Native American camping ground for Utes for over 5,000 years. Frisco Historic Park depicts the town's mining and logging heyday.

Caravan Inn

1826 Grand Avenue
Glenwood Springs, CO 81601
800-945-5495 • 970-945-7451
www.caravaninn.com
caravan@soprzs.net

Type of Lodging: Hotel

Room Rates: $59–$119, including continental breakfast. AAA and AARP discounts.

Pet Charges & Deposits: $5 per day. $50 refundable deposit.

Pet Policy: Designated rooms only. Manager's prior approval required.

Amenities: Cable TV, refrigerators, microwaves, safes, pool, whirlpool, Jacuzzi, hot tubs.

Pet Amenities: List of nearby veterinarians maintained. Dog runs. Exercise area. Sayer Park is next door to the hotel.

Rated: 3 Paws — 70 rooms and 6 suites.

The Caravan Inn has several large units, many with mountain views. The lodgings are in two-story buildings and there is dining nearby. The Caravan Inn is close to Glenwood Hot Springs Pool, one of the world's largest outdoor mineral hot pools (two city blocks long). You can go rafting on the Colorado River. The world-famous ski resorts of Aspen-Snowmass and Vail are close by. Glenwood Caverns, originally called Fairy Caves, is noteworthy—one passageway leads to a spectacular cliff-side overlook.

West Gate Inn

2210 Highways 6 & 50
Grand Junction, CO 81505-9402
800-453-9253 • 970-241-3020
www.gj.net/wgi
wgi@gj.net

Type of Lodging: Motel

Room Rates: $49–$70. AAA discount.

Pet Charges & Deposits: $25 refundable.

Pet Policy: Designated rooms only. Pets must not be left unattended.

Amenities: Cable TV, pool, guest laundry, restaurant, lounge, free local calls.

Pet Amenities: List of nearby veterinarians maintained. Exercise area. Colorado National Monument nearby.

Rated: 2 Paws — 100 rooms.

The West Gate Inn is located in a captivating valley surrounded by three incomparable mountain ranges. From high desert to high mesa, Grand Junction is a distinctive, thoroughly "Western" town. Early check-in, late checkout and free local calls are special amenities. Dinosaur Valley Museum displays dinosaur bones and other fossils from the surrounding region. The Colorado National Monument, an easy drive away, is lined with canyons more than 600 feet deep and isolated monoliths such as Independence Monument, Balanced Rock, Coke Ovens and Pipe Organ. The Rim Rock Drive, which takes you around the edges of the canyons, can be quite narrow.

Microtel Inn & Suites

5630 West Tenth Street
Greeley, CO 80634
881-771-7171 • 970-392-1530
www.microtelinn.com
microtelelgc@uswest.net

Type of Lodging: Hotel

Room Rates: $46–$83, including continental breakfast and afternoon cookies. AAA, AARP, AKC, ABA, Corporate and Government discounts.

Pet Charges & Deposits: $5 per day. $50 refundable deposit.

Pet Policy: None. All Pets Welcome.

Amenities: Cable TV, refrigerators, microwaves, dataports, coffeemakers.

Pet Amenities: List of nearby veterinarians maintained. Exercise area. Park nearby.

Rated: 3 Paws — 55 rooms and 14 suites.

When Horace Greeley exhorted, "Go West, young man!" a group of New England teetotalers, the Union Colony, went west and established an agricultural community in 1869. The Centennial Village Museum is a wonderful display of what Greeley truly looked like in 1876. Microtel Inn & Suites features attractive, newly built rooms in a three-story structure connected by interior corridors. It's 45 miles to Rocky Mountain National Park and five miles to downtown Greeley. There are numerous restaurants nearby.

River's Edge

110 Seventh Avenue
P.O. Box 472
Ouray, CO 81427
970-325-4621
www.riversedgeouray.com
rivredge@rmi.net

Type of Lodging: Motel

Room Rates: $40–$100, including coffee.

Pet Charges & Deposits: $10 per day.

Pet Policy: Sorry, no cats.

Amenities: Cable TV, refrigerators, microwaves, Jacuzzi, hot tubs.

Pet Amenities: List of nearby veterinarians maintained. Hot Springs Park is located on Highway 550.

Rated: 2 Paws — 18 rooms.

The River's Edge has a quiet and peaceful location in the cottonwoods on the banks of the Uncompahgrie River. This motel has well-kept rooms that vary from compact to large. Ouray, the Switzerland of America, has breathtaking four-wheel drive roads. Ouray is located on the scenic San Juan Highway, a land of silver mines, gold mines and hot springs. It's almost too beautiful for its own good. Recreational activities include cross-country skiing, ice-skating, snowmobiling, world-renowned ice climbing park, gold-medal trout fishing and every outdoor activity you can imagine.

Avalanche Ranch

12863 Highway 133
Redstone, CO 81623
877-963-9339 • 970-963-2846
www.avalancheranch.com
aranch@rof.net

Type of Lodging: Guest Ranch

Cabin Rates: $70–$395.

Pet Charges & Deposits: $10 per day.

Pet Policy: None. All Pets Welcome.

Amenities: Fully equipped kitchens, BBQs, picnic tables, pond, hot tubs.

Pet Amenities: Welcome treats and towels available. List of nearby veterinarians maintained. Exercise area. White River National Forest adjacent to property.

Rated: 4 Paws — 1 ranchhouse and 12 cabins.

Avalanche Ranch is often described as a Vermont picture postcard in the heart of the Rockies. The Ranch resides on 45 acres, overlooking the Crystal River, surrounded by forest and wilderness land. Each of the guest cabins presents a different decor. Some have wood-burning stoves, clawfooted tubs and lofts. They range in size from a studio to two bedrooms and a loft. A spacious three-bedroom ranchhouse sleeps up to ten. All cabins and the ranchhouse have private yards with BBQ grills and picnic tables. On the grounds, there is an apple orchard and a variety of trees and greenery. A hiking trail skirts the upper boundaries of the ranch. Tucked away up high, a small pond offers premier views and a canoe for floating in the moonlight. Volleyball and horseshoes are available near the cabins.

Aspen Leaf Lodge

7350 West U.S. Highway 50
Salida, CO 81201
888-315-2378 • 719-539-6733
www.bestvalueinn.com

Type of Lodging: Motel

Room Rates: $40–$70. AAA, AARP, AKC, ABA, Government, Commercial and *10% Pets Welcome*™ discounts.

Pet Charges & Deposits: $6 per day. Credit card refundable deposit.

Pet Policy: Sorry, no cats. No pets over 30 lbs. Designated rooms only. Manager's prior approval required.

Amenities: Cable TV, refrigerators, microwaves, hot tub, hot springs pool nearby.

Pet Amenities: List of nearby veterinarians maintained. Dog runs. Centennial Park is located on Rainbow Boulevard.

Rated: 2 Paws — 18 rooms.

Aspen Leaf Lodge was completely remodeled in the Spring of 2000 and thus has a new "feel" about it. The guestrooms are exceptionally well-kept and located in a single-story structure. There's a landscaped island with benches, a fountain and a sun deck, as well as a riverside deck with grill. Because of the cool, comfortable summers and mild winters (for Colorado), Salida has been called the banana belt of Colorado. There's fine hunting for rock hounds, with aquamarine, garnet, sapphire, turquoise, topaz and Native American arrowheads in the area. The Salida Museum displays exhibits devoted to pioneer and Native American life, railroading and mining.

Rainbow Inn

105 East Highway 50
Salida, CO 81201
800-539-4447 • 719-539-4444
rainbows@lynx.sni.net

Type of Lodging: Motel

Room Rates: $35–$95, including continental breakfast. AAA discount.

Pet Charges & Deposits: $5 per day.

Pet Policy: Pets must be on leash and must not be left unattended.

Amenities: Cable TV, Jacuzzi.

Pet Amenities: List of nearby veterinarians maintained. Exercise area. Park nearby.

Rated: 2 Paws — 21 rooms.

The Rainbow Inn has lovely landscaped grounds with shaded outdoor picnic areas. Special amenities include early check-in, late checkout and free local calls. The Arkansas River cuts through the nearby mountains and there are several passes in the vicinity. The arrival of the railroad in 1880 fostered the growth of a permanent community. In spring, the melting snow on Mount Shavano assumes a unique shape called the "Angel of Dhavano."

Salida Super 8

525 West Rainbow Boulevard
Salida, CO 81201
800-800-8000 • 719-539-6689
www.salidasuper8.com
salsuper8@aol.com

Type of Lodging: Motel
Room Rates: $60–$100. AAA and AARP discounts.
Pet Charges & Deposits: None.
Pet Policy: None. All Pets Welcome.
Amenities: Cable TV, pool, whirlpool, hot tubs, beautiful sun deck.
Pet Amenities: List of nearby veterinarians maintained. Dog runs. Exercise area. Centennial Park is right across the street.
Rated: 3 Paws — 52 rooms

The Salida Super 8 has a picnic area with a lovely mountain view and a small heated pool. The Arkansas River, fed by melting mountain snows, swells to near-flood stage in mid-June. Champion kayakers challenge a 26-mile downstream course in the FIB-Arkansas River Boat Race. Salida Hot Springs Swimming Pool and Baths has mineral waters piped in from a locale five miles away.

Woodland Motel

903 West "F" Street
Salida, CO 81201
800-488-0456 • 719-539-4980
www.woodlandmotel.com
info@woodlandmotel.com

Type of Lodging: Motel
Room Rates: $39–$100.
Pet Charges & Deposits: None.
Pet Policy: None. All Pets Welcome.
Amenities: Cable TV, refrigerators, microwaves, spas.
Pet Amenities: Treats and freshly laundered bed available. List of nearby veterinarians maintained. Exercise area. Marvin Park is across the street. Walk your dog between the river and the far side of Marvin Park.
Rated: 4 Paws — 14 rooms and 4 suites. Salida Tree Board 2000 Commercial Landscape Award Winner.

The Woodland Motel has some units with full kitchens and two-bedroom condos. Some rooms have a mountain view. The Mount Shavano State Fish Hatchery covers 25 acres and produces more than 4 million fish each year, including brook, brown, cutthroat and rainbow trout. Salida, and its sister towns of Buena Vista and Poncha Springs, contain shopping, art galleries, hot springs, performing arts, ghost towns and the largest historic district in Colorado.

Inn at Silver Creek

P.O. Box 4222
Silver Creek, CO 80446
800-926-4 FUN • 970-887-2131
www.silvercreeklodging.com
reeser@nwco.quik.com

Type of Lodging: Hotel

Room Rates: $79–$399. AAA and AARP discounts.

Pet Charges & Deposits: $12 per stay.

Pet Policy: Sorry, no cats. Designated rooms only

Amenities: Refrigerators, microwaves, safety deposit boxes, pool, whirlpool, hot tubs, spas.

Pet Amenities: Hotel has an annual K9 5K event that is a charity race for dogs and their humans. List of nearby veterinarians maintained. Exercise area. City park nearby.

Rated: 3 Paws — 200 rooms and suites.

The Inn at Silver Creek, a resort within a resort, offers lodging from hotel rooms to suites—many with fireplaces, kitchenettes and meadow views. The athletic club contains a year-round heated pool, hot tubs, sauna, weight room and racquetball court. Many shops, a gourmet restaurant and bar are all located under one roof. Whitewater rapids are nearby. If you're feeling frisky enough, play a round of golf at 10,000 feet above sea level. Ski at Silver Creek or Winter Park resorts, visit Rocky Mountain National Park, fish in mountain lakes, it's your choice. Silver Creek is located near Granby in Grand County, between Winter Park Resort and Grand Lake, and is approximately 90 minutes northwest of Denver.

Mountain Vista Bed & Breakfast

358 Lagoon Lane
P.O. Box 1398
Silverthorne, CO 80498
800-333-5165 • 970-468-7700
www.colorado-mtnvista.com
mtnvistabnb@juno.com

Type of Lodging: B&B

Room Rates: $50–$100, including full breakfast.

Pet Charges & Deposits: None.

Pet Policy: Sorry, no cats. Designated rooms only. Manager's prior approval required.

Amenities: Cable TV, refrigerators, microwaves.

Pet Amenities: List of nearby veterinarians maintained. Rainbow Park nearby. Many bike paths for walking and national forests nearby.

Rated: 3 Paws — 3 rooms.

Welcome to Mountain Vista Bed & Breakfast. There's a robe in the room for each guest and a fully equipped guest kitchen for preparation of light meals. The home is located near the town recreation center and Dillon Reservoir. Excellent skiing is so close you can almost reach out and touch it—nine miles to Keystone, 15 miles to Arapahoe Basin, 11 miles to Copper Mountain, 13 miles to Breckenridge, 30 miles to Vail.

The Wyman Hotel & Inn

1371 Greene Street
P.O. Box 780
Silverton, CO 81433
800-609-7845 • 970-387-5372
www.thewyman.com
thewyman@frontier.net

Type of Lodging: B&B
Room Rates: $95–$185, including full breakfast and afternoon tea with cookies. AAA, AARP, AKC, ABA and **10% off-season Pets Welcome™** discounts.
Pet Charges & Deposits: $15 per day.
Pet Policy: Designated rooms only.
Amenities: Cable TV, refrigerators, whirlpool.
Pet Amenities: Dog biscuits at tea time. List of nearby veterinarians maintained. Exercise area. Memorial Park is 2 blocks away. Mesa Verde National Park and Black Canyon of the Gunnison National Park are 1½ hours away.
Rated: 3 Paws — 15 rooms and 3 suites. 2000 B&B Innkeepers Association of Colorado Excellence Award Winner.

The Wyman Hotel & Inn, a completely refurbished, very romantic 1902 hotel, has high ceilings, king- and queen-sized beds and mountain views from every room. It's on the Durango and Silverton Narrow Gauge Railroad, which skirts the San Juan Mountain Range. The lure of the D & S Railroad lures visitors from all over the world to western Colorado each year. There's something about the romance of the rails, going through the mountains…and the Wyman may just be the most romantic place of all.

Snowmass Mountain Chalet

P.O. Box 566
Snowmass Village, CO 81615
800-843-1579 • 970-923-3900
www.mountainchalet.com
stay@mountainchalet.com

Type of Lodging: Hotel
Room Rates: $89–$299, including full breakfast and hot soup lunch in winter only. AAA and *10% Pets Welcome™* discounts.
Pet Charges & Deposits: $20 per stay. $20 nonrefundable deposit.
Pet Policy: None. All Pets Welcome.
Amenities: Cable TV, refrigerators, pool, hot tubs, fitness room, hairdryers.
Pet Amenities: List of nearby veterinarians maintained. Exercise area. Snowmass ski area adjacent to the hotel.
Rated: 3 Paws — 64 rooms.

Ski in and ski out right from your hotel! Snowmass Mountain Chalet is adjacent to Snowmass Village and Aspen is only 12 miles away. Over half the rooms have slope side balconies with spectacular views from Mount Daly to the Continental Divide. Summer is filled with mountain hikes, music festivals, white water rafting, biking and horseback riding. The Mountain Chalet features a spacious outdoor hot tub and large heated pool. The hotel advertises itself as "Bordering on Perfection…" and it just may be at that.

Rabbit Ears Motel

201 Lincoln Avenue
Steamboat Springs, CO 80477
800-828-7702 • 970-879-1150
www.rabbitearsmotel.com
ski-rabbit-ears@toski.com

Type of Lodging: Motel

Room Rates: $59–$149, including continental breakfast. AAA and *10% Pets Welcome*™ discounts.

Pet Charges & Deposits: None.

Pet Policy: Pets must not be left unattended.

Amenities: Cable TV, refrigerators.

Pet Amenities: Yampa River Park is located next door to the motel.

Rated: 3 Paws — 65 rooms.

Old-fashioned charm with all the modern comforts. Guests can choose from attractive units in a variety of sizes and scenic Yampa River views. The Rabbit Ears has been a popular landmark since 1952—its highly visible sign with the playful pink ears is one of the most photographed subjects in Northwest Colorado. The motel is situated right near the Yampa River, where you can enjoy rafts and kayaks negotiating the bubbling currents from their windows, picnic in nearby Yampa Park, then bicycle, stroll or jog with your pet along the scenic riverfront path.

Antlers at Vail

680 West Lionshead Place
Vail, CO 81657
800-843-8245 • 970-476-2471
www.antlersvail.com
info@antlersvail.com

Type of Lodging: Condominium Hotel

Room Rates: $95–$731. AAA discount

Pet Charges & Deposits: $10–$15 per day.

Pet Policy: Designated rooms only.

Amenities: Cable TV, refrigerators, microwaves, pool, hot tubs, hairdryers, humidifiers, irons and ironing boards.

Pet Amenities: List of nearby veterinarians maintained. Exercise area.

Rated: 3 Paws — 68 rooms.

The Antlers at Vail is located only 150 yards from Vail's only gondola. There are sparkling stream or gorgeous mountain views from your bedroom window. The seven-story structure has exterior corridors, a heated pool, saunas and whirlpool. There's an adjacent restaurant. Flourishing Vail is an international resort center, renowned for its extensive winter recreation facilities and its Alpine style. Vail shifted into high gear after WWII, when paratroopers who had trained nearby returned to see if all that beauty was for real. It was…and the rest is history.

Lift House Condominiums

555 East Lionshead Circle
Vail, CO 81652
800-654-0635 • 970-476-2340
www.toski.com/lifthouse
lifthouse@vail.net

Type of Lodging: Condominium

Apartment Rates: $75–$265. AAA, AARP and *10–15% Pets Welcome™* discounts.

Pet Charges & Deposits: $25–$100 per stay.

Pet Policy: None. All Pets Welcome.

Amenities: Cable TV, refrigerators, microwaves, Jacuzzi, two restaurants.

Pet Amenities: List of nearby veterinarians maintained. There are numerous places nearby that you can take your pet, including walking areas and creeks where your pet can swim.

Rated: 4 Paws — 43 condominiums.

The Lift House in Vail, one of the world's finest resorts, is 40 seconds away from the creek, less than a minute to the Gondola and lifts, in the very heart of the expanded village. It has sweeping views of the surrounding valley. You'll find amenities galore in your condominium: an efficiency kitchen, fireplace, private balconies, cable television and two queen-sized beds. The Lift House contains two ski shop/boutiques, a full service bank and two outstanding restaurants. The whole world knows Vail as a winter wonderland, but Vail's best kept secret is summer! There's a nearby 18-hole golf course, Jeep and mountain biking trips, white water rafting, fishing, hiking and tennis under a sky that averages 300 days of sunshine a year. When in Vail, be sure to visit the Betty Ford Alpine Gardens, the Colorado Ski Museum and Ski Hall of Fame.

CONNECTICUT

Nicknames: Constitution State; Nutmeg State

Population: 3,282,031

Area: 5,554 square miles

Climate: Moderate; winters average slightly below freezing; warm, humid summers.

Capital: Hartford

Entered Union: January 9, 1788

Motto: *Qui Transtulit Sustinet* (He who transplanted still sustains).

Song: Yankee Doodle

Flower: Mountain Laurel

Tree: White Oak

Bird: American Robin

Famous Nutmeggers: Ethan Allen, Phineas T. Barnum, Katherine Hepburn, Robert Mitchum, J.P. Morgan, Mark Twain, Noah Webster, Eli Whitney.

 History: The Algonquin peoples inhabited the land at the time the first Europeans arrived. By 1634, settlers from Plymouth Bay had started colonies along the Connecticut River. In 1637, they defeated the Pequots. The colony of Connecticut was chartered by England in 1662. New Haven was added in 1665. Connecticut Patriots fought in most major engagements in the Revolutionary War, while Connecticut Privateers captured British merchant ships. Connecticut was the 5th of the original 13 states to sign the Constitution. Tourist attractions include the Mark Twain House in Hartford, the P.T. Barnum Museum in Bridgeport, and the U.S.S. Nautilus Memorial, commemorating the first nuclear powered submarine.

Ramada Inn Danbury

116 Newtown Road
Danbury, CT 06810
203-792-3800
locde@primehospitality.com

Type of Lodging: Hotel

Room Rates: $139–$175, including continental breakfast. AAA, AARP and *10% Pets Welcome™* discounts.

Pet Charges & Deposits: Credit card imprint required.

Pet Policy: No pets over 100 lbs. Designated rooms only.

Amenities: Cable TV, pool, restaurant.

Pet Amenities: List of nearby veterinarians maintained. Exercise area. Capellaro's Grove nearby.

Rated: 2 Paws — 181 rooms and 10 suites.

Centrally located in Danbury, within easy driving distance of White Plains, N.Y., Stamford and Hartford, Ramada Inn is housed in two- to five-story buildings with interior corridors. For nearly two centuries, Danbury was the "Hat City of the World." Since the early 1950s, Danbury's economic base has undergone a dramatic change and now finds itself host to businesses related to metal fabrication, high technology products, pharmaceuticals, biomedical products, paper, publishing, energy and aerospace product development. The Danbury Museum includes houses from the late 18th century, the Charles Ives birthplace, exhibits on the Danbury Hatting industry and a one-room schoolhouse. The Danbury Railway Museum is a restored 1903 railroad station.

Red Roof Inn

5 Hazard Avenue
Enfield, CT 06082
800-THE ROOF • 860-741-2571
www.redroof.com
io105@redroof.com

Type of Lodging: Motel

Room Rates: $50–$107. AAA and AARP discounts.

Pet Charges & Deposits: None.

Pet Policy: Limit two pets per room. Pets must be leashed on the property.

Amenities: Cable TV, refrigerators, microwaves.

Pet Amenities: List of nearby veterinarians maintained. Exercise area inclued a large field behind motel.

Rated: 3 Paws — 108 rooms.

Red Roof Inn is perfectly placed for your Hartford-Springfield holiday or business trip. Six Flags Amusement Park is nearby, you're within ten minutes of Springfield, Massachusetts' Big-E Fairgrounds and Hartford is a mere 17 miles away. The motel offers comfortable rooms, cable television, newspaper and free local calls. Nine restaurants are in the immediate vicinity and close-by attractions include Riverside Amusement Park, the Basketball Hall Of Fame, Webb-Deane-Stevens Museum in Hartford, the Mark Twain House and the Harriet Beecher Stowe House.

Inn at Iron Masters

229 Main Street
Route 44
P.O. Box 690
Lakeville, CT 06039
860-435-9844
www.innatironmasters.com
ironmstr@discovernet.net

Type of Lodging: Motor Lodge

Room Rates: $95–$185, including continental breakfast. AAA discount.

Pet Charges & Deposits: None.

Pet Policy: Sorry, no cats. Designated rooms only. Manager's prior approval required. Pets must be leashed at all times per local regulations.

Amenities: Cable TV, pool.

Pet Amenities: List of nearby veterinarians maintained. Exercise area. Many city and state parks nearby.

Rated: 4 Paws — 27 rooms and 1 suite.

Known as the "Southern Berkshire's best-kept secret," the Inn at Iron Masters offers elegant accommodations in scenic Lakeville, in the heart of the Litchfield Hills. Each guest-room has a sitting area and private bath. Relax by the outdoor swimming pool or warm yourself by the large fieldstone fireplace in the Hearth Room Water sports, mountain climbing, biking, horseback riding and hiking abound in the area. Enjoy a round of golf in the Berkshires, soar above it all in a hot air balloon, or explore the caves of the Berkshire Mountains with experienced spelunkers. During winter, skating, skiing and snowboarding are close by at Cata-mount, Mohawk and Butternut Mountains. Do you love music and the performing arts? Tanglewood, Jacob's Pillow, the Norfolk Chamber Music Festival, Shakespeare & Company, Music Mountain and live theater venues are within easy reach.

Applewood Farm Inn Bed & Breakfast

528 Colonel Ledyard
Mystic / Ledyard, CT 06339
800-717-4262 • 860-536-2022
www.visitmystic.com
applewoodfarmsinn@worldnet.att.net

Type of Lodging: B&B

Room Rates: $125–$290, including full breakfast.

Pet Charges & Deposits: None.

Pet Policy: Manager's prior approval required.

Amenities: Hot tub.

Pet Amenities: Two bassets in residence. List of nearby veterinarians maintained. Dog runs. Exercise area includes 33 acres for your pet to enjoy. Many city and state parks nearby.

Rated: 3 Paws — 4 rooms and 1 suite. Listed on National Register of Historic Places.

The Applewood Farms Inn B&B is circa an 1826 restored farmhouse. The guestrooms are individually furnished with antique and period furniture and feature fireplaces, air conditioning and private baths. The B&B is two hours from Boston and 2½ hours from New York. Nearby Mashantucket Pequot Museum and Research Center, devoted to the history and culture of the Pequot Native American tribe, includes a recreated 16th century Pequot village and an 18th century farmstead. The fastest clipper ships in the country were built in nearby Mystic by the middle of the 19th century. You can visit Mystic Seaport, redolent of the sights and aromas of yesteryear, or spend time with more than 3,500 living sea creatures at Mystic Aquarium.

DELAWARE

Nicknames: First State; Diamond State
Population: 753,538
Area: 2,396 square miles
Climate: Moderate
Capital: Dover
Entered Union: December 7, 1787
Motto: Liberty and independence.
Song: Our Delaware
Flower: Peach Blossom
Tree: American Holly

Bird: Blue Hen Chicken
Famous Delawareans: Thomas F. Bayard, Henry Seidel Canby, E. I. DuPont, John P. Marquand, Howard Pyle, Caesar Romney.

 History: The Lenni Lenape (Delaware) people lived in the region at the time of European contact. Henry Hudson located the Delaware River in 1609. English explorer Samuel Argall named the area after Virginia's governor, Lord De La Warr. In 1631, Native Americans destroyed the first Dutch settlement. The Dutch returned in 1651 only to lose the whole of Delaware to the British nine years later. After 1682, Delaware became part of Pennsylvania. In 1704, it was granted its own Assembly. In 1787, it was the first state to sign the United States Constitution. Although it remained in the Union during the Civil War, it did not abolish slavery until 1865. Most large American corporations are domiciled in Delaware because of favorable tax and other laws.

DEWEY BEACH, DELAWARE (Pop. 500)

Atlantic Oceanside Motel

1700 Highway One
Dewey Beach, DE 19971
302-227-8811
www.atlanticoceanside.com

Type of Lodging: Motel
Room Rates: $35–$119.
Pet Charges & Deposits: $5 per day.
Pet Policy: None. All Pets Welcome.
Amenities: Cable TV, refrigerators, microwaves, pool.
Pet Amenities: Delaware Seashore State Park nearby.
Rated: 3 Paws — 60 rooms and suites.

If you are planning a vacation at the beach in Dewey Beach, the Atlantic Oceanside Motel offers swimming pool, complimentary coffee, remote control cable television and touch-tone phones. All rooms have microwaves and refrigerators, while most suites have full kitchens. It offers easy access to the Jolly Trolley for a quick ride into downtown Rehoboth or Dewey, and is in close proximity to area attractions including: clean and safe beaches, restaurants, night clubs, tax-free outlet shopping, windsurfing, sailing, fishing, tennis, golf, state parks and historical sites.

Sea-Esta Motels

713 Rehoboth Avenue
Rehoboth Beach, DE 19971
800-436-6591 • 302-227-4343
www.seaesta.com

Type of Lodging: Motel
Room Rates: Call for rate information. AAA discount.
Pet Charges & Deposits: $10 per day.
Pet Policy: None. All Pets Welcome.
Amenities: Cable TV, refrigerators, microwaves.
Pet Amenities: List of nearby veterinarians maintained. Delaware Seashore Park nearby.
Rated: 3 Paws — Rooms and suites vary.

All four Sea-Esta Motels offer accommodations ranging from budget rooms to deluxe units. The deluxe units include cooking facilities (you provide dishes) and private balconies. Relaxation on the beach is only a short walk away from any of the four locations. Centrally located in beautiful Rehoboth Beach, there are many night spots, dining, water sports, golf and outlet shopping nearby. Quaint and historic Lewes is eight short miles north.

DISTRICT OF COLUMBIA

Major Attractions in Our Nation's Capital

- Bureau of Engraving & Printing
- United States Capitol
- Federal Bureau of Investigation
- Folger Shakespeare Library
- Holocaust Memorial Museum
- Jefferson Memorial
- John F. Kennedy Center
- Korean War Veterans Memorial
- Library of Congress
- Lincoln Memorial
- National Archives and Records
- National Gallery of Art
- Franklin Delano Roosevelt Memorial
- Smithsonian Institution
- Vietnam Veterans Memorial
- Washington Monument
- White House
- Arlington National Cemetery (VA)
- Mount Vernon (VA)
- The Pentagon (VA)

Hereford House Bed and Breakfast

604 South Carolina Avenue Southeast
Washington, D.C. 20003
202-543-0102
herefordhs@aol.com

Type of Lodging: B&B

Room Rates: $58–$82, including full breakfast.

Pet Charges & Deposits: $50 refundable deposit.

Pet Policy: Manager's prior approval required.

Amenities: Guest laundry.

Pet Amenities: None.

Rated: 2 Paws — 4 rooms.

Hereford House Bed and Breakfast, is an early 1900s brick townhouse that has been converted into a private home, bed and breakfast and guest cottage on an attractive, quiet, residential avenue on Capitol Hill, one block from the underground subway train. Guestrooms are clean, well furnished and economical. Three blocks away from the Hereford House is the guest house—a two-bedroom, two-bath cottage with living room. Hereford House prides itself on having no phones, televisions, computer terminals or fax machines in the rooms. This ideal location is a ten-minute walk to the U.S. Capitol, Supreme Court and Library of Congress. Easily reached on foot or by public transportation are the Mall, art galleries and Smithsonian museums.

Sofitel - Washington, D.C.

1914 Connecticut Avenue Northwest
Washington, DC 20009
800-424-2464 • 202-797-2000
www.sofitel.com

Type of Lodging: Hotel

Room Rates: $129–$359. AAA and AARP discounts.

Pet Charges & Deposits: $20 per stay.

Pet Policy: Designated rooms only. Manager's prior approval required.

Amenities: Cable TV, honor bar, safes, fitness room.

Pet Amenities: List of nearby veterinarians maintained. Exercise area. Rock Creek Park and Kalorama Park nearby.

Rated: 3 Paws — 105 rooms and 39 suites.

Rising serenely above the city's fashionable Embassy Row, Hotel Sofitel offers travelers a haven of old world refinement amidst the modern-day bustle of the nation's capital. From the inviting ambiance of its finely appointed lobby, to the gracious arrangement of its rooms, to the personal attentiveness of its professionally trained staff, every aspect of Hotel Sofitel has been carefully arranged to meet your highest requirements. National Zoo is a ten-minute walk from the hotel. All of the major D.C. attractions are within a 25-minute walk or a ten-minute drive: the Smithsonian Museums, the White House, the U.S. Capitol and the Performing Arts Complex of Kennedy Center.

Swiss Inn

1204 Massachusetts Avenue Northwest
Washington, DC 20005
800-955-7947 • 202-371-1816
www.theswissinn.com
swissinndc@aol.com

Type of Lodging: Inn
Room Rates: Call for rates. AAA, AARP, AKC, ABA and *10% Pets Welcome™* discounts.
Pet Charges & Deposits: None.
Pet Policy: Manager's prior approval required.
Amenities: Kitchenettes.
Pet Amenities: List of nearby veterinarians maintained. There are numerous parks within walking distance.
Rated: 3 Paws — 7 rooms.

The Swiss Inn is a small inn located in the heart of the city. You can walk to virtually every major attraction in the downtown D.C. area. The Corcoran Gallery has an extensive collection of American art. Explorers Hall at the National Geographic Society has an interactive geography science center featuring the world's largest freestanding painted globe. The United States Holocaust Memorial Museum commemorates the history of the six million Jews and millions of others, including Romany (gypsies), Soviet prisoners of war, Poles, dissidents, homosexuals, Jehovah's Witnesses, disabled and others who perished at the hands of the Nazis between 1933 and 1945.

FLORIDA

Nicknames: Sunshine State
Population: 15,111,244
Area: 59,928 square miles
Climate: Subtropical north of Lake Bradenton-Okeechobee line; tropical south of the line.
Capital: Tallahassee
Entered Union: March 3, 1845
Motto: In God We Trust.
Song: Old Folks At Home

Flower: Orange Bossom
Tree: Sabal Palmetto Palm
Bird: Mockingbird
Famous Floridians: Jeb Bush, Dave Barry, Henry M. Flagler, MacKinlay Cantor, Carl Hiaasen, Chief Osceola, Claude Pepper, Marjorie Kinnan Rawlings, Joseph W. Stillwell.

 History: The Seminoles were the dominant people in the area when Juan Ponce de Leon, searching for the Fountain of Youth, saw Florida in 1513. France established a failed colony in 1564. The following year, the Spanish settled St. Augustine. In 1763, Spain ceded Florida to Great Britain, which held the area briefly before returning it to Spain in 1783. After Andrew Jackson led an invasion in 1818, Spain ceded Florida to the United States. The Seminole War (1835-42) resulted in the removal of most Native Americans to the Oklahoma Territory. Florida seceded from the Union in 1861 and was readmitted in 1868. Henry Flagler's railroad extension through the Florida Keys signaled the first of many land booms that continue today.

Boca Raton Doubletree Guest Suites

701 Northwest 53rd Street
Boca Raton, FL 33487
800-222 TREE • 561-997-9500
www.doubletree.com

Type of Lodging: Hotel

Suite Rates: $69–$219, including continental breakfast. AAA and AARP discounts.

Pet Charges & Deposits: $50 nonrefundable deposit.

Pet Policy: No pets over 80 lbs.

Amenities: Cable TV, refrigerators, microwaves, pool, Jacuzzi, hot tubs.

Pet Amenities: List of nearby veterinarians maintained. Patch Reef Park is located at Yamato and Military.

Rated: 3 Paws — 183 suites.

Situated in the heart of the Boca Raton business district and five minutes from the sun-drenched beaches, Doubletree Guest Suites is a fine choice for business or pleasure. Visit nearby tourist attractions and enjoy fabulous shopping in Boca Raton Town Center and Mizner Park. The Doubletree is 20 miles from Palm Beach and Fort Lauderdale International Airport and Miami International Airport are less than an hour away. Each of the suites is beautifully appointed with two televisions, refrigerator, microwave, coffeemaker and wet bar. Play a few sets of tennis, enjoy nearby championship golf or work out at a state-of-the-art Scandinavian Fitness Center just minutes away. Then relax in the outdoor heated pool and whirlpool.

Radisson Suite Hotel Boca Raton

7920 Glades Road
Boca Raton, FL 33434
800-333-3333 • 561-483-3600
www.radisson.com

Type of Lodging: Hotel

Suite Rates: $99–$239, including full breakfast and evening cocktail hour. AAA and AARP discounts.

Pet Charges & Deposits: $100 per stay.

Pet Policy: Designated rooms only.

Amenities: Cable TV, microwaves, honor bar, pool, Jacuzzi, lakeside restaurants.

Pet Amenities: List of nearby veterinarians maintained. Dog runs. Exercise area. Patch Reef Park is located at Yamato and Military.

Rated: 3 Paws — 200 suites.

At Radisson Suite Hotel, each suite is designed with your comfort in mind. You'll find two remote control cable televisions, hairdryer, iron and ironing board, two telephones with voicemail, dataport, coffeemaker, microwave, mini bar and a private balcony. A variety of restaurants are just outside the door. Take a dip in the heated outdoor swimming pool; relieve stress in the fitness area, whirlpool and a lakeside-jogging course. Golf, tennis, beaches, water sports and world-class shopping are all within easy reach.

Ramada Inn at Boca Raton

2901 North Federal Highway
Boca Raton, FL 33408
561-395-6850

Type of Lodging: Hotel

Room Rates: $60–$140, including coffee and mini muffins in lobby. AAA and AARP discounts.

Pet Charges & Deposits: $10 per day. $100 refundable deposit.

Pet Policy: Sorry, no puppies or kittens. Designated rooms only. Manager's prior approval required. Dogs must be kept on leashes.

Amenities: Cable TV, safes, pool, Jacuzzi.

Pet Amenities: Exercise area. City parks nearby.

Rated: 3 Paws – 97 rooms and 30 suites.

Escape to the breathtaking beauty of Boca Raton. Enjoy some of Florida's most beautiful beaches or the Ramada's ocean pool, invigorating whirlpool and spa. A wealth of shopping opportunities await you, from Town Mall Center, the largest indoor shopping mall in Palm Beach County, to Mizner Park, a cluster of specialty stores, arenas, theaters, arts and music. The Ramada features rooms with direct dial phones, cable television, large closets, dataports, executive work areas, refrigerators and coffee.

Tortuga Inn

1325 Gulf Drive North
Bradenton Beach, FL 34217
877- TORTUGA • 941-778-6611
www.tortugainn.com
tortuga.inn@worldnet.att.net

Type of Lodging: Hotel

Room Rates: $100–$300. AAA, AARP and *10% Pets Welcome*™ discounts.

Pet Charges & Deposits: $35 per stay.

Pet Policy: Designated rooms only.

Amenities: Cable TV, VCRs, refrigerators, microwaves, pool, Jacuzzi.

Pet Amenities: List of nearby veterinarians maintained.

Rated: 3 Paws – 38 rooms.

All rooms have a private patio at Tortuga Inn. The grounds are beautifully landscaped and there are fountains in the pool area. There are three heated pools and a boat dock. Bradenton is one of the loveliest areas on Florida's west coast. The Art League of Manatee County displays works of local artists. Pirate City is spring training camp for the Pittsburgh Pirates. Manatee Village Historical Park includes an 1860 courthouse, 1912 settler's house, 1903 general store and 1908 one-room schoolhouse.

Tradewinds Resort of Anna Maria

1603 Gulf Drive North
Bradenton Beach, FL 34217
888-686-6716 • 941-779-0010
www.tradewindsresort.com
tradewin@gate.net

Type of Lodging: Resort
Room Rates: $89–$210, including continental breakfast. AAA, AARP and *10% Pets Welcome™* discounts.
Pet Charges & Deposits: $25 per stay.
Pet Policy: Designated rooms only.
Amenities: Cable TV, VCRs, fully equipped kitchens, pool, guest laundry, BBQ areas.
Pet Amenities: List of nearby veterinarians maintained. Working on dog runs. Exercise area.
Rated: 3 Paws — 34 rooms.

Tradewinds Resort has a Key West appearance, set on the Intercoastal Waterway. It has a private beach and private boat dock, making it an ideal self-contained destination resort. In Bradenton, Hunsader Farms is geared toward educating children about farming and farm life, featuring a petting zoo, with chickens, cows, ducks, emus, goats, llamas, pheasants, pigs and turkeys. Hayrides and pony rides are available. The South Florida Museum, Bishop Planetarium and Parker Manatee Aquarium shows varied aspects of southwest Florida history, including a collection of Stone Age relics, Civil War memorabilia and pioneer artifacts.

Behind the Fence Bed & Breakfast

1400 Viola Drive at Countryside
Brandon, FL 33511
813-685-8201

Type of Lodging: B&B
Room Rates: $79–$99, including continental breakfast. AAA and *10% Pets Welcome™* discounts.
Pet Charges & Deposits: None.
Pet Policy: Small pets only.
Amenities: Cable TV, refrigerators, microwaves, pool.
Pet Amenities: List of nearby veterinarians maintained. Dog runs. Exercise area. J.C. Handley Park (largest county park) is located right behind the property.
Rated: 3 Paws — 5 rooms and 1 suite.

To get a sense of Behind the Fence B&B, you must come behind the fence. Just 15 minutes east of Tampa, you lose all sense of the modern world beyond its doors. Owners Carolyn and Larry Yoss constructed the Connecticut-style dwelling in 1977, after an unsuccessful search for a Florida home that would display their early 19th century American antiques. They recycled lumber salvaged from late 19th century Tampa Bay-area buildings slated for demolition. Eager to share their passion for the lifestyle of the early 1800s, the Yosses opened their inn to school tours and invite spinners, weavers and blacksmiths to demonstrate old-fashioned trades and crafts of all styles.

La Quinta Inn & Suites - Brandon

310 Grand Regency Boulevard
Brandon, FL 33510
800-687-6667 • 813-643-0574
www.laquinta.com

Type of Lodging: Hotel

Room Rates: $69–$149, including continental breakfast. AAA and AARP discounts.

Pet Charges & Deposits: None.

Pet Policy: No pets over 20 lbs. Designated rooms only. Manager's prior approval required.

Amenities: Cable TV, refrigerators, microwaves, safes, pool, Jacuzzi, guest laundry, fitness room.

Pet Amenities: List of nearby veterinarians maintained. Exercise area.

Rated: 3 Paws — 123 rooms and 5 suites.

A semi-high-rise lodging, the comfortable La Quinta Inn is situated near Tampa Bay, a place that combines all the necessary ingredients for a fabulous vacation. There are water parks, theme parks, museums, recreational pursuits and sports galore. Tampa-St. Petersburg, and surrounding areas such as Brandon, can occupy a full holiday. Busch Gardens, the Florida Aquarium and the Museum of Science and Industry are only three of a galaxy of stellar attractions.

Moorings at Carrabelle

1000 U.S. Highway 98
Carrabelle, FL 32322
850-697-2800
www.mooringscarrabelle.com
moorings@mooringscarrabelle.com

Type of Lodging: Marina Resort

Suite Rates: $75–$95. AAA, AARP and *10% Pets Welcome*™ discounts.

Pet Charges & Deposits: $10 per day. $50 refundable deposit.

Pet Policy: None. All Pets Welcome.

Amenities: Cable TV, refrigerators, microwaves, pool.

Pet Amenities: List of nearby veterinarians maintained. Dog runs. Exercise area. St. George Island State Park nearby.

Rated: 3 Paws — 22 suites.

Just east of the bridge, the Moorings enjoys a wonderful location on the Carrabelle River. The two-story building housing the resort is spacious and has outdoor corridors. There's a boat ramp and a marina. Fishing, including charter fishing, is a main draw to this sportsman's area.

Park Place Hotel

P.O. Box 613
Cedar Key, FL 32625
800-868-7963 • 352-543-5737
www.parkplaceincedarkey.com
parkplace@inktw.net

Type of Lodging: Motel

Room Rates: $65–$150. AAA and AARP discounts.

Pet Charges & Deposits: $7 per day

Pet Policy: Designated rooms only. Call for breed restrictions.

Amenities: Cable TV, refrigerators, microwaves.

Pet Amenities: Cedar Key City Park is located at Second and "A" Streets.

Rated: 2 Paws — 32 rooms and 4 suites.

Cedar Key, located on a small barrier island off Florida's Gulf Coast, was a strategic point from which blockade-runners exported cotton and lumber and imported food supplies for the Confederacy during the Civil War. After the war, lumbering and shipbuilding continued to dominate the town's industry until 1896, when a hurricane destroyed much of the area. Today, Cedar Key, a resort area, relies on commercial fishing, crabbing, clam farming and oystering to bolster its economy. Park Place Hotel features some third floor bi-level units with sleeping loft and gulf-view private balconies.

Econo Lodge Space Center

3220 North Cocoa Boulevard (U.S. 1)
Cocoa, FL 32926
888-721-9423 • 321-632-4561

Type of Lodging: Hotel

Room Rates: $44–$150. AAA, AARP and *10% Pets Welcome*™ discounts.

Pet Charges & Deposits: $10 per stay. $30 refundable deposit.

Pet Policy: No pets over 40 lbs. Designated rooms only.

Amenities: Cable TV, refrigerators, microwaves, pool, restaurant, lounge.

Pet Amenities: List of nearby veterinarians maintained. Exercise area.

Rated: 2 Paws — 150 rooms.

Econo Lodge Space Center is centrally located on Florida's Space Coast at the junction of the Beeline Expressway and U.S. 1. It's eight minutes from the Kennedy Space Center, ten minutes from Port Canaveral and Cocoa Beach. Orlando International Airport is 40 minutes away and within an hour you can be at Walt Disney World®, Universal Studios®, Sea World® and a plethora of other great central Florida attractions. At Econo Lodge, you have your choice of tastefully decorated rooms with cable television. Amenities include a large outdoor pool, guest laundry facilities, shuffleboard and a large sun deck.

Econo Lodge Resort

1275 North Atlantic Avenue
Cocoa Beach, FL 32931
800-795-2252 • 321-783-2252

Type of Lodging: Hotel
Room Rates: $65–$105. AAA and AARP discounts.
Pet Charges & Deposits: None.
Pet Policy: Designated rooms only.
Amenities: Cable TV, safes, pool, restaurant, lounge.
Pet Amenities: Exercise area. Park nearby.
Rated: 3 Paws — 128 rooms.

Econo Lodge Resort, formerly Cape Colony Inn, was built and owned by the original seven astronauts! The news media was a common sight at the former convention center, now a large beachwear and gift shop. After the moon landing, the news media conference was held here. Econo Lodge is only 20 minutes from Kennedy Space Center, a three-minute walk from Atlantic Beach, the closest beach to Disney World®, Sea World®, Universal Studios® and several other central Florida attractions. Oh, and just in case you're wondering who the seven original owners were, they were Alan Shepard, Jr., Virgil "Gus" Grissom, John Glenn, Jr., Scott Carpenter, Walter Shirra, Gordon Cooper, Jr., and Donald "Deke" Slayton.

South Beach Inn-on-the-Sea

1701 South Atlantic Avenue
Cocoa Beach, FL 32931
800-546-6835 • 321-784-3333
www.southbeachinn.com
info@southbeachinn.com

Type of Lodging: Motel
Apartment Rates: $70–$140, including coffee. AAA discount.
Pet Charges & Deposits: $10 per day. $50 refundable deposit.
Pet Policy: No pets over 20 lbs. Manager's prior approval required.
Amenities: Cable TV, full kitchens.
Pet Amenities: List of nearby veterinarians maintained. City park is located next door.
Rated: 2 Paws — 16 apartments.

South Beach Inn is located on the Atlantic Ocean. NASA's Kennedy Space Center is nearby. Port Canaveral, only minutes away, is home to the second largest cruise port in the nation, as well as charter fishing boats. The Inn is within easy driving distance to Walt Disney World®, Epcot Center®, Sea World® and other Orlando attractions. All units have complete kitchens, remote control cable television and telephone. A large deck awaits you for sunbathing and enjoying the beach view of space shots from the Cape. A pavilion and BBQ area is provided for cooking steaks, sizzling hamburgers and fresh fish caught in the sea.

Breakers Beach Oceanfront Motel

27 South Ocean Avenue
Daytona Beach, FL 32118
800-441-8459 • 904-252–863
www.breakersbeach.com
motelwizz@aol.com

Type of Lodging: Motel
Room Rates: $47–$167. AAA and AARP discounts.
Pet Charges & Deposits: $10 per day
Pet Policy: Sorry, no cats. No pets over 50 lbs.
Amenities: Cable TV, refrigerators, microwaves, pool.
Pet Amenities: List of nearby veterinarians maintained. Dog runs. Exercise area. Park nearby.
Rated: 2 Paws — 22 rooms and 1 suite.

Breakers Beach Oceanfront Motel is a premium oceanfront hotel with accommodations for every type of traveler. There are several room options: deluxe oceanfront, ocean view, courtyard rooms or efficiencies. There's a host of outdoors activities close by: fishing at the Main Street Pier or offshore from Ponce Inlet, volleyball at the Boardwalk, golfing at one of Volusia County's 30 golf courses, windsurfing, jet ski rentals on the Halifax River, tennis, surfing, swimming in the year-round heated pool, or miniature golf with the kids. "Just around the corner," you'll find Adventure Landing Water Park, Daytona Beach Ocean Center, Daytona Beach Main Street Fishing Pier, Daytona Beach Boardwalk. Daytona International Speedway and Daytona Beach Kennel Club.

Manatee Suites

3167 South Atlantic Avenue
Daytona Beach Shores, FL 32118
800-378-6826 • 904-761-1121

Type of Lodging: Motel
Suite Rates: $39–$89.
Pet Charges & Deposits: $5 per day or $10 per week.
Pet Policy: Sorry, no puppies. Manager's prior approval required.
Amenities: Cable TV, fully equipped kitchens, pool, BBQ area, guest laundry.
Pet Amenities: List of nearby veterinarians maintained. Exercise area. Lighthouse Point Park nearby.
Rated: 3 Paws — 38 suites.

Experience the beauty of the Atlantic at the newly remodeled, oceanfront Manatee Suites. Spacious one-bedroom suites with fully equipped kitchens are designed with all the comforts of home. In-room coffeemakers and guest laundry facilities are located on the premises. Within walking distance of the motel, you will find a wide variety of restaurants and shops. Tennis courts are nearby and golf can be arranged on any of the ten championship Daytona Beach courses.

Luxury On The Ocean

2815 South Oceanshore Boulevard
Flagler Beach, FL 32136
904-439-1826
www.floridaocean.com

Type of Lodging: Inn
Suite Rates: $150. Two-day minimum stay required.
Pet Charges & Deposits: $10 per day.
Pet Policy: None. All Pets Welcome.
Amenities: Cable TV, refrigerators, microwaves, spas.
Pet Amenities: List of nearby veterinarians maintained. Exercise area. Gamble Rogers State Park nearby. Pet friendly beach right out the back door.
Rated: 3 Paws — 4 suites.

Luxury on the Ocean is the ultimate in intimate resorting. There are four suites, and each suite is located on the resort's private beach. Your door is approximately 12 yards from the water line. These are not motel or hotel rooms—they are luxurious 900 square foot suites with individual climate controls. Complimentary bicycles and lounge chairs are available. Watch dolphins, sea turtles and an occasional whale from your back door.

Flamingo Lodge in Everglades National Park

Everglades National Park
Flamingo, FL 33034
800-600-3813 • 941-695-3101
www.flamingolodge.com
info@flamingolodge.com

Type of Lodging: Motel
Room Rates: $65– $145.
Pet Charges & Deposits: None.
Pet Policy: No pets over 40 lbs. Pets are not allowed on park boardwalks or trails and must be on leash at all times. Pets are allowed in canoe and skiff rentals.
Amenities: Pool, restaurant.
Pet Amenities: Inside Everglades National Park.
Rated: 3 Paws — 126 rooms and 1 suite.

Less than an hour from the Miami metropolitan area, the Everglades National Park is the largest mangrove ecosystem in the Western Hemisphere. This subtropical wilderness—1½ million acres of saw grass prairie and mangrove forests, is one of the country's largest parks and a treasure of biological diversity. Located 38 miles southwest of the main park entrance, the motel features air-conditioned rooms plus cottages with kitchen facilities. Flamingo Lodge Restaurant has an extensive and varied selection of seafood, steak, chicken, vegetarian dishes and local specialties. The Everglades is the only place in the world where alligators and American crocodiles co-exist side by side.

Courtyard Villa On the Ocean

4312 El Mar Drive
Fort Lauderdale, FL 33308
800-291-3560 • 954-776-1164
www.courtyardvilla.com

Type of Lodging: Hotel
Room Rates: $105–$190, including full breakfast. AAA and *10% Pets Welcome*™ discounts.
Pet Charges & Deposits: $10 per day. $100 refundable deposit.
Pet Policy: Sorry, no pit bulls, dobermans or rotweilers. Manager's prior approval required.
Amenities: Cable TV, refrigerators, microwaves, pool, spa, BBQ grill, guest laundry.
Pet Amenities: List of nearby veterinarians maintained. Beach nearby.
Rated: 3 Paws — 10 rooms.

A romantic little hideaway directly on the beach, Courtyard Villa offers true charm and luxury throughout elegantly furnished accommodations. The hotel is within easy walking distance to restaurants, shops and the world-famous fishing pier. The hotel's newly remodeled and redecorated apartments and efficiencies are tastefully furnished. In-room amenities include cable television, VCR, coffeepot, hairdryer, direct dial phone with 24-hour message center and air conditioning.

Best Western Springs Resort

18051 Tamiami Trail
Fort Myers, FL 33908
800-344-9794 • 941-267-7900
www.bestwesternhotels.com
springs@olsusa.com

Type of Lodging: Hotel
Room Rates: $55–$120. AAA and AARP discounts.
Pet Charges & Deposits: $8 per day for the first pet, $4 each additional pet.
Pet Policy: No pets over 50 lbs.
Amenities: Cable TV, refrigerators, microwaves, safes, pool, restaurant, bar, fitness room, mineral water spa.
Pet Amenities: List of nearby veterinarians maintained. Exercise area.
Rated: 2 Paws — 50 rooms.

Best Western Springs Resort, formerly known as San Carlos Inn and Warm Mineral Spa, might seem like a conventional hotel at the side of the road in Fort Myers. The warm springs in the hotel's own backyard is another story. Unlike some springs, "which are stagnant and of poor flow," as the management puts it, these springs are crystal clear and bursting with energy. They deliver millions of gallons of mineral-high water every day. Besides drinking from it and collecting its natural chlorides, you may sit in or under its fountain, letting the mineral showers play on your body. Best Western Springs Resort is centrally located between Fort Myers and Naples, near Bonita Springs Beaches. The great location provides guests easy access to all that Southwest Florida has to offer.

Days Inn

6651 Darter Court
Fort Pierce, FL 34945
800-329-7466 • 561-466-4066
www.daysinn.com
fpdaysinn@aol.com

Type of Lodging: Motel

Room Rates: $55–$84. AAA, AARP, Government and Corporate discounts.

Pet Charges & Deposits: $10 per stay.

Pet Policy: None. All Pets Welcome.

Amenities: Cable TV, refrigerators, microwaves, pool, restaurant.

Pet Amenities: Dog treats with dog walk information on check-in. List of nearby veterinarians maintained. Exercise area. Fort Pierce Inlet State Park is located at 905 Shorewinds Drive on the Southern tip of North Hutchinson Island. North Pepper Beach is located on AIA North.

Rated: 3 Paws — 125 rooms and 13 suites.

Fort Pierce is more than just a pretty place. The New York Mets Spring Training Camp is held here each year, the Treasure Coast beaches are ten miles away, it's two hours to both Disney World® and Miami, and Harbor Branch Oceanographic Institution and manatee viewing are close by. Days Inn boasts newly-renovated rooms with in-room coffee, dataport, hairdryer, iron and ironing board. Kids stay free with their parents. There are meeting facilities for up to 80 people and a heated swimming pool.

Royal Inn

222 Hernando Street
Fort Pierce, FL 34949
561-464-0405

Type of Lodging: Motel

Room Rates: $50–$80, including cookies and coffee. AAA and AARP discounts.

Pet Charges & Deposits: $15–$20 per stay. $25 refundable deposit.

Pet Policy: Sorry, no cats. Designated rooms only. Manager's prior approval required.

Amenities: Cable TV, free local telephone calls.

Pet Amenities: Park nearby.

Rated: 2 Paws — 18 rooms.

Fort Pierce was established as an army outpost in 1838. Today, Fort Pierce serves as a marketing center, with its key location along the Indian River. The world's fastest ball game can be seen at Fort Pierce Jai Alai. The UDT-Seal (Frogman) Museum depicts the history and development of the U.S. Navy's UDT's (Underwater Demolition Teams), SEALS (Sea, Air and Land Teams), and other specialized arms of the Navy, through photographs, dioramas and outdoor displays. All guestrooms have balconies and some rooms have views of the water and sun decks.

Howard Johnson Inn

203 Miracle Strip Parkway
Fort Walton Beach, FL 32548
850-244-8663

Type of Lodging: Hotel

Room Rates: $50–$99. AAA, AARP and *10% Pets Welcome*™ discounts.

Pet Charges & Deposits: $25 nonrefundable deposit.

Pet Policy: None. All Pets Welcome.

Amenities: Cable TV, refrigerators, microwaves, safes, pool.

Pet Amenities: List of nearby veterinarians maintained.

Rated: 3 Paws — 102 rooms.

Fort Walton Beach, on the western edge of the Florida panhandle, is surprisingly close to many points of interest. The beaches are two miles away. Hulburt Air Field and Eglin Air Force Base are five and 15 miles away. You'll find golf and chartered fishing less than half an hour away. It's three miles to the Air Force and Naval Museum, even less to an outlet mall. The Alabama border is close by. Howard Johnson Inn features complimentary coffee, kitchenettes, adjacent restaurant and lounge.

La Quinta Gainesville

920 Northwest 69th Terrace
Gainesville, FL 32605
800-531-5900 • 352-332-6466
www.laquinta.com

Type of Lodging: Hotel

Room Rates: $69–$99, including continental breakfast. AAA and AARP discounts.

Pet Charges & Deposits: None.

Pet Policy: No pets over 25 lbs.

Amenities: Cable TV, pool.

Pet Amenities: None.

Rated: 3 Paws — 130 rooms and 4 suites.

The La Quinta's new guestrooms feature a fresh décor, rich wood furniture, large desks, bright bathrooms, televisions, coffeemakers and alarm clock radios. Opportunities to observe wildlife and geological formations are within a few miles of town. To the northwest is the 6,500-acre San Felasco Hammock State Preserve. In Micanopy, not far away, you'll find the 20,000-acre Paynes Prairie State Preserve. Walk your pet along the Gainesville to Hawthorne Rail Trail, a 17-mile trail designed for walking, bicycling and horseback riding. The Florida Museum of Natural History on the University of Florida campus exhibits Native American artifacts. A highlight of Gainesville is the Fred Bear Museum, which features natural history exhibits, archery artifacts, bow hunting trophies and items Fred Bear collected on bow hunting adventures from around the world.

La Quinta Inn & Suites

2620 North 26th Avenue
Hollywood, FL 33020
800-531-5900 • 954-922-2295
www.laquinta.com
lq0985dos1@laquinta.com

Type of Lodging: Hotel

Room Rates: $79–$129, including continental breakfast. AAA and AARP discounts.

Pet Charges & Deposits: None.

Pet Policy: No pets over 50 lbs. Designated rooms only.

Amenities: Cable TV, refrigerators, microwaves, pool, whirlpool, fitness center.

Pet Amenities: Exercise area. Ann Klob Nature Park and T.V. Park are both located on Sheridan Street.

Rated: 3 Paws — 125 rooms and 6 suites.

La Quinta Inn & Suites is only three miles to Fort Lauderdale Airport and Port Everglades. The hotel creates a relaxing, residential feel with a sun-drenched lobby, beautiful courtyard, spa, pool, flexible meeting facilities and a fitness center. King rooms have a king-sized bed, microwave, refrigerator, recliner or sleeper sofa, swivel tilt desk chair and speaker phone. Hollywood is wonderfully located between Fort Lauderdale and Miami Beach, in the middle of all the fun and activity travelers have come to expect of southeastern Florida.

Casablanca Inn

1805 North A1A Highway
Indialantic, FL 32903
800-333-7273 • 321-728-7188

Type of Lodging: Motel

Room Rates: $45–$85, including coffee and pastry. AAA and AARP discounts.

Pet Charges & Deposits: $5 per day.

Pet Policy: Sorry, no cats. No pets over 25 lbs. Manager's prior approval required.

Amenities: Cable TV, refrigerators, microwaves, pool, guest laundry.

Pet Amenities: List of nearby veterinarians maintained. Sebastian State Park is located off A1A Highway. No animals are allowed on beaches in Brevard County.

Rated: 2 Paws — 34 rooms.

Mrs. Clean lives at the Casablanca Inn, and the Superior Small Lodging as well as AAA approves this lovely motel. Indialantic is the closest beach to the Disney® complex, within one hour's drive to Disney®, Universal Studios® and Orlando International Airport. Indialantic is 25 minutes from Port Canaveral and Kennedy Space Center.

Oceanfront Cottages & Vacation Homes

612 Wavecrest Avenue
Indialantic, FL 32903
800-785-8080 • 321-725-8474
www.oceanfrontcottages.com

Type of Lodging: Cottages

Suite Rates: $99–$145.

Pet Charges & Deposits: $15 per day. Refundable deposit.

Pet Policy: Small pets only. No pets over 25 lbs.

Amenities: Satellite TV, fully equipped kitchens, pool, fireplaces.

Pet Amenities: List of nearby veterinarians maintained. Sebastian State Park is located off AIA Highway. No animals are allowed on beaches in Brevard County.

Rated: 3 Paws — 6 suites.

Oceanfront Cottages are located on the boardwalk, overlooking the Atlantic Ocean. The suites have luxurious king- or queen-sized beds, individual climate controls, ceiling fans and plantation shutters that capture the feel of the islands. The floors are Mexican tile. Each suite has large sliding glass doors that lead to your own private patio surrounded by beautiful tropical plants, old-style porch swings, wicker rockers and BBQ grills. Surf fishing and shell collecting can be found almost outside your door. Kennedy Space Center, Disney®, Universal Studios®, MGM and Orlando are all less than an hour away.

Bed & Breakfast of Islamorada

81175 Old Highway
Islamorada, FL 33036-3710
305-664-9321

Type of Lodging: B&B

Room Rates: $50–$65, including full breakfast.

Pet Charges & Deposits: $10 per day.

Pet Policy: No pets over 35 lbs.

Amenities: Cable TV

Pet Amenities: List of nearby veterinarians maintained. Harry Harris Park is located at Mile Marker 92.5. Anne's Beach is located at Mile Marker 73.5.

Rated: 2 Paws — 2 rooms.

Bed & Breakfast of Islamorada offers all the comforts of home in an island paradise: clean, relaxing rooms, air conditioning, private baths, a friendly atmosphere and snorkeling gear. Islamorada is a fishing resort on Upper Matecumbe Key. The wreck of the Spanish galleon Herrera, 2½ miles off Whale Harbour Bridge, offers opportunities for underwater exploration and photography. Indian Key State Historic Site, half a mile southeast of Lower Matecumbe Key, is a ten-acre uninhabited island. Lignumvitae Key State Botanical Site can be reached only by private or chartered boat from the marinas at the western end of Islamorada.

White Gate Court Resort

76010 Overseas Highway
P.O. Box 1528
Islamorada, FL 33036
800-645 GATE • 305-664-4136
www.whitegatecourt.com
whitegatecourt@worldnet.att.net

Type of Lodging: Hotel
Room Rates: $105–$230.
Pet Charges & Deposits: $5–$10 per day.
Pet Policy: No pets over 100 lbs. Manager's prior approval required.
Amenities: Cable TV, refrigerators, private dock.
Pet Amenities: List of nearby veterinarians maintained. Dog runs. Exercise area. Several state parks nearby. Hotel has 3 acres for your pet to enjoy.
Rated: 3 Paws — 7 rooms on 3 acres.

White Gate Court Resort offers you and your pet unique accommodations: simple, but pretty, definitely with barefoot elegance. And, of course, all the comfort you are used to. There are seven recently remodeled units in five cottages, sitting on the ground floor, scattered on three acres of tropical beauty. They combine old time charm with modern comfort: full efficiency, completely equipped kitchens, cable television, direct phone lines and individual climate controls. White Gate Court Resort wants your pet around, running, swimming, having fun with you.

Holiday Inn Airport

Interstate 95 and Airport Road
Jacksonville, FL 32229
800-HOLIDAY • 904-741-4404
www.holiday-inn.com

Type of Lodging: Hotel
Room Rates: $80–$164. AAA, AARP and **20% Pets Welcome**™ discounts.
Pet Charges & Deposits: None.
Pet Policy: Designated rooms only.
Amenities: Cable TV, safes, pools, tennis and basketball courts, fitness room, game room.
Pet Amenities: List of nearby veterinarians maintained. Exercise area.
Rated: 3 Paws — 489 rooms. Holiday Inn Excellence Award Winner.

Jacksonville's Holiday Inn Airport is a premier lodging with all manner of amenities, a full service dining room, golf shop and 15 multipurpose rooms, which accommodate anything from a small working breakfast to a gala banquet for 450. Jacksonville Zoo is only four miles away and Jaguar Stadium is 12 miles away. Only 15 minutes away from the beaches, yet it's convenient to one of Florida's most enticing cities. Minutes away from the airport, the hotel provides a shuttle.

La Quinta Inn & Suites

4686 Lenoir Avenue South
Jacksonville, FL 32216
904-296-0703
Email lqo9691@laquinta.com

Type of Lodging: Hotel

Room Rates: $79–$125, including continental breakfast. AAA and AARP discounts.

Pet Charges & Deposits: None.

Pet Policy: Small pets only.

Amenities: Cable TV, refrigerators, microwaves, pool, Jacuzzi.

Pet Amenities: Dog runs. Exercise area. Parks nearby.

Rated: 3 Paws — 131 rooms.

Jacksonville is a wonderful introduction to the Sunshine State. The wonderful riverfront walk gives you a preview of what gracious living is all about. The Cummer Gallery of Art contains decorative and fine arts dating from 2000 B.C. and includes a superlative collection of 18th century Meissen porcelain tableware. The Cummer's setting is exquisite: a formal garden, modeled after the Villa Gamberaia in Florence, Italy, extends from the museum to the river. The Karpeles Manuscript Museum has a changing collection, which includes letters from Napoleon Bonaparte and George Washington, musical notations of Mozart, Beethoven and Wagner, even a copy of the Emancipation Proclamation signed by Abraham Lincoln. La Quinta Inns have well-appointed rooms and fine amenities.

River Palm Cottages & Fish Camp

2325 Northeast Indian River Drive
Jensen Beach, FL 34957
800-305-0511 • 561-334-0401
www.riverpalmcottages.com
rivpalm@aol.com

Type of Lodging: Motel

Room Rates: $55–$199. AAA and **10% Pets Welcome™** discounts.

Pet Charges & Deposits: $10 per day or $50 per week or $100 per month.

Pet Policy: None. All Pets Welcome.

Amenities: Cable TV, refrigerators, microwaves, pool.

Pet Amenities: List of nearby veterinarians maintained. Exercise area. Langford Park is located on Northeast Dixie Highway.

Rated: 3 Paws — 19 suites and 4 rooms.

The grounds at River Palm Cottages & Fish Camp are planted with lush tropical palms and native plants. You'll find hammocks hanging in the trees for your relaxation and enjoyment. Just a short drive or bicycle pedal from River Palm, historic Old Jensen Beach offers all types of vacationing fun: ocean beaches, golf, shopping, tennis, wind surfing, jet skiing, kayaking and boat rentals. River Palm Cottages & Fish Camp is located on the western bank of the Indian River Lagoon. The lodging has modernized old cabins that date back to the 1920s, 40s and 60s.

Howard Johnson Resort Hotel–Key Largo

Bayside at Mile Marker 102 Overseas Highway
P.O. Box 1024
Key Largo, FL 33037
305-451-1400

Type of Lodging: Hotel
Room Rates: $99–$225. AAA and AARP discounts.
Pet Charges & Deposits: $10 per day.
Pet Policy: Limit two pets per room. Designated rooms only. Manager's prior approval required or there is a $50 penalty for unregistered pets.
Amenities: Cable TV, refrigerators, safes.
Pet Amenities: John Pennekamp Coral Reef State Park is located Oceanside at Mile Marker 103 Overseas Highway.
Rated: 3 Paws – 100 rooms.

Just off the tip of Southern Florida, you and your pet will find the tropical Howard Johnson Resort Hotel. Located just one hour from Miami International Airport, you are surrounded by a chain of beautiful coral isles connected by a series of scenic bridges. The comfortable rooms offer coffeemakers, refrigerators, cable television and microwaves. Nearby is the famous John Pennekamp Coral Reef State Park, the only living coral reef in the continental United States. Dive or snorkel the clear waters with over 600 varieties of tropical fish or tour the deep blue sea aboard a glass bottom boat.

Atlantic Shores Resort

510 South Street
Key West, FL 33040
305-296-2491
www.atlanticshoresresort.com
info@atlanticshoresresort.com

Type of Lodging: Resort
Room Rates: $75–$375
Pet Charges & Deposits: $200 refundable deposit.
Pet Policy: Sorry, no cats. Designated rooms only.
Amenities: Cable TV, refrigerators, microwaves, pool, ocean access.
Pet Amenities: List of nearby veterinarians maintained. Higgs Beach Park nearby.
Rated: 2 Paws – 71 rooms and 1 suite.

Atlantic Shores Resort is Key West's only oceanfront, adult, alternative resort—one of the most open, inclusive and entertaining environments on the island. The pool area offers a "clothing optional" sunning deck and pier. For those guests who may be uncomfortable in the "clothing optional" environment, the resort can arrange for use of a "clothing required" beach and pool next door. The resort's clean, affordable rooms are located on the south, ocean side of Key West in the historic old town area. You and your pet are only minutes away from the heart of downtown, Duval Street, and within walking distance of all area bars, attractions, restaurants and other places of interest.

Casa Alante Guest Cottages

1435 South Roosevelt Boulevard
Key West, FL 33040
800-688-3942 • 305-293-0702
www.casaalante.com
casa-alante@aol.com

Type of Lodging: B&B

Room Rates: $80–$165, including continental breakfast. *10% Pets Welcome*™ discount.

Pet Charges & Deposits: $5 per day.

Pet Policy: Designated rooms only. Manager's prior approval required.

Amenities: Cable TV, refrigerators, pool.

Pet Amenities: Guests have continental breakfast served on their private terrace, including a ribbon-wrapped Milk Bone® treat for their dog. There is a private gated terrace so pets may sit with their owners. List of nearby veterinarians maintained. Key West as a "dog" beach nearby.

Rated: 4 Paws — 10 rooms.

The ultimate Key West vacation experience! What could be more charming and relaxing than a group of historic cottages nestled amongst lush tropical foliage on a small island—each designed to be your own personal gateway to paradise? All cottages are decorated in soothing tones with cool ceramic tiles and ceiling fans. Each has its own kitchen, private bathroom, air conditioning, and telephone. Additional amenities include BBQ, picnic table, guest laundry, exchange-a-book library, free use of bicycles, German spoken and concierge service.

Courtney's Place - Historic Cottages & Inn

720 Whitmarsh Lane
Key West, FL 33040
800-869-4639 • 305-294-3480
www.keywest.com/Courtney.html
cplacekw@keysdigital.com

Type of Lodging: B&B

Room Rates: $75–$295, including extended continental breakfast. AAA and AARP discounts.

Pet Charges & Deposits: Call for refundable deposit.

Pet Policy: Designated rooms only.

Amenities: Cable TV, refrigerators, microwaves, pool, outdoor BBQ area, bike rentals.

Pet Amenities: Treats and bed blankets available. List of nearby veterinarians maintained. Park nearby.

Rated: 2 Paws — 8 rooms and 8 suites.

Stay in Key West like a native. Courtney's Place Historic Cottages & Inn is located in the heart of Old Key West, 1½ blocks from world-famous Duval Street, seven blocks ocean-to-ocean, yet situated on a quiet lane in an authentic Conch neighborhood. Their breakfast motto, "If you go away hungry, it's your own fault," is meaningful. There are full kitchens in most cottages and efficienciess with dishes, silverware, pots, pans, etc. Choose a private room, efficiencies, or a great one-, two- or three-bedroom cottage. It's an ideal place to kick back, relax and get the real flavor of Key West.

Cuban Club Suites

1108 Duval Street
Key West, FL 33040
800-432-4849 • 305-296-0465
www.keywestcubanclub.com

Type of Lodging: All-Suites Hotel

Suite Rates: $139–$399. *10% Pets Welcome*™ discount.

Pet Charges & Deposits: $200 refundable deposit.

Pet Policy: Sorry, no cats. Pets must not be left unattended.

Amenities: Cable TV, fully equipped kitchens, safes, pool.

Pet Amenities: Pet walkers available. List of nearby veterinarians maintained. Fort Zachary Taylor State Park is located on Southard Street. Dog beach is only 5 blocks away.

Rated: 3 Paws — 8 suites.

The Cuban Club is the best of then and now. Built in the style of Old Key West and located in the heart of paradise on legendary Duval Street, guests are within easy access to the island's fabled and unforgettable historical sites, galleries, attractions, dining and shopping. Cuban cigar makers and their families founded the building in 1900 as their home away from home. They used it as a place of meeting, playing games, music, dance and culture. It was built with 50 cents on a dollar from each man's paycheck as dues. Today, the Cuban Club Suites offer such amenities as cathedral ceilings with fans, fully equipped kitchens with tile counter tops and floors, tiled baths and airy rooms for up to six people, ranging from 900 to 1,900 square feet.

Frances Street Bottle Inn

535 Frances Street
Key West, FL 33040
800-294-850 • 305-294-8530
www.bottleinn.com

Type of Lodging: B&B

Room Rates: $80–$225, including continental breakfast, social hour and beach passes. AAA discount.

Pet Charges & Deposits: None.

Pet Policy: Designated rooms only.

Amenities: Cable TV, refrigerators, microwaves, safe, Jacuzzi.

Pet Amenities: List of nearby veterinarians maintained. Fort Zachary Taylor State Park is located on Southard Street.

Rated: 3 Paws — 8 rooms.

Frances Street Bottle Inn is centrally located in Old Town Key West, within easy walking distance to Duval Street, the historic seaport, museums and beaches. Built in the traditional Conch blend of European and Caribbean architecture, with gracious porches and a lovely brick patio, nestled under tropical Poinciana trees, the Bottle Inn is only steps away from spectacular restaurants, intriguing galleries, colorful shopping and the historic waterfront.

Travelers Palm Tropical Suites

815 Catherine Street
Key West, FL 33040
800-294-9560 • 305-294-9560
www.travelerspalm.com

Type of Lodging: Cottages and Apartments

Room Rates: $75–$400, including continental breakfast. AAA discount.

Pet Charges & Deposits: $10 per day

Pet Policy: Sorry, no cats. No pets over 20 lbs. Designated rooms only. Limit two pets per room.

Amenities: Cable TV, refrigerators, microwaves, pool, Jacuzzi, hammocks, grill area.

Pet Amenities: List of nearby veterinarians maintained. Exercise area. Bayview Park and Dog's Beach nearby.

Rated: 3 Paws — 19 rooms and 2 suites.

Charles Kuralt called Travelers Palm, "eclectic…laid back accommodations…a small Eden." Travelers Palm features unique one and two bedroom accommodations, all containing air conditioning, kitchens and private garden/patio areas. The units are beautifully furnished with a tropical flair. Located just three blocks from Duval Street and six blocks from the Atlantic beaches, you can walk or bike anywhere from this Old Town oasis. Bicycles are available for rent on the premises.

Homewood Suites by Hilton on the Parkway

3100 Parkway Boulevard
Kissimmee, FL 34747
800-255-4543 • 407-396-2229
www.homewood-suites.com

Type of Lodging: Hotel

Suite Rates: $109–$169, including continental breakfast and weekday Manager's Reception. AAA, AARP and *10% Pets Welcome™* discounts.

Pet Charges & Deposits: $75 per stay. $250 deposit of which $175 is refundable.

Pet Policy: None. All Pets Welcome.

Amenities: Cable TV, fully equipped kitchens, safes, pool, Jacuzzi.

Pet Amenities: List of nearby veterinarians maintained. Exercise area.

Rated: 3 Paws — 156 suites.

It's a scant 1½ miles from Homewood Suites to the Walt Disney World® resort area. In fact, Homewood Suites provides a complimentary scheduled shuttle to all four Walt Disney World® theme parks. There's a 24-hour convenience store, guest laundry, exercise facilities, a sport court and some of the roomiest accommodations you'll find anywhere.

Howard Johnson Kissimmee Hotel

2323 U.S. 192 East
Kissimmee, FL 34744
800-521-4656 • 407-846-4900
www.hojohotel.com
hjkissfl@aol.com

Type of Lodging: Hotel
Room Rates: $50–$66. AAA, AARP, AKC, ABA and *10% Pets Welcome*™ discounts.
Pet Charges & Deposits: $10 per day.
Pet Policy: Designated rooms only.
Amenities: Cable TV, refrigerators, microwaves, safes, pool.
Pet Amenities: List of nearby veterinarians maintained. Dog runs. Exercise area. Lakefront Park nearby.
Rated: 2 Paws — 200 rooms. Gold Medal Award Winner

This unit of the Howard Johnson chain is 15 minutes from EPCOT® Center, 20 minutes from Universal Studios® and Islands of Adventure®, 20 minutes from Seaworld® and 15 minutes to Walt Disney World®. In fact, the hotel provides free transportation to the Disney® theme parks. Kids stay and eat free, a free weekday newspaper and over-sized, newly renovated rooms are just a few of the amenities. Howard Johnson couldn't be more centrally located for mid-Florida's fun center.

Summerfield Condo Resort

2425 Summerfield Way
Kissimmee, FL 34741
800-207-9582 • 407-847-7222
www.summerfieldcondo.com

Type of Lodging: Condominiums
Condominium Rates: $99–$129, including weekday continental breakfast. AAA discount.
Pet Charges & Deposits: $25 per day for small pets. Call for large pets.
Pet Policy: Manager's prior approval required.
Amenities: Cable TV, refrigerators, microwaves, pool, hot tubs, playground, picnic tables, guest laundry.
Pet Amenities: List of nearby veterinarians maintained. Exercise area. Lakefront Park nearby.
Rated: 3 Paws — 37 condominiums.

These lovely townhouses, each of which contains two bedrooms, has spacious living and dining areas, remote control cable television and fully equipped kitchen with full-sized appliances. There's a clubhouse on the grounds. This resort is centrally located within 15 minutes of all the major attractions— Walt Disney World®, Universal Studios®, Sea World®, etc. You're an hour away from the Kennedy Space Center and the beaches of Florida's east and west coasts.

Royalty Inn

3425 U.S. Highway 98 North
Lakeland, FL 33809
800-633-4305 • 863-858-4481
www.lakelandhotel.com
royinn@aol.com

Type of Lodging: Motel

Room Rates: $60–$100, including coffee. AAA and AARP discounts.

Pet Charges & Deposits: $10 per day.

Pet Policy: None. All Pets Welcome.

Amenities: Refrigerators, microwaves, safes, pool.

Pet Amenities: List of nearby veterinarians maintained. Lake Hollingsworth nearby.

Rated: 3 Paws — 63 rooms.

Lakeland's 13 lakes provide wonderful opportunities for fishing, boating and water skiing, as well as golf and tennis. The city is a processing and distribution center for citrus fruits and other agricultural products. A majority of the world's phosphate, the primary ingredient in fertilizer, is mined in the Lakeland area. The city is spring training headquarters for the Detroit Tigers. Explorations V Children's Museum is a wonderful place for kids with hands-on exhibits. Disney's theme parks and Tampa's Busch Gardens are within easy driving distance.

Wellesley Inn & Suites

3520 U.S. Highway 98 North
Lakeland, FL 33809
863-859-3399
www.wellesleyinnandsuites.com

Type of Lodging: Hotel

Room Rates: $79–$119, including continental breakfast. AAA, AARP and *10% Pets Welcome™* discounts.

Pet Charges & Deposits: $10 per stay. $75 refundable deposit.

Pet Policy: No pets over 15 lbs.

Amenities: Cable TV, safes, pool.

Pet Amenities: Lake Parker is located on Lakeland Hills Boulevard.

Rated: 3 Paws — 83 rooms and 23 suites.

Lakeland is halfway between Tampa Bay and Orlando—turn right or turn left, proceed east or west, and you're in the middle of central Florida's exciting tourist attractions. In Lakeland's Polk Museum of Art, you can see changing exhibits of contemporary and historical art. The world's largest group of buildings designed by Frank Lloyd Wright is on the Florida Southern College campus. At Lakeland Center, there are ice hockey games, concerts, ballet performances and trade shows.

Amerisuites Miami/Kendall

11520 Southwest 88th Street
Miami, FL 33176
800-833-1516 • 305-279-8688
www.amerisuites.com

Type of Lodging: Hotel

Suite Rates: $129–$169, including free Bountiful Breakfast Buffet. AAA, AARP and *20% Pets Welcome™* discounts.

Pet Charges & Deposits: None.

Pet Policy: No pets over 30 lbs. Pets must not be left unattended.

Amenities: Cable TV, refrigerators, microwaves, safes, pool, guest laundry, hairdryer.

Pet Amenities: None.

Rated: 3 Paws — 67 suites.

Amerisuites Miami/Kendall, just south of Miami, is within 15 minutes of Monkey Jungle, Parrot Jungle, Dadeland Mall, Coral Castle and Miccosukee Native American Village and Gaming complex. It's convenient to Miami International Airport. Amerisuites features modern suites with iron and ironing board, guest laundry facility, hairdryer and free weekday newspaper. The meeting facility will accommodate up to 50 people.

Baymont Inn & Suites Miami/Cutler Ridge

10821 Caribbean Boulevard
Miami, FL 33189
800-301-0200 • 305-278-0001
www.baymontinns.com

Type of Lodging: Hotel

Room Rates: $65–$119, including continental breakfast. AAA, AARP and *10% Pets Welcome™* discounts.

Pet Charges & Deposits: $50 refundable deposit.

Pet Policy: No pets over 50 lbs. Designated rooms only.

Amenities: Cable TV, refrigerators, microwaves, pool.

Pet Amenities: Many county and state parks nearby.

Rated: 3 Paws — 92 rooms and 11 suites.

Baymont delivers a clean room loaded with amenities. There's a long, luxurious bed, a cable television, coffeemaker and complimentary coffee, but that's just the beginning. There's an iron and ironing board, a hairdryer, voicemail, a large desk, free local telephone calls—and that's just in the rooms. The hotel is located 20 miles from Miami International Airport, three miles to Miami Zoo, near Monkey Jungle, Parrot Jungle, Homestead Air Force Base, Dadeland Mall and Florida Keys factory outlet shops.

Hampton Inn Miami Airport West

3620 Northwest 79th Avenue
Miami, FL 33166
305-513-0777
miawe01@hi-hotel.com

Type of Lodging: Hotel

Room Rates: $80–$150, including continental breakfast. AAA discount.

Pet Charges & Deposits: $25 per stay.

Pet Policy: No pets over 40 lbs.

Amenities: Cable TV, irons and ironing boards, hairdryers, pool.

Pet Amenities: None.

Rated: 3 Paws — 127 rooms.

The Hampton Inn has contemporary décor. The hotel is situated on attractive grounds in a six-story main building. Miami and Miami Beach combine natural beauty with contemporary entertainment. Swaying palm trees share space with tall, modern buildings; exotic bougainvillea and hibiscus mix with major league sporting events; and the worlds of Dave Barry, Little Havana and Miami Beach all come together to make this an utterly unique international metropolis.

Hotel Ocean

1230 Ocean Drive
Miami Beach, FL 33139
800-783-1725 • 305-672-2579
www.hotelocean.com
info@hotelocean.com

Type of Lodging: Hotel

Room Rates: $200–$600, including continental breakfast. *10%
Pets Welcome*™ discount.

Pet Charges & Deposits: $15 per day.

Pet Policy: None. All Pets Welcome.

Amenities: Cable TV, refrigerators, safes, Jacuzzis.

Pet Amenities: A turndown treat is provided for your pet. List of
nearby veterinarians maintained. Dog runs. Exercise area. Lummus
Park is located across the street, along the beach. The Hotel Ocean
was ranked #7 of the Top Ten in the United States and Canada in
Pet-Friendly Properties (Food & Wine Magazine, February, 1998).

Rated: 5 Paws – 11 rooms and 16 suites.

The Hotel Ocean wins a coveted Pets Welcome™ Five-Paw award because
of its special, extra attention to pets. This small, pet-friendly luxury bou-
tique hotel combines the amenities of the 21st century with timeless
European tradition in service. The accommodations are bright, sound-
proofed, filled with light and ocean views. It's located at one of the world's
most desirable addresses, Ocean Drive in South Beach. French-owned
and operated, it's a Mediterranean oasis in a dense urban environment.
Hotel Ocean is in the heart of the Art Deco Historic District, among fashionable boutiques, great restaurants, theaters, trendy clubs, museums, art
galleries, ballet, cinemas, golf—with all of Miami at your feet.

Loews Miami Beach Hotel

1601 Collins Avenue
Miami Beach, FL 33139
800-23-LOEWS • 305-604-1601
www.loewshotels.com
loewsmiamibeach@loewshotels.com

Type of Lodging: Hotel

Room Rates: $369–$409. AAA and AARP discounts.

Pet Charges & Deposits: None.

Pet Policy: None. All Pets Welcome.

Amenities: Cable TV, honor bar, safes, pool, Jacuzzi.

Pet Amenities: List of nearby veterinarians maintained. Dog runs. Exercise area. Flamingo Park nearby.

Rated: 4 Paws — 800 rooms.

Smack-dab in the middle of it all on legendary Collins Avenue, the hotel is an Art Deco masterpiece, and all rooms follow this theme. The 18-story high-rise building insures that you will have ocean or city rooms. Naturally, there are dining, entertainment and gift shops on the premises. Loews Miami Beach Hotel is one of the premier addresses in a decidedly upscale area. Indoor and outdoor entertainments of all kinds abound within 30 minutes.

Main Stay Suites

101 Fairway Drive
Miami Springs, FL 33166
305-870-0448
www.mainstaysuites.com

Type of Lodging: Hotel

Suite Rates: $80–$130, including weekday continental breakfast and social hour. AAA and AARP discounts.

Pet Charges & Deposits: $5 per day. $100 refundable deposit.

Pet Policy: None. All Pets Welcome.

Amenities: Cable TV, fully equipped kitchens, safes, pool.

Pet Amenities: List of nearby veterinarians maintained. Dog runs. Exercise area. Virginia Gardens Park is located ½ mile away. Miami Springs Park is located a mile away. Dog walking trail nearby.

Rated: 3 Paws — 102 suites. 1999 Hotel Of The Year Award

This brand new Main Stay Suites opened in January 1999 and proceeded to win the 1999 Hotel Of The Year Award! Each suite comes with a fully equipped kitchen, direct dial, two-line speaker telephone with dataport and voicemail, generous work space, outdoor pool and fitness room, courtyard with BBQ area and a 100% satisfaction guarantee. Main Stay Suites is located just off the Airport Perimeter Road, near Miami International Airport.

Econo Lodge

7631 U.S. Highway 19
New Port Richey, FL 34652
800-889-9083 • 727-845-4990
www.hotelchoice.com/res/hotel/FL466

Type of Lodging: Motel

Room Rates: $45–$90, including continental breakfast. AAA, AARP, Corporate and *Pets Welcome*™ discounts.

Pet Charges & Deposits: $10 per day.

Pet Policy: No pets over 20 lbs. Designated rooms only.

Amenities: Cable TV, refrigerators, microwaves, guest laundry, picnic and BBQ area, free local phone calls.

Pet Amenities: List of nearby veterinarians maintained. Exercise area. Sims Park is located on Main Street and North Boulevard. Starkey Wilderness Park nearby.

Rated: 2 Paws — 104 rooms.

Econo Lodge has newly renovated ground-floor rooms with king-sized beds and kitchenettes. New Port Richey is near Weeki Wachee and it is known for their underwater shows, yet it's less than an hour to Tampa Airport. There's a casino boat next door, ample restaurants and shopping nearby, Tarpon Springs, Green Key and Clearwater Beaches in the vicinity and Tampa-St. Petersburg an easy hour's drive away.

Holiday Inn SunSpree Resort

13351 State Route 535
Orlando, FL 32821
800-366-6299 • 407-239-4500
www.kidsuites.com

Type of Lodging: Resort

Room Rates: $69–$139. AAA, AARP, AKC, Government, Airline, Military, ESM and *20% Pets Welcome*™ discounts.

Pet Charges & Deposits: $25 nonrefundable deposit.

Pet Policy: No pets over 25 lbs. Manager's prior approval required.

Amenities: Cable TV, refrigerators, microwaves, safes, whirlpool, Jacuzzi, fitness room, nightly entertainment.

Pet Amenities: Welcome Goodie bag at check-in with dog treats and ID collar. List of nearby veterinarians maintained. Exercise area. Little Lake Bryan nearby. Beepers provided if guests leave resort property.

Rated: 4 Paws — 507 rooms and 231 suites. Featured in USA Today as a "Best for Vacationing Pets."

The award-winning Holiday Inn SunSpree Resort, less than a mile from the Walt Disney World® resorts, offers a convenient and wonderful pet program. The Resort treats pets with the same first-class service that human guests receive. A welcome goodie bag and ID band are pleasant amenities, as are window signs, notifying other guests and employees that there's a pet in the room.

Portofino Bay Hotel at Universal Orlando   A Loews Hotel

5601 Universal Boulevard
Orlando, FL 32819
800-UESCAPE • 407-503-1000
www.loewshotels.com

Type of Lodging: Hotel

Room Rates: $235–$2,000. AAA discount.

Pet Charges & Deposits: $50 per stay. $100 refundable deposit.

Pet Policy: Designated rooms only. Pets restricted from restaurant and pool areas.

Amenities: Cable TV, honor bar, safes, pool, hot tubs, coffeemakers, irons and ironing boards, voicemail.

Pet Amenities: Welcome amenities include "Loews Loves Pets" Placemat, bowl and treats. List of nearby veterinarians maintained. Exercise area. Lake Marsha Park is located at Turkey Lake and Conroy-Windemere Roads.

Rated: 4 Paws — 750 rooms including 48 suites.

Portofino Bay Hotel, a Loews hotel, is a wonderful destination hotel located in the Universal-Orlando area. It's strikingly close to all of the Orlando attractions—Walt Disney World®, Wet N' Wild, Sea World®—and within an easy 45-minute drive to Kennedy Space Center. This is truly a wonderful place to spend a holiday.

Brazilian Court Hotel

301 Australian Avenue
Palm Beach, FL 33480
800-552-0335 • 561-655-7740
www.braziliancourt.com
info@braziliancourt.com

Type of Lodging: Hotel

Room Rates: $150–$875.

Pet Charges & Deposits: $75 nonrefundable deposit.

Pet Policy: No pets over 35 lbs.

Amenities: Cable TV, refrigerators, honor bar, pool.

Pet Amenities: Excellent pet menu and special VIPet Amenities. Veterinarians on call and grooming services available. Exercise area. City and county parks nearby.

Rated: 3 Paws — 108 rooms and 38 suites.

The Brazilian Court is located in the heart of fashionable Palm Beach, two blocks from the Atlantic Beaches and three blocks from world-class shopping on tree-shaded Worth Avenue. It has all the amenities you'd expect from a first-class lodging establishment. Well worth seeing is the Flagler Museum, a 1902 Gilded Age mansion that railroad magnate and developer Henry Flagler built for his bride. The grandeur of this 55-room house earned it the title "Taj Mahal of North America." Among the highlights are a marble entrance hall, Louis XIV music room and Louis XV ballroom.

Chesterfield Hotel

363 Cocoanut Row
Palm Beach, FL 33480
800-243-7871 • 561-659-5800
www.redcarnationhotels.com
chesterpb@aol.com

Type of Lodging: Hotel
Room Rates: $99–$1,500. AAA discount.
Pet Charges & Deposits: $150 refundable deposit.
Pet Policy: No pets over 40 lbs.
Amenities: Cable TV, safes, pool, Jacuzzi, restaurant, lounge.
Pet Amenities: Pet beds, pet treats and pet bowls upon arrival. List of nearby veterinarians maintained. Exercise area. Park is located on Lake Drive and Chilean Avenue.
Rated: 4 Paws — 43 rooms and 11 suites.

The Chesterfield Hotel is a distinguished member of Small Luxury Hotels of the World. It's located in the center of Palm Beach, two blocks from Worth Avenue and three blocks from the ocean. The Chesterfield Hotel offers individually designed suites and rooms, an award-winning restaurant, and a private courtyard and pool where pets can feel at home. Luxurious style, exquisite furnishings, constant attention to the provision of thoughtful extras and a commitment to exceptional personal service make this hotel a special "find" in an area of upscale lodgings.

Heart of Palm Beach Hotel

160 Royal Palm Way
Palm Beach, FL 33480
800-523-5377 • 561-655-5600
www.heartofpalmbeach.com
reservations@heartofpalmbeach.com

Type of Lodging: Hotel
Room Rates: $89–$259. AAA, AARP and *10% Pets Welcome*™ discounts.
Pet Charges & Deposits: None.
Pet Policy: None. All Pets Welcome.
Amenities: Cable TV, refrigerators, pool, restaurant.
Pet Amenities: Exercise area. Lots of open space and parks nearby.
Rated: 4 Paws — 88 rooms.

The Heart of Palm Beach Hotel is located on the island of Palm Beach, half a block from the ocean. This intimate hotel offers large rooms featuring a balcony or terrace. Dine at the island-acclaimed "Pleasant Peasant" Restaurant on the premises. Complimentary underground self-parking, limousine and bicycle rentals on the property, kids stay free with their parents are some of the amenities offered. Golf, tennis, water sports and shopping are all nearby. A multilingual staff is a wonderful bonus.

Plaza Inn

215 Brazilian Avenue
Palm Beach, FL 33480
800-233-2632 • 561-832-8666
www.plazainnpalmbeach.com
plazainn@aol.com

Type of Lodging: Hotel

Room Rates: $125–$325, including full breakfast. AAA, AARP and **5% Pets Welcome™** discounts.

Pet Charges & Deposits: None.

Pet Policy: No pets over 80 lbs. Designated rooms only.

Amenities: Cable TV, refrigerators, safes, pool, Jacuzzi.

Pet Amenities: List of nearby veterinarians maintained. Exercise area. Phipps Park is located on A1A Highway.

Rated: 3 Paws — 41 rooms and 3 suites.

The management of this fine hotel has indicated that they are delighted to receive guests from our Pets Welcome™ guide. They have proudly accommodated numerous "celebrity pets," and with good reason. The Plaza Inn is a warm, friendly place in a restored three-story art-deco building. Right in the middle of Palm Beach, it has been featured in Travel & Leisure Magazine, in U.S. Airways Magazine and in all major travel books, such as Fodor's, Frommer's, Mobil and other international travel guides. A wonderful choice for a wonderful destination city.

Ramada Inn Bayview

7601 Scenic Highway
Pensacola, FL 32504
800-282-1212 • 850-477-7155
www.ramadabayview.com
rsvtns@ramadabayview.com

Type of Lodging: Hotel

Room Rates: $57–$78, including continental breakfast. AAA, AARP and **10% Pets Welcome™** discounts.

Pet Charges & Deposits: None.

Pet Policy: No pets over 25 lbs. Designated rooms only.

Amenities: Cable TV, refrigerators, microwaves, safes, pool, whirlpool, Jacuzzi.

Pet Amenities: List of nearby veterinarians maintained. Exercise area. Fort Pickens, YMCA Park and Scenic Bluffs Parks nearby.

Rated: 3 Paws — 140 rooms and 10 suites.

Ramada Inn Bayview is beautifully landscaped, featuring a secluded courtyard with pool and gazebo. Well-appointed guestrooms and executive suites with private balcony or patio, free local phone calls, in-room coffee and complimentary newspaper, a private hot tub and fitness room and a full service restaurant and piano bar are among the many amenities you'll find here. The Ramada Inn Bayview is near the U.S. Naval Air Museum, restaurants, malls, beaches and so much more. Just minutes away from Pensacola Airport, the Ramada is perfectly placed.

Ramada Limited

8060 Lavelle Way
Pensacola, FL 32526
800-2 RAMADA • 850-944-0333
www.ramada.com

Type of Lodging: Motel
Room Rates: $54–$75, including continental breakfast. AAA and AARP discounts.
Pet Charges & Deposits: $25 per stay.
Pet Policy: None. All Pets Welcome.
Amenities: Cable TV, refrigerators, microwaves, safes, pool.
Pet Amenities: Exercise area.
Rated: 3 Paws — 93 rooms.

Ramada Limited is a fine, cost-conscious choice for your stay in Pensacola. Although an attempt was made to establish a settlement at Pensacola as early as 1559, it was not until 1698 that Fort San Carlos was actually built. In 1814, the British used the harbor as their base in the war with the United States, but withdrew when General Andrew Jackson attacked the city. It was here that Jackson completed the transaction where Spain sold Florida to the United States. Historic Pensacola Village is a complex of 19th century buildings well worth seeing. The National Museum of Naval Aviation rates a star on anyone's list of things to see. Among its stellar attractions are the NC-4 Flying Boat, which in 1919 became the first plane to cross the Atlantic. Other attractions include the F6F Hellcat, a WWII fighter plane and the Skylab Command Module.

Allison House Inn

215 North Madison
Quincy, FL 32351
888-904-2511 • 850-895-2511

Type of Lodging: B&B
Room Rates: $80–$95, including continental or full breakfast. AAA and AARP discounts.
Pet Charges & Deposits: None.
Pet Policy: Sorry, no cats. No pets over 20 lbs. Manager's prior approval required.
Amenities: Cable TV.
Pet Amenities: List of nearby veterinarians maintained. Exercise area.
Rated: 3 Paws — 5 rooms.

When you stay at Allison House Inn, you are truly absorbing history, even as you sleep and gaze about you. A former Florida governor built this Greek Revival home in 1843. Quincy owed its early prosperity to the tobacco industry. The Quincy State Bank eventually persuaded its patrons to invest in a fledgling Georgia company called Coca Cola. This resulted in economic fortune for the town and its citizens. Allison House is within the 36-block historic district, which features landscaping, period lighting and Victorian-style buildings.

Waterside Inn on the Beach

3033 West Gulf Drive
Sanibel, FL 33957
800-741-6166 • 941-472-1345
www.watersideinnonthebeach.com
watersideinn@iline.com

Type of Lodging: Motel & Resort

Room Rates: $113–$314. AAA discount.

Pet Charges & Deposits: $5 per day.

Pet Policy: No pets over 30 lbs. Designated rooms only. Manager's prior approval required.

Amenities: Cable TV, refrigerators, microwaves, pool.

Pet Amenities: List of nearby veterinarians maintained. Exercise area. Parks and beach nearby.

Rated: 2 Paws — 27 rooms.

Waterside Inn's goal is to exceed your expectations—and they just might do it. Of course, that's not the only reason Sanibel is one of Florida's premier tourist destinations. This barrier island is known for its lighthouse, lush vegetation, extensive beaches and abundant birdlike. Oh, did we forget to mention seashells? Sanibel is, of course, known worldwide for its seashells and each tide brings thousands of shells onto the fine sand beaches. Superstar attractions include the Bailey-Matthews Shell Museum and the J.N. "Ding" Darling National Wildlife Refuge.

Coquina On The Beach

1008 Ben Franklin Drive
Sarasota, FL 34236
800-833-2141 • 941-388-2141
www.coquinaonthebeach.com
coquina@earthlink.net

Type of Lodging: Hotel

Room Rates: $89–$319. AAA, AARP and *10% Pets Welcome™* discounts.

Pet Charges & Deposits: $25 per stay.

Pet Policy: None. All Pets Welcome.

Amenities: Cable TV, full kitchens, pool.

Pet Amenities: List of nearby veterinarians maintained. Dog runs. Exercise area.

Rated: 3 Paws — 26 rooms and 8 suites directly on the beach.

Once you settle in at Coquina On The Beach, you may never want to leave. However, if you decide to venture out, the surrounding city of Sarasota offers plenty of excitement. European St. Armand's Circle, reminiscent of Europe, contains unique boutiques, award-winning dining, relaxing carriage rides and exciting nightclubs. Known as Florida's cultural capital, Sarasota features theaters, museums, art galleries and more. Coquina on the Beach is beautifully landscaped in a tropical motif, with tiki huts, a BBQ area, private beach, water sports, beach cabanas, blue skies, swaying palm trees and seemingly endless white sand beaches.

Holiday Inn Express

6600 South Tamiami Trail
Sarasota, FL 34231
800-HOLIDAY • 941-924-4900
www.floridatravelnet.com

Type of Lodging: Hotel

Room Rates: $89–$139, including continental breakfast. AAA, AARP and **20% Pets Welcome™** discounts.

Pet Charges & Deposits: $30 nonrefundable deposit.

Pet Policy: No pets over 20 lbs.

Amenities: Cable TV, refrigerators, safes, pool, whirlpool.

Pet Amenities: List of nearby veterinarians maintained. Exercise area. Oscar Shearer State Park is located off Route 41 in Osprey.

Rated: 3 Paws — 130 rooms.

Holiday Inn Express guestrooms feature king or double-double rooms, coffeemakers, alarm clocks, safes, two separate phone lines with voicemail and dataports, hairdryers, iron and ironing board. It's less than one mile from Siesta Key Beach, world-famous for the finest, whitest sand on the planet. The Ringling Circus Museum, the airport and the dog track are nine miles away. It's only six miles to the Mote Marine Aquarium, eight miles to Sarasota Outlet Mall. Kick back, relax, and enjoy a wonderful holiday at the Holiday Inn Express.

Surfrider Motel & Beach Apartments

6400 Midnight Pass Road
Sarasota, FL 34242
941-349-2121

Type of Lodging: Motel / Apartments

Room Rates: $65–$150 daily or $410–$900 weekly.

Pet Charges & Deposits: None.

Pet Policy: None. All Pets Welcome.

Amenities: Cable TV, refrigerators, pool, hot tubs, dinner restaurant.

Pet Amenities: Exercise area. City parks nearby.

Rated: 4 Paws — 7 rooms and 14 suites.

Surfrider Motel & Beach Apartments affords you your own private beach, directly on the Gulf of Mexico. The Surfrider offers you a choice of motel rooms or completely private one- and two-bedroom apartments overlooking the beautiful Gulf of Mexico. Fascinating specialty shops and services are located within walking distance at Stickney Point. The lodgings are located on Siesta Key. There are more than 30 golf courses within minutes of downtown Sarasota. An array of performing arts groups, including the Asolo Theatre Company, The Players, Sarasota Opera, the Florida West Coast Symphony, Sarasota Ballet of Florida, Florida String Quartet and the Florida Symphonic Band provide year-round cultural entertainment.

Tropical Breeze Inn

140 Columbus Boulevard
Siesta Key
Sarasota, FL 34242
800-300-2492 • 941-349-1125
www.tropicalbreezeinn.com
info@tropicalbreezeinn.com

Type of Lodging: Inn

Room Rates: $79–$295. AAA, AARP, AKC and ABA discounts.

Pet Charges & Deposits: Call for charges and deposit information.

Pet Policy: Designated rooms only. Manager's prior approval required.

Amenities: Cable TV, refrigerators, microwaves, pool, Jacuzzi.

Pet Amenities: None.

Rated: 2 Paws — 21 rooms and suites.

Tropical Breeze Inn, situated on Siesta Key, is a complex of one-story units, some of which are right across the street from the beach. Early check-in, late checkout and free local calls are among the friendlier amenities at this fine lodging. Sarasota, including the offshore islands of Lido Key, Longboat Key, St. Armand Key and Siesta Key, is a beach resort and art community. There are 35 miles of fine, white sand beaches for your enjoyment.

Tropical Shores Beach Resort

6717 Sara Sea Circle
Siesta Key
Sarasota, FL 34242
800-235-3493 • 941-349-3330
www.tropicalshores.com
tropshores@aol.com

Type of Lodging: Hotel

Room Rates: $99–$395. AAA, AARP, AKC, ABA and *10% Pets Welcome™* discounts.

Pet Charges & Deposits: $50 per stay. Call for deposit information.

Pet Policy: Designated rooms only. Manager's prior approval required.

Amenities: Cable TV, refrigerators, microwaves, pool, Jacuzzi, private beach access, tiki hut, BBQ grills, shuffleboard courts.

Pet Amenities: List of nearby veterinarians maintained. Paw Park is located at 17th Street and Tuttle. Island Park is located at 41st and Main Streets. Pets are not allowed on the beach.

Rated: 3 Paws — 22 rooms and 8 suites.

Tropical Shores Beach Resort has won a beautification award, adding its own individual touch to one of the Top Ten Beaches in the World. Of all 50 states, only Alaska has more islands than Florida, and we'll wager that none are more beautiful than Siesta Key, over the causeway from (and a part of) mainland Sarasota, former home of the Ringling Brothers and Barnum & Bailey Circus. While in Sarasota, be sure to see the John & Mable Ringling Museum of Art, built in the Italian Renaissance style. Among other works, this fine museum has reproductions of many world famous sculptures (including the bronze cast of Michelangelo's David), paintings from the 14th through 19th centuries and an extensive collection of Peter Paul Rubens.

Flamingo Beach House

110, 124, 129, 135 Avenida Veneccia
Siesta Key, FL 34242
800-899-0230 • 941346-8079
www.4sarasota.com/flamingohouse
siestarent@home.com

Type of Lodging: Apartments
Room Rates: $413–$995 per week.
Pet Charges & Deposits: $200 refundable deposit.
Pet Policy: No pets over 40 lbs. Manager's prior approval required.
Amenities: Cable TV, fully equipped kitchenettes, pool, hot tub, BBQ grill, guest laundry.
Pet Amenities: Siesta Beach Park is within walking distance.
Rated: 2 Paws — 1 room and 10 suites.

Designed for long, leisurely stays, this group of apartment properties is perfect for families and pets. You can enjoy the tropical beach life to the fullest on gorgeous Siesta Key, yet be within minutes of all the cultural amenities of the "big city"—Sarasota—just across the causeway. Long, idyllic beach walks, swimming in the pool or in the Gulf, stars so close at night you can reach out and grab them. Who would want more?

Gulf Lookout

69 Avenida Messina
Siesta Key, FL 34242
800-899-0230 • 941-346-8079
siestarent@home.com

Type of Lodging: Apartments
Suite Rates: $567–$995 per week.
Pet Charges & Deposits: $200 refundable deposit.
Pet Policy: No pets over 40 lbs. Manager's prior approval required.
Amenities: Cable TV, fully equipped kitchenettes, Jacuzzi, BBQ grills, guest laundry.
Pet Amenities: None.
Rated: 2 Paws — 9 suites.

Gulf Lookout consists of comfortable apartments just steps away from the brilliant white sand beach of Siesta Key. It's an easy walk to shops and restaurants on the island, and a hop, skip and jump to the relaxed bustle and activity of the cultural capital of the Florida Gulf Coast. These well-kept units are designed for leisurely visits, providing you and your pet with a home base to numerous central Florida destinations.

Heron Lagoon Club

8212 Midnight Pass Road
Siesta Key, FL 34242
800-889-3582 • 941-518-5445
siestarent@home.com

Type of Lodging: Apartments

Suite Rates: $399–$850 per week.

Pet Charges & Deposits: $200 refundable deposit.

Pet Policy: No pets over 40 lbs. Manager's prior approval required.

Amenities: Cable TV, fully equipped kitchenettes, pool, BBQ grills.

Pet Amenities: Exercise area. Turtle Beach is located 2 miles south.

Rated: 2 Paws — 10 suites.

Housekeeping has never been easier than in paradise. The Heron Lagoon Club has beautifully landscaped gardens in a perfect location, close to the magnificent Siesta Key beaches, shopping and restaurants, and a stone's throw from all the wonders of Sarasota. Very convenient to all of mid-Florida's plethora of vacation activities.

Waterside Place (formerly Mangrove Bay)

9240 Midnight Pass Road
Siesta Key, FL 34242
800-661-6551 • 941-923-6354
www.4sarasota.com/mangrovebay
siestarent@home.com

Type of Lodging: Apartments

Suite Rates: $485– $995 per week.

Pet Charges & Deposits: $200 refundable deposit.

Pet Policy: No pets over 40 lbs. Manager's prior approval required.

Amenities: Cable TV, fully equipped kitchenettes, pool, BBQ grills, guest laundry.

Pet Amenities: List of nearby veterinarians maintained. Turtle Beach is located ½ mile north.

Rated: 2 Paws — 8 suites.

Waterside Place contains a series of vacation apartment units on nicely landscaped grounds. There's a beach just steps away. A few more steps and you come to shops and restaurants. In addition, you're so close to Sarasota. While in the "big city," see the Florida State University Center for the Performing Arts, a reconstruction of a 1903 Scottish opera house, or the Gulf Coast Wonder and Imagination Zone at Airport Mall, filled with physical science and nature exhibits. Myakka Wildlife Tours offers narrated tram tours through the wildlife habitats in Myakka River State Park.

Best Western Ocean Inn

101 Sandpiper Boulevard
St. Augustine Beach, FL 32080
800-528-1234 • 904-471-8010
www.bestwestern.com
gholiday@aug.com

Type of Lodging: Motel

Room Rates: $50–$190, including continental breakfast. AAA, AARP and *10% Pets Welcome™* discounts.

Pet Charges & Deposits: $10 per day

Pet Policy: Sorry, no cats. No pets over 30 lbs. Designated rooms only.

Amenities: Cable TV, refrigerators, microwaves, pool, whirlpools, free local calls.

Pet Amenities: List of nearby veterinarians maintained. Dog runs. Exercise area. Dog beach is located only 800 yards from motel.

Rated: 2 Paws — 30 rooms and 5 suites.

Best Western Ocean Inn is a very well run, pet-friendly motel that is located near all major attractions. Two excellent restaurants are within walking distance. St. Augustine, a premier tourist destination, not only in Florida but also in the United States, is the oldest continuously occupied European settlement in the United States. Juan Ponce de Leon, searching for the legendary Fountain of Youth, landed in this area in spring, 1513. The Privateer (translation Pirate) was sent to colonize what became St. Augustine in 1565. You absolutely cannot miss the Castillo de San Marcos National Monument, a Spanish fortress, and the oldest masonry fort in the United States, built between 1672 and 1695.

Holiday Inn – St. Augustine Beach

860 A1A – Beach Boulevard
St. Augustine Beach, FL 32080
800-626-SAND • 904-471-2555
www.holidayinnstaugustine.com

Type of Lodging: Hotel

Room Rates: $79–$130. AAA and AARP discounts.

Pet Charges & Deposits: $10 per day.

Pet Policy: Designated rooms only.

Amenities: Cable TV, pool, hairdryers, irons and ironing boards.

Pet Amenities: List of nearby veterinarians maintained. Exercise area. Anastasia State Park is located on A1A Highway.

Rated: 3 Paws — 151 rooms.

You feel the sense of days long since past everywhere you go in St. Augustine. It makes for magical days that you sometimes wish would go on forever. There's so much to do in romantic St. Augustine: sunny days and soft white beaches, the charm and character of every quaint shop, museum and outdoor café. Holiday Inn is located five miles from the historic district. The only thing between the Holiday Inn and the beach is the hotel pool! You can sip exotic tropical concoctions at Crabbie's Poolside Bar & Grill (seasonal) or enjoy Scores Sports Bar.

Bay Street Villas & Resort Marina

7201 Bay Street
St. Pete Beach, FL 33706
800-566-8358 • 727-360-5591
www.baystreetvillas.com
baystr@aol.com

Type of Lodging: Resort
Villa Rates: $75–$135.
Pet Charges & Deposits: $5 per day.
Pet Policy: No pets over 25 lbs. Designated rooms only.
Amenities: Cable TV, full kitchens, pool, gas BBQ grills, fishing and boat dock, water bikes, paddleboats and canoes, gym room, guest laundry.
Pet Amenities: Pet treats, dishes and some beds available. List of nearby veterinarians maintained. Fort DeSoto Park nearby.
Rated: 3 Paws — 20 villas.

Bay Street Villas and Resort Marina asks, "Why stay in a motel when you can have the comforts of home?" The spacious one- and two-bedroom villas contain lovely modern furnishings, fully equipped kitchens, and, most important for our purposes, allocated rooms for pet-friendly stays. You will find yourself among friends in this tropical island retreat, so close to Tampa-St. Petersburg, but a world away. Start to unwind the island way, feel the sun caressing you as you lie sunning beside the waterfront pool or sit beneath the swaying palms, lounging with a tall, cool drink and listening to the parrots sing as they fly overhead.

Steinhatchee Landing & Resort

228 Northeast Highway 51
Steinhatchee, FL 32359
800-584-1709 • 352-498-3513
www.steinhatcheelanding.com
slr@inetw.net

Type of Lodging: Resort
Cottage Rates: $120–$385, including continental breakfast. AAA discount.
Pet Charges & Deposits: $100 refundable deposit.
Pet Policy: Sorry, no cats. No pets over 30 lbs. Designated rooms only.
Amenities: Cable TV, refrigerators, microwaves, pool, Jacuzzi, hot tubs, children's playground, petting zoo.
Pet Amenities: List of nearby veterinarians maintained. Dog runs. Exercise area. Manatee Springs State Park is located in nearby Chiefland. There are 35 acres of landscaped grounds with lots of brilliant squirrels. Many dog owners take their pets canoeing and swimming in the river.
Rated: 3 Paws — 25 cottages.

Florida's natural beauty extends far beyond the sandy white beaches, for which it has become famous. Steinhatchee Landing has become a natural retreat for outdoor enthusiasts and sportsmen alike: bird watching, fishing, scalloping, canoeing, horseback riding, swimming, tennis, volleyball, shuffleboard, bicycling, badminton, basketball—even a children's playground—are among the activities you can enjoy right on the property. Steinhatchee Landing includes 20 beautifully furnished Victorian and Florida cracker-style cottages, located along 35 acres on the banks of the Steinhatchee River. These quaint cottages accommodate from four to ten people each, and all are fully furnished.

Best Western All Suites Hotel Behind Busch Gardens

3001 University Center Drive
Tampa, FL 33612
800-786-7446 • 813-971-8930
www.thatparrotplace.com

Type of Lodging: Hotel

Suite Rates: $89–$129, including full breakfast. AAA, AARP, AKC, ABA and *Pets Welcome*™ discounts.

Pet Charges & Deposits: $10 per day.

Pet Policy: No pets over 75 lbs. No pets allowed at the pool, hot tub or in the restaurants.

Amenities: Cable TV, refrigerators, microwaves, pool, hot tubs, restaurant.

Pet Amenities: List of nearby veterinarians maintained. Hills River State Park is located 9 miles north of Fowler on Highway 301. Lettuce Lake Park is located at 6920 East Fletcher Avenue in Tampa.

Rated: 3 Paws — 150 suites. Tampa's Small Business of the Year.

Best Western All Suites Hotel Behind Busch Gardens is in the center of everything. Busch Gardens is right behind the hotel—"So close, the parrots escape to our trees." All suites come with a hairdryer and iron and ironing board. Tampa is a vigorous, young city on the go. There's much more than the Devil Rays Baseball Team and the Buccaneers. Check out the Museum of Science and Industry, which contains more than 254,000 square feet of exhibits, including hand-on displays, demonstrations and even a simulated Gulf Coast Hurricane.

Holiday Inn Tampa near Busch Gardens

2701 East Fowler Avenue
Tampa, FL 33612
800-206-2747 • 813-971-4710
www.holiday-inn.com

Type of Lodging: Hotel

Room Rates: $76–$100, including continental breakfast. AAA, AARP and *10% Pets Welcome*™ discounts.

Pet Charges & Deposits: $25 refundable deposit.

Pet Policy: No pets over 25 lbs.

Amenities: Cable TV, pool, refrigerators, microwaves, restaurant.

Pet Amenities: List of nearby veterinarians maintained. Flatwoods Park is located at Interstate 75 and Bruce B. Downs Boulevard.

Rated: 3 Paws — 408 rooms and 3 suites.

Located just half a mile from Busch Gardens, Holiday Inn-Tampa welcomes travelers to Florida's Gulf Coast with handsome guestrooms and family-friendly Kidsuites™. The Marketplace Café serves a daily breakfast buffet with seating around the pool and waterfall. T.G.I. Friday's restaurant is located in the hotel, while Tampa's largest shopping mall is right across the street. The Inn has over 8,000 square feet of event space, making it a conference center as well as a vacation destination.

La Quinta Inn – Tampa Airport

4730 Spruce Street
Tampa, FL 33607
813-287-0440
www.laquinta.com
lq0597gm@laquinta.com

Type of Lodging: Motel
Room Rates: $59–$125, including continental breakfast. AAA, AARP and **Pets Welcome™** discounts.
Pet Charges & Deposits: None.
Pet Policy: Small pets only.
Amenities: Cable TV, refrigerators, microwaves, safes, pool.
Pet Amenities: List of nearby veterinarians maintained. Dog runs.
Rated: 3 Paws — 122 rooms and 1 suite.

La Quinta Inn, which guarantees 100% satisfaction, is located immediately across the street from Tampa International Airport. New guestrooms feature a fresh décor, rich wood furniture, built-in closets, large desks, bright bathrooms, cable televisions, coffeemakers and alarm clock radios. You're afforded free local calls and dataports, free airport shuttle service, workout privileges at a nearby health club and a meeting space that accommodates groups of up to 25 people. Downtown Tampa, and the Tampa Convention Center are only five miles away; double that to Busch Gardens and MacDill Air Force Base.

Days Inn Kennedy Space Center

3755 Cheney Highway
Titusville, FL 32780
877-767-3297 • 321-269-4480
www.daysinn.com

Type of Lodging: Hotel
Room Rates: $59–$135, including continental breakfast. AAA and AARP discounts.
Pet Charges & Deposits: $10 per day.
Pet Policy: Designated rooms only.
Amenities: Cable TV, pool, refrigerators, microwaves, fitness center, guest laundry.
Pet Amenities: Exercise area.
Rated: 2 Paws — 148 rooms and 1 suite. Days Inn Five Sunbursts Award Winner.

Days Inn Kennedy Space Center has a perfect location: 20 minutes to Port Canaveral beaches and one hour to all the Orlando attractions. There's a whirlpool room, a wading pool and a restaurant on the premises. And it's one of the closest venues to Kennedy Space Center and all the thrills of the space age.

Anchor Inn Motel & Apartments

10133 Gulf Boulevard
Treasure Island, FL 33706
727-360-1871
www.anchorinn.com
info@anchorinn.com

Type of Lodging: Motel

Suite Rates: $45–$125. AAA, AARP, AKC and *5% Pets Welcome*™ discounts.

Pet Charges & Deposits: Call for charges & deposits.

Pet Policy: Sorry, no cats. No pets over 30 lbs. Designated rooms only. Manager's prior approval required. Pets must be on leash or subject to voice command.

Amenities: Cable TV, refrigerators, microwaves.

Pet Amenities: List of nearby veterinarians maintained. Exercise area. City park is located 2 blocks north of motel.

Rated: 2 Paws — 10 suites.

Anchor Inn Motel and Apartments is located right on the Bay. It's 100 feet to Gulf Beach. The units have docks and fishing nearby, with fine views of the city in the distance. Accommodations range from a small efficiency to a fully equipped two-bedroom home that comfortably sleeps up to eight people.

Howard Johnson

4431 West New Haven Avenue
West Melbourne, FL 32909
321-768-8439

Type of Lodging: Inn

Room Rates: $55–$89. AAA and *15% Pets Welcome*™ discounts.

Pet Charges & Deposits: $20 per stay.

Pet Policy: None. All Pets Welcome.

Amenities: Cable TV, refrigerators, microwaves, safes, pool.

Pet Amenities: None.

Rated: 3 Paws — 119 rooms.

Howard Johnson's Inn is a fine cost-conscious choice in the neighborhood of the Kennedy Space Center. West Melbourne's first resident were free African-Americans who established a settlement in the 1860s. The adjacent town of Melbourne was named after the Australian postmaster's hometown. Today, the town is home to the Florida Marlins baseball team during spring training. Highlights include the Brevard Museum of Arts & Science and the Brevard Zoo.

Hibiscus House Bed & Breakfast

501 30th Street
West Palm Beach, FL 33407
800-203-4927 • 561-863-5633
www.hibiscushouse.com
hibiscushouse@mymailstation.com

Type of Lodging: B&B
Room Rates: $65–$270, including full breakfast. AAA discount.
Pet Charges & Deposits: None.
Pet Policy: None. All Pets Welcome.
Amenities: Cable TV, pool.
Pet Amenities: List of nearby veterinarians maintained. Exercise area. McArthur State Park nearby.
Rated: 3 Paws — 5 rooms and 3 suites.

Hibiscus House was built in 1922 by Mayor David Dunkle during the Florida land boom in the heart of Old Northwood, a National Register Historic District. Once badly neglected, the home has been lovingly restored and offers elegant surroundings for your comfort, both indoors and out. Relax by the home's secluded heated pool and sip complimentary cocktails. Lush landscaping and tropical gardens complete the backdrop, offering you a variety of private areas to sit and soak in the Florida sun. Each guestroom is individually furnished to provide an intimate, relaxed atmosphere. All rooms have private baths, terraces, air conditioning, paddle fans, televisions and phones.

GEORGIA

Population: 7,778,240
Area: 58,977 square miles
Climate: Marine tropical air mass dominates in summer; polar air masses in winter; east central area is drier.
Capital: Atlanta
Entered Union: January 2, 1788
Motto: Wisdom, Justice & Moderation.
Song: Georgia On My Mind
Flower: Cherokee Rose

Tree: Live Oak
Bird: Brown Thrasher
Famous Georgians: James Brown, Jimmy Carter, Ray Charles, Joel Chandler Harris, Martin Luther King, Jr., Margaret Mitchell, Flannery O'Connor, Jackie Robinson, Ted Turner, Alice Walker, Joanne Woodward.

History: Creek and Cherokee people were early inhabitants. The earliest European settlement was the Spanish Mission of Santa Catalina in 1566. In 1733, Gen. James Oglethorpe established a colony at Savannah for the poor and religiously prosecuted. The Cherokee were removed to the Oklahoma Territory from 1832-1838, in a trek known as the Trail of Tears. Georgia seceded from the Union in 1861 and was invaded in 1864. It was readmitted in 1870. Atlanta, billed as "the town too busy to hate," has been a leader in southern civil rights, and has had several African-American mayors. The smaller, more southern portions of the state remain troubled.

1906 Pathway Inn

501 South Lee Street
Americus, GA 31709
800-889-1466 • 229-928-2078
www.1906pathwayinn.com
info@1906pathwayinn.com

Type of Lodging: B&B

Room Rates: $85–$125, including full breakfast. AAA discount.

Pet Charges & Deposits: $20 per day. $50 refundable deposit.

Pet Policy: No pets over 25 lbs. Designated rooms only. Manager's prior approval required.

Amenities: Cable TV, whirlpool.

Pet Amenities: List of nearby veterinarians maintained. Park nearby.

Rated: 3 Paws – 5 rooms.

Relax and recapture the scent of magnolias, stroll the historic district and fall in love all over again. There's plenty to see and do—if only you can pull yourself away from your lovely room, which features a king- or queen-sized bed, ceiling fan, individual climate controls, remote control television and so many other amenities. Spend your time rambling through the Civil War town of Andersonville or visit Plains, home of former President Jimmy Carter. Try hiking across Providence Canyon, locally known as "Little Grand Canyon." Step back in time at Westville, a functioning living history village from the 1850s. Even one day in this gracious small town will revive your spirits and leave you with fond memories.

University Inn at Emory

1767 North Decatur Road
Atlanta, GA 30307
800-654-8591 • 404-634-7327
www.univinn.com
info@univinn.com

Type of Lodging: Motel

Room Rates: $73–$124, including continental breakfast. AAA and AARP discounts.

Pet Charges & Deposits: $15 per stay.

Pet Policy: None. All Pets Welcome.

Amenities: Cable TV, refrigerators, microwaves, pool.

Pet Amenities: Dog treats at check-in. List of nearby veterinarians maintained. Parks are located within a 5 minute walking distance.

Rated: 4 Paws – 47 rooms and 2 suites.

The University Inn offers guestrooms in two facilities—the Inn and the Guesthouse. The Inn is more like a "bed and breakfast," with spacious, beautifully decorated deluxe rooms featuring a microwave and refrigerator. Guesthouse rooms are designed for those seeking economical accommodations with a residential atmosphere. The University Inn is located in the center of the quiet Druid Hills neighborhood, adjacent to Emory University campus. The vibrant world of Atlanta is ten minutes away. You're close to the CNN Center, the Martin Luther King National Historic Site, Centennial Olympic Park and Stadium, the Georgia Dome and so much more. It's a smart choice for you and your pet if you're in, or close to, the capital of the New South.

7 Creeks Housekeeping Cabins

5109 Horseshoe Cove Road
Blairsville, GA 30512
706-745-4753
www.7creeks.com
cabins@7creeks.com

Type of Lodging: Cabins
Cabin Rates: $70–$100.
Pet Charges & Deposits: None.
Pet Policy: Designated rooms only. Manager's approval required.
Amenities: Fully equipped kitchens, fireplaces, guest laundry, BBQ grills, picnic tables, covered porches.
Pet Amenities: List of nearby veterinarians maintained. Exercise area. Vogel State Park is located at U.S. Highway 129 and Georgia Highway 180.
Rated: 3 Paws — 6 cabins.

Located near Brasstown Bald, Georgia's highest mountain, and one of the South's most beautiful areas, is 7 Creeks Housekeeping Cabins. These cabins provide guests with everything you'll need, except linens and food, and are set in the middle of 70 acres of mountainous terrain, offering a tranquil setting with breathtaking views from your private covered porch. A crystal-clear lake is stocked for fishing. Guests may fish (no license required), spend the day relaxing on the lake or picnicking in the covered pavilion. Rental boats are available. You may also want to take a moment to visit the goats and other farm animals on the property, as well as the resident dog.

Misty Mountain Inn & Cottages

4376 Misty Mountain Lane
Blairsville, GA 30512
888-647-8966 • 706-745-4786
www.jwww.com/misty
mistyinn@whitelion.net

Type of Lodging: B&B & Cottages
Room Rates: $60–$90. AAA and *10% Pets Welcome™* discounts.
Pet Charges & Deposits: $10–$20 per stay.
Pet Policy: Designated rooms only. Manager's prior approval required. Stable nearby for boarding horses.
Amenities: Satellite TV, refrigerators, microwaves, fully equipped kitchens (cottages).
Pet Amenities: Basset Hound in residence. Exercise area. Vogel State Park is located at U.S. Highway 129 and Georgia Highway 180. Many hiking trails nearby.
Rated: 4 Paws — 4 rooms and 6 cottages.

Misty Mountain Inn's brochure proudly reads, "Awarded Four-Paws by Pets Welcome," and this place doesn't disappoint! The delightful innkeeper insures that mountainside cottages provide a romantic décor or family-style atmosphere, with lofted bedrooms, tin-roofed cabins, individual climate controls, wood-burning fireplaces, a full bath and equipped eat-in kitchens. Bed and breakfast rooms feature private bath, fireplaces and balconies. The wrap-around porch, replete with wicker furniture, hanging plants, bird feeders, and perhaps a resident Basset Hound taking a nap, make you feel you've arrived pretty close to Heaven. Misty Mountain Inn is located in Blairsville's Trackrock area, with mountains full of activities at Lake Winfield Scott, Lake Nottely, Lake Chatuge and, of course, Vogel State Park, one of Georgia's oldest and most popular state parks, with 17 miles of wonderful trails.

Blue Ridge Mountain Cabins

P.O. Box 1182
Blue Ridge, Georgia 30513
706-632-8999
www.blueridgemtncabins.com

Type of Lodging: Cabins

Cabin Rates: $95–$170. Call for weekly rates.

Pet Charges & Deposits: $20 per stay. $50 refundable deposit.

Pet Policy: Weight restrictions vary by cabin. Designated cabins only. Manager's prior approval required.

Amenities: Cable TV, fully equipped kitchens, fireplaces, guest laundry.

Pet Amenities: List of nearby veterinarians maintained. Chattahoochee National Forest, Benton Mackaye Trail and Cohutta Wilderness Area nearby. Vogel State Park is located at U.S. Highway 129 & Georgia Highway 180.

Rated: 3 Paws — 45 cabins.

Escape to the beautiful north Georgia mountains and relax on the front porch of one of the Blue Ridge Mountain Cabins. These completely furnished cabins have fully equipped kitchens and supplies you need for a weekend getaway or a relaxing vacation. All you need to bring is your food and your spirit of adventure. The cabins are located either on the mountainside or set in the woods, all with beautiful views, near a lake, stream, creek or river. There are plenty of places to enjoy tubing or white-water rafting on the Toccoa or Ocoee rivers, or go swimming, boating or fishing on Lake Blue Ridge. You and your pet can commune with nature while enjoying a picnic in the Chattahoochee National Forest.

Embassy Suites Hotel - Brunswick of the Golden Isles

500 Mall Boulevard
Brunswick, GA 31525
800-432-3229 • 912-264-6100
www.embassysuites.com/es/brunswick
embassy@darientel.net

Type of Lodging: Hotel

Suite Rates: $99–$149. AAA and AARP discounts.

Pet Charges & Deposits: $10 per day.

Pet Policy: None. All Pets Welcome.

Amenities: Refrigerators, microwaves, pool.

Pet Amenities: List of nearby veterinarians maintained. Exercise area.

Rated: 3 Paws — 130 suites.

Embassy Suites Hotel is conveniently located just two miles from Interstate 95 along Georgia's Colonial Coast. It's attached to Colonial Mall at Glynn Place, coastal Georgia's finest regional mall. Embassy Suites is minutes from St. Simons and Jekyll Island beaches and championship golfing. It's just 15 minutes from historic plantation homes and the Emerald Princess Dinner Cruise & Casino, 20 minutes to Millionaires' Village and an hour to the Okefenokee Swamp. The Hofwyl-Broadfield Plantation is a standout.

Holiday Inn Interstate 95

5252 New Jesup Highway
Brunswick, GA 31523
912-264-4033
www.holiday-inn.com\brunswickga
gmbrw@lodgian.com

Type of Lodging: Hotel

Room Rates: $69–$89. AAA, AARP and *10% Pets Welcome*™ discounts.

Pet Charges & Deposits: $10 per day.

Pet Policy: "No elephants, horses or camels in rooms."

Amenities: Cable TV, safes, pool, dining room, lounge, fitness room.

Pet Amenities: List of nearby veterinarians maintained. Selden Park is located at 4th Street and Highway 341.

Rated: 4 Paws — 126 rooms.

Holiday Inn might only rate Three-Paws, except for its exceptionally friendly, whimsical and pet-loving atmosphere. That, along with mature, attractive landscaping, a small scenic pool, a dedication to service, and a "can do" attitude bumps this Holiday Inn up to Four-Paws. Shrimp and crabmeat processing plants are clustered in Bay Street, between Gloucester and Prince streets. Boats unload shrimp onto the street's docks most weekdays in the late afternoon. Charter fishing trips are available.

Forest Cabins

151 Azalea Drive
Ellijay, GA 30540
706-636-1945
www.forestcabins.com

Type of Lodging: Log cabins

Cabin Rates: $100.

Pet Charges & Deposits: None.

Pet Policy: None. All Pets Welcome.

Amenities: Cable TV, refrigerators, microwaves, Jacuzzi.

Pet Amenities: List of nearby veterinarians maintained. Dog runs. Exercise area. Amicalola Falls State Park nearby.

Rated: 4 Paws — 2 cabins.

Where's Ellijay, Georgia? It's well north of Atlanta, a little west of Dahlonega in the north central part of the state. It's a faraway place with a strange sounding name, and if you long for the simple, rustic charm of a log cabin, you cannot find a better place. One of the cabins is situated on a trout stream. The other is located on a small lake.

Helendorf River Inn

33 Munichstrasse
P.O. Box 305
Helen, GA 30545
800-445-2271 • 706-878-2271
www.helendorf.com

Type of Lodging: Motel

Room Rates: $34–$180, including continental breakfast.

Pet Charges & Deposits: $10 per day.

Pet Policy: Designated rooms only. Pets must not be left unattended.

Amenities: Cable TV, refrigerators, pool, Jacuzzi.

Pet Amenities: List of nearby veterinarians maintained. Exercise area. Unicoi State Park is located 6 miles north on Highway 356.

Rated: 3 Paws – 94 rooms and 6 suites.

Helen was a nearly deserted lumber mill town in 1969. It was remodeled to resemble an Alpine village, complete with crafts and antique shops specializing in foreign items. Half of the Museum of the Hills is devoted to life in Georgia's hilly northern regions. The other half recreates imaginative settings from fairy tales and nursery rhymes. This is one of the hidden treasures of travel within the United States and the Helendorf River Inn makes your mountain vacation a special event you'll long remember. Located in the center of town on the banks of the Chattahoochee River, ideal for canoeing, tubing, fishing and swimming. The Helendorf River Inn is incredibly atmospheric. If you can find vacancy in the Top of the Tower, grab it! Romance personified.

Holiday Inn Beach Resort

200 South Beachview Drive
Jekyll Island, GA 31527
800-753-5955 • 912-635-3311
www.jekyllisland.com
dosjekyll@netscape.net

Type of Lodging: Hotel

Room Rates: $59–$139. AAA and AARP discounts.

Pet Charges & Deposits: $10 per day.

Pet Policy: Designated rooms only.

Amenities: Cable TV, pool, tennis courts, fitness room, restaurant, lounge, boardwalk.

Pet Amenities: Treats available. List of nearby veterinarians maintained. Dog runs. Sea dunes are adjacent to hotel.

Rated: 3 Paws – 199 rooms and 6 suites only 30 yards from sandy beaches.

Located in the Golden Isles, the Holiday Inn Beach Resort features brightly decorated rooms and suites with modern conveniences and all the comforts of home. Business executives appreciate its copiers, secretarial and facsimile services. Leisure travelers and families enjoy an outdoor pool, wading pool, playground, seasonal snack bar, tennis courts and bicycle rentals. There are miles of white sand beaches and history: Jekyll Island, after all, was the place that millionaires Henry Goodyear, Edwin and George Gould, J.P. Morgan, Joseph Pulitzer and William Rockefeller bought for a family getaway! The President of AT&T made the first transcontinental telephone call from Jekyll Island and the first draft of the nation's Federal Reserve Act was drawn up here. Today, it remains one of Georgia's premier resort areas.

Red Roof Inn

520 Roberts Court
Kennesaw, GA 30144
800-RED ROOF • 770-429-0323

Type of Lodging: Inn

Room Rates: $50–$53, including coffee. AAA and AARP discounts.

Pet Charges & Deposits: None.

Pet Policy: No pets over 85 lbs. Pets must not be left unattended.

Amenities: Refrigerators, microwaves, safes.

Pet Amenities: Exercise area.

Rated: 3 Paws — 136 rooms.

Red Roof Inn offers comfortable and cost-conscious lodgings. The Walt Disney movie, "The Great Locomotive Chase," was based on a true Civil War incident that took place in 1862. Major James Andrews and 21 Union soldiers hijacked a Confederate train and headed north to Chattanooga, Tennessee. The conductor and crew chased the stolen train on foot, by handcar and with commandeered engines. They caught Andrews just five miles from his goal and returned him to Atlanta, where he was executed as a spy.

Days Inn

744 Georgia 155 South
McDonough, GA 30253
800-DAYS INN • 770-957-5261
www.daysinn.com

Type of Lodging: Motel

Room Rates: $53–$65, including continental breakfast. AAA, AARP and *10% Pets Welcome™* discounts.

Pet Charges & Deposits: $7 per day.

Pet Policy: No pets over 20 lbs.

Amenities: Refrigerators, microwaves, pool, coffeemakers, hairdryers, irons and ironing boards.

Pet Amenities: List of nearby veterinarians maintained. Exercise area. Cedar Park and McDonough City Park nearby.

Rated: 2 Paws — 60 rooms.

At Days Inn, you can check in early and check out late. The Tanger Outlet is nearby, and so is O.B.'s BBQ—head to the woods and get a taste of authentic, slow-cooked hickory pit barbecue in a rustic log cabin with a large stone fireplace. Fried catfish and ribs are favorites. After all, you're talking the Deep South here.

Amberley Suite Hotel

5885 Oakbrook Parkway
Norcross, GA 30093
800-365-0659 • 770-263-0515

Type of Lodging: Hotel

Suite Rates: $69–$129, including full breakfast and complimentary cocktails. AAA and AARP discounts.

Pet Charges & Deposits: $50 nonrefundable deposit.

Pet Policy: Manager's prior approval required.

Amenities: Cable TV, refrigerators, microwaves, safes, pool, whirlpool, Jacuzzi, fitness room, sauna.

Pet Amenities: List of nearby veterinarians maintained. Dog runs. Exercise area. Stone Mountain State Park is located 25 miles east on Highway 78.

Rated: 3 Paws — 76 suites.

Amberley Suite Hotel is indeed a "sweet" place to stay. It's modern, pet-friendly and close to all the activities and attractions of Atlanta. The Hotel is located in the Fortune 500 office park. Stone Mountain Park and the North Atlanta Trade Center are nearby.

La Quinta Inn

6187 Dawson Boulevard
Norcross, GA 30093
800-531-5900 • 770-448-8686

Type of Lodging: Motel

Room Rates: $55–$65, including continental breakfast. AAA and AARP discounts.

Pet Charges & Deposits: None.

Pet Policy: No pets over 25 lbs.

Amenities: Cable TV, safes, pool.

Pet Amenities: Exercise area. Stone Mountain State Park is located 25 miles east on Highway 78.

Rated: 3 Paws — 130 rooms.

Welcome to the dynamic South and to Atlanta, the most dynamic city in the South. Atlanta, home of Delta Airlines, Coca Cola, CNN and UPS, boasts a fine symphony, Broadway shows, exciting nightlife at Buckhead and Underground Atlanta and year-round professional sports. La Quinta Inn is located just northeast of Atlanta, 25 miles from Stone Mountain Park, Underground Atlanta and the Coca Cola Museum. Totally new rooms feature fresh décor, floor-length draperies, built-in closets, expanded bathrooms, televisions, free local phone calls and kids stay in their parents' room.

Quality Inn Perry

P.O. Drawer 1012
Perry, GA 31069
478-987-1345
www.qualityinn.com/hotel/GA049

Type of Lodging: Motel

Room Rates: $50–$75, including continental breakfast. AAA, AARP and *10% Pets Welcome™* discounts.

Pet Charges & Deposits: $7.50 per day. $10 per day during Dog Shows.

Pet Policy: None. All Pets Welcome.

Amenities: Cable TV, pool, refrigerators, microwaves.

Pet Amenities: List of nearby veterinarians maintained. Exercise area. Rozar Park, Calhoun Park and Veterans State Park nearby.

Rated: 3 Paws — 65 rooms and 3 suites on 13 acres of gardens.

Do not expect "ordinary" when you pull into the parking lot at Perry's Quality Inn. This is one of the finest motels in Georgia, built especially for your comfort and pleasure in mind. Flowers bloom all year. The extensive grounds have Koi Ponds, a Bamboo Tea House with ferns and exotic plants, and the charm of early American furnishings. The old Plantation House, now situated in the beautiful gardens surrounding the motel, was built in 1855 and has been tastefully redecorated and furnished. Bring your camera—the motel and gardens are among the most photographed spots in Georgia.

Goodbread House B&B

209 Osborne Street
St. Mary's, GA 31558
912-882-7490
www.stmaryswelcome.com

Type of Lodging: B&B

Room Rates: $75–$95, including full breakfast.

Pet Charges & Deposits: None.

Pet Policy: None. All Pets Welcome.

Amenities: Cable TV, refrigerators, honor bar.

Pet Amenities: List of nearby veterinarians maintained. Exercise area. Fenced yard. Crooked River State Park nearby.

Rated: 4 Paws — 5 rooms.

The Goodbread House was built in 1870. In 1918, the Brandon sisters bought the house to provide for overflow from the popular Riverview Hotel. Most recently, the house served as Dixon's Boarding House, serving family-style lunches and dinners to locals and visitors. It was renovated in the early 1980s and converted to a bed and breakfast a few years later. The Brandon Sisters' great nephew, Jerry Brandon and his wife Gaila, now own it. Gaila's sister, Michele Becnel, serves as innkeeper-hostess, while Jerry is attending to his other duties—as Mayor of St. Mary's. Wander through St. Mary's historic district and along the waterfront or take an excursion to Cumberland Island and the Okefenokee Swamp or Georgia's Golden Isles. Osprey Cove Golf Course and Laurel Island Links are minutes away. Jacksonville (Florida) International Airport is less than an hour away.

Baymont Inn & Suites

8484 Abercorn Street
Savannah, GA 31406
912-927-7660

Type of Lodging: Hotel
Room Rates: $59–$69, including continental breakfast. AAA and AARP discounts.
Pet Charges & Deposits: None. All Pets Welcome.
Pet Policy: No pets over 45 lbs. Designated rooms only. Two-day minimum stay.
Amenities: Cable TV, dataports, irons and ironing boards, hairdryers, pool.
Pet Amenities: Exercise area. Park nearby.
Rated: 3 Paws — 102 rooms and suites.

Baymont Inn & Suites Savannah gives you a choice of single, double, king or business rooms, or, if you prefer, a Leisure Suite or Ambassador Suite. Amenities include free local phone calls, dataports, irons and ironing boards, hairdryers and free continental breakfast. Savannah, like Charleston, is one of the cities that exemplify the Old South at its charming best. Historic downtown Savannah is only six miles away and Hilton Head, South Carolina a mere 25 miles distant. While in Savannah, be sure to see the Owens-Thomas House & Museum, an elegant 1816-built English-style villa, furnished with genuine period pieces.

Best Western Central

45 Eisenhower Drive
Savannah, GA 31406
912-355-1000

Type of Lodging: Hotel
Room Rates: $49–$79, including continental breakfast. AAA and AARP discounts.
Pet Charges & Deposits: $15–$25 per stay.
Pet Policy: No pets over 25 lbs.
Amenities: Refrigerators, microwaves, pool.
Pet Amenities: Local vet located ⅛ mile from the property. Lake Mayer is located on the corner of Sally Mood Drive and Montgomery Crossroads.
Rated: 2 Paws — 129 rooms.

Best Western Savannah features clean rooms, with remote control television, outdoor swimming pool, dataport phones and free local calls. There's a meeting and banquet facility on the premises. It's near beautiful beaches and convenient to historic Fort Jackson, Fort Pulaski and River Street. Golf, tennis, fishing and the charm of Savannah surround you.

Joan's on Jones B&B

17 West Jones Street
Savannah, GA 31401
800-407-3863 • 912-234-3863
www.bbonline.com/ga/joans
joansonjones@aol.com

Type of Lodging: B&B

Suite Rates: $145–$165, including continental breakfast.

Pet Charges & Deposits: $50 per stay.

Pet Policy: Sorry, no cats. No pets over 100 lbs. Designated rooms only. Manager's prior approval required.

Amenities: Cable TV, refrigerators, microwaves.

Pet Amenities: List of nearby veterinarians maintained. Exercise area. Fenced-in courtyard. Forsyth Park is located 2 blocks away from B&B.

Rated: 3 Paws — 2 suites.

Joan's on Jones—with a name like that how could you not be intrigued? And you will be. This exquisite jewel is located in an 1883 Victorian townhouse that's been right in the center of Savannah's National Historic Landmark District for generations. Both suites feature antique furnishings, ground level access with private entrance, wine and fruit, private baths and luxury firm mattresses.

Super 8 Motel

15 Fort Argyle Road
Savannah, GA 31419
800-800-8000 • 912-927-8550
Website www.innworks.com

Type of Lodging: Motel

Room Rates: $45–$65, including continental breakfast. AAA and AARP discounts.

Pet Charges & Deposits: $10 per stay.

Pet Policy: Sorry, no cats. Manager's prior approval required.

Amenities: Cable TV, safes, pool, one free 8-minute long distance call each night.

Pet Amenities: Exercise area.

Rated: 2 Paws — 61 rooms.

Super 8 affords cost-conscious lodgings of the quality you've come to expect from this fine chain. General James Oglethorpe and his settlers founded Savannah, England's 13th and last colony, in February 1733. Although this lovely old city has seen more than one ruination, both economic and physical, today's Savannah preserves 22 of Ogelthorpe's original 24 squares, bordered by handsome townhouses and landscaped with live oaks, azaleas, fountains and statues. This was not an accident. A lost fight to save the old vegetable and fish market from the modernization by developers in 1955, led to the founding of the Historic Savannah Foundation. This dedicated group of women organized one of the country's first and most successful restoration programs, buying hundreds of properties and selling them to private parties with covenants to restore and repair them.

Inn at Statesboro

106 South Main Street
Statesboro, GA 30459
800-846-9466 • 912-489-8628
www.statesboroinn.com

Type of Lodging: Inn
Room Rates: $85–$135, including full breakfast. AAA discount.
Pet Charges & Deposits: $10 per day.
Pet Policy: No pets over 25 lbs. Designated rooms only. Manager's prior approval required.
Amenities: Cable TV.
Pet Amenities: List of nearby veterinarians maintained. Exercise area. Park nearby.
Rated: 3 Paws — 18 rooms and 2 suites. Listed on the National Register of Historic Places.

The two-story Inn at Statesboro is housed in a 1904 late Victorian-Neoclassical home with a charming wraparound porch. Some rooms come with operable fireplace and a private screened porch. Statesboro was established in 1803. A hundred years later, it was shipping one-eighth of the world's supply of cotton. Today, Georgia Southern University is situated in Statesboro. While in the town, don't miss the Georgia Southern Botanical Gardens and the Georgia Southern Museum.

Best Western Peach Inn

2739 Watson Boulevard
Warner Robins, GA 31093
800-528-1234 • 478-753-3800
www.bestwestern.com

Type of Lodging: Motel
Room Rates: $56–$99, including continental breakfast. *10% Pets Welcome™* discount.
Pet Charges & Deposits: $5 per day. $10 refundable deposit.
Pet Policy: Sorry, no cats. No pets over 15 lbs. Designated rooms only. Manager's prior approval required.
Amenities: Cable TV, refrigerators, microwaves, safes, pool, whirlpools, hairdryers.
Pet Amenities: List of nearby veterinarians maintained. Dog runs. Exercise area. PetSmart next door.
Rated: 2 Paws — 50 rooms and 5 suites.

Best Western Peach Inn is a comfortable, well-located establishment, four miles east of the city center. You can make free local phone calls. A standout in Warner Robins is the Air Force Museum of Aviation, only three miles from the Inn. More than 85 historical aircraft are housed in four buildings, including a Soviet MIG-17 and a 60-feet cutaway replica of a B-17 bomber. Comfortable walking shoes are advised and allow three hours minimum to see it all.

HAWAII

Nicknames: Aloha State
Population: 1,185,497
Area: 6,459 square miles
Climate: Subtropical with wide variations in rainfall.
Capital: Honolulu
Entered Union: August 21, 1959
Motto: The life of the land is perpetuated in righteousness.
Song: Hawaii Pono'i

Flower: Yellow Hibiscus
Tree: Kukui (Candlenut)
Bird: Hawaiian Goose
Famous Islanders: Don Ho, Duke Kahanamoku, King Kamehameha, Queen Liliuokalani, Bette Midler.

 History: Polynesians settled the islands between 300 and 600 A.D. The first European visitor, British Captain James Cook, came in 1778. Between 1790 and 1810, the islands were united under King Kamehameha the Great. Missionaries arrived in 1820, bringing a western constitution and a legislature that set up the public school system. Sugar production began in 1835 and became the dominant industry. In 1893, Queen Liliuokalani was deposed. The U.S. annexed Hawaii in 1898. The Japanese attacked Pearl Harbor, near Honolulu, on December 7, 1941 and brought the U.S. into World War II. Since then, Hawaii has become a world tourist destination. Although it is the farthest away from any other landmass on Earth, its beauty delights millions each year.

Pet quarantine laws

Hawaii has stringent pet control laws. Before you consider bringing your pet, it is best to contact local authorities listed below, who may be very helpful.

For more information, please contact:

Hawaii Tourism Authority
Hawaii Convention Center
1801 Kalakaua Avenue
Honolulu, Hawaii 96815
Telephone: 808-973-2255
Fax: 808-973-2253

or

Hawaii Visitors and Convention Bureau
Royal Hawaiian Shopping Center
2201 Kalakaua Avenue, Suite A401A
Honolulu, HI 96815
Telephone: 808-924-0266
www.hawaii.gov/tourism

Tourist Attractions:

Hawaii Volcanoes National Park
Haleakala National Park
National Memorial Cemetery of the Pacific
Waikiki Beach
Diamond Head, Honolulu
U.S.S. Arizona Memorial
Pearl Harbor
Hanauma Bay
Polynesian Cultural Center
Waimea Canyon
Wailoa and Wailuku State Parks
Old town Lahaina
Hana and The Seven Falls
Maui's Beaches
Akaka Falls State Park
Iao Needle
Kona

IDAHO

Nickname: Gem State
Population: 1,251,700
Area: 83,574 square miles
Climate: Tempered by Pacific westerly winds; drier, colder climate in southeast; altitude an important factor.
Capital: Boise
Entered Union: July 3, 1890
Motto: *Esta perpetua* (It is perpetual).
Song: Here We Have Idaho

Flower: Syringa
Tree: White Pine
Bird: Mountain Bluebird
Famous Idahoans: William Borah, Frank Church, Fred Dubois, Chief Joseph, Ezra Pound, Sacajawea.

 History: Shoshone, Northern Paiute, Bannock and Nez Perce people were early inhabitants. Lewis and Clark explored the area in 1805-1806. Fur traders set up posts between 1809 and 1834. The missionaries arrived in the decades between 1830 and 1850. Mormons made their first permanent settlement at Franklin in 1860. Idaho's gold rush began the same year and brought thousands of settlers. In 1877, Chief Joseph led his Nez Perce people 1,700 miles, pursued through three states and was captured just short of the Canadian border. The Idaho territory was organized in 1863 and became a state in 1890. World famous potatoes and onions are grown here. Hell's Canyon, the deepest gorge in the world, is found in Idaho.

BOISE, IDAHO (Pop. 125,600)

Rodeway Inn of Boise

1115 North Curtis Road
Boise, ID 83706
208-376-2200
www.rodewayinn.com

Type of Lodging: Hotel
Room Rates: $74–$84, including breakfast coupon. AAA, AARP and **20% Pets Welcome™** discounts.
Pet Charges & Deposits: $10 per stay. $25 deposit of which $15 is refundable.
Pet Policy: Pets must not be left unattended.
Amenities: Cable TV, pool, sauna, restaurant, lounge.
Pet Amenities: Exercise area.
Rated: 3 Paws — 86 rooms and 12 suites.

Conveniently located near Boise Towne Square Mall, downtown, and St. Alphonsus Regional Medical Center, Rodeway Inn is a decidedly upscale, full service facility with a friendly, helpful staff, spacious guestrooms, free airport shuttle and a year-round heated pool. Boise, "the City of Trees," is Idaho's capital and largest metropolitan area. Boise's steady economic growth is largely occasioned by its quality of life, low cost of living and liberal tax advantages. The city is protected from unduly harsh weather by the Owyhee Mountains, and thus provides year-round opportunities for leisure and recreation.

Shilo Inn Boise Airport

411 Broadway Avenue
Boise, ID 83705
800-222-2244 • 208-343-7662
www.shiloinns.com

Type of Lodging: Hotel
Room Rates: $55–$105, including continental breakfast. AAA and AARP discounts.
Pet Charges & Deposits: $10 per day.
Pet Policy: Designated rooms only.
Amenities: Cable TV, refrigerators, microwaves, safes, pool, Jacuzzi, spas, hairdryers, irons and ironing boards, coffeemakers, sauna, steam room, fitness room.
Pet Amenities: None.
Rated: 3 Paws — 126 rooms.

Newly remodeled Shilo Inn Boise Airport, a hotel that justifiably advertises "Affordable Excellence," is a fine choice when you're in Idaho's capital. It's a clean, beautiful property. The Boise Greenbelt, a 25-mile long bicycle and pedestrian path, follows the Boise River. May through August is horse racing season at LeBois Park on the Western Idaho Fairgrounds. Once used as a Native American lookout, Table Rock rises 1,100 feet above the surrounding valley, east of Boise.

Shilo Inn Boise Riverside

3031 Main Street
Boise, ID 83702
800-222-2244 • 208-344-3521
www.shiloinns.com

Type of Lodging: Hotel
Room Rates: $55–$95, including continental breakfast. AAA and AARP discounts.
Pet Charges & Deposits: $10 per day.
Pet Policy: Designated rooms only.
Amenities: Cable TV, refrigerators, microwaves, safes, indoor pool, Jacuzzi, spas, hairdryers, irons and ironing boards, sauna, steam room, fitness room.
Pet Amenities: Treats available. Exercise area. Ann Morrison Park and Julia Davis Park are located along the Boise River Greenbelt.
Rated: 3 Paws — 112 rooms.

Shilo Inn Boise Riverside is an attractive hotel located on the banks of the Boise River. Accommodations are clean, spacious, quiet and hospitable. There are a lot of free amenities: local calls, fresh fruit, popcorn, ice and a newspaper. The Basque Museum and Cultural Center celebrates the legacy of the Basques. Exhibits focus on traditional music, dance, sports, food, history and culture. The State Capitol, the most impressive of Boise's public buildings, is built of sandstone from Idaho and marble from Italy, Vermont, Georgia and Alaska.

Super 8 Motel

2773 Elder Street
Boise, ID 83705
800-800-8000 • 208-344-8871
www.super8.com

Type of Lodging: Motel

Room Rates: $44–$81, including continental breakfast. AAA, AARP and *10% Pets Welcome™* discounts.

Pet Charges & Deposits: $25 refundable deposit.

Pet Policy: Manager's prior approval required.

Amenities: Cable TV, safes, pool.

Pet Amenities: Owyhee Park nearby.

Rated: 2 Paws — 108 rooms.

Super 8 Motel is a great budget choice in Boise. The Discovery Center of Idaho is a science museum with more than 200 exhibits, including numerous hands-on displays. The World Center for Birds of Prey is a 7,200 square foot interpretive center with exhibits about birds of prey, ecology and conservation.

Shilo Inn Nampa Boulevard

617 Nampa Boulevard
Nampa, ID 83687
800-222-2244 • 208-466-8993
www.shiloinns.com

Type of Lodging: Hotel

Room Rates: $50–$99, including continental breakfast. AAA and AARP discounts.

Pet Charges & Deposits: $10 per day.

Pet Policy: Designated rooms only.

Amenities: Cable TV, refrigerators, microwaves, safes, pool, Jacuzzi, spas, hairdryers, irons and ironing boards, fitness center.

Pet Amenities: None.

Rated: 2 Paws — 61 rooms.

Shilo Inn Nampa Boulevard—the original Shilo Inn—is a neat, newly remodeled lodging, conveniently located off Interstate 84, Nampa-Marsing Exit 35, near the Nampa Civic Center. There are numerous amenities and it's a fine place to stay when you're in Nampa. Just a stone's throw away from Boise, Nampa is very much its own community. Givens' Hot Springs is 17 miles south, on the banks of the Snake River. Celebration Park, with impressive Native American rock art, is nine miles south. This is a great recreation area.

Shilo Inn Nampa Suites

1401 Shilo Drive
Nampa, ID 83487
800-222-2244 • 208-465-3250
www.shiloinns.com

Type of Lodging: Mini-Suite Hotel

Mini-Suite Rates: $75–$105, including continental breakfast. AAA and AARP discounts.

Pet Charges & Deposits: $10 per day

Pet Policy: Designated rooms only.

Amenities: Cable TV, refrigerators, microwaves, safes, pool, Jacuzzi, hairdryers, irons and ironing boards, spa, fitness area.

Pet Amenities: None.

Rated: 3 Paws — 83 mini-suites

Shilo Inn Nampa Suites is a fine, newly remodeled property that affords conference facilities for up to 200 people. It provides spacious rooms, free 24-hour shuttle to Boise or Nampa Airports by appointment, free local calls and a restaurant adjacent to the hotel. Deer Flat National Wildlife Refuge, four miles southwest of Nampa, consists of Lake Lowell and 107 islands in the Snake River. Lake Lowell, itself a popular recreation area, provides beaches, docks and boat ramps. Silver City, high in the Owyhee Mountains, was a "world class" place during the gold and silver mining days in the area, during the late 19th century. It went from a population of 3,000 in its heyday to 100 by the 1920s. A walk down Silver City's unpaved streets is a living history tour. Today, 75 buildings remain of the once boisterous mining town.

Sleep Inn of Post Falls

100 North Pleasantview Road
Post Falls, ID 83854
800-851-3178 • 208-777-9394
sleepinnid611@aol.com

Type of Lodging: Motel

Room Rates: $50–$100, including continental breakfast. AAA, AARP and *10% Pets Welcome*™ discounts.

Pet Charges & Deposits: $15 per stay.

Pet Policy: No pets over 50 lbs. Pets must not be left unattended.

Amenities: Cable TV, pool, Jacuzzi.

Pet Amenities: List of nearby veterinarians maintained. Exercise area. Centennial Trail is adjacent to the motel.

Rated: 2 Paws — 84 rooms.

Sleep Inn of Post Falls is a pet-friendly lodging choice that is right on the Idaho-Washington border. It's five minutes away from Coeur d'Alene and ten minutes away from Spokane, Washington. Frederick Post founded Post Falls in the late 1800s when he harnessed the falls to generate power for his sawmill. Treaty Rock Historic Park commemorates the spot where Coeur d'Alene Native American Chief Andrew Seltice transferred land to Frederick Post. Beautiful Lake Coeur d'Alene is only eight miles away and factory outlet malls are adjacent to the hotel property.

Comfort Inn

1565 West Main Street
Rexburg, ID 83440
800-228-5150 • 208-359-1311

Type of Lodging: Motel

Room Rates: $50–$100, including continental breakfast. AAA, AARP, Corporate and Government discounts.

Pet Charges & Deposits: None.

Pet Policy: None. All Pets Welcome.

Amenities: Cable TV, refrigerators, microwaves, pool, hot tubs.

Pet Amenities: Yellowstone and Grand Teton National Parks nearby.

Rated: 3 Paws — 48 rooms and 4 suites.

Comfort Inn is a pleasant property, housed in a two-story structure with secure interior corridors. In 1976, the Teton Dam collapsed and sent eight billion gallons of water into the valley below the town. The Teton Flood Museum commemorates the event. Travelers normally don't associate Idaho with Yellowstone and Grand Teton National Parks in Wyoming, but these parks are very, very close to Rexburg, which in extreme eastern Idaho, near the Wyoming and Idaho borders.

Mountain Village Resort

Corner of Highway 75 & 21
P.O. Box 83278
Stanley, ID 83278
800-843-5475 • 208-774-3661
www.mountainvillage.com
info@mountainvillage.com

Type of Lodging: Hotel

Room Rates: $50–$75. AAA and AARP discounts.

Pet Charges & Deposits: $8 per day.

Pet Policy: None. All Pets Welcome.

Amenities: Satellite TV, refrigerators, microwaves, hot tubs, natural hot springs.

Pet Amenities: Sawtooth National Recreation Area surrounds the city.

Rated: 3 Paws — 61 rooms and 3 suites.

Mountain Village Resort is housed in a rustic two-story structure and affords rooms with coffeemakers, telephones, satellite television and use of the hotel's private enclosed natural hot spring. Stanley is in the heart of the Sawtooth Mountains and the views from your room are nothing short of spectacular. Stanley, situated on the Salmon River (the "River of No Return"), is at the center of the Sawtooth National Recreation Area—a four-season wonderland in the geographical center of Idaho.

Teton Mountain View Lodge

510 Egbert Avenue
P.O. Box 8
Tetonia, ID 83452
800-625-2232 • 208-456-2741
www.tetonmountainlodge.com
tetonmvl@pdt.net

Type of Lodging: Motel

Room Rates: $39–$110, including continental breakfast. AAA and AARP discounts.

Pet Charges & Deposits: $10 per day. Call for refundable deposit.

Pet Policy: Designated rooms only. Manager's prior approval required.

Amenities: Refrigerators, microwaves, hot tub, horseshoe pit, picnic tables, fire pit.

Pet Amenities: List of nearby veterinarians maintained. Exercise area includes 5 acres that your pet may enjoy.

Rated: 3 Paws — 24 rooms.

Teton Mountain View Inn is situated on the Idaho-Wyoming border, convenient to Grand Teton National Park, Jackson Hole and Yellowstone. Rooms are cozy, romantic and comfortable, at a price that makes the Tetons look very attractive indeed. In summer, there are day horseback trips to the Grand Tetons. Winter is the season for snowmobile rentals and sleigh rides. Hiking, nature walks, glider rides and fishing—virtually every outdoor activity is at your doorstep when you're at this pristine holiday destination. Moreover, with five acres, you and your pet have plenty of exercise area.

Shilo Inn Twin Falls

1586 Blue Lakes Boulevard North
Twin Falls, ID 83301
800-222-2244 • 208-733-7545
www.shiloinns.com

Type of Lodging: Hotel

Room Rates: $90–$169, including continental breakfast. AAA and AARP discounts.

Pet Charges & Deposits: $10 per day.

Pet Policy: Designated rooms only.

Amenities: Cable TV, refrigerators, microwaves, safes, pool, Jacuzzi, hairdryers, irons and ironing boards, spa, fitness area.

Pet Amenities: None.

Rated: 3 Paws — 128 rooms.

Shilo Inns Twin Falls has extraordinarily spacious rooms. The "Magic Valley" area, of which Twin Falls is the dominant city, is one of the nation's most productive agricultural areas. Twin Falls and Shoshone Falls, both on the Snake River, are notable scenic attractions. Perrine Memorial Bridge spans the spectacular Snake River Gorge. The 1,500-feet long bridge rises 486 feet above the water. The Herrett Center for Arts & Science contains pre-Columbian and other artifacts from Native American civilizations of the Western Hemisphere.

Best Western Wallace Inn

P.O. Box 867
Wallace, ID 83873
800-643-2386 • 208-752-1252
www.bestwestern.com

Type of Lodging: Hotel

Room Rates: $72–$225. AAA, AARP and **5% *Pets Welcome*™** discounts.

Pet Charges & Deposits: $10 per day.

Pet Policy: No pets over 80 lbs. Designated rooms only.

Amenities: Cable TV, pool, Jacuzzi, spa, steam room, fitness room, restaurant.

Pet Amenities: List of nearby veterinarians maintained. Exercise area. Day Park and John Mullan Park nearby.

Rated: 3 Paws — 59 rooms and 4 suites.

Best Western Wallace Inn is a modern, comfortable, upscale hotel, a fine home away from home when you're in Wallace. The Wallace area, a great lead and silver mining region at the junction of four major canyons, has several of the world's deepest silver mines. The Sierra Silver Mine Tour takes you on a trip through a working mine. Afterwards, attend a performance at the Sixth Street melodrama. The Wallace District Mining Museum displays local mining equipment, historic photographs and artifacts of the area's mining past.

ILLINOIS

Nickname: Prairie State

Population: 12,128,370

Area: 57,918 square miles

Climate: Temperate; cold, snowy winters, hot summers.

Capital: Springfield

Entered Union: December 3, 1818

Motto: State Sovereignty–National Union.

Song: Illinois

Flower: Native Violet

Tree: White Oak

Bird: Cardinal

Famous Illinoisians: Jane Addams, Saul Bellow, Ray Bradbury, William Jennings Bryan, Herb Chelner, Hillary Rodham Clinton, Betty Friedan, Benny Goodman, Ulysses S. Grant, Ernest Hemingway, Abraham Lincoln, Oscar Mayer, Ronald Reagan, Carl Sandburg, Adlai Stevenson, Frank Lloyd Wright.

 History: Peoria, Illinois, Kaskaskia and Tamaroa lived in the region at the time of the first European contact. Marquette and Joliette explored the area in 1673, followed by LaSalle in 1680. In 1778, American General George Rogers Clark took Kaskaskia from the British without firing a shot. Growth of the railroads brought expansion of the area. Post Civil War Illinois became a center of the labor movement (1885-86). Chicago experienced immigration of one of the greatest numbers of ethnic Americans. Al Capone held sway in the 1920s. Chicago is one of the most diverse cities in the U.S.

Baymont Inn Alsip

12801 South Cicero
Alsip, IL 60803
800-301-0200 • 708-597-3900
www.baymont.net/alsip.com

Type of Lodging: Hotel

Room Rates: $70–$140, including continental breakfast. AAA, AARP and *10% Pets Welcome*™ discounts.

Pet Charges & Deposits: $20 refundable deposit.

Pet Policy: Designated rooms only.

Amenities: Cable TV, refrigerators, microwaves, Jacuzzi.

Pet Amenities: List of nearby veterinarians maintained. Alsip Park is at Pulaski and 123rd Streets.

Rated: 3 Paws — 95 rooms and 6 suites.

Alsip's location, just southwest of Chicago, adjacent to the Tri-State Tollway, is convenient to America's third largest city. It's less than eight miles south of Midway Airport and a gateway to all the thrills of the Windy City. The Baymont Inn is situated in a three-story structure with interior corridors for convenience and security. Rooms are an excellent value.

Best Western Carriage Inn

1304 South Main Street
Altamont, IL 62411
800-528-1234 • 618-483-6101
www.bestwestern.com

Type of Lodging: Motel

Room Rates: $45–$65, including continental breakfast. AAA, AARP and *10% Pets Welcome*™ discounts.

Pet Charges & Deposits: $5 per day.

Pet Policy: Designated rooms only.

Amenities: Cable TV, pool.

Pet Amenities: None.

Rated: 2 Paws — 36 rooms and 8 suites.

Best Western Carriage Inn satisfies your need for a good, old-fashioned motel at a cost-conscious price: unpretentious, traditional design inside and out, yet clean and comfortable. There's a restaurant and lounge on the premises, RV or truck parking available, and kids stay free in their parents' room. Four golf courses are within eight miles of the motel. Thompson Mill covered bridge is 25 miles away and Coles Memorial Airport is less than an hour's drive from your lodgings.

Exel Inn of Bridgeview

9625 South 76th Avenue
Bridgeview, IL 60455
800-367-3435 • 708-430-1818
www.exelinns.com

Type of Lodging: Hotel

Room Rates: $55–$77, including continental breakfast. AARP discount.

Pet Charges & Deposits: $100–$200 refundable deposit for extended stays.

Pet Policy: No pets over 25 lbs. Designated rooms only. Manager's prior approval required. Limit two pets per room.

Amenities: Hairdryers, irons, coffeemakers, full-length mirrors.

Pet Amenities: None.

Rated: 2 Paws — 113 rooms.

Bridgeview, less than four miles from Midway Airport, is a fine value if you're in the Chicagoland area. The hotel affords interior corridors and free local calls. Among Chicago's outstanding attractions is the Adler Planetarium and Astronomy Museum, just east of Lake Shore Drive in Northerly Island Park on the lakefront. All kinds of exhibits, from ancient timepieces to space age models, lead you to the StarRide Theater, a virtual reality space journey. The Sky Show Theater displays the night sky, laden with stars, planets and views of the galaxy. There's even a show for children.

House of the Blues Hotel, a Loews Hotel

333 North Dearborn Street
Chicago, IL 60610
877-569-3742 • 312-245-0333
www.loewshotels.com
HouseofBlues@loewshotels.com

Type of Lodging: Hotel

Room Rates: $159–$329. AAA discount.

Pet Charges & Deposits: None.

Pet Policy: None. All Pets Welcome.

Amenities: Cable TV, honor bar, CD players, in-room fax, guest laundry, bowling alley, fitness center, House of Blues Music Hall.

Pet Amenities: Pet beds, bowls, mats and snacks available. List of nearby veterinarians maintained. Lake Michigan waterfront nearby. Grant Park is located on the lakefront between Randolph Street and Roosevelt Road.

Rated: 4 Paws — 367 room including 22 suites.

This high-rise hotel is as centrally situated as you can get. It's on the Chicago River between Dearborn and State Streets. Grant Park, in the immediate vicinity, contains Saint-Gaudens' Seated Statute of Lincoln, a yacht basin, a rose garden and formal gardens. It's home to free evening concerts at the bandshell from June through August. Across the street is the fabulous Field Museum, a superstar attraction containing more than nine acres of exhibits, including the most recent phenomenon, "Sue," the full skeleton of a tyrannosaurus rex.

Ritz-Carlton Chicago – A Four Seasons Hotel

160 East Pearson Street
Chicago, IL 60611
800-621-6906 • 312-266-1000

Type of Lodging: Hotel
Room Rates: $360–$570.
Pet Charges & Deposits: None.
Pet Policy: No pets over 30 lbs.
Amenities: Cable TV, spas, guest laundry, hairdryers, safes, business center, restaurants.
Pet Amenities: Welcome amenities with dog toys, pet food, in-room pet dining menu, almost too many pet amenities to mention as part of the "The Ritz Pet Program." Park is located at Mies Vanderroh and Pearson Streets.
Rated: 5 Paws – 435 rooms and suites. 1999 Best Hotel in North America by Conde Nast Traveler magazine.

This Hotel rates Five Diamonds for humans and Five-Paws for Pets Welcome™ readers. It's not simply that it's located at the junction of North Michigan Avenue and East Pearson Streets, in Water Tower Place, smack dab in the middle of one of America's most exciting cities. The Ritz Pet Program is about as welcoming as you can get. The Ritz Pet's "Gour-r-r-met" In-Room Service Menu includes "Our Lovable" Chopped Filet Mignon and "Tail Waggin' Good" Grilled Breast of Chicken for dogs, Chicken Liver Paté (Morris' favorite meal after an exhausting nap), Filet of Salmon "Chopped Charlie" and a Side Order of Anchovies for cats. Then there's the *piece de resistance*—for $65 if your cat is a discriminating diner, she or he can enjoy Beluga Caviar—with or without garnish! On the more "mundane" side, the Ritz-Carlton offers a dog walking service through the concierge department, a "Ritz Pet Corner" in The Shop, featuring gourmet dog biscuits, collars and cat toys, a complimentary gift sent to every room, even pet celebrations on the pet's special days. This is Pets Welcome at its very cushiest.

Exel Inn of Elk Grove Village

1000 West Devon Avenue
Elk Grove Village, IL 60007
800-367-3935 • 847-895-2085
www.exelinns.com

Type of Lodging: Hotel

Room Rates: $62–$69, including continental breakfast. AARP discount.

Pet Charges & Deposits: $100–$200 refundable deposit on extended stays.

Pet Policy: No pets over 25 lbs. Designated rooms only. Manager's prior approval required. Limit two pets per room.

Amenities: Irons, coffeemakers, full-length mirrors.

Pet Amenities: Busse Wood Park is located at Higgins and Arlington Heights Roads.

Rated: 2 Paws – 113 rooms.

Elk Grove Village a few miles west of O'Hare International Airport, combines the best of both possible worlds: it's "out in the country," yet convenient to the greater Chicagoland area. It's an excellent value—three stories, interior corridors and pleasant rooms. Chicago's John G. Shedd Aquarium exhibits more than 8,000 animals. Its Oceanarium, said to be the largest indoor marine pavilion in the world, contains Beluga whales, Pacific whiteside dolphins, sea otters, harbor seals and a colony of penguins. Don't think you can see all there is to see in Chicago's Museum of Science and Industry in one day—we've tried. You can't. It's that fascinating.

Exel Inn of O'Hare

2881 Touhy Avenue
Elk Grove Village, IL 60007
800-3673935 • 847-803-9400
www.exelinns.com

Type of Lodging: Hotel

Room Rates: $67–$86, including continental breakfast. AARP discount.

Pet Charges & Deposits: $100–$200 refundable deposit on extended stays.

Pet Policy: No pets over 25 lbs. Designated rooms only. Manager's prior approval required.

Amenities: Hairdryers, irons, coffeemakers, full-length mirrors

Pet Amenities: None.

Rated: 2 Paws – 123 rooms.

Exel Inn bills itself as "Exellent and Innexpensive," and this closest of the chain's units to Chicago O'Hare International Airport is no exception. Guest laundry, free local phone calls and an ideal location make this hotel worthy for your stay. In Chicago, the Navy Pier is a fabulous place to stroll (although our editors wondered what the heck the U.S. Navy was doing stationed in Chicago since "we own the lake"). The pier originally served as an amusement park when it was opened in 1916. Today, it's filled with retail shops, restaurants, the Chicago Shakespeare Theater, a one-acre indoor botanical garden, the Chicago Children's Museum, sightseeing and dinner tours on Lake Michigan.

Best Western Quiet House & Suites

9923 U.S. Route 20 West
Galena, IL 61036
800-528-1234 • 815-777-2577
www.quiethouse.com

Type of Lodging: Motel

Room Rates: $91–$190, including coffee and hot cocoa. AAA and AARP discounts.

Pet Charges & Deposits: $15 per day

Pet Policy: Designated rooms only. Manager's prior approval required. Pets must not be left unattended.

Amenities: Cable TV, pool, whirlpool, Jacuzzi, hot tubs, refrigerators.

Pet Amenities: List of nearby veterinarians maintained. Dog runs. Grant Park is located on Park Street, Highway 20 West, approximately a mile from the motel.

Rated: 3 Paws — 41 rooms and 1 suite.

Best Western Quiet House carries on a tradition established in the 1800s when Julius Vogt established the original Quiet House in Milwaukee, Wisconsin. More than 100 years later, this Quiet House blends that tradition of hospitality with fine contemporary service and modern amenities. Galena, the former home of President Ulysses S. Grant, was once the largest Mississippi River port north of St. Louis. Belvedere Mansion, Dowling House, the Galena/Jo Daviess County History Museum and the Old Market House State Historic Site are well worth seeing. The Ulysses S. Grant Home State Historic Site is a standout.

Travel Inn

834 U.S. Highway 24 West
Gilman, IL 60938
815-265-7283

Type of Lodging: Motel

Room Rates: $45–$50, including continental breakfast. AAA and AARP discounts

Pet Charges & Deposits: $5 per day

Pet Policy: Small pets only. Designated rooms only. Manager's prior approval required.

Amenities: Cable TV.

Pet Amenities: List of nearby veterinarians maintained. Dog runs.

Rated: 2 Paws — 16 rooms.

Travel Inn is a budget-priced, convenient, small motel, located in a typical, small Midwestern town 75 miles south of Chicago, about the same distance northeast of Bloomington. It's a fine rest stop if you're "on the road" when the sun goes down.

Super 8 Motel

211 Ohren Drive
Litchfield, IL 62056
217-324-7788

Type of Lodging: Motel

Room Rates: $44–$73, including continental breakfast. AAA, AARP, AKC, ABA and *10% Pets Welcome*™ discounts.

Pet Charges & Deposits: $25 refundable deposit.

Pet Policy: Designated rooms only.

Amenities: Cable TV, refrigerators, microwaves, safes.

Pet Amenities: List of nearby veterinarians maintained. Walton Park is located on State Street.

Rated: 2 Paws — 61 rooms and 2 suites.

Super 8 Motel combines the cleanliness we've come to expect of this fine chain with a convenient location. It's close to Interstate 55, 35 miles south of Springfield and 45 minutes south of the St. Louis Metropolitan area. Area attractions include Lake Lou Yaeger, Litchfield Airport, Litchfield Industrial Park, Sportsman Park and a Mini-Golf & Mini Race Track nearby. Super 8 affords you free local calls, cable television, 24-hour desk and wake-up service, fax and copy machine availability and kids stay free when accompanied by an adult.

Exel Inn of Moline

2501 52nd Avenue
Moline, IL 61265
800-367-3935 • 309-797-5580
www.exelinns.com

Type of Lodging: Hotel

Room Rates: $40–$70, including continental breakfast. AARP discount.

Pet Charges & Deposits: $100–$200 refundable deposit on extended stays.

Pet Policy: No pets over 25 lbs. Designated rooms only. Manager's prior approval required.

Amenities: None.

Pet Amenities: None.

Rated: 2 Paws — 102 rooms.

Unpretentious, budget-conscious motel located near the Quad Cities Airport. The Quad Cities area, a commercial and manufacturing complex on the Mississippi, includes Moline and Rock Island on the Illinois side, and Bettendorf and Davenport, Iowa on the west side of the Mighty Mississippi. There are three major floating casinos anchored in the Mississippi—between the states. Moline is famous as the home of the John Deere works and the John Deere Pavilion is a glass-encased showcase for vintage and modern day John Deere products.

Holiday Inn Express

6910 27th Street
Moline, IL 61265
309-762-8300

Type of Lodging: Hotel
Room Rates: $54–$82, including continental breakfast. AAA, AARP, ABA and **10% Pets Welcome™** discounts.
Pet Charges & Deposits: None.
Pet Policy: None. All Pets Welcome.
Amenities: Cable TV.
Pet Amenities: List of nearby veterinarians maintained. Blackhawk State Park, located on Blackhawk Road, Rock Island, is 8 miles away.
Rated: 4 Paws — 110 rooms and 1 suite.

Holiday Inn Express, "America's New Bed & Breakfast Hotel," offers a warm welcome, a comfortable night's sleep and a value conscious experience. Rooms are decorated and furnished in "Holiday Inn-style," and guests have a choice of king or double bed rooms. Amenities include free local calls and kids stay free when sharing a room with an adult. Quad City Municipal Airport is nearby. Three riverboat casinos are within a 15-minute drive and there's a restaurant and lounge adjacent to the hotel.

Exel Inn of Naperville

1585 Naperville-Wheaton Road
Naperville, IL 60563
800-367-3935 • 630-357-0022
www.exelinns.com

Type of Lodging: Hotel
Room Rates: $50–$70, including continental breakfast. AARP discount.
Pet Charges & Deposits: $100–$200 refundable deposit on extended stays.
Pet Policy: No pets over 25 lbs. Designated rooms only. Manager's prior approval required. Limit two pets per room.
Amenities: Hairdryers, irons, coffeemakers, full-length mirrors.
Pet Amenities: None.
Rated: 2 Paws — 123 rooms.

Exel Inn is a fine, budget-conscious choice in the Naperville area. Naperville was founded in 1831 and has numerous restored Victorian homes in the historic downtown area. The Naper Settlement, in old Naperville, is a living historical museum occupying some 13 acres in the style of a 19th century village. It's educational fun for the whole family with costumed interpreters demonstrating work, play and crafts reminiscent of early 1800s life in Northern Illinois. Riverwalk, a brick walkway with fountains and covered bridges, begins at the foot of Chicago Avenue and Main Street and follows the DuPage River for several miles.

Exel Inn of Prospect Heights

540 Milwaukee Avenue
Prospect Heights, IL 60070
800-367-3935 • 847-459-0545
www.exelinns.com

Type of Lodging: Hotel

Room Rates: $40–$73, including continental breakfast. AARP discount.

Pet Charges & Deposits: $100–$200 refundable deposit for extended stays.

Pet Policy: No pets over 25 lbs. Designated rooms only. Manager's prior approval required. Limit two pets per room.

Amenities: Hairdryers, irons, coffeemakers, full-length mirrors.

Pet Amenities: The Nature Center is located on Milwaukee Avenue.

Rated: 2 Paws — 123 rooms.

Exel Inn gives you great value for your dollar. The Prospect Heights member of the chain is housed in a three-story structure with interior corridors for security. Nearby Chicagoland has so many activities it's a full vacation in itself. The Merchandise Mart, on the North Bank of the Chicago River between Wells and Orleans Streets, is one of the world's largest commercial buildings. Over seven miles of corridors link hundreds of wholesale showrooms that display millions of dollars worth of home furnishings, gifts, etc. The shops on the first and second floors are open to the public. The Museum of Contemporary Art, at 220 East Chicago Avenue, features all manner of visual art forms created since 1945 and is well worth a visit.

Fanmarker Inn

200 Linden
Rantoul, IL 61866
217-893-1234

Type of Lodging: Hotel

Room Rates: $40–$48, including continental breakfast. AAA, AARP and *10% Pets Welcome™* discounts.

Pet Charges & Deposits: $25 refundable deposit.

Pet Policy: None. All Pets Welcome.

Amenities: Cable TV, refrigerators, microwaves, pool.

Pet Amenities: Exercise area. Numerous parks surround the hotel.

Rated: 3 Paws — 200 rooms and 1 suite.

Fanmarker Inn has wonderful amenities at a pet-friendly and human-friendly price, particularly if you're planning on spending awhile in Rantoul. The Inn is housed in the former Visiting Officers' Quarters and Officers' Club of Chanute Air Force Base. Nearby attractions include the Octave Chanute Air Force Museum, which includes historic uniforms, interactive displays and 30 aircraft. You can even sit in the cockpit of a B-52, one of America's first "Big Jets," which is still on active duty more than 45 years after the first of these behemoths rolled off the production line.

Exel Inn of Rockford

220 South Lyford Road
Rockford, IL 61108
800-367-3935 • 815-332-4915
www.exelinns.com

Type of Lodging: Hotel

Room Rates: $40–$64, including continental breakfast. AARP discount.

Pet Charges & Deposits: $100–$200 refundable deposit on extended stays.

Pet Policy: No pets over 25 lbs. Designated rooms only. Manager's prior approval required. Limit two pets per room.

Amenities: Hairdryers, irons, coffeemakers, full-length mirrors.

Pet Amenities: None.

Rated: 2 Paws — 100 rooms.

Another fine budget choice in a well-run budget chain, this well-maintained property has unpretentious rooms, with ample truck parking and a whirlpool room. Rockford, a short way from the Wisconsin border, was founded by African American slave Lewis Lemon, his master Germanicus Kent, and Thatcher Blake, who built a sawmill near the ford in 1834. Scots, Swedes, Italians, African-Americans, Germans, Irish and Eastern Europeans settled Rockford and the ethnic heritage of those who came survives today. The late 19th century Village that makes up Midway Village and Museum Center occupies 137 acres and contains 24 historic buildings. On the other hand, the Anderson Japanese Gardens boasts five acres of formal gardens based on the style popular during the Kamakura Period (1183-1333 A.D.).

Days Inn

16733 Intersection of Interstate 80 and
Highway 40, Exit 45
Sheffield, IL 61361
815-454-2361

Type of Lodging: Motel

Room Rates: $60–$90. AAA, AARP and *10% Pets Welcome™* discounts.

Pet Charges & Deposits: $7 per day.

Pet Policy: Designated rooms only.

Amenities: Cable TV, refrigerators, microwaves, Jacuzzi, restaurant.

Pet Amenities: List of nearby veterinarians maintained. Dog runs. Exercise area. Hennipen State Park nearby.

Rated: 2 Paws — 51 rooms and 5 suites.

Well-situated halfway between Chicago to the East and Moline to the West, Days Inn has spacious guestrooms with upscale touches. The two-story structure has interior corridors and a dinner restaurant on the premises. Early check-in and late checkout is a special convenience, as is the winter plug-in service. Nearby La Salle is home to Starved Rock State Park, 2,630 acres of wooded bluff land. The park has 18 canyons, formed by glaciers over 15,000 years ago. Waterfalls form at the head of each canyon in early spring. There are more than 15 miles of marked hiking trails within the park.

Ramada Limited

902 West Killarney Street
Urbana, IL 61801
800-272-6232 • 217-328-4400
www.ramada.com

Type of Lodging: Hotel

Room Rates: $59–$140, including continental breakfast. AAA, AARP, Ramada Club, Corporate and *10% Pets Welcome*™ discounts.

Pet Charges & Deposits: $50 refundable deposit.

Pet Policy: No pets over 30 lbs.

Amenities: Cable TV, refrigerators, microwaves, pool, whirlpool, Jacuzzis, guest laundry, coffeemakers.

Pet Amenities: List of nearby veterinarians maintained. Exercise area. Crystal Lake Park is located on Park Street. Westside Park is located on Church Street.

Rated: 3 Paws — 53 rooms and 20 suites. 1998 Ramada Limited Hotel of the Year and Gold Key Award Winner.

The Urbana Ramada Limited prides itself on wonderful amenities and as friendly a staff as you'll find anywhere. Located just north of the University of Illinois campus, Assembly Hall and Memorial Stadium, Ramada Limited is convenient to Carle and Covenant Hospitals, the Market Place Shopping Center, a variety of restaurants and many area businesses. There's a state of the art fitness room, an indoor heated pool and whirlpool. The Krannert Art Museum and Krannert Center for the Performing Arts are worthwhile attractions in the Urbana-Champaign area. And with the University of Illinois School of Veterinary Medicine is close by, you and your pet will find the veterinary care is among the best in the country.

Jay's Inn

720 Gochenour Street
Vandalia, IL 62471
618-283-1200
www.hiddentravel.com

Type of Lodging: Motel

Room Rates: $34–$52. AAA and AARP discounts.

Pet Charges & Deposits: None.

Pet Policy: None. All Pets Welcome.

Amenities: Cable TV, refrigerators, microwaves, hairdryers, restaurant, lounge.

Pet Amenities: List of nearby veterinarians maintained. Exercise area. Park nearby.

Rated: 3 Paws — 21 rooms.

You can take advantage of early check-ins, in-room coffee, free local phone calls and winter plug-ins at friendly Jay's Inn. A traditional two-story motel structure houses guestrooms at an affordable price. Abraham Lincoln received his license to practice law and gained his first experience as a legislator in Vandalia, which served as Illinois' state capital from 1819 to 1839. In that year, Lincoln spearheaded a movement to move the capital to Springfield. The Old State Capitol was the last of three Vandalia buildings to serve as the state Capitol. The Little Brick House, a simple, 19th century Italianate residence, contains furnishings from the capital period.

Baymont Inn & Suites

855 79th Street
Willowbrook, IL 60521
630-654-0077

Type of Lodging: Hotel

Room Rates: $79–$120, including continental breakfast. AAA and AARP discounts.

Pet Charges & Deposits: None.

Pet Policy: No pets over 30 lbs. Designated rooms only.

Amenities: Cable TV, refrigerators, microwaves, fitness room, hairdryers, irons and ironing boards.

Pet Amenities: Exercise area.

Rated: 3 Paws — 130 rooms and 15 suites.

Baymont Inn & Suites promises that you'll be happy with everything. If your room isn't right, they'll make it right—or you don't pay! With this ironclad guarantee, you're sure to enjoy your stay in this bright and very attractive lodging. It's a hop, skip and jump to Interstate 55, and from there it's 15 miles into downtown Chicago, with its myriad of superlatives and activities for every age group. DellRhea's Chicken Basket, Porterhouse, Balducci's, Denny's and Kerry Piper Restaurants are within one block.

INDIANA

Nickname: Hoosier State

Population: 5,942,901

Area: 36,420 square miles

Climate: Four distinct seasons with a temperate climate.

Capital: Indianapolis

Entered Union: December 11, 1816

Motto: Crossroads of America.

Song: On the Banks of the Wabash

Flower: Peony

Tree: Tulip Poplar

Bird: Cardinal

Famous Hoosiers: Larry Bird, Hoagy Carmichael, James Dean, Eugene V. Debs, Theodore Dreiser, David Letterman, Jane Pauley, Cole Porter, Dan Quayle, Red Skelton, Kurt Vonnegut, Wilbur Wright.

History: When the Europeans arrived, Miami, Potowatomi, Kickapoo and Shawnee peoples were already there. A French fort was built here in 1717 and a French trading post was built in 1731, but France ceded the area to Britain in 1763. At the end of the Revolutionary War, Britain ceded the area to the United States. Native Americans defeated U.S. troops twice in 1790, but were beaten at Fallen Timbers in 1794. General William Henry Harrison defeated Tecumseh's Native American confederation at Tippecanoe in 1811. The Delaware, Potowatomi, and Miami were moved further west between 1820-1850 Indiana is best known for the "Indy 500" auto race at Indianapolis.

Days Inn

1033 North 13th Street
Decatur, IN 46733
800-930-6545 • 219-728-2196

Type of Lodging: Inn

Room Rates: $47–$60, including continental breakfast. AAA, AARP and *10% Pets Welcome™* discounts.

Pet Charges & Deposits: $5 per day

Pet Policy: Sorry, no cats. Small pets only. Manager's prior approval required.

Amenities: Cable TV, refrigerators, microwaves, safes, pool, Jacuzzi, hairdryers.

Pet Amenities: List of nearby veterinarians maintained.

Rated: 2 Paws — 42 rooms. 1999 Days Inn Chairman's Award for Quality.

Days Inn has truck and motor coach parking and there are restaurants and attractions nearby. Winter plug-ins are available. Located in eastern Indiana near the Ohio border, Decatur is convenient to all major highways. You won't leave hungry if you stop at the Back Forty Junction Restaurant, which features large lunch and dinner buffets.

Holiday Inn Express

592 South County Road 200 West
Frankfort, IN 46041
800-HOLIDAY • 765-659-4400

Type of Lodging: Hotel

Room Rates: $58–$105, including continental breakfast. AAA and AARP discounts.

Pet Charges & Deposits: None.

Pet Policy: Designated rooms only.

Amenities: Cable TV, pool, hairdryers, irons and ironing boards.

Pet Amenities: Exercise area.

Rated: 3 Paws — 63 rooms.

Holiday Inn Express, housed in a two-story structure, has interior corridors for security and relaxing guestrooms. Located between Monticello and Morocco, in northwestern Indiana, Frankfort is on the border of the Central and Eastern time zones. It's scarcely an hour north to Indiana Dunes National Lakeshore, 15,000 acres on the southernmost shore of Lake Michigan. The area has an unusual ecosystem of dunes, plants and animals. Its surface is constantly changed because of sand dropped by continuous winds. The largest dune, 123-feet high Mount Baldy, moves four to five feet south from the lake each year.

Patoka Lake Village Log Cabin Rentals (The Pines)

Lake Village Drive
7900 West County Road 1025 South
French Lick, IN 47432
800-324-5350 • 812-936-9854
http://patokalakevillage.webjump.com
patokalakelogcabins@iname.com

Type of Lodging: Cabins

Cabin Rates: $60–$89.

Pet Charges & Deposits: None.

Pet Policy: Manager's prior approval required.

Amenities: Fully equipped kitchens, spa.

Pet Amenities: List of nearby veterinarians maintained. Exercise area. Newton Stewart Recreation Area is located at 3084 Dillard Road in Birdseye.

Rated: 3 Paws — 12 cabins.

The Pines at Patoka Lake Village is the perfect spot to get away from it all. Located ten miles south of French Lick, in the heart of the Patoka Lake recreation area, these modern, luxury log cabins near the lake are surrounded by acres of pines and hardwood trees, providing a perfect opportunity to experience the wonders of nature without giving up the comforts of home. All cabins sleep six, have individual climate controls, television and a fully equipped kitchen. Braided rugs and oak furnishings provide a comfortable, cozy décor. A covered deck, cedar picnic table and barbecue grill are provided for each cabin. Located in southern Indiana, the cabins are convenient the Dome at West Baden Springs, the French Lick Railway Museum, Lincoln's Boyhood Home, numerous caves, scenic canoe trips and Holiday World.

Best Western Pines Inn

2317 North State Road 3
Greensburg, IN 47240
800-528-1234 • 812-663-6055
www.bestwestern.com

Type of Lodging: Hotel

Room Rates: $59–$135, continental breakfast. AAA, AARP and *10% Pets Welcome*™ discounts.

Pet Charges & Deposits: $5 per day.

Pet Policy: None. All Pets Welcome.

Amenities: Cable TV, pool, Jacuzzi, spas.

Pet Amenities: List of nearby veterinarians maintained. Exercise area. Greensburg City Park nearby.

Rated: 3 Paws — 72 rooms and 2 suites.

Best Western Pines Inn, home of the famous "Tree in the Courthouse Tower," is located 60 miles from both Indianapolis and Cincinnati. The fine accommodations and friendly staff make you and your pet feel right at home. Meeting rooms at this lodging accommodate up to 150 people. Free local telephone calls are a convenient amenity.

Holiday Inn Chicago Southeast – Hammond

3830 179th Street
Hammond, IN 46323
800-HOLIDAY • 219-844-2140

Type of Lodging: Hotel
Room Rates: $86–$96. AAA, AARP and *10% Pets Welcome*™ discounts.
Pet Charges & Deposits: $25 refundable deposit.
Pet Policy: Designated rooms only. Manager's prior approval required.
Amenities: Cable TV, safes, pool, fitness room, bar, restaurant.
Pet Amenities: List of nearby veterinarians maintained. Exercise area. Hessville Park is located at Kennedy Avenue and 173rd Street. Oxbow Nature Park is located down the street from the hotel.
Rated: 2 Paws – 152 rooms and 2 suites.

Although technically across the border in Indiana, the Holiday Inn is very convenient to Chicago. The Riverboat Casinos are only seven minutes away. It's half an hour to downtown Chicago's Magnificent Mile. Hammond is the oldest city in the Calumet region, dating back to 1851. Originally called Hohmanville after a German immigrant who built a log cabin on the northern bank of the Grand Calumet, the town was renamed in 1868 after George Hammond, who brought the first major industry, a meat packing plant, to the city.

Pickwick Farms Airport

25 Beachway Drive
Indianapolis, IN 46224
800-869-7368 • 317-240-3567
www.pickwickairport.com

Type of Lodging: Apartments
Apartment Rates: $30–$85. AAA and *10% Pets Welcome*™ discounts.
Pet Charges & Deposits: $40 per month; daily rates vary. $150 deposit, of which $100 is refundable.
Pet Policy: None. All Pets Welcome.
Amenities: Cable TV, fully equipped kitchens, pool.
Pet Amenities: Lodging will recommend nearby veterinarians. Park nearby.
Rated: 3 Paws – 124 apartments.

One of two wonderful finds in Indianapolis, both under the same management. Here you'll find very nicely furnished studio, one-, two-, and three-bedroom apartments with dining areas, fully equipped kitchens, free local calls and voicemail. Although you think of the "Indy 500" when you think of Indianapolis, there's so much more to see and do in the exciting, vibrant Midwestern city. The Children's Museum of Indianapolis, the largest such museum in the world, has exhibits pertaining to history, foreign cultures, physical and natural science, arts, paleontology and everything intriguing to the budding polymath. Plan on spending the better part of a full day there.

Pickwick Farms North

9300 North Ditch Road
Indianapolis, IN 46260
800-869-7368 • 317-872-6506
www.pickwicknorth.com

Type of Lodging: Apartments

Apartment Rates: $30–$85. AAA and
10% Pets Welcome™ discounts.

Pet Charges & Deposits: $40 per
month; daily rates vary. $150 deposit,
of which $100 is refundable.

Pet Policy: None. All Pets Welcome.

Amenities: Cable TV, fully equipped
kitchens, pool.

Pet Amenities: Lodging will recommend nearby veterinarians. Park
nearby.

Rated: 3 Paws — 340 apartments.

Pickwick Farms North short-term furnished
apartments is most convenient if you're
traveling with pets or children—or both.
Comfortable and very affordable studios,
one-, two- and three-bedroom apartments
with full kitchens and dining areas await you
when you stay in one of the Midwest's premier cities, home to the Indianapolis Colts
football team. You can't go to Indianapolis
without at least a "courtesy" stop at the
Indianapolis Motor Speedway; or you might
wish to pay homage to James Whitcomb
Riley by visiting his Victorian home, where
the poet lived from 1893-1916.

Red Roof Inn - South

5221 Victory Drive
Indianapolis, IN 46203
800-THE ROOF • 800-RED ROOF
317-788-9555
www.redroof.com
10013@redroof.com

Type of Lodging: Hotel

Room Rates: $40–$100, including
coffee. AAA and AARP discounts.

Pet Charges & Deposits: None.

Pet Policy: Designated rooms only.
Manager's prior approval required.

Amenities: Cable TV.

Pet Amenities: Park nearby.

Rated: 3 Paws — 107 rooms.

Red Roof Inn features newly renovated
rooms, free local calls, free newspaper on
weekdays and kids stay free in their parents'
rooms. Nearby attractions include the Indianapolis Motor Speedway, the RCA Dome,
Indianapolis Convention Center, the Fairgrounds, Indianapolis Zoological Gardens
and numerous shopping centers. Restaurants
are within easy walking distance of the hotel
and there's ample tractor/trailer and bus
parking.

Red Roof Inn

Rural Route 3, Box 27
Montgomery, IN 47558
800-THE ROOF • 812-486-2600

Type of Lodging: Hotel
Room Rates: $35–$75, including continental breakfast. AAA, AARP and *10%
Pets Welcome™* discounts.
Pet Charges & Deposits: $50 refundable deposit.
Pet policy: Pets must not be left unattended.
Amenities: Cable TV, refrigerators, microwaves, safes.
Pet Amenities: List of nearby veterinarians maintained. Exercise area. The hotel has a large field and yard area immediately surrounding it. Glendale Fish & Wildlife Area nearby.
Rated: 3 Paws — 80 rooms and 2 suites.

Red Roof Inn is situated on the shores of a small lake, adjacent to an Amish village. A restaurant, craft shop, bakery and gift shop are all nearby in a rural lakeview setting. This fresh, clean property has many upscale features. The lodging provides winter plug-ins.

Radisson Hotel Roberts

420 South High Street
Muncie, IN 47305
800-333-3333 • 765-741-7777

Type of Lodging: Hotel
Room Rates: $72–$225, including breakfast buffet. AAA, AARP, AKC and ABA discounts.
Pet Charges & Deposits: $25 refundable deposit.
Pet Policy: No pets over 20 lbs.
Amenities: Cable TV, refrigerators, microwaves, pool, Jacuzzi, hot tubs, restaurant, lounge.
Pet Amenities: None.
Rated: 3 Paws — 130 rooms and 29 suites. Listed on the National Register of Historic Places.

Reflecting the architecture and ambiance of the Roaring 20s, the Roberts is listed in the National Register of Historic Places. From its beautiful facade and imposing portico of Indian limestone and brick, to the lobby's sunny glass atrium and ornate architectural details, the Roberts meet the high expectations of today's lodging and dining guests. Many of the guestrooms feature a sitting area, dressing area and bath accented with a sophisticated mix of brass, wood and wall coverings. An indoor pool, whirlpool, free parking and an exclusive concierge level—the Grand Quarters—are just a few of the amenities available to guests.

Holiday Inn

Interstate 65 and State Route 43 North
West Lafayette, IN 47906
765-567-2131
www.holiday-inn.com
hinwla@indy.net

Type of Lodging: Motel

Room Rates: $75–$99. AAA and AARP discounts.

Pet Charges & Deposits: None.

Pet Policy: None. All Pets Welcome.

Amenities: Cable TV, safes, irons and ironing boards, hairdryers.

Pet Amenities: List of nearby veterinarians maintained. Exercise area. Columbian City Park is located at 1915 Scott Street.

Rated: 3 Paws — 149 rooms and 1 suite.

Holiday Inn starts out with spacious, attractive guestrooms accessed by interior corridors. Then it adds a large indoor heated swimming pool, versatile banquet space with seating up to 1,200 people. Its location is superb: five minutes to the Tippecanoe Battlefield, ten minutes to Purdue University, shopping, theaters, golf, tennis and local attractions. Indianapolis is an hour away and Chicago is 2½ hours away. This is the Midwest at its best.

IOWA

Nickname: Hawkeye State
Population: 2,869,413
Area: 56,276 square miles
Climate: Humid, continental
Capital: Des Moines
Entered Union: December 28, 1846
Motto: Our liberties we prize, and our rights we will maintain.
Rock: Geode
Flower: Wild Rose

Tree: Oak
Bird: Eastern Goldfinch
Famous Iowans: Johnny Carson, Marquis Childs, Buffalo Bill Cody, Mamie Doud Eisenhower, George Gallup, Herbert Hoover, Ann Landers, Lillian Russell, William Shirer, John Wayne, Meredith Willson, Grant Wood.

History: Early inhabitants were mound builders. Then came the Iowa and Yankton Sioux. The first Europeans, Marquette and Joliet, gave France its claim to Iowa in 1673. In 1762, France ceded the area to Spain, but Napoleon took it back in 1800, only to sell it to the U.S. in 1803 as part of the Louisiana Purchase. Native American Sauk and Fox tribes moved into the area from states farther east, but relinquished the land after being defeated in the uprising of 1832. Iowa became a territory in 1838 and entered the union as a free state in 1846. Iowa is the penultimate "small town USA," celebrated in Meredith Willson's "The Music Man" and in Grant Wood's "American Gothic."

Fillenwarth Beach

P.O. Box 536
Arnolds Park, IA 51331
712-332-5646
www.fillenwarthbeach.com

Type of Lodging: Resort

Room Rates: $50–$500. Seasonal discounts.

Pet Charges & Deposits: None.

Pet Policy: None. All Pets Welcome.

Amenities: Cable TV, refrigerators, microwaves, pool, whirlpool.

Pet Amenities: List of nearby veterinarians maintained. Exercise area. Several parks nearby.

Rated: 4 Paws — 50 rooms and 43 suites.

Fillenwarth Beach Resort is a wonderful vacation location on the southeast shore of West Lake Okoboji. Okoboji, a spring-fed lake, covers 17 square miles and is 132 feet deep. There are so many things to do here: go water-skiing, take a ski lesson, sail in Fillenwarth Beach's 28-feet racing sailboat or enjoy a special Jungle Cruise. Arnolds Park Amusement Park is the oldest continually operating amusement park west of the Mississippi. The Legend Roller Coaster is one of the oldest operating wooden coasters in the country.

Best Western Pzazz! Motor Inn

3001 Winegard Drive
Burlington, IA 52601
800-373-1223 • 319-753-2223
pzazzbw@aol.com

Type of Lodging: Inn

Room Rates: $69–$115, including full breakfast. AAA, AARP and *10% Pets Welcome™* discounts.

Pet Charges & Deposits: None.

Pet Policy: Guest must sign a pet responsibility form.

Amenities: Cable TV, refrigerators, microwaves, safes, pool, whirlpool, Jacuzzi, game room, restaurant, sports bar, night club.

Pet Amenities: List of nearby veterinarians maintained.

Rated: 3 Paws — 145 rooms and 6 suites.

Best Western Pzazz! Motor Inn is aptly named. In addition to roomy, classy rooms, you'll find three restaurants, three lounges, a dance club, live entertainment—the list goes on and on! The Pzazz! Motor Inn is two blocks from professional class-A baseball, three miles from Steamboat Days riverboat gambling, two miles from Snake Alley (6th Street), which *Ripley's Believe It Or Not* dubbed the "crookedest" street in the world. The 29-block Heritage Hill Judicial District is a showcase for Victorian, Greek, Gothic Revival, Queen Anne and Italian Villa houses.

University Inn

4711 University Avenue
Cedar Falls, IA 50613
800-962-7784 • 319-277-1412
www.skyport.com/uni-inn
uni-inn@kca.net

Type of Lodging: Motel

Room Rates: $39–$130, including continental breakfast. AARP discount.

Pet Charges & Deposits: $30 refundable deposit.

Pet Policy: Designated rooms only.

Amenities: Cable TV, refrigerators, microwaves, safes, whirlpool, Jacuzzi, hot tubs, spas.

Pet Amenities: List of nearby veterinarians maintained. Dog runs. Exercise area. Blackhawk State Park and George Wyth State Park nearby.

Rated: 2 Paws — 53 rooms and 6 suites.

University Inn was completely refurbished in 1996 with new carpet, new furniture and fresh paint. It's beautifully maintained; the owner lives on the premises to assure your comfort. There's a friendly, homey atmosphere with the amenities you'd expect from a pricier chain, but at prices you can afford. Kids stay free, and with eight nights lodging, you get the ninth night free. University Inn is close to the University of Northern Iowa (2 miles), the John Deere Tractor Works, and the Iowa State Trap Shoot, the largest trap shoot in the United States.

Exel Inn of Cedar Rapids

616 33rd Avenue Southwest
Cedar Rapids, IA 52404
800-367-3935 • 319-366-2475
www.exelinns.com

Type of Lodging: Hotel

Room Rates: $36–$58, including continental breakfast. AARP discount.

Pet Charges & Deposits: $100–$200 refundable deposits on extended stays.

Pet Policy: No pets over 25 lbs. Designated rooms only. Manager's prior approval required. Limit two pets per room.

Amenities: Hairdryers, coffeemakers, irons, full-length mirrors.

Rated: 2 Paws — 102 rooms.

Exel Inn is a perfect locale for budget conscious travelers. Cedar Rapids, which started as a log cabin in 1838, developed into Iowa's leading manufacturing center as well as a distribution point for the surrounding agricultural counties. The city has a wondrous ethnic heritage and has produced more than its share of players on the world stage. Artist Grant Wood grew up in Cedar Rapids and moved to Paris in the 1920s to be part of the Paris Scene. Not quite realizing the success he sought, this shy man came back to his roots in Cedar Rapids, and shortly thereafter gained immortality. William Shirer (The Rise & Fall of the Third Reich), the noted foreign correspondent, who both wrote and broadcast from the 1920s into the 1970s, grew up in Cedar Rapids. The National Czech & Slovak Museum is well worth seeing.

Sheraton Four Points Hotel & Convention Center

525 33rd Avenue Southwest
Cedar Rapids, IA 52404
800-325-3535 • 319-366-8671
www.sheratoncr.com
sheraton-zeus@la.net

Type of Lodging: Hotel

Room Rates: $69–$98, including fruit in lobby. AAA and AARP discounts.

Pet Charges & Deposits: $50 refundable deposit.

Pet Policy: No pets over 100 lbs. Designated rooms only.

Amenities: Cable TV, refrigerators, microwaves, pool, Jacuzzi.

Pet Amenities: List of nearby veterinarians maintained. Exercise area. Hotel has a 4½ acres that many guests use to walk their pets. The hotel is two blocks away from Hawkeye Downs Fairgrounds, which has many dog and cat shows.

Rated: 3 Paws — 157 rooms and 4 suites.

Sheraton Four Points Hotel & Convention Center is a premier address in Cedar Rapids. The beautiful six-story hotel offers tastefully appointed guestrooms, including luxurious suites with sunken baths. Relax and enjoy Zazza's Restaurant for breakfast, lunch or dinner. For an evening of entertainment, visit the Gaslight Pub. There's 12,360 square feet of meeting space when it's time to get down to business. The Cedar Rapids Museum of Art displays the work of native son Grant Wood, as well as Marvin Cone, Malvina Hoffman, Betha Jaques, Mauricio Lasansky and James Swann.

Lake Country Inn

518 Highway 18 West
Clear Lake, IA 50428
888-357-2185 • 641-357-2184
www.netmation.com/lci

Type of Lodging: Motel

Room Rates: $30–$60, including continental breakfast. AAA, Seniors and *10% Pets Welcome™* discounts.

Pet Charges & Deposits: None.

Pet Policy: None. All Pets Welcome.

Amenities: Cable TV.

Pet Amenities: List of nearby veterinarians maintained. Exercise area includes a nice grass area. MacGowan Park is located at West 10th Avenue North and Buddy Holly Place. City park is located at Main Avenue and North Shore Drive. McIntosh Woods State Park is located at North Shore Drive and McIntosh Road.

Rated: 4 Paws — 28 rooms.

Lake Country Inn bills itself as offering "Big Name Quality at a Small Name Price." It features tidy rooms, all located on the ground floor. Winter plug-ins are a welcome service. The motel is located five blocks from the Surf Ballroom—the last venue for Buddy Holly, Ritchie Valens and The Big Bopper. It's just blocks from beautiful Clear Lake with its 3,600 acres of boating and fishing, public access boat ramps, state parks and public swimming areas. There are no less than 13 charming antique shops in the area.

Travelodge

2325 Avenue North
Council Bluffs, IA 51501
712-328-3881

Type of Lodging: Motel
Room Rates: $50–$60. AAA, AARP, AKC, ABA, Travelodge Employees, Government and *10% Pets Welcome™* discounts.
Pet Charges & Deposits: $5 per day.
Pet Policy: No pets over 30 lbs. Manager's prior approval required.
Amenities: Cable TV, safes, pool, spa, fitness room.
Pet Amenities: List of nearby veterinarians maintained. Roberts Park is located on 25th Street and Big Lake is located a mile east on Nash Boulevard.
Rated: 2 Paws — 141 rooms.

Travelodge features restful rooms in a four-story structure. Council Bluffs is on the Missouri River and is almost a "twin city" with Omaha, Nebraska. As such, it's close to the Ameristar Casino and Harvey's Hotel Casino, 24-hour riverboat gambling and entertainment venues. Among historic attractions are the General Dodge House, the Potowatomi County Jail, Kanesville Tabernacle, from which Brigham Young left for Utah, and the Railwest Railroad Museum

Days Inn

3202 East Kimberly Road
Davenport, IA 52807
800-329-7466 • 319-355-1190
www.daysinn.com

Type of Lodging: Hotel
Room Rates: $55–$85, including continental breakfast. AAA discount.
Pet Charges & Deposits: $5 per stay.
Pet Policy: No horses, sheep, etc.
Amenities: Cable TV, refrigerators, microwaves, pool, Jacuzzi, hot tubs.
Pet Amenities: List of nearby veterinarians maintained. Exercise area. Middle Road Park is located right off of East Kimberly Road.
Rated: 3 Paws — 65 rooms and 5 suites.

Days Inn is a convenient choice in the Quad Cities area. Winter plug-ins are a fine convenience. The Quad Cities are a unique community consisting of Bettendorf and Davenport, Iowa and Moline and Rock Island, Illinois. Davenport's regional heritage is preserved at East Davenport Village and Walnut Grove Pioneer Village. The Quad Cities area is the largest metropolis between Minneapolis-St. Paul and St. Louis.

Exel Inn of Davenport

6310 North Brady Avenue
Davenport, IA 52806
800-367-3935 • 319-386-6350
www.exelinns.com

Type of Lodging: Hotel

Room Rates: $39–$66, including continental breakfast. AARP discount.

Pet Charges & Deposits: $100–$200 refundable deposit on extended stays.

Pet Policy: No pets over 25 lbs. Designated rooms only. Manager's prior approval required. Limit two pets per room.

Amenities: None.

Pet Amenities: None.

Rated: 2 Paws — 103 rooms.

Exel Inn has unpretentious rooms and is a good value for cost conscious travelers. Davenport is on the Mississippi, so why not take a Celebration River Cruise, which offers non-gaming sightseeing tours on the mightiest river in America? Of course, there are casinos on the Mississippi, if you're so disposed, or you can raise your level of cultural awareness at the Davenport Museum of Art or the Putnam Museum of History and Natural Science.

Ramada Limited

450 Evansdale Drive
Evansdale, IA 50707
800-2 RAMADA • 319-235-1111
www.ramada.com

Type of Lodging: Motel

Room Rates: $55–$200, including continental breakfast. AAA, AARP and *10% Pets Welcome™* discounts.

Pet Charges & Deposits: $25 refundable deposit.

Pet Policy: None. All Pets Welcome.

Amenities: Cable TV, pool, whirlpool, free local calls.

Pet Amenities: List of nearby veterinarians maintained. Deerwood Park is located on River Forest Road, approximately a mile from the motel.

Rated: 2 Paws — 46 rooms and 4 suites.

Ramada Limited is conveniently located halfway between Cedar Falls and Waterloo. It's a fresh, crisp, comfortable place offering all the necessities, conveniences and luxuries for the business or vacation traveler, including a free indoor pool and whirlpool, and free executive continental breakfast. In nearby Waterloo, visit the Bluedorn Science Imaginarium that highlights interactive exhibits on physics, light, sound and momentum. At the Grout Museum of History & Science, the Discovery Zone is a hands-on area that explores biology, physics and anthropology through computer games and scientific experiments.

Days Inn

1605 West 19th Street South
Newton, IA 50208
515-792-2330

Type of Lodging: Hotel

Room Rates: $35– $70, including continental breakfast. AAA and AARP discounts.

Pet Charges & Deposits: $7 per stay.

Pet Policy: None. All Pets Welcome.

Amenities: Cable TV, refrigerators, microwaves.

Pet Amenities: List of nearby veterinarians maintained. Exercise area. Maytag Park is within a mile from the hotel.

Rated: 3 Paws — 59 rooms and 1 suite.

Nestled among the cornfields of Central Iowa, Days Inn is conveniently located on Interstate 80, just 35 miles east of Des Moines. With such a location, Days Inn has access to big city activities as well as small town charm and security. Built in 1979, the Inn was completely remodeled in 1999. Nearby restaurants include Country Kitchen, the Golden Corral and Perkins.

Hotel Pattee

11112 Willis Avenue
P.O. Box 307
Perry, IA 50220
888-424-4268 • 515-465-3511
www.hotelpattee.com
hotlpattee@aol.com

Type of Lodging: Hotel

Room Rates: $95–$230. AAA and AARP discounts.

Pet Charges & Deposits: $200 per stay. $200 refundable deposit.

Pet Policy: Sorry, no cats. Manager's prior approval required.

Amenities: Cable TV, refrigerators, safes, Jacuzzi, bowling alley, fitness center.

Pet Amenities: List of nearby veterinarians maintained. Pattee Park, Wiese Park and Forest Park and Museum nearby.

Rated: 2 Paws — 36 rooms and 4 suites.

Walk into the Hotel Pattee and walk into The Music Man. This is early 20th century Midwest America at its genuine best. Each room is individually hand-decorated to honor a person or craft that made the town of Perry what it is today. The three-story "anything-but-contemporary" Hotel is an icon to an earlier, more peaceful time that still exists in this place where time stood still. If you think this isn't so, challenge your mate or friend to a game in the original 1913 bowling alley! While in Perry, you're convenient to the honest-to-gosh Bridges of Madison County, the John Wayne Birthplace Home and Museum and Iowa State University.

Sleep Inn at Living History Farms

11211 Hickman Road
Urbandale, IA 50322
877-233-0333 • 515-270-2424
www.hoari.com

Type of Lodging: Hotel

Room Rates: $59–$159, including continental breakfast. AAA, AARP and *10% Pets Welcome*™ discounts.

Pet Charges & Deposits: $5 per day.

Pet Policy: None. All Pets Welcome.

Amenities: Cable TV, pool, whirlpool, recreation room.

Pet Amenities: List of nearby veterinarians maintained. Exercise area. Park nearby.

Rated: 3 Paws — 107 rooms and 5 suites.

Sleep Inn couldn't be better situated: it's right next-door to the superstar Living History Farms. Prairie Meadows Racetrack and Casino is 16 miles distant. The hotel has upscale rooms, with a 100% satisfaction guarantee. The 600-acre Living History Farms is an open-air agricultural museum that depicts the story of farming in the Midwest and preserves pioneer farming skills. There's a 1700 Ioway Native American village, an 1850 working pioneer farm, an 1875 frontier town, a horse-powered 1900 farm and a modern crop center. We recommend allowing a minimum of three hours to relive history.

Comfort Inn

1945 Laporte Road
Waterloo, IA 50702
800-228-5150 • 319-234-7411

Type of Lodging: Hotel

Room Rates: $50–$80, including continental breakfast. AAA, AARP and *10% Pets Welcome*™ discounts.

Pet Charges & Deposits: None.

Pet Policy: Sorry, no cats. No pets over 50 lbs. Designated rooms only.

Amenities: Cable TV, refrigerators, microwaves, safes, pool, hot tubs.

Pet Amenities: Exercise area. George Wyth State Park is located at Highways 218 and 58.

Rated: 3 Paws — 53 rooms and 3 suites.

Comfort Inn has a 100% guarantee that you'll be happy here. You get a free newspaper on weekdays, in-room coffee, iron and ironing board and cold weather plug-ins. Local Waterloo attractions include the Cattle Congress, John Deere tours and the Rensselaer Russell House Museum, a restored 1861 Victorian mansion.

Exel Inn of Waterloo

3350 University Avenue
Waterloo, IA 50701
800-367-3935 • 319-235-2165
www.exelinns.com

Type of Lodging: Hotel

Room Rates: $39–$62, including continental breakfast. AARP discount.

Pet Charges & Deposits: $100–$200 refundable deposit on extended stays.

Pet Policy: No pets over 25 lbs. Designated rooms only. Manager's prior approval required. Limit two pets per room

Amenities: None.

Pet Amenities: George Wyth State Park is located at Highways 218 and 58.

Rated: 2 Paws — 104 rooms.

Exel Inn, a harbinger of good value for the money, is a pet-friendly Midwest chain that offers guestrooms in a two-story structure with interior corridors. Waterloo boasts 150 industries, including substantial tractor works. Iowa's second largest fair, the National Cattle Congress, is held for ten days each September. The Convention Center is named in honor of the five Sullivan brothers, Waterloo natives, who perished at sea when their ship was sunk during the WWII battle for Guadalcanal. The Cedar Valley Nature Trail extends 52 miles along the abandoned Illinois Central Gulf Railroad.

AmericInn

628 South Gear Avenue
West Burlington, IA 52655
800-634-3444 • 319-758-9000
www.americinn.com

Type of Lodging: Motel

Room Rates: $66–$106, including continental breakfast. AAA and AARP discounts.

Pet Charges & Deposits: $25 refundable deposit.

Pet Policy: No pets over 100 lbs. Designated rooms only.

Amenities: Cable TV, pool, whirlpool.

Pet Amenities: List of nearby veterinarians maintained. Exercise area. Geode State Park is located 10 miles from the motel on Highway 79.

Rated: 3 Paws — 45 rooms and 10 suites.

AmericInn boasts upscale rooms, including suites and meeting space. Its recreation area features a large indoor pool and whirlpool, plus video games and a pool table. West Burlington's AmericInn is conveniently located off Interstate 34 at the Gear Avenue Exit (Exit 260). It's five minutes away from the Mississippi River Front, Catfish Bend Casino, Burlington Municipal Auditorium, downtown Burlington, Southeastern Community College and Snake Alley, said to be the world's "crookedest" street.

Best Western Quiet House & Suites

1708 North Highland Street
Williamsburg, IA 52361
800-528-1234 • 319-668-9777
www.quiethouse.com

Type of Lodging: Motel

Room Rates: $76–$155, including continental breakfast. AAA and AARP discounts.

Pet Charges & Deposits: $15 per day.

Pet Policy: No pets over 30 lbs. Designated rooms only. Manager's prior approval required.

Amenities: Cable TV, whirlpools, pool.

Pet Amenities: List of nearby veterinarians maintained.

Rated: 3 Paws — 31 rooms and 2 suites.

Best Western Quiet House subscribes to the tradition of elegant comfort established by its founder, Julius Vogt, in the late 1800s. Rooms are spacious, beautifully furnished and amenable to long stays. Less than an hour away are the Amana Colonies—seven historic villages famous for their quality woolens, crafts and home-style cooking. Across the street from the Quiet House, you'll find Tanger Outlet Mall.

Super 8 Motel

1708 North Highland Street
Williamsburg, IA 52361
800-800-8000 • 319-668-9718

Type of Lodging: Motel

Room Rates: $59–$79, including coffee. AAA and AARP discounts.

Pet Charges & Deposits: $15 per day.

Pet Policy: Designated rooms only. Manager's prior approval required.

Amenities: Cable TV.

Pet Amenities: List of nearby veterinarians maintained. Exercise area.

Rated: 3 Paws — 18 rooms and 2 suites.

Super 8 Motel is one of the pet-friendliest chains we've found. This lodging features large, spotless rooms and an alert, accommodating staff. It's located within easy driving distance of the fabled Amana Colonies. Adventureland is an hour away. It's 26 miles to the University of Iowa and Hospital, two miles from the nearest golf course and there's a convenient restaurant nearby.

KANSAS

Nicknames: Sunflower State
Population: 2,654,052
Area: 82,282 square miles
Climate: Temperate but continental, with great extremes between summer and winter.
Capital: Topeka
Entered Union: January 29, 1861
Motto: *Ad astra per aspera* (To the stars through difficulties).
Song: Home on the Range

Flower: Native Sunflower
Tree: Cottonwood
Bird: Western Meadowlark
Famous Kansans: Roscoe "Fatty" Arbuckle, Ed Asner, George Washington Carver, Wilt Chamberlain, Walter Chrysler, Robert Dole, Amelia Earhart, Wyatt Earp, Dwight D. Eisenhower, William Inge, Buster Keaton, Emmett Kelly, Vivian Vance, William Allen White.

History: When Coronado first explored the area, Kansa and Osage peoples lived there. The U.S. took over most of the territory in 1803 as part of the Louisiana Purchase. Kansas became a territory in 1854. Violence between pro-slavery and anti-slavery forces caused the territory to be known as "Bleeding Kansas." It entered the Union as a free state in 1861. Abilene and Dodge City became terminals for cattle drives from Texas after the Civil War. The song "I'm as corny as Kansas in August" is not quite accurate. Kansas' principal crop is wheat.

COLBY, KANSAS (Pop. 5,400)

Best Western Crown Motel

2320 South Range Avenue
Colby, KS 67701
785-462-3943

Type of Lodging: Motel
Room Rates: $50–$80. AAA, AARP and **10% Pets Welcome™** discounts.
Pet Charges & Deposits: None.
Pet Policy: None. All Pets Welcome.
Amenities: Cable TV, refrigerators, microwaves, safes, pool.
Pet Amenities: List of nearby veterinarians maintained. Exercise area includes 3½ acres where you can walk your pet. City park is located 1½ miles from the motel.
Rated: 3 Paws — 29 rooms.

Best Western Crown Motel is so pet-friendly, their motto is, "If your pet will vouch for you, we'll let you stay, too!" All rooms are on the ground floor with coffeemakers in each room. Free local telephone calls, modem lines and kids stay free with their parents are added conveniences. There's on-site bird watching and an outlet center. The Prairie Museum of Art and History is a 24-acre complex that features bisque and china dolls, ceramics, glass, textiles, furniture and Asiatic artifacts. There's a house restored to its 1930s appearance, a furnished sod house, a windmill, a country church and a one-room schoolhouse. Colby is true Middle America—it's a distribution center for the wheat-producing area around it.

Super 8 Motel

2913 North Highway 50
Emporia, KS 66801
800-800-8000 • 316-342-7567
www.innworks.com

Type of Lodging: Motel

Room Rates: $45–$65, including continental breakfast. AAA and AARP discounts.

Pet Charges & Deposits: $10 per stay.

Pet Policy: Sorry, no cats. Manager's prior approval required.

Amenities: Cable TV, safes, one free 8-minute long distance call each night.

Pet Amenities: Exercise area.

Rated: 2 Paws — 46 rooms.

Super 8 Motel is a budget-conscious choice in Emporia, a city known for its fiercely outspoken journalistic tradition. In celebration of the "Sage of Emporia," the William Allen White Library is housed at Emporia State University. The Gazette is still published by the White family. The National Teachers Hall of Fame depicts the heritage of education in America and honors teachers who have been recognized for their commitment and dedication to teaching grades K-12.

Best Western Red Baron Hotel

Highway 50 and 83 Junction, East Side
Garden City, KS 67846
800-333-4164 • 316-275-4164

Type of Lodging: Hotel

Room Rates: $47–$75, including continental breakfast. AAA, AARP, AKC, ABA and *10% Pets Welcome*™ discounts.

Pet Charges & Deposits: None.

Pet Policy: None. All Pets Welcome.

Amenities: Cable TV, refrigerators, pool, restaurant.

Pet Amenities: List of nearby veterinarians maintained. Exercise area.

Rated: 4 Paws — 68 rooms.

Best Western Red Baron is the closest motel to Garden City Airport. Rooms are newly remodeled and feature either queen- or king-sized beds, electronic door locks, cable television and kids stay free with an adult. There's a heated outdoor swimming pool and playground. Two of Western Kansas' best golf courses are within one mile. The 24-hour restaurant is decorated in the Red Baron WW I theme. The Red Baron Hotel is one mile from Garden City Community College, two miles from the Santa Fe Railway and the Lee Richardson Zoo.

Best Western Wheat Lands Hotel & Conference Center

1311 East Fulton Street
Garden City, KS 67846
800-333-2387 • 316-276-2387
www.wheatlands.com

Type of Lodging: Hotel

Room Rates: $51–$87, including full breakfast. AAA, AARP, AKC, ABA and *10% Pets Welcome™* discounts.

Pet Charges & Deposits: None.

Pet Policy: None. All Pets Welcome.

Amenities: Cable TV, refrigerators, pool, restaurant.

Pet Amenities: List of nearby veterinarians maintained. Exercise area.

Rated: 4 Paws — 98 rooms and 9 suites.

Best Western Wheat Lands Hotel affords rooms with king- or queen-sized beds, modem lines, coffeemakers and cable television. The Hotel amenities include the Wheat Lands Restaurant and Lounge, meeting and banquet facilities, complimentary newspaper and a beauty salon. The Hotel is only one mile away from the zoo, Garden City Community College and the Finney Company Exhibit Building.

Garden City Days Inn

1818 Comanche
Garden City, KS 67846
316-275-5095
daysinn@gcnet.com

Type of Lodging: Hotel

Room Rates: $56–$65, including continental breakfast. AAA, AARP and *10% Pets Welcome™* discounts.

Pet Charges & Deposits: None.

Pet Policy: None. All Pets Welcome.

Amenities: Cable TV, refrigerators, microwaves, pool.

Pet Amenities: List of nearby veterinarians maintained.

Rated: 3 Paws — 72 rooms and 4 suites.

Garden City Days Inn has pleasant rooms housed in a two-story structure. Winter plug-ins are a nice convenience. The Lee Richardson Zoo, two miles away, is one of the largest in the state. From huge elephants to tiny birds in the well-planned aviary, you'll find a variety of species here. Recreational facilities in surrounding Finnup Park include a large swimming pool, horseshoe pits, tennis courts, picnic sites, a playground and a historical museum.

Super 8 Motel

3500 Tenth Street
Great Bend, KS 67530
800-800-8000 • 316-793-8486
www.innworks.com

Type of Lodging: Motel

Room Rates: $45–$65, including continental breakfast. AAA and AARP discounts.

Pet Charges & Deposits: $10 per stay.

Pet Policy: Sorry, no cats. Manager's prior approval required.

Amenities: Cable TV, safes, pool, one free 8-minute long distance call each evening.

Pet Amenities: Exercise area.

Rated: 2 Paws — 42 rooms.

Super 8 is certainly a wise budget choice in Great Bend. Rooms are attractive and comfy. Great Bend is located on the Arkansas River in central Kansas. It is, indeed, the bounteous land. Wheat is harvest from the fields, while oil is pumped from below the land. Founded around the shell of Fort Zarah in 1871, the rowdiness of a typical western railway town exploded when the railroad arrived a year later. To establish order, the state passed a law that Texas herds could move no closer than a point 30 miles west of town. Fort Zarah Park occupies nine acres at the site of the old fort.

Super 8 Motel

1315 East 11th Avenue
Hutchinson, KS 67501
800-800-8000 • 316-662-6394
www.innworks.com

Type of Lodging: Motel

Room Rates: $45–$65, including continental breakfast. AAA and AARP discounts.

Pet Charges & Deposits: $10 per stay.

Pet Policy: Sorry, no cats. Manager's prior approval required.

Amenities: Cable TV, safes, one free 8-minute long distance call each night.

Pet Amenities: Exercise area.

Rated: 2 Paws — 46 rooms.

Super 8 is conveniently located near the downtown area of Hutchinson, home of the superstar Kansas Cosmosphere and Space Center. We recommend allowing three hours minimum to see it all: the Hall of Space Museum, IMAX Dome Theater and Justice Planetarium Theater. An affiliate of the Smithsonian Institution, it features one of the largest collections of international space artifacts, including the largest collection of Russian space artifacts outside Moscow. Salt mining and processing has been a major industry in Hutchinson since 1887, when a bed of salt and salt shale between 300 and 350 feet thick and 600 feet below the surrounding wheat fields was discovered.

Super 8 Motel

515 McDonald Drive
Lawrence, KS 66049
800-800-8000 • 785-842-5721
www.innworks.com

Type of Lodging: Motel
Room Rates: $45–$65, including continental breakfast. AAA and AARP discounts.
Pet Charges & Deposits: $10 per stay.
Pet Policy: Sorry, no cats. Manager's prior approval required.
Amenities: Cable TV, safes, one free 8-minute long distance call each night.
Pet Amenities: Exercise area.
Rated: 2 Paws — 49 rooms.

Budget-alert travelers flock to comfortable Super 8 Motel. Lawrence is best known as the home of the University of Kansas, which contains the Kenneth Spencer Research Library, the Museum of Anthropology and the Watkins Community Museum of History. Two particularly noteworthy attractions are the Spencer Museum of Art, which ranks as one of the finest university art museums in the country, and the Natural History Museum and Biodiversity Research Center.

Liberal Inn

603 East Pancake Boulevard
Liberal, KS 67901
800-458-4667 • 316-624-7254

Type of Lodging: Motel
Room Rates: $49–$67. AAA, AARP, Military, Commercial and *15% Pets Welcome*™ discounts.
Pet Charges & Deposits: None.
Pet Policy: None. All Pets Welcome.
Amenities: Cable TV, pool, whirlpool, restaurant, lounge, free local calls.
Pet Amenities: List of nearby veterinarians maintained. Exercise area. Park is located 2 blocks west of the motel.
Rated: 4 Paws — 120 rooms and 3 suites.

Liberal Inn has quite lovely rooms at a very affordable price. It's close to Liberal's two primary attractions. The first, Mid America Air Museum, is Kansas' largest aviation museum with more than 80 military and civilian aircraft. Visitors can see WWII fighters and bombers, as well as "golden age" aircraft used in the Korean and Vietnam wars. Dorothy's House simulates the farmhouse from which Dorothy and Toto were whisked off to the magical land of Oz. Dorothy's Room is a twin of the set used in the 1939 movie.

Best Western Holiday Manor

2211 East Kansas Avenue
McPherson, KS 67460
316-241-5343
bwhm@midusa.net

Type of Lodging: Motel

Room Rates: $52–$64, including continental breakfast. AAA and AARP discounts.

Pet Charges & Deposits: $10 per day

Pet Policy: Small pets only.

Amenities: Cable TV, pools, hot tubs, restaurant, lounge.

Pet Amenities: List of nearby veterinarians maintained. Exercise area. Lakeside Park is located at Kansas Avenue and Lakeside.

Rated: 3 Paws — 110 rooms.

Best Western Holiday Manor, located at the junction of Interstate 35 and U.S. Highway 56, is nicely situated and boasts large rooms. The two-story structure has both interior and exterior corridors. Kids stay free of charge, an indoor pool and an outdoor pool, a whirlpool and sauna are just a few of the extra amenities. The Sirloin Stockade Restaurant and Manor Club Lounge are located on the premises. McPherson Museum, in a restored 1920s house, displays vintage furniture, antique tools, fossils, Native American artifacts, farm equipment, pioneer household items, gems and minerals.

Super 8 Motel

2110 East Kansas Avenue
McPherson, KS 67460
800-800-8000 • 316-241-8881
www.innworks.com

Type of Lodging: Motel

Room Rates: $45–$65, including continental breakfast. AAA and AARP discounts.

Pet Charges & Deposits: $10 per stay.

Pet Policy: Sorry, no cats. Manager's prior approval required.

Amenities: Cable TV, safes, one free 8-minute long distance call each night.

Pet Amenities: Exercise area.

Rated: 2 Paws — 42 rooms.

Super 8 is a clean, budget-oriented place, well located at the intersection of Interstate 35 and U.S. Highway 56. McPherson was named after a Civil War general who was killed in the Battle of Atlanta in 1864. He never visited the city named after him, but a bronze statue of the general has been sitting astride a bronze horse in Memorial Park since 1917. Most early settlers to McPherson were lured by the prospect of free land. They stayed and became farms. The 1890s McPherson County Courthouse with its 105-feet high clock tower is a highlight of this medium-sized prairie town.

Super 8 Motel

1620 East Second Street
Newton, KS 67114
800-800-8000 • 316-283-7611
www.innworks.com

Type of Lodging: Motel
Room Rates: $45–$65, including continental breakfast. AAA and AARP discounts.
Pet Charges & Deposits: $10 per stay.
Pet Policy: Sorry, no cats. Manager's prior approval required.
Amenities: Cable TV, safes, one free 8-minute long distance call each night.
Pet Amenities: Exercise area.
Rated: 2 Paws — 38 rooms.

Super 8 Newton is part of one of the pet-friendliest chains in this area of the United States. After the wildness of Newton's site as a terminus for the Atchison, Topeka and Santa Fe Railroad wore off, Russian Mennonites looked for a new home on the North American prairie. Today, Newton is the largest Mennonite settlement in the United States. Mennonite farmers imported Turkey Red Winter Wheat, which had flourished in the Eastern European and Western Asian steppes. Soon, Kansas became the wheat capital of the world. Newton's best-known attraction is the Kaufman Museum. The five-acre site consists of woods and a prairie reconstruction depicting the arrival of the Russian Mennonites in the 1870s. Buildings include a late 19th century homesteader's log cabin, a Kansas farmstead with an 1875 house and an 1886 barn.

Best Western Mid America Inn

1846 North Ninth Street
Salina, KS 67401
800-528-1234 • 785-827-0356

Type of Lodging: Motel
Room Rates: $47–$90, including continental breakfast. AARP discount.
Pet Charges & Deposits: None.
Pet Policy: None. All Pets Welcome.
Amenities: Cable TV, pools, whirlpool, Jacuzzi, hot tubs, restaurant, lounge.
Pet Amenities: House cat lives here. List of nearby veterinarians maintained. Exercise area. Thomas Park is ½ block from the motel on North 9th Street.
Rated: 3 Paws — 108 rooms and 2 suites.

Best Western is a excellent inn with many up-scale amenities. There's a restaurant, cocktail lounge, meeting rooms and computer jacks in each room. It's conveniently located at Exit 252 off Interstate 70. When in Salina, consider visiting the Central Kansas Flywheel Historical Museum, located in, of all places, a large metal warehouse. There's a vast collection of historical implements here, including barbershop, print shop and general store exhibits, a 500-piece dog figurine collection (talk about Pets Welcome!), an old post office, filling station, schoolhouse and library, not to mention farm machinery and equipment.

La Quinta Inn

7700 East Kellogg
Wichita, KS 67207
800-531-5900 • 316-681-2881
www.laquinta.com
lq0532gm@laquinta.com

Type of Lodging: Inn

Room Rates: $69–$89, including continental breakfast. AAA, AARP and Sam's Travel Club discounts.

Pet Charges & Deposits: None.

Pet Policy: Sorry, no cats. No pets over 30 lbs. Designated rooms only. Pets must not be left unattended. Manager's prior approval required on larger pets.

Amenities: Cable TV, refrigerators, microwaves, pool.

Pet Amenities: List of nearby veterinarians maintained. City park is located at Lincoln and Webb Road, a mile from the inn.

Rated: 3 Paws — 120 rooms and 2 suites.

La Quinta Inn features new guestrooms with fresh décor, rich wood furniture, large desks, bright bathrooms, coffeemakers and alarm clock radios. Free local phone calls and dataport phones are an added benefit. In Wichita, you'll find all the cultural amenities of a large city. The Wichita Center for the Arts houses two galleries, an art school and a professional community theater. Sedgwick County Zoo contains more than 2,000 animals on 247 acres. Wichita State University boasts the Corbin Education Center, designed by Frank Lloyd Wright, while the Old Cow Town Museum highlights Wichita's "humble" beginnings.

KENTUCKY

Nicknames: Bluegrass State

Population: 3,960,825

Area: 40,411 square miles

Climate: Moderate with plentiful rainfall.

Capital: Frankfort

Entered Union: June 1, 1792

Motto: United we stand, divided we fall.

Song: My Old Kentucky Home

Flower: Goldenrod

Tree: Tulip Poplar

Bird: Cardinal

Famous Kentuckians: Muhammad Ali, John James Audubon, Daniel Boone, Louis D. Brandeis, Kit Carson, Henry Clay, Jefferson Davis, D.W. Griffith, Abraham Lincoln, Carry Nation, Colonel Harland Sanders, Diane Sawyer, Adlai Stevenson, Zachary Taylor, Whitney Young, Jr.

History: Kentucky was the first area west of the Alleghenies settled by American pioneers. Before that, it had been home to the Shawnee, Wyandot, Delaware and Cherokee peoples. Daniel Boone blazed a trail through the Cumberland Gap in 1775. In 1792, Virginia dropped its claim to the region and Kentucky became a state. Although officially union, the state witnessed strongly divided loyalties. Arguable the world's most famous horse race, the Kentucky Derby is held each year at Churchill Downs in Louisville. The area is famous for its horse breeding farms and its bourbon distilleries.

Hampton Inn - Bardstown

985 Chambers Boulevard
Bardstown, KY 40004
502-349-0100
www.hamptoninn.com/hi/bardstown
bdstwol@hi-hotel.com

Type of Lodging: Hotel
Room Rates: $59–$75, including continental breakfast. AAA discount.
Pet Charges & Deposits: None.
Pet Policy: No pets over 60 lbs.
Amenities: Cable TV, pool.
Pet Amenities: My Old Kentucky Home State Park is 2 miles distant from the hotel.
Rated: 3 Paws — 106 rooms and 3 suites.

Nestled deep in the heart of Bluegrass country lies Bardstown, a gem of a town, which was founded in 1780. Here you'll find famous whiskey distilleries—after all, this is the Bourbon Capital of the World. My Old Kentucky Home State Park, where it is believed Stephen Foster wrote "My Old Kentucky Home," actually contains a mansion, originally built in 1795, furnished with heirlooms and old portraits. "Stephen Foster The Musical," is a musical drama that captures the spirit of the famed American composer's works, presented in an outdoor amphitheater.

King Creek Resort & Marina

972 King Creek Resort
Benton, KY 42025
800-733-6710 • 270-354-8268
www.kentuckylake.com

Type of Lodging: Cottages
Cottage Rates: $100–$220.
Pet Charges & Deposits: $40 per stay.
Pet Policy: Sorry, no cats. Manager's prior approval required.
Amenities: Cable TV, fully equipped kitchens.
Pet Amenities: List of nearby veterinarians maintained. Exercise area. Many parks nearby, including Land Between the Lakes (between Kentucky Lake and Lake Barkley) and Benton Park, at the south end of Poplar and 16th Streets. There's also a grass yard and a lake swimming area in which to play.
Rated: 2 Paws — 9 cottages.

You're close to a rustic paradise when you rent one of these vacation cottages on beautiful Kentucky Lake—everything you need to set up housekeeping is right here. Activities include horseshoes, beach volleyball, a playground, a sand bottom swim area and beach, pontoons and pedal boats, ski boats, fishing boats, rowboats, and many more. It's time for a relaxed, wonderful vacation.

Moors Resort and Marina

570 Moors Road
Gilbertsville, KY 42044
800-626-5472 • 270-362-8361
www.moorsresort.com
info@moorsresort.com

Type of Lodging: Resort
Room Rates: $47–$75.
Cottage Rates: $60–$257.
Pet Charges & Deposits: $50 refundable deposit.
Pet Policy: Designated cottages only. Pets not allowed in lodge rooms.
Amenities: Fully equipped kitchens, pool, hot tubs, restaurant.
Pet Amenities: None.
Rated: 3 Paws — 24 rooms and 30 cottages and duplexes.

Enjoy log-cabin lodging, nestled on Buckhorn Bay. The large deck overlooking Kentucky Lake provides a front-row seat for one of the most beautiful sunsets you can imagine. The Moors also offers lakeside cottages, duplexes and four-plexes with a wide range of choices. The fleet of Jamestowner Houseboat rentals includes all the comforts of home. Fuel-efficient motors provide economical power to experience more of Kentucky Lake. The houseboats feature air conditioners, VCRs, cellular phones and complete kitchens with four-burner ranges, ovens, microwaves and refrigerators.

La Quinta Inn

1919 Stanton Way
Lexington, KY 40511
800-NU ROOMS • 859-231-7551
www.laquinta.com

Type of Lodging: Hotel
Room Rates: $65–$125, including continental breakfast. AAA and *10% Pets Welcome*™ discounts.
Pet Charges & Deposits: $5 per day.
Pet Policy: None. All Pets Welcome.
Amenities: Cable TV, pool.
Pet Amenities: Exercise area. Kentucky Horse Park is located at Interstate 75, Exit 120.
Rated: 3 Paws — 129 rooms.

La Quinta Inn's new guestrooms feature a fresh décor, floor-length draperies, built-in closets, ceiling molding and rich wood furniture. Large desks, expanded bathrooms, cable televisions, coffeemakers and alarm clock radios complete the picture. La Quinta Inn is close to Ashland and the Henry Clay Memorial, yet you are only seven miles from Red Mile Race Track and eight miles from the University of Kentucky. You'll find the Cracker Barrel and Waffle House Restaurants, as well as Subway and McDonald's within walking distance.

Marriott's Griffin Gate Resort

1800 Newtown Pike
Lexington, KY 40511
800-228-9290 • 859-231-5100

Type of Lodging: Hotel

Room Rates: $79–$149. AARP discount.

Pet Charges & Deposits: $40 per stay.

Pet Policy: Designated rooms only.

Amenities: Cable TV, coffeemakers, hairdryers, irons and ironing boards, pools, Jacuzzi, spas, championship golf course, tennis courts, restaurants.

Pet Amenities: Room service menu available. List of nearby veterinarians maintained. Exercise area. Nearby Masterson Station and Jacobs Park both have dog run areas.

Rated: 4 Paws — 408 rooms and 21 suites.

Marriott's Griffin Gate Resort, Kentucky's only AAA Four-Diamond resort, has hosted several dog groups that have had shows in Lexington. The three restaurants, indoor and outdoor pools, a full service spa with massage, 18-hole championship golf course, two lighted tennis courts, lighted basketball court, sand volleyball court and jogging and cycling trails make this such a complete resort that you may never want to leave the property. Lexington, in the middle of Blue Grass horse country, is convenient to Louisville, Cincinnati, Ohio and Charleston, West Virginia.

Red Roof Inn

1090 Haggard Court
Lexington, KY 40356
800- RED ROOF • 859-293-2626
www.redroof.com

Type of Lodging: Inn

Room Rates: $50–$70. AAA discount.

Pet Charges & Deposits: None.

Pet Policy: None. All Pets Welcome.

Amenities: Cable TV.

Pet Amenities: List of nearby veterinarians maintained. Exercise area. Kentucky Horse Park and Masterson Station Park nearby.

Rated: 4 Paws — 108 rooms.

Red Roof Inn features clean rooms at a budget-conscious price. In addition to a variety of restaurants nearby, you'll find Red Mile Race Track and Keeneland Horse Racing within easy driving distance. Fascinated by horse auctions, or, perhaps, interested in buying a new, useful, large pet? There are numerous horse auctions in the Bluegrass horse country surrounding Lexington.

Aleksander House Bed & Breakfast

1213 South First Street
Louisville, KY 40203
502-637-4985
www.bbonline.com/ky/aleksander
alekhouse@aol.com

Type of Lodging: B&B

Room Rates: $85–$149, including full breakfast. AAA, AARP and AKC discounts.

Pet Charges & Deposits: None.

Pet Policy: Designated rooms only. Manager's prior approval required.

Amenities: Refrigerators, fireplaces.

Pet Amenities: List of nearby veterinarians maintained. Exercise area. Central Park is located between 4th and 5th Streets and Magnolia and Park.

Rated: 3 Paws — 5 rooms and 1 suite. Listed on the National Register of Historic Landmarks.

Originally owned by the president of the Presbyterian Theological Seminary, the Aleksander House is a gracious 1882 Victorian Italianate home. Located in historic "Old Louisville," the three-story brick building, which features 14-feet ceilings, original fireplaces, stained glass, hardwood floors and moldings, has been completely restored. Louisville, Kentucky's largest city, is most famous for its running of the Kentucky Derby at Churchill Downs, but this wonderful, friendly city offers so much more than that, whether you pronounce it "Lou-uh-vull," "Louville," "Loueyville" or "Lewisville." The Actor's Theater, Louisville Orchestra, Louisville Ballet and Louisville Opera Company are of the highest caliber. If that's not enough, there's the annual Blue Grass, Blues, and Jazz Festivals, the St. James Art Show, the Shakespeare Festival in Central Park and Victorian House and Garden Tours.

Days Inn - Mt. Sterling

705 Maysville Road
Mt. Sterling, KY 40353
800-329-7466 • 606-498-4680
www.daysinnmtsterling.com

Type of Lodging: Motel

Room Rates: $30–$53, including continental breakfast. AAA, AARP, ABA, Government, Commercial and *10% Pets Welcome™* discounts.

Pet Charges & Deposits: $5 per day.

Pet Policy: None. All Pets Welcome.

Amenities: Cable TV, pool, restaurant, lounge.

Pet Amenities: Exercise area. Easy Walker Park is 7 miles away from the motel.

Rated: 2 Paws — 94 rooms.

Days Inn Mount Sterling features a restaurant, lounge and ample bus and truck parking. The Ruth Hunt Old Time Confectionary, Civil War Tours, Antique Walking Mall and the Historic Machpelah Cemetery are all within a half-mile radius. Farther afield, it's 20 miles to Cable Run Lake, 30 miles to Kentucky Horse Park in Lexington, 35 miles to Keeneland Race Track and 35 miles to Natural Bridge State Park.

Bryce Inn

Interstate 65, Exit 38
P.O. Box 153
Smiths Grove, KY 42171
270-563-5141
http://bg.ky.net/bryceinn
bryceinn@aol.com

Type of Lodging: Inn
Room Rates: $45–$59, including coffee. AAA, AARP and *10% Pets Welcome*™ discounts.
Pet Charges & Deposits: None.
Pet Policy: No pets over 20 lbs. Manager's prior approval required.
Amenities: Cable TV, refrigerators, pool.
Pet Amenities: List of nearby veterinarians maintained. Dog runs. Exercise area. Mammoth Cave National Park is off Interstate 65, Exit 48, approximately 10 miles from the Inn.
Rated: 3 Paws — 25 rooms.

Caves, Corvettes and Antiques, stay close to it all at Bryce Inn. Bob and Jackie Lightfoot invite you to share their unassuming inn, which has been featured in newspaper articles and television spots for its unique style and hospitality, and for the many Corvette clubs and reunions Bob and Jackie have hosted over the years. Enjoy the relaxed country atmosphere and the quiet comfort of "white glove clean" rooms. The Inn is centrally located between Mammoth Cave National Park, the National Corvette Museum, and the fine antique shops and historic homes of Smiths Grove—each just ten minutes away.

1823 Historic Rose Hill Inn

233 Rose Hill
Versailles, KY 40383
800-307-0460 • 859-873-5957
www.rosehillinn.com
innkeepers@rosehillinn.com

Type of Lodging: B&B
Room Rates: $99–$139, including full breakfast.
Pet Charges & Deposits: None.
Pet Policy: Sorry, no cats. Designated rooms only. Manager's prior approval required.
Amenities: Cable TV, refrigerators, microwaves, Jacuzzis.
Pet Amenities: List of nearby veterinarians maintained. Exercise area. Big Springs Park and Rose Hill Park nearby.
Rated: 3 Paws — 4 rooms and 2 suites.

Sharon and Marianne Amberg, mother and daughter innkeepers, welcome you to an exquisite slice of genuine Americana. Relax, romance, renew and reflect at Rose Hill—the porch swing is ready for you. The 7,800-square-foot mansion was originally built for the Terrell family. It was used as a hospital during the Civil War, and then altered in the 1880s when Miss Lucie transformed it from Federal-style to the present Victorian Gothic. It's one of the most charming places we've found anywhere. Versailles, it's pronounced Ver-sayles, by the way (sorry, Francophiles), is within easy driving distance to the Labrot and Graham Bourbon Distillery, Shaker Village, the Kentucky Horse Park (Lexington), Keeneland Race Track, Buckley Wildlife Sanctuary, the Historic Homes of Jack Jouett, Henry Clay and Mary Todd Lincoln, and various horse farms, which you can visit by appointment.

LOUISIANA

Nickname: Pelican State
Population: 4,372,035
Area: 49,659 square miles
Climate: Subtropical, affected by continental weather patters.
Capital: Baton Rouge
Entered Union: April 30, 1812
Motto: Union, Justice, and Confidence.
Song: Give Me Louisiana
Flower: Magnolia

Tree: Cypress
Bird: Eastern Brown Pelican
Famous Louisianans: Louis Armstrong, Judah P. Benjamin, Antoine "Fats" Domino, Lillian Helman, Grace King, Huey Long, Wynton Marsalis, Anne Rice, Britney Spears.

History: Europeans first visited the area in 1530. LaSalle claimed it for France in 1682. France ceded the region to Spain in 1762, took it back in 1800, and sold it to the U.S. in 1803. Admitted as a state in 1812, Louisiana was the scene of the Battle of New Orleans in 1815, the last major battle of the War of 1812. Louisiana Creoles are descendants of early French/Spanish settlers. The British forcibly transported about 4,000 Acadians ("Cajuns") from Nova Scotia to Louisiana in 1755. Another group, the Islenos, is descended from Canary Islanders. Louisiana is the only state that subscribes to the Code Napoleon rather than English common law.

CROWLEY, LOUISIANA (Pop. 13,600)

Best Western of Crowley

9571 Egan Highway
Crowley, LA 70526
800-940-0003 • 337-783-2378
www.bestwestern.com

Type of Lodging: Hotel
Room Rates: $61–$109, including continental breakfast. AAA, AARP and *10% Pets Welcome*™ discount.
Pet Charges & Deposits: $10 per day. $25 refundable deposit.
Pet Policy: Designated rooms only. Manager's prior approval required.
Amenities: Cable TV, pool.
Pet Amenities: None.
Rated: 2 Paws — 46 rooms and 12 suites.

Located in the heart of Cajun Country, you will find the Best Western of Crowley. Here you and your pet may enjoy Cajun music, dancing, festivals and world-famous Cajun restaurants all within just a few blocks of the property. Crowley is also the home of the International Rice Festival and just two miles from the rice processing plants. Video Poker Casino, Rodeo and Equestrian horse attractions are just one to two blocks away. You and your pet are within a 30-minute drive of the Evangeline area.

Hilton New Orleans Airport

901 Airline Drive
Kenner, LA 70062
800-872-5914 • 504-469-5000
www.hilton.com

Type of Lodging: Hotel

Room Rates: $69–$289. AAA, AARP and **20% Pets Welcome™** discounts.

Pet Charges & Deposits: $25 nonrefundable deposit.

Pet Policy: No pets over 30 lbs.

Amenities: Cable TV, pool, Jacuzzi, tennis courts, jogging track, putting green, fitness center.

Pet Amenities: Kenner Park is located on Williams Boulevard at West Metairie.

Rated: 3 Paws — 317 rooms and 2 suites.

At the Hilton New Orleans Airport it's "Beyond Business As Usual." There is nothing typical about this Hotel except its location. It is an ideal site for conferences and business travel. Its outdoor pool, tennis court and health club provide an ideal spot for the leisure traveler. As the premier full service hotel in the airport area, the Hilton New Orleans Airport features well-appointed guestrooms, fine dining in Cafe La Salle and the ever-popular Second Line Sports Edition. Other hotel amenities include a fitness center, hot tub, lighted tennis court and putting green. For meetings or conventions, there is 18,200 square feet of meeting space, and a full service business center. New Orleans must-sees include the French Quarter, Treasure Chest Casino and the Esplanade Mall.

Essem's House – New Orleans' First Bed & Breakfast

3660 Gentilly Boulevard
New Orleans, LA 70122
504-947-3401
www.neworleansbandb.com
info@neworleansbandb.com

Type of Lodging: B&B

Room Rates: $65–$95, including continental breakfast.

Pet Charges & Deposits: None.

Pet Policy: Sorry, no cats. Small pets only. Designated rooms only. Manager's prior approval required.

Amenities: Refrigerators.

Pet Amenities: Exercise area. Park nearby.

Rated: 2 Paws — 3 rooms and 1 cottage.

Essem's House, a ten-room brick home on a tree-shaded boulevard, has three bedrooms. The large master bedroom is striking in rose, black and ivory, with king-sized bed and private bath. The other two rooms may form a suite, with a large bath between the rooms. Both have double beds. A pretty cottage has a king-sized or two twin beds, living area, kitchen and bath. Essem's House is only 15 minutes from New Orleans' world-famous French Quarter. There's a city bus at the corner and plenty of off-street parking. Owners and pets are accommodated in a private cottage behind the main home and pets can watch activities in backyard.

The Chimes Bed and Breakfast of New Orleans

1146 Constantinople Street
New Orleans, LA 70115
800-729-4640
www.historiclodging.com/chimes

Type of Lodging: B&B

Room Rates: $107–$149, including continental breakfast.

Pet Charges & Deposits: $10 per day.

Pet Policy: Designated rooms only. Manager's prior approval required.

Amenities: Cable TV, refrigerators, microwaves, honor bars.

Pet Amenities: List of nearby veterinarians maintained.

Rated: 3 Paws — 3 rooms and 2 suites.

Uptown in the largest historical neighborhood in the United States is The Chimes Bed and Breakfast of New Orleans. This 1876 inn offers guests individually decorated rooms reflecting the flavor of New Orleans, with private entries, beautiful antique iron beds, claw-foot bathtubs, high ceilings, wooden or slate floors and a friendly atmosphere. Only minutes from the famed French Quarter, the inn's neighborhood of antebellum homes will take you back in time. You can even get a little help with dog-walking duties if you ask. Three blocks from St. Charles Avenue, The Chimes is minutes away from major New Orleans attractions including the Audubon Zoological Gardens, antique shops and the famous restaurants, jazz clubs and art galleries.

Shreveport Super 8 Motel

5204 Monkhouse Drive
Shreveport, LA 71109
318-635-8888

Type of Lodging: Motel

Room Rates: $42–$67, including continental breakfast. AAA, AARP, AKC, ABA and *10% Pets Welcome*™ discounts.

Pet Charges & Deposits: $25 refundable deposit.

Pet Policy: No pets over 12 lbs. Designated rooms only.

Amenities: Cable TV, safes, pool.

Pet Amenities: List of nearby veterinarians maintained. Airport Park Recreation is located at Airport and Kennedy Drive.

Rated: 2 Paws — 143 rooms and 6 suites.

Life's great at Shreveport's Super 8. There's an outdoor heated pool, airy rooms, large meeting rooms, free airport shuttle service, restaurants nearby and kids stay free when accompanied by an adult. Super 8 is adjacent to Shreveport Regional Airport. Harrah's, Isle of Capri and Horseshoe Casinos are nearby, as are the American Rose Garden, Louisiana State Fairgrounds, Hamel's Amusement Park, Watertown USA and Louisiana Downs Racetrack.

La Quinta Inn Slidell

794 East Interstate 10 Service Road
Slidell, LA 70461
800-531-5900 • 504-643-9770
www.laquinta.com
lq910gm@laquinta.com

Type of Lodging: Motel

Room Rates: $59–$100. AAA and AARP discounts.

Pet Charges & Deposits: None.

Pet Policy: No pets over 20 lbs.

Amenities: Cable TV, pool.

Pet Amenities: None.

Rated: 3 Paws — 172 rooms.

La Quinta Slidell, just north of New Orleans, features crisp, fresh rooms. There are new in-room entertainment systems, dataports and free local phone calls. Swamp tours are a scant two miles away and the Cracker Barrel Restaurant is adjacent to the property. Casinos are 20 miles away. Drive the same distance, and you'll come to the Funny Faces Mardi Gras Mask Factory. New Orleans' fabled French Quarter is 25 miles distant.

Butler Greenwood Plantation

8345 U.S. Highway 61
St. Francisville, LA 70775
225-635-6312
www.butlergreenwood.com
butlergree@aol.com

Type of Lodging: B&B

Cottage Rates: $110, including continental breakfast.

Pet Charges & Deposits: None.

Pet Policy: Small pets only. Designated rooms only. Manager's prior approval required.

Amenities: Cable TV, fully equipped kitchens, pool, fireplaces, large decks or porches

Pet Amenities: List of nearby veterinarians maintained. Exercise area includes 45 acres with lots of oak trees and a pond. Clark Creek Natural Area nearby.

Rated: 3 Paws — 7 cottages.

Butler Greenwood Plantation provides a classic bed and breakfast experience in seven secluded, romantic cottages scattered across the plantation grounds. There are four-poster beds, decks down into steep wooded ravines or porches overlooking a peaceful pond. Guided bird walks and ballooning are available by reservation. You can enjoy tours through the historic, antique-filled antebellum home of this early 1790s plantation. Located between New Orleans and Natchez, in scenic, unspoiled English Louisiana, where John J. Audubon painted nearly one-third of his Birds of America studies.

MAINE

Nickname: Pine Tree State
Population: 1,253,040
Area: 33,741 square miles
Climate: Southern interior and coastal influenced by air masses from south and west; northern area harsher, averages over 100" of snow in winter.
Capital: Augusta
Entered Union: March 15, 1820
Motto: *Dirigo* (I direct).
Song: State of Maine Song

Flower: White Pine Cone and Tassel
Tree: Eastern White Pine
Bird: Chickadee
Famous "Down Easters": James G. Blaine, Stephen King, Henry Wadsworth Longfellow, Edna St. Vincent Millay, Edmund Muskie, Edward Arlington Robinson.

 History: Algonquin peoples inhabited Maine when the Europeans arrived. The Cabots are believed to have explored Maine's rocky coast in 1498-1499. French settlers arrived in 1604 and the English arrived in 1607, but both settlements failed. In 1691, Maine was made a part of the Massachusetts colony. In 1820, Maine broke off and became a separate state. The Kennebunks, Bar Harbor and Boothbay Harbor are summertime tourist destinations. L.L. Bean is headquartered in Maine, and the Pine Tree State is very "patriotic" about any product "Made in Maine." Almost all of Stephen King's stories either take place entirely in Maine, or use Maine as a "jumping off point."

AUGUSTA, MAINE (Pop. 20,000)

Best Western Senator Inn

*284 Western Avenue at Interstate 95
Augusta, ME 04330
877-772-2224 • 207-622-5804*

Type of Lodging: Hotel
Room Rates: $59–$119, including full breakfast. AAA and AARP discounts.
Pet Charges & Deposits: None.
Pet Policy: Sorry, no cats. Manager's prior approval required.
Amenities: Cable TV, pool, whirlpools, full service health spa, restaurant and oyster bar.
Pet Amenities: None.
Rated: 3 Paws — 80 rooms and 20 suites.

Warmth greets you as you enter the Senator Inn, conveniently located in Augusta, the capital of Maine. The guestrooms feature luxurious accommodations, with a second TV, phone and refrigerator in the bathroom next to the huge, inviting tub. The spa includes a gym, aerobic classes and services such as facials, manicures and pedicures. The Senator Inn is consistently voted Greater Augusta's Best Hotel and is conveniently located near the scenic coast, L.L. Bean Retail Outlet and Freeport Outlet Shops. Enjoy year-round outdoor activities with on-site nature trails and the nearby the Augusta Arboretum.

Best Western White House Inn

155 Littlefield Avenue
Bangor, ME 04401
800-WESTERN • 207-862-3737
www.bestwestern.com/whitehouseinnb
angor

Type of Lodging: Motel

Room Rates: $58–$116, including continental breakfast. AARP discount.

Pet Charges & Deposits: Credit card imprint required.

Pet Policy: None. All Pets Welcome.

Amenities: Cable TV, refrigerators, safes, pool, sauna.

Pet Amenities: List of nearby veterinarians maintained. Exercise area including seasonal walking path located on 30 acres of fields.

Rated: 4 Paws — 61 rooms and 5 suites.

Best Western White House Inn is the perfect headquarters for day trips to Camden, Acadia National Park and the beautiful Bar Harbor region. Enjoy Mount Katahdin, the Moosehead Lake region and beautiful fall foliage tours. Bangor Mall, downtown Bangor and numerous discount stores are just a short drive away. A pet-friendly, family-run Maine inn, Best Western White House offers attractive rooms with many amenities including a seasonal walking path, gas grill, cocktail lounge, volleyball, tetherball, badminton and a 24-hour restaurant across the street on 35 acres of field.

Days Inn Hotel

250 Odlin Road
Bangor, ME 04401
800-835-4667 • 207-942-8272
daysinn@midmaine.com

Type of Lodging: Hotel

Room Rates: $49–$79, including continental breakfast. AAA, AARP and 10% Pets Welcome™ discounts.

Pet Charges & Deposits: $6 per stay.

Pet Policy: No pets allowed in pool area.

Amenities: Cable TV, safes, pool, Jacuzzi.

Pet Amenities: List of nearby veterinarians maintained. Exercise area.

Rated: 2 Paws — 101 rooms. Days Inn Five-Sunburst Award Winner.

Days Inn Hotel boasts an exceptional location and service, as well as numerous attractions within easy driving distance. Blackbeard's Family Fun Park is across the street. The 110-store Bangor Mall is five miles away while Bangor itself is just two miles distant. It's 45 miles to Bar Harbor and 12 miles to the University of Maine at Orono.

Holiday Inn Civic Center

500 Main Street
Bangor, ME 04401
800-799-8651 • 207-947-8651
www.holiday-inn.com/bangor-civic

Type of Lodging: Hotel

Room Rates: $60–$200. AAA, AARP and *15% Pets Welcome*™ discounts.

Pet Charges & Deposits: None.

Pet Amenities: None. All Pets Welcome.

Amenities: Cable TV, coffeemakers, hairdryers, irons and ironing boards, pool, fitness center, restaurant, lounge.

Pet Amenities: List of nearby veterinarians maintained. Exercise area. Paul Bunyan Park is located at the corner of Main and Dutton Streets.

Rated: 4 Paws — 121 rooms and 8 suites.

The superior level of service offered at Holiday Inn has earned it an outstanding reputation. All guestrooms have individual climate controls, dataports, irons and ironing boards, coffeemakers and hairdryers. A free morning newspaper is delivered to the room. On-site, you'll find Killarney's Fine Dining, a full service restaurant with an Irish cottage atmosphere, Fitzgerald's lounge and the high energy Bounty Tavern Nightclub. Acadia National Park is 50 miles away and Sugarloaf Ski Resort is 100 miles away, but there's plenty to do in Bangor, nearby Orono (ten miles away), home of the University of Maine and Bangor Auditorium & Civic Center, less than a mile away.

Hutchins Mountain View Cottages

Rural Route 2, Box 1190
Bar Harbor, ME 04609
800-775-4833 • 207-288-4833
www.hutchinscottages.com
hutchins@acadia.net

Type of Lodging: Cottages

Cottage Rates: $68–$136. Open June-October.

Pet Charges & Deposits: None.

Pet Policy: Manager's prior approval required.

Amenities: Cable TV, refrigerators, pool.

Pet Amenities: List of nearby veterinarians maintained. Exercise area. Acadia National Park is located Route 3, a mile away.

Rated: 2 Paws — 25 cottages on 20 acres of land.

Hutchins Mountain View Cottages is the perfect spot to enjoy "Down East" Maine at its best. It's located in a beautiful pine grove with a magnificent view of majestic Cadillac Mountain. Family-owned and operated for three generations, it's only four miles north of Bar Harbor and one mile from Acadia National Park. Many restaurants and stores are nearby. The one- and two-bedroom cottages include complete kitchens, shower baths, cable television, individual climate controls and screened porches.

Bethel Inn & Country Club

P.O. Box 49
Bethel, ME 04217
800-654-0125 • 207-824-2175
www.bethelinn.com
info@bethelinn.com

Type of Lodging: Guest Ranch & Resort

Room Rates: $99–$209, including full breakfast, full four-course dinner, unlimited golf and Sunday River skiing.

Pet Charges & Deposits: $10 per day.

Pet Policy: Sorry, no cats. Designated rooms only. Manager's prior approval required.

Amenities: Cable TV, refrigerators, microwaves, pool, whirlpool, Jacuzzi.

Pet Amenities: List of nearby veterinarians maintained.

Rated: 3 Paws — 58 rooms and 80 suites.

Bethel Inn & Country Club dates from 1913 and it is truly special. The inn is a cluster of four colonial buildings and a modern health club surrounding the main Inn. In the summer, there's golf, tennis and a health club with pool, saunas, fitness and game rooms. There are miles of trails to walk. Across the village common, you will find the shops, museum and National Historic District of Bethel, founded in 1796. In winter, Bethel is Maine's cross-country ski capital. Ranked at the top of northeastern ski areas, Sunday River Ski Area offers eight mountain peaks to ski with 120 trails and 15 lifts.

Briar Lea Inn & Restaurant

150 Mayville Road
Bethel, ME 04217
877-311-1299 • 207-824-4717
www.briarleainnrestaurant.com
briarlea@megalink.net

Type of Lodging: Inn

Room Rates: $59–$119, including full breakfast.

Pet Charges & Deposits: $10 per day.

Pet Policy: Manager's prior approval required. Pets must not be left unattended.

Amenities: Cable TV, restaurant.

Pet Amenities: List of nearby veterinarians maintained. Exercise area. Grafton Notch State Park and White Mountain National Forest nearby.

Rated: 3 Paws — 6 rooms.

Experience the comfort and ambience of a 150-year-old renovated Maine farmhouse. The six cozy rooms all have private baths, cable televisions, phones, air conditioning and casual antique décor. The restaurant, relaxed and casual, serves breakfast and dinner. The Briar Lea is located in the Mahoosuc Mountains, a mile outside the quaint historic village of Bethel, five miles from the renowned New England ski area, Sunday River and six miles from Ski Mount Abram. In summer, you can hike the Appalachian Trail in the White Mountain National Forest.

Lawnmeer Inn & Restaurant

65 Hendricks Hill Road
P.O. Box 505
Boothbay Harbor, ME 04575
800-633-7645 • 207-633-2544
www.lawnmeerinn.com

Type of Lodging: Inn

Room Rates: $95–$195. AARP discount.

Pet Charges & Deposits: $10 per day.

Pet Policy: No pets over 75 lbs. Designated rooms only. Manager's prior approval required.

Amenities: Cable TV, private deck on water.

Pet Amenities: List of nearby veterinarians maintained. Dog runs. Exercise area. Numerous Land Trust parks nearby.

Rated: 2 Paws — 32 rooms.

Lawnmeer is celebrating 103 years in 2001! Tucked away at the water's edge on serene Southport Island, it's just a five-minute drive across a unique swing bridge to the mainland and bustling Boothbay Harbor. The Lawnmeer is the oldest operating inn in the region. While you're here, visit Boothbay Harbor, explore spectacular Pemaquid Point and its beautiful lighthouse, go on a harbor cruise to see the seals, perhaps even take a day trip to fabled Monhegan Island. Freeport, home of the famous L.L. Bean Store, is located less than an hour away.

Inn By The Sea

40 Bowery Beach Road
Cape Elizabeth, ME 04107
800-888-4287 • 207-799-3134
www.innbythesea.com
innmaine@aol.com

Type of Lodging: Inn

Suite Rates: $189–$549. AAA and AARP discounts.

Pet Charges & Deposits: None.

Pet Policy: Designated rooms only.

Amenities: Cable TV, refrigerators, microwaves, pool, coffeemakers, two-line phones with voicemail and modem jacks.

Pet Amenities: Full pet menu. Free dog tags, pictures taken at check-in, bowls, beds & throws in suites, turn down treats, towels for use of pets. List of nearby veterinarians maintained. Exercise area. Two Lights State Park, Crescent Beach State Park and Fort Williams State Park nearby.

Rated: 5 Paws — 43 suites.

The pet-friendly Inn By The Sea doesn't just welcome pets, or as they say, "our little people in fur coats," but offers many very special amenities. Registration cards include space for the pet's name. Special stickers are put on the guest directory board, to show where "our special friends" are. When making a reservation, the pet's name is entered directly into the computer. The Inn provides dog dishes, bones, pooper-scoopers, oversized towels for drying dogs, and a special gourmet pet menu. Pet sitting or grooming are available with advance notice. Of course, the Inn occupies one of the most splendid locations along Maine's entire 3,000-mile coast. Framed by the same breathtaking scenery immortalized in Winslow Homer's paintings, the Inn is a Maine masterpiece. Pets Welcome is proud to award this sumptuous Inn a well-deserved Five-Paws once again.

Jasper's Restaurant & Motel

200 High Street
Ellsworth, ME 04605
207-667-5318
www.jaspersmaine.com
info@jaspersmaine.com

Type of Lodging: Motel
Room Rates: $44–$98, including full breakfast. AAA and AARP discounts.
Pet Charges & Deposits: $10 per stay.
Pet Policy: No pets over 200 lbs. Pets must not be left unattended.
Amenities: Cable TV, restaurant.
Pet Amenities: List of nearby veterinarians maintained. Exercise area includes 5 acres of woods behind motel for your pets' enjoyment. Park nearby.
Rated: 2 Paws – 32 rooms and 1 suite.

Some come to eat, some come to sleep, but come you must! Locals eat at Jasper's regularly, and when they have company they bring them to Jasper's because they know the menu offers lobster ten delicious ways. When people come from afar, they often spend the night. Jasper's is on Route 1 in Ellsworth, about 20 minutes from the entrance to Bar Harbor's Acadia National Park.

Freeport Inn

31 U.S. Route 1
Freeport, ME 04032
800-99 VALUE • 207-865-3106
www.freeportinn.com
info@freeportinn.com

Type of Lodging: Inn
Room Rates: $60–$120.
Pet Charges & Deposits: None.
Pet Policy: Designated rooms only.
Amenities: Cable TV, pool, restaurants.
Pet Amenities: List of nearby veterinarians maintained. Exercise area. Wolf's Neck State Park and Winslow Park nearby.
Rated: 3 Paws – 80 rooms.

Anchored by L.L.Bean, Freeport has become "The Shopping Mecca of the Northeast." In addition to the fabulous Bean headquarters, there are over 110 factory outlets. Set high on a hill, the Inn overlooks 25 acres of windswept lawns and a tidal river flowing through the property. All guestrooms are tastefully decorated and have private baths, cable television, individual climate controls and phones. Two of Freeport's finest restaurants, the Café and the Muddy Rudder, are located on the premises. Freeport is surprisingly close to Portland, the South Coast, the Mid-Coast and inland attractions.

Colony Hotel

Ocean Avenue
P.O. Box 511
Kennebunkport, Maine 04046-0511
800-552-2363 • 207-967-3331
www.thecolonyhotel.com
reservations@thecolonyhotel.com

Type of Lodging: Hotel

Room Rates: $125–$430, including full breakfast in dining room and afternoon tea. Open mid-May through mid-October.

Pet Charges & Deposits: $25 per day.

Pet Policy: Manager's prior approval required.

Amenities: Pool, private beach, restaurant.

Pet Amenities: Designated dog-walking area. Pet blankets, treats available.

Rated: 4 Paws — 125 rooms.

The majestic Colony Hotel, built on a rocky promontory at the mouth of the Kennebunk River in 1914, is a nautical landmark. Its fine Gregorian architecture epitomizes the elegance of the era. Gracious service and friendly pampering complete this unique and rare retreat. Handmade pet blankets, embroidered with a doggie bone, are provided upon check-in. The heated, filtered saltwater swimming pool delights guests with a warmer version of the same Atlantic waters as the private sandy beach. The pool has spectacular views of the breakwater and southern Maine's Mount Agamenticus. There is plenty of room to roam, both on the property and nearby. Honored as Maine's first environmentally responsible hotel, the Colony Hotel is the only "U.S. backyard wildlife habitat" in the Northeast. A staff naturalist leads guided tours on coastal Maine ecology along the sandy beaches and tidal pools that are free for hotel guests.

Lodge at Turbat's Creek

7 Turbat's Creek Road
P.O. Box 2722
Kennebunkport, ME 04046
207-967-8700
www.visitkennebunkport.com
info@visitkennebunkport.com

Type of Lodging: Hotel

Room Rates: $75–$139, including continental breakfast. AAA discount.

Pet Charges & Deposits: None.

Pet Policy: Designated rooms only. Manager's prior approval required.

Amenities: Cable TV, refrigerators, pool, bikes.

Pet Amenities: Exercise area. Park nearby.

Rated: 3 Paws — 26 rooms.

The Lodge at Turbat's Creek is a family place, just like Maine itself: unpretentious, comfortable abnd always glad to see you. You're only a stone's throw from the cool, salty waters of the Atlantic, where fishermen pull in some of the best lobster, clams and shrimp in the country. The Lodge has superior rooms, each with two chintz-covered double beds, open-air deck and private bath. The Lodge is only minutes away from the historic shipbuilding and fishing village of Kennebunkport, now an energetic town with great restaurants, wonderful shops, quaint streets, bright shop windows and the wharves of the river still lined with boats, just as they were in the 17th century.

Enchanted Nights Bed and Breakfast

29 Wentworth Street
Kittery, ME 03904
207-439-1489
www.enchanted-nights-bandb.com
info@enchanted-nights-bandb.com

Type of Lodging: B&B

Room Rates: $56–$200, including full breakfast.

Pet Charges & Deposits: Call for information.

Pet Policy: Manager's prior approval required.

Amenities: Whirlpools.

Pet Amenities: Exercise area.

Rated: 3 Paws — 6 rooms and 2 suites.

Enchanted Nights is a Victorian fantasy bordering New Hampshire's romantic Portsmouth Harbour area. Each guestroom is uniquely decorated with whimsical furnishings, complete with fanciful feather bedding and private bath. Antique claw-footed and whirlpool tubs and elegant French-Victorian decor, including a wrought-iron bed, grace the guest quarters. It is centrally located with easy access to the Kittery Outlet Malls, Boston, Portland and Scenic Route 103's ocean drive. Dine and dance, beach and bike, cliff walk or cruise in a whale-watching craft. Enjoy concerts in the park, quaint shops and outdoor cafes. Water Country, the Children's Museum, the Strawbery Banke Museum of historic homes and Prescott Park Gardens are all nearby.

Gateway Inn

Route 157
P.O. Box 637
Medway, ME 04460
207-746-3193

Type of Lodging: Motel

Room Rates: $45–$100, including continental breakfast. AAA, AARP and **10% Pets Welcome™** discounts.

Pet Charges & Deposits: None.

Pet Policy: None. All Pets Welcome.

Amenities: Refrigerators, pool, hot tubs.

Pet Amenities: List of nearby veterinarians maintained. Exercise area. Baxter State Park nearby.

Rated: 3 Paws — 30 rooms and 8 suites.

Located at the foot of Mount Katahdin, with breathtaking views and a country setting, Gateway Inn offers travelers modern facilities. Rooms are clean, quiet and equipped with queen- and king-sized beds. Some have private decks where guests can relax and enjoy the view. After a hard day on the road or exploring Maine's beautiful wilderness, enjoy the fully equipped fitness room or take a couple of laps in the heated pool. Finish unwinding in the bubbling hot tub. The Inn is located directly on a trail for snowmobilers and is minutes from Baxter State Park.

Small Point Bed & Breakfast

312 Small Point Road
Phippsburg, ME 04562
207-389-1716

Type of Lodging: B&B

Room Rates: $75–$140, including full breakfast.

Pet Charges & Deposits: None.

Pet Policy: Sorry, no cats. Manager's prior approval required.

Amenities: Cable TV, refrigerators, microwaves.

Pet Amenities: Dog bedding, water bowl, a beach towel, biscuits and dog sitting available. List of nearby veterinarians maintained. Fenced yard and doggy door in the Carriage House. Popham Beach and Head Beach nearby.

Rated: 3 Paws — Carriage House

Nestled among the pines and vistas of scenic Cape Small is a lovely 1890s coastal farmhouse, the Small Point Bed & Breakfast. Over the years, owners David & Jan have lovingly restored the old homestead and have been sharing the sound of the surf and the aroma of fresh sea air with their guests. Come and share the porch swing with them. Nearby attractions and activities include Popham Beach State Park, miles of unspoiled beaches, Hermit Island and Head Beach, L.L. Bean and the Freeport Outlets, boating, sailing, fishing and sightseeing charters.

Craignair Inn

533 Clark Island Road
Spruce Head, ME 04859
800-320-9997 • 207-594-7644
www.craignair.com
innkeeper@craignair.com

Type of Lodging: Inn

Room Rates: $48–$120, including full breakfast.

Pet Charges & Deposits: $8.50 per day.

Pet Policy: Designated rooms only. Manager's prior approval required. **Pets must not be left unattended.**

Amenities: Cable TV.

Pet Amenities: List of nearby veterinarians maintained. Exercise area.

Rated: 3 Paws — 21 rooms on 4 acres.

Craignair Inn at Clark Island is situated on four acres of shorefront within the 3500 miles of bays, peninsulas, inlets and headlands which form a coastline unmatched anywhere for its beauty and activity. The guestrooms are furnished simply but comfortably with quilt-covered beds, colorful wall coverings and hooked rugs on the floor. The Vestry Annex has eight bedrooms, all with private baths, and is furnished with antiques. Spruce Head, Rockland, Port Clyde, Thomaston Camden/Rockport and Owls Head are all nearby.

Budget Host Airport Inn

400 Kennedy Memorial Drive
Waterville, ME 04901
800-87 MAINE • 207-873-3366
http://members.mint.net/budget
budget@mint.net

Type of Lodging: Inn

Room Rates: $40–$110, including continental breakfast. AAA, AARP and *10% Pets Welcome*™ discounts.

Pet Charges & Deposits: $5 per stay.

Pet Policy: Manager's prior approval required.

Amenities: Cable TV, irons and ironing boards, restaurant.

Pet Amenities: List of nearby veterinarians maintained. Exercise area.

Rated: 2 Paws — 45 rooms.

A budget inn with many of the conveniences of a full service hotel, Budget Host Airport Inn features recently renovated rooms, a restaurant, free continental breakfast, free local calls, fax service, irons and ironing boards and a host of upscale amenities. The Inn is convenient to the Belgrade Lakes Region, Colby College, Thomas College and the Waterville Airport. It's located off Interstate 95, between Augusta and Bangor.

Ne'r Beach Motel

395 Post Road, Route 1
Wells, ME 04090
207-646-2636

Type of Lodging: Motel

Room Rates: $39–$109.

Pet Charges & Deposits: $8 per day.

Pet Policy: Designated rooms only.

Amenities: Cable TV, refrigerators, pool.

Pet Amenities: List of nearby veterinarians maintained. Exercise area.

Rated: 2 Paws — 43 rooms.

Ne'r Beach Motel is centrally located on U.S. Route 1, 1½ miles north of Ogunquit and five miles south of Kennebunkport. It's a "ne'r" ten-minute walk to beautiful Moody-Ogunquit Beach, one of the nicest sand beaches on the East Coast, and a two-minute drive from Wells Beach. During the summer, Ne'r Beach Motel is a trolley stop for service to beaches and shops in Ogunquit and Wells. A variety of available accommodations have individual climate controls, cable television, telephones and refrigerators. Picnic tables under large trees make it a great place for you and your pet. Or go for a relaxing walk to the nearby beach.

Whispering Pines Motel & Gift Shop

183 Lake Road
P.O. Box 649
Wilton, ME 04294
800-626-7463 • 207-645-3721
whpmotel@exploremaine.com

Type of Lodging: Motel
Room Rates: $39–$88. AAA discount.
Pet Charges & Deposits: $3 per day.
Pet Policy: Designated rooms only.
Manager's prior approval required.
Pets must not be left unattended.
Amenities: Cable TV, refrigerators,
microwaves, guest laundry, free boat
use.
Pet Amenities: Treats available. List
of nearby veterinarians maintained.
Exercise area. Kineowatha Park is
located on High Street. Mount Blue
State Park is located in Weld, Maine.
Rated: 2 Paws — 29 rooms and 4
suites.

Whispering Pines Motel & Gift Shop is situated on beautiful Wilson Lake. It's 1½ hours from Portland Jetport and three hours from Logan International Airport, Boston. Whispering Pines has newly remodeled rooms and suites. There's a children's play area, a big backyard for picnics, baseball or horseshoes. Recreational activities nearby include golf, parks, hiking, skiing, snowmobiling, rafting, kayaking, fishing and you can even pan for gold in the Coos Canyon area of the Swift River.

MARYLAND

Nicknames: Old Line State; Free State
Population: 5,171,634
Area: 12,297 square miles
Climate: Continental in the west; humid subtropical in the east
Capital: Annapolis
Entered Union: April 28, 1788
Motto: *Fatti Maschii, Parole Femine*
(Manly deeds, womanly words).
Song: Maryland, My Maryland

Flower: Black-eyed Susan
Tree: White Oak
Bird: Baltimore Oriole
Famous Marylanders: John Astin, Benjamin Bannaker, Tom Clancy, Jonathan Demme, Francis Scott Key, H.L. Mencken, Edgar Allan Poe, Babe Ruth, Upton Sinclair, Roger B. Taney.

History: Europeans encountered Algonquin peoples when they first visited the area. Italian explorer Verrazano visited the area in the early 16th century. Captain John Smith explored the area in 1608. The first trading post was set up in the Chesapeake in 1631. King Charles granted land to Cecilius Calvert, Lord Baltimore, in 1632. In the War of 1812, when a British fleet tried to take Fort McHenry, Marylander Francis Scott Key wrote "The Star Spangled Banner" (1814). Although it was a slave-holding state, Maryland remained with the Union during the Civil War. Maryland was the site of the Battle of Antietam, 1862, which halted General Lee's march north.

Loews Annapolis Hotel

126 West Street
Annapolis, MD 21401
800-526-2593 • 410-263-7777
www.loewsannapolis.com
info@loewsannapolis.com

Type of Lodging: Hotel

Room Rates: $109–$379. AAA and AARP discounts.

Pet Charges & Deposits: None.

Pet Policy: Designated rooms only.

Amenities: Cable TV, honor bar, limited fitness center.

Pet Amenities: Welcome amenities include mat, bowl, door hanger, information services and "Loews Loves Pets Program." List of nearby veterinarians maintained. Dog runs. Exercise area. Quiet Waters Park is located on Hillsmere Drive.

Rated: 5 Paws — 217 rooms and 13 suites.

Loews Annapolis Hotel subscribes to the Loews Loves Pets Program and it shows. The Hotel is everything you'd expect a world-class lodging to be and its location could not be better. Annapolis is a fabulous walking city, whether you're here to see the U.S. Naval Academy, historic Annapolis, the narrow, tree-lined streets or the equally charming shops. This is one of the editors' favorite places in the country—a wondrous mélange of everything that makes you feel good to be alive.

Comfort Inn-BWI

6921 Baltimore Annapolis Boulevard
Baltimore, MD 21225
888-826-1055 • 410-789-9100
www.comfortinn.com/hotel/MD410
cibwi@aol.com

Type of Lodging: Hotel

Room Rates: $119–$175, including full breakfast. AAA and *10% Pets Welcome™* discounts.

Pet policy: No pets over 25 lbs. Manager's prior approval required.

Amenities: Cable TV, Jacuzzi, fitness room, restaurant/lounge, airport shuttle.

Pet Amenities: List of nearby veterinarians maintained. Exercise area.

Rated: 3 Paws — 185 rooms and 3 suites. Eleven-consecutive-time Choice Hotels Gold Hospitality Award Winner.

The Choice Hotels Gold Hospitality is awarded to only 6% of the hotels in the chain. Comfort Inn-BWI had won the award eleven consecutive times. The hotel features large rooms with cable television, voicemail, hairdryer, iron and ironing board, two-line dataport speakerphones and oversized desks. The Rose Restaurant and lounge, a fitness center and 8,000 feet of meeting and banquet space complete the picture. Kids stay free with parents or grandparents. Nearby attractions include the shops and eateries at Baltimore's Inner Harbor, PSINet Stadium, home of the Baltimore Ravens, and all the delights of both Baltimore and our nation's capital. The Maryland Light Rail is right across the street from the hotel.

Sleep Inn & Suites - BWI Airport

6055 Belle Grove Road
Baltimore, MD 21225
888-826-1055 • 410-789-7223
www.sleepinn.com/hotel/MD128
sleepbwi@aol.com

Type of Lodging: Hotel

Room Rates: $99–$149, including continental breakfast. AAA and *10% Pets Welcome™* discounts.

Pet Charges & Deposits: None.

Pet Policy: No pets over 25 lbs. Manager's prior approval required.

Amenities: Cable TV, fitness room, airport shuttle, restaurant.

Pet Amenities: List of nearby veterinarians maintained. Exercise area.

Rated: 3 Paws — 145 rooms and 34 suites.

Sleep Inn BWI is the newest hotel in the Baltimore Washington International area and it's a beauty. Local free phone calls, The Rose Restaurant and plethora of amenities make this hotel a quality lodging at an affordable price. It's ten minutes to Camden Yards, home of the Baltimore Orioles, only seven miles to Baltimore's Inner Harbor and the National Aquarium. Annapolis is 20 minutes away and Washington D.C. can be reached in half an hour. Great location, pet-friendliness, what more can you ask for?

Comfort Inn Shady Grove

16216 Frederick Road
Gaithersburg, MD 20877
888-605-9100 • 301-330-0023
www.comfortinn.com/hotel/MD413
cisg@aol.com

Type of Lodging: Hotel

Room Rates: $69–$119, including full breakfast buffet. AAA, AARP and *10% Pets Welcome*™ discounts.

Pet Charges & Deposits: None.

Pet Policy: None. All Pets Welcome.

Amenities: Cable TV, pool, picnic area.

Pet Amenities: List of nearby veterinarians maintained. Exercise area. Seneca Park is located on Clopper Road.

Rated: 3 Paws — 127 rooms. Five-time Choice Hotels Gold Hospitality Award Winner.

Comfort Inn Shady Grove has won the coveted Choice Hotels Gold Hospitality Award five times. This extraordinarily first-class hotel features guestrooms with everything you can think of, including a full buffet breakfast. The hotel has an outstanding location in the D.C. suburb closest to the Interstate 270 Technology Corridor. Washington, D.C. has almost too many attractions to count, from the Smithsonian Institute Museums to fun-and-funky Georgetown, from the White House to the Capitol, and from the Washington Monument and Lincoln Memorial to the Vietnam Wall.

Walnut Ridge Bed & Breakfast

92 Main Street
P.O. Box 368
Grantsville, MD 21536
888-419-2568 • 301-895-4248
www.walnutridge.net
walnutridge@usa.net

Type of Lodging: B&B

Room Rates: $85–$135, including full breakfast.

Pet Charges & Deposits: $10 per day.

Pet Policy: Sorry, no cats. Designated rooms only. Manager's prior approval required.

Amenities: Cable TV, fireplaces, wood-fired hot tub.

Pet Amenities: List of nearby veterinarians maintained. Savage River Forest nearby.

Rated: 3 Paws — 2 rooms, 1 suite and 1 cabin.

Walnut Ridge Bed & Breakfast, one of the most romantic places we've found, is located in tiny Grantsville. It's just about as northwest as you can get in Maryland, almost on the Pennsylvania border and close to the West Virginia State Line as well. There's plenty to see and do in the area: Fallingwater, the historic Casselman Bridge (1813), the Scenic Railroad, Deep Creek Lake, Ohio Pyle (white water rafting) and nearby Wisp Ski and Golf Resort.

Waterloo Country Inn

28822 Mount Vernon Road
Princess Anne, MD 21853
410-651-0883
www.waterloocountryinn.com
innkeeper@waterloocountryinn.com

Type of Lodging: B&B

Room Rates: $105–$245, including full breakfast.

Pet Charges & Deposits: None.

Pet Policy: Designated rooms only. Manager's prior approval required.

Amenities: Cable TV, pool, whirlpool, Jacuzzi, fireplaces, canoes, bicycles.

Pet Amenities: List of nearby veterinarians maintained. Exercise area. Manokin River Park nearby.

Rated: 3 Paws — 4 rooms and 2 suites.

Retreat to the Waterloo Country Inn and find yourself in another world, a more relaxed world, a world where time loses meaning. Prominent Somerset County landowner Henry Waggaman built this luxurious, pre-Revolutionary waterfront estate in the 1750s. It has been lovingly restored to its 18th century elegance. The Inn is situated on a tidal pond that is a habitat for wildlife and birds, with trails for walking. Princess Anne is 12 miles south of Salisbury on Maryland's Eastern Shore. Chincoteague, Assateague, Ocean City and Crisfield are close by.

Huntingfield Manor B&B

4928 Eastern Neck Road
Rock Hall, MD 21661
410-639-7779
www.huntingfield.com
ManorLord@Juno.com or
* ManorLady@Juno.com*

Type of Lodging: B&B

Room Rates: $95–$145, including continental breakfast. AAA discount.

Pet Charges & Deposits: None.

Pet Policy: Designated room only.

Amenities: Refrigerators, microwaves, honor bar, pool.

Pet Amenities: Exercise area. Eastern Neck Wildlife Refuge is located on Route 445.

Rated: 3 Paws — 4 rooms, 1 suite and 1 cottage.

Huntingfield Manor, one room wide and 136-feet-long, is a working farm that dates back to the mid-1600s. In the 1850s, the 70-acre farm on the Eastern Shore of Chesapeake Bay was called, "The Prevention of Inconvenience." A visit to Rock Hall would not be complete without eating crabs, oysters, rockfish or clams. Explore the unspoiled shoreline of Chesapeake Bay, the Chester and Sassafras Rivers and numerous creeks in the area. This is a veritable paradise for pets and their companions.

River House Inn

201 East Market Street
Snow Hill, MD 21863
410-632-2722
www.riverhouseinn.com
innkeeper@riverhouseinn.com

Type of Lodging: Inn

Room Rates: $140–$220, including full breakfast. AAA, AARP, AKC and **10% Pets Welcome™** discounts.

Pet Charge & Deposits: None.

Pet Policy: Sorry, no cats. Manager's prior approval required.

Amenities: Cable TV, refrigerators, microwaves, Jacuzzi.

Pet Amenities: List of nearby veterinarians maintained. Exercise area including 2½ acres of fenced lawns and gardens. Sturgis Park is located a block away.

Rated: 3 Paws — 5 rooms and 4 suites. Listed on the National Register of Historic Homes.

Treat yourself to a casual yet elegant getaway at the River House Inn, a spacious National Register Victorian home on the beautiful Pocomoke River. Located on the Eastern Shore in the village of Snow Hill, where you can be as active or relaxed as you choose, the possibilities are endless. The River House Inn has three guest buildings in a lovely rambling setting on more than two acres of rolling lawn leading down to the river. All guestrooms have air conditioning, queen-sized beds and private baths.

Five Gables Inn & Spa

209 North Talbot Street
St. Michaels, MD 21663
877-466-0100 • 410-745-0100
www.fivegables.com
fivegables@crosslink.net

Type of Lodging: Inn

Room Rates: $195–$425, including expanded continental breakfast and afternoon refreshments.

Pet Charges & Deposits: Call for deposit information.

Pet Policy: None. All Pets Welcome.

Amenities: Cable TV, CD players, hairdryers, pool, sauna, steam room, Aveda Concept Spa.

Pet Amenities: List of nearby veterinarians maintained. Exercise area.

Rated: 3 Paws — 16 rooms.

Run away to a charming bit of yesterday. Guests have their choice of rooms in one of two completely renovated buildings: the colonial-style Five Gables or the traditional, historical Brick House. The original buildings are circa 1860 and have historic significance in this lovely eastern shore hamlet. St. Michaels developed as a noted shipbuilding center during the American Revolution. Ask locals why the town is known as "The Town that fooled the British?" Seafood and agricultural processing industries now sustain the economy. Visitors are rediscovering the region's unspoiled heritage. One of the better-known East Coast yachting centers, St. Michaels draws thousands of sailing enthusiasts each summer.

Rambler Inn

426 North Church Street
Thurmont, MD 21788
301-271-2424

Type of Lodging: Motel

Room Rates: $46–$76. AAA discount.

Pet Charges & Deposits: None.

Pet Policy: Small pets only. Manager's prior approval required. Pets must not be left unattended.

Amenities: Cable TV, refrigerators, microwaves.

Pet Amenities: List of nearby veterinarians maintained. Exercise area. Catoctin Mountain Park nearby.

Rated: 3 Paws – 30 rooms.

Rambler Inn, also known as Rambler Motel, has tastefully decorated rooms, all at ground level with at-door parking, direct dial phones and exceptional housekeeping. Parks and sports activities in the area include Catoctin Mountain National Park, Cunningham Falls State Park, ski resorts and golf courses. It's covered bridge country and Camp David is close by. You're just over the border from either Pennsylvania or West Virginia with Frederick, Harpers Ferry, the Gettysburg and Antietam Battlefields an easy day trip, and, of course, Washington, D.C. and Baltimore.

MASSACHUSETTS

Nicknames: Bay State; Old Colony

Population: 6,175,169

Area: 9,241 square miles

Climate: Temperate with colder and drier climate in western region.

Capital: Boston

Entered Union: February 6,1788

Motto: *Ence Petit Placidam Sub Libertate Quietem* (By the sword we seek peace, but peace only under liberty).

Song: All Hail to Massachusetts

Flower: Mayflower

Tree: American Elm

Bird: Chickadee

Famous "Bay Staters": John Adams, John Quincy Adams, Louisa May Alcott, Horatio Alger, Susan B. Anthony, Clara Barton, Alexander Graham Bell, George Bush, Emily Dickinson, Ralph Waldo Emerson, John Hancock, Nathaniel Hawthorne, Oliver Wendell Holmes, John F. Kennedy, Samuel F.B. Morse, Paul Revere, Dr. Seuss, Henry David Thoreau.

 History: The Algonquin peoples predated the Pilgrims, who settled in Plymouth in 1620, giving thanks for their survival on their first Thanksgiving Day in 1621. Between 1630 and 1640, 20,000 new settlers arrived. Native American relations with the colonists deteriorated. By 1676, Native Americans ceased to be a threat. Massachusetts was the hotbed of the American Revolution—the Boston Massacre in 1770 and the Boston Tea Party in 1773 led to the first bloodshed of the American Revolution at Lexington in 1775.

Lord Jeffery Inn

30 Boltwood Avenue
Amherst, MA 01003
800-742-0358 • 413-253-2576
www.pinnacle-inns.com/lordjefferyinn
lordjefferyinn@pinnacle-inns.com

Type of Lodging: Inn
Room Rates: $79–$189, including complimentary morning tea and coffee. AAA and AARP discounts.

Pet Charges & Deposits: $10 per day

Pet Policy: Designated rooms only. Pets must not be left unattended.

Amenities: Cable TV, dataports, restaurant.

Pet Amenities: Amherst Common out front.

Rated: 3 Paws — 40 rooms and 8 suites.

A visit to the Lord Jeffery Inn is a journey back to a time when a good inn and tavern stood at the center of most New England villages. Overlooking the town common, these inns were the heart and soul through which the pulse of village life flowed. Within, the day's reminiscence mingled with future dreams over hearty meals, stout ales and precious imported wines. Travelers, guided by the light beckoning from a windowed hearth, brought tales from afar to these tables, knowing that a good meal, a hot bath and a comfortable bed awaited them. Each of the guestrooms and suites offers handcrafted furnishings, fine cotton linens and quilt bed coverings. It's within easy walking distance to the Amherst Town Common, downtown shops, the Emily Dickinson Home, bike trails and Amherst College.

Cape Cod's Lamb & Lion Inn

2504 Main Street
Barnstable, MA 02630
800-909-6923 • 508-362-6823
www.lambandlion.com
info@lambandlion.com

Type of Lodging: Inn
Room Rates: $85–$225, including continental breakfast.

Pet Charges & Deposits: $15 per day.

Pet Policy: Manager's prior approval required. Pets must not be left unattended.

Amenities: Cable TV, refrigerators, microwaves, pool, hot tubs.

Pet Amenities: List of nearby veterinarians maintained. Cape Cod National Seashore nearby.

Rated: 3 Paws — 5 rooms and 5 suites.

The original section of the Lamb and Lion Inn was built as a private home in 1740. It features multiple fireplaces and that old Cape Cod charm you've longed for all these years. The Inn is centrally located on Old King's Highway—which isn't really a highway at all. It's a peaceful, beautiful New England road made famous in the history books when the American Patriots marched down it on their way to join the Revolutionary War. The Inn is 1½ miles from quaint Barnstable Harbor and whale watching, walking distance to the beach, two minutes from golf courses, eight minutes from the Island ferries and a little over an hour from Boston and Providence. Nearby Cape Cod National Seashore has plenty of hiking trails and beaches for you and your pet.

Jenkins Inn & Restaurant

7 West Street, Route 122
Barre, MA 01005
800-378-7373 • 978-355-6444
www.bbhost.com/jenkinsinn
jenkinsinn@juno.com

Type of Lodging: Inn

Room Rates: $110–$150. AARP discount.

Pet Charges & Deposits: $5 per day.

Pet Policy: Designated rooms only. Manager's prior approval required.

Amenities: Cable TV.

Pet Amenities: List of nearby veterinarians maintained. Exercise area. North Park is located across the street from the Inn. Rutland State Park is located on Route 122.

Rated: 4 Paws — 5 rooms.

Whether your getaway is a fall foliage retreat, a winter ski vacation, and "antiquing" weekend or time away just to unwind, the 1834 Jenkins Inn in historic Barre provides all the comforts and amenities of a home away from home. Conveniently located in central Massachusetts, the Inn is just 1½ hours from Boston and southern Maine, an hour to the Berkshires and western Massachusetts and close to shopping and theaters in Worcester or sightseeing in Old Sturbridge Village. From in-room televisions to a delicious home cooked breakfast, lunch and dinner in the cozy dining room, the Jenkins Inn's friendly and professional innkeepers anticipate your every desire.

Colonnade Hotel

120 Huntington Avenue
Boston, MA 02116
800-962-3030 • 617-424-7000
www.colonnadehotel.com

Type of Lodging: Hotel

Room Rates: $225–$425, AAA and AARP discounts.

Pet Charges & Deposits: None.

Pet Policy: None. All Pets Welcome.

Amenities: Pool, guest laundry, irons and ironing boards, restaurant, lounge.

Pet Amenities: "Cause for Paws" package available.

Rated: 5 Paws – 285 rooms and suites.

The Colonnade, located in Boston's Back Bay, is an independent luxury hotel in the European tradition, catering to the discriminating traveler. Lauded for its bold, modern architecture, the building's facade is defined by a series of exterior columns that provide a look of contemporary grace and elegance.

The guest rooms are classically furnished and thoughtfully designed with seating areas and work desks. The amenities range from plush bathrobes to telephones in the bathrooms. The suites feature Jacuzzi baths, stereo CD systems and wide-screen televisions. The resort-style swimming area commands stunning views of Boston and includes lounge chairs, tables for poolside dining and changing rooms. For indoor recreation, enjoy the fully equipped fitness room.

Colonnade Hotel is located in Back Bay, across from the Hynes Convention Center and the Prudential Center, next to Copley Place, and steps from Newbury Street. Symphony Hall, Fenway Park, the Museum of Fine Arts and Faneuil Hall are minutes away. Special packages, including the special pet package "Cause for Paws," cater to every lifestyle.

Bertram Inn

92 Sewall Avenue
Brookline, MA 02146
800-295-3822 • 617-566-2234

Type of Lodging: Inn

Room Rates: $84–$219, including expanded continental breakfast and afternoon tea.

Pet Charges & Deposits: $10 per day. $150 refundable deposit.

Pet Policy: No pets over 85 lbs. Manager's prior approval required. Limit one pet per room.

Amenities: Cable TV, hairdryers, irons and ironing boards.

Pet Amenities: Charles River nearby. Pet stores, groomers and veterinarians are only minutes away.

Rated: 3 Paws — 14 rooms and suites.

A stay at the Bertram Inn offers the opportunity to step back into another era. The handsome building was constructed by fine artisans, with oak panels and a sweeping stairway, masterpieces of lead and glass and fireplaces in the tradition of the Old World. Typical of a large Victorian home, no two rooms are alike. Each of the guestrooms has its own character and size. The elegant Victorian home is located near the Commonwealth Mall, Boston Commons and Charles River Esplanade.

Bay Motor Inn

223 Main Street
Buzzards Bay, MA 02532
508-759-3989
www.capecodtravel.com/baymotorinn
bmotorinn@capecod.net

Type of Lodging: Motor Lodge

Room Rates: $46–$99, including coffee. AAA and AARP discounts.

Pet Charges & Deposits: $5 per day

Pet Policy: Manager's prior approval required. Pets must not be left unattended.

Amenities: Cable TV, pool.

Pet Amenities: List of nearby veterinarians maintained. Exercise area. Buzzards Bay Town Park is adjacent to the motor lodge.

Rated: 2 Paws — 17 rooms.

The Bay Motor Inn features cottage-style and motel units with free local telephone calls. There's plenty of space to walk your pet on the property. Cape Cod Road nearby provides seven miles of road for walking and biking. Buzzards Bay is on the mainland, right near Heritage Plantation and Otis Air National Guard Station. It's less than a hour from Plymouth Rock.

Charles Hotel

One Bennett Street
Cambridge, MA 02138
800-882-1818 • 617-661-5052
www.charleshotel.com
reservations@charleshotel.com

Type of Lodging: Hotel

Room Rates: $250–$500. AAA and AARP discounts.

Pet Charges & Deposits: None.

Pet Policy: Pets must not be left unattended.

Amenities: Cable TV, refrigerators, honor bar, safes, pool, Jacuzzi, spas, full concierge services.

Pet Amenities: Exercise area. JFK Park is located at Memorial Drive and JFK Street.

Rated: 3 Paws — 249 rooms and 44 suites.

When in the Boston area, it would be hard to find a more convenient place to stay than the Charles Hotel. Its immediately adjacent to Harvard Square and Harvard University, a short ride from historic downtown Boston and all the attractions of the fabulous city. The Charles features charming and cozy country-style room décor. Harvard University was founded in 1636 and is America's oldest, and perhaps its most prestigious center of learning. Not to be outshone, Massachusetts Institute of Technology (MIT) is also located in Cambridge, as is the house of Henry Wadsworth Longfellow. It's a great walking town, no matter your mood.

Best Western at Historic Concord

740 Elm Street
Concord, MA 01742
978-369-6100
www.bestwestern.com

Type of Lodging: Inn

Room Rates: $104–$144, including continental breakfast. AAA and AARP discounts.

Pet Charges & Deposits: $10 per day.

Pet Policy: None. All Pets Welcome.

Amenities: Cable TV, pool, whirlpool.

Pet Amenities: List of nearby veterinarians maintained. Exercise area.

Rated: 3 Paws — 106 rooms.

Best Western at Historic Concord is a fine lodging if you're in the Boston-Concord area. There's an upscale, yet casual, North Italian restaurant and lounge next door, dataports in each room, interior corridors, a fitness facility and guest laundry facilities. It could not be more centrally located. Historic Concord and the Concord Museum are 2½ miles away while Walden Pond is four miles distant. It's 22 miles to the middle of downtown Boston and less than a half hour to Logan Airport.

The Bed & Biscuit

Rural Route 1, Box 71B
Edgartown, MA 02539
508-627-3666

Type of Lodging: B&B

House Rates: $2,000–$2,500 per week.

Pet Charges & Deposits: None.

Pet Policy: Manager's prior approval required.

Amenities: Cable TV.

Pet Amenities: List of nearby veterinarians maintained. Exercise area.

Rated: 3 Paws — A rental residence with four bedrooms, family room and kitchen.

Nestled on Martha's Vineyard, The Bed & Biscuit offers a peaceful setting where you can escape and relax with your family and pet. Enjoy the unique ambience of each of the four bedrooms, family room and kitchen. The large deck is a wonderful place for outdoor cookouts and there's a big fenced-in yard for you and your pet. Also nearby are tranquil walking trails to enjoy and lots of freedom for your pet to roam. The innkeeper makes certain that this spotless home is the perfect locale for your location on romantic Martha's Vineyard.

Cape Ann Motor Inn

33 Rockport Road
Gloucester, MA 01966
800-464-8439 • 978-281-2900
www.capeannmotorinn.com
camotor@tiac.net

Type of Lodging: Motel

Room Rates: $60–$200, including continental breakfast.

Pet Charges & Deposits: None.

Pet Policy: None. All Pets Welcome.

Amenities: Cable TV, refrigerators.

Pet Amenities: Halibut State Park, Ravenswood Park and Dogtown Park nearby.

Rated: 3 Paws — 29 rooms and 1 suite.

Enjoy a vacation right on the beach. Cape Ann Motor Inn is located directly on the sands of beautiful Long Beach, on the Gloucester-Rockport line. An easy drive from Boston, Salem, Lexington and Concord, the town of Gloucester, which was settled in 1623, has remained a fishing center. There are numerous whale watching cruises available in the area.

Brandt House

29 Highland Avenue
Greenfield, MA 01301
800-235-3329 • 413-774-3329
www.brandthouse.com
info@brandthouse.com

Type of Lodging: B&B

Room Rates: $115–$205, including continental breakfast on weekdays and full breakfast on weekends. AAA discount.

Pet Charges & Deposits: $20 per stay. Call for deposit information.

Pet Policy: Sorry, no cats. Manager's prior approval required. Pets must not be left unattended.

Amenities: Cable TV, fireplaces, Jacuzzis, skylights.

Pet Amenities: List of nearby veterinarians maintained. Exercise area. Highland Park nearby. Walking and hiking trails with map.

Rated: 3 Paws — 8 rooms and 2 suites.

The Brandt House is a turn-of-the-century Revival mansion with wraparound porch in a quiet neighborhood. Each guestroom has a luxurious featherbed, down comforter, private bath, private telephone, bathrobes and air conditioning. Antiques and fresh flowers are everywhere. In the morning, join other guests for a delicious breakfast at the great oak table, or have an intimate breakfast for two in the living room or outside on the patio. The Brandt House is conveniently located in western Massachusetts, where magnificent views of the Berkshire Mountains greet you on arrival.

Harbor Village

160 Marston Avenue
P.O. Box 635
Hyannis Port, MA 02647
508-775-7581
www.harborvillage.com

Type of Lodging: Cottages

Cottage Rates: $90 per night to $1,600 per week.

Pet Charges & Deposits: $15 per day or $100 per week.

Pet Policy: Sorry, no cats. Manager's prior approval required.

Amenities: Cable TV, VCRs, fully equipped kitchens, fireplaces, deck.

Pet Amenities: List of nearby veterinarians maintained. Exercise area. Mickerson State Forest nearby.

Rated: 2 Paws — 4 rooms and 15 suites.

Harbor Village is a quiet, secluded village of Cape-style homes located on the south shore of Cape Cod at the edge of Hyannis Port (Kennedy country). The 17-acre peninsula is studded with pine trees and laced with cool, sandy paths leading to the ocean beach. The historic sights of Plymouth are within an hour, as is Provincetown at the very tip of Cape Cod. See the John F. Kennedy Museum and the Kennedy Compound, take a horse and buggy ride down Main Street and see the Aquarium and other sites.

Seven Hills Country Inn & Restaurant

40 Plunkett Street
Lenox, MA 01240
800-869-6518 • 413-637-0060
www.sevenhillsinn.com
7hills@berkshire.net

Type of Lodging: B&B
Room Rates: $75–$325, including continental or full breakfast. AAA, AARP, AKC, ABA and *5% Pets Welcome™* discounts.
Pet Charges & Deposits: $20 per day
Pet Policy: Designated rooms only.
Amenities: Cable TV, pool, fireplaces.
Pet Amenities: List of nearby veterinarians maintained. Exercise area. Kennedy Park nearby.
Rated: 4 Paws — 56 rooms and 2 suites on 27 acres.

Jim Eder and Patrica Flores Eder, two of the friendliest people a pet will ever meet, have extensively renovated this imposing Baronial mansion, once the summer home of the Spencer family, prominent members of Boston society. The bed and breakfast is like stepping into the England of the last century— elegant, opulent and charming. Its chef graduated "top of his class" from both Cordon Bleu in Paris and the Culinary Institute of America. The Seven Hills Country Inn is two hours from Boston, 2½ hours from New York City. Tanglewood is a cultural mecca and is summer home to the Boston Symphony Orchestra. Situated in the Berkshire Mountains, this is as close to a perfect vacation spot as you'll find in New England.

Safe Harbor

2 Harborview Way
Nantucket, MA 02554
508-228-3222
www.beesknees.net/safeharbor
sharbor@nantucket.net

Type of Lodging: B&B
Room Rates: $170–$200, including continental breakfast.
Pet Charges & Deposits: $10 per day
Pet Policy: Sorry, no cats. Manager's prior approval required.
Amenities: None.
Pet Amenities: List of nearby veterinarians maintained. Exercise area. Children's Beach nearby.
Rated: 2 Paws — 5 rooms.

Safe Harbor offers a fine headquarters for your vacation on Nantucket Island, whose history dates from 1659 when a group of colonists seeking economic opportunity formed a partnership with Thomas Mayhew of Martha's Vineyard to purchase Nantucket from Native Americans for 30 British pounds and two beaver hats. Nantucket retains much of its whaler days charm, with cobblestone main streets, small lanes, plain Quaker-style homes and handsome houses from the 19th century. Nantucket, 30 miles off the mainland, is reached by air or boat. It's the quintessential New England "escape."

Five Bridge Inn

154 Pine Street
Rehoboth, MA 02769-0462
508-252-3190
www.fivebridgeinn.com
fbicom1@ma.ultranet.com

Type of Lodging: B&B

Room Rates: $88–$125, including full breakfast. *Seasonal Pets Welcome*™ discount.

Pet Charges & Deposits: $10 per stay.

Pet Policy: Designated rooms only. Manager's prior approval required. Pets must not be left unattended.

Amenities: Cable TV, refrigerators, microwaves, pool, Jacuzzi, tennis court, gazebo.

Pet Amenities: List of nearby veterinarians maintained. Exercise area. Slater Park, Capron Park and Roger Williams Park are all within an eight mile radius.

Rated: 3 Paws — 4 rooms and 1 suite on 60 acres.

Five Bridge Farm Inn bills itself as "one of southern New England's best kept secrets," and a wonderful secret it is. This stately Georgian Colonial mansion is secluded on 60 acres of forest and fields. There's a private tennis court, lap pool, jogging track and hiking trails. Riding stables are right next door. In nearby Fall River, you'll find Battleship Cove, which harbors 20th century vessels of the U.S. Navy, a Russian built Corvette, and two PT boats, as well as a Bell Huey helicopter that served in Vietnam.

Hawthorne Hotel

18 Washington Square West
Salem, MA 01970
800-729-7829 • 978-744-4080
www.hawthornehotel.com
info@hawthornehotel.com

Type of Lodging: Hotel

Room Rates: $115–$295. AAA, AARP and *10% Pets Welcome*™ discounts.

Pet Charges & Deposits: $15 per stay.

Pet Policy: None. All Pets Welcome.

Amenities: Cable TV, refrigerators.

Pet Amenities: List of nearby veterinarians maintained. Exercise area. Salem Commons adjacent to the hotel.

Rated: 3 Paws — 83 rooms and 6 suites.

This classic six-story circa 1925 hotel faces Salem Common. Mention Salem and the words "Witch trials" invariably follow. Now adjacent to Boston, Salem was the capital of the Massachusetts Bay Company from 1626 to 1630. The Witch House built in 1642 and located at 310½ Essex Street, was the home of Jonathan Corwin, one of the judges in the witchcraft trials, and was the site of preliminary witchcraft examinations. Just across the Common from the Hotel is the Salem Witch Museum.

Salem Inn

7 Summer Street
Salem, MA 01970
800-446-2995 • 978-741-0680
www.saleminnma.com
saleminn@earthlink.net

Type of Lodging: Inn

Room Rates: $119–$290, including continental breakfast. AAA discount.

Pet Charges & Deposits: $15 per stay.

Pet Policy: Designated rooms only.

Amenities: Cable TV, refrigerators, microwaves, Jacuzzi.

Pet Amenities: List of nearby veterinarians maintained.

Rated: 3 Paws — 39 rooms.

You don't even have to step inside the Salem Inn to know you're taking a trip into the 19th century. This elegant hostelry is made up of converted 1834 townhouses. Each of the individually decorated guestrooms features antiques, period details and homey touches. You're only 18 miles from the center of Boston, yet there's so much to see in Salem as well. The New England Pirate Museum, the House of the Seven Gables Historic Site, the Peabody Essex Museum and the Witch Dungeon Museum are only a few of the cultural and haunting venues that await you in Salem.

Days Inn

66-68 Haynes Street
P.O. Box 185
Sturbridge, MA 01566
800-DAYS INN • 508-347-3391

Type of Lodging: Motel

Room Rates: $75–$120, including continental breakfast. AAA and AARP discounts.

Pet Charges & Deposits: $7 per day

Pet Policy: Pets must not be left unattended.

Amenities: Cable TV, refrigerators.

Pet Amenities: Dog runs. Exercise area. Wells State Park is located on Route 49. Nature trails nearby.

Rated: 2 Paws — 32 rooms.

Nestled among beautiful pine trees, Days Inn has cable television, air conditioning and a swimming pool. It's only about a mile from Old Sturbridge Village, where you can literally step back in time to the early 19th century. This 200-acre living history museum authentically recreates life in a rural New England community around the early 1800s. In addition to sightseeing, Sturbridge and the surrounding area boasts numerous fine antique, gift and specialty shops. The motel is within easy access to major highways and cities in New England: Boston is 59 miles away, Hartford 39 miles distant, Worcester is 22 miles away and Providence, Rhode Island is only 45 miles away.

Cape Cod Claddagh Country Inn

77 Main Street West
West Harwich, MA 02671-0667
800-356-9628 • 508-432-9628
www.capecodcladdaghinn.com
claddagh@capecod.net

Type of Lodging: Irish Inn
Room Rates: $120–$150, including full or continental breakfast. AAA, AARP, AKC, ABA and *10% (3 or more nights only) Pets Welcome™* discount.
Pet Charges & Deposits: Call for charges and deposit information.
Pet Policy: Sorry, no cats. Small pets only. Designated rooms only. Manager's prior approval required. Pets must not be left unattended.
Amenities: Cable TV, refrigerators, pool, Irish Pub.
Pet Amenities: Exercise area. Conservation Lands Park and National Seashore Park nearby.
Rated: 2 Paws — 9 rooms.

This is surely one of the most unusual and charming lodgings we've found in New England, reminiscent of a small Irish manor. Comfortably decorated with antiques, oriental rugs and lace curtains "like Grandma's house," it is an eclectic mix of the best of New England. The Claddagh, a delightfully Irish, intimate pub serves homemade meals—a place where good craic (conversation) prevails. It's right in the middle of Cape Cod, "just at the dimple before the crook of the elbow." It's 1½ hours from Boston or Providence and you can make an easy day trip to Nantucket, Martha's Vineyard, Plymouth or Provincetown.

Jericho Valley Inn

2541 Hancock Road
Williamstown, MA 01267
800-537-246 • 413-458-9511
www.jerichovalleyinn.com
jvinn@bcn.net

Type of Lodging: Motel
Room Rates: $138–$258, including continental breakfast. AAA discount.
Pet Charges & Deposits: None.
Pet Policy: Designated rooms only. Manager's prior approval required.
Amenities: Cable TV, refrigerators, pool, full kitchens, fireplaces.
Pet Amenities: List of nearby veterinarians maintained. Exercise area. Park nearby.
Rated: 3 Paws — 10 rooms and 25 cottages.

Jericho Valley Inn, located in the Berkshires in a quiet mountain setting, has lovely views. It's secluded, with miles of hiking trails for you and your pet. In winter, you'll find skiing at Jiminy Peak Mountain Resort. The Sterling and Francine Clark Art Institute, near the Williams College campus, houses an impressive collection of 15th through 19th century works of art, including paintings by Corot, Degas, Fragonard, Francesca, Gainsborough, Goya, Winslow Homer, Manet, Monet, Renoir, John Singer Sargent and Gilbert Stuart, as well as sculptures by Rodin and Degas.

MICHIGAN

Nicknames: Great Lakes State; Wolverine State
Population: 9,863,775
Area: 96,705 square miles
Climate: Well-defined seasons tempered by the Great Lakes
Capital: Lansing
Entered Union: January 26, 1837
Motto: *Si Quaeris Peninsulam Amoenam, Circumspice* (If you seek a pleasant peninsula, look around you).
Song: Michigan, My Michigan

Flower: Apple Blossom
Tree: White Pine
Bird: Robin
Famous Wolverines: Ralph Bunche, Thomas Edison, Edna Ferber, Gerald Ford, Henry Ford, Aretha Franklin, Lee Iacocca, Magic Johnson, Elmore Leonard, Charles Lindbergh, Joe Louis, Madonna, Diana Ross, Glenn Seaborg, Tom Selleck, Lily Tomlin.

History: Ojibwa, Ottawa, Miami, Potawatomi and Huron peoples predated European fur traders and missionaries, who visited the area in 1616. French settlements were taken over by the British in 1763. The Treaty of Paris ceded Michigan to the United States in 1783. The British seized Fort Mackinac in 1812, but after Perry's Lake Erie victory and William Henry Harrison's victory near the Thames River in 1813, the British retreated to Canada. In the 20th century the advent of the automobile and the "Motown Sound" made Detroit a household word.

BATTLE CREEK, MICHIGAN (Pop. 53,500)

Hampton Inn of Battle Creek

1150 Riverside Drive
Battle Creek, MI 49017
888-313-8991 • 616-979-5577
www.hampton-inn.com

Type of Lodging: Hotel
Room Rates: $68–$84, including continental breakfast. AAA, AARP and *10% Pets Welcome™* discounts.
Pet Charges & Deposits: Call for refundable deposit information.
Pet Policy: No pets over 40 lbs. Designated rooms only.
Amenities: Cable TV, pool, whirlpool, coffeemakers, irons and ironing boards.
Pet Amenities: List of nearby veterinarians maintained. Willard Beach is located at Goquac Lake on Capital Avenue. Friendship Park is located on McAmley and Capital Avenue.
Rated: 3 Paws — 64 rooms and 8 suites.

Hampton Inn is a great hotel with upscale accommodations. Cable television, heated indoor pool and whirlpool, free local calls and kids staying free are among some of the amenities. Across the street from Lakeview Square Mall and several popular restaurants, the Hampton Inn is near Kellogg's Cereal City, Full Blast and Binder Park Zoo. The latter features exotic animals in a natural park setting. The Zoo has wooden boardwalks and a conservation adventure station with hands-on activities.

Pointes North Inn

101 Michigan Avenue
Charlevoix, MI 49720
231-547-0055
www.pointesnorthcharlevoix.com
pointes@voyager.net

Type of Lodging: Hotel-Motel

Room Rates: $75–$250, including continental breakfast. AARP discount.

Pet Charges & Deposits: $5 per day.

Pet Policy: None. All Pets Welcome.

Amenities: Cable TV, refrigerators, microwaves, pool, Jacuzzi.

Pet Amenities: List of nearby veterinarians maintained. Exercise area. Park nearby.

Rated: 3 Paws — 19 suites.

Pointes North Inn is a fine choice if you're in the area of Charlevoix, which is way up the Peninsula on the western side of Lake Michigan. Charlevoix's early history is linked to the intriguing machinations of the Mormon monarchy on Beaver Island. Today, it's a resort center that offers excellent boating and beaches. The city has musical entertainment during the summer months. There's ferry service to Beaver Island.

Best Western Royal Crest Motel

803 South Otsego Avenue
Gaylord, MI 49735
800-876-9252 • 517-732-6451

Type of Lodging: Motel

Room Rates: $59–$99, including continental breakfast. AAA and AARP discounts.

Pet Charges & Deposits: None.

Pet Policy: No pets over 35 lbs. Pets must not be left unattended. Limit one pet per room.

Amenities: Cable TV, pool, whirlpool, hot tubs, spas.

Pet Amenities: List of nearby veterinarians maintained. Dog runs. Exercise area. City park and trails are located at the end of Commerce Boulevard.

Rated: 3 Paws — 44 rooms.

Best Western Royal Crest Motel is situated on beautifully landscaped grounds in the center of Michigan's scenic North Woods. Championship golf courses, pristine lakes and streams, peaceful remote forests, fabulous winter sports and recreation areas surround it. The guestrooms have touch-tone phones and dataports, coffeemakers, free local calls and kids stay free in their parents' room. While in Gaylord, be sure to see the Call Of The Wild Museum, which displays more than 150 lifelike North American wild animals, complete with sound effects.

Exel Inn of Grand Rapids

4855 28th Street Southeast
Grand Rapids, MI 49512
800-367-3935 • 616-957-3000
www.exelinns.com

Type of Lodging: Hotel

Room Rates: $46–$70, including continental breakfast. AARP discount.

Pet Charges & Deposits: $100–$200 refundable deposit on extended stays.

Pet Policy: No pets over 25 lbs. Designated rooms only. Manager's prior approval required. Limit two pets to each room.

Amenities: Cable TV, hairdryers, coffeemakers, irons, full-length mirrors.

Pet Amenities: None.

Rated: 2 Paws — 109 rooms.

Exel Inn offers price conscious and tidy accommodations in Grand Rapids, a vigorous industrial and convention center. Grand Center on Monroe Avenue has large convention and exhibit halls. The Voigt House, an opulent 19th century Victorian, retains the original furnishings of the first owners. The Gerald Ford Museum displays the private life and public career of President Gerald Ford, including a re-creation of the Ford Paint and Varnish Company where he had worked as a boy.

Hampton Inn

4981 28th Street Southeast
Grand Rapids, MI 49513
616-956-9304

Type of Lodging: Hotel

Room Rates: $65–$85, including continental breakfast. AAA and AARP discounts.

Pet Charges & Deposits: None.

Pet Policy: Pets must not be left unattended.

Amenities: Cable TV, pool, free local calls.

Pet Amenities: None.

Rated: 3 Paws — 120 rooms.

Hampton Inn has a 100% satisfaction guarantee. Lovely rooms assure you a good night's rest. Start your day off right with a variety of breakfast rolls, cereals, milk, juice, coffee and more. It's adjacent to Carlos Murphy's Restaurant and Lounge and has a conference room that accommodates up to 40 people. The Van Andel Museum Center has exhibits depicting the heritage and manufacturing traditions of Grand Rapids, including a partially operational reconstruction of an early 20th century furniture factory.

North Country Lodge

615 Interstate 75 Business Loop
P.O. Box 290
Grayling, MI 49738
800-475-6300 • 517-348-8471
ncl@grayling-mi.com

Type of Lodging: Motel

Room Rates: $50–$160, including coffee and juice. AAA, AARP and **8%** *Pets Welcome*™ discounts.

Pet Charges & Deposits: None.

Pet Policy: Designated rooms only.

Amenities: Cable TV, refrigerators, microwaves, whirlpool, kitchenettes.

Pet Amenities: List of nearby veterinarians maintained. Dog runs. Exercise area. Hartwick Pines State Park nearby.

Rated: 3 Paws — 20 rooms and 4 suites.

North Country Lodge has been serving the public for 30 years. Beautiful knotty pine paneling covers the walls in the original section of the Lodge. Hand-painted pictures by Judy Craft, who, along with husband Carl serve as hosts, are displayed in the Lodge as well as in all the rooms. Open year-round, North Country Lodge offers air conditioning and cable television in all rooms. Grayling is on the Au Sable River, about ⅔ of the way up the Peninsula. Although the grayling no longer inhabits nearby rivers, the town remains an embarkation point for trout fishing, canoeing, cross-country skiing and snowmobiling expeditions.

Harbor Springs Cottage Inn

145 Zoll Street
Harbor Springs, MI 49740
213-526-5431
www.harborsprings-mi.com/cottage
cottage@freeway.net

Type of Lodging: Inn

Room Rates: $62–$185, including continental breakfast. Senior discount.

Pet Charges & Deposits: $5 per day.

Pet Policy: None. All Pets Welcome.

Amenities: Refrigerators, microwaves.

Pet Amenities: Great Danes in residence.

Rated: 3 Paws — 21 rooms and 3 suites.

This traditional, one-story Inn offers the convenience of separate entrances and private baths with warm atmosphere including breakfast treats and the morning newspaper. A variety of guestrooms offer brass beds with antiques, refrigerators and efficiency kitchens or full kitchens. Unique shops and restaurants of Harbor Springs, the beach, the harbor and shoreline sights, the deer park and duck pond are all within an easy walk of the inn. The two resident Harlequin Great Danes are always ready for a W-A-L-K and the iced tea is always cold.

Blue Mill Inn

409 South U.S. 31
Holland, MI 49423
888-258-3140 • 616-392-7073

Type of Lodging: Motel
Room Rates: $35–$80. AAA, AARP, AKC, ABA and *10% Pets Welcome™* discounts.
Pet Charges & Deposits: $5 per day.
Pet Policy: Designated rooms only.
Amenities: Cable TV.
Pet Amenities: List of nearby veterinarians maintained. Exercise area. Van Ralte Farm is located at 16th and Country Club Drive.
Rated: 2 Paws — 81 rooms.

Calling itself "a motel with a Dutch touch," the Blue Mill Inn wants you to have a relaxed and enjoyable stay. All rooms have individual climate controls, direct dial phones, cable television, full tile bath and showers, with extra-long double and king-sized beds. Keep in shape by walking to nearby restaurants, shopping centers, miniature golf and the Wooden Shoe Factory. Within a mile or two, you'll find Dutch Village, Windmill Island, Poll Museum, the Veldeer Tulip Farm, DeKlomp Wooden Shoe & Delft factory, the Netherland Museum and the Baker Museum. If you haven't guessed by now, Holland, settled by Dutch immigrants in 1847, remains the quintessential Dutch town in America.

Days Inn

6692 Newark Road
Imlay City, MI 48444
800-DAYS INN • 810-724-8005
www.daysinn.com

Type of Lodging: Hotel
Room Rates: $50–$85, including continental breakfast. AAA, AARP and *10% Pets Welcome™* discounts.
Pet Charges & Deposits: $8 per day. $50 refundable deposit.
Pet Policy: Pets must not be left unattended.
Amenities: Cable TV, refrigerators, microwaves, pool, hot tubs.
Pet Amenities: List of nearby veterinarians maintained. Dog runs. Exercise area. Lion's Park is located on Black Corners Road.
Rated: 3 Paws — 60 rooms and 6 suites. Days Inn Chairman's Award Winner

Days Inn is located in Imlay City, the self-styled "Gateway to the Thumb" in eastern Michigan. The motel is a scant quarter mile from Eastern Michigan Fairgrounds, within an easy drive of Flint or Port Huron, not that far from Detroit.

Super 8 Motel

6951 Newark Road
Imlay City, MI 48444
810-724-8700

Type of Lodging: Motel

Room Rates: $49–$62, including continental breakfast. AAA, AARP and *10% Pets Welcome™* discounts.

Pet Charges & Deposits: $4–$8 per day. $50 refundable deposit or credit card imprint.

Pet Policy: None.

Amenities: Cable TV, refrigerators, whirlpool, spas, playground, BBQ picnic area.

Pet Amenities: Dog runs.

Rated: 3 Paws — 60 rooms, 2 suites and 3 whirlpool rooms. Super 8 Blue Ribbon Award Winner.

Super 8's Imlay City lodging has tidy, comfortable and modern rooms in a two-story facility with interior corridors. It features a spa and fitness room, a hospitality/meeting suite, free local calls, coffee and kids stay free in their parents' room. Shopping and restaurants are within walking distance and it's easily accessible to Interstate 69.

Days Inn

West 8176 South U.S. 2
Iron Mountain, MI 49801
800-883-5335 • 906-774-2181
www.daysinn.com

Type of Lodging: Hotel

Room Rates: $43–$100, including continental breakfast. AAA, AARP and *10% Pets Welcome™* discounts.

Pet Charges & Deposits: $6 per day.

Pet Policy: Sorry, no male cats. Designated rooms only.

Amenities: Cable TV, refrigerators, microwaves, pool, whirlpools.

Pet Amenities: List of nearby veterinarians maintained. Exercise area. City park nearby.

Rated: 2 Paws — 44 rooms and 5 suites.

The Days Inn features large rooms with free local calls, computer modem hookup and many modern conveniences. Iron Mountain was established in 1879, following the discovery of rich iron deposits. Mines continued to operate into the 1940s. Area attractions include Lake Antoine Park, Pine Mountain Ski Jump, Fumee Lake Natural Area and shopping complexes.

White Rabbit Inn Bed & Breakfast

14634 Red Arrow Highway
P.O. Box 725
Lakeside, MI 49116-0725
800-967-2224 • 616-469-4620
www.whiterabbitinn.com
info@whiterabbitinn.com

Type of Lodging: B&B

Room Rates: $95–$200, including continental breakfast.

Pet Charges & Deposits: None.

Pet Policy: Designated rooms only. Manager's prior approval required.

Amenities: Cable TV, refrigerators, microwaves, hot tubs, wood-burning stoves.

Pet Amenities: List of nearby veterinarians maintained.

Rated: 3 Paws — 6 rooms and 2 cabins.

The White Rabbit Inn is a small bed and breakfast located in the lovely little village of Lakeside, only 90 minutes from the hustle and bustle of downtown Chicago, 3½ hours from Detroit or Indianapolis. Six rooms each feature a whirlpool bath, two have gas fireplaces, and all are uniquely decorated with rustic furniture. The two knotty pine cabins each have a kitchen, wood burning stove and a private outdoor hot tub. Antique stores, art galleries, gourmet restaurants and wineries surround it. Nearby are majestic dunes, wooded trails and Lake Michigan. This is the ultimate romantic spot.

Holiday Inn Express

5323 U.S. Highway 10 West
Ludington, MI 49431
888-845-7004 • 231-845-7004

Type of Lodging: Hotel

Room Rates: $79–$169, including continental breakfast. AAA, AARP and *10% Pets Welcome™* discounts.

Pet Charges & Deposits: $10 per stay.

Pet Policy: Designated rooms only.

Amenities: Cable TV, refrigerators, microwaves, safes, pool, whirlpool, spas.

Pet Amenities: List of nearby veterinarians maintained. Dog runs. Exercise area. Ludington City Park is located on Ludington Avenue. Ludington State Park is located on M 116.

Rated: 3 Paws — 100 rooms and 2 suites.

Holiday Inn Express is a fine lodging with upscale amenities. The Badger Car Ferry crossing to Wisconsin is close by. Beautifully restored, two-century-old White Pine Village contains the entertaining and informative Lumbering and Maritime Museums, an authentic one-room schoolhouse, a fully-functioning general store, blacksmith's shop and much more. Ludington State Park features sandy beaches on Lake Michigan, a beautiful skyline trail overlooking 5,300 acres of rolling sand dunes and the 1867 Big Sable Point Lighthouse.

Naders Lakeshore Motor Lodge

612 North Lakeshore Drive
Ludington, MI 49431
800-968-0109 • 231-843-8757

Type of Lodging: Motor Lodge

Room Rates: $45–$100, including free coffee. AARP and *5% (off-season)* *Pets Welcome™* discounts.

Pet Charges & Deposits: None.

Pet Policy: Manager's prior approval required. Pets must be leashed and must not be left unattended.

Amenities: Cable TV, refrigerators, microwaves, pool, Jacuzzi.

Pet Amenities: List of nearby veterinarians maintained. Exercise area. Ludington State Park is on located on M 116.

Rated: 2 Paws — 22 rooms and 3 suites.

Every room at Naders Lakeshore Motor Lodge is spacious and elegantly furnished. Sliding glass doors open to your own patio. The Lodge is close to charter boat services, dune scooter rides, Lake Michigan Car Ferry Boat Trips and the pleasures of Michigan's "Gold Coast."

The Beach House

P.O. Box 141
Mackinaw City, MI 49701
800-262-5353 • 231-436-5353
www.mackinawcity.com/beachhouse
beach@freeway.net

Type of Lodging: Motel

Room Rates: $39–$150, including continental breakfast. AAA discount. Open May to October.

Pet Charges & Deposits: $10 per stay.

Pet Policy: Manager's prior approval required.

Amenities: Cable TV, refrigerators, pool, whirlpool.

Pet Amenities: List of nearby veterinarians maintained. Dog runs.

Rated: 2 Paws — 28 rooms.

The Beach House features a variety of units on Lake Huron. Clean, cozy cottages and kitchenette units are available. There's a sandy swimming beach, indoor pool, whirlpool, picnic area and views of Mackinac Bridge and Mackinac Island. For a relatively small city, the "Guardian of the Straits of Mackinac" has spectacular attractions. Colonial Michilimackinac is on the site of the fort of the same name and reenacts the history of the fort. Historic Mill Creek features an 18th century industrial complex with a water-powered sawmill. Mackinac City is at the very top of Michigan's "Lower Peninsula."

Westwood Suites

2782 U.S. Highway 41 West
Marquette, MI 49855
877-226-2314 • 906-226-2314

Type of Lodging: Motel

Suite Rates: $55. AAA, AARP, AKC and *10% Pets Welcome*™ discounts.

Pet Charges & Deposits: $6 per stay.

Pet Policy: None. All Pets Welcome.

Amenities: Cable TV, refrigerators, microwaves, restaurant.

Pet Amenities: List of nearby veterinarians maintained. Mattson Park is located on Lakeside Boulevard.

Rated: 3 Paws — 25 suites.

Westwood Suites features newly renovated rooms, a full service restaurant and weekly rates. There are banquet and meeting rooms. Marquette is on Michigan's Upper Peninsula, a finger peninsula that separates Superior, Michigan and Huron Great Lakes. Nearby, at Negaunee, is the Michigan Iron Industry Museum, site of the first forge in the Lake Superior region.

Howard Johnson Express Inn

2516 Tenth Street
Menominee, MI 49858
906-863-4431

Type of Lodging: Motel

Room Rates: $40–$70, including continental breakfast. AAA and AARP discounts.

Pet Charges & Deposits: None.

Pet Policy: None. All Pets Welcome.

Amenities: Cable TV, whirlpool.

Pet Amenities: List of nearby veterinarians maintained. Exercise area. Henes Park is located on Henes Park Drive.

Rated: 3 Paws — 50 rooms and 3 suites.

The Menominee Howard Johnson Inn is five minutes from the downtown Menominee waterfront and from Marinette, Wisconsin. There are five restaurants within walking distance. All rooms feature king- or queen-sized beds and cable television. Menominee is on the shores of Green Bay, adjacent to the Menominee River.

Comfort Inn

6500 East Albain
Monroe, MI 48161
734-384-1500

Type of Lodging: Motel
Room Rates: $69–$124, including continental breakfast. AAA and AARP discounts.
Pet Charges & Deposits: $10 per day.
Pet Policy: Designated rooms only.
Amenities: Cable TV, safes, pool, whirlpools.
Pet Amenities: Sterling State Park nearby.
Rated: 3 Paws – 64 rooms.

Great rooms are guaranteed at Comfort Inn. It's located a mile from historic downtown Monroe, across from the Horizon Outlet Center, adjacent to the New Golf Course and a mile from charter fishing. The French at the site of a Native American village founded one of the oldest communities in the state, Monroe in 1780. The settlement, originally called Frenchtown, was the site of the River Raisin Massacre in 1813. General George Custer lived in Monroe for several years before starting his army career. Monroe, at the southeast corner of the state, is convenient to Detroit and the surrounding areas.

Quality Inn & Suites - Paw Paw

153 Ampey Road
P.O. Box 228
Paw Paw, MI 49079
800-228-5151 • 616-655-0303
www.choicehotels.com/hotel/MI154

Type of Lodging: Hotel
Room Rates: $55–$120, including continental breakfast. AAA, AARP and *10% Pets Welcome™* discounts.
Pet Charges & Deposits: $10 refundable deposit.
Pet Policy: Designated rooms only. Pets must be on leashes and must not left unattended.
Amenities: Cable TV, refrigerators, microwaves, pool, hot tubs.
Pet Amenities: List of nearby veterinarians maintained. Exercise area. Maple Island nearby.
Rated: 3 Paws – 48 rooms and 17 suites. Quality Inn Gold Hospitality Award Winner.

Quality Inn is delightfully upscale, with double queen rooms, king rooms, king suites with microwaves and refrigerators, free local calls, dataports and a fitness center. Paw Paw, in the southwest corner of the Lower Peninsula, is the heart of Michigan's wine country! St. Julian Winery and Warner Winery are within ½ mile of the Inn. Timber Ridge & Swiss Valley Ski Areas are a scant 15 miles away.

Budget Host Inn

700 North State Street
St. Ignace, MI 49781
800-872-7057 • 906-643-9666
www.stignacebudgethost.com
stay@stignacebudgethost.com

Type of Lodging: Motel

Room Rates: $44–$158, including continental breakfast. AAA and AARP discounts.

Pet Charges & Deposits: $20 refundable deposit.

Pet Policy: Designated rooms only. Pets must not be left unattended.

Amenities: Cable TV, refrigerators, microwaves, pool, Jacuzzi, guest laundry, game room.

Pet Amenities: List of nearby veterinarians maintained. City park is located on Ferry Lane.

Rated: 2 Paws — 41 rooms and 17 suites. Budget Host Inn of the Year for six years running.

Budget Host – St. Ignace is located at the bottom tip of the Upper Peninsula, practically at the junction of Lakes Superior, Huron and Michigan. Every room opens to an enclosed hall for easy access to the indoor pool, whirlpool spa, video game arcade, guest laundry and snack area. See and do everything in the area—the majestic Mackinac Bridge, Mackinac Island, museums, forts, quaint shops, casinos, beaches and fine dining. Each season brings opportunities to enjoy a different aspect of this remarkable area.

Firefly Resort

15657 Lake Shore Road
Union Pier, MI 49129
616-469-0245
www.fireflyresort.com
info@fireflyresort.com

Type of Lodging: Resort

Room Rates: $75–$135. *10% Pets Welcome™* discount.

Pet Charges & Deposits: $20 per stay.

Pet Policy: None. All Pets Welcome.

Amenities: Cable TV, stoves, refrigerators.

Pet Amenities: List of nearby veterinarians maintained. Exercise area.

Rated: 2 Paws — 16 rooms, 2 suites, 1 guesthouse and 1 cottage.

Firefly Resort, only 1½ hours from Chicago, has been voted "Best of the Best" by Chicago Magazine. It's directly across the street from Lake Michigan. The resort's private grounds feature outdoor grills, picnic areas, perennial gardens and a tennis court. Firefly Resort is minutes from Harbor County's diverse restaurants and activities which include golfing, horseback riding, shopping, fishing, boating, cross-country skiing, snowmobiling trails and much more. Not to be missed are the famous antique shops, galleries, fresh fruit and vegetable stands, local vineyards, Warren Dunes and Michigan's most beautiful beaches.

Sweethaven Resort

9517 Union Pier Road
Union Pier, MI 49129
616-469-0332
www.sweethavenresort.com

Type of Lodging: Resort
Cottage Rates: $135–$215.
Pet Charges & Deposits: None.
Pet Policy: Limit two pets per cottage.
Amenities: Fully equipped kitchens, Jacuzzi, hot tubs, decks, screened porches.
Pet Amenities: Buster, the host dog, in residence. List of nearby veterinarians maintained. Exercise area.
Rated: 5 Paws — 5 cottages.

Imagine a beautiful country cottage, a great room with valued ceiling and fireplace, a private deck, a well-equipped kitchen, roomy baths and sunny bedrooms with quilt-covered beds. Sweethaven's community of three acres plus six acres of woods offer its guests privacy, lots of year-round outdoor activities and room to roam. Just minutes from Lake Michigan, restaurants, golf courses, horseback riding and shopping, it's open all year and welcomes you, your children and your pets. The host dog, Buster, is Sweethaven's official greeter. His other duties include charming the pants off the two-legged guests and wearing out the four-legged guests so they sleep at night. Buster gets lots of fan mail.

MINNESOTA

Nicknames: North Star State; Gopher State
Population: 4,775,508
Area: 86,943 square miles
Climate: Northern part lies in the moist Great Lakes storm belt; western border lies at the edge of the semi-arid Great Plains.
Capital: St. Paul
Entered Union: May 11,1858
Motto: *L'Etoile du Nord* (The star of the North).
Song: Hail! Minnesota.

Flower: Pink and White Lady's Slipper
Tree: Red Pine
Bird: Common Loon
Famous Minnesotans: Warren Burger, William O. Douglas, Bob Dylan, F. Scott Fitzgerald, Judy Garland, Garrison Keilor, Sinclair Lewis, William and Charles Mayo, Eugene McCarthy, Walter Mondale, Charles Schultz, Jesse Ventura.

 History: Dakota Sioux were early inhabitants of the area. In the 16th century, Ojibwa moved in. French fur traders entered the area in the mid-17th century. Britain took the area east of the Mississippi in 1763. The U.S. took over that portion after the Revolutionary War, and, in 1803, gained the remainder through the Louisiana Purchase. The Territory of Minnesota was created in 1849. Always a maverick state in politics, Minnesota's current governor, former professional wrestler Jesse "The Body" Ventura, is emblematic.

ALBERT LEA, MINNESOTA (Pop. 18,300)

Countryside Inn Motel

2101 East Main Street
Albert Lea, MN 56007
800-373-1188 • 507-373-2446

Type of Lodging: Motel
Room Rates: $34–$65, including continental breakfast. AAA and AARP discounts.
Pet Charges & Deposits: Call for charges information.
Pet Policy: Designated rooms only. Manager's prior approval required.
Amenities: Cable TV, refrigerators, microwaves, free local phone calls.
Pet Amenities: List of nearby veterinarians maintained. Exercise area.
Rated: 2 Paws — 49 rooms.

Countryside Inn is a good budget-conscious choice in Albert Lea. There are varied room sizes and vintages. Albert Lea is practically on the Iowa border. The construction of a dam for a water-powered mill in 1855 led to the creation of Fountain Lake. The city of Albert Lea soon grew up around that lake and today it is an attractive southern Minnesota venue. Freeborn County Historical Society and Pioneer Village is a collection of 19th century buildings that depict life, as it was when the city was founded.

Timber Bay Lodge and Houseboats

8347 Timber Bay Road
P.O. Box 248
Babbitt, MN 55706
800-846-6821 • 218-827-3682
www.timberbay.com

Type of Lodging: Resort

Cabin & Houseboat Rates: Call for daily and/or weekly rates.

Pet Charges & Deposits: $10 per day. $50 per week.

Pet Policy: None. All Pets Welcome.

Amenities: Vary from cabins to houseboats.

Pet Amenities: None.

Rated: 3 Paws — 12 private cabins and 5 houseboats.

If you enjoy camping, boating and fishing, you'll love Timber Bay Houseboats. Explore 20-mile-long Birch Lake with its many miles of forested shoreline and rocky islands. Take your small boat to the base of the foaming rapids of the Stony River or paddle a canoe up the Kawishiwi River. At night, anchor in a secluded bay and sleep with the sounds of wind in the pines and the gentle motion of your floating home. Houseboats range in size from 30 feet to 44 feet, accommodating 2 to 10 people. The boats are completely modern with hot and cold running water, propane gas stove, oven and refrigerator, microwave, pollution-free toilet and shower. Furnishings include pillows, blankets, cooking utensils, linens, deck furniture, a charcoal grill and even the ice chest. The deluxe log-sided, knotty-pine cabins feature wood-burning fireplaces, color TVs, showers and decks.

Best Western Bemidji Inn

2420 Paul Bunyan Drive
Bemidji, MN 56601
218-751-0390
www.bestwestern.com/bemidjiinn

Type of Lodging: Motel

Room Rates: $49–$70, including continental breakfast. AAA, AARP and *10% Pets Welcome*™ discounts.

Pet Charges & Deposits: Call for deposit information.

Pet Policy: Small pets only. Designated rooms only.

Amenities: Cable TV, pool, whirlpool.

Pet Amenities: Park nearby.

Rated: 2 Paws — 58 rooms and 2 suites.

Conveniently located at the intersection of two highways, Best Western is a fine choice if you're traveling in Paul Bunyan country. Paul Bunyan Amusement Park is three miles distant. Bemidji State University is 1½ miles away. Bemidji, from the Chippewa word "lake with river flowing through," is the legendary home of the mythical Paul Bunyan and Babe the Blue Ox. There are massive statues of the pair on the lakefront. Bemidji is the first city on the Mississippi River.

Best Western Thunderbird Hotel & Convention Center

2201 East 78th Street
Bloomington, MN 55425-1228
800-328-1931 • 952-854-3411

Type of Lodging: Hotel

Room Rates: $88–$150. AAA and AARP discounts.

Pet Charges & Deposits: None.

Pet Policy: Designated rooms only.

Amenities: Cable TV, pool, whirlpool, Jacuzzi, fitness room, sauna, game room, restaurants, lounge.

Pet Amenities: List of nearby veterinarians maintained. Exercise area. Fort Snelling State Park nearby.

Rated: 3 Paws — 248 rooms and 15 suites on 15 acres.

Best Western Thunderbird is an upscale, modern, beautifully maintained lodging on a 15-acre site. It is precisely two blocks away from the Mall of America. Inside the mall, there is a full-scale amusement park, Knott's Camp Snoopy, which includes a roller coaster! There are dozens of restaurants, sports bars and nightclubs. UnderWater World, in the Mall, features a 1.2 million gallon walk-through aquarium. Bloomington is within the suburban limits of Minnesota's twin cities, Minneapolis and St. Paul, and the Hotel is only four miles from Minneapolis-St. Paul International Airport.

Exel Inn of Minneapolis

2701 East 78th Street
Bloomington, MN 55425
800-367-3935 • 612-854-7200
www.exelinns.com

Type of Lodging: Hotel

Room Rates: $65–$89, including continental breakfast. AARP discount.

Pet Charges & Deposits: $100–$200 refundable deposit on extended stays.

Pet Policy: No pets over 25 lbs. Designated rooms only. Manager's prior approval required. Limit two pets per room.

Amenities: Hairdryers, irons, coffeemakers, full-length mirrors.

Pet Amenities: None.

Rated: 2 Paws — 203 rooms.

Exel Inn is a fine, budget-conscious chain, and the Minneapolis-Bloomington unit is no exception. It's conveniently located right near the Mall Of America, the Twin Cities' primary magnet. You'll spend a wonderfully wacky time at Minneapolis' Museum of Questionable Medical Devices, which contains more than 200 quack medical devices dating from 1790. The scope and range of these artifacts is limited only by your imagination.

Super 8 Motel

1101 Burnsville Parkway
Burnsville, MN 55337
800-800-8000 • 952-894-3400
www.innworks.com

Type of Lodging: Motel

Room Rates: $55–$75, including continental breakfast. AAA and AARP discounts.

Pet Charges & Deposits: $10 per stay.

Pet Policy: Sorry, no cats. Manager's prior approval required.

Amenities: Cable TV, safes, one free 8-minute long distance call each night

Pet Amenities: Exercise area.

Rated: 2 Paws – 67 rooms.

Super 8 is a budget-friendly choice for lodging in the greater Minneapolis-St. Paul area. Although the pioneers arrived in 1850, Burnsville did not become an incorporated city until 1965. The Twin Cities offer all the entertainment, educational and cultural facilities of a major metropolitan area, while retaining small town friendliness. The Walker Art Center in Minneapolis is one of the premier venues for American art of the past two centuries, while the Minnesota Children's Museum and the State Capitol are highlights of St. Paul. Jesse Ventura, perhaps America's most colorful political figure, is easily reachable—he conducts a call-in "Lunch with the Governor" radio show.

Best Western Edgewater

2400 London Road
Duluth, MN 55812
800-777-7925 • 218-728-3601
www.bestwestern.com/edgewatereast
bestwesternedgewater@zmchotels.com

Type of Lodging: Motel

Room Rates: $49–$139, including continental breakfast and cocktail party. AAA and AARP discounts.

Pet Charges & Deposits: None.

Pet Policy: Designated rooms only. Pets must not be left unattended.

Amenities: Cable TV, refrigerators, pool, whirlpool, playground.

Pet Amenities: Exercise area. Duluth Lakewalk is adjacent to the parking lot. Park nearby.

Rated: 3 Paws – 262 rooms and 20 suites.

The Best Western Edgewater allows you to treat yourself to the finest accommodations, even on a family budget. The lodging is at the edge of the water, yet in the heart of the city. Duluth is strategically positioned on the extreme western corner of Lake Superior. While in Duluth, be sure to visit the new Great Lakes Aquarium, America's only all-freshwater aquarium, which features five habitats from around Lake Superior filled with countless species of fish, mammals, reptiles, amphibians and birds.

Holiday Inn Express Hotel & Suites

1950 Rahncliff Court
Eagan, MN 55122
800-681-5290 • 651-681-9266
www.holidayinneagan.com

Type of Lodging: Hotel
Room Rates: $80–$190, including continental breakfast. AAA and AARP discounts.
Pet Charges & Deposits: $10 per day. Call for deposit information.
Pet Policy: None. All Pets Welcome.
Amenities: Cable TV, safes, pool, fitness room, whirlpools.
Pet Amenities: Small park is located a block from the hotel.
Rated: 3 Paws — 60 rooms and 60 suites.

You get much more than just a good night's sleep at Holiday Inn Express in Eagan. There's an indoor swimming pool, whirlpool, 24-hour airport transportation and Mall of America shuttle service. There are conference facilities and the high Holiday Inn standards of cleanliness and comfort. Eagan is just 15 minutes east of Minneapolis-St. Paul Airport. While it is convenient to the Twin Cities, Eagan has its own prime attraction—Caponi Art Park with contemporary sculptures set in 60 acres of rolling hills and woods. The Scherer Flower Garden, within the park, contains six acres of perennials, annuals, shrubs and trees on a private residence on Thomas Lake.

Gunflint Pines Resort & Campgrounds

217 South Gunflint Lake Road
Grand Marais, MN 55604
800-533-5814 • 218-388-4454
www.gunflintpines.com
play@gunflintpines.com

Type of Lodging: Resort
Cabin Rates: $110–$135. Call for weekly rates.
Pet Charges & Deposits: $10 per day. $50 per week.
Pet Policy: None. All Pets Welcome.
Amenities: Fully equipped kitchens, fireplaces, decks.
Pet Amenities: None.
Rated: 3 Paws — 6 cabins.

Nestled in the pine-crested high country of northern Minnesota and at the doorstep of a federal wilderness area is Gunflint Pines Resort. The resort has both modern, A-frame housekeeping cabins and complete campground facilities. Each cabin is fully carpeted, with your choice of three or four bedrooms, 1½ baths and a fully equipped kitchen. A fireplace and large picture window overlooking Gunflint Lake complete the vacation atmosphere. Gunflint Lake and connecting waterways offer the fisherman abundant opportunity to catch walleyes, lake trout, smallmouth bass and northerns. Try a leisurely canoe paddle to Little Rock Falls and have a picnic. Photography and wildlife watching can also be rewarding here. Or just sit back and revel in nature's beauty at its finest.

Country Inn by Carlson

2601 South Highway 169
Grand Rapids, MN 55744
800-456-4000 • 218-327-4960

Type of Lodging: Hotel

Room Rates: $60–$74, including continental breakfast. AAA and AARP discounts.

Pet Charges & Deposits: None.

Pet Policy: None. All Pets Welcome.

Amenities: Pool, whirlpool, irons and ironing boards.

Pet Amenities: None.

Rated: 3 Paws — 46 rooms.

Here you will find cozy rooms, a complimentary breakfast and great rates. You'll feel the country charm throughout, in the fireplace, hardwood floors and personal touches of home. Country Inn by Carlson offers small-town hospitality while offering area attractions such as the Judy Garland House, Forest History Center, golf and cross-country skiing.

Hinckley Gold Pine Inn

Route 2, Box 384
Hinckley, MN 55037
888-384-6112 • 320-384-6112
www.goldpinebw.com
goldpine@pinenet.com

Type of Lodging: Motel

Room Rates: $52–$109, including coffee and cookies. AAA and AARP discounts.

Pet Charges & Deposits: $5 per day.

Pet Policy: No pets over 30 lbs. Pets must not be left unattended.

Amenities: Cable TV, refrigerators, microwaves, Jacuzzis.

Pet Amenities: List of nearby veterinarians maintained. Exercise area. Westside Park is located a block west of Highway 61. St. Croix State Park is located off Highway 48.

Rated: 2 Paws — 50 rooms.

Hinckley Gold Pine Inn offers pleasant accommodations, a free daily newspaper, early check-in and late checkout options. Rooms vary in size with the larger ones being in the one-story section of the lodging. There are winter plug-ins and the motel is a mile from the Grand Casino. A huge forest fire destroyed the city in 1894 and the tragedy is commemorated at the Hinckley Fire Museum. Hinckley is at the eastern end of the state, near the Wisconsin border, halfway between the northern and southern borders of Minnesota.

Solbakken Resort

4874 West Highway 61
Lutsen, MN 55612
800-435-3950 • 218-663-7566
www.solbakkenresort.com

Type of Lodging: Resort

Room Rates: $48–$227. AAA discount.

Pet Charges & Deposits: $5 per day.

Pet Policy: Designated rooms only. Manager's prior approval required.

Amenities: Full kitchens, whirlpool, sauna.

Pet Amenities: None.

Rated: 3 Paws — 18 guest units including the lodge, condos, cabins or lake homes.

Small, peaceful and quiet, Solbakken Resort's shoreline is ledge rock that slopes into Lake Superior. Bird migrations usually begin in early to mid-May here, where a variety of birds and majestic eagles nest in the Superior National Forest. An array of wildflowers begin to bloom in late May through summer, right up to the October frosts. This is a place to relax and recharge. Guest accommodations include kitchenettes and cabins that are tucked along the shoreline, close enough so the sound of the waves lulls you to sleep. Lodge suites offer scenic lake views and each has its own fireplace and fully equipped kitchen. The Joan House and Olof House are two- and three-bedroom lakefront homes with wood-burning stoves, antiques and handmade quilts.

Comfort Inn

1511 East College Drive
Marshall, MN 56258
800-228-5150 • 507-532-3070
www.comfortinn.com/hotel/mn016

Type of Lodging: Motel

Room Rates: $59–$120, including continental breakfast. AAA and AARP discounts.

Pet Charges & Deposits: None.

Pet Policy: None. All Pets Welcome.

Amenities: Cable TV, pool, whirlpools, Jacuzzi.

Pet Amenities: Camden State Park is located off Highway 23. Independent Park is located on East Lyon Street.

Rated: 3 Paws — 46 rooms and 3 suites.

In addition to its clean, comfortable rooms, Comfort Inn features an indoor pool and hot tub, whirlpool suites, free newspaper, free local calls, guest laundry and a meeting room with a 40-person capacity. Within walking distance, you will find a shopping mall, restaurants, Southwest State University and the William Whipple Art Gallery. Since it's not far to the South Dakota state border, why not visit nearby Pipestone National Monument?

Radisson Hotel South & Plaza Tower

7800 Normandie Boulevard
Minneapolis, MN 55439
800-333-3333 • 952-835-7800
www.radisson.com

Type of Lodging: Hotel

Room Rates: $139–$169. AAA and AARP discounts.

Pet Charges & Deposits: $40 per stay. $100 refundable deposit.

Pet Policy: None. All Pets Welcome.

Amenities: Cable TV, pool, whirlpool, gift shop, health center, business center, game room.

Pet Amenities: List of nearby veterinarians maintained. Dog walking area.

Rated: 3 Paws — 565 rooms.

The high-rise Radisson Hotel South towers 22 stories above Bloomington's bustling business and entertainment corridor. It's a great hotel with a prime location and offers soundproof rooms and a wonderful array of world-class amenities. For the ultimate in comfort, Plaza Tower accommodations are generously oversized and include many special amenities. The elegant ballroom accommodates up to 2,500 persons. The Hotel is located just north of the Ring Interstate 494, close to the airport, Mall Of America and all the major attractions of the Twin Cities.

Budget Host Inn

745 State Avenue
Owatonna, MN 55060
800-283-4678 • 507-451-8712

Type of Lodging: Motel

Room Rates: $36–$66, including continental breakfast. AAA, AARP, AKC and ABA discounts.

Pet Charges & Deposits: $7 per day.

Pet Policy: Designated rooms only. Manager's prior approval required.

Amenities: Cable TV, refrigerators, microwaves.

Pet Amenities: List of nearby veterinarians maintained. City parks nearby.

Rated: 2 Paws — 27 rooms.

Budget Host Inn is an affordable, pleasant lodging housed in a two-story building with exterior corridors. It affords guests winter plug-ins. The frail, sickly Owatonna, daughter of the great Chief Wabena, was restored to health by drinking the local curative waters. Travelers still come to the northeast side of town to drink the water and look at the statue of the Native American princess in Mineral Springs Park. The Village of Yesteryear displays 19th and early 20th century buildings. Owatonna is also the home of the 1880 locomotive, "Old 201," once driven by the legendary engineer Casey Jones.

Oakdale Motel

1418 South Oak Avenue
Owatonna, MN 55060
507-451-5480

Type of Lodging: Motel
Room Rates: $36–$110, including continental breakfast. AAA, AARP, AKC, ABA and *10% Pets Welcome*™ discounts.
Pet Charges & Deposits: $7 per day. $25 refundable deposit.
Pet Policy: Designated rooms only. Manager's prior approval required.
Amenities: Cable TV, refrigerators, microwaves.
Pet Amenities: List of nearby veterinarians maintained. Minot Brown Park nearby.
Rated: 2 Paws — 25 rooms.

Early check-in, late checkout, free local telephone calls and winter plug-ins are welcome amenities at budget-friendly Oakdale Motel. There are comfy rooms in this two-story, exterior-corridor facility. Famed architect Louis Sullivan designed Norwest Bank in the middle of the city. The Owatonna Arts Center, housed in an 1887 Romanesque building, displays works by local and regional artists as well as traveling shows.

Best Western Quiet House & Suites

725 Withers Harbor Drive
Red Wing, MN 55066
800-528-1234 • 651-388-1577
www.quiethouse.com

Type of Lodging: Motel
Room Rates: $86–$169, including coffee. AAA and AARP discounts.
Pet Charges & Deposits: $15 per day.
Pet Policy: Designated rooms only. Manager's prior approval required. Pets must not be left unattended.
Amenities: Cable TV, pool.
Pet Amenities: List of nearby veterinarians maintained. Bay Point Park and Levee Park are located on Levee Road. Frontenac State Park is located off Highway 61 and Cannon Valley Trail.
Rated: 3 Paws — 51 rooms and 7 suites.

The Best Western Quiet House is part of a wonderful chain-within-a-chain, carrying on the tradition of Julius Vogt, who established the original Quiet House in Milwaukee, Wisconsin. The Quiet House features a large indoor pool connected to a heated, year-round outdoor pool. There are seven "luxury whirlpool for two" suites, each offering a unique, elegant experience in a different setting. Red Wing is an historic town on the Mississippi River—there's the historic Pottery Place, the Cannon Valley Trail, casino gambling, downhill and cross-country skiing and the antique and outlet-shopping district.

Ramada Limited

435 16th Avenue Northwest
Rochester, MN 55901
507-288-9090

Type of Lodging: Hotel

Room Rates: $69–$125, including continental breakfast. AAA and AARP discounts.

Pet Charges & Deposits: $5 per day. Call for refundable deposit information.

Pet Policy: Designated rooms only.

Amenities: Refrigerators, pool, whirlpool.

Pet Amenities: List of nearby veterinarians maintained. Park is located right behind the hotel.

Rated: 2 Paws — 99 rooms and 20 kitchenettes.

The Ramada Limited is a three-story structure with interior corridors and a shuttle to area transportation. Think Rochester and the first thing that pops into your head is undoubtedly the Mayo Clinic. The Clinic offers guided tours, enabling you to visit several floors in the Mayo Building as well as the historical area in the Plummer Building. Mayo Park includes the Mayo Memorial, Mayo Civic Center and Rochester Art Center. Concerts are given from the tower of the Rochester Carillon, whose 56 bells were cast in England and the Netherlands.

Americinn Motel of Sauk Centre

1230 Timberland Drive
Sauk Center, MN 56378
800-634-3444 • 320-352-2800

Type of Lodging: Motel

Room Rates: $60–$118, including continental breakfast. AAA and AARP discounts.

Pet Charges & Deposits: $10 per stay. $50 refundable deposit.

Pet Policy: Designated rooms only. Manager's prior approval required.

Amenities: Cable TV, pool, whirlpool, sauna, internet access.

Pet Amenities: List of nearby veterinarians maintained. Park nearby.

Rated: 3 Paws — 37 rooms and 5 suites.

Americinn represents a fine value: spacious, masonry-constructed rooms, welcoming lobbies with fireside seating, free continental breakfast and kids stay free in their parents' room. There's a meeting room that accommodates up to 30 people. Sauk Centre was Sinclair Lewis' boyhood home and the prototype for many settings in his novels. Garrison Keillor's imaginary town that "time forgot and decades cannot improve" is celebrated along the 28-mile long Lake Wobegon Bike Trail.

Holiday Inn Hotel & Suites

75 South 37th Avenue
St. Cloud, MN 56301
320-253-9000
www.holiday-inn.com/stcloudmn
innsc@cloudnet.com

Type of Lodging: Hotel
Room Rates: $75–$200. AAA and AARP discounts.
Pet Charges & Deposits: None.
Pet Policy: Pets must not be left unattended.
Amenities: Cable TV, pools, whirlpool, Jacuzzi, spas, restaurants, fitness center.
Pet Amenities: Exercise area. Heritage Park is located at 225 33rd Avenue South. Wilson Park is located at 625 Northeast Riverside Drive.
Rated: 3 Paws — 257 rooms and 43 suites.

Holiday Inn Hotel & Suites has all the amenities and the high quality you expect of a Holiday Inn. There are two full service restaurants, two full-size pools, two Jacuzzis, wading pool, playland gym, fitness center, sauna, two volleyball courts and two half-size basketball courts. John Wilson paid only $250 for the 325 acres that now constitutes downtown St. Cloud, which he named after Napoleon's birthplace in France. The area is famed for its fine-grained, colored granite, ranging from coal black to pink, which has been used in many of the nation's finest buildings. St. John's University, the College of St. Benedict and St. Cloud State University contribute mightily to the city's cultural life.

Exel Inn of St. Paul

1739 Old Hudson Road
St. Paul, MN 55106
800-367-3935 • 651-771-5566
www.exelinns.com

Type of Lodging: Hotel
Room Rates: $50–$74, including continental breakfast. AARP discount.
Pet Charges & Deposits: $100–$200 refundable deposit on extended stays.
Pet Policy: No pets over 25 lbs. Designated rooms only. Manager's prior approval required. Limit two pets per room.
Amenities: Cable TV.
Pet Amenities: List of nearby veterinarians maintained. Exercise area.
Rated: 2 Paws — 100 rooms.

Exel Inn of St. Paul is a budget-conscious choice for travelers in the Twin Cities. The hotel is housed in a three-story structure with interior corridors. St. Paul, Minnesota's capital, is a charming city, from its Skywalk to the large campus of the University of Minnesota. The immense Cathedral of St. Paul, styled after St. Peter's Cathedral in Rome, seats 3,000 people. The City Hall and Courthouse is an example of Art Deco architecture. Each of the 18 floors is finished in a different wood from around the world. Fort Snelling State Park occupies 3,300 acres on the Mississippi and Minnesota Rivers.

Ramada Inn & Conference Center

1870 Old Hudson Road
St. Paul, Minnesota 55119
800-211-0778 • 651-735-2333

Type of Lodging: Hotel

Room Rates: $69–$124. AAA and AARP discounts.

Pet Charges & Deposits: $25 refundable deposit.

Pet Policy: None. All Pets Welcome.

Amenities: Cable TV, pool, whirlpool, Jacuzzi, video arcade, fitness center, coffeemakers, hairdryers, irons and ironing boards.

Pet Amenities: List of nearby veterinarians maintained. Dog runs. Exercise area. Battle Creek Park is located at McKnight and Interstate 94. Conway Park is located at Ruth and Conway.

Rated: 3 Paws — 144 rooms and 8 suites.

Ramada Inn is tidy and decidedly upscale. Lush foliage provides a spectacular setting for its large indoor pool. Ramada Inn is adjacent to the 3M World Headquarters and only five minutes away from downtown St. Paul. The Afton Alps ski area, Omni Theater and Mall of America are just minutes away. The Inn provides complimentary transportation to Minneapolis-St. Paul International Airport.

Travelodge Mall Of America

1870 Old Hudson Road
St. Paul, MN 55119
877-864-5808 • 651-735-2337
www.travelodge.com
11986@hotelcendant.com

Type of Lodging: Hotel

Room Rates: $59–$109. AAA and AARP discounts.

Pet Charges & Deposits: $25 refundable deposit.

Pet Policy: None. All Pets Welcome.

Amenities: Cable TV, safes, pool, whirlpool, Jacuzzi, video arcade, fitness center, coffeemakers.

Pet Amenities: List of nearby veterinarians maintained. Dog runs. Exercise area. Battle Creek Park is located at McKnight and Interstate 94. Conway Park is located at Ruth and Conway.

Rated: 2 Paws — 88 rooms and 3 suites.

Travelodge Mall Of America is located just three miles from downtown St. Paul and moments away from the Mall of America, Minneapolis and 3M World Headquarters. There are nearly 1,000 small lakes in the Greater Minneapolis-St. Paul Area. For those who feel uncomfortable when winter's chill brings on inclement weather, both Minneapolis and St. Paul offer an extensive, glass-enclosed walkway system called the Skyway, which connects shops, restaurants and offices one story above the ground. Nicollet Mall, a pedestrian mall in downtown Minneapolis, has heated sidewalks and bus shelters with piped-in classical music.

Superior Shores Resort

10 Superior Shores Drive
Two Harbors, MN 55616
800-242-1988 • 218-834-5671
www.superiorshores.com
supshores@norshor.dst.mn.us

Type of Lodging: Resort

Room Rates: $49–$429. Call for discounts.

Pet Charges & Deposits: $25 refundable deposit.

Pet Policy: Designated rooms only. Manager's prior approval required.

Amenities: Fully equipped kitchens, pool, whirlpool, Jacuzzi, hot tub, tennis courts, restaurant, lounge.

Pet Amenities: None.

Rated: 5 Paws — 144 rooms, suites and lakefront homes.

Imagine taking all that Lake Superior's North Shore has to offer. The massive rock formations and pebbled beaches. The pines and the birches. The turbulent majesty of the "Big Lake." Now imagine an extraordinary resort placed right in the middle. A resort with beautiful lodge suites, gorgeous townhouses, stone fireplaces, fully equipped kitchens and warm pine woodwork, along with down comforters. Well, you can stop imagining, because we've just introduced you to Superior Shores Resort.

The Resort is open year-round, providing guests four seasons of activities. Premier downhill skiing is an hour's drive away at Lutsen Mountain, with more than twenty runs. Over 500 kilometers of cross-country ski trails await you on the North Shore. During summer, numerous rivers and streams are home to brook and brown trout. Or pass the time on one of six different golf courses.

Quality Inn of Winona

956 Mankato Avenue
Winona, MN 55987
800-562-4544 • 507-454-4390
winquinn@luminet.net

Type of Lodging: Hotel

Room Rates: $50–$140. AAA and AARP discounts.

Pet Charges & Deposits: None.

Pet Policy: Designated rooms only.

Amenities: Cable TV, pool, whirlpool.

Pet Amenities: List of nearby veterinarians maintained. Exercise area. Whitewater State Park and Winona Lake Park nearby.

Rated: 3 Paws — 109 rooms and 3 suites.

Quality Inn has rooms with both inside and outside entrances, which makes it far easier to take your pet out for exercise. Winona is located on an island in the Mississippi River Valley. Limestone from its quarries is equal to Italy's finest. Sugar Loaf, a 500-feet bluff at the southeast edge of town is a dramatic limestone formation. Garvin Heights Park affords a panorama of the Mississippi Valley. Visit the Polish Cultural Institute, which has displays of local Polish history and culture.

Days Inn

207 Oxford Street
Worthington, MN 56187
800-329-7466 • 507-376-6155

Type of Lodging: Motel

Room Rates: $46–$129, including continental breakfast. AAA, AARP, Seniors, Corporate, Trucker and *10% Pets Welcome*™ discounts.

Pet Charges & Deposits: $6 per day.

Pet Policy: None. All Pets Welcome.

Amenities: Cable TV, pool, refrigerators, microwaves, Jacuzzis, guest laundry.

Pet Amenities: List of nearby veterinarians maintained. Exercise area. Olson Park nearby.

Rated: 2 Paws — 30 rooms and 3 suites.

Days Inn provides pleasant accommodations. Kids stay free in their parents' rooms, free local calls, guest laundry, remote control cable television and large vehicle parking are convenient amenities. The Nobles County Pioneer Village, one mile southeast of Worthington, contains about 40 restored or replicated structures that reflect prairie life in the late 1800s and early 1900s. Lake Okabena affords boating, fishing and swimming opportunities.

MISSISSIPPI

Nickname: Magnolia State
Population: 2,788,619
Area: 48,286 square miles
Climate: Semitropical with abundant rainfall, long growing season, and extreme temperatures unusual.
Capital: Jackson
Entered Union: Dec. 10, 1817
Motto: *Virtute et Armis* (By virtue and arms).
Song: Go, Mississippi!

Flower: Magnolia
Tree: Magnolia
Bird: Mockingbird
Famous Mississippians: Dana Andrews, Jimmy Buffett, Hodding Carter, Bo Didley, William Faulkner, Brett Favre, Morgan Freeman, John Grisham, Jim Henson, James Earl Jones, B.B. King, Elvis Presley, Leontyne Price, Charley Pride, Eudora Welty, Tennessee Williams, Oprah Winfrey, Tammy Wynette.

 History: Early inhabitants of the area were Choctaw, Chickasaw and Natchez peoples. LaSalle claimed the area for France in 1682. The first French settlement followed in 1699. The area was ceded to Britain in 1763. During the American Revolution, Spain seized part of the area, but moved out in 1798, after the new United States had acquired title to the area. Mississippi entered the Union in 1817, seceded in 1861, and was readmitted in 1870. Long viewed as the poorest of the United States, tourism has been hampered by its reputation as a backward area of Civil Rights repression.

BILOXI, MISSISSIPPI (Pop. 46,300)

Breakers Inn

2506 Beach Boulevard
Biloxi, MS 39531
800-624-5031 • 228-388-6320
www.biloxibreakersinn.com

Type of Lodging: Condos
Suite Rates: $55–$171. AAA and AARP discounts.
Pet Charges & Deposits: Call for charges information. $20 nonrefundable deposit.
Pet Policy: Sorry, no cats. No pets over 20 lbs.
Amenities: Cable TV, refrigerators, microwaves, pool, tennis court, playground.
Pet Amenities: None.
Rated: 2 Paws — 50 suites.

Biloxi is Mississippi's premier Gulf Coast city and the Breakers Inn is adjacent to the beach. The Breakers has everything you need to create your home away from home: full-sized condominiums with upstairs and downstairs, 2½ baths, fully equipped kitchen and dinette. Tree-lined gardens surround the Breakers' accessible, yet restful grounds. Casinos as well as many golf courses are only a few minutes away. A leisurely drive takes you to New Orleans. While in Biloxi, be sure to visit Beauvoir—the Jefferson Davis home, presidential library and museum.

Crowne Plaza Hotel

200 East Amite Street
Jackson, MS 39201
601-969-5100

Type of Lodging: Hotel

Room Rates: $59–$89. AAA and AARP discounts.

Pet Charges & Deposits: $25 per stay. $100 refundable deposit.

Pet Policy: Manager's prior approval required.

Amenities: Cable TV, refrigerators, microwaves, pool, fitness room, guest laundry, restaurant, lounge.

Pet Amenities: None.

Rated: 3 Paws — 354 rooms.

The Crowne Plaza Hotel towers over the heart of metropolitan Jackson. This 23-story luxury hotel and convention center caters to business travelers and families on vacation. You will enjoy the personal, pet-friendly service traditionally associated with Crowne Plaza Hotels, with the added benefit of Southern hospitality. In addition to elegantly appointed rooms, guest amenities include a corporate floor with a fitness center, a swimming pool, a gift shop for those little extras you might need, plus a panoramic view of the city.

Oliver-Britt House Inn

512 Van Buren Avenue
Oxford, MS 38655
662-234-8043
eoliver@ebicom.net

Type of Lodging: Inn

Room Rates: $50–$70, including full breakfast on weekends. AAA and AARP discounts.

Pet Charges & Deposits: None.

Pet Policy: None. All Pets Welcome.

Amenities: Cable TV.

Pet Amenities: List of nearby veterinarians maintained.

Rated: 4 Paws — 5 rooms.

The Oliver-Britt House Inn is only a short walk from the University of Mississippi campus and only a few minutes away from Rowan Oak, the home of William Faulkner, and Oxford Square. The restored manor house offers five guestrooms, uniquely decorated with period antiques and reproductions, with queen- or king-sized beds, private baths, cable television and individual climate controls. On weekends, guests are treated to a full Southern-style breakfast.

Key West Inn

1004 Central Drive
Philadelphia, MS 39350
800-833-0555 • 601-656-0052

Type of Lodging: Motel

Room Rates: $50–$89, including continental breakfast. AAA and AARP discounts.

Pet Charges & Deposits: $5 per day

Pet Policy: No pets over 25 lbs.

Amenities: Cable TV, refrigerators, microwaves, pool.

Pet Amenities: None.

Rated: 3 Paws — 44 rooms and 6 suites.

There's real lodging value to be found at Key West Inn. It's amazingly affordable, yet surprisingly stylish. Clean, affordable rooms, cable television and guest laundry are welcome amenities. Key West Inn is minutes away from the Silver Star Casino, downtown Philadelphia and the Neshoba County Fairgrounds.

Shoney's Inn of Jackson

839 Ridgewood Road
Ridgeland, MS 39157
800-222-2222 • 601-956-6203
www.shoneysinn.com

Type of Lodging: Inn

Room Rates: $48–$70, including continental breakfast. AAA, AARP, AKC, ABA and *10% Pets Welcome*™ discounts.

Pet Charges & Deposits: $25 refundable deposit.

Pet Policy: None. All Pets Welcome.

Amenities: Cable TV, refrigerators, microwaves, pool.

Pet Amenities: List of nearby veterinarians maintained. Exercise area. Natchez Trace Park is located a mile from the Inn.

Rated: 3 Paws — 125 rooms and 12 suites.

Shoney's Inn provides budget-conscious accommodations near Mississippi's capital and largest city. There's a meeting room, free local phone calls, complimentary newspaper in the lobby and kids stay free in their parents' room. The Mississippi Agriculture and Forestry Museum, combined with the National Agricultural Aviation Museum, exhibits three eras of transportation and tells the story of Mississippi's farmers and lumbermen. The city is filled with museums and buildings commemorating its status as one of the industrial and distribution centers of the Deep South.

Key West Inn

11635 Highway 62 North
Robinsonville, MS 38664
662-363-0021

Type of Lodging: Motel

Room Rates: $40–$99, including coffee and donuts. AAA and AARP discounts.

Pet Charges & Deposits: $5 per day. $15 refundable deposit.

Pet Policy: Small pets only. Designated rooms only.

Amenities: Cable TV, refrigerators, microwaves.

Pet Amenities: None.

Rated: 2 Paws — 38 rooms and 6 suites.

Key West Inn is budget-friendly and accommodating. The two-story structure has exterior corridors allowing for easy entry and exit. Robinsonville, in the northwest corner of the state, is on the Mississippi River. Of course, that means major league riverboat gambling and there are no less than nine of the big names, including Bally's, Harrah's, Sam's Town and the Sheraton, in the immediate vicinity.

Duff Green Mansion Inn

1114 First East Street
Vicksburg, MS 39183
800-992-0037 • 601-636-6968
www.duffgreenmansion.com

Type of Lodging: B&B

Room Rates: $95–$125, including full breakfast and cocktail hour.

Pet Charges & Deposits: None.

Pet Policy: None. All Pets Welcome.

Amenities: Cable TV, pool, garden area, guest laundry.

Pet Amenities: List of nearby veterinarians maintained. Exercise area. Vicksburg National Military Park is located on Clay Street.

Rated: 4 Paws — 5 rooms and 1 suite.

Built in 1856 by Duff Green, a wealthy merchant, the mansion was used simultaneously as a Confederate and Union hospital during the siege of Vicksburg. During one of five attacks on the house, Mary Green gave birth to a son in a nearby shelter and named him Siege. The restored Palladian mansion, now a bed and breakfast establishment, is furnished with antiques, including a chandelier from 1730. The Gray and Blue Naval Museum in Vicksburg presents the naval history of the War Between the States, using paintings, reference materials, artifacts and model ships. Vicksburg maintains much of its Civil War flavor and is a worthy vacation stop.

The Corners Bed & Breakfast Inn

607 Klein Street
Vicksburg, MS 39180
800-444-7421 • 601-636-7421
www.thecorners.com
cornersb@magnolia.com

Type of Lodging: B&B

Room Rates: $90–$130, including full breakfast. AAA discount.

Pet Charges & Deposits: None.

Pet Policy: None All Pets Welcome.

Amenities: Cable TV, refrigerators, microwaves, whirlpool, Jacuzzi.

Pet Amenities: Exercise area. Vicksburg National Military Park is located on Clay Street.

Rated: 4 Paws — 15 rooms and 2 suites.

Step back in time to the gracious Vicksburg home of the Whitneys. Built in 1873 as a wedding gift, The Corners sits atop a bluff overlooking the Mississippi Valley and River in the distance. Soak in the magnificent sunsets in a high-back rocker on the 68-feet front gallery. Enjoy Victorian elegance in the large double parlor filled with period antiques and a grand piano. Vicksburg was called the Gibraltar of the Confederacy. In 1863, after a 47-day siege pitting General Ulysses S. Grant and Admiral David Dixon Porter against the Confederate forces of General John Pemberton, the city surrendered. Slaves built the Old Court House Museum in 1858. Harrah's Casino, the Isle of Capri and the Rainbow Casino at Vicksburg Landing assure gaming and allied entertainment year-round.

MISSOURI

Nickname: Show Me State

Population: 5,468,388

Area: 68,709 square miles

Climate: Continental, susceptible to cold Canadian air, moist, warm gulf air, and drier southwest air.

Capital: Jefferson City

Entered Union: Aug. 10, 1821

Motto: *Salutis Populi Supreme Lex Esto* (The welfare of the people shall be the supreme law).

Song: Missouri Waltz

Flower: Hawthorn

Tree: Dogwood

Bird: Bluebird

Famous Missourians: Maya Angelou, Josephine Baker, Thomas Hart Benton, Tom Berenger, Chuck Berry, George Washington Carver, Walter Cronkite, Walt Disney, T.S. Elliot, James Garner, Betty Grable, Jesse James, J.C. Penney, John J. Pershing, Brad Pitt, Joseph Pulitzer, Harry S. Truman, Tina Turner, Mark Twain, Shelley Winters, Dick Van Dyke.

 History: Algonquian, Sauk & Fox, and Illinoisian Native Americans populated the land when deSoto visited in 1541. French hunters and miners settled the area in 1735. The territory was sold to the U.S. three years later as part of the Louisiana Purchase. Most Native American tribes were driven out of the area by 1836. The fur trade and the Santa Fe Trail added to the state's prosperity, and St. Louis became the gateway to the west. Missouri entered the Union as a slave state in 1841, but remained with the Union during the Civil War.

Days Inn

3524 Keeter Street
Branson, MO 65616
417-334-5544
www.bransonusa.com
hotelinfo1@aol.com

Type of Lodging: Hotel

Room Rates: $45–$90, including continental breakfast. AAA and AARP discounts.

Pet Charges & Deposits: $10 per day.

Pet Policy: No pets over 50 lbs.

Amenities: Cable TV, pool, whirlpool, kiddie pool, restaurant.

Pet Amenities: Exercise area.

Rated: 3 Paws — 423 rooms.

Days Inn features newly remodeled rooms and a recreation complex with pool, spas and playground. Kids eat free at the Green Mountain Café. The hotel is one block off the "76 Strip." Early check-in, late checkout and free local phone calls are appreciated amenities. Branson has been a popular tourist mecca since 1900, when Harold Bell Wright's *The Shepherd Of The Hills* was published. Today, the glittery show venues of "76 Country Boulevard" or "The Strip" have almost eclipsed the Shepherd Of The Hills homestead and the Shepherd Of The Hills outdoor theater.

Ramada Limited

2316 Shepherd of the Hills Expressway
Branson, MO 65616
800-856-0730 • 417-337-5207
www.branson-ramada.com

Type of Lodging: Motel

Room Rates: $40–$100, including continental breakfast. AAA, AARP, AKC, ABA and *10% Pets Welcome*™ discounts.

Pet Charges & Deposits: $5 per day

Pet Policy: Designated rooms only.

Amenities: Cable TV, refrigerators, pool.

Pet Amenities: List of nearby veterinarians maintained. Exercise area. Stockstill Park is located at Roark Valley and Epps Road.

Rated: 3 Paws — 90 rooms. Ramada Gold Key Award Winner.

Ramada Limited Branson is close to all major Branson attractions. Silver Dollar City combines the atmosphere of an 1880s Ozark pioneer village and a 21st century theme park, complete with flume, rafting, coaster rides, daily music and comedy shows, and the Geyser Gulch children's area, which includes a giant tree house and Splash Harbor, a water cannon play area.

Red Roof Inn

220 Wildwood Drive
Branson, MO 65616
800-351-4644 • 417-335-4500
www.bransonusa.com
hotelinfo1@aol.com

Type of Lodging: Motel

Room Rates: $39–$105, including continental breakfast. AAA, AARP and *10% Pets Welcome™* discounts.

Pet Charges & Deposits: $10 per day

Pet Policy: No pets over 50 lbs.

Amenities: Cable TV, pool.

Pet Amenities: List of nearby veterinarians maintained. Exercise area.

Rated: 2 Paws — 104 rooms and 1 suite.

Red Roof Inn is located directly behind the Grand Palace and 1½ blocks from Andy Williams Theater. The major theaters of Branson are within walking distance. Among Branson's top show venues are the Andy Williams Moon River Theater, the Wild West Theater, the Bobby Vinton Blue Velvet Theater and the Wayne Newton Theater—and that's just for starters! There are no less than 32 theaters in Branson!

Settle Inn

3050 Green Mountain Drive
Branson, MO 65616
800-677-6906 • 417-335-4700
www.bransonsettleinn.com
bsettleinn@aol.com

Type of Lodging: Hotel

Room Rates: $50–$130, including continental breakfast. AAA, AARP, AKC, ABA and *10% Pets Welcome™* discounts.

Pet Charges & Deposits: $8 per day.

Pet Policy: None. All Pets Welcome.

Amenities: Cable TV, pool, Jacuzzi, hot tubs, fitness center, game room.

Pet Amenities: List of nearby veterinarians maintained. Exercise area.

Rated: 3 Paws — 250 rooms and 50 suites.

Settle Inn, home of the whirlpool theme rooms, free morning shows and a lot more, bills itself as "Branson's Theme Hotel." Conference rooms and catering is available. Marvel Cave, below Silver Dollar City, has three miles of explored passageways and a room that is over 400 feet long and 20 stories high. There's even a winery in Branson, competing as it does with the likes of the Osmond Family Theater, the Roy Clark Celebrity Theater and the Shoji Tabuchi Theater.

Colonial Mountain Inn

Route 76
Branson West, MO 65737
417-272-8414

Type of Lodging: Motel

Room Rates: $45–$55.

Pet Charges & Deposits: $5 per day.

Pet Policy: Sorry, no cats, pit bulls or rottweilers. Designated rooms only.

Amenities: Cable TV, pool.

Pet Amenities: List of nearby veterinarians maintained. Exercise area. Park nearby.

Rated: 3 Paws — 52 rooms and 2 suites.

The Colonial Mountain Inn offers you the very best in a family-oriented setting. No matter what time of the year you visit the beautiful Ozark Mountains, the Colonial Mountain Inn is ready to accommodate you. An added extra is a 70-feet waterslide with large pool. Shopping is within walking distance and you're minutes away from all popular mountain attractions, including Branson.

Goodnite Inn

642 South Ash
P.O. Box 409
Buffalo, MO 65622
417-345-2345
http://goodniteinn.todays-tech.com
goodniteinn@todays-tech.com

Type of Lodging: Motel

Room Rates: $30–$75. AAA, AARP, AKC, ABA, Seniors, Corporate, Truckers and *10% Pets Welcome*™ discounts.

Pet Charges & Deposits: $5 per day. $25 refundable deposit.

Pet Policy: No pets over 50 lbs. Designated rooms only. Manager's prior approval required.

Amenities: Cable TV, pool.

Pet Amenities: List of nearby veterinarians maintained. Exercise area. Buffalo City Park and Bennett Springs National Park are within 15 miles of the motel.

Rated: 2 Paws — 15 rooms.

Goodnite Inn is a clean, comfortable place for cost-conscious travelers. There's early check-in, late checkout and free local calls. Buffalo is situated in the very heart of the Ozarks, 70 miles from Branson, 50 miles from Lake of the Ozarks and 15 miles to Bennett Springs National Park. It's a land of many lakes and a great vacationland.

Grand River Inn

606 West Highway 36
Chillicothe, MO 64601
888-317-8290 • 660-646-6590

Type of Lodging: Hotel

Room Rates: $61–$89, including continental breakfast. AAA, AARP and *10% Pets Welcome*™ discounts.

Pet Charges & Deposits: None.

Pet Policy: Pets must not be left unattended.

Amenities: Cable TV, refrigerators, pool.

Pet Amenities: List of nearby veterinarians maintained. Exercise area. Simpson Park is located on Highway 65, approximately 2 miles from the hotel.

Rated: 3 Paws — 60 rooms and 5 suites.

Grand River Inn is close to everything, yet away from it all. It's conveniently located at the crossroads of U.S. Highways 65 and 36. In addition to spacious rooms, there are business facilities for up to 300 persons. There's a heated pool, sauna, hot tub and the Inn's famous Sunday Champagne Buffet is rated the best in Northern Missouri. Chillicothe is near the Jamesport Amish Community and antique shops. It's 45 minutes from Swan Lake National Wildlife Refuge aka "the Goose Capital of the World," 30 minutes from J.C. Penney's Birthplace and 45 minutes from the Walt Disney Boyhood Home at Marceline.

Daniele Hotel

216 North Meramec
Clayton, MO 63105
800-325-8302 • 314-721-0101

Type of Lodging: Hotel

Room Rates: $129–$295. Call for discounts.

Pet Charges & Deposits: None.

Pet Policy: Sorry, no cats.

Amenities: Pool, fitness center, guest laundry, complimentary limousine service, restaurant.

Pet Amenities: City park is located a block from hotel.

Rated: 3 Paws — 82 rooms and 6 suites.

Located in the heart of Clayton, the Daniele is an elegant, European-style hotel with personalized service. Guestrooms are private, intimate and relaxing. At the popular health club, you will enjoy complimentary workouts with expert trainers. Continue relaxing by the Olympic-sized pool and enjoy your favorite snack or cocktail. The staff is available 18 hours a day to fulfill your needs or to chauffeur you to Clayton destinations and shopping malls. Your personal wake-up service greets you at the door with fresh hot coffee, orange juice and the newspaper.

Days Inn

1900 Interstate 70 Drive Southwest
Columbia, MO 65203
573-445-8511
http://members.aol.com/daysinn.col

Type of Lodging: Motel

Room Rates: $50–$90, including full breakfast. AAA, AARP, Military, Corporate and *10% Pets Welcome™* discounts.

Pet Charges & Deposits: $5 per day.

Pet Policy: No pets over 50 lbs. Designated rooms only.

Amenities: Cable TV, refrigerators, microwaves, restaurant, lounge.

Pet Amenities: List of nearby veterinarians maintained.

Rated: 2 Paws — 156 rooms and 10 suites.

Days Inn affords comfy accommodations, free local calls, a pool, fitness room and free hot breakfast. The University of Missouri, the first public university west of the Mississippi River, opened its doors in 1839 after 900 patrons raised subscriptions of $117,000, a truly generous sum at the time, to obtain the state university campus. The city began its life as Smithton in 1819; it was renamed and made the county seat of Boone County two years later. The University of Missouri campus includes the George Caleb Bingham Gallery, the Museum of Anthropology, the Museum of Art & Archaeology and the State Historical Society of Missouri.

Travelodge

900 Van Diver Drive
Columbia, MO 65202
800-456-1065 • 573-449-1065
http://members.aol.com/tlodsccol

Type of Lodging: Motel

Room Rates: $40–$80, including continental breakfast. AAA, AARP, Military, Corporate and *10% Pets Welcome™* discounts.

Pet Charges & Deposits: $5 per day.

Pet Policy: Sorry, no large pets. Designated rooms only.

Amenities: Cable TV, refrigerators, microwaves, free local calls.

Pet Amenities: List of nearby veterinarians maintained. Exercise area. Oakland Park is located at 1900 Blue Ridge Road. Douglas Park is located at 400 North Providence.

Rated: 2 Paws — 160 rooms and 3 suites.

Travelodge is the perfect place to stay if you're visiting students or faculty at the University of Missouri. Although U of M is the big attraction, Columbia College and Stephens College establish Columbia as a college town. Stephens College has theater performance throughout the year. The insurance industry and medical services industry are economic mainstays of Columbia.

Rock Eddy Bluff Farm

10245 Maries Co. Road #511
Dixon, MO 65459
800-335-5931 • 573-759-6081
www.rockeddy.com

Type of Lodging: B&B & Cabins

Room Rates: $70–$110, including continental or full breakfast.

Pet Charges & Deposits: None.

Pet Policy: Designated rooms only. Manager's prior approval required. Horses welcome.

Amenities: Refrigerators, microwaves, hot tubs.

Pet Amenities: Exercise area and plenty of room to roam.

Rated: 4 Paws — 1 suite, 2 cottages and 1 cabin on 150 acres.

Rock Eddy Bluff Farm offers the consummate get-away-from-it-all vacation. It offers picturesque bed and breakfast rooms, two secluded cottages and a cozy 1880s cabin on 150 acres of scenic Ozark forest. Here, the Gasconade River enters the Farm's valley, sweeps between an island and willowed gravel bar, and relaxes into a pool or "eddy." Viewed from the bluff, meadows appear below, wooded ridges stretch to the horizon. It is located on a river and offers canoeing, fishing, hiking, even horse-drawn wagon rides. This is a quiet place with a sense of, "Nothing must I do but please myself."

Serendipity Bed and Breakfast

116 South Pleasant Street
Independence, MO 64050
800-203-4299 • 816-833-4719

Type of Lodging: B&B

Room Rates: $30–$85, including full breakfast.

Pet Charges or Deposits: $10 per day.

Pet Policy: Designated rooms only. Manager's prior approval required.

Amenities: BBQ grill, 1926 car rides.

Pet Amenities: None.

Rated: 3 Paws — 6 rooms.

This delightful 1887 three-story brick home transports you back to the Victorian era, with antique walnut furniture, rugs and period lighting. The details include Victorian children's books and toys, a myriad of china figurines and vividly colored glassware adorning shelves and tables. The dining room is filled with the luxuries that a middle-class family could obtain from the latest Sears and Wards catalogues of the 1890s. From century-old books to antique medicine bottles and shaving paraphernalia in the bathrooms—this house is overflowing with genuine articles of daily life from the turn-of-the-century era. Outside, a three-tiered fountain provides a glorious bath for the many birds that flock to the flower-bedecked gardens. A full breakfast of quiche, fruit, muffins, juice and coffee or tea is served on antique china, graced by lace tablecloths and candlelight.

Hallmark Inn

3600 South Rangeline Road
Joplin, MO 64804
800-825-2378 • 417-624-8400

Type of Lodging: Motel

Room Rates: $40–$54, including continental breakfast. AAA, AARP and *15% Pets Welcome*™ discounts.

Pet Charges & Deposits: $10 refundable deposit.

Pet Policy: Pets must not be left unattended.

Amenities: Cable TV, safes, pool, guest laundry.

Pet Amenities: List of nearby veterinarians maintained. Exercise area. Lodging is across the street from the convention center where dog shows are held.

Rated: 2 Paws — 95 rooms and 1 suite.

Hallmark Inn is a two-story motel that affords free breakfasts and local phone calls. Following the Civil War, mining companies divided Joplin into two cities, each controlled by competing companies. In 1873, the state assembly stepped in and incorporated the two towns as one. The railroad arrived shortly afterward and zinc soon overtook lead production. Today, Joplin is the home of Missouri Southern State College, which boasts a 310-acre campus. The Post Memorial Library features a 2,500-piece collection of art reference material. The Dorothea Hoover Historical Museum boasts a miniature animated circus, antique dolls, an 18th century tavern and historic photographs of the area.

Baymont Inn & Suites Kansas City South

8601 Hillcrest
Kansas City, MO 64138
816-822-7000

Type of Lodging: Inn

Room Rates: $59–$150, including continental breakfast. AAA, AARP and *10% Pets Welcome*™ discounts.

Pet Charge & Deposits: None.

Pet Policy: None. All Pets Welcome.

Amenities: Cable TV.

Pet Amenities: Exercise area. Swope Park nearby.

Rated: 3 Paws — 90 rooms and 12 suites.

Baymont Inn & Suites is a wonderful choice in one of the Midwest's premier and most livable cities. Kansas City is filled with a plethora of wondrous activities, including riverboat gambling and entertainment, museums, shopping—a "European" city-within-a-city! One of our favorite "off the beaten track" activities is the "Save A Connie" exhibit at Kansas City's close-in downtown airport. You actually go to a privately supported museum of aviation, then get to visit a genuine Lockheed Constellation and a Martin 341 late-1940s vintage commercial airliner, totally restored by a volunteer staff of folks who worked on these beauties when they were the "Queens of the Air."

Su Casa Bed & Breakfast

9004 East 92nd Street
Kansas City, MO 64138
816-965-5647
www.sucasabb.com
sucasa@swbell.net

Type of Lodging: B&B

Room Rates: $50–$95, including continental breakfast on weekdays and full breakfast on weekends. AARP and *10% Pets Welcome™* discounts.

Pet Charges & Deposits: $10 per day for most animals. $25 per day for horses.

Pet Policy: Sorry, no cats. Designated rooms only. Manager's prior approval required. Horses welcome.

Amenities: Cable TV, refrigerators, microwaves, pool, Jacuzzi, game room.

Pet Amenities: Lots of horses, llamas, goats and ducks on property. List of nearby veterinarians maintained. Dog runs. Exercise area. Longview Lake nearby.

Rated: 3 Paws — 3 rooms and 1 suite on 5 acres.

Bienvenidos a Su Casa! (Welcome to Su Casa!) There are unique rooms that are decorated Southwestern-style. There's a warm hearth room with wood-burning stove and office facilities. The Su Casa is located in south-eastern Kansas City, 15 miles from Crown Center, Science City, Union Station and the Harry Truman Home, 18 miles from the Riverboat Casinos.

Kimberling Arms Resort

Highway 13
P.O. Box 429
Kimberling City, MO 65686
888-899-5070

Type of Lodging: Resort

Room Rates: $49–$109. AAA, AARP and *10% Pets Welcome™* discounts.

Pet Charges & Deposits: None.

Pet Policy: No pets over 15 lbs. Pets must not be left unattended.

Amenities: Cable TV, refrigerators, microwaves, pool, Jacuzzi.

Pet Amenities: Designated walking area. List of nearby veterinarians maintained. Mark Twain National Forest nearby.

Rated: 3 Paws — 9 rooms and 29 suites.

Kimberling Arms Resort features deluxe accommodations on beautiful Table Rock Lake. It boasts the most central location in the Ozarks with Silver Dollar City only 15 miles away, Branson, 25 minutes to the east, Springfield, 45 minutes to the north, and Eureka Springs, Arkansas, 45 minutes to the southwest. However, with all this activity surrounding you, you'll stay in the serenity and beauty of Table Rock Reservoir, a Corps of Engineers impoundment that sprawls over 42,100 acres at conservation pool and occupies nearly 80 miles of the original White River channel.

Whiteman Inn

2340 West Irish Lane
Knob Noster, MO 65336
800-563-3321 • 660-563-3000

Type of Lodging: Motel

Room Rates: $44–$80, including continental breakfast. AAA, AARP and *10% Pets Welcome™* discounts.

Pet Charges & Deposits: $3 per day. $20 refundable deposit.

Pet Policy: Designated rooms only. Pets must not be left unattended.

Amenities: Cable TV, refrigerators, microwaves, pool.

Pet Amenities: List of nearby veterinarians maintained. Exercise area. Knob Noster State Park is across the street from the motel.

Rated: 3 Paws — 87 rooms.

Whiteman Inn provides accommodations that stand proudly apart from other economy lodging facilities in mid-Missouri. It's 60 miles southeast of Kansas City, nestled among the rolling hills of West Central Missouri. It's also near the bustling community of Whiteman Air Force Base, home of the B-2 Stealth Bomber. Group tours of Whiteman AFB are available. Central Missouri State University is also located at Knob Noster, which is near Sedalia, home of the Missouri State Fair.

Days Inn

2232 Taney Street
North Kansas City, MO 64116
800-DAYS INN • 816-421-6000
www.innworks.com

Type of Lodging: Motel

Room Rates: $50–$75, including continental breakfast. AAA and AARP discounts.

Pet Charges & Deposits: $10 per stay.

Pet Policy: Sorry, no cats. Manager's prior approval required.

Amenities: Cable TV, safes, one free 8-minute long distance phone call each night.

Pet Amenities: Exercise area.

Rated: 2 Paws — 89 rooms.

Days Inn provides cost-conscious accommodations in the greater Kansas City area. Harrah's North Kansas City Riverboat Casino offers riverboat gaming and entertainment galore. While in the area, visit the Harry S. Truman Library and Museum in nearby Independence. Or, cross the border into Kansas City, Kansas, just to have the opportunity of placing one foot in each state.

Comfort Inn

1900 West Evangel
Ozark, MO 65721
800-228-5150 • 417-485-6688

Type of Lodging: Motel
Room Rates: $53–$69, including continental breakfast. AAA and AARP discounts.
Pet Charges & Deposits: $10 nonrefundable deposit.
Pet Policy: None. All Pets Welcome.
Amenities: Cable TV, safes, pool, whirlpool, Jacuzzi, hot tubs.
Pet Amenities: List of nearby veterinarians maintained. Ozark City Park nearby.
Rated: 3 Paws — 46 rooms and 2 suites.

Comfort Inn provides dependable accommodations in the midst of the Ozarks. Scottish mountaineers and homesteaders from Kentucky, Virginia, the Carolinas and Tennessee settled the Ozark Mountains after the Civil War. In the isolation of the hills and hollows, farmers started an underground business with moonshine stills and birthing country music. The Ozarks are one of the oldest mountain ranges in North America. Hardwood forests conceal approximately 4,000 caves in the vicinity.

Days Inn South

621 West Sunshine
Springfield, MO 65807
800-DAYS INN • 417-862-0153

Type of Lodging: Hotel
Room Rates: $60–$95, including continental breakfast. AAA, AARP and *10% Pets Welcome™* discounts.
Pet Charges & Deposits: $10 per day.
Pet Policy: None. All Pets Welcome.
Amenities: Cable TV, refrigerators, microwaves, pool, whirlpool, spas.
Pet Amenities: List of nearby veterinarians maintained. Exercise area. Fassnight Park is located on Grant Street.
Rated: 3 Paws — 69 rooms. Days Inn Five Sunburst Award Winner.

Days Inn South is a refreshing and restful place. It's located ½ block from Bass Pro Shops Outdoor World, which houses a 140,000-gallon game fish aquarium, a four-story waterfall, huge largemouth bass, a fishing museum, a 30,000-gallon saltwater aquarium, a wildlife art gallery and a trout pond. Union spy/scout James Butler Hickok, better known as Wild Bill Hickok, stayed in Springfield after the Civil War. He achieved fame as a gunfighter, making national news in 1865 when he killed Dave Tutt in the public square. He was later acquitted.

Ramada Limited

3404 East Ridgeview
Springfield, MO 65804
800-2 RAMADA • 417-882-2220
Ramada2@aol.com

Type of Lodging: Hotel

Room Rates: $59–$74, including continental breakfast. AAA, AARP, ABA, Star-Basic and *10% Pets Welcome*™ discounts.

Pet Charges & Deposits: $10 per day.

Pet Policy: None. All Pets Welcome.

Amenities: Cable TV, refrigerators, microwaves, pool.

Pet Amenities: List of nearby veterinarians maintained. Exercise area. Property is on and next to a large field and residential area.

Rated: 3 Paws — 52 rooms and 6 suites.

Ramada Limited is a fine choice should you find yourself in bustling Springfield with recently-constructed, upscale rooms that are meticulously maintained. There's an open atrium lobby with "Living Room" setting, a conference room and board rooms, and a three-story indoor corridor with elevator. Ramada Limited is located near all of Springfield's major attractions: Bass Pro Shop Outdoor World, Battlefield Civil War Park, Springfield Nature Center, Japanese Stroll Gardens, Butterfield Mall and, of course, the universities.

Red Roof Inn

2655 North Glenstone
Springfield, MO 65803
800-733-7663 • 417-831-2100
www.redroof.com
i0175@redroof.com

Type of Lodging: Motel

Room Rates: $37–$53. AAA discount.

Pet Charges & Deposits: None.

Pet Policy: None. All Pets Welcome.

Amenities: Cable TV.

Pet Amenities: List of nearby veterinarians maintained. Smith Park is located at Glenstone and Division.

Rated: 3 Paws — 112 rooms.

Red Roof is a great choice when you're in Springfield. Fantastic Caverns, 1½ miles north of the junction of Interstate 44 and State Route 3, then three miles west on Fantastic Caverns Road is one of Missouri's largest caves. Twelve women first explored it in 1867. In the 1920s, the cave was outfitted with a dance floor, gambling tables and a bar—it was a speakeasy. It was a country music theater in the 1960s and '70s. The Springfield Little Theater on historic Walnut Street was built in 1909 and saw the likes of John Philip Sousa and Lillian Russell perform there. Today, it offers performances by the Springfield civic theater, ballet and regional opera companies.

outh I-55

...o • 314-894-0700
...w.midamcorp.com
holinsouth@stlnet.com

Type of Lodging: Hotel

Room Rates: $70–$170. AAA, AARP, AKC and *15% Pets Welcome*™ discounts.

Pet Charges & Deposits: $4 per day. $55 refundable deposit.

Pet Policy: Pets must not be left unattended.

Amenities: Cable TV, refrigerators, microwaves, honor bar, safes, pool, whirlpool.

Pet Amenities: List of nearby veterinarians maintained. Dog runs. Exercise area. Arnold City Park and Susan Park nearby.

Rated: 3 Paws — 140 rooms and 23 suites.

The upscale quality you've come to expect at Holiday Inn venues is very much evident in this first-class lodging. "Meet me in St. Louis" was the rallying cry of this sophisticated city on the Mississippi, even before the famous World's Fair and the Movie Musical that gave it worldwide fame. The St. Louis Art Museum, the St. Louis Zoo, huge Forest Park and, of course, the Gateway Arch are superstar attractions. However, for our purposes, you could do a lot worse than visiting the American Kennel Club Museum of the Dog in Queeny Park.

University Inn Conference Center

Junction at Highways 13 & 50
P.O. Box 415
Warrensburg, MO 64093
877-99 MULES • 660-747-5125
www.theinnbythepond.com
university-inn@hotmail.com

Type of Lodging: Inn

Room Rates: $50–$70, including full breakfast, complimentary drink and meal discounts. AAA and AARP discounts.

Pet Charges & Deposits: $5 per day.

Pet Policy: Sorry, no cats. No pets over 30 lbs.

Amenities: Cable TV, pool, restaurant, lounge.

Pet Amenities: List of nearby veterinarians maintained. Exercise area.

Rated: 3 Paws — 80 rooms.

University Inn & Conference Center, aka The Inn by the Pond, is a well-kept inn. There's an outdoor pool, family restaurant, lounge and two meeting rooms for up to 150 people. Free local phone calls, cable television, complimentary newspaper and dataports in all rooms makes this a wonderful choice. It's ten miles to Whiteman Air Force Base, an hour to Kansas City, and only a mile to Central Missouri State University. There's an eight-screen movie theater next door to the Inn.

Ramada Inn & Figuro's Fine Eatery

1301 Preacher Roe Boulevard
West Plains, MO 65775
800-2 RAMADA • 417-256-8191
www.figuros.com

Type of Lodging: Hotel

Room Rates: $43–$57. AAA, AARP and **15% Pets Welcome™** discounts.

Pet Charges & Deposits: $10 per day.

Pet Policy: None. All Pets Welcome.

Amenities: Cable TV, pool, restaurant.

Pet Amenities: List of nearby veterinarians maintained. Exercise area. Mark Twain National Forest nearby.

Rated: 2 Paws — 79 rooms and 2 suites.

The Ramada Inn gives you a choice of either ground-level guestrooms with individual outside access or upstairs guestrooms with secured corridor entrances. Figuro's is the only Four-Star restaurant in the area as well as the only eatery in Missouri with three Nationally Certified Chefs under one roof. The lodging is located in the South Central Ozarks Heritage Region of the State, surrounded by the Mark Twain National Forest. Traveling a few miles in any direction, you'll find numerous historic, turn-of-the-century gristmills. Whether you enjoy classic cars, auto racing, antiques, bluegrass music, lakes or rivers, you'll find endless side trips that will make your stay unforgettable.

MONTANA

Nicknames: Treasure State; Big Sky Country

Population: 882,779

Area: 147,046 square miles

Climate: Colder continental climate with low humidity.

Capital: Helena

Entered Union: Nov. 8,1889

Motto: *Oro y Plata* (Gold & Silver).

Song: Montana

Flower: Bitterroot

Tree: Ponderosa Pine

Bird: Western Meadowlark

Famous Montanans: Gary Cooper, Chet Huntley, Myrna Loy, Mike Mansfield, Brent Mussburger, Jeannette Rankin, Charles M. Russell.

 History: Cheyenne, Blackfoot, Crow, Assinboin, Salish, Kootenai and Kalispell Native Americans populated the area long before French explorers visited the region in 1742. The U.S. acquired the area partly through the Louisiana Purchase in 1803 and partly through the explorations of Lewis & Clark in 1805-06. Fur traders and missionaries established posts in the early 19th century. Gold was discovered in 1863 and the Montana Territory was established. Native American uprisings reached their peak with the Battle of Little Big Horn in 1876. Chief Joseph and the Nez Perce people surrendered in 1877, after a long trek across the state. Mining activity and the coming of the railway in 1883 brought prosperity and growth.

Rimview Inn

1025 North 27th Street
Billings, MT 59101
800-551-1418 • 406-248-2622

Type of Lodging: Motel
Room Rates: $40–$60, including conti-nental breakfast. AAA, AARP and *$2 off Pets Welcome*™ discounts.
Pet Charges & Deposits: $5 per stay.
Pet Policy: Sorry, no cats. Manager's prior approval required.
Amenities: Cable TV, refrigerators, microwaves, hot tubs.
Pet Amenities: Pioneer Park is a mile from the motel.
Rated: 2 Paws — 54 rooms.

Rimview Inn takes pride in providing quali-ty service and affordable rates. The guest-rooms come with a full range of extras, including hot tubs, king- or queen-sized beds and family accommodations. Cowboy mo-tion picture star William S. Hart posed for a bronze statue of a cowboy, the Range Rider of the Yellowstone, which commands an im-pressive view of the city. The Rimrocks, Billings' most striking natural feature, rise 400 feet above the Yellowstone Valley, run-ning the length of the city and beyond. Pictograph Cave State Park, seven miles southeast of the city, features caverns that have sheltered people of many Native Amer-ican cultures. Pictorial records adorn the walls of one cave.

Ramada Limited

2020 Wheat Drive
Bozeman, MT 59715
800-272-6232 • 406-585-2626

Type of Lodging: Hotel
Room Rates: $39–$139, including continental breakfast. AAA, AARP and *10% Pets Welcome*™ discounts.
Pet Charge & Deposits: None.
Pet Policy: Designated rooms only.
Amenities: Cable TV, safes, pool, Jacuzzi, 90-feet indoor waterslide.
Pet Amenities: None.
Rated: 3 Paws — 44 rooms and 6 suites.

Located in the heart of the Rockies and near Yellowstone National Park, the Ramada Inn is clean, comfortable and commands a view of the magnificent Big Sky countryside. It's convenient to the Bridger Bowl and Big Sky ski areas, the Museum of the Rockies, Crystal Caverns and numerous ghost towns. It's also close to fishing, camping, hiking and outdoor activities almost beyond counting, including white water rafting.

Ramada Inn Copper King

4655 Harrison Avenue
Butte, MT 59701
800-332-8600 • 406-494-6666
www.ramadainncopperking.com
www.info@ramadainncopperking.com

Type of Lodging: Hotel

Room Rates: $80–$100, including full buffet breakfast. AAA, AARP and *10% Pets Welcome*™ discounts.

Pet Charges & Deposits: $10 per day.

Pet Policy: No pets over 100 lbs. Designated rooms only.

Amenities: Cable TV, safes, pool, Jacuzzi, alarm clocks, dataports.

Pet Amenities: List of nearby veterinarians maintained.

Rated: 3 Paws — 144 rooms and 2 suites.

Ramada Inn has Butte's largest and most beautiful guestrooms. It offers many wonderful amenities, two excellent restaurants and a lounge featuring weekend entertainment and complimentary shuttle to the airport. Butte is halfway between Glacier and Yellowstone National Parks, with convenient access to all of Montana's natural wonderlands. It has a unique mining history. Special sights include the Berkeley Pit, the Copper King Mansion and Our Lady of the Rockies, a 90-feet high statue of the Virgin Mary, which took six years to build and was airlifted into place in 1985.

Coleman-Fee Mansion Bed & Breakfast

500 Missouri Avenue
Deer Lodge, MT 59722
888-888-2507 • 406-846-2922
stiehlmansion@in-tch.com

Type of Lodging: B&B

Room Rates: $65–$150, including full breakfast. AAA discount.

Pet Charges & Deposits: $10 per day. $20 nonrefundable deposit.

Pet Policy: Sorry, no cats. Manager's prior approval required.

Amenities: Cable TV, refrigerators.

Pet Amenities: List of nearby veterinarians maintained. Exercise area. Grant Khors Ranch nearby.

Rated: 3 Paws — 3 rooms and 1 suite. Listed on the National Register of Historic Places.

Built in 1891 and nestled in the heart of gold country in western Montana, the Coleman-Fee Mansion stands as a gold miner's tribute to a gentleman's lifestyle in the rugged western town of Deer Lodge. Deer Lodge, the second oldest township in Montana, is located halfway between Yellowstone and Glacier National Parks, 80 miles southeast of Missoula, 40 miles northwest of Butte. At one time, the Grant Khors Ranch National Historic Site occupied 27,000 acres and its owners controlled more than a million acres in the U.S. and Canada. Today, although it has been reduced to "only" 1,500 acres, it still has 80 buildings, from bunkhouse row to the big ranch house.

Guest House Inn & Suites

580 Sinclair Street
Dillon, MT 59725
800-214-8378 • 406-683-3636
www.orchardhospitality.com
dillongh@bmt.net

Type of Lodging: Motel

Room Rates: $54–$99, including continental breakfast. AAA, AARP and *$10 off Pets Welcome™* discounts.

Pet Charges & Deposits: Call for charges information. $10 nonrefundable deposit.

Pet Policy: Small pets only.

Amenities: Cable TV, refrigerators, microwaves, safes, pool, whirlpool, Jacuzzi, fitness room, business center, dataports, irons and ironing boards, hairdryers.

Pet Amenities: Exercise area.

Rated: 3 Paws — 58 rooms and 2 suites.

Guesthouse Inn & Suites offers six kinds of rooms, including Spa Suites, two-room kids' suites with bunk beds, kitchenettes and rooms with special accessibility features. Dillon was named for the president of the Union Pacific Railroad and today it's important as the central focus of five stock raising valleys. Bannack State Historic Park, 21 miles west, was Montana's first territorial capital and one of the first Gold Rush towns of the area. The park includes the remains of the first capitol building, a jail, a hotel and log cabins.

Best Western by Mammoth Hot Springs

South Highway 89
P.O. Box 646
Gardiner, MT 59030
800-828-9080 • 406-848-7311
www.bestwestern.com/mammothhotsprings

Type of Lodging: Hotel

Room Rates: $45–$104. AARP discount.

Pet Charges & Deposits: $5 per day.

Pet Policy: Designated rooms only. Pets must not be left unattended.

Amenities: Cable TV, refrigerators, microwaves, pool, whirlpool, Jacuzzi, hot tubs, spas, hairdryers, irons and ironing boards, free local calls.

Pet Amenities: List of nearby veterinarians maintained. Exercise area. Yellowstone National Park and Town Park nearby.

Rated: 3 Paws — 81 rooms and 4 suites.

Best Western by Mammoth Hot Springs is a superior lodging with a superlative location on the banks of the Yellowstone River, just one mile from the north entrance to Yellowstone National Park. It's 52 miles to Old Faithful and five miles to Mammoth Hot Springs. While there, enjoy the Yellowstone Mine—fine dining in an old time mine atmosphere; the Rusty Rail Lounge and Casino, where you can relax in front of a fireplace and enjoy your favorite cocktail or indulge yourself in Keno, live poker or pool; or visit Gold Strike Gifts, which specializes in Black Hills gold, pottery and unique Montana-made gifts.

Cottonwood Inn

45 First Avenue Northeast
Glasgow, MT 59230
800-321-8213 • 406-228-8213
cwinn@nemontel.net

Type of Lodging: Hotel

Room Rates: $50–$65. AAA and AARP discounts.

Pet Charges & Deposits: None.

Pet Policy: Manager's prior approval required.

Amenities: Cable TV, refrigerators, pool, whirlpool, Jacuzzi, hot tubs, dining room, lounge.

Pet Amenities: List of nearby veterinarians maintained. Exercise area.

Rated: 3 Paws — 92 rooms.

Glasgow's in the middle of the Milk and Missouri River Valleys and the Cottonwood Inn bills itself as Northeastern Montana's premier hotel and convention center. It boasts quiet rooms with valet and room service. Executive rooms have a full-sized desk, computer and fax outlets, recliner and a telephone in the bathroom. The building began its life as a railroad station. The Pioneer Museum, five miles west, displays 19th century Native American and pioneer artifacts. The Cottonwood Inn is minutes from Fort Peck Lake, developed when Fort Peck Dam was built by the U.S. Army Corps of Engineers in the 1930s. It has more miles of shoreline than California.

Days Inn

101 14th Avenue Northwest
Great Falls, MT 59404
800-329-7466 • 406-727-6565
www.the.daysinn.com/greatfalls05845

Type of Lodging: Motel

Room Rates: $46–$76, including continental breakfast. AAA, AARP and *10% Pets Welcome™* discounts.

Pet Charges & Deposits: $5 per day.

Pet Policy: Designated rooms only.

Amenities: Cable TV, refrigerators, microwaves.

Pet Amenities: List of nearby veterinarians maintained. Exercise area. Gibson Park nearby.

Rated: 2 Paws — 62 rooms. Days Inn Five-Sunburst Award Winner.

Days Inn is an excellent choice for affordable lodging in Montana's second largest city. Lewis and Clark first saw the Great Falls of the Missouri River in 1805. However, the city of that name was not developed until 78 years later. Malmstrom Air Force Base and agriculture are the two pillars on which the city's economy is built. The C.M. Russell Museum of Western Art, his home, and his log cabin studio are highlights of any trip to the area.

Great Falls Inn

1400 28th Street South
Great Falls, MT 59405
800-454-6010 • 406-453-6000
www.greatfallsinn.com
tgfi@mcn.net

Type of Lodging: Inn

Room Rates: $55–$70, including continental breakfast. AAA, AARP and *10% Pets Welcome™* discounts.

Pet Charges & Deposits: $5 per day.

Pet Policy: Designated rooms only.

Amenities: Cable TV, refrigerators, microwaves, safes.

Pet Amenities: List of nearby veterinarians maintained. Dog runs. Lions Park is located at 27th Street and 10th Avenue South.

Rated: 3 Paws — 61 rooms.

The Great Falls Inn is most accommodating to pets. It's conveniently located in the center of town, near Benefits Health Care and the Great Falls Clinic. Rivers Edge Trail, which begins north of U.S. Highway 89 on River Drive and meanders along the Missouri River for 13 miles, ten of which are paved, is great for walking your pet or bicycling. The Great Falls Historic Trolley offers two-hour guided tours of the city, including the Historic Home District, the Railroad Area and downtown Great Falls.

Barrister Bed & Breakfast

416 North Ewing Street
Helena, MT 59601
800-823-1148 • 406-443-7330
www.wtp.net/go/montana/sites/barrister.
  html
barister@rcisys.net

Type of Lodging: B&B

Room Rates: $90–$105, including full breakfast and wine & hors d'oeuvres. AAA discount.

Pet Charges & Deposits: None.

Pet Policy: None. All Pets Welcome.

Amenities: Cable TV, business center.

Pet Amenities: Pet sitting available. List of nearby veterinarians maintained. Exercise area. Hill Park is located at Neill Avenue and Park Avenue.

Rated: 4 Paws — 5 rooms.

The Barrister Bed & Breakfast is an 1874 Victorian mansion, centrally located in Montana's lovely capital city. The guestrooms are carefully decorated to provide warmth and comfort. The Barrister is located directly across the street from the extraordinarily beautiful Cathedral of St. Helena, a neo-Gothic structure modeled after the Votive Church of Vienna, Austria. The Last Chance Gulch Tour takes you through one of America's most charming capital cities on an automotive tour train.

Best Western Outlaw Hotel

1701 Highway 93 South
Kalispell, MT 59901
800-325-4000 • 406-751-5050
www.westcoasthotels.com

Type of Lodging: Motel

Room Rates: $75–$150. AAA and AARP discounts.

Pet Charges & Deposits: $10 per day.

Pet Policy: Designated rooms only.

Amenities: Cable TV, safes, pool, whirlpool.

Pet Amenities: List of nearby veterinarians maintained.

Rated: 3 Paws — 196 rooms and 24 suites.

The Best Western Outlaw Hotel is home not only to upscale rooms but also to Hennessy's Steakhouse, Lounge & Casino. Kalispell, in the Flathead Valley, is only a 35-minute drive from Glacier National Park—over one million acres of unspoiled wilderness and dramatic mountains and waterfalls. Adjoining Waterton Lakes National Park in southwestern Alberta, Canada, the two have been designated Waterton-Glacier International Peace Park. Kalispell is near Flathead Lake, the largest natural freshwater lake in the Western United States. Outdoor recreation opportunities are limitless in this gorgeous country,

Kalispell Grand Hotel

100 Main Street
Kalispell, MT 59901
800-858-7422 • 406-755-8100
www.kalispellgrand.com
grand@kalispellgrand.com

Type of Lodging: Hotel

Room Rates: $58–$125, including continental breakfast. AARP discount.

Pet Charges & Deposits: None.

Pet Policy: None. All Pets Welcome.

Amenities: Cable TV, dataports, fitness room, restaurant.

Pet Amenities: List of nearby veterinarians maintained. Woodland Park is on the corner of Woodland Avenue and Conrad Drive, just 6 blocks east of the hotel.

Rated: 4 Paws — 38 rooms and 2 suites.

Located just 30 minutes from Glacier National Park in Montana's magnificent Flathead Valley, this historic accommodation offers a glimpse into the past with its original high, pressed-tin ceilings, terrazzo floor and grand oak staircase. Complimentary continental breakfast is an every morning occasion in the Grand Lobby. You'll climb the royal oak stairway to enjoy your room furnished with the warmth of Victorian cherry wood-style. Guestrooms vary in size, including family suites and jetted tub suites. All rooms feature private baths with showers, cable television with remote and telephones equipped with dataports.

WestCoast Kalispell Center Hotel

20 North Main
Kalispell, MT 59901
800-325-4000 • 406-751-5050
www.westcoasthotels.com

Type of Lodging: Motel

Room Rates: $75–$150. AAA and AARP discounts.

Pet Charges & Deposits: $10 per day

Pet Policy: Designated rooms only.

Amenities: Cable TV, safes, pool, Jacuzzi, hot tubs, sauna

Pet Amenities: List of nearby veterinarians maintained. Exercise area.

Rated: 3 Paws — 119 rooms and 13 suites.

WestCoast Kalispell Center Hotel, sister lodging of the Best Western Outlaw Hotel immediately above, is Northwest Montana's only lodging and shopping complex under one roof. It's a full service hotel with all the amenities you'd expect of a first-class lodging. Kalispell defines what you always dreamed "the Wild West" would look like. It's one mile to the historic Conrad Mansion, only eight miles to Flathead Lake, a region noted for the production of cherries. Located in the heart of the Rocky Mountains, dense forests, lakes, rivers and dramatic mountains surround Kalispell. The Hockaday Museum of Art houses noteworthy works of local, regional and national artists.

Best Inn - North

4953 North Reserve Street
Missoula, MT 59808
800-272-9500 • 406-542-7500
www.bestinn.com
mtgs-4-u@bigsky.net

Type of Lodging: Motel

Room Rates: $59–$79, including continental breakfast. AAA and AARP discounts.

Pet Charges & Deposits: $6 per day.

Pet Policy: No pets over 100 lbs. Designated rooms only.

Amenities: Cable TV, refrigerators, microwaves, coffeemakers, hairdryers, dataports, hot tubs, guest laundry, free local phone calls.

Pet Amenities: None.

Rated: 2 Paws — 67 rooms

Best Inn – North affords cable television, airport van service and deluxe rooms featuring sleeper sofas, microwaves, refrigerators, coffeemakers, hairdryers and dataports. Missoula is a great place to stay as a short drive in any direction will take you into a national forest or wilderness area. The Historical Museum at Fort Missoula, housed in the center of the old fort, features displays about the Native American presence in the vicinity, as well as galleries depicting the role of the lumber industry, a major industry as well as a major concern, in the area.

Best Inn & Conference Center - South

3803 Brooke Street
Missoula, MT 59804
800-272-9500 • 406-251-2665
www.bestinn.com
mtgs-4-u@bigsky.net

Type of Lodging: Motel

Room Rates: $59–$79, including continental breakfast. AAA and AARP discounts.

Pet Charges & Deposits: $6 per day.

Pet Policy: No pets over 100 lbs. Designated rooms only.

Amenities: Cable TV, hot tubs, free local phone calls, guest laundry.

Pet Amenities: Fort Missoula is located on South Avenue.

Rated: 2 Paws – 81 rooms.

Best Inn & Conference Center – South features standard rooms, as well as deluxe rooms with substantial upscale amenities. Its Evergreen Rooms provide air purification systems to guarantee an odor-free, allergen-free atmosphere. An in-lodge conference center accommodates up to 250 people. The Smokejumpers Base Aerial Fire Depot, next to Missoula's Johnson-Bell Airport, displays dioramas, historic photographs and artifacts relating to the history of firefighting in the Forest Service. The Art Museum of Missoula contains art of the western states, as well as changing exhibits throughout the year.

Elkhorn Mountain Inn

One Jackson Creek Road
Montana City, MT 59634
406-442-6625

Type of Lodging: Hotel

Room Rates: $50–$99, including continental breakfast. AAA and *10% Pets Welcome™* discounts.

Pet Charges & Deposits: $5 per day

Pet Policy: Manager's prior approval required.

Amenities: Cable TV, refrigerators.

Pet Amenities: List of nearby veterinarians maintained. Exercise area with plenty of room for pets to romp. Montana City Soccer Field and Elkhorn Roodlers Area nearby.

Rated: 3 Paws – 20 rooms and 2 suites.

Elkhorn Mountain Inn demonstrates justifiable pride. Hosts Joe & Mariann Calnan sum up their philosophy as follows, "We're not just innkeepers, we're a local family. We know the area—things to do, short-cut directions, local entertainment and events, and the best dining facilities. Making your stay comfortable with great accommodations and real Montana hospitality is part of our lifestyle, not just a job." Montana City is outside the "big city" of Helena, but still close to all major points of interest there. It's midway between Yellowstone and Glacier National Parks, in the heart of historic vigilante and mining country.

Comfort Inn

612 North Broadway
P.O. Box 1970
Red Lodge, MT 59068
888-733-4661 • 406-446-4469
www.wtp.net/comfortinn
1stpic@wtp.net

Type of Lodging: Hotel

Room Rates: $50–$100, including continental breakfast. AAA and AARP discounts.

Pet Charges & Deposits: $25 refundable deposit.

Pet Policy: Designated rooms only.

Amenities: Cable TV, pool, whirlpool, hot tubs.

Pet Amenities: List of nearby veterinarians maintained. Exercise area. Lions Club Park is a 5-minute walk from the hotel.

Rated: 3 Paws — 53 rooms. 1999 Comfort Inn Gold Award Winner.

Comfort Inn is a fine, value-priced choice when you're in this all-year resort town at the base of the Beartooth Mountains. The highly scenic Bear Tooth Pass leads you to the northeast entrance to Yellowstone National Park. Area attractions include skiing at Red Lodge Mountain, the Peaks to Prairie Museum, Little Bighorn Battlefield, ice caves and whitewater rafting.

O'Haire Manor Motel

204 Second Street South
Shelby, MT 59474
800-541-5809 • 406-434-5555

Type of Lodging: Motel

Room Rates: $35–$60. AAA and AARP discounts.

Pet Charges & Deposits: $5 per day.

Pet Policy: Designated rooms only.

Amenities: Cable TV, refrigerators, microwaves, hot tubs.

Pet Amenities: List of nearby veterinarians maintained. Exercise area. Shelby City Park nearby.

Rated: 2 Paws — 37 rooms.

O'Haire Manor Motel offers relaxing guest-rooms designed to maximize your comfort and convenience. The motel has three- and four-bed family units, complete with microwave ovens and refrigerators. Shelby in its heyday was a Wild West fun town, where cowboys celebrated being in "the big city" after months on the range. It's also been a railroad, farming and ranching center. In 1922, oil was discovered nearby. A year later, the 1923 Dempsey-Gibbons prizefight nearly bankrupted the community. Shelby is near the intersection of Interstate 15 and U.S. Highway 2, 70 miles southeast of Glacier National Park.

Pine Lodge

920 Spokane Avenue
Whitefish, MT 59937
800-305-8463 • 406-862-7600
www.thepinelodge.com
info@thepinelodge.com

Type of Lodging: Motor Lodge

Room Rates: $55–$160, including continental breakfast. AAA, AARP and *10% Pets Welcome™* discounts.

Pet Charges & Deposits: None.

Pet Policy: Pets must not be left unattended.

Amenities: Cable TV, pool, hot tubs, microwaves, refrigerators.

Pet Amenities: Although there are no formal runs or exercise areas, one can take a pet virtually anywhere in the area. Riverside Park is located at Fifth Street and Baker.

Rated: 3 Paws — 50 rooms and 26 suites.

The Pine Lodge reflects the grandeur of Montana. Set on the Whitefish River, with views of the Big Mountain Ski and Summer Resort and Glacier National Park, the Pine Lodge is romantic and inviting. Its rooms are decorated with rich fabrics, Montana-made furniture and artifacts. Whitefish, which adjoins Kalispell, is only a short 25-mile drive to Glacier National Park. In the city itself, the Great Northern Railway Depot has been restored to its 1927 chalet-like appearance and contains historical and railroad memorabilia.

Super 8 Motel

800 Spokane Avenue
Whitefish, MT 59937
800-800-8000 • 406-862-8255

Type of Lodging: Motel

Room Rates: $38–$77, including toast bar. AAA, AARP and *10% Pets Welcome™* discounts.

Pet Charges & Deposits: $5 per day.

Pet Policy: No pets over 40 lbs. Designated rooms only. Manager's prior approval required.

Amenities: Cable TV, hot tubs.

Pet Amenities: Exercise area. Riverside City Park is located at Fifth Street and Central Avenue.

Rated: 2 Paws — 40 rooms and 1 suite.

Super 8 – Whitefish is an excellent budget-conscious choice for lodging in the Kalispell-Whitefish-Glacier National Park area. You'll have a wonderful time and a wonderful meal at 'Stube & Chuckwagon Grill at Big Mountain Ski & Summer Resort. It is a Western-style barbecue dinner followed by an evening of Western songs, poems and tall tales with a cowboy band. This is the "sort of tamed" Wild West of your imagination.

NEBRASKA

Nickname: Cornhusker State
Population: 1,666,028
Area: 77,358 square miles
Climate: Continental, semi-arid.
Capital: Lincoln
Entered Union: March 1,1867
Motto: Equality before the law.
Song: Beautiful Nebraska
Flower: Goldenrod
Tree: Cottonwood

Bird: Western Meadowlark
Famous Nebraskans: Fred Astaire, Marlon Brando, William Jennings Bryan, Warren Buffett, Johnny Carson, Willa Cather, Dick Cavett, "Buffalo Bill" Cody, Henry Fonda, Nick Nolte, Robert Taylor, Darryl F. Zanuck.

 History: Pawnee, Ponca, Omaha and Oto peoples lived in the region before the coming of the Europeans. The U.S. acquired the area as part of the Louisiana Purchase in 1803. The first permanent settlement was Bellevue, near Omaha, in 1823. The region was gradually settled, despite the 1834 Indian Intercourse Act, which declared Nebraska to be Native American country and precluded White settlement. Conflicts with settlers eventually caused the Native Americans to settle on reservations. Many Civil War veterans settled in Nebraska under the free land terms of the 1862 Homestead Act. As agriculture grew, struggles followed between ranchers and homesteaders.

COLUMBUS, NEBRASKA (Pop. 19,500)

Sleep Inn & Suites

3030 23rd Street
Columbus, NE 68601
402-562-5200
www.megavision.net/sleepinn
sleepinn@megavision.com

Type of Lodging: Motel
Room Rates: $55–$120, including continental breakfast. AAA, AARP, Corporate and *10% Pets Welcome™* discounts.
Pet Charges & Deposits: $10 per day.
Pet Policy: Designated rooms only.
Amenities: Cable TV, safes, pool, whirlpool.
Pet Amenities: None.
Rated: 3 Paws — 99 rooms and suites.

Whether you and your pet are just visiting, passing through, or a business traveler, the Sleep Inn located in Columbus, will be the place you will want for your stay. Located on Highway 30 (the historic Lincoln Highway and Mormon Trail), it is convenient to restaurants, golf courses, airport, industrial district and the agricultural park. The rooms have oversized showers, large work desks, remote control cable television, dataports and a 100% guest satisfaction guarantee.

Super 8 Motel

401 Platte River Drive
Gothenburg, NE 69138
308-537-2684

Type of Lodging: Motel

Room Rates: $40–$125, including continental breakfast. AAA and AARP discounts.

Pet Charges & Deposits: Credit card imprint required.

Pet Policy: Manager's prior approval required.

Amenities: Cable TV, refrigerators, pool, whirlpool.

Pet Amenities: List of nearby veterinarians maintained. Exercise area.

Rated: 3 Paws — 37 rooms and 5 suites.

Super 8 Motel offers rooms and suites that are spacious, well appointed and decidedly upscale. Recreational amenities include an indoor pool and fitness room. Other amenities consist of free parking, guest laundry services, cable television and continental breakfast.

Midlands Lodge

910 West J
Hastings, NE 68901
800-237-1872 • 402-463-2428
www.midlandslodge.com

Type of Lodging: Motel

Room Rates: $30–$64, including free coffee. AAA and Senior Citizens discounts.

Pet Charges & Deposits: None.

Pet Policy: Designated rooms only. Manager's prior approval required. Pets must not be left unattended.

Amenities: Cable TV, refrigerators, microwaves, pool, hairdryers, vanities.

Pet Amenities: List of nearby veterinarians maintained. Exercise area. Lincoln Park is adjacent to the motel.

Rated: 2 Paws — 45 rooms and 2 suites.

Originally built in 1963 by a local contractor, Midlands Lodge's guestrooms are enhanced by prints from the renowned Nebraskan photographer, Tom Mangelson. Other amenities include cable television, refrigerator and hairdryers. Free coffee and an outdoor heated pool are awaiting you at Midlands Lodge. Centrally located at the junction of Highways 281, 34 and 6, the motel is adjacent to Dykeman's Camper Place and Lincoln Park. Other area attractions and events include Bill Smith Softball Complex, Lied IMAX Theatre, Champions Sports and Recreation Center, Cottonwood Prairie Festival, Nebraska Country Music Festival, Kool-Aid Days, Adams County Fairfest and Labor Day Weekend Rodeo.

Super 8 Motel

15 West Eighth Street
Kearney, NE 68847
800-800-8000 • 308-234-5513
www.innworks.com

Type of Lodging: Motel
Room Rates: $45–$65, including continental breakfast. AAA and AARP discounts.
Pet Charges & Deposits: $10 per stay.
Pet Policy: Sorry, no cats. Manager's prior approval required.
Amenities: Cable TV, safes, one free 8-minute long distance call each night.
Pet Amenities: Exercise area.
Rated: 3 Paws — 60 rooms.

This Super 8 Motel is a great place to stay for those who need access to Kearney, Grand Island, University of Nebraska, Amherst, Axtell, Elm Creek, Funk, Gibbon, Hazard, Heartwell, Hildrith, Kennesaw, Minden, Norman, Overton, Pleasanton, Prosser, Riverdale, Shelton, Wilcox and downtown Hastings. It offers you and your pet many amenities designed to keep you happy in your home away from home.

Microtel Inn and Suites

2505 Fairfield Street
Lincoln, NE 68521
888-771-7171 • 402-476-2591
microtelinn@sprintmail.com

Type of Lodging: Motel
Room Rates: $43–$66, including continental breakfast. AAA discount.
Pet Charges & Deposits: $6 per day. $20 refundable deposit.
Pet Policy: Designated rooms only. Manager's prior approval required.
Amenities: Cable TV, refrigerators, microwaves.
Pet Amenities: List of nearby veterinarians maintained. Exercise area.
Rated: 3 Paws — 40 rooms and 8 suites.

Microtel Inn and Suites is a good choice for travelers who wish to have access to Folsom Children's Zoo, Lincoln Airport, University of Nebraska, State Park, shopping, Nebraska State Historical Society, State Fairgrounds, SAC Museum and downtown Lincoln.

Red Roof Inn & Suites

6501 North 28th Street
Lincoln, NE 68504
800-733-7663 • 402-438-4700

Type of Lodging: Motel
Room Rates: $64–$73, including
continental breakfast. AAA, AARP and
10% Pets Welcome™ discount.
Pet Charges & Deposits: $10 refund-
able deposit.
Pet Policy: No pets over 60 lbs.
Designated rooms only.
Amenities: Cable TV, refrigerators,
microwaves, safes, pool, hot tubs.
Pet Amenities: List of nearby veteri-
narians maintained. Exercise area.
Dog runs and park are 3 miles away.
Rated: 3 Paws — 64 rooms and 14
suites.

The Red Roof Inn & Suites offers an indoor
heated pool, hot tub, basic cable television,
and free continental breakfast. This Inn is
located within miles of Pershing Municipal
Auditorium, Devaney Sports Center,
Lincoln Children's Museum, Nebraska State
Capitol, University of Nebraska, Nebraska
State Fairgrounds, Memorial Stadium and
Folsom Zoo. There are many special events
in Lincoln including Jazz in June, July Jamm,
Lincoln Marathon, Nebraska Football and
the Nebraska State Fair.

Villager Courtyard & Gardens Hotel

5200 "O" Street
Lincoln, NE 68510
800-356-4321 • 402-464-9111
www.bestwestern.com
villagerne@aol.com

Type of Lodging: Hotel
Room Rates: Call for rates. AAA, AARP
and *10% Pets Welcome*™ discounts.
Pet Charges & Deposits: $25 refund-
able deposit.
Pet Policy: None. All Pets Welcome.
Amenities: Cable TV, pool, whirlpool,
Jacuzzi, hot tubs.
Pet Amenities: List of nearby veterinar-
ians maintained. Dog runs. Exercise
area. Holms Park is located at 70th and
Van Horn.
Rated: 3 Paws — 186 rooms.

The Villager Courtyard & Gardens is in the
heart of Lincoln, accessible to all areas of
Nebraska's capital city. The beautifully landscaped hotel is a full service lodging facility
with two restaurants and a country nightclub. All the attractions of Lincoln are
nearby, which include the State Capitol,
University of Nebraska campus, State
Fairgrounds, shopping centers, state govern-
ments and downtown Lincoln.

Norfolk Country Inn

1201 South 13th Street
Norfolk, NE 68701
800-233-0733 • 402-371-4430
www.norfolkcountryinn.com
ncinn@uswest.net

Type of Lodging: Motel
Room Rates: $50–$56. AAA and AARP discounts.
Pet Charges & Deposits: None.
Pet Policy: Designated rooms only.
Amenities: Cable TV, pool.
Pet Amenities: Exercise area. Ta-ha-zooka Park is located off Highway 81 South.
Rated: 3 Paws — 120 rooms and 6 suites.

At the Norfolk Country Inn, they are committed to providing the service you and your pet deserve during your stay with them. Don't let their down-home, small town charm fool you, Norfolk Country Inn offers all the amenities you'd expect to find at a big-city motel. Enjoy a restful night in one of the uniquely decorated guestrooms and suites. Just minutes away is a shopper's delight with everything from major department store chains to novelty boutiques. Norfolk offers many nearby attractions including the Elkhorn Valley Museum, Cuthills Vineyard, Ashfall Fossil Beds and it's the home of Johnny Carson.

Best Western Chalet Lodge

920 North Jeffers
North Platte, NE 691001
800-622-2313 • 308-532-2313

Type of Lodging: Motel
Room Rates: $45–$66, including continental breakfast. AAA and AARP discounts.
Pet Charges & Deposits: $3 per day.
Pet Policy: Designated rooms only.
Amenities: Cable TV, refrigerators, pool.
Pet Amenities: List of nearby veterinarians maintained. Dog runs. Cody Park nearby.
Rated: 3 Paws — 38 rooms.

The Best Western Chalet Lodge offers newly remodeled guestrooms with cable television, in-room coffee and air conditioning. Wake up to the delights of the complimentary continental breakfast and relax in the heated outdoor pool. Explore North Platte, home of legendary Buffalo Bill Cody and tour the Cody Park and area museums. Outdoors excitement includes: public golf courses, tennis courts, parks, fishing, water-skiing, boating and swimming. Local attractions include Buffalo Bill's Ranch State Park, Factory Outlet Mall, Bailey Yards Observation Point and Visitors Center.

Days Inn

601 Stagecoach Trail
Ogallala, NE 69153
308-284-6365

Type of Lodging: Motel

Room Rates: $45–$75, including continental breakfast. AAA, AARP, AKC, ABA and *10% Pets Welcome™* discounts.

Pet Charges & Deposits: $6 per day.

Pet Policy: Designated rooms only. Manager's prior approval required.

Amenities: Cable TV, refrigerators, microwaves, safe.

Pet Amenities: List of nearby veterinarians maintained. Exercise area. Park is adjacent to the motel.

Rated: 3 Paws — 31 rooms and 1 suite.

The Days Inn Ogallala is conveniently located on Interstate Highway 80 off of Exit 126. They offer many amenities to their guests. In the morning, they serve a complimentary continental breakfast, and they also have complimentary coffee in the lobby. Free parking is also available on property. Ogallala is America's Cowboy Capital where the Platte River Forks for the Christi, Oregon, Norman and Denver trails. There is excellent fishing, boating, and water sports on Lake McConaughy and Lake Ogallala. Or watch eagles from the enclosed Kingsley Dam viewing facility, or visit Historical Boot Hill and The Mansion on the Hill.

Trade Winds Lodge

HC 37, Box 2
Valentine, NE 69201
800-341-8000 • 402-376-1600
www.bestvalueinn.com

Type of Lodging: Motel

Room Rates: $39–$61. AAA and AARP discounts.

Pet Charges & Deposits: $5 per stay.

Pet Policy: None. All Pets Welcome.

Amenities: Cable TV.

Pet Amenities: List of nearby veterinarians maintained. Exercise area. Park nearby.

Rated: 3 Paws — 32 rooms.

The Trade Winds Lodge offers spacious, remodeled rooms with king- and queen-sized beds and reclining chairs. There is an indoor fish cleaning area and deep freeze available for guests to use. Recreational activities include fishing, canoeing and hiking.

NEVADA

Nicknames: Sagebrush State; Silver State; Battle Born State
Population: 1,809,253
Area: 110,567 square miles
Climate: semi-arid and arid
Capital: Carson City
Entered Union: Oct. 31, 1864
Motto: All for our country.
Song: Home Means Nevada
Flower: Sagebrush

Tree: Single Leaf Pinon and Bristlecone Pine
Bird: Mountain Bluebird
Famous Nevadans: Walter Van Tilburg Clark, George Feris, Sarah Winnemucca Hopkins, Paul Laxalt, Pat McCarran.

History: Shoshone, Paiute, Bannock and Washoe peoples lived in the area at the time of European contact. Hudson's Bay Trappers explored the area in 1825. A year later, Jedediah Smith crossed the state. The area was acquired by the U.S. in 1848. In 1859, the discovery of the Comstock Lode (gold and silver) spurred a population boom, but it was nothing compared to the post-1980s explosion of Las Vegas, which now adds 5,000 new inhabitants each month. The net change between 1990 and 1999 was 50.6%! Legalized gambling, a "Disney World for Adults," the state is a tourist mecca, featuring not only Las Vegas, but Virginia City, the liveliest ghost town in the U.S., and Reno, "Biggest Little City in the World."

CARSON, NEVADA (Pop. 53,000)

Days Inn

3103 North Carson Street
Carson City, NV 89706
775-883-3343

Type of Lodging: Motel
Room Rates: Call for rates. AAA and AARP discounts.
Pet Charges & Deposits: $5 per day. $100 refundable deposit.
Pet Policy: None. All Pets Welcome.
Amenities: Cable TV, refrigerators, microwaves.
Pet Amenities: List of nearby veterinarians maintained. Dog runs. Exercise area. Mills Park nearby.
Rated: 3 Paws — 61 rooms and 2 suites.

When traveling to Carson City, whether to visit the Governor's Mansion, the Nevada State Museum, the Nevada State Railroad Museum or Virginia City, the Days Inn is the place to stay. The rooms and suites have all the modern day conveniences. Other nearby attractions include golfing, fishing, horseback riding, boating, water and snow-skiing. Ghost towns can also be reached on a brief ride.

Topaz Lodge and Casino

P.O. Box 187
Gardnerville, NV 89410
800-962-0732 • 775-266-3338
www.enterit.com/topaz3338.htm
topazlodge@aol.com

Type of Lodging: Motel
Room Rates: $39– $55.
Pet Charges & Deposits: $5 per day.
Pet Policy: Sorry, no cats. Designated rooms only.
Amenities: Cable TV, pool, restaurant.
Pet Amenities: Douglas County Park nearby.
Rated: 2 Paws – 102 rooms.

If you are looking for 24-hour Nevada-style entertainment for you and your pet, Topaz Lodge and Casino is the place for you. Not only is there gambling, but also Topaz Lake produces some trophy-case worthy-rainbow trout. The larger ones (7 to 8 pounders) are mostly caught from January to March. Guests are encouraged to enter the annual Rainbow Trout Contest which runs from January to mid-April. The rest of the year brings great stream trout fishing in the Walker River.

Hawthorn Suites Las Vegas Strip

5051 Duke Ellington Way
Las Vegas, NV 89119
800-811-2450 • 702-739-7000
www.hawthorn.com
lvsuite@aol.com

Type of Lodging: Hotel
Suite Rates: $89–$165, including full buffet breakfast, Wednesday evening dinner and weekday social hour. AAA, AARP, AKC, AMA and *10% Pets Welcome*™ discounts.
Pet Charges & Deposits: $125 deposit of which $100 is refundable.
Pet Policy: Designated rooms only.
Amenities: Cable TV, refrigerators, microwaves, pool, Jacuzzi.
Pet Amenities: Treats available. List of nearby veterinarians maintained. Exercise area. Paradise Park is located on Tropicana and Paradise Roads.
Rated: 3 Paws – 281 suites. Only non-gaming hotel adjacent to the Las Vegas Strip.

Just steps away from the Strip, this is the ideal resort for both the leisure and business traveler. All suites offer fully equipped kitchens, bedrooms and baths. While minutes away from major casinos such as the MGM and New York-New York, Hawthorn Suites is three miles away from the Las Vegas Convention Center and only two miles from the Airport. Your pet will enjoy the peaceful atmosphere as well as the treats.

Best Western North Shore Inn

520 North Moapa Valley Boulevard
Overton, NV 89040
702-397-6000
www.bestwesternnsi.com
nsinn@bestwesternnsi.com

Type of Lodging: Hotel

Room Rates: $57–$67, including continental breakfast. AAA, AARP and *10% Pets Welcome™* discounts.

Pet Charges & Deposits: $50 refundable deposit.

Pet Policy: Sorry, no cats. Designated rooms only. Horse boarding facilities.

Amenities: Cable TV, refrigerators, microwaves, pool, Jacuzzi.

Pet Amenities: List of nearby veterinarians maintained. Exercise area. Lake Mead National Park and Valley of Fire State Park nearby.

Rated: 3 Paws — 43 rooms and 2 suites.

While the Best Western North Shore Inn is located less than one hour from Las Vegas, it feels a world away. That's because of Lake Mead and its crystal blue waters offering beauty, peace and serenity. Other nearby attractions include Hoover Dam, Red Rock Canyon, Lost City Museum, Valley of Fire State Park and Wildlife Refuge.

Saddle West Hotel Casino and RV Park

1220 South Highway 160
Pahrump, NV 89048
800-433-3987 • 775-727-1111
www.saddlewest.com
swsam@saddlewest.com

Type of Lodging: Hotel

Room Rates: $44–$150, including full breakfast. AAA, AARP, Good Sam, Senior, FMCA and *10% Pets Welcome™* discounts.

Pet Charges & Deposits: $100 refundable deposit.

Pet Policy: No pets over 75 lbs. Pets must not be left unattended.

Amenities: Cable TV, refrigerators, safes, whirlpool, Jacuzzi, hot tubs, coffeemakers.

Pet Amenities: Death Valley National Park, Spring Mountain Recreation Areas and Red Rock Canyon nearby.

Rated: 3 Paws — 145 rooms and 10 suites.

Pahrump is a rapidly growing community just 63 miles from Las Vegas. It is the gateway to Death Valley National Park. The Spring Mountain Recreation Area covers both sides of the majestic Spring Mountain Range between Pahrump and Las Vegas. Also, the Red Rock Canyon Park is about 45 minutes away. The Saddle West Hotel is centrally located, with easy access to shopping and other services in town. There is a large desert area at the rear of the property that provides ample space to walk and exercise your pet. There are a variety of outdoor activities and day hiking in the surrounding areas.

Meadow Wood Courtyard

5851 South Virginia Street
Reno, NV 89502
800-797 RENO • 775-825-2940
www.meadowwoodcourtyard.com
10149@hotel.cendant.com

Type of Lodging: Motor Lodge

Room Rates: $45–$119, including continental breakfast. AAA, AARP and *10% Pets Welcome*™ discounts.

Pet Charges & Deposits: $10 per day.

Pet Policy: Designated rooms only.

Amenities: Satellite TV, refrigerators, microwaves, safes, pool, whirlpool, Jacuzzi, guest laundry.

Pet Amenities: List of nearby veterinarians maintained. Dog run. Exercise area.

Rated: 3 Paws — 155 rooms.

Centrally located in Reno is the Meadow Wood Courtyard. Ideally suited for those in town for business or pleasure (or both), guestrooms feature all modern conveniences including direct-dial phones with voicemail, dataports and remote satellite television. Just steps away are a heated pool and year-round spa, situated around a beautifully landscaped courtyard.

Residence Inn by Marriott

9845 Gateway Drive
Reno, NV 89511
800-331-3131 • 775-853-8800
www.residenceinn.com

Type of Lodging: Hotel

Suite Rates: $104–$179, including continental breakfast and weekday Hospitality Hour. AAA and AARP discounts.

Pet Charges & Deposits: $6 per day. $80–$100 nonrefundable deposit.

Pet Policy: None. All Pets Welcome.

Amenities: Cable TV, refrigerators, microwaves, pool, whirlpool, SportCourt®.

Pet Amenities: List of nearby veterinarians maintained.

Rated: 3 Paws — 120 suites.

Whether traveling on business or pleasure, the Residence Inn by Marriott is the next best thing to being home. The suites provide you and your pet with all the comforts and conveniences you'll need, including fully equipped kitchen, large living room, fireplace, efficient work space and laundry facilities.

NEW HAMPSHIRE

Nickname: Granite State
Population: 1,201,134
Area: 9,283 square miles
Climate: Highly varied, due to its nearness to high mountains and ocean.
Capital: Concord
Entered Union: June 21,1788
Motto: Live free or die.
Song: Old New Hampshire
Flower: Purple Lilac

Tree: White Birch
Bird: Purple Finch
Famous New Hampshirites: Salmon P. Chase, Mary Baker Eddy, Robert Frost, Horace Greeley, Franklin Pierce, David H. Souter, Daniel Webster.

History: Algonquin-speaking people were the earliest inhabitants of the region. The first European explorers to visit the area were England's Martin Pring in 1603 and France's Champlain in 1605. Before the American Revolution, New Hampshire residents seized a British fort at Portsmouth and drove the royal governor out in 1774. New Hampshire became the first colony to adopt its own constitution in 1776. Tourist attractions include Mt. Washington, highest peak in the Northeast, White Mountain National Forest, and numerous eastern ski areas. The chief industries in New Hampshire are tourism, manufacture, agriculture, trades and mining.

CONCORD, NEW HAMPSHIRE (Pop. 36,000)　　　

Comfort Inn

71 Hall Street
Concord, NH 03301
603-226-4100

Type of Lodging: Inn
Room Rates: $59–$169, including continental breakfast. AAA discount.
Pet Charges & Deposits: $10 per day.
Pet Policy: Designated rooms only.
Amenities: Cable TV, pool, whirlpool, sauna.
Pet Amenities: List of nearby veterinarians maintained. Memorial Field and White's Park nearby.
Rated: 3 Paws – 97 rooms and 3 suites.

Located in the New Hampshire capital of Concord, the Comfort Inn promises pleasant accommodations offered by a warm and friendly staff. Each room has a large bath area and plenty of space to relax or work. If you have a taste for royal luxury, check into one of the two-room suites, offering a separate living and bedroom area, a wet bar, an oversized whirlpool and a step-in shower. The Inn is situated minutes from downtown with historical sites, shops, restaurants, state capitol buildings, antiques, golf and tennis. Visit the New Hampshire International Speedway or the Christy McAuliffe Planetarium. Both Memorial Field and Rollins Park are nearby for your pet's pleasure.

Foothills Farm Bed & Breakfast

P.O. Box 1368
Conway, NH 03818
207-935-3799
foothillsbb@landmarknet.net

Type of Lodging: B&B

Room Rates: $58–$125, including full breakfast. AAA discount.

Pet Charges & Deposits: $25 refundable deposit.

Pet Policy: No pets over 100 lbs. Manager's prior approval required.

Amenities: Refrigerators, microwaves.

Pet Amenities: List of nearby veterinarians maintained. Dog runs. Exercise area consists of 50 acres of fields, forests and streams for swimming. White Mountain National Forest nearby.

Rated: 4 Paws — 3 rooms and 1 suite.

Situated in an unspoiled region of the White Mountains, the Foothills Farm Bed & Breakfast offers the charm of a bygone era with all the modern amenities of nearby Conway and the bustling Mount Washington Valley. The 50 acres of forest, fields and streams provide the opportunity for leisurely walks or secluded picnics. Excellent bicycling, hiking, cross-country skiing, fishing and snowmobiling can be found just outside the door. Swimming, canoeing, skiing, fine dining and tax-free shopping are just minutes away.

Tanglewood Motel & Cottages

Route 16
R.F.D. 1 Box 108
Conway, NH 03818
603-447-5932
www.seene.com/
   tanglewoodmotelandcottages
tanglewood@landmarknet.net

Type of Lodging: Motel

Room Rates: $56 and up.

Pet Charges & Deposits: None.

Pet Policy: Designated rooms only. Manager's prior approval required.

Amenities: Fully equipped kitchens, screened porches, picnic tables, BBQ grills.

Pet Amenities: List of nearby veterinarians maintained. Exercise area consists of many acres to roam. White Mountain National Forest nearby.

Rated: 3 Paws — 15 rooms.

Tanglewood Motel & Cottages is a "Kick off your shoes and relax kinda place" located on a stream by the entrance of the White Mountains, away from the hustle and bustle of modern day life, yet still close to all attractions and restaurants. The one and two room efficiency cottages with fully equipped kitchens sleep two to six. They feature screened porches, picnic tables and grills, children's swing set and play area. Enjoy fishing and swimming in the stream, hiking on the property or on one of the many trails of the nearby Kancamagus Highway. Experience the many pleasures of New England living at Tanglewood.

Days Inn

481 Central Avenue
Dover, NH 03820
800 DAYS INN • 603-742-0400
www.dover-durham-daysinn.com
sleepwell@dover-durham-daysinn.com

Type of Lodging: Motel
Room Rates: $76–$175, including continental breakfast. AAA, AARP and *10% Pets Welcome™* discounts.
Pet Charges & Deposits: $50 refundable deposit.
Pet Policy: Designated rooms only.
Amenities: Cable TV, refrigerators, microwaves, pool, spa, irons & ironing boards, hairdryers.
Pet Amenities: List of nearby veterinarians maintained. Henry Law Park nearby.
Rated: 3 Paws — 50 rooms and 13 suites. Days Inn Five-Sunbursts Award Winner and Chairman's Award for Excellence Winner.

Days Inn has a staff dedicated to ensuring an enjoyable stay for each of their guests—including the four-legged kind. Each guestroom offers individual climate controls, remote control cable television and telephones. There is ample off-street, free parking at your door. The University of New Hampshire, southern Maine and New Hampshire beaches, Portsmouth, Pease International Trade Port and the famed Kittery Outlets are all within a 30-minute drive.

Gale River Motel

One Main Street
Franconia, NH 03580
800-255-7909 • 603-823-5655
galermtl@together.net

Type of Lodging: Motel
Room Rates: $50–$82. AAA and AARP discounts.
Pet Charges & Deposits: $5 per day.
Pet Policy: Designated rooms only. Manager's prior approval required.
Amenities: Cable TV, refrigerators, pool, Jacuzzi.
Pet Amenities: List of nearby veterinarians maintained. Exercise area. Franconia Notch State Park and White Mountain National Forest nearby.
Rated: 3 Paws — 10 rooms.

Located in the picturesque village of Franconia, the Gale River Motel offers the ideal year-round location for enjoying the White Mountains and many other attractions. Each room offers two double beds, coffeemaker, refrigerator, cable television, individual thermostats and spectacular views of Mount Lafayette, Mount Lincoln, Haystack and Cannon Mountain Ski area. Just minutes away you will find the Old Man of the Mountains, Flume Gorge, Cannon Mountain Aerial Tramway, Echo Lake, Mount Washington Cog Railway, Lost River, Appalachian Trail, Clark's Trading Post, Santa's Village, Story Land, Whale's Tale Waterpark and N.E. Ski Museum.

Royalty Inn

130 Main Street
Gorham, NH 03581
800-437-3529 • 603-466-3312
www.royaltyinn.com
innkeeper@royaltyinn.com

Type of Lodging: Hotel

Room Rates: $42–$96, including complimentary coffee.

Pet Charges & Deposits: $5 per day.

Pet Policy: Designated rooms only.

Amenities: Cable TV, pool, whirlpool, game room, sauna, weight room, restaurant, bar.

Pet Amenities: List of nearby veterinarians maintained. Exercise area. White Mountain National Forest nearby.

Rated: 3 Paws — 90 rooms and 2 suites.

Three generations of the King family have been accommodating guests at the Royalty Inn, in a continuing tradition of warm hospitality. It is located in the center of the charming village of Gorham, within walking distance to shopping, the "town common," tennis courts and a playground. Golfers will appreciate the 18-hole golf course three minutes away, as well as nearby Mount Washington and the majestic Presidential Range, offering challenging hiking, climbing, skiing and a host of year-round activities.

Topnotch Motor Inn

265 Main Street
Gorham, NH 03581
800-228-5496 • 603-466-5496
www.top-notch.com

Type of Lodging: Motel

Room Rates: $44–$140, including restaurant discount. AAA, AARP, AKC, ABA and *10% Pets Welcome™* discounts.

Pet Charges & Deposits: None.

Pet Policy: Sorry, no cats. No pets over 50 lbs.

Amenities: Cable TV, refrigerators, microwaves, pool, spa, coffeemakers.

Pet Amenities: List of nearby veterinarians maintained. Exercise area. White Mountain National Forest nearby.

Rated: 3 Paws — 36 rooms.

The Top Notch Motor Inn is a quality motel in a perfect location to enjoy a vacation in the White Mountains, or stay a day or two on your way to and from the seacoast and other destinations. They offer quality motel rooms and newly decorated country inn-style rooms. All guestrooms include king-sized or double beds, refrigerators, telephones, coffeemakers and cable television. Nearby attractions include the Mount Washington Auto Road, Story Land, Santa's Village, Six Gun City and Tuckerman Ravine. One of the most popular attractions in Gorham is Moose Tours, a great opportunity to see these marvelous creatures in their natural habitat. The Appalachian Mountain Club, a number of hiking trails, fishing, golf and other outdoor activities are all nearby.

Hampton Falls Inn

11 Lafayette Road
Hampton Falls, NH 03844
800-356-1729 • 603-926-9545

Type of Lodging: Hotel

Room Rates: $59–$169. AAA and AARP discounts.

Pet Charges & Deposits: $50 refundable deposit.

Pet Policy: Sorry, no cats. No pets over 40 lbs. Designated rooms only. Manager's prior approval required. Pets must not be left unattended.

Amenities: Cable TV, refrigerators, microwaves, pool, Jacuzzi, coffee shop.

Pet Amenities: List of nearby veterinarians maintained. Exercise area including a large walking area. Hampton Beach State Park is located on Highway 101 and IA.

Rated: 3 Paws — 33 rooms and 14 suites.

Hampton Falls Inn, strategically located along New Hampshire's seacoast, offers guestrooms equipped with queen-sized beds, cable television, refrigerators and private balconies. Enjoy a day of recreation, then unwind in the large indoor heated swimming pool and hot tub. Other guest amenities include the in-house coffee shop offering both breakfast and lunch. The Inn is located minutes away from year-round recreation—whether it is the sea, mountains, top entertainment, fine dining, ski slopes, tennis or golf.

Swiss Chalets Village Inn

Route 16A
P.O. Box 279
Intervale, NH 03845
800-831-2727 • 603-356-2232
www.swisschaletsvillage.com
stay@swisschaletsvillage.com

Type of Lodging: Motor Lodge

Room Rates: $49–$299, including coffee and doughnuts.

Pet Charges & Deposits: $15 per day.

Pet Policy: Designated rooms only.

Amenities: Cable TV, refrigerators, pool, whirlpool, hot tub.

Pet Amenities: List of nearby veterinarians maintained. Dog runs. Generous exercise area. Hampton Beach State Park nearby.

Rated: 3 Paws — 42 rooms on 12 acres.

Swiss Chalets Village Inn offers shelter and lots of Swiss charm right in the midst of New Hampshire's spectacular White Mountains. The entire village has just been completely renovated. The guestrooms offer wall-to-wall carpeting, individual climate controls, refrigerators, telephones and cable television. The Swiss Chalets Village Inn is located on 12 tranquil acres close to all the natural wonders and family attractions of the White Mountains. Not to be missed are Mount Washington and the Cog Railway, Attitash Alpine Slide, Story Land, Conway Scenic Railroad and the Kancamaugus Highway.

Dana Place Inn

Route 16, Pinkham Notch
Jackson, NH 03846
800-537-9276 • 603-383-6822
www.danaplace.com
contact@danaplace.com

Type of Lodging: Inn

Room Rates: $95–$155, including full breakfast and afternoon tea or après ski refreshment. AAA, AARP and *10% Pets Welcome*™ discounts.

Pet Charges & Deposits: None.

Pet Policy: Sorry, no cats. Designated rooms only. Pets not allowed in common areas.

Amenities: Cable TV, pool, Jacuzzi, pub.

Pet Amenities: List of nearby veterinarians maintained. Exercise area along the river. White Mountain National Forest abuts the property.

Rated: 4 Paws – 35 rooms.

Experience more than 100 years of hospitality at historic Dana Place Inn, situated on 300 acres in Pinkham Notch, nestled at the base of the highest mountain in the northeast, Mount Washington. Surrounded by the 750,000-acre White Mountain National Forest, this rural retreat is dotted with apple orchards and mountain pools on the sparkling Ellis River. Accommodations include a variety with king-, double- or queen-sized beds, most with a private bath. The Inn features fine dining, pub, heated indoor pool, Jacuzzi and a library with a fireplace. Cross-country ski from the doorsteps in winter or choose from four downhill ski mountains within 15 miles. Visit Jackson Village for antique shops and galleries or enjoy outlet shopping in North Conway. The Inn is located minutes from the White Mountain attractions that offer year-round recreational fun.

Whitneys' Inn

Five Mile Circuit Road
Jackson, NH 03846
800-677-5737 • 603-373-8916
www.whitneysinn.com
whitneys@ncia.net

Type of Lodging: Inn

Room Rates: $95–$150, including full breakfast. AAA and *10% Pets Welcome*™ discounts.

Pet Charges & Deposits: $25 per stay.

Pet Policy: Designated rooms only.

Amenities: Cable TV, pool, hot tub, fishing pond.

Pet Amenities: List of nearby veterinarians maintained. Exercise area. White Mountain National Forest abuts the property.

Rated: 3 Paws – 20 rooms and 10 suites.

When you're ready to escape, let Whitneys' Inn, an authentic country inn located in the scenic foothills of Mount Washington at the base of Black Mountain Ski Area, show you a slower, more relaxed beat. The guestrooms grace the restored New England farmhouse that dates back to the 1840s. In the summer, enjoy picnics, swimming, tennis, lobster bakes, hiking and relaxing on the porch rocker with a good book. During the winter, skiing, ice-skating, sledding and sleigh rides abound.

Parker's Motel

Route 3, Box 100
Lincoln, NH 03251
800-766-6835 • 603-745-8341
www.parkersmotel.com
parkersmotel@linwoodnet.com

Type of Lodging: Motel

Room Rates: $39–$89. AAA, AARP and *10% Pets Welcome™* discounts.

Pet Charges & Deposits: $5 per day. $25 refundable deposit.

Pet Policy: Designated rooms only.

Amenities: Cable TV, pool, Jacuzzi.

Pet Amenities: Franconia Notch State Park nearby.

Rated: 2 Paws – 27 rooms.

Parker's Motel is located in the heart of the White Mountains right next to Franconia Notch State Park and the Flume. A perfect place to stay when visiting Whales Tale Waterpark, Clark's Trading Post, Lost River, Hobo Railroad, Cannon Mountain Tramway, Loon Mt. Gondola, Old Man of the Mountains, Echo and Profile Lakes, North Country Center for the Arts and the Appalachian Trail. Activities to enjoy include hiking, kayaking, golfing and, of course, skiing.

Lovejoy Farm Bed & Breakfast

268 Lovejoy Road
Loudon, NH 03307
800-783-4007 • 603-783-4007
www.lovejoy-inn.com

Type of Lodging: B&B

Room Rates: $69–$97, including full breakfast.

Pet Charge & Deposits: None.

Pet Policy: No pets over 50 lbs. Designated rooms only. Manager's prior approval required.

Amenities: None.

Pet Amenities: List of nearby veterinarians maintained. The property has a very rural setting with 8 acres for your pet to enjoy.

Rated: 3 Paws – 8 rooms and 1 suite.

Located on a quiet country road and surrounded by acres of fields and woods, Lovejoy Farm Bed & Breakfast offers accommodations in an elegant, 1790 Georgian Colonial and attached carriage house complete with beamed ceilings for a rustic charm. Originally constructed by one of Loudon's founding fathers, it later became the country retreat for industrialist Elwyn Lovejoy. Located only ten miles from Concord, Lovejoy Farm is easily accessible. Guests enjoy hiking, mountain biking, cross-country skiing, snowmobiling, downhill skiing, canoeing, golfing, horseback riding, antiquing and tax-free shopping.

Comfort Inn

298 Queen City Avenue
Manchester, NH 03102
800-228-5150 • 603-668-2600

Type of Lodging: Hotel

Room Rates: $80–$160, including continental breakfast. AAA and AARP discounts.

Pet Charges & Deposits: Credit card imprint required as deposit.

Pet Policy: Designated rooms only.

Amenities: Cable TV, refrigerators, microwaves, pool, saunas, hairdryers.

Pet Amenities: Exercise area. Eastman Park, Howell Park and Singer Park nearby.

Rated: 3 Paws — 100 rooms.

Conveniently located near Interstate 293 and offering airport shuttle service, the Inn is situated in the heart of Manchester. Whether the nature of your visit is business, pleasure or just passing through, guests will find a cheerful staff and comfortable accommodations. The Manchester area is situated for a convenient visit to the Currier Gallery of Art, Anheuser-Busch Brewery, home of the world-famous Clydesdale horses and the Canterbury Shaker Village. Visitors can also enjoy the Palace Theater's drama, orchestras, Broadway musicals and comedy shows.

Red Roof Inn

77 Spit Brook Road
Nashua, NH 03060
800 RED ROOF • 603-888-1893
www.redroof.com
i01zz@redroof.com

Type of Lodging: Motel

Room Rates: $50–$95. AAA discount.

Pet Charges & Deposits: None.

Pet Policy: None. All Pets Welcome.

Amenities: Satellite TV, refrigerators, microwaves.

Pet Amenities: Exercise area. Roby Park is located on Spit Brook Road, approximately ½ mile west of the Inn.

Rated: 3 Paws — 115 rooms.

Red Roof Inn has clean, tastefully decorated rooms with cable television, free local calls and fresh coffee. It is a great base for those visiting Lockheed/Martin, Pheasant Lane Mall, St. Joseph's Hospital, Budweiser Clydesdales, Minuteman National Historic Park and New Hampshire International Speedway.

Mt. Washington Valley Motor Lodge

1567 White Mt. Highway
P.O. Box 3180
North Conway, NH 03860
800-634-2383 • 603-356-5486
www.motorlodge.com
mwvml@ncia.net

Type of Lodging: Hotel

Room Rates: $59–$159.

Pet Charges & Deposits: $50 refundable deposit.

Pet Policy: Sorry, no cats. No pets over 40 lbs. Designated rooms only. Pets must not be left unattended.

Amenities: Cable TV, refrigerators, microwaves, safe, pool, whirlpool, hot tub, restaurant.

Pet Amenities: Treats available. List of nearby veterinarians maintained. Exercise area. White Mountain National Forest, Schuler Park and Whitaker Woods nearby.

Rated: 3 Paws — 68 rooms and 2 suites.

The Mt. Washington Valley Motor Lodge is in a prime location for enjoying the Mt. Washington Valley and the White Mountains. All guestrooms include private baths with hairdryers and newspapers delivered to your door each morning. There are over 150 shops and outlets within walking distance. Settlers Green, the largest mall in the area, is right behind the building. Skiing, snowboarding, cross-country skiing, hiking, golf, canoeing, kayaking, rock climbing and swimming are just some of the many outdoor adventures awaiting you and your pet.

Tamworth Inn

15 Cleveland Hill Road
Tamworth, NH 03886
800-642-7352 • 603-323-7721
www.tamworth.com
inn@tamworth.com

Type of Lodging: Inn

Room Rates: $115–$250, including full breakfast. AAA discount.

Pet Charges & Deposits: $10 per day.

Pet Policy: Sorry, no cats. Pets must not be left alone.

Amenities: Pool, microwaves, restaurant, lounge.

Pet Amenities: List of nearby veterinarians maintained. Town Park is across the street from the Inn. Hemenway State Park is located on Great Hill Road, approximately 2 miles from the Inn. White Mountain National Forest is located 15 minutes from the Inn.

Rated: 4 Paws — 16 rooms and 7 suites.

Surround yourself with the essence of New England hospitality. Each guestroom is tastefully accented with a country flavor and the Inn's public areas offer a warm invitation to relax and enjoy the comforts of an authentic New England village inn. There are picturesque mountains with miles of hiking trails and acres of green lawns. Located within a short drive are the tall peaks of the White Mountain National Forest and the beautiful Lake Winnipesaukee waterfront. Excellent cross-country skiing is at the front door and the oldest professional theater in the United States is down the lane. Here you can enjoy the river bordering the back lawn with some of the best fishing around, cocktails in the pub or a leisurely dinner.

Airport Economy Inn

45 Airport Road
West Lebanon, NH 03784
800-433-3466 • 603-298-8888

Type of Lodging: Hotel

Room Rates: $50–$95, including continental breakfast. AAA discount.

Pet Charges & Deposits: $10 per day.

Pet Policy: Designated rooms only. Pets must not be left unattended.

Amenities: Cable TV, refrigerators, pool.

Pet Amenities: List of nearby veterinarians maintained. Exercise area.

Rated: 3 Paws — 56 rooms.

Airport Economy Inn has luxury rooms at economical rates. The top quality rooms feature double or queen-sized beds, telephones, cable television and individual climate controls. Located within one hour of Hanover, Woodstock (Vermont), White Mountain or Vermont ski slopes, Dartmouth College, Dartmouth-Hitchcock Medical Center and fine dining and shopping, this is a great place for you and your pet to rest.

NEW JERSEY

Nickname: Garden State

Population: 8,143,412

Area: 8,215 square miles

Climate: Moderate, with marked difference between NW and SE extremities.

Capital: Trenton

Entered Union: Dec. 18, 1787

Motto: Liberty and prosperity

Flower: Purple Violet

Tree: Red Oak

Bird: Eastern Goldfinch

Famous New Jerseyans: Count Basie, Judy Blume, Bill Bradley, Aaron Burr, Grover Cleveland, James Fennimore Cooper, Stephen Crane, Thomas Edison, Albert Einstein, Alexander Hamilton, Whitney Houston, Buster Keaton, Thomas Paine, Dorothy Parker, Philip Roth, Frank Sinatra, Bruce Springsteen, Meryl Streep, Walt Whitman, Woodrow Wilson.

 History: The native people had peaceful relations with early European settlers. The British took New Netherlands in 1664. Many historical American Revolutionary battles were fought here. Princeton University is one of the most prestigious centers of higher education in the United States. New Jersey is more than Newark Airport and stories of Mafia infiltration. Travel a few miles west from the Turnpike and you'll see why it's called the Garden State.

AmeriSuites

3565 U.S. Route 1
Princeton, NJ 08540
609-720-0200

Type of Lodging: Hotel
Suite Rates: $165–$210, including continental breakfast. AAA and AARP discounts.
Pet Charges & Deposits: None.
Pet Policy: No pets over 10 lbs. Manager's prior approval required.
Amenities: Cable TV, refrigerators, microwaves, safes, pool.
Pet Amenities: List of nearby veterinarians maintained. Mercer County Park is located 15 miles from the hotel.
Rated: 3 Paws — 124 suites.

AmeriSuites is housed in an impressive high-rise building. The suites are spacious, homey and quite luxurious, with just about every amenity you can think of. Princeton University/Palmer Square is only a mile away. The Market Fair Mall is adjacent to the hotel. Numerous 18th century houses present themselves when you make a walking tour of the city. Brochures concerning these tours can be found at Bainbridge House, the birthplace of the commander of the U.S.S. Constitution during the War of 1812.

Residence Inn by Marriott at Greate Bay Golf Club

900 Mays Landing Road
Somers Point, NJ 08244
800-788-8234 • 609-927-6400
www.residenceinnac.com or
www.adnetint.com/residence
resinnnj@aol.com

Type of Lodging: Hotel
Suite Rates: $99–$259, including full buffet breakfast and evening hospitality reception. AAA, AARP, AKC and ABA discounts.
Pet Charges & Deposits: $75 per stay.
Pet Policy: None. All Pets Welcome.
Amenities: Cable TV, refrigerators, microwaves, pool.
Pet Amenities: List of nearby veterinarians maintained.
Rated: 3 Paws — 120 suites.

Residence Inn offers newly renovated suites with fully equipped kitchens, living rooms and fireplaces in most suites. There's even complimentary grocery shopping service, along with meeting rooms, a complimentary evening hospitality reception, complimentary newspapers, mini-sport court and BBQ areas. It's only 11 miles from the Inn to the bustle and frolic of the "Queen of the Coast," Atlantic City, where family-oriented attractions such as the Boardwalk, a broad beach, and cultural and historical museums compete with the big-name, big-time gambling casinos and their concomitant 24-hour entertainment.

Holiday Inn

304 Route 22 West
Springfield, NJ 07081
973-376-9400

Type of Lodging: Hotel

Room Rates: $116–$125, including full buffet breakfast. AAA, AARP, AKC, ABA and *10% Pets Welcome*™ discounts.

Pet Charges & Deposits: None.

Pet Policy: If not a dog or a cat, manager's prior approval required. Limit two pets per room.

Amenities: Cable TV, pool, restaurant, lounge.

Pet Amenities: List of nearby veterinarians maintained. Ecno Lake Park is located on Route 22.

Rated: 3 Paws — 189 rooms

The Springfield Holiday Inn is housed in an impressive four-story structure with interior corridors. All rooms and amenities are of the highest quality, and the guestrooms are quite spacious.

NEW MEXICO

Nickname: Land of Enchantment

Population: 1,739,844

Area: 121,598 square miles

Climate: dry, with temperatures rising or falling 5 degrees Fahrenheit with every 1,000 feet elevation.

Capital: Santa Fe

Entered Union: Jan. 6, 1912

Motto: *Crescit Eundo* (It grows as it goes).

Song: O, Fair New Mexico

Flower: Yucca

Tree: Piñon

Bird: Roadrunner

Famous New Mexicans: Billy (the Kid) Bonney, Kit Carson, Bill Mauldin, Georgia O'Keeffe, Kim Stanley, Al Unser, Bobby Unser, Lew Wallace.

 History: The Navajo and Apache tribes arrived in the 15th century, scarcely a hundred years before the coming of the Franciscan Monk Marcos de Niza and a former African slave, Estevanico in 1539. The first Spanish settlement was at San Juan Pueblo in 1598. Settlers alternately traded and fought with the numerous Native American tribes in the area. Trade on the Santa Fe Trail to Missouri stated in 1821. Pancho Villa raided Columbus in 1916. Certain parts of New Mexico vacillated between the United States and Mexico when the southern boundary, the Rio Grande, overflowed its banks and changed course. The world's first atomic bomb was detonated south of Alamogordo in 1945.

Brittania and W.E. Mauger Estate Bed and Breakfast

701 Roma Avenue Northwest
Albuquerque, NM 87102
800-719-9189 • 505-242-8755
www.maugerbb.com
maugerbb@aol.com

Type of Lodging: B&B

Room Rates: $99–$179, including full breakfast. AAA and *10% Pets Welcome*™ discounts.

Pet Charges & Deposits: $30 per stay.

Pet Policy: Sorry, no cats. No pets over 50 lbs. Designated rooms only.

Amenities: Cable TV.

Pet Amenities: Dog bed, bowl, food, bones and other treats available. List of nearby veterinarians maintained. Dog run. Exercise area. Roma Avenue Park nearby.

Rated: 3 Paws — 8 rooms.

The Mauger (pronounced Major) Estate Bed and Breakfast Inn is one of New Mexico's grand old homes, a classic example of Queen Anne architecture. The interior of the inn features a cozy parlor, a stunning suite with a fireplace, finely restored woodwork and a breakfast room in what was once the home's sleeping porch. The feeling here is uncomplicated; it's an invitation to relax and unwind. Do things at your own pace. Enjoy summer mornings reading or writing in the parlor and evenings watching the sunset on the old-fashioned, 30-foot-long front porch. See the many sights in Albuquerque that are practically at your doorstep. Business and leisure travelers alike couldn't find a more convenient address.

Days Inn - West

6031 Iliff Road Northwest
Albuquerque, NM 87121
800 DAYS INN • 505-836-3279

Type of Lodging: Hotel

Room Rates: $60-$1,100. AAA and AARP discounts.

Pet Charges & Deposits: $5 per day. Deposit required if paying in cash.

Pet Policy: None. All Pets Welcome.

Amenities: Cable TV, safe, pool, Jacuzzi, hot tubs, spa.

Pet Amenities: List of nearby veterinarians maintained. Park nearby.

Rated: 3 Paws — 80 rooms.

If you and your pet are looking for great accommodations at a great price, Days Inn is the answer. It offers bright and airy rooms decorated in a contemporary Southwestern-style. The hotel is conveniently located off Coors and Interstate 40, which makes travel to anywhere in Albuquerque a snap. You are minutes away from historical Old Town, the Aquarium, Botanic Gardens, Rio Grande Zoo and various museums and parks.

Days Inn Hotel Circle

10321 Hotel Avenue Northeast
Albuquerque, NM 87123
800 DAYS INN • 606-275-3297

Type of Lodging: Hotel
Room Rates: $55–$1,150. AAA and AARP discounts.
Pet Charges & Deposits: $5 per day. Deposit required if paying in cash.
Pet Policy: None. All Pets Welcome.
Amenities: Cable TV, safe, pool, Jacuzzi, hot tubs, spa.
Pet Amenities: List of nearby veterinarians maintained. City park nearby.
Rated: 3 Paws — 76 rooms.

The Days Inn Hotel Circle is conveniently located on Hotel Avenue just off Interstate 40 seven miles from the downtown business district and the Albuquerque International Airport. The hotel features an indoor atrium pool, hot tub, dry sauna and continental breakfast. The guestrooms are furnished with a dining table with two chairs, individual climate controls, armoire dressers with wall-mounted mirrors and cable television. Skiing and the world's longest tramway are just a short drive away. Other nearby attractions includes historic Old Town, Rio Grande Zoo, Museum of Natural History, Rio Grande Nature Center and sports facilities. There are also a variety of restaurants, nightspots and shopping centers to enjoy. Albuquerque enjoys more than 330 days of sunshine allowing you to take advantage of all it has to offer.

Holiday Inn Express Hotel Circle

10330 Hotel Avenue Northeast
Albuquerque, NM 87123
800 HOLIDAY • 606-275-8900
www.holiday-inn.com

Type of Lodging: Hotel
Room Rates: $65–$75. AAA and AARP discounts.
Pet Charges & Deposits: $5 per day. Deposit required if paying in cash.
Pet Policy: None. All Pets Welcome.
Amenities: Cable TV, microwaves, safe, pool Jacuzzi, hot tubs, spa.
Pet Amenities: List of nearby veterinarians maintained. Los Altos Park nearby.
Rated: 3 Paws — 104 rooms.

Friendly service is what you will find at the Holiday Inn Express Hotel Circle in Albuquerque. They offer a more intimate environment than big hotels and more amenities than most small ones. The guestroom suites are designed for both vacationers and business travelers in mind: voicemail, dual phone jacks for in-room faxing, VCR, cable television, hairdryer, individual climate controls, valet and dry cleaning service. There are lots of recreational activities to enjoy including golfing, tennis, racquetball, handball, bicycling, fishing, skiing, hiking, horseback riding and walking. Within a ten-mile radius, you will find Sandia National Laboratory, Kirtland Air Force Base, New Mexico State Fairgrounds, Albuquerque Convention Center and the University of New Mexico.

Howard Johnson Express

7630 Pan American Northeast
Albuquerque, NM 87109
800 I GO HOJO • 505-828-1600
www.hojo.com

Type of Lodging: Hotel
Room Rates: $55–$69, including deluxe continental breakfast. AAA, AARP and *10% Pets Welcome*™ discounts.
Pet Charges & Deposits: $5 per day.
Pet Policy: None. All Pets Welcome.
Amenities: Cable TV, safes, pool, fitness room, coffeemakers.
Pet Amenities: Parks nearby.
Rated: 3 Paws — 85 rooms.

The Howard Johnson Express offers you and your pet clean, comfortable rooms with cable television, alarm clock radio and deluxe continental breakfast. It's located minutes from Sandia Peak Tramway, Rio Rancho, Old Town and the Balloon Fiesta Park. Santa Fe is 45 minutes away.

Plaza Inn Albuquerque

900 Medical Arts Northeast
Albuquerque, NM 87102
800-237-1307 • 505-243-5693
www.plazainnabq.com
plxinabq@aol.com

Type of Lodging: Hotel
Room Rates: $59–$109, including continental breakfast. AAA, AARP, AKC, ABA and *20% Pets Welcome*™ discounts.
Pet Charges & Deposits: None.
Pet Policy: No pets over 50 lbs. Designated rooms only.
Amenities: Cable TV, pool, whirlpool, spa.
Pet Amenities: List of nearby veterinarians maintained. Exercise area.
Rated: 3 Paws — 120 rooms.

Rising on a hillside, the Plaza Inn overlooks the downtown skyline and Albuquerque's West Valley. The hotel is conveniently located just minutes from the Albuquerque International Airport, downtown business district, University of New Mexico, Medical Center, Albuquerque Convention Center and historic Old Town. During your stay, you can ride the courtesy shuttle to any of these locations!

Residence Inn by Marriott

3300 Prospect Avenue Northeast
Albuquerque, NM 87107
800-331-3131 • 505-881-2661

Type of Lodging: Inn

Suite Rates: $85–$179, including full breakfast and weekday Hospitality Hour. AAA and AARP discounts.

Pet Charges & Deposits: $50 for the first day, $10 each additional day; not to exceed $150.

Pet Policy: None. All Pets Welcome.

Amenities: Cable TV, fully equipped kitchens, pool, hot tubs, fireplaces.

Pet Amenities: List of nearby veterinarians maintained. Exercise area. Petroglyph National Monument, Sandia National Park and Cibola National Forest nearby.

Rated: 3 Paws — 112 suites.

At Residence Inn, the extended-stay experience is combined with all of the comforts of home in order to make every guest—two- and four-legged—feel welcome. The roomy suites offer living and sleeping areas with plenty of space for relaxing, entertaining or meeting with colleagues and fully equipped kitchens. Take advantage of the pool, heated spa and SportCourt® to melt tensions away. Don't forget to stop by and visit the Acoma Pueblo, Aquarium, Botanical Gardens, Beach Water Park, Sandia Peak Tramway, National Atomic Museum, University of New Mexico and the Zoo.

Angels' Ascent Bed & Breakfast & Retreat Center

P.O. Box 4
Cedar Crest, NM 87008
505-286-1588
www.angelsascent.com
angelsasc1@aol.com

Type of Lodging: B&B

Room Rates: $85–$150, including full breakfast. AAA, AARP and *10% (midweek only) Pets Welcome™* discounts.

Pet Charges & Deposits: $30 per stay. $150 refundable deposit.

Pet Policy: Manager's prior approval required.

Amenities: Cable TV, refrigerators, Jacuzzi.

Pet Amenities: List of nearby veterinarians maintained. Exercise area includes ½ acre-fenced yard. Cibola National Forest nearby.

Rated: 4 Paws — 2 rooms and 1 suite.

Angels' Ascent Bed and Breakfast claims they are so close to Heaven, you can almost hear the rustle of angel wings—and guess what? They are not exaggerating. Your visit to the Land of Enchantment is enhanced by the warmth, ambiance and gracious hospitality that can only be found at Angels' Ascent. This cozy two-story cedar chalet is nestled among pine, pinion and juniper with magnificent views and a peaceful retreat which encourages rest, relaxation and rejuvenation. The decor is English Country with lace curtains, fine linens, beautiful quilts and, of course, an angel theme. There is an outdoor deck and a Jacuzzi, perfect for taking advantage of the magnificent views. While in Cedar Crest, enjoy downhill and cross-country skiing, scenic train rides, hiking, golfing, shopping, museums, historic tours, wine tastings, art galleries and theater.

Deming Motel

500 West Pine Street
Deming, NM 88030
505-546-2737
demingmotel2@zianet.com

Type of Lodging: Motel
Room Rates: $28–$65, including coffee. AAA, AARP, Military and *5% Pets Welcome*™ discounts.

Pet Charges & Deposits: $3 per day.

Pet Policy: Designated rooms only. Manager's prior approval required.

Amenities: Cable TV, pool.

Pet Amenities: Exercise area. Eighth Street Park is located at 8th and Spruce Streets. Deming Recreation Area is located on Nickel Street.

Rated: 3 Paws — 28 rooms and 1 suite.

The Deming Motel, located just four blocks west of the business district, offers clean, quiet and comfortable rooms at reasonable rates. The guestrooms have individual climate controls, cable television, phones and plenty of parking.

Holiday Inn

Interstate 10, Exit 85
P.O. Box 1138
Deming, NM 88031
888-546-2661 • 505-546-2661
www.holiday-inn.com/demingnm
hidem@zianet.com

Type of Lodging: Inn
Room Rates: $50–$100. AAA, AARP and *10% Pets Welcome*™ discounts.

Pet Charges & Deposits: None.

Pet Policy: None. All Pets Welcome.

Amenities: Cable TV, refrigerators, pool, Jacuzzi, weight room, lounge.

Pet Amenities: List of nearby veterinarians maintained. Exercise area. Deming Park is located a mile from the Inn.

Rated: 4 Paws — 116 rooms and 1 suite.

The Holiday Inn offers accommodations decorated in Southwestern décor with individual climate controls, cable television, irons and ironing boards, coffeemakers, hairdryers and dataport telephones. Guests can enjoy lounging by the large heated swimming pool or having a cocktail in the lounge. Deming is a great home base to explore the many points of interest in the Land of Enchantment. The Deming Museum is a must-see to view exhibits of how life really was in the pioneering days of the "Old West."

Best Western Inn & Suites

700 Scott Avenue
Farmington, NM 87401
505-327-5221
swibw@cyberport.com

Type of Lodging: Hotel

Room Rates: $79–$89, including express breakfast. AAA, AARP, AKC, ABA and *10% Pets Welcome*™ discounts.

Pet Charges & Deposits: $10 per stay.

Pet Policy: Designated rooms only.

Amenities: Cable TV, refrigerators, microwaves, safes, pool, Jacuzzi, fitness center, coffeemakers, guest laundry, restaurant, lounge.

Pet Amenities: List of nearby veterinarians maintained. Exercise area.

Rated: 3 Paws — 154 rooms and 38 suites.

Farmington thrives amidst spectacular scenery, ancient history and modern technology. The Best Western Inn & Suites is your overnight headquarters for The Four Corners. Extra large rooms, Executive Suites, a heated indoor pool, sauna and Jacuzzi in a tropical setting, a full service dining room and lounge are all part of the package…as is great service. Popular attractions include Navajo National Reservation, ancient Indian ruins, "Anasazi: The Ancient Ones," outdoor summer musical drama, annual sporting and rodeo events, and cultural and special events. Outdoor recreation includes fishing, golfing at the Five-Star Pinor Hills Golf Course (rated by Golf Digest), hiking and mountain biking. Shop for Native American jewelry, rugs, sand paintings, folk art and other artifacts at local trading posts or at the daily flea market in nearby Shiprock, located on the Navajo Nation Reservation.

Best Western Inn & Suites

3009 West Highway 66
Gallup, NM 87301
800-722-6399 • 505-722-2221
swibw@cyberport.com

Type of Lodging: Hotel

Room Rates: $59–$69, including express breakfast. AAA, AARP, AKC, ABA and *10% Pets Welcome*™ discounts.

Pet Charges & Deposits: $10 per stay.

Pet Policy: Designated rooms only.

Amenities: Cable TV, refrigerators, microwaves, safes, pool, Jacuzzi, fitness center, coffeemakers, guest laundry, restaurant, lounge.

Pet Amenities: List of nearby veterinarians maintained. Exercise area. Red Rock State Park and Petrified Forest National Park nearby.

Rated: 3 Paws — 154 rooms and 38 suites.

Offering quality lodging in this world capital of Native American jewelry and arts and crafts is the Best Western Inn & Suites. Located on Historic Route 66, just one mile off Interstate 40, the hotel is easily accessible to the town and many recreational activities of the area. Gallup is the trading hub of western American Indian arts and crafts. This is the city where Indian craftsmen from the Navajo, Zuni, Acoma, Laguna and Hopi Indian nations sell their wares. In dozens of trading posts and galleries, you will discover the world's finest collection of traditional and modern jewelry, rugs, carvings, sand paintings and fine art. Many festivals and ceremonies reflecting the Old West origins of the town are held, including the annual Inter-Tribal Indian Ceremonial, the annual Route 66 Festival and the Native American Film Festival.

Sleep Inn

3820 East Highway 66
Gallup, NM 87301
505-863-3535

Type of Lodging: Motel
Room Rates: $48–$65, including continental breakfast. AAA, AARP and *10% Pets Welcome™* discounts.
Pet Charges & Deposits: $5 per stay.
Pet Policy: Small pets only. Designated rooms only. Manager's prior approval required.
Amenities: Cable TV, refrigerators, pool, spas.
Pet Amenities: Red Rock State Park nearby.
Rated: 2 Paws — 61 rooms.

Whether visiting one of the local corporate offices or simply enjoying many of Gallup's tourist attractions, the Sleep Inn is the perfect home away from home. This stylish, modern hotel features an indoor heated pool and whirlpool, conference room, free local calls, guest laundry, plenty of parking, dataport phones, signature walk-in showers and remote control cable television. Within a short drive, you will find Kit Carson Cave, Navajo Reservoir, Red Rock State Park, Window Rock, Zuni Indian Reservation, Fort Wingate Army Depot, Rehoboth McKinley and University of New Mexico campus. Take a longer drive and you will find Canyon de Chelly, Chaco Canyon, Monument Valley, Painted Desert and the Petrified Forest.

Best Western Inn & Suites

1501 East Santa Fe Avenue
Grants, NM 87020
505-287-7901
swibw@cyberport.com

Type of Lodging: Hotel
Room Rates: $59–$69, including express breakfast. AAA, AARP, AKC, ABA and *10% Pets Welcome™* discounts.
Pet Charges & Deposits: $10 per stay.
Pet Policy: Small pets only. Designated rooms only.
Amenities: Cable TV, refrigerators, microwaves, safes, pool, Jacuzzi, fitness center, coffeemakers, guest laundry, restaurant, lounge.
Pet Amenities: List of nearby veterinarians maintained. Exercise area.
Rated: 3 Paws — 88 rooms and 24 suites.

Cradled in the shadow of majestic Mount Taylor, the Best Western Inn & Suites is a welcome sight to the weary traveler or enthusiastic visitor. Ideally located just off Interstate 40 on East Grants Spur Highway (historic Route 66), the hotel is a great place to launch excursions to one of the many nearby attractions that the area is famous for. Grants sits square in the heart of western New Mexico, and that means there is a greater variety of scenery and culture within an hour of Grants than almost anywhere else in the Southwest. Visit ancient Anasazi ruins or experience boomtown-mining adventures, see exquisite Native American pottery and art, and enjoy spectacular mountains, lakes and mesas.

Holiday Inn Express

1496 East Santa Fe Avenue
Grants, NM 87020
800 HOLIDAY • 505-285-4676
www.basshotels.com/hiexpress
hexpress@7cities.net

Type of Lodging: Motel

Room Rates: $50–$70, including continental breakfast. AAA and AARP discounts.

Pet Charges & Deposits: None.

Pet Policy: None. All Pets Welcome.

Amenities: Cable TV, safes, pool, Jacuzzi.

Pet Amenities: List of nearby veterinarians maintained.

Rated: 3 Paws — 58 rooms.

Holiday Inn Express is a strikingly attractive lodging with wonderful, upscale rooms and suites. It is a short drive from Sky City (the Oldest Inhabited Pueblo), El Malpais, Mining Museum, Bluewater Lake, Chaco Canyon, Coyote del Malpais, Dinamation Dinosaur Museum, Laguna Pueblo, Mount Taylor and Ice Caves. Any one is worth a special trip.

Sands Motel

112 McArthur
Grants, NM 87020
800-424-7679 • 505-287-2996

Type of Lodging: Motel

Room Rates: $35–$50, including continental breakfast. AAA, AARP and *10% Pets Welcome™* discounts.

Pet Charges & Deposits: $5–$10 per day.

Pet Policy: Small pets only. Designated rooms only.

Amenities: Cable TV, refrigerators.

Pet Amenities: List of nearby veterinarians maintained. Exercise area. Several city parks within a 1-mile radius. Three national parks within a 30-mile radius.

Rated: 3 Paws — 25 rooms.

The Sands Motel invites you and your pet to come and enjoy their hospitality. Guestrooms feature refrigerators, direct-dial phones, remote control cable television, tubs, showers and plenty of truck and RV parking.

Royal Host Motel

2146 West Picacho Avenue
Las Cruces, NM 88005
505-524-8536
woodcoral@yahoo.com

Type of Lodging: Motel

Room Rates: $30–$54. AAA and AARP discounts.

Pet Charges & Deposits: $7 per stay.

Pet Policy: No pets over 40 lbs. Manager's prior approval required. Pets must not be left unattended.

Amenities: Cable TV, refrigerators, pool, restaurant.

Pet Amenities: List of nearby veterinarians maintained. Exercise area. Rio Grande River and Burn Lake nearby.

Rated: 3 Paws — 26 rooms.

The Royal Host Motel offers quality spacious rooms with ground-floor convenience. Other amenities include restaurant, outdoor pool and free local calls. Las Cruces is adjacent to the charming Mexican-flavored town of Mesilla, which became a part of Old Mexico for a time in the 1880s when the Rio Grande flooded and changed course, putting the town on the "other side" of the border. You're less than two hours from El Paso and Ciudad Juarez, one of Old Meixco's largest cities.

T.R.H. Smith Mansion Bed & Breakfast

909 North Alameda Boulevard
Las Cruces, NM 88005
800-526-1914 • 505-525-2525
www.smithman.com
smithmansion@zianet.com

Type of Lodging: B&B

Room Rates: $60–$132, including full breakfast.

Pet Charges & Deposits: $15 per day.

Pet Policy: No pets over 50 lbs. Designated rooms only. Manager's prior approval required.

Amenities: Cable TV, pool table, air purifiers.

Pet Amenities: Resident 12-year-old Keeshond is co-manager. List of nearby veterinarians maintained. Exercise area. Lions Park is located at Picacho and Melendres. Pioneer Park is located Las Cruces and Reymond. Johnson Park is located at Main and Picacho.

Rated: 3 Paws — 4 rooms.

T.R.H. Smith Mansion Bed & Breakfast is the largest residence in the bustling city of Las Cruces and stands prominently in the heart of the historic Alameda Depot District. The Prairie-style architecture features high-beamed ceilings, hardwood floors, stained glass windows and a brick-and-stucco exterior surrounds you in an atmosphere of early 20th century elegance in the lush, 4000-feet high Mesilla Valley. The oversized guestrooms are each decorated with its own distinctive mood and style. All this and you are within easy walking distance to restaurants, outdoor pool, tennis courts, a country-western nightclub and many other conveniences of this wonderful city.

Plaza Hotel

230 Old Town Plaza
Las Vegas, NM 87701
800-328-1882 • 505-425-3591
www.worldplaces.com/plaza
plazahotel@worldplaces.com

Type of Lodging: Hotel
Room Rates: $73–$129, including continental breakfast. AAA and AARP discounts.
Pet Charges & Deposits: $10 per day.
Pet Policy: Small pets only.
Amenities: Cable TV, safes, restaurant, bar.
Pet Amenities: List of nearby veterinarians maintained. Bridge Street Park nearby.
Rated: 3 Paws — 32 rooms and 4 suites.

Located on the historic Old Town Plaza in Las Vegas, the Plaza Hotel has been a gathering place for locals and visitors since 1882. More than a place to sleep, the Plaza's tastefully renovated rooms offer today's comfort in yesterday's setting. The Plaza Hotel's Landmark Grill offers delightful menu selections, from Southwestern favorites to daily specials, and is open for breakfast, lunch and dinner. Your favorite libation and lively conversation await you in Byron T's Saloon, named for a past owner and alleged ghost.

Hacienda de Placitas Inn of the Arts

491 Highway 165
Placitas, NM 87043
505-867-0082
www.haciendainnofthearts.com

Type of Lodging: B&B
Room Rates: $99–$199, including full breakfast.
Pet Charges & Deposits: Call for refundable deposit.
Pet Policy: Manager's prior approval required.
Amenities: Cable TV, refrigerators, microwaves, pool, Jacuzzi, hot tubs, VCRs, coffeemakers, hairdryers.
Pet Amenities: Leashes available. List of nearby veterinarians maintained. Dog runs. Exercise area. Cibola National Forest is located off Highway 165.
Rated: 3 Paws — 3 houses and 4 suites.

Hacienda de Placitas Inn of the Arts captures the charm of the Old West. At day's end, enjoy nature's palette celebrated in spectacular sunsets and views of the Sandia, Jemez and Sangre de Cristo Mountains, Taylor Mountain and San Luis de Cabezon Volcano. Late evening hours invite moonlight swims with the shimmer of distant city lights and the sound of plaintive coyotes. Parts of the Hacienda are over 100 years old, while the acreage dates to a 1700s land grant. Surrounded by 300 high desert acres, the Hacienda has miles of hiking trails, wildlife and bird watching. Santa Fe is a 40-minute drive, while shorter drives will lead you to Albuquerque and the Balloon Fiesta Field. There are many historical and archaeological sites nearby including Chaco Canyon, Puye Cliff Dwellings and Bandelier National Monument.

Best Western Sally Port Inn & Suites

2000 North Main Street
Roswell, NM 88201
505-622-6430
swibw@cyberport.com

Type of Lodging: Hotel
Room Rates: $79–$89, including express breakfast. AAA, AARP, AKC, ABA and *10% Pets Welcome*™ discounts.
Pet Charges & Deposits: $10 per stay.
Pet Policy: Designated rooms only.
Amenities: Cable TV, refrigerators, microwaves, safes, pool, Jacuzzi, fitness center, coffeemakers, guest laundry, restaurant, lounge.
Pet Amenities: List of nearby veterinarians maintained. Exercise area. Bottomless Lakes State Park is located only 15 minutes from the hotel.
Rated: 3 Paws — 99 rooms and 25 suites.

Located just steps from the prestigious New Mexico Military Institute, the Best Western Sally Port Inn & Suites is a contemporary facility that complements Roswell's historic past, steeped in tradition and honor. From the bold handsome exterior to the elegant touches of the fine guestrooms, attention to detail is exemplary. The oversized guestrooms and suites will make you and your pet feel at home and you will enjoy the inviting indoor heated pool, Jacuzzi, sauna and fitness center. Roswell is the home of the 1947 UFO sighting.

Alexander's Inn Bed and Breakfast

529 East Palace Avenue
Santa Fe, NM 87501
888-321-5123 • 505-986-1431
www.alexanders-inn.com
alexandinn@aol.com

Type of Lodging: B&B
Room Rates: $80–$175, including continental breakfast and afternoon tea. *10% Pets Welcome*™ discount.
Pet Charges & Deposits: $20 per stay.
Pet Policy: Manager's prior approval required.
Amenities: Cable TV, refrigerators, microwaves, hot tubs.
Pet Amenities: List of nearby veterinarians maintained. Exercise area. Santa Fe National Forest nearby.
Rated: 3 Paws — 5 rooms and 5 suites.

For a romantic stay in Santa Fe, nestle into this delightful bed and breakfast in the town's historic residential east side. Quiet and peaceful, yet just a short walk from the famous central plaza and the multitude of galleries on Canyon Road, this 1903 Craftsman-style home has been lovingly decorated. Hand-stenciling, dried flowers and family antiques create a warm, relaxing and nurturing atmosphere. The country cottage feel is enhanced by dormer windows and carefully restored architectural details. Sunlight streams through stained glass windows or lace curtains onto gleaming hardwood floors. Fresh flowers grace every room throughout the house.

Best Western Inn of Santa Fe

3650 Cerrillos Road
Santa Fe, NM 87505
800-528-1234 • 505-438-3822
www.bestwestern.com

Type of Lodging: Motel

Room Rates: $50–$95, including continental breakfast. AAA, AARP, AKC, ABA and *10% Pets Welcome*™ discounts.

Pet Charges & Deposits: None.

Pet Policy: None. All Pets Welcome.

Amenities: Cable TV, refrigerators, safes, pool, Jacuzzi.

Pet Amenities: List of nearby veterinarians maintained. Exercise area. Park is located on Camino Carlos Rey and Rodeo Road.

Rated: 4 Paws — 97 rooms and 21 suites.

Enjoy the flavor of Santa Fe and the comforts of home at the Best Western Inn of Santa Fe. The hotel offers a wide variety of room types, from economy priced standard rooms to deluxe suites with Jacuzzis. Guests will appreciate amenities such as a complimentary continental breakfast, 24-hour coffee, indoor pool, Jacuzzi and guest laundry. Located just minutes away from the historic plaza district, the Best Western Inn of Santa Fe offers easy access to museums, shopping, restaurants, skiing, Indian pueblos and the many art galleries for which Santa Fe is famous.

El Paradero

220 West Manhattan Avenue
Santa Fe, NM 87501
505-988-1177
www.elparadero.com
info@elparadero.com

Type of Lodging: B&B

Room Rates: $75–$140, including full breakfast.

Pet Charges & Deposits: $10 per day.

Pet Policy: Designated rooms only.

Amenities: Cable TV, kitchenettes.

Pet Amenities: List of nearby veterinarians maintained. Hyde Park nearby.

Rated: 2 Paws — 12 rooms and 2 suites.

El Paradero offers you the opportunity to experience the real New Mexico. From the moment you and your pet walk into the reception room with its thick adobe walls, see the folk art furnishings and smell muffins baking, you'll know this is a place for relaxation and enjoyment. From El Paradero's location on a downtown side street, you and your pet may explore the historic heart of Santa Fe.

Hacienda Nicholas Bed & Breakfast Inn

320 East Marcy Street
Santa Fe, NM 87501
888-284-3170 • 505-992-8385
www.haciendanicholas.com
haciendanicholas@aol.com

Type of Lodging: B&B

Room Rates: $95–$160, including full breakfast and afternoon tea. *10% Pets Welcome*™ discount.

Pet Charges & Deposits: $20 per stay.

Pet Policy: Manager's prior approval required.

Amenities: Cable TV, homemade baked goodies.

Pet Amenities: List of nearby veterinarians maintained. Small park across the street from the B&B. Triangle Park and Santa Fe National Forest nearby.

Rated: 3 Paws — 5 rooms and 2 suites.

Walking into Hacienda Nicholas is like stepping back into time. The old adobe home in the heart Santa Fe features a central "great room" with 20-feet ceilings, thick wooden Vigas, softly colored hand-troweled plaster walls and a fireplace large enough to cook in. The historic home is built around a garden courtyard filled with roses, wisteria, iris, daisies, pansies and geraniums, providing an ideal setting for leisurely breakfasts or afternoon tea. The bedrooms feature wrought iron or carved wood four-poster beds, private baths decorated with unique and charming Mexican tiles, telephones, cable television and air conditioning.

Inn of the Turquoise Bear

342 East Buena Vista Street
Santa Fe, NM 87501
800-396-4104 • 505-983-0798
www.turquoisebear.com
bluebear@roadrunner.com

Type of Lodging: B&B

Room Rates: $95–$210, including continental breakfast and afternoon wine & cheese hour. AAA and AARP discounts.

Pet Charges & Deposits: $20 per stay.

Pet Policy: Designated rooms only. Manager's prior approval required.

Amenities: Cable TV, fireplaces, VCRs.

Pet Amenities: None.

Rated: 4 Paws — 9 rooms and 1 suite. Sunset Magazine's "Best Inns of the West." Heritage Preservation Award. Out & About Editors' Choice Award.

This rambling adobe house, constructed in Spanish-Pueblo Revival-style from a core of rooms that date to the mid-1800s, is considered one of Santa Fe's most important historical buildings. Adobe walls and coyote fences enclose an acre of terraced gardens, with old stone benches, meandering flagstone paths and soaring ponderosa pines. Guestrooms with Kiva fireplaces and Viga ceilings are reached through private entrances and romantic courtyards. Fluffy robes, fresh flowers and fruit are enjoyed in each of the Southwestern-style guestrooms at Inn of the Turquoise Bear. Complimentary off-street parking is available.

Madeleine Bed & Breakfast Inn

106 Faithway Street
Santa Fe, NM 87501
888-877-7622 • 505-982-3465
www.madeleineinn.com
madeleineinn@aol.com

Type of Lodging: B&B

Room Rates: $70–$165, including full breakfast and afternoon tea. *10% Pets Welcome*™ discount.

Pet Charges & Deposits: $20 per stay.

Pet Policy: Manager's prior approval required.

Amenities: Cable TV, refrigerators, hot tubs, homemade baked goodies.

Pet Amenities: List of nearby veterinarians maintained. Exercise area. Park nearby.

Rated: 3 Paws — 6 rooms and 2 suites.

The Madeleine is a Queen Anne-style house, built in 1886, featuring all the original classic Victorian touches: stained glass windows, window seats, dark wood molding, brick and tile fireplaces, and a large front porch complete with wooden rocking chairs. The interior, painted in warm and sunny hues, is filled with period antiques. The three-story gingerbread house is tucked away on a quiet street on Santa Fe's famous east side and is just blocks away from the historic Plaza and the galleries of Canyon Road.

Residence Inn by Marriott

1698 Galisteo Street
Santa Fe, NM 87505
800-331-3131 • 505-988-7300
www.ri-destinations.com or
  www.residenceinn.com
sales@ri-destinations.com

Type of Lodging: Hotel

Suite Rates: $89–$199, including hot breakfast buffet and weekday Hospitality Hour. AAA and AARP discounts.

Pet Charges & Deposits: $10 per day. $150 flat fee for extended stays. $150 refundable deposit.

Pet Policy: None. All Pets Welcome.

Amenities: Cable TV, fully equipped kitchens, pool, Jacuzzi, Sportcourt®.

Pet Amenities: Treats upon check-in. List of nearby veterinarians maintained. Exercise area. Salvador Perez Park is located ½ mile from the hotel.

Rated: 4 Paws — 120 suites.

No matter what brings you to Santa Fe, the Residence Inn by Marriott, will always give you and your pet the "room to relax, room to work, room to breathe," that you need and deserve! Experience the magic of Santa Fe, where echoes from a rich Spanish and Native American history mingle with world-class cuisine and art, creating a timeless symphony promising to captivate any visitor. Outdoor enthusiasts—enjoy skiing down the snow-covered slopes of the Sangre de Cristo mountains, hiking, mountain biking, horseback riding or white water rafting along the picturesque Rio Grande River.

Adobe and Stars Bed and Breakfast Inn

P.O. Box 2285
Taos, NM 87571
800-211-7076 • 505-776-2776
www.taosadobe.com
stars@taos.newmex.com

Type of Lodging: B&B
Room Rates: $115–$180, including full breakfast. AAA discount.
Pet Charges & Deposits: $20 per stay. $50 refundable deposit.
Pet Policy: Manager's prior approval required.
Amenities: Kiva fireplaces.
Pet Amenities: None.
Rated: 4 Paws — 8 rooms and 1 suite.

Adobe and Stars opened its doors in 1996 for guests seeking striking accommodations and a high level of hospitality in a majestic setting. Surrounded by the ancient Sangre de Cristo Mountains, this contemporary, luxurious Inn was designed with the views in mind. Big windows, decks and patios invite star-gazing, sunset viewing and the pleasure of contemplation. Many traditional Pueblo-style features have been included to create warmth and Southwestern ambiance. Such features include high, Viga-beamed ceilings, Kiva fireplaces tucked into the corners of rooms and outdoor portals to shade the strong sun.

Quality Inn

1043 Paseo del Pueblo Sur
P.O. Box 2319
Taos, NM 87571
800-845-0648 • 505-758-2200
www.taoshotels.com/qualityinn
quality@newmex.com

Type of Lodging: Hotel
Room Rates: $60–$99, including full breakfast. AAA and AARP discounts.
Pet Charges & Deposits: $7 per day.
Pet Policy: Designated rooms only.
Amenities: Cable TV, pool, Jacuzzi.
Pet Amenities: List of nearby veterinarians maintained.
Rated: 2 Paws — 98 rooms and 2 suites.

When venturing into the history, culture and recreation of Taos, you and your pet will need a good home base and the newly remodeled Quality Inn is happy to be that base. Enjoy all the unique shops, art galleries, museums, historic homes, Indian Pueblos, alpine and cross-country skiing, fishing, bicycling, horseback riding, windsurfing, river rafting, hot springs hopping, country music two-steppin' and fine New Mexican dining that Taos has to offer.

Sagebrush Inn

1508 Paseo del Pueblo Sur
P.O. Box 557
Taos, NM 87571
800-428-3626 • 505-758-2254
www.sagebrushinn.com
sagebrush@newmex.com

Type of Lodging: Hotel
Room Rates: $85–$140, including full breakfast. AAA, AARP, AKC, ABA and *10% Pets Welcome™* discounts.
Pet Charges & Deposits: None.
Pet Policy: Designated rooms only.
Amenities: Cable TV, refrigerators, pool, hot tubs.
Pet Amenities: List of nearby veterinarians maintained. Exercise area encompasses 14 acres of open field.
Rated: 4 Paws — 48 rooms and 52 suites.

Sagebrush Inn is a Taos landmark, built in 1929 of adobe and huge, hand-hewn timbers called Vigas. The Inn catered to visitors traveling between New York and Arizona, offering them authentic Southwestern charm along with an extensive regional art collection. The original adobe structure, now the cantina and lobby, still houses an impressive collection of Indian rugs and artifacts, New Mexican paintings and original R.C. Gorman works. Many rooms have their own wood-burning fireplaces and all the rooms feature handmade furniture and local art. Enjoy a complimentary full breakfast each morning in the Sagebrush dining room or on one of the patios. An outdoor pool and two hot tubs are available for guests.

Zuni Mountain Lodge

40 Perch Drive
P.O. Box 5114
Thoreau, NM 87323
505-862-7616
www.cia-g.com/~zuniml
zuniml@cia-g.com

Type of Lodging: B&B
Room Rates: $55–$85, including full breakfast and dinner. AAA discount.
Pet Charges & Deposits: None.
Pet Policy: Manager's prior approval required.
Amenities: Refrigerators, microwaves.
Pet Amenities: List of nearby veterinarians maintained. Exercise area. Cibola National Forest and Bluewater Lake State Park nearby.
Rated: 3 Paws — 7 rooms.

Just up the mountainside from Bluewater Lake is the Zuni Mountain Lodge, providing all the comforts of modern living amidst the rugged beauty of the mountains, with spectacular lake and mountain scenery. Comfortably furnished public areas provide places for quiet meditation and relaxation, or a place to view the very latest on cable or video in the lounge. An intimate dining room seats 24 people, while the kitchen prepares the most delicious meals in two counties. Landscaped lawns and gardens surround an outdoor gazebo.

Safari Motel

722 East Tucumcari Boulevard
Tucumcari, NM 88401
877-388 WARM • 505-461-3642

Type of Lodging: Motel

Room Rates: $35–$65, including coffee. AAA, AARP, AKC, ABA and *10% Pets Welcome™* discounts.

Pet Charges & Deposits: $4 per day.

Pet Policy: None. All Pets Welcome.

Amenities: Cable TV, refrigerators, microwaves, pool.

Pet Amenities: List of nearby veterinarians maintained. Dog runs. Exercise area. Several Parks nearby.

Rated: 3 Paws — 24 rooms.

The newly refurbished Safari Motel offers lovely, well-furnished guest units with cable televisions, carpeting, air conditioning and telephones. Tucumari is a stop in the old "Route 66"—the gateway to the Texas Panhandle.

NEW YORK

Nickname: Empire State

Population: 18,196,601

Area: 53,989 square miles

Climate: Variable; the southeast portion is moderated by the Atlantic Ocean.

Capital: Albany

Entered Union: July 26, 1788

Motto: *Excelsior* (Ever Upward).

Song: I Love New York

Flower: Rose

Tree: Sugar Maple

Bird: Bluebird

Famous New Yorkers: Woody Allen, Lucille Ball, Humphrey Bogart, Aaron Copland, Lou Gehrig, George & Ira Gershwin, Ruth Bader Ginsburg, Washington Irving, Fiorello LaGuardia, Herman Melville, J.P. Morgan, Eugene O'Neil, Colin Powell, Nancy Reagan, John D. Rockefeller, Eleanor Roosevelt, Franklin D. Roosevelt, Theodore Roosevelt, Jerry Seinfeld, Paul Simon, Barbara Streisand, Donald Trump, Gore Vidal, Elizabeth Wharton.

History: New Amsterdam, later to become New York City, was settled by the Dutch in 1626. A British fleet seized it in 1664. Over 90 of the 300 engagements of the Revolutionary War took place in New York. This is a land with the most superlative city in America, yet it is also a place of mountain beauty, small villages, and abundant educational facilities. It is a magnificent tourist destination.

Mansion Hill Inn

115 Philip Street at Park Avenue
Albany, NY 12202
888-299-0455 • 518-465-2038
www.mansionhill.com
Inn@mansionhill.com

Type of Lodging: Inn
Room Rates: $145–$165, including full breakfast. AAA and *10% Pets Welcome*™ discounts.
Pet Charges & Deposits: None.
Pet Policy: None
Amenities: Cable TV, refrigerators.
Pet Amenities: List of nearby veterinarians maintained. Exercise area. Lincoln Park is located at Eagle and Park Avenue.
Rated: 4 Paws — 8 rooms.

Mansion Hill Inn is an "urban inn nestled in the heart of a residential neighborhood." It is located just south of the Governor Nelson A. Rockefeller Empire State Plaza, within a few minutes' walk of the State Capitol, government offices, Knickerbocker Arena and downtown Albany business and shopping districts. Nearby historic sites include Ten Broeck Mansion, Historic Cherry Hill, the Schuyler Mansion and the New York State Executive Governor's Mansion.

Riveredge Resort Hotel & Conference Center

17 Holland Street
Alexandria Bay, NY 13607
800-365 ENJOY US • 315-482-9917
www.riveredge.com
enjoyus@riveredge.com

Type of Lodging: Resort
Room Rates: $74–$368. AAA, AARP and *10% Pets Welcome*™ discounts.
Pet Charges & Deposits: $10 per day.
Pet Policy: No pets over 70 lbs. Manager's prior approval required.
Amenities: Cable TV, safes, pool, hot tubs, spas, fitness room, lounge, dockage facilities.
Pet Amenities: List of nearby veterinarians maintained. Keewaydin State Park, Grasse Point State Park and Krings State Park nearby.
Rated: 4 Paws — 88 rooms and 41 suites.

The Riveredge Resort Hotel & Conference Center is located in the heart of one of the most beautiful settings in New York, the incomparable Thousand Islands on the international border between the United States and Canada. This world-class lodging rises four floors above the St. Lawrence River and overlooks Boldt Castle, a turreted stone castle begun in 1900 but never completed and never occupied. It has been under restoration since 1977. Numerous boat-tour sightseeing cruises may be found in this well-and-deservedly touristy area.

Red Roof Inn

42 Flint Road
Amherst, NY 14226
800-RED ROOF • 716-689-7474

Type of Lodging: Hotel

Room Rates: $35–$100. AAA and *10% Pets Welcome™* discounts.

Pet Charges & Deposits: None.

Pet Policy: Small pets only. Manager's prior approval required. Limit one pet per room. Pets must not be left unattended.

Amenities: Cable TV.

Pet Amenities: List of nearby veterinarians maintained. Exercise area.

Rated: 2 Paws — 108 rooms.

Red Roof Inn gives you roomy accommodations at cost conscious prices when you're in the Buffalo-Amherst area. Amherst is most convenient to Buffalo-Niagara Falls International Airport. There's a State University of New York (SUNY) campus in Amherst. Buffalo, with 311,000 people, is a "Queen City." The Buffalo Museum of Science takes you back to the days of the dinosaurs. Catch Matisse, Monet, Picasso, Renoir and Van Gogh at the Allbright-Knox Art Gallery. The Naval and Military Park lets you board the U.S.S. Croaker and see what life was like on a WWII submarine.

Ramada Limited

65 Front Street
Binghampton, NY 13905
607-724-2412

Type of Lodging: Motel

Room Rates: $52–$89, including continental breakfast. AAA, AARP and *10% Pets Welcome™* discounts.

Pet Charges & Deposits: $10 refundable deposit.

Pet Policy: Sorry, no large pets. Designated rooms only. Pets must not be left unattended.

Amenities: Cable TV, refrigerators, pool, night club.

Pet Amenities: List of nearby veterinarians maintained. Park nearby.

Rated: 2 Paws — 130 rooms.

Ramada Limited affords nice guestrooms in a convenient downtown location. There are banquet and meeting facilities, voicemail and the Eclipse night club on the premises. Railroads, photography and cigar making were the town's major industries before 1900, but shoe manufacturing became the dominant enterprise in the early 20th century. Today, Universal Instruments, Link Flight Simulation and IBM occupy the forefront of Binghampton's economy. The Binghampton area has six genuine old-time carousels. The Roberson Museum and Science Center has exhibits of 19th and 20th century art, history, folk life and science.

Econo Lodge

170 Eastern Boulevard
Canandaigua, NY 14424
800-797-1222 • 716-394-9000

Type of Lodging: Motel
Room Rates: $39–$99, including coffee, juice and donuts. AAA, AARP and *10% Pets Welcome™* discounts.
Pet Charges & Deposits: None.
Pet Policy: Manager's prior approval required. Pets must not be left unattended.
Amenities: Cable TV, refrigerators, microwaves.
Pet Amenities: List of nearby veterinarians maintained. Park nearby.
Rated: 3 Paws — 65 rooms.

Econo Lodge is a fine budget chain and the Canandaigua unit is no exception. The modern town of Canandaigua stands on the site of the Seneca Native American village of Kan-an-dargue, which was destroyed by General John Sullivan in 1779. Canadaigua Lake, 17 miles long, is reputedly one of the most beautiful of the Finger Lakes. Thoroughbred horse racing takes place Friday through Tuesday from early April through early December. The lovely Sonnenberg Gardens is a 50-acre estate with gardens and an 1887 Victorian mansion.

Buena Vista Motel

HC 74, Box 212
Andes Road
Delhi, NY 13753
607-746-2135
www.buenavistamotel.com
motel@catskill.net

Type of Lodging: Motel
Room Rates: $55–$98, including continental breakfast. AAA discount.
Pet Charges & Deposits: $5 per day.
Pet Policy: Manager's prior approval required. Pets must not be left unattended.
Amenities: Cable TV, refrigerators, microwaves.
Pet Amenities: List of nearby veterinarians maintained. Dog runs. Exercise area. Pets may walk in the back of the motel to the nearby river.
Rated: 2 Paws — 32 rooms.

Your hosts at the Buena Vista Motel make sure that you are treated to very clean rooms with a modern telephone system and cable television. There are many antique stores in Delhi and antique auctions take place almost every weekend. There are three skiing centers nearby. The Delaware County Historical Association Museum offers seven restored rural buildings, including the 1790s Frisbee House, a blacksmith shop, timber-frame barn, schoolhouse and gun shop. It's covered bridge country and you shouldn't miss the fall foliage season.

Lake House on Lake George

P.O. Box 195
Diamond Point, NY 12824
518-668-5545
www.lakehouseonlakegeorge.com

Type of Lodging: House
Room Rates: $500–$3,500.
Pet Charges & Deposits: $40 per stay.
Pet Policy: Manager's prior approval required.
Amenities: Cable TV, boat house with docking space, full kitchen, linens, dining table for 12, gas grill, playhouse, campfire, swimming.
Pet Amenities: Bedding available. List of nearby veterinarians maintained. Exercise area. Lake George is found within Adirondack Park. There is a short walking trail in the woods.
Rated: 3 Paws — Lakefront house and grounds.

Lake House is a 3,000-square-foot contemporary house with private lakefront. It has five bedrooms, four baths and is furnished and arranged for a party of ten people, including children and babies. There's plenty of skiing (Gore Mountain), fishing, golfing, whitewater rafting, kayaking, mountain biking and other outdoor activities, yet you're close enough to enjoy the Saratoga Performing Arts Center ballets and concerts, the Lake George Dinner Theater, and the variety of museums in Glens Falls, Blue Mountain Lake and the Adirondack Mountains.

Super 8 Motel

6620 Old Collamer Road
East Syracuse, NY 13087
800-800-8000 • 315-432-5612
www.super8.com

Type of Lodging: Motel
Room Rates: $35–$100, including 24-hour coffee. AAA, AARP, AKC, ABA, VIP, Military, Entertainment and *10% Pets Welcome*™ discounts.
Pet Charges and Deposits: $10 per day. $25 refundable deposit.
Pet Policy: Small pets only. No pets over 25 lbs. Manager's prior approval required.
Amenities: Cable TV, refrigerators, microwaves, safes.
Pet Amenities: List of nearby veterinarians maintained. Exercise area. Court Street Park nearby.
Rated: 2 Paws — 52 rooms and 1 suite.

Super 8 Motel, a clean and fine value, is situated in East Syracuse. Downtown Syracuse offers the historic Armory Square District, with quaint shops and restaurants. You can take a walking tour of the downtown area—interpretive signs describing the history of the city are signposted everywhere. Sainte Marie Among the Iroquois recreates a 17th century Jesuit mission, featuring costumed interpreters who demonstrate traditional building, harvesting, and cooking techniques and a recreated Iroquois fishing village.

Jefferson Inn

3 Jefferson Street
P.O. Box 1566
Ellicottville, NY 14731-1566
800-577-8451 • 716-699-5869
www.thejeffersoninn.com
jeffinn@eznet.net

Type of Lodging: B&B

Room Rates: $65–$180. AAA discount.

Pet Charges & Deposits: $10 per day.

Pet Policy: Sorry, no cats. Designated rooms only.

Amenities: Cable TV, kitchenettes.

Pet Amenities: List of nearby veterinarians maintained. Allegany State Park, Finger Lakes Trail and Village Park nearby.

Rated: 2 Paws — 4 rooms, 2 efficiency units and 3 suites.

The serenity of a small town in Western New York allows for quiet family day-strolls or romantic evenings along the streets of Ellicottville. The Jefferson Inn was built circa 1835 and offers an elegant living room with an inviting fireplace and tastefully decorated guest accommodations. Located centrally, behind Ellicottville's Town Hall, the Jefferson Inn is only minutes away from the Holiday Valley and HoliMont Ski Resorts. Just an hour south of Buffalo, in the foothills of the Allegheny Mountains and close to Allegany State Park, the Inn is also close to the Nannen Arboretum, B&B Buffalo Ranch, Amish country and the Chautauqua Institution.

Coachman Motor Lodge

908 Pennsylvania Avenue
Elmira, NY 14904
607-733-5526

Type of Lodging: Motel

Room Rates: $65–$85. AAA and AARP discounts.

Pet Charges & Deposits: None.

Pet Policy: Manager's prior approval required. Pets must not be left unattended.

Amenities: Cable TV, refrigerators, microwaves.

Pet Amenities: List of nearby veterinarians maintained. Dog runs. Exercise area.

Rated: 2 Paws — 18 rooms and 18 suites.

The Coachman Motor Lodge features rooms that are updated and immaculate with remote control cable television. The Lodge has been family-owned and operated for more than a quarter century. Samuel Clemens (Mark Twain) married an Elmira native, Olivia Langdon, in 1870 and the family spent many summers thereafter at Olivia's sister's farm. While in Elmira, Twain wrote *The Adventures of Huckleberry Finn*. Woodlawn National Cemetery contains more than 3,000 graves of Confederate soldiers who died in the local prisoner-of-war camp. Mark Twain's grave is in Elmira, as is the National Soaring Museum, which has movies and exhibits about gliding. If you're adventurous, sailplane rides are available at Schweizer Soaring School at Elmira-Corning Regional Airport.

Wellesley Inn

20 Schuyler Boulevard
Fishkill, NY 12524
800-444-8888 • 845-896-4995
www.wellesleyinnandsuites.com

Type of Lodging: Hotel
Room Rates: $79–$109, including continental breakfast. AAA and AARP discounts.
Pet Charges & Deposits: $10 per day.
Pet Policy: No pets over 50 lbs. Designated rooms only. Pets must not be left unattended.
Amenities: Cable TV, refrigerators, microwaves, safes.
Pet Amenities: Park is located ¼ mile down the street from the hotel.
Rated: 2 Paws — 81 rooms and 1 suite.

Moderately priced Wellesley Suites advertises, "Value Never Looked This Good," and this lovely, homey place proves that statement true. There are nice amenities everywhere you look. It's 20 miles from Fishkill to West Point Military Academy, nine miles to the Poughkeepsie Galleria and 15 miles each to the Vanderbilt Mansion and the FDR Mansion. "Big Blue," aka IBM, has plants in Fishkill and in Poughkeepsie, 15 minutes away. Vassar University is 12 miles distant and a 13-mile drive will bring you to the Culinary Institute of America.

Days Inn

10455 Bennett Road
Route 60
Fredonia, NY 14063
800-329-7466 • 716-673-1351
www.the.daysinn.com/fredonia05551

Type of Lodging: Motel
Room Rates: $43–$120, including continental breakfast and newspaper. AAA and AARP discounts.
Pet Charges & Deposits: None.
Pet Policy: Designated rooms only.
Amenities: Cable TV.
Pet Amenities: Courtyard area on the property. Barker Commons is located on Main Street.
Rated: 2 Paws — 125 rooms and 10 suites.

Days Inn, roughly halfway between Buffalo and Erie, Pennsylvania, provides quality at a budget price. There are guestrooms with secure interior corridors. The Dunkirk Historical Lighthouse and Veterans Park Museum was built in 1875. Woodbury Vineyards Winery is well worth a visit. It's a scant two miles to Lake Erie and Dunkirk Harbor. For those so inclined, Seneca Nation Native American Bingo is 15 miles distant.

Sandy Creek Manor House

1960 Redman Road
Hamlin, NY 14464
800-594-0400 • 716-964-7528
www.sandycreekbnb.com
agreatbnb@aol.com

Type of Lodging: B&B

Room Rates: $70–$95, including full breakfast. AAA and *10% Pets Welcome*™ discounts.

Pet Charges & Deposits: $5 per day.

Pet Policy: None. All Pets Welcome.

Amenities: Refrigerators, hot tubs, player piano, creek.

Pet Amenities: List of nearby veterinarians maintained. Exercise area. Hamlin Beach State Park is located 3½ miles north of the B&B. Property has 6 acres with creek for your pet's pleasure. The Genesee Valley Dog Show takes place three times a year in Hamlin.

Rated: 4 Paws – 4 rooms.

Escape the rigors of life at this quiet European-style bed & breakfast. Reminisce about days gone by while listening to the Inn's antique player piano. Snuggle into the warmth of Amish quilts and feather pillows. The inn is located near Hamlin Beach State Park, the historic Erie Canal and SUNY Brockport. Take day trips to Niagara Falls, the Finger Lake Wineries, Corning and downtown Rochester.

Best Western Marshall Manor

3527 Watkins Road
Horseheads, NY 14845
800-528-1234 • 607-739-3891

Type of Lodging: Hotel

Room Rates: $44–$78, including continental breakfast. AAA, AARP and *10% Pets Welcome*™ discounts.

Pet Charges & Deposits: $4 per stay.

Pet Policy: None. All Pets Welcome.

Amenities: Cable TV, refrigerators, microwaves, safes, pool.

Pet Amenities: List of nearby veterinarians maintained. Exercise area. Watkins Glen State Park is located on Route 14. Mark Twain State Park is located at 201 Middle Road.

Rated: 3 Paws – 40 rooms.

The Best Western Marshall Manor has newly renovated guestrooms and many appreciated amenities. Horseheads is named for the remains of the packhorses that General John Sullivan used to transport his men from Pennsylvania to Western New York to fight the Six Nations of the Iroquois. The National Warplane Museum, at Elmira-Corning Regional Airport, contains transport planes, fighters and seaplanes from 1919 to the present. Horseheads is immediately adjacent to Elmira and Corning, and convenient to Lake Ontario.

Ithaca Holiday Inn

222 South Cayuga Street
Ithaca, NY 14850
800 HOLIDAY • 607-272-1000
www.harthotels.com

Type of Lodging: Hotel

Room Rates: $84–$350. AAA and AARP discounts.

Pet Charges & Deposits: $15 per stay. $15 nonrefundable deposit.

Pet Policy: Designated rooms only.

Amenities: Cable TV, pool.

Pet Amenities: List of nearby veterinarians maintained. Park nearby.

Rated: 3 Paws — 180 rooms and 3 suites.

Ithaca Holiday Inn has all the accommodating amenities you'd expect in a first-class hotel. It's immaculate and classy. Ithaca, at the southern tip of Cayuga Lake, is the home of Cornell University and Ithaca College. The Sciencenter is an interactive science museum. Numerous cultural pursuits may be found in this mid-sized university town.

Comfort Inn

2800 North Main Street Extension
Jamestown, NY 14701
800-228-5150 • 716-664-5920
www.comfortinn.com/hotel/ny403
cijamestown@hudsonhotels.com

Type of Lodging: Hotel

Room Rates: $70–$140, including continental breakfast. AAA, AARP and *10% Pets Welcome™* discounts.

Pet Charges & Deposits: $10 refundable deposit.

Pet Policy: No pets over 25 lbs. Designated rooms only. Pets must not be left unattended.

Amenities: Cable TV, refrigerators, microwaves, safes, Jacuzzi.

Pet Amenities: Falconer Park nearby.

Rated: 3 Paws — 101 rooms.

Slick, spotless and moderately priced, Jamestown's Comfort Inn is a wonderful choice when you and your pet are in the area. The Chautauqua Belle, on the Chautauqua Lake waterfront, is a replica of an old-fashioned, steam-powered stern-wheeler, which affords 1½ hour cruises. An unusual Jamestown attraction is the Lucy-Desi Museum. Its exhibits describe the lives and careers of Desi Arnaz and Jamestown-native Lucille Ball.

Balmoral Motel

444 Canada Street
Lake George, NY 12845
800-457-2673 • 518-668-2673
www.balmoralmotel.com

Type of Lodging: Motel

Room Rates: $69–$169.

Pet Charges & Deposits: $10 per day.

Pet Policy: Sorry, no cats. No pets over 40 lbs. Designated rooms only. Manager's prior approval required. Pets must not be left unattended.

Amenities: Cable TV, refrigerators, pool.

Pet Amenities: You can take a dog most anywhere in Lake George if on a leash.

Rated: 2 Paws — 28 rooms and 2 suites.

The Balmoral, a nifty, friendly place, is located in the heart of Lake George Village. It boasts a 55-feet heated Island Pool or you can walk 300 yards to the beach. There are three restaurants adjacent to the Motel. You can also stroll to cruise ships, amusements parks, nightclubs, churches or you can ride the Trolley that stops at the Motel. The village is at the southern end of a 32-mile-long lake that contains some 365 islands. The Lake George Steamship Company, Shoreline Cruises and others provide wonderful narrated tours of the lake.

Lake Placid Resort, Hotel & Golf Club

One Olympic Drive
Lake Placid, NY 12946
800-874-1980 • 518-523-2556
www.lakeplacidresort.com
info@lpresort.com

Type of Lodging: Hotel

Room Rates: $59–$259. AARP discount

Pet Charges & Deposits: $100 refundable deposit.

Pet Policy: Pets must not be left unattended.

Amenities: Cable TV, refrigerators, microwaves, pool, whirlpool, Jacuzzi.

Pet Amenities: List of nearby veterinarians maintained. Exercise area. Adirondack Park nearby.

Rated: 3 Paws — 201 rooms.

The Lake Placid Resort, Hotel & Golf Club presents first-class, upscale rooms and guest amenities in a wonderful vacation atmosphere. Host of the 1932 and 1980 Winter Olympics, Lake Placid's Whiteface Mountain is a magnificent ski center. Many of the city's premier tourist sites are geared to the history of the Olympics, including the Olympic Center, 1932 & 1980 Lake Placid Olympic Museum, the Olympic Jumping Complex, the Olympic Sports Complex at Mount Van Hoevenberg and the United States Olympic Training Center.

Lake Ontario Motel

3330 Lockport-Olcott Road
Newfane, NY 14108
800-446-5767 • 716-778-5004
http://members.aol.com/lakeontmot
lakeontmot@aol.com

Type of Lodging: Motel

Room Rates: $37–$87. AAA discount.

Pet Charges & Deposits: $5 per day,
$10 maximum per stay.

Pet Policy: None. All Pets Welcome.

Amenities: Cable TV, refrigerators,
microwaves, coffeemakers.

Pet Amenities: List of nearby veterinarians maintained. Exercise area. Krull Park is located 6 miles from the motel.

Rated: 2 Paws – 11 rooms.

Lake Ontario Motel is a charming, small, traditional motel—in fact, it's a converted 19th century country barn. One of the nicest things about the Motel is that it's minutes away from Niagara Falls but in a much less pricey area. It's only 24 miles to Niagara Falls, six miles south of Olcott on Lake Ontario. Of course, once in Niagara Falls, take the Cave of the Winds Trip, Old Fort Niagara, the Maid of the Mist (on the Canadian side) and the entire hullabaloo that attends this world magnet destination.

Metropolitan Hotel, a Loews Hotel

569 Lexington Avenue
New York City, NY 10022
866- METRO NY • 212-752-7000
www.metropolitanhotelnyc.com

Type of Lodging: Hotel

Room Rates: $179–$409. AAA discount.

Pet Charges & Deposits: None.

Pet Policy: Small pets only. No pets over 40 lbs.

Amenities: Cable TV, refrigerators, safes, complimentary health club.

Pet Amenities: Treats, bowls, leashes, pet closet and "Metropet Pet Program" available. List of nearby veterinarians maintained. Central Park is located 2 blocks from the hotel.

Rated: 4 Paws – 722 rooms and 40 suites.

What can you say about New York City other than it is the pounding heart that, more than any other major metropolis, defines America to the world? The Metropolitan Hotel, sometimes known as the Loews New York Hotel, could not be more centrally located in midtown Manhattan. It's rock-throwing distance to mammoth Central Park, an easy walk (or taxi ride) to the theaters on the Great White Way, convenient to the Metropolitan Museum of Art. Then there's Greenwich Village, Washington Square, Grand Central Station, and on, and on, and on. The City that Never Sleeps is a 7/24/365 wonderland that never fails to thrill.

The Regency Hotel

540 Park Avenue
New York City, NY 10021
800-23 LOEWS • 212-759-4100
www.loewshotels.com

Type of Lodging: Hotel

Room Rates: $279–$495.

Pet Charges & Deposits: None.

Pet Policy: None. All Pets Welcome.

Amenities: Cable TV, refrigerators, microwaves, honor bar, safes.

Pet Amenities: Bowls, mats, beds and special in-room pet menus available. Exercise areas and dog runs in Central Park.

Rated: 5 Paws — 351 rooms and 74 suites.

Located on trendy Park Avenue, the Regency Hotel offers top-of-the-line rooms and suites in an elegant setting. It's smack dab in the middle of the best part of midtown Manhattan. There's more to see and do in this city than almost any place else on Earth. The Metropolitan Museum of Art is close by, the Empire State Building a little farther away. Why not take a boat out to see the Statue of Liberty herself? Or pay one fare and ride the subways all day and night if that's your thing. After all, this is a city so big, so boisterous and so grandiose that they had to name it twice—New York, New York!

Darien Lakes Econo Lodge

8493 State Route 77
Pembroke, NY 14036
716-599-4681
econolodge@adelphia.net

Type of Lodging: Hotel
Room Rates: $39–$80, including coffee. AAA, AARP and *10% Pets Welcome*™ discounts.
Pet Charges & Deposits: None.
Pet Policy: None. All Pets Welcome.
Amenities: Cable TV, refrigerators, microwaves.
Pet Amenities: List of nearby veterinarians maintained. Exercise area. Darien State Park nearby.
Rated: 3 Paws — 73 rooms.

Darien Lakes Econo Lodge is a great budget-conscious choice with nice rooms and well-thought-out amenities. Six Flags Darien Lake is five minutes away. It features more than 100 rides, including five roller coasters and live shows. Niagara Falls is 35 minutes away. It's 15 miles to Buffalo Airport and a 20-mile drive to watch the Buffalo Bills football team in action. If you want to shimmy and shake, visit the Jell-O Gallery Museum, located 24 miles east of the motel.

Holiday Inn Rochester Airport

911 Brooks Avenue
Rochester, NY 14625
800 HOLIDAY • 716-328-6000
www.holiday-inn.com

Type of Lodging: Hotel
Room Rates: $89–$128. AAA, AARP and *20% Pets Welcome*™ discounts.
Pet Charges & Deposits: $25 refundable deposit.
Pet Policy: No pets over 80 lbs.
Amenities: Cable TV, pool, whirlpool, coffeemakers, hairdryers, irons and ironing boards, voicemail, dataports, restaurant, lounge.
Pet Amenities: List of nearby veterinarians maintained. Genesee Valley Park nearby.
Rated: 3 Paws — 280 room and 3 suites.

The Holiday Inn Airport is conveniently located off major expressways, adjacent to the Rochester International Airport and only five minutes from downtown Rochester and the New York State Thruway. Guest facilities include newly renovated rooms with upgraded amenities, Greenhouse Cafe Restaurant, Players Sports Bar & Dance Club, heated indoor pool with sauna and whirlpool, fitness center, flexible meeting rooms which can accommodate up to 400 people and ample complimentary parking.

Holiday Inn

173 Sunrise Highway
Rockville Centre, NY 11570
877-241-7544 • 516-678-1300
www.holiday-inn.com/rockvilleny

Type of Lodging: Hotel

Room Rates: $130–$179. AAA and AARP discounts.

Pet Charges & Deposits: $15 per day.

Pet Policy: None. All Pets Welcome.

Amenities: Pool.

Pet Amenities: List of nearby veterinarians maintained. Exercise area. Hempstead Lake State Park nearby

Rated: 3 Paws — 100 rooms.

Holiday Inn Rockville Centre offers deluxe, upscale accommodations on Long Island. It's one of the closest quality lodgings to New York City's JFK Airport. Its meeting facilities can accommodate a general session of 250 people or an executive board meeting of ten people. While it's a world away from the hustle and bustle of the City, the Long Island Railway that whisks you into Manhattan is moments away from the hotel. Need we say more?

Ontario Place Hotel

103 General Smith Drive
P.O. Box 540
Sackets Harbor, NY 13685
800-564-1812 • 315-646-8000
www.ontarioplacehotel.com
hotel@imcnst.net

Type of Lodging: Hotel

Room Rates: $49–$375, including full breakfast, coffee and doughnuts in lobby.

Pet Charges & Deposits: None.

Pet Policy: Designated rooms only. Manager's prior approval required.

Amenities: None.

Pet Amenities: List of nearby veterinarians maintained. Exercise area.

Rated: 3 Paws — 40 rooms.

Ontario Place Hotel is a small, utterly charming hotel located on the harbor in beautiful, historic Sackets Harbor. This is one of New York State's premier summer resort areas and with good reason. Sackets Harbor, on eastern Lake Ontario, witnessed one of the first battles of the War of 1812, when one U.S. ship and a group of farmers onshore who, between them, shared a single cannon defeated five British battleships. The only British shot to land near the farmers was loaded into the cannon and, when it was fired, it obliterated the mast of the British flagship. It was "one of those days." The Sackets Harbor Battlefield State Historic Site commemorates the two battles of the War of 1812 fought here. It is a living history encampment and Naval exhibit depicting a sailor's life during that long-ago war.

Hotel Saranac of Paul Smith's College

101 Main Street
Saranac Lake, NY 12983
800-937-0211 • 518-891-2200
www.hotelsaranac.com
hsaranac@paulsmiths.edu

Type of Lodging: Hotel
Room Rates: $59–$119. AAA, AARP and *10% Pets Welcome™* discounts.
Pet Charges & Deposits: $5 per day.
Pet Policy: None. All Pets Welcome.
Amenities: Cable TV, refrigerators, honor bar, hairdryers, alarm clocks, dataport, voicemail, coffeemakers.
Pet Amenities: List of nearby veterinarians maintained. Adirondack Park nearby
Rated: 3 Paws – 92 rooms.

Opened in 1927, the Hotel Saranac has been owned and operated by Paul Smith's College since 1961. The Hotel offers a gourmet restaurant, boathouse lounge, International Student Buffet, gift shop, bakery and numerous other unique amenities. The Hotel is in the heart of Saranac Lake, recently ranked #1 Small Town in New York State by The 100 Best Small Towns In America. It's located in the Adirondacks, in a land of evergreen forests and mountains that provide year-round activity. It's hard to believe this is the same New York in which you'll find Manhattan, for although there's plenty of culture to be found here, from fine dining to theaters, to special events for each month of the year, and you're only a few footsteps from the pristine wilderness.

Union Gables Bed and Breakfast

55 Union Avenue
Saratoga Springs, NY 12866
800-398-1558 • 518-584-1558
www.uniongables.com
information@uniongables.com

Type of Lodging: B&B
Room Rates: $125–$300, including continental breakfast.
Pet Charges & Deposits: None.
Pet Policy: Manager's prior approval required. No pets during racing season.
Amenities: Cable TV, refrigerators, hot tubs.
Pet Amenities: List of nearby veterinarians maintained.
Rated: 3 Paws – 10 rooms.

The Union Gables is an utterly charming 1901 Queen Anne home restored to its Victorian splendor. It has all the allure and curves of a turn-of-the-century mansion and all the amenities you look for while you're away from home. Saratoga Springs is renowned for its beautiful setting, the reputed health-enhancing properties of its waters and the intensity of its summer life. The Lake George Opera Festival has numerous high-powered and local performances during its season, which runs in June and July.

Best Western Rotterdam Motor Inn

2788 Hamburg Street
Schenectady, NY 12302
888-371-3316 • 518-355-1111

Type of Lodging: Hotel

Room Rates: $65–$125. AAA and AARP discounts.

Pet Charges & Deposits: $10 per day.

Pet Policy: No pets over 15 lbs.

Amenities: Cable TV, pool.

Pet Amenities: List of nearby veterinarians maintained. Large area in back of the hotel where pets can walk. Central Park nearby.

Rated: 2 Paws – 44 rooms and 6 suites.

The Best Western Rotterdam Motor Inn is a fine, moderately priced choice of lodging in Schenectady. Founded in 1661 by Dutch settlers, the Dutch influence is evident in buildings throughout the city. Scenic attractions include the Rose Garden in Central Park and Jackson's Gardens on the Union College campus. Touring Broadway shows find their home in the 1926 Proctor's Theater. Schenectady Museum features a planetarium, a hands-on science exploration area and a plethora of intriguing exhibits. Center City features a large indoor ice-skating rink and exhibit hall.

Bird's Nest Motel & Suites

1601 East Genesee Street
Skaneateles, NY 13152
315-685-5641
www.skaneateles.com/birdsnest
birdsnest@aubcom.com

Type of Lodging: Motel

Room Rates: $39–$69. AAA, AARP and AKC discounts.

Pet Charges & Deposits: $150 refundable deposit.

Pet Policy: Sorry, no cats. Designated rooms only.

Amenities: Cable TV, refrigerators, pool, whirlpool.

Pet Amenities: Dog runs. Exercise area. Austin Park is located on State Street.

Rated: 2 Paws – 25 rooms and 10 suites.

Bird's Nest Motel & Suites offers affordable accommodations. Skaneateles is near Syracuse, but located amid numerous small and mid-size lakes in its own right. Mid-Lakes Navigation Company offers many types of cruises including sightseeing, dinner, lunch and wine tasting. In nearby Geneva, you'll find the elegant Rose Hill Mansion, a beautifully restored 1839 edifice situated on 30 acres overlooking Seneca Lake. Furnished in the Empire style, the house is one of America's finest examples of Greek Revival architecture.

John Milton Inn

6578 Thompson Road
Syracuse, NY 13206
800-352-1061 • 315-463-8555

Type of Lodging: Motel
Room Rates: $35–$70, including continental breakfast.
Pet Charges & Deposits: $6 per day.
Pet Policy: Designated rooms only. Pets must not be left unattended.
Amenities: Cable TV, refrigerators.
Pet Amenities: Exercise area. Park nearby.
Rated: 2 Paws — 54 rooms and 2 suites.

The John Milton Inn is a fine budget-conscious choice in bustling Syracuse, a city that owes its prominence to its geographic location and geologic wealth. The Erie Canal Museum, housed in a unique 1850 building, demonstrates an intriguing chapter of early travel in America. Not to be outdone, the Museum of Automobile History displays more than 10,000 pieces of automotive memorabilia.

Ramada Limited

6590 Thompson Road
Syracuse, NY 13206
800-2 RAMADA • 315-463-0202

Type of Lodging: Motel
Room Rates: $59–$129, including continental breakfast. *15% Pets Welcome™* discount.
Pet Charges & Deposits: $10 per stay.
Pet Policy: Sorry, no dogs. No pets over 20 lbs. Manager's prior approval required. Pets must not be left unattended.
Amenities: Cable TV.
Pet Amenities: None.
Rated: 2 Paws — 74 rooms and 13 suites.

Ramada Limited is an excellent, moderately priced motel that gives fine value for the money. The city of Syracuse, founded in 1805 on the former site of the capital of the Iroquois Confederacy, supplied the bulk of the salt used in America for several years. Syracuse University, founded in 1870, occupies a 640-acre campus. Burnett Park Zoo displays domestic and exotic animals in a simulated natural setting. The Milton J. Rubenstein Museum of Science and Technology is a wonderful hands-on science museum.

Ledge Rock at Whiteface

HCR 2, Box 34
Whiteface Mountain, NY 12997
800-336-4754 • 518-946-2379
ledge-rock@yahoo.com

Type of Lodging: Motel
Room Rates: $59–$159. AAA discount.
Pet Charges & Deposits: $50 per stay.
Pet Policy: Designated rooms only.
Amenities: Cable TV, refrigerators, microwaves, pool, pond with paddle boating, grills and picnic tables, playground.
Pet Amenities: List of nearby veterinarians maintained. Exercise area.
Rated: 3 Paws — 19 rooms.

Awake each morning to a breathtaking view of majestic Whiteface Mountain, site of the 1980 Winter Olympics. The long, two-story lodge-like building is affordably priced and the outdoor amenities are never-ending, whatever season you come. On a clear night, you are bathed in the light of stars so close you could almost reach out and touch them. The Ledge Rock is nestled on a hill directly across from Whiteface Ski Center, only a few scenic miles from Bobsled Run, Ski Jumping Complex, Ice Skating Arena and Lake Placid. Sledding hills and snowshoe trails, cross-country ski and snowmobile trails are almost at your door.

NORTH CAROLINA

Nicknames: Tarheel State; Old North State
Population: 7,650,689
Area: 52,672 square miles
Climate: Subtropical in southeast, mid-continental in mountain region; tempered by the gulf stream and mountains in the west.
Capital: Raleigh
Entered Union: Nov. 21, 1789
Motto: *Esse Quam Videri* (To be rather than to seem).
Song: The Old North State

Flower: Dogwood
Tree: Pine
Bird: Cardinal
Famous Tarheels: David Brinkley, Elizabeth Dole, Ava Gardner, Billy Graham, Andy Griffith, O. Henry, Andrew Jackson, Andrew Johnson, Dolley Madison, Arnold Palmer, James K. Polk, Carl Sandburg, Wilbur & Orville Wright.

History: Algonquian, Souian and Iroquoian were here to greet Sir Walter Raleigh when he attempted to set up the first colony—Roanoke Island—in 1585 and 1587. The first group returned to England, the second was the "Lost Colony." The Colonists drove out the Royal Governor in 1775 and North Carolina was the first to vote for independence. The state seceded from the Union in 1861 and furnished more Confederate troops than any other state. North Carolina was readmitted to the Union in 1868. Today, North Carolina is the largest tobacco producing state.

Comfort Inn Riverridge

800 Fairview Road
Asheville, NC 28803
828-298-9141
www.comfortinn.com
ashcomrr@aol.com

Type of Lodging: Hotel
Room Rates: $69–$149, including deluxe continental breakfast. AAA, AARP, AKC, ABA and *10% Pets Welcome*™ discounts.
Pet Charges & Deposits: None.
Pet Policy: Pets must not be left unattended.
Amenities: Cable TV, refrigerators, microwaves, pool, Jacuzzi, coffeemakers, hairdryers.
Pet Amenities: List of nearby veterinarians maintained. Dog runs and exercise area on 6 acres of land. Blue Ridge Parkway nearby.
Rated: 3 Paws — 154 rooms and 24 suites on 35 acres.

Comfort Inn is located on 35 acres of rolling hills, surrounded by the Great Smoky Mountains. Guest quarters are well appointed and decidedly upscale. You simply cannot visit Asheville without seeing America's closest approach to a true palace, the 250-room Biltmore Estate, the largest private home in America. The home and grounds are stunning, inside and out. Inside, you'll find priceless antiques and art. Outside, the formal gardens and a working winery delight visitors.

Days Inn Asheville Mall

201 Tunnel Road
Asheville, NC 28805
800-DAYS INN

Type of Lodging: Inn
Room Rates: $35–$129, including full breakfast. AAA, AARP and *10% Pets Welcome*™ discounts.
Pet Charges & Deposits: $5 per day. $15 nonrefundable deposit.
Pet Policy: Designated rooms only.
Amenities: Cable TV, refrigerators, microwaves, safes, pool.
Pet Amenities: Exercise area. Great Smoky National Park is located 30 miles and Blue Ridge Parkway is located 2 miles away from the hotel.
Rated: 2 Paws — 130 rooms and 10 suites.

Days Inn, located next to, and within walking distance of, Asheville's largest shopping mall, boasts pleasant rooms, a heated outdoor swimming pool and conference rooms for up to 200 persons. Biltmore Estate is three miles away. Asheville is justifiably one of the most popular resorts in the East. The Great Smoky and Blue Ridge Mountains surround it. Scenic highways pass through the city. Chimney Rock Park is a 1,000-acre park with exceptional views. Three different trails lead to Hickory Nut Falls, which drops 404 feet, twice the height of Niagara. Other points of interest in the park include the Chimney, Lake Lure, Devil's Head, Moonshiner's Cave and Needle's Eye.

Travelodge Asheville Mall

199 Tunnel Road
Asheville, NC 28805
800-578-7878 • 828-254-4311

Type of Lodging: Motel
Room Rates: $35–$95, including continental breakfast. AAA and AARP discounts.
Pet Charges & Deposits: $20 nonrefundable deposit.
Pet Policy: Designated rooms only.
Amenities: Cable TV, safes, guest laundry.
Pet Amenities: Great Smoky National Park is located 30 miles from the motel.
Rated: 2 Paws — 77 rooms.

Travelodge is a fine cost-conscious choice when you're in tourist-laden Asheville. While you can't mention Asheville without mentioning the Biltmore Estate, there are numerous other attractions in or near the city, including the Homespun Shops, Grovewood Gallery & Museums, established to preserve the Old World wool manufacturing skills of mountain people. Mount Mitchell State Park includes the 6,684-foot summit of Mount Mitchell, the highest peak east of the Mississippi River.

Siena Hotel

1505 East Franklin Street
Chapel Hill, NC 27514
800-223-7379
www.sienahotel.com

Type of Lodging: Hotel
Room Rates: $149–$250, including full breakfast. AAA and AARP discounts.
Pet Charges & Deposits: $50 nonrefundable deposit.
Pet Policy: None. All Pets Welcome.
Amenities: Cable TV, refrigerators, safes, restaurant.
Pet Amenities: Exercise area. City park is located ¼ mile from the hotel on Estes Street.
Rated: 3 Paws — 68 rooms and 12 suites.

The Siena Hotel is surely one of the city's most elegant hostelries. Among other things, Il Palio, an elegant Northern Italian ristorante, is situated within the confines of the hotel. The University of North Carolina, dominant center of this thriving community, was chartered in 1789. The outstanding Moorhead Planetarium, on campus, served as the NASA training center for the Mercury, Gemini, Apollo and Skylab astronauts.

Clarion Hotel

*321 West Woodlawn Road
Charlotte, NC 28217
800 CLARION• 704-523-1400
www.clarionhotelcharlotte.com*

Type of Lodging: Hotel

Room Rates: $90–$110. AAA, AARP and *10% Pets Welcome*™ discounts.

Pet Charges & Deposits: $25 on first day, $10 each additional day.

Pet Policy: None. All Pets Welcome.

Amenities: Cable TV, refrigerators, microwaves, safes, pool, Jacuzzi, restaurant, bar, convenience store.

Pet Amenities: Renaissance Park is located on Tyvola Road.

Rated: 3 Paws — 174 rooms.

A moderately priced hotel with substantial touches of elegance, the Clarion Hotel situated five miles from Charlotte-Douglas International Airport. It has a 24-hour convenience store right on the premises, as well as a restaurant. Charlotte combines the graciousness of the Old South and the sophistication of a city very much on the move. Colonial and Victorian homes jostle skyscrapers that house the nation's second largest financial center. Charlotte, North Carolina's largest city, spreads its tentacles well into South Carolina, just over the border.

Drury Inn & Suites

*415 West W.T. Harris Boulevard
Charlotte, NC 28262
800-378-7946
www.druryinn.com*

Type of Lodging: Hotel

Room Rates: $70–$113, including "Quickstart" continental breakfast and weekday Manager's Reception. AAA and AARP discounts.

Pet Charges & Deposits: None.

Pet Policy: Pets must not be left unattended.

Amenities: Cable TV, refrigerators, microwaves, safe, pools, Jacuzzi.

Pet Amenities: List of nearby veterinarians maintained. Exercise area. Reedy Creek Park is located 8 miles from the hotel.

Rated: 3 Paws — 143 rooms and 14 suites.

Drury Inn & Suites is an immaculate, impressive lodging at Exit 45A off Interstate 85. Most of the rooms are non-smoking rooms. Kids stay free in their parents' rooms and there's a 100% satisfaction guarantee. It's five miles from the hotel to Lowe's Motor Speedway and its NASCAR stock car racing. Whatever your taste in theater and concerts, you'll find it in Charlotte. There are several performing arts companies, the Charlotte Philharmonic Orchestra, the Charlotte Repertory Theatre, Charlotte Symphony Orchestra, the North Carolina Dance Theatre and Opera Carolina.

Sheraton Charlotte Airport Plaza Hotel

3315 Interstate 85 at Billy Graham Parkway
Charlotte, NC 28208
704-392-1200

Type of Lodging: Hotel

Room Rates: $69–$179. AAA and AARP discounts.

Pet Charges & Deposits: None.

Pet Policy: Designated rooms only. Manager's prior approval required.

Amenities: Cable TV, pools, hot tub, coffeemakers, hairdryers, irons and ironing boards, restaurant.

Pet Amenities: Freedom Park is located 7 miles from the hotel.

Rated: 3 Paws — 222 rooms and 2 suites.

From its striking architecture to its newly renovated guestrooms, from the impressive lunch buffet and terrace dining of Oscar's Restaurant to the 20 public meeting venues, including the 7,000-square-foot Grand Ballroom, the Sheraton Charlotte Airport Plaza Hotel is magnificent. Discovery Place at 301 North Tryon Street, is a hand-on complex incorporating an exhibition hall, planetarium and Omnimax theater. The Greek Revival Mint Museum of Art, which housed the first branch of the United States Mint from 1837-61 and later served as a Confederate hospital, an assay office, and a federal courthouse, features Art in the Americas and an exquisite collection of pottery and porcelain.

La Quinta Inn & Suites Durham

4414 Chapel Hill Boulevard
Durham, NC 27707
800-531-5900 • 919-401-9660
www.laquinta.com
LQ0183GM@laquinta.com

Type of Lodging: Hotel

Room Rates: $70–$85, including deluxe continental breakfast. AAA, AARP and *10% Pets Welcome*™ discounts.

Pet Charges & Deposits: None.

Pet Policy: No pets over 30 lbs.

Amenities: Cable TV, refrigerators, microwaves, safes, pool, Jacuzzi, fitness center, irons and ironing boards, coffeemakers, hairdryers.

Pet Amenities: List of nearby veterinarians maintained. Duke Park is located 7 miles from the hotel.

Rated: 3 Paws — 118 rooms and 12 suites.

La Quinta represents one of the best values in all of North Carolina. Its elegantly appointed rooms, complimentary breakfast and numerous amenities, including kids staying free in their parents' rooms, make this a truly superior choice. Convenient to both Chapel Hill and Durham, it's centrally located in a high caliber education and technology area. Duke University Chapel is the central and dominant structure of the university buildings.

Comfort Inn Interstate 95

1957 Cedar Creek Road
Fayetteville, NC 28301
800-621-6596 • 910-323-8333

Type of Lodging: Motel

Room Rates: $65–$80, including full breakfast. AAA and AARP discounts.

Pet Charges & Deposits: None.

Pet Policy: Designated rooms only.

Amenities: Cable TV, refrigerators, microwaves, pool, free car wash.

Pet Amenities: Exercise area. Mazarick Park is located at 1368 Belvedere Avenue. PetSmart is located at 2061 Skibo Road.

Rated: 3 Paws — 120 rooms and suites.

Comfort Inn represents quality and great value in an attractive setting. Its new guestrooms include 25 new luxury king suites. Wake up to a hot Southern-style breakfast in the lodging's beautifully appointed breakfast nook. Fayetteville is North Carolina's most inland port, on the Cape Fear River. It's home to Fort Bragg, one of the country's largest and most important military installations. It's also home to the Old Market House, built in 1832, the First Presbyterian Church (present structure dates from 1832) and Pope Air Force Base.

Microtel Inn & Suites

81 Allman Drive
Franklin, NC 28734
888-403-1700 • 828-349-9000
www.microtelfranklinnc.com
microtel@dnet.net

Type of Lodging: Hotel

Room Rates: $40–$100, including continental breakfast. AAA, AARP and *10% Pets Welcome™* discounts.

Pet Charges & Deposits: $20 per stay.

Pet Policy: Sorry, no cats.

Amenities: Cable TV, refrigerators, microwaves, safes.

Pet Amenities: List of nearby veterinarians maintained. Macon County Recreational Park is located on Allman Drive.

Rated: 2 Paws — 52 rooms and 9 suites.

The hallmark of this chain is compact rooms with no wasted space, fine amenities and immaculate cleanliness. Franklin is famous for the mining of gemstones, including rubies, sapphires, amethyst, garnet, rose quartz and topaz. The town is on a ridge overlooking the Little Tennessee River, and the numerous mines serve as wonderful tourist sites. In addition, the town is a center for textile production, sawmilling, talc and mica mining and grinding. It's 30 miles to Harrah's Cherokee Casino and 60 miles to Asheville's Biltmore Estate.

Mountainside Vacation Lodging

8356 Sylva Road
Franklin, NC 28734
828-524-6209
mtsidel@aol.com

Type of Lodging: Guest Ranch

Apartment Rates: $70–$85.

Pet Charges & Deposits: $5 per day.

Pet Policy: No pets over 40 lbs.
Designated rooms only. Manager's prior approval required.

Amenities: Cable TV, refrigerators, microwaves, porches.

Pet Amenities: List of nearby veterinarians maintained. Great Smoky Mountains National Park nearby.

Rated: 3 Paws — 5 apartments and 5 suites.

Get away from the routines and stress of everyday life. Visit the high country of Western North Carolina and relax in the mountains. There are spectacular views from your front porch. Franklin is called the "Gem Capital of the World" in these parts, but there's also whitewater rafting, golfing, hiking and horseback riding for outdoor-minded visitors and their pets.

River House Country Inn & Restaurant

1896 Old Field Creek Road
Grassy Creek, NC 28631
336-982-2109
www.riverhousenc.com
riverhouse@skybest.com

Type of Lodging: Inn

Room Rates: $115–$150, including full breakfast.

Pet Charges & Deposits: None.

Pet Policy: None. All Pets Welcome.

Amenities: Bar, restaurant.

Pet Amenities: List of nearby veterinarians maintained. Exercise area.

Rated: 4 Paws — 7 rooms on 125 acres.

Situated on 125 acres next to By River House, a community of 46 acres in the Blue Ridge Mountains on the North Fork of the New River (so named by Thomas Jefferson's father, Peter) is the River House Inn. It was founded in 1989 by Gayle Winston, a restaurant entrepreneur who returned to her native Ashe County after many years as a producer in the theater in New York City. Amenities include handsome guestrooms, many in reclaimed outbuildings from the old farm, and a wonderful full service restaurant. The Blue Ridge Parkway is minutes away and it's only an hour to half a dozen ski resorts and several cross-country ski trails.

Biltmore Greensboro Hotel

111 West Washington Street
Greensboro, NC 27401
800-332-0303 • 336-272-3474
www.biltmorehotelgreensboro.com
thebiltmore@juno.com

Type of Lodging: Hotel
Room Rates: $85– $135, including continental breakfast and Manager's evening reception. AAA, AARP and *10% Pets Welcome*™ discounts.
Pet Charges & Deposits: None.
Pet Policy: Sorry, no cats. Designated rooms only.
Amenities: Cable TV, refrigerators, hairdryers.
Pet Amenities: List of nearby veterinarians maintained. Dog runs. Exercise area. Park nearby.
Rated: 3 Paws — 27 rooms and 4 suites.

Built in 1895, The Biltmore Hotel captures the essence of 19th century architecture and furniture, while at the same time providing modern day facilities. Recently renovated after its acquisition by the Biltmore Suites chain, accommodations include guestrooms with Victorian furniture and four-poster beds. Greensboro became a major textile center after the Civil War. It was home to William Sydney Porter (O. Henry) and Dolley Madison. The Greensboro Historical Museum contains an extensive military history collection, Dolley Madison and O. Henry memorabilia and a depiction of the 1960s civil rights movement lunch counter sit-ins.

Beechtree Inn

948 Pender Road
Hertford, NC 27944
252-426-7815
www.hobbsfurniture.com
jhobbs@hobbsfurniture.com

Type of Lodging: B&B
Room Rates: $55–$90, including full breakfast.
Pet Charges & Deposits: None.
Pet Policy: Designated rooms only. Manager's prior approval required.
Amenities: Cable TV, refrigerator, microwaves, reproduction furniture classes.
Pet Amenities: List of nearby veterinarians maintained. Exercise area. Missing Mill Park nearby.
Rated: 3 Paws — 1 room and 3 cottages.

Over the past 28 years, the Hobbs family has assembled a collection of 14 pre-Civil War buildings, restored them, and furnished them with period antiques and reproductions made by Ben Hobbs. Three houses are now ready for guests. The cottages have all modern amenities while sustaining their great sense of history. And the Beechtree Inn offers a very unique amenity—week-long furniture classes are offered each month. The Beechtree Inn is located in Northeast North Carolina, ten miles north of Edenton, five miles south of Hertford. The Newbold-White House in Hertford is the oldest brick house in North Carolina. Originally built in 1730, it has been painstakingly reconstructed to its pre-Revolutionary War appearance.

Fire Mountain Inn

P.O. Box 2772
Highlands, NC 28741
800-775-4446 • 828-526-4446
www.firemt.com
reservations@firemt.com

Type of Lodging: Inn & Cabins

Room Rates: $130–$410.

Pet Charges & Deposits: $25 per day. $150 refundable deposit.

Pet Policy: Sorry, no cats. No pets over 40 lbs. Designated rooms only. Manager's prior approval required.

Amenities: Refrigerators, microwaves, Jacuzzi, hot tubs, library, art gallery.

Pet Amenities: List of nearby veterinarians maintained. Exercise area. Nearby parks: Nantahala National Forest, Sumter National Forest, Great Smoky Mountains National Park, three hiking trails, hundreds of acres with ponds and waterfalls.

Rated: 5 Paws — 6 rooms, 6 cabins and 3 suites.

The extraordinary physical setting of unsurpassed beauty on top of Fire Mountain inspired the Inn. The Inn sits at the very summit; spectacular views abound from every single room and suite. The Inn consists of the Lodge, the Treehouses, the Gallery, the Big Dipper (aromatherapy in an eight-person outdoor hot tub). There are rooms, suites and cabins to accommodate every taste and budget. Founded in 1875, Highlands quickly became an escape from the summer heat for aristocratic southern families. The Highlands are at the headwaters of four major rivers, in the midst of a land of waterfalls. The year-round village population of 2,500 swells to 15,000 during the high season months of the year. The village boasts 25 renowned and critically acclaimed restaurants, 150 shops of every kind (with not a neon sign in sight), a live theater and chamber music concerts.

Super 8 Motel

2149 North Marine Boulevard
Jacksonville, NC 28546
800-800-8000 • 910-455-6888
www.innworks.com

Type of Lodging: Motel

Room Rates: $45–$65, including continental breakfast. AAA and AARP discounts.

Pet Charges & Deposits: $10 per stay.

Pet Policy: Sorry, no cats. Manager's prior approval required.

Amenities: Cable TV, safes, pool, one free 8-minute long distance call each night.

Pet Amenities: Exercise area.

Rated: 2 Paws — 60 rooms.

Super 8 Motel replicates clean and value-priced rooms inherent throughout this fine chain. Jacksonville, at the mouth of the New River, has a plethora of water activities. Camp Lejeune is one of the major U.S. Marine bases on the eastern seaboard. Its 153,000 acres house the Expeditionary Forces in Readiness, 2nd Marine Division, 6th Marine Expeditionary Brigade, 2nd Force Service Support Group and the 2nd Marine Expeditionary Force. The Greatest Story Retold is a museum housing religious objects, artifacts from the Holy Land, Biblical dolls, a 1702 hand-printed Bible and numerous religious paintings.

Best Western Inn

201 Jackson Court
Lumberton, NC 28358
800-WESTERN • 910-618-9799
www.bestwestern.com

Type of Lodging: Motel

Room Rates: $55–$85, including continental breakfast. AAA, AARP and **10% Pets Welcome™** discounts.

Pet Charges & Deposits: $10 per day.

Pet Policy: No pets over 20 lbs.

Amenities: Cable TV, refrigerators, microwaves, hairdryers, free local calls.

Pet Amenities: Exercise area.

Rated: 3 Paws — 58 rooms and 4 suites.

Best Western Inn, the newest motel on Interstate 95, Exit 22, lives up to the high standards set by the chain. It has an airy and open feeling created by large rooms. The city of Lumberton, founded in 1787 by a Revolutionary War officer, bases its economy on tobacco, textiles and farm produce. Situated directly off Interstate 95, it's halfway between New York and Florida. The Robeson County Showcase Museum displays stuffed birds and mammals, guns from the early 19th century and fossils found near the Lumber River.

Country Cabins

171 Bradley Street
Maggie Valley, NC 28751
888-222-4611 • 828-926-0612

Type of Lodging: Cabins
Cabin Rates: $100–$125. *10% Pets Welcome™* discount.
Pet Charges & Deposits: $10 per stay.
Pet Policy: Sorry, no large pets.
Amenities: Cable TV, refrigerators, microwaves, whirlpool, hot tubs, spas.
Pet Amenities: List of nearby veterinarians maintained. Exercise area. Great Smoky Mountains National Park nearby.
Rated: 2 Paws — 6 cabins.

If you're looking for an Appalachian holiday, look no farther. These authentic log cabins are situated on 2½ acres with two small streams. Yet, once inside, these cabins afford modern comfort in the midst of rustic ambience. Each cabin has a wood-burning fireplace with cozy, furnished kitchens. The Country Cabins make a great base camp to allow travel to tourist attractions. But, as far as our editors are concerned, the absolute "must" experience is Ghost Town In The Sky. A chairlift and incline railway carry you almost 3,400 feet up the mountain to the main part of the park—saloon shows, thrill rides, gunfights, a country music show and then you ride the very steep transport back down the mountain. This is vacationing at its best.

Marshall House Bed & Breakfast Inn

100 Hill Street
P.O. Box 865
Marshall, NC 28753
828-649-9205
www.geocities.com/madisonavenue/
  2501/marshallpage.html

Type of Lodging: B&B
Room Rates: $30–$85, including full breakfast.
Pet Charges & Deposits: None.
Pet Policy: Manager's prior approval required.
Amenities: Refrigerators, microwaves, free live music at the depot in town of Marshall every Friday night.
Pet Amenities: Innkeepers have a large dog and cat. Pet sitting available. List of nearby veterinarians maintained. Schoolyard within walking distance. National Parks and trails nearby. Pets can walk all around the area of the property.
Rated: 2 Paws — 8 rooms.

Imagine a quaint town on the banks of the French Broad River and the timeless Appalachian Mountains—the kind of sleepy little place that seems to be missing from the daily grind of life. That's Marshall, and that's the view you get from the 50-feet veranda of the Marshall House, a 1903 bed and breakfast with eight guestrooms. In the parlor is an original watercolor of innkeeper Ruth Boylan as a child, painted by no less than Liberace! Co-host Jim Boylan, an award-winning sculptor, has a few of his original works on display. Marshall House is only 18 miles northwest of Asheville. It's a center for white water rafting, hiking and is only minutes away from the Appalachian Trail.

La Quinta Inn & Suites

1001 Hospitality Court
Morrisville, NC 27560
800-531-5900 • 919-461-1771
lg0944gm@laquinta.com

Type of Lodging: Hotel

Room Rates: $69–$175, including continental breakfast. AAA and AARP discounts.

Pet Charges & Deposits: None.

Pet Policy: No pets over 20 lbs. Designated rooms only.

Amenities: Cable TV, refrigerators, microwaves, safes, pool, whirlpool.

Pet Amenities: Exercise area. William B. Umstead State Park and Lake Crabtree nearby.

Rated: 3 Paws — 135 rooms and 8 suites.

La Quinta Inn & Suites provides upscale accommodations with rich wood furniture, bright bathrooms, cable televisions, large desks, coffeemakers, dataport phones, alarm clock radios, hairdryers, irons and ironing boards. It's two miles from Raleigh-Durham International Airport, minutes away from all the area attractions, downtown Raleigh and the State Capitol, University of North Carolina at Chapel Hill, the Research Triangle Park and the State Fairgrounds.

Anchorage Inn & Marina

P.O. Box 880
Ocracoke, NC 27960
252-928-1101
www.theanchorageinn.com
info@theanchorageinn.com

Type of Lodging: Hotel

Room Rates: $69–$135, including continental breakfast. AAA discount.

Pet Charges & Deposits: $10 per day.

Pet Policy: Designated rooms only. Pets must not be left unattended.

Amenities: Cable TV, pool.

Pet Amenities: There is only one veterinarian on the island who is there two days a week. Cape Hatteras National Seashore nearby.

Rated: 2 Paws — 35 rooms and 2 suites.

Anchorage Inn & Marina, in the heart of Ocracoke Village, is right on the water and the views from here must be experienced to be believed. The Outer Banks is a chain of barrier islands, situated in a 100-mile arc. Driving Highway 12 is like driving a road across the sea. Many believe the nation was born in the Outer Banks—The "Lost Colony" of Roanoke was founded on nearby Roanoke Island in 1585. The area is also home to Kill Devil Hill (Wright Brothers National Memorial), where the Wright Brothers changed world history with their first flight of a heavier-than-air machine. Ocracoke, the southernmost major island in the chain, is adjacent to Cape Hatteras National Seashore and its plethora of wondrous lighthouses.

Red Roof Inn

3201 Wake Forest Road
Raleigh, NC 27609
800-716-6406 • 919-878-9310
www.redroofinn.com

Type of Lodging: Motel
Room Rates: $50–$70, including continental breakfast. AAA, AARP and **10% Pets Welcome™** discounts.
Pet Charges & Deposits: None.
Pet Policy: No pets over 80 lbs. Designated rooms only.
Amenities: Cable TV, pool.
Pet Amenities: Exercise area.
Rated: 2 Paws — 147 rooms.

Red Roof Inn provides excellent value in North Carolina's capital. It's spotless and possesses many fine amenities. There's also a meeting facility for up to 25 people. Just about everything in Raleigh is less than five miles away—the State Capitol, the North Carolina Museum of Art, the North Carolina Museum of History, several colleges and universities. Mordecai Historic Park, north of town, features a 1785 plantation house with original furnishings, portraits and books. The park also contains the 1795 house in which President Andrew Johnson was born.

Woodlands Inn of Sapphire

1305 U.S. 64-A
Sapphire, NC 28774
828-966-4709
www.woodlandsinn.net
woodlandsinn@citcom.net

Type of Lodging: B&B
Room Rates: $75–$125, including full breakfast.
Pet Charges & Deposits: $5 per day.
Pet Policy: Sorry, no cats. No pets over 25 lbs. Designated rooms only. Manager's prior approval required.
Amenities: Cable TV, refrigerators, microwaves, pool, Jacuzzi, gas log fireplaces.
Pet Amenities: List of nearby veterinarians maintained. Gorges State Park nearby.
Rated: 2 Paws — 12 rooms and 3 suites.

Snuggled in the heart of the Blue Ridge Mountains, the Woodlands Inn is a special place with a home-like feeling. Each room has its own décor and modern amenities. Breakfast is served each morning in the cedar and glass dining room. Sapphire is a tiny town in the mountains, close to Asheville and Highlands. There are over 250 waterfalls nearby, along with horseback riding, hiking, white water rafting, boating, golfing and numerous other outdoor activities.

Mountain Creek Bed & Breakfast

146 Chestnut Walk
Waynesville, NC 28786
800-557-9766 • 828-456-5509
www.bbonline.com/nc/mcbb

Type of Lodging: B&B
Room Rates: $85–$130, including full breakfast.
Pet Charges & Deposits: $20 per day.
Pet Policy: Sorry, no cats. No pets over 100 lbs. Designated rooms only. Manager's prior approval required.
Amenities: Cable TV, refrigerators, Jacuzzis, honor bars, private balconies, private baths.
Pet Amenities: Bowls, food, biscuits and rawhide chews available. List of nearby veterinarians maintained. Dog runs. Exercise area. Pisgah National Forest and Great Smoky Mountains National Park nearby.
Rated: 2 Paws — 7 rooms.

With only seven rooms, Mountain Creek Bed & Breakfast has all the amenities you'd expect from a mountain retreat. Choose from tree top balcony suites with king-sized beds and cedar lined closets or newly renovated Jacuzzi suites with queen-size beds and whirlpool tubs. Named in honor of Revolutionary War general "Mad Anthony" Wayne, Waynesville was settled by English, Scotch-Irish, German and Dutch immigrants who came from the coast to the mountains in search of better hunting and farming. The World Methodist Council is headquartered three miles from Waynesville. Close to Great Smoky Mountains National Park, it's a mountain haven.

Anderson Guest House

520 Orange Street
Wilmington, NC 28401
888-865-1216 • 910-343-8128
anderlancon@aol.com

Type of Lodging: B&B
Room Rates: $70–$90, including full breakfast.
Pet Charges & Deposits: None.
Pet Policy: None. All Pets Welcome.
Amenities: Fireplace.
Pet Amenities: Greenfield Park nearby
Rated: 3 Paws — 2 rooms.

Anderson Guest House is a charming, private guesthouse overlooking its own garden in historic downtown Wilmington. Each bedroom has a private bath, working fireplace, ceiling fan and individual climate controls. Wilmington, situated on the Cape Fear River, is North Carolina's primary deepwater port. The city was the colonial capital in 1743, and was the scene of the Stamp Act Resistance in 1765. British forces established their headquarters here during the winter of 1780-81, and during the Civil War, it was one of the principal ports of the Confederacy. There are numerous plantations in the area. The Battleship North Carolina, anchored on the Cape Fear River, served in every major U.S. naval offensive in the Pacific during World War II.

Augustus T. Zevely Inn

803 South Main Street
Winston-Salem, NC 27101
800-928-9299 • 336-748-9299
www.winston-salem-inn.com

Type of Lodging: B&B

Room Rates: $80–$205, including continental breakfast or full breakfast. AAA and *10% Pets Welcome*™ discounts.

Pet Charges & Deposits: None.

Pet Policy: No pets over 25 lbs. Designated rooms only. Manager's prior approval required.

Amenities: Cable TV, refrigerators, microwaves, whirlpool, steam baths, two-story heated outdoor porch.

Pet Amenities: This Inn was featured on Good Morning America as a pet-friendly Bed & Breakfast. List of nearby veterinarians maintained. Exercise area. Old Salem Historical Area and Salem College field within the nearby area.

Rated: 3 Paws — 12 rooms and 1 suite.

The Augustus T. Zevely Inn, the only lodging in the Old Salem Historic District, has been meticulously and accurately restored to its mid-19th century appearance. Guestrooms are individually decorated to reflect their property's original uses. The Historic District of Old Salem was designated a Registered National Historic Landmark by the U.S. Department of the Interior in 1966. It's a living history restoration of the Moravian church town that was founded in 1766. The city is unashamedly a tobacco center. The R.J. Reynolds Tobacco Manufacturing Center produces 265 million cigarettes a day—this activity helped, in part, to found the Reynolds House Museum of American Art, built in 1916-17 by R.J. Reynolds. Wake Forest University is situated in Winston-Salem.

NORTH DAKOTA

Nickname: Peace Garden State

Population: 633,666

Area: 70,704 square miles

Climate: Continental, with wide range of temperature and moderate rainfall.

Capital: Bismarck

Entered Union: Nov. 2, 1889

Motto: Liberty and union, now and forever, one and inseparable.

Song: North Dakota Hymn

Flower: Wild Prairie Rose

Tree: American Elm

Bird: Western Meadowlark

Famous North Dakotans: Maxwell Anderson, Angie Dickinson, John Bernard Flannigan, Phil Jackson, Louis L'Amour, Peggy Lee, Eric Sevareid, Lawrence Welk.

 History: Ojibwa, Yanktonai and Teton Sioux, Mandan, Arikara, and Hidatsa Native American tribes inhabited the area at the time of the first European contact. The U.S. acquired the territory in the Louisiana Purchase in 1805. Lewis and Clark explored the new territory in 1803. The first permanent settlement was at Pembina in 1812. Missouri River steamboats plied the area twenty years later. The first railroads came in 1873, bringing many homesteaders. This was followed by a farming boom in the mid-1870s and 1880s. North Dakota was the first state to hold a Presidential primary in 1912. The Theodore Roosevelt National Park is a major tourist draw for the state.

Buckboard Inn

1191 First Avenue Northwest
Beach, ND 58621
888-449-3599 • 701-872-4794

Type of Lodging: Motel

Room Rates: $33–$51, including continental breakfast. AARP and *10% Pets Welcome™* discounts.

Pet Charges & Deposits: None.

Pet Policy: Designated rooms only. Manager's prior approval required.

Amenities: Cable TV, microwaves.

Pet Amenities: List of nearby veterinarians maintained. Exercise area. Theodore Roosevelt National Park is located 25 miles from the motel.

Rated: 3 Paws — 39 rooms.

The Buckboard Inn has cozy and convenient accommodations, with refrigerators, microwaves and cable television. There is plenty of room for you and your pet to go on long walks around the motel. Located within a short drive is Theodore Roosevelt National Park, where you can enjoy hiking, cross-country horseback riding, camping and canoeing on the Little Missouri River.

Comfort Inn

215 Highway 2 East
Devils Lake, ND 301
888-266-3948 • 701-662-6760

Type of Lodging: Motel

Room Rates: $55–$75, including deluxe continental breakfast. AAA, AARP and *10% Pets Welcome™* discounts.

Pet Charges & Deposits: $10 refundable deposit.

Pet Policy: None. All Pets Welcome.

Amenities: Cable TV, refrigerators, microwaves, pool, whirlpool, hot tubs.

Pet Amenities: List of nearby veterinarians maintained. Exercise area. Roosevelt Park nearby.

Rated: 4 Paws — 87 rooms and 6 suites.

Devils Lake Comfort Inn has guestrooms with microwaves, refrigerators and cable televisions. Devils Lake is a great fishing lake. Other attractions include Black Tiger Bay State Park, Fort Trotten Calvary Square, Fort Trotten Historic Site and Lakeside Bingo.

Best Western Kelly Inn

1510 26th Avenue Southwest
Minot, ND 58701
800-735-5868 • 701-852-4300

Type of Lodging: Hotel
Room Rates: $60–$125, including continental breakfast. AAA, AARP and *10% Pets Welcome*™ discounts.
Pet Charges & Deposits: None.
Pet Policy: Small pets only. Designated rooms only. Manager's prior approval required.
Amenities: Cable TV, pool, whirlpool, hot tubs.
Pet Amenities: None.
Rated: 3 Paws — 90 rooms and 10 suites.

Whether traveling on business or pleasure, you can expect the best in hospitality from the Best Western Kelly Inn. With modern amenities, friendly service, and a convenient location, you get affordable value that adds up to a very enjoyable stay. You will want to return to the Best Western Kelly Inn time and time again. Located in the heart of the city, guests are minutes away from miniature golf, an amusement park, museums, Minot State University, Nodak Speedway and Roosevelt Park and Zoo.

OHIO

Nickname: Buckeye State
Population: 11,256,654
Area: 44,828 square miles
Climate: Temperate but variable, subject to much precipitation
Capital: Columbus
Entered Union: March 1, 1803
Motto: With God, all things are possible.
Song: Beautiful Ohio
Flower: Scarlet Carnation

Tree: Buckeye
Bird: Cardinal
Famous Ohioans: Sherwood Anderson, Neil Armstrong, Erma Bombeck, Clarence Darrow, Thomas Edison, Clark Gable, John Glenn, Bob Hope, Toni Morrison, Jesse Owens, John D. Rockefeller, Sr. & Jr., Roy Rogers, Steven Spielberg, Gloria Steinem, William Howard Taft.

 History: The area was sparsely populated when Lafayette explored the area in 1679. France claimed the area in 1682. Around 1730, traders from Pennsylvania and Virginia entered what is now Ohio. The French and their Native American allies attempted to drive them out. France ceded its claim to Britain in 1763, but Americans occupied Ohio during the Revolutionary War and Britain ceded the territory to the U.S. in 1783. The first organized settlement was at Marietta in 1788. Today, Ohio is heavily industrialized. Cincinnati, Columbus, Cleveland, Dayton and Akron are among its major cities.

Aurora Inn

30 Shawnee Trail
Aurora, OH 44202
800-444-6121 • 330-563-6121
aurorainn@aol.com

Type of Lodging: Hotel
Room Rates: $69–$199. AAA discount.
Pet Charges & Deposits: $50 refundable deposit.
Pet Policy: Designated rooms only. Pets must not be left unattended.
Amenities: Satellite TV, safe, pool, restaurant, lounge.
Pet Amenities: List of nearby veterinarians maintained. Sunny Lake Park is located on East Mennonite Road.
Rated: 2 Paws — 69 rooms.

Though secluded, the Aurora Inn is within minutes from SeaWorld of Cleveland, Six Flags Amusement Park, cross-country ski trails, Dankorona Winery, golf and many other unique attractions. The Inn offers group discounts and privileges at the Pine Lake Trout Club, its sister property, an exclusive discount to Mario's International Spa and VIP discount certificates to the Aurora Premium Outlets. They feature a full service restaurant, lounge, banquet facilities, indoor and outdoor pools as well as Jacuzzi, saunas and tennis courts. Another Time…Another Place…

Microtel Inn

7393 South Avenue
Boardman, OH 44512
800-804-8385 • 330-788-3337
www.microtelinn.com
microtel@cboss.com

Type of Lodging: Hotel
Room Rates: $30–$60, including continental breakfast. Call for discounts.
Pet Charges & Deposits: None.
Pet Policy: None. All Pets Welcome.
Amenities: Cable TV, safes, meeting room, adjoining rooms.
Pet Amenities: Mill Creek Park nearby.
Rated: 3 Paws — 92 rooms.

Microtel Inn is centrally located in Boardman just off Interstate 680. It's surrounded by some of the finest restaurants and retail establishments in the area. Within 20 miles, guests will find Southern Park Mall, Butler Institute of American Art, Youngstown State University, Mill Creek Park, Canfield Fairgrounds, Youngstown-Warren Regional Airport and a plethora of other great Ohio attractions. At Microtel Inn you have your choice of tastefully decorated rooms with cable television, fitness facilities, desks, "reach anywhere" phones with modem hook-up, individual climate controls and complimentary morning coffee.

Amerisuites Cincinnati North

12001 Chase Plaza Drive
Cincinnati, OH 45240
800-833-1516 • 513-825-9035
www.amerisuites.com

Type of Lodging: Hotel

Suite Rates: $69–$129, including continental breakfast. AAA, AARP and *10% Pets Welcome™* discounts.

Pet Charges & Deposits: None.

Pet Policy: None. All Pets Welcome.

Amenities: Cable TV, VCRs, refrigerators, microwaves, pool, fitness room, business center, guest laundry, hairdryers, irons and ironing boards.

Pet Amenities: List of nearby veterinarians maintained. Exercise area. Winton Woods County Park is located only 5 minutes south of the hotel.

Rated: 4 Paws — 126 suites.

Amerisuites offers fine upscale accommodations at reasonable prices. You and your pet may enjoy a free bountiful breakfast buffet, indoor heated pool, guest laundry, voicemail service, internet access, a fitness center and state-of-the-art business center. Nearby attractions include the Golf Center, Surf Cincinnati Waterpark, Museum Center, Cincinnati Zoo, Paramount's Kings Island, Argosy Casino, Riverfront Stadium & Coliseum and three large shopping malls.

Ramada Inn North

4079 Little York Road
Dayton, OH 45414
800-860-7666 • 937-890-9500
www.ramada.com

Type of Lodging: Motel

Room Rates: $60–$80, including continental breakfast. AAA and AARP discounts.

Pet Charges & Deposits: None.

Pet Policy: Designated rooms only.

Amenities: Cable TV, refrigerators, pool, fitness room, guest laundry, free airport transportation.

Pet Amenities: Exercise area.

Rated: 3 Paws — 136 rooms and 3 suites.

If you and your pet's travel plans take you to Dayton, you are certain to find Ramada Inn North a value choice for the travelers seeking great service from a friendly, well-trained staff. Centrally located off Interstate 75, you are a short drive to many major attractions, businesses and shopping areas in the Dayton area. They are only five miles from downtown Dayton, Dayton Convention Center, Salem Mall and Dayton Airport. The Wright Patterson Air Force Museum is only eight miles away.

Econo Lodge

6161 US 127 North
Eaton, OH 45320
800-55 ECONO • 437-456-5959

Type of Lodging: Motel

Room Rates: $43–$65, including continental breakfast. AAA, AARP, AKC, ABA and *10% Pets Welcome*™ discounts.

Pet Charges & Deposits: $5 per day.

Pet Policy: Designated rooms only.

Amenities: Cable TV, refrigerators, microwaves.

Pet Amenities: Dog runs. Exercise area.

Rated: 3 Paws — 51 rooms.

The Econo Lodge has easy access to Interstate 70. All guestrooms are large and clean. Guests receive a free continental breakfast. The adjoining restaurant gives a ten percent discount to guests. Area attractions include Eldora Speedway, Miami University, Preble County Pork Festival and Reed Memorial Hospital. So whether Eaton is your final destination or you're just passing through, Econo Lodge is a great choice for you and your pet.

Heartland Country Resort

2994 Chesterville-Sparta Road
Fredericktown, OH 43019
800-230-7030 • 419-768-9300
www.heartlandcountryresort.com

Type of Lodging: B&B

Room Rates: $85–$195, including full breakfast. AAA discount.

Pet Charges & Deposits: $15 per day.

Pet Policy: Sorry, no cats. Designated rooms only. Manager's prior approval required. Horses welcome.

Amenities: Refrigerators, microwaves, honor bar, pool, Jacuzzi, pool table, fireplaces.

Pet Amenities: List of nearby veterinarians maintained. Dog runs. Exercise area. Mount Gilead State Park, Mohican State Park and Malabar Farm State Park nearby.

Rated: 5 Paws — 7 rooms and 5 suites on a farm with other animals, including horses.

Welcome to Heartland Country Resort, a sprawling haven for families and couples alike. The Heartland is peacefully nestled amidst the beautiful rolling hills and shady woodlands northeast of Columbus. Everyone loves their friendly chickens, horses, cattle, golden retriever dogs, cats and a variety of indoor and outdoor activities. Relax and enjoy the outdoor swimming pool, basketball, ping pong, croquet and volleyball. Or visit the Mid-Ohio Raceway, Mohican and Malabar Farms State Parks and Kingwood Garden Center. Then return to the remodeled 1878 farmhouse and newly constructed log building, situated on over 100 acres, providing a private country retreat with all the modern amenities. The main farmhouse is completely refurbished for your comfort and has private bathrooms, air conditioning, a spacious deck and a screened porch. A Five-Paw getaway for you and your pet!

Shawnee Inn

30916 Lake Logan Road
Logan, OH 43138
740-385-5675
www.shawneeinn.ohgolly.com

Type of Lodging: Motel
Room Rates: $45–$85. AAA and AARP discounts.
Pet Charges & Deposits: $5 per stay.
Pet Policy: Small pets only. Designated rooms only. Manager's prior approval required.
Amenities: Cable TV.
Pet Amenities: Exercise area. Hocking Hills State Park nearby.
Rated: 2 Paws — 22 rooms.

Imagine the discovery of a hidden jewel…a hideaway place where you will experience breathtaking sunsets and majestic, unspoiled vistas. Shawnee Inn is enchantment, and once experienced, you and your pet will be compelled by its magic to return. The Inn is one block from Lake Logan where you and your pet can enjoy walking along the beach, fishing and boating. Golfing, horseback riding, Old Man's Cave parks, Hocking Scenic Railroad, Hocking College and Ohio University Athens are within 30 minutes.

Knights Inn Marietta

506 Pike Street
Marietta, OH 45750
800-526-5947 • 740-373-7373

Type of Lodging: Motel
Room Rates: $45–$59, including coffee and tea. AAA discount.
Pet Charges & Deposits: $5 per day.
Pet Policy: None. All Pets Welcome.
Amenities: Cable TV, refrigerators, microwaves, pool, Jacuzzi, free health club visits.
Pet Amenities: List of nearby veterinarians maintained. Exercise area. VFW Park is only 2 blocks away from the motel.
Rated: 3 Paws — 97 rooms.

The Knights Inn Marietta provides outstanding value through a friendly, helpful staff, well-maintained accommodations and inviting, up-to-date surroundings—all at a great price! Guest amenities includes alarm clock, 24-hour front desk service, free local calls, modem, free parking, free newspaper, pool, RV or truck parking, cable television and laundry/valet services. Nearby, guests will find fishing, golfing, tennis and shopping. There are many local attractions to choose from including the Fenton Glass Factory, Famous Middleton Doll Factory, Historic Harmar Village, Coca-Cola Museum and Harmar Railroad Station.

Red Roof Inn

1570 South Reynolds Road
Maumee, OH 43537
800-843-7663 • 419-893-0292
www.redroof.com

Type of Lodging: Motel
Room Rates: $40–$70. AAA and AARP discounts.
Pet Charges & Deposits: None.
Pet Policy: None. All Pets Welcome.
Amenities: Cable TV.
Pet Amenities: List of nearby veterinarians maintained. Exercise area.
Rated: 4 Paws — 110 rooms.

Red Roof Inn affords a clean, comfortable room that gives you a welcomed feeling. Maumee Sports Mall Adjacent, Lucas County Recreation Center, Masonic Auditorium, Medical College, Toledo Botanical Gardens, Toledo Zoo, Seagate Convention Center and Bowling Green State University are all within a short drive. The motel is located 12 miles southwest of downtown Toledo.

Comfort Inn East

2930 Navarre Avenue
Oregon, OH 43616
419-691-8911

Type of Lodging: Hotel
Room Rates: $69–$129, including continental breakfast. AAA, AARP and *Pets Welcome*™ discounts.
Pet Charges & Deposits: None.
Pet Policy: Designated rooms only.
Amenities: Cable TV, refrigerators, microwaves, pool.
Pet Amenities: Pearson Park is located at 4600 Starr Avenue.
Rated: 3 Paws — 79 rooms and 17 suites. Gold Award Winner.

Comfort Inn East is a cost-conscious and delightfully pet-friendly establishment. You and your pet are an easy drive away from Anchor Point, Lake Erie, Maumee Bay State Park, Meinke's Marina, Seagate Convention Center, Toledo Sports Arena, Toledo Museum of Art, University of Toledo, Toledo Zoo and downtown Toledo. For outdoor enthusiasts, the area is a mecca for bird watching and fishing.

Knights Inn

51260 National Road
St. Clairsville, OH 43950
800-835-9628 • 740-695-5038

Type of Lodging: Motel

Room Rates: $40–$67. AAA, AARP and *10% Pets Welcome™* discounts.

Pet Charges & Deposits: $5 per day.

Pet Policy: None. All Pets Welcome.

Amenities: Cable TV, refrigerators, microwaves, pool, Jacuzzi.

Pet Amenities: List of nearby veterinarians maintained. Exercise area.

Rated: 3 Paws — 104 rooms.

This beautiful, one-floor Knights Inn is situated at Exit 218 on Interstate 70 and Exit 1 on 470, next to the Ohio Valley Mall and the new Ohio Valley Plaza. Offering a variety of rooms, it is only eight miles from Wheeling, West Virginia and the Capital Music Hall and Wheeling Downs Dog Track.

Red Roof Inn

68301 Red Roof Lane
St. Clairsville, OH 43950
800 RED ROOF • 740-695-4057
www.redroof.com

Type of Lodging: Motel

Room Rates: $40–$80, including coffee and tea. AAA and AARP discounts.

Pet Charges & Deposits: None.

Pet Policy: None. All Pets Welcome.

Amenities: Cable TV, refrigerators, microwaves, voicemail.

Pet Amenities: List of nearby veterinarians maintained. Exercise area. Oglebay Park is located 10 miles from the motel. Wheeling Park is located 8 miles from the motel.

Rated: 3 Paws — 108 rooms. Hospitality Star Award and Guest Satisfaction Award.

Red Roof Inn is located adjacent to Ohio Valley Plaza and half a mile from the Ohio Valley Mall. The Inn is only nine miles west of Wheeling, Wheeling Civic Center, Capital Music Hall, Wheeling Downs Greyhound Track and Video Slots. This is a great place for you and your pet to stay. This motel offers cable television, microfridges and refrigerators for a nominal charge.

Stow Inn

4601 Darrow Road
Stow, OH 44224
330-688-3508

Type of Lodging: Motel

Room Rates: $50–$110. AAA and AARP discounts.

Pet Charges & Deposits: None.

Pet Policy: None. All Pets Welcome.

Amenities: Cable TV, safe, pool, whirlpool.

Pet Amenities: List of nearby veterinarians maintained. Exercise area. Cuyahoga Valley National Recreation Area nearby.

Rated: 3 Paws — 32 rooms.

The Stow Inn is a great budget-choice in Stow. The pet-friendly, family atmosphere will make you and your pet feel very welcome. The motel is located on a public par 3 golf course. Only 20 minutes to the many local attractions including Sea World, Six Flags Ohio, Inventor's Hall of Fame, Football Hall of Fame and the Akron Zoo.

Best Western Downtown Motor Inn

777 Mahoning Avenue Northwest
Warren, OH 44483
800 WESTERN • 330-392-2515
www.bestwestern.com/downtownmotor
inn
bwwarrenohio@earthlink.net

Type of Lodging: Motel

Room Rates: $49–$150, including continental breakfast. AAA and AARP discounts.

Pet Charges & Deposits: None.

Pet Policy: Manager's prior approval required.

Amenities: Cable TV, pool.

Pet Amenities: List of nearby veterinarians maintained. Exercise area. Perkins Park is a block from the motel via Perkins Drive.

Rated: 3 Paws — 71 rooms and 2 suites.

Guestrooms at the Best Western Downtown Motor Inn have cable television and air conditioning. It is a great place to stay when visiting Warren. Visitors will find many great attractions a short drive away including Packard Music Hall & Convention Center, Packard Electric, Mosquito Lake State Park, Eastwood Expo Center, General Motors Lordstown, Ledges Racetrack, Sea World and Geauga Lake Amusement Park.

Cleveland/Willoughby Travelodge

346 Maplegrove Road
Willoughby, OH 44094
440-585-1900

Type of Lodging: Motel
Room Rates: $49–$89. AAA, AARP, AKC, ABA and *10% Pets Welcome™* discounts.
Pet Charges & Deposits: $25 refundable deposit.
Pet Policy: None. All Pets Welcome.
Amenities: Cable TV, safe, pool.
Pet Amenities: List of nearby veterinarians maintained. Exercise area. Metropolitan Park nearby.
Rated: 3 Paws — 110 rooms.

The Cleveland/Willoughby Travelodge is just 20 minutes from downtown Cleveland and features a quiet, park-like setting with restaurants, shops and attractions nearby. Guests will find outstanding value in such amenities as free in-room coffee, free weekday lobby newspaper, free incoming faxes and no long distance access charges.

OKLAHOMA

Nickname: Sooner State
Population: 3,358,944
Area: 69,903 square miles
Climate: Temperate. Southern humid belt merging with colder northern continental; humid eastern and dry western zones.
Capital: Oklahoma City
Entered Union: Nov. 16, 1907
Motto: *Labor Omnia Vincit* (Labor conquers all things).
Song: Oklahoma!

Flower: Mistletoe
Tree: Redbud
Bird: Scissor-tailed Flycatcher
Famous Oklahomans: Troy Aikman, Carl Albert, Gene Autry, Johnny Bench, Garth Brooks, William "Hopalong" Cassidy, Lon Chaney, Walter Cronkite, James Garner, Woody Guthrie, Paul Harvey, Ron Howard, Reba McEntire, Tony Randall, Oral Roberts, Will Rogers.

 History: Native Americans sparsely inhabited the region when Coronado arrived in 1541. Oklahoma was part of the Louisiana Purchase. It was established as "Indian Territory," but not given territorial government. It became home to the so-called "Civilized Tribes"— Cherokee, Choctaw, Chickasaw, Creek, and Seminole—after the forced removal of Native Americans from the Eastern U.S The land was also used by Comanche, Osage, and other Plains tribes. Land was opened for homesteading by runs and lottery, the first run in 1889. The most famous run was the Cherokee Outlet in 1893.

Best Western Altus

2804 North Main Street
Altus, OK 73521
800-528-1234 • 580-482-9300
www.zmchotels.com

Type of Lodging: Motel

Room Rates: $51–$61, including continental breakfast and cocktails. AAA, AARP and *10% Pets Welcome*™ discounts.

Pet Charges & Deposits: None.

Pet Policy: None. All Pets Welcome.

Amenities: Cable TV, refrigerators, pool, Jacuzzi, lounge.

Pet Amenities: List of nearby veterinarians maintained. Exercise area. City park is located on North Main Street.

Rated: 4 Paws — 100 rooms.

The Best Western Altus provides all travelers with the amenities needed to make your stay a nice experience. The motel features a free continental breakfast, cable television, in-room coffee and free local telephone calls. You can enjoy your favorite refreshment in the Candlelight Lounge. Local points of interest include Western Oklahoma State College, Altus Air Force Base, Quartz Mountain State Park, golfing, fishing and boating facilities. The Best Western looks forward to having you and your pet as their guests during your stay in Altus.

Comfort Inn & Suites

2112 West Main
Durant, OK 74701
580-924-8881

Type of Lodging: Inn

Room Rates: $59–$139, including continental breakfast. AAA, AARP and *10% Pets Welcome*™ discounts.

Pet Charges & Deposits: $10 per day.

Pet Policy: None. All Pets Welcome.

Amenities: Cable TV, refrigerators, microwaves, Jacuzzi, pool.

Pet Amenities: List of nearby veterinarians maintained. Exercise area. City park is only 5 minutes away from the Inn.

Rated: 3 Paws — 46 rooms and 16 suites.

Comfort Inn & Suites is a budget-priced, convenient, small inn, located in a typical, small Midwestern town. It's a fine rest stop if you're "on the road" when the sun goes down. But don't forget to visit the Antique Craft Mall, Choctaw Bingo, Medical Center of Southern Oklahoma, Southeastern Oklahoma State and Lake Texoma while in the area.

Days Inn

1100 Highway 34 and Interstate 40
Elk City, OK 73644
580-225-9210

Type of Lodging: Motel & Inn

Room Rates: $50–$60, including continental breakfast. AAA, AARP and *15% Pets Welcome™* discounts.

Pet Charges & Deposits: $5 per day.

Pet Policy: Designated rooms only.

Amenities: Cable TV, refrigerators, pool.

Pet Amenities: List of nearby veterinarians maintained. Dog runs. Exercise area.

Rated: 3 Paws — 100 rooms and 25 suites.

The Days Inn has a very pet-friendly staff more than willing to help in any way possible. A courtyard of trees and flowers beautifully surrounds the outdoor pool. They offer continental breakfast in the lobby each morning. Some guestrooms have a full kitchen area. These rooms are spacious with plenty of living area. Some have easy chairs. The two-room suites provide guests with a bedroom adjacent to a living/kitchen area. Other amenities include 24-hour front desk, guest laundry, safe-deposit boxes, cable television and a restaurant adjacent to the hotel.

Holiday Inn

1010 Meadow Ridge
Elk City, OK 73644
800 HOLIDAY • 580-225-6637
holidayinnelk@itlnet.net

Type of Lodging: Motel

Room Rates: $55–$75, including full breakfast. AAA, AARP, AKC, ABA and *10% Pets Welcome™* discounts.

Pet Charges & Deposits: None.

Pet Policy: None. All Pets Welcome.

Amenities: Cable TV, hot tubs, pool, Holidome, miniature golf, ping pong, fitness room.

Pet Amenities: List of nearby veterinarians maintained. Exercise area. Lake Elk is located 2 miles south of the motel.

Rated: 4 Paws — 147 rooms and 3 suites.

While a guest at Holiday Inn, you will be able to enjoy the indoor swimming pool and whirlpool; play miniature golf and ping pong in the Holidome, enjoy meals at the Gazebo Restaurant, real racing excitement in the Payzone Club and relax in the comfort of the rooms. Conveniently located halfway between Oklahoma City and Amarillo (Texas) on Interstate 40, Elk City is located in the heart of the American oil and natural gas production region. This hotel has become the preferred "home away from home" for all of the major oil company executives. While in Western Oklahoma, stop by Ackley Park, Elk City Golf & Country Club, Black Kettle Museum, Paul Peeler Sports Complex, Elk City Speedway, Rodeo Arena, Foss Lake and Resort, Erick Honey Farm and Quartz Mountain Resort.

Residence Inn by Marriott

2681 Jefferson Avenue
Norman, OK 73072
800-331-3131 • 405-366-0900
www.whghotels.com

Type of Lodging: Hotel
Suite Rates: $79–$119, including expanded continental breakfast and weekday evening Hospitality Hour. AAA, AARP, AKC and ABA discounts.
Pet Charges & Deposits: $75 per stay.
Pet Policy: None. All Pets Welcome.
Amenities: Cable TV, refrigerators, microwaves, pool, Jacuzzi.
Pet Amenities: List of nearby veterinarians maintained. Exercise area. Norman Riverside Park is located on 24th Avenue.
Rated: 3 Paws — 126 suites.

Encounter heartland hospitality at its finest at the Residence Inn by Marriott. Enjoy all the comforts of home in their elegant suites which feature fully equipped kitchens, living room areas (most with fireplaces), voicemail, dataport phones, guest laundry facilities and complimentary daily newspapers. Conveniently located at the corner of Interstate 35 and Highway 9 East, making it easy for you to find, Residence Inn is less than three miles away from the University of Oklahoma. Other tourist attractions include Thunder Valley Raceway, Cleveland County Historical Museum, Firehouse Art Center, Fred Jones, Jr. Museum of Art, Jacobson House Native American Cultural Center, Oklahoma Museum of Natural History, Little River Zoo, Lake Thunderbird State Park and Westwood Water Park.

Best Western Saddleback Inn

4300 Southwest Third
Oklahoma City, OK 73108
800-228-3903 • 405-947-7000
www.bestwestern.com/saddlebackinn
bwsaddleback@msn.com

Type of Lodging: Hotel
Room Rates: $69–$92. AAA and AARP discounts.
Pet Charges & Deposits: $25 refundable deposit.
Pet Policy: None. All Pets Welcome.
Amenities: Cable TV, refrigerators, pool, whirlpool, lounge, restaurant, voicemail, dataports.
Pet Amenities: Will Rogers Park is located at 3201 North Grand.
Rated: 3 Paws — 186 rooms and 34 suites.

Discover southern hospitality with a personal touch at Oklahoma City's finest full service hotel—the Best Western Saddleback Inn. Nearby attractions include the Oklahoma City State Fairgrounds, Oklahoma City Art Museum, Route 66 Trading Post, Overholser Mansion, Oklahoma Heritage Center, Oklahoma Governor's Mansion, Oklahoma City Zoo, 45th Infantry Division, Cowboy Hall of Fame and the University of Oklahoma.

Howard Johnson Express Inn - Airport

400 South Meridian Avenue
Oklahoma City, OK 73108
800-458-8186 • 405-943-9841
www.the.hojo.com
hojookc@aol.com

Type of Lodging: Hotel

Room Rates: $42–$68, including continental breakfast. AAA, AARP and *10% Pets Welcome™* discounts.

Pet Charges & Deposits: $6 per day.

Pet Policy: None. All Pets Welcome.

Amenities: Cable TV, refrigerators, microwaves, fitness room, free local phone calls, pool.

Pet Amenities: Exercise area is a large courtyard where you walk or play with your pet. Will Rogers Park, Wheeler Park and Woodlawn Park are all located within 6 miles of the hotel.

Rated: 3 Paws — 96 rooms. Howard Johnson Gold Medal Property and President's Award Winner.

The Oklahoma City Howard Johnson Express is conveniently located off Interstate 40 at Meridian Avenue, Exit 145, serving business and vacation travelers. They are within five minutes of downtown Oklahoma City, local attractions and Will Rogers World Airport, and one mile west of the State Fairgrounds.

Motel 6

4200 West Interstate 40, Service Road
Oklahoma City, OK 73108
800-4 MOTEL 6 • 405-947-6550
www.motel6.com

Type of Lodging: Motel

Room Rates: $39–$58, including free coffee. AARP discount.

Pet Charges & Deposits: None.

Pet Policy: No pets over 30 lbs.

Amenities: Cable TV, refrigerators, microwaves, pool, whirlpool, hot tubs.

Pet Amenities: List of nearby veterinarians maintained.

Rated: 2 Paws — 114 rooms and 5 suites.

This pet-friendly Motel 6 affords rooms with free local phone calls and cable television. The Motel is only miles away from Oklahoma State Capitol, Convention Center, Waterpark, Fairgrounds, Oklahoma City Bombing Memorial and Brick Town & Baseball Stadium.

OREGON

Nickname: Beaver State
Population: 3,316,154
Area: 97,132 square miles
Climate: Coastal mild and humid climate; continental dryness and extreme temperatures in the interior.
Capital: Salem
Entered Union: Feb. 14, 1859
Motto: She flies with her own wings.
Song: Oregon, My Oregon

Flower: Oregon Grape
Tree: Douglas Fir
Bird: Western Meadowlark
Famous Oregonians: Ernest Bloch, Raymond Carver, Chief Joseph, Bob Packwood, Linus Pauling, Steve Prefontaine, Alberto Salazar.

 History: More than 100 Native American tribes occupied the area at the time of the first contact with Europeans. Lewis and Clark wintered at the mouth of the Columbia in 1805-6. John Jacob Astor established a trading post in 1811. The first large wave of settlers came over the Oregon Trail and arrived in 1845. Oregon adopted such forward-looking ideas as the initiative, referendum, recall, the direct primary, and women's suffrage in the early 1900s. It is a land that possesses all the best that is America—tall, volcanic mountains, Crater Lake, peaceful, astoundingly beautiful beaches, the wonderful cities of Portland, Eugene, Salem and Ashland, and even the high desert.

ASHLAND, OREGON (Pop. 16,200)

Ashland Patterson House

639 North Main Street
Ashland, OR 97520
888-482-9171 • 541-482-9171

Type of Lodging: B&B
Room Rates: $65–$115, including full breakfast.
Pet Charges & Deposits: $10 per day.
Pet Policy: Sorry, no cats. Designated rooms only. Pets must not be left unattended.
Amenities: None.
Pet Amenities: List of nearby veterinarians maintained.
Rated: 2 Paws – 4 rooms.

The Ashland Patterson House, a spacious craftsman-style bungalow built circa 1910, remained in the original family until the late forties. In the early 1990s, when the property was subdivided, the house was converted to a casual, comfortable bed and breakfast. It's easy to spot the Patterson House—a Williamsburg blue bungalow with white trim and a red front door. Ashland, just over the border from California, is home to a world famous Shakespeare Festival, complete with an Elizabethan stage house and two indoor theaters. It is one of the oldest such festivals in the Western Hemisphere and runs each year from late February until November.

Green Springs Box-R Ranch

16799 Highway 66
Ashland, OR 97520
541-482-1873
www.boxrranch.com
boxr@internetcds.com

Type of Lodging: Guest Ranch

Cabin Rates: $75–$175.

Pet Charges & Deposits: None.

Pet Policy: None. All Pets Welcome.

Amenities: Completely furnished cabins.

Pet Amenities: The ranch consists of 1,500 acres, most of which is forest and woodlands, which guests can roam. The Pacific Crest Trail is within 5 miles of the ranch.

Rated: 5 Paws — 3 cabins.

Authentic Old West buildings, covered wagons and carriages surround the Green Springs Box-R Ranch property, and provide guests with a look at one of the most extensive collections of Old West artifacts in the area. The log guesthouses are designed for family living and equipped for comfort with modern amenities. The Green Springs Box-R Ranch is a working ranch with over 1,500 acres. Enjoy family-style dining at the Pinehurst Inn. The Ranch is located on Highway 66, 23 miles east of Ashland and 39 miles west of Klamath Falls. It's a vacation destination all its own.

Crest Motel

5366 Leif Erickson Drive
Astoria, OR 97103
800-421-3141 • 503-325-3141
www.crest-motel.com
thecrest@pacifier.com

Type of Lodging: Motel
Room Rates: $58–$105, including continental breakfast. AAA discount.
Pet Charges & Deposits: None.
Pet Policy: None. All Pets Welcome.
Amenities: Cable TV, refrigerators, microwaves, coffeemakers, spa.
Pet Amenities: List of nearby veterinarians maintained. Exercise area. Two acres of dog walking on property. Parks nearby.
Rated: 3 Paws – 40 rooms.

Well-appointed rooms with coffeemakers and many other amenities greet you at the Crest Motel. Of course, that's after its sweeping view of the incredible Oregon Coast gets your attention. Astoria sits on a peninsula where the Columbia River meets the Pacific Ocean at Youngs Bay, in the extreme northwest corner of the state. Dozens of historical sites are within minutes of the Motel, including the Astoria Column, with its magnificent views, the Columbia River Maritime Museum, the Flavel House Museum, and Fort Clatstop National Memorial, where the Lewis & Clark Expedition wintered in 1805-1806.

Driftwood Motel

460 Highway 101
Bandon, OR 97411
888 DRIFTWD • 541-347-9022

Type of Lodging: Motel
Room Rates: $45–$65, including continental breakfast.
Pet Charges & Deposits: $5 per day.
Pet Policy: Sorry, no cats. Designated rooms only. Manager's prior approval required.
Amenities: Refrigerators, safes.
Pet Amenities: Bandon is a very pet-friendly town. Bullards Beach, Bandon City Park and beach access within 5 miles of the motel.
Rated: 2 Paws – 20 rooms and 2 suites.

Driftwood Motel is directly across the street from Old Town Bandon. The guestrooms occupy a two-story building with exterior corridors. Rooms are contemporary in motif and feature original sea-themed paintings. Bandon is home to Bullards Beach State Park. The Coquille River Lighthouse, once known as the "guardian of the navigator's nightmare," is on the north jetty. The West Coast Game Park Walk-Thru Safari, located seven miles south of town, features more than 75 species of wildlife from around the world on over 20 acres.

Sleep Inn

600 Northeast Bellevue
Bend, OR 97701
800 SLEEP INN • 541-330-0050

Type of Lodging: Motel

Room Rates: $56–$79, including continental breakfast. AAA discount.

Pet Charges & Deposits: $8 per stay.

Pet Policy: Household pets only. Pets must not be left unattended.

Amenities: Cable TV, pool, whirlpool.

Pet Amenities: Dog runs. Exercise area. Lots of vacant space adjacent to property for walking pets.

Rated: 2 Paws — 50 rooms.

Sleep Inn is affordably priced and offers king-, queen- or double-sized rooms, and several appreciated amenities, including free newspaper, free local calls, microwaves and refrigerators. Bend's best-known attractions include the Cascade Lakes Highway, an 87-mile scenic drive through the Deschutes National Forest (Mount Bachelor, Three Sisters, Broken Top, Fall River), and the High Desert Museum, a hands-on museum, with a wide variety of indoor and outdoor exhibits and 20 acres of outdoor trails.

Days Inn Ponderosa

577 West Monroe
Burns, OR 97720
800-303-2047 • 541-573-2047

Type of Lodging: Motel

Room Rates: $43–$65, including deluxe continental breakfast. AAA, AARP and *10% Pets Welcome*™ discounts.

Pet Charges & Deposits: None.

Pet Policy: None. All Pets Welcome.

Amenities: Cable TV, refrigerators, microwaves, pool.

Pet Amenities: List of nearby veterinarians maintained. Triangle Park is located at Highway 78 and Foley Drive.

Rated: 3 Paws — 52 rooms and 4 suites.

Days Inn Ponderosa features newly remodeled rooms in a two-story structure. Nonsmoking and ADA accessible rooms, as well as airport pickup, are appreciated conveniences. Burns was cowboy country during the 19th century and cattle barons might run a million head of cattle on a million acre spread. Old Camp Casino is within walking distance of the motel. Malheur National Wildlife Refuge, 30 miles from Burns, is situated on 186,000 acres of marsh, ponds, lakes, meadows and desert. It's a major nesting and feeding stop along the Pacific flyway.

Inn at Arch Rock

70 Southwest Sunset Street
P.O. Box 1516
Depoe Bay, OR 97341
800-767-1835 • 541-765-2560
www.innatarchrock.com
archrock@wcn.net

Type of Lodging: B&B

Pet Room Rates: $99–$109, including continental breakfast. AAA, AARP and **5% Pets Welcome™** discounts.

Pet Charges & Deposits: $10 per day.

Pet Policy: Designated rooms only. Pets must not be left unattended.

Amenities: Cable TV, refrigerators, microwaves.

Pet Amenities: List of nearby veterinarians maintained. Sunset Park is located a block from the B&B.

Rated: 3 Paws — 13 rooms.

Discover the serenity of a beautiful oceanfront setting overlooking Depoe Bay, charming accommodations (some kitchens) with touches of home and pet-friendly hosts—the Inn at Arch Rock. Along the sea wall north of Depoe Bay, natural rock tubes are flooded by the incoming tide, causing them to spout geyser-like sprays. There are wondrous views of the Oregon Coast at its very best throughout the area, from Boiler Bay to Devil's Punch Bowl and from Fogarty Creek to Rocky Creek.

Hilton Eugene & Conference Center

66 East Sixth Avenue
Eugene, OR 97402
800-937-6660 • 541-342-2000
www.hiltoneugene.com
gm@hiltoneugene.com

Type of Lodging: Hotel

Room Rates: $88–$181. AAA and AARP discounts.

Pet Charges & Deposits: $25 per stay.

Pet Policy: No pets over 20 lbs.

Amenities: Cable TV, refrigerators, microwaves, safes, pool, Jacuzzi, irons and ironing boards, hairdryers, valet service.

Pet Amenities: Spencer Butte Park is located on High Street nearby.

Rated: 3 Paws — 272 rooms and suites.

The Hilton Eugene & Conference Center is the largest full service facility between San Francisco and Portland. The hotel allows you to choose from comfortable double and king rooms, or parlor or alcove suites, all with business class amenities, such as an executive desk, two two-line phones with voicemail and dataport. Eugene is noted for its fine parks, miles of bicycle trails and opportunities for water sports. Hult Center for the Performing Arts is noted for its fine architecture and acoustic design.

Travelodge Eugene

1859 Franklin Boulevard
Eugene, OR 97403
800-444-6383 • 541-342-6383
www.travelodge.com

Type of Lodging: Motel

Room Rates: $53–$110, including continental breakfast.

Pet Charges & Deposits: None.

Pet Policy: No pets over 45 lbs. Designated rooms only.

Amenities: Cable TV, safes, whirlpool, sauna.

Pet Amenities: Exercise area.

Rated: 3 Paws — 56 rooms and 4 suites.

Free continental breakfast, free morning paper and free local calls are only a few of the many amenities you'll find at Travelodge Eugene. Modern rooms have all the comforts of home, without you having to do the housekeeping. The motel is only one block from the University of Oregon campus. It's walking distance to Autzen Stadium and Mac Court. Miles of biking and jogging trails await you right outside your door. A winery in Oregon? Yes, indeed. You'll find Hinman Vineyards, seven miles southwest of the city.

Park Motel

85034 Highway 101 South
Florence, OR 97439
800-392-0441 • 541-997-2634

Type of Lodging: Motel

Room Rates: $41–$139. AAA and AARP discounts.

Pet Charges & Deposits: $6 per day.

Pet Policy: Designated rooms only. Pets must not be left unattended.

Amenities: Cable TV, refrigerators, microwaves.

Pet Amenities: List of nearby veterinarians maintained. Dog runs. Exercise area. Honeyman State Park is located off Highway 101.

Rated: 2 Paws — 13 rooms and 4 suites.

Nestled back off the highway in a grove of giant fir trees, Park Motel is a fine choice of lodging in the Florence area. From standard motel rooms to a quaint and private three-bedroom A-frame chalet, Park Motel will fulfill or exceed your highest expectations. Florence is sand dune country—sometimes they reach a height of 300 feet. Sea Lion Caves, 11 miles north of the motel, is the only year-round mainland home for wild Steller sea lions. A flight of stairs and an elevator descend 208 feet, providing access to a 1,500-foot-long cavern.

Steelhead Run B&B and Fine Art Gallery

23049 North Umpqua
Glide, OR 97443
800-348-0563 • 541-496-0563
www.steelheadrun.com
steelhead@steelheadrun.com

Type of Lodging: B&B

Room Rates: $68–$115, including full breakfast. AAA discount.

Pet Charges & Deposits: $10 per day. $20 refundable deposit.

Pet Policy: Small pets only. Designated rooms only. Manager's prior approval required.

Amenities: Refrigerators, pool table, VCRs, private bathrooms, river views.

Pet Amenities: Property has 5 acres on the North Umpqua River with beach, swimming hole and woods nearby. Waterfalls nearby. Exercise area. Whistler Park is located at Whistler Road and Highway 138.

Rated: 3 Paws – 3 studio apartments and 1 large apartment.

Steelhead Run B&B is a rambling home perched on a bluff overlooking the North Umpqua River. Different theme rooms offer a unique lodging experience; and there's an American heritage art gallery on the premises of the two-story main building. Glide is convenient to world-famous Crater Lake, the deepest lake in the United States. A drive-around road leads to a visitor's center situated, as is the lake, in the caved-in crater of an extinct volcano.

Ireland's Rustic Lodges

29330 Ellensburg Avenue
P.O. Box 774
Gold Beach, OR 97444
541-247-7718

Type of Lodging: Motel

Room Rates: $50–$70.

Pet Charges & Deposits: $10 per day.

Pet Policy: No pets over 100 lbs. Designated rooms only. Manager's prior approval required. Pets must not be left unattended.

Amenities: Cable TV.

Pet Amenities: Exercise area. Property is in a nice, park-like setting.

Rated: 2 Paws – 37 rooms and 3 suites.

At Ireland's Rustic Lodges, all cottages have open fireplaces, and the lodging furnishes wood. The Lodges are situated on Highway 101, on the south side of Gold Beach. The town is named after the placer mining prevalent in the area until a flood in 1861 swept the gold deposits out to sea. Numerous jet boat trips allow you to explore the whitewater areas of the Rogue River, or, if you are not so vigorously inclined, comb the beach for agates and driftwood.

Jot's Resort

94360 Wedderburn Loop
P.O. Box 1200
Gold Beach, OR 97444
800-367-5687 • 541-247-6676
www.jotsresort.com
jotsresort@harborside.com

Type of Lodging: Resort

Room Rates: $90–$295. AAA, AARP, AKC, ABA and *10% Pets Welcome*™ discounts.

Pet Charges & Deposits: $10–$15 per day.

Pet Policy: Designated rooms only. Manager's prior approval required.

Amenities: Cable TV, refrigerators, microwaves, pool, sauna, fitness room, restaurant.

Pet Amenities: List of nearby veterinarians maintained. Dog runs. Exercise area. Buffington Memorial Park is located at Highway 1 and West Caughell.

Rated: 3 Paws — 100 rooms.

Jot's Resort affords river views from each guestroom. There are two pools, an indoor heated sauna and a boat ramp, as well as a gift shop and restaurant. Jet boat tours, boat rentals and guided fishing complete the picture of a perfect place to enjoy an outdoor vacation. The 37-mile drive south on U.S. Highway 101 to the California border offers wonderfully scenic photographic opportunities. Cape Sebastian State Scenic Viewpoint, seven miles south of the Resort, covers 1,104 acres of forested land. Cape Sebastian itself is a dramatic headland that rises 700 feet above sea level.

Motel 6

94433 Jerry's Flat Road
P.O. Box 1336
Gold Beach, OR 97444
800-759-4533 • 541-247-4533

Type of Lodging: Motel

Room Rates: Call for room rates. AAA, AARP, AKC, ABA and *10% Pets Welcome*™ discounts.

Pet Charges & Deposits: None.

Pet Policy: None. All Pets Welcome.

Amenities: Cable TV.

Pet Amenities: List of nearby veterinarians maintained. Dog runs. Exercise area. Cape Sebastian State Park nearby.

Rated: 3 Paws — 50 rooms.

The Gold Beach unit of French-owned Accor's Motel 6 chain affords surprisingly large rooms with contemporary décor. Some have river views and several have at-door parking. As with all Motel 6 properties, this one offers good value for the money. Gold Beach treats you to numerous fine restaurants, beachcombing, whale watching, windsurfing and kayaking. This is the great Oregon outdoors at its legendary best.

Riverside Inn Resort

971 Southeast Sixth Street
Grants Pass, OR 97526
800-334-4567 • 541-476-6873
www.riverside-inn.com
info@riverside-inn.com

Type of Lodging: Hotel

Room Rates: $69–$360. AAA and *Pets Welcome*™ discounts.

Pet Charges & Deposits: $15 per stay.

Pet Policy: Designated rooms only.

Amenities: Cable TV, pools, whirlpools, Jacuzzi, river front rooms, launching docks for the Hellgate Jetboat excursions.

Pet Amenities: List of nearby veterinarians maintained. River Inn Park is directly across the river and easily accessible.

Rated: 3 Paws — 157 rooms and 13 suites.

Riverside Inn Resort is the largest hotel on the Rogue River. Guestrooms have recently been upgraded with custom designed furnishings featuring Pacific Northwest fabrics. Many rooms overlook the Rogue River. Grants Pass enjoys a key crossroads location on Interstate 5. You can raft the Rogue River or take a jet boat excursion. Oregon Caves National Monument, 480 acres of marble caves with calcite pillars, columns and curtains, is an hour's drive west. Ashland, with many restaurants and the world-acclaimed Shakespeare Festival, is 45 minutes south, and there are six popular wineries in the southern Oregon area, just waiting for you to explore.

Pine Valley Lodge

163 North Main Street
P.O. Box 712
Halfway, OR 97834
541-742-2027
www.neoregon.net/pinevalleylodge
skytel@pinetel.com

Type of Lodging: Inn

Room Rates: $85–$110, including continental breakfast.

Pet Charges & Deposits: $10 per stay.

Pet Policy: Designated rooms only. Manager's prior approval required.

Amenities: Refrigerators, microwaves.

Pet Amenities: List of nearby veterinarians maintained. Exercise area. Wallowa Lake, Whitman National Forest and Hells Canyon Recreational Area nearby.

Rated: 3 Paws — 8 rooms and 1 suite.

Pine Valley Lodge owners Dale and Babette are two of the friendliest, most accommodating hosts in the Pacific Northwest. They're justifiably proud of their establishment, which was recently lauded in Sunset Magazine as one of the five best small inns in the northwest. While the Lodge itself has three rooms, the remaining bedrooms are housed in the Love Shack (no snide comments, please), the oldest building in Halfway. Halfway, in Northeast Oregon, is the closest town to Hells Canyon National Recreation Area, nearly 653,000 acres that encompass North America's deepest gorge abutting the Snake River. From desert to Alpine forest, Hells Canyon presents a unique and varied opportunity to witness the grandeur of the North American continent. Be sure to visit the National Historic Oregon Trail Interpretive Center in nearby Baker City.

Oxford Suites

1050 North First
Hermiston, OR 97838
888-545-7848 • 541-564-8000
www.oxfordsuites.com

Type of Lodging: Hotel

Suite Rates: $59–$109, including full buffet breakfast and evening snacks. AAA and AARP discounts.

Pet Charges & Deposits: $20 per stay for up to two pets.

Pet Policy: No pets over 100 lbs. Designated rooms only. Limit two pets per room.

Amenities: Cable TV, refrigerators, microwaves, irons and ironing boards, safes, pool, whirlpool, Jacuzzi.

Pet Amenities: List of nearby veterinarians maintained. Exercise area. Numerous parks nearby.

Rated: 3 Paws — 92 suites.

Oxford Suites is a fine, upscale choice for accommodations in the Hermiston area. Housed in three-story structures with interior corridors for security, it's clean, comfortable, and possessed of a wide variety of upscale amenities. Hermiston is an outdoor enthusiast's dream, with lots of fishing in the area.

Wellesley Inn & Suites

19311 Northwest Cornell Road
Hillsboro, OR 97124
503-439-0706
lochp@primehospitality.com

Type of Lodging: Hotel

Room Rates: $99–$109, including continental breakfast. AAA and AARP discounts.

Pet Charges & Deposits: None.

Pet Policy: No pets over 35 lbs.

Amenities: Cable TV, fully equipped kitchens, safes, workout room.

Pet Amenities: Exercise area.

Rated: 3 Paws — 55 rooms and 82 suites.

Wellesley Inn & Suites gives you wonderfully spacious living and sleeping areas. The suites have fully equipped kitchens and a plethora of upscale amenities. Downtown Portland is 15 miles from the lodging. It's 60 miles to the coast, 80 miles to dramatic Mount Hood. Portland, "the City of Roses," is one of the most livable large cities in the United States. Gardens proliferate throughout the city, trees drape its streets, downtown features world-class museums and funky restaurants. Oregon Zoo replicates the natural environments of its inhabitants.

Westcoast Hillsboro Hotel

3500 Northeast Cornell Road
Hillsboro, OR 97124
503-648-3500
www.westcoasthotels.com

Type of Lodging: Hotel

Room Rates: $59–$90, including continental breakfast. AAA and AARP discounts.

Pet Charges & Deposits: $5 per day. $75 nonrefundable deposit.

Pet Policy: None. All Pets Welcome.

Amenities: Cable TV, refrigerators, microwaves, pool, Jacuzzi, hot tubs, restaurant.

Pet Amenities: List of nearby veterinarians maintained. Shute Park nearby.

Rated: 3 Paws – 123 rooms.

The Westcoast Hillsboro Hotel welcomes you to any of its deluxe guestrooms and suites. All rooms feature king- or queen-sized beds, coffeemakers, irons, hairdryers and dataports. There's a full service restaurant, lounge, a fitness center and 3,000 square feet of meeting and banquet facilities. The climate of Hillsboro is similar to that of the grape-growing region of France; thus, the area produces thousands of gallons of berry and fruit wine annually. Hillsboro is the center of a high tech corridor known as the Silicon Forest. It's 20 miles west of Portland, halfway between the Cascade Mountains and the Pacific Ocean.

Columbia Gorge Hotel

4000 Westcliff Drive
Hood River, OR 97031
800-345-1921 • 541-386-5566
www.columbiagorgehotel.com
cghotel@gorge.net

Type of Lodging: Inn

Room Rates: $159–$279, including their "World-Famous Farm Breakfast."

Pet Charges & Deposits: $25 per day.

Pet Policy: None. All Pets Welcome.

Amenities: Cable TV, restaurant, lounge, massage spa.

Pet Amenities: "Pet Package" upon check-in. List of nearby veterinarians maintained. Exercise area. Rutherton Park is ½ mile west of property.

Rated: 5 Paws — 40 rooms. Award-winning restaurant.

High atop a cliff overlooking the extraordinary Columbia River Gorge is the Columbia Gorge Hotel with its acres of manicured gardens. Built in 1921 by a Portland lumber baron, the Hotel has maintained its legendary reputation for hospitality for more than 75 years. This 11-acre oasis offers a wide selection of distinctive guestrooms. Each guestroom features antique furnishings and a view of either the gardens rimming Phelps Creek or the spectacular Columbia River Gorge. The unique rooms have polished brass or canopy beds, and some of the larger suites have fireplaces. Upon check-in, four-legged guests will receive a special "Pet Package" consisting of a toy, a chew bone, treats and a special dish with the Hotel's logo, to make their stay more enjoyable.

Dreamers Lodge

144 North Canyon Boulevard
John Day, OR 97845
800-654-2849 • 541-575-0526
www.grantcounty.cc/business/johnday
/dreamers/index.htm
dreamers@oregontrail.net

Type of Lodging: Motel
Room Rates: $42–$85.
Pet Charges & Deposits: None.
Pet Policy: Designated rooms only.
Amenities: Cable TV, refrigerators, microwaves, kitchenettes.
Pet Amenities: List of nearby veterinarians maintained. John Day City Park nearby.
Rated: 3 Paws — 25 rooms and 1 suite.

Dreamers Lodge features excellently kept and well-maintained units set well back from the highway in a two-story structure with exterior corridors. Lying in a broad valley in east central Oregon, John Day, named after a scout of the Astor expedition in 1811, is surrounded by steep hills and rugged peaks. The Kam Wah Chung Museum was a Chinese doctor's office and store in the mid-1880s. Today, it's a repository for more than 1,000 herbs, Western and Chinese medicines used by an herbal doctor.

Best Western Klamath Inn

4061 South Sixth Street
Klamath Falls, OR 97603
877-882-1200 • 541-882-1200

Type of Lodging: Motel
Room Rates: $69–$89, including continental breakfast. AAA, AARP and *10% Pets Welcome*™ discounts.
Pet Charges & Deposits: None.
Pet Policy: Small pets only. Designated rooms only.
Amenities: Cable TV, refrigerators, microwaves, pool, Jacuzzi.
Pet Amenities: Convenient to Crater Lake and Lava Beds.
Rated: 3 Paws — 52 rooms.

Best Western Klamath Inn features contemporary décor and pleasant guestrooms in a two-story facility with exterior corridors. Upper Klamath Lake is the largest body of fresh water in Oregon. It's home to several national wildlife refuges. The white pelican is the county mascot and is a familiar sight on nearby lakes and rivers. The Baldwin Hotel Museum contains original hotel furnishings from the early 1900s.

Cimarron Motor Inn

3060 South Sixth Street
Klamath Falls, OR 97603
800-742-2648 • 541-882-4601
www.oxfordsuites.com

Type of Lodging: Motel
Room Rates: $69–$89, including continental breakfast. AAA, AARP and *12% Pets Welcome*™ discounts.
Pet Charges & Deposits: $5 per stay. $5 nonrefundable deposit.
Pet Policy: None. All Pets Welcome.
Amenities: Cable TV, refrigerators, microwaves, safes, pool, restaurant, lounge.
Pet Amenities: List of nearby veterinarians maintained. Exercise area.
Rated: 3 Paws — 164 rooms and suites.

Cimarron Motor Inn is conveniently located on South Sixth Street, close to all traveler's services, approximately two miles east of downtown Klamath Falls. It contains tastefully appointed guestrooms and kitchen suites. There's a restaurant and lounge on the premises. The Favell Museum of Western Art in downtown Klamath Falls displays arrowheads, baskets, bead work and stone carvings, as well as coins, minerals and pioneer relics.

Howard Johnson Inn

2612 Island Avenue
LaGrande, OR 97850
541-963-7195

Type of Lodging: Hotel
Room Rates: $52–$77, including continental breakfast. AAA, AARP and *10% Pets Welcome*™ discounts.
Pet Charges & Deposits: $10 per stay. $10 nonrefundable deposit.
Pet Policy: Designated rooms only.
Amenities: Cable TV, refrigerators, safes, pool, whirlpool, Jacuzzi, spas.
Pet Amenities: List of nearby veterinarians maintained. Exercise area. Riverside Park nearby.
Rated: 2 Paws — 146 rooms and 24 suites.

Housed in two-story structures, the Howard Johnson Inn affords well-priced accommodations when in LaGrande, a particularly scenic, productive agricultural area in northeastern Oregon. LaGrande is on the western edge of the Grande Ronde Valley, at the foot of the Blue Mountains. The Oregon Trail Visitor Park at Blue Mountain Crossing provides three interpretive walking tails along preserved portions of the Old Emigrant Road. LaGrande is also home to Eastern Oregon State University.

Coho Inn

1635 Northwest Harbor Drive
Lincoln City, OR 97367
800-848-7006 • 541-994-3681
www.thecohoinn.com

Type of Lodging: Motel

Room Rates: $60–$170, including morning coffee.

Pet Charges & Deposits: $8 per day.

Pet Policy: No pets over 25 lbs. Designated rooms only.

Amenities: Cable TV, refrigerators, microwaves, oceanfront Jacuzzi, sauna, oceanfront views.

Pet Amenities: List of nearby veterinarians maintained. Exercise area. Beach access is only ½ block from the hotel. There is a park approximately 2 blocks away and numerous parks and dock in vicinity

Rated: 2 Paws — 30 rooms and 20 suites.

Coho Inn offers a variety of accommodations in a variety of price ranges. The units are housed in three-story buildings with exterior corridors. Lincoln City, with 7½ miles of public beaches, is a popular Oceanside resort destination with all manner of water sports.

Sailor Jack's Oceanfront Motel

1035 Northwest Harbor Avenue
Lincoln City, OR 97367
888-432-8346 • 541-994-3696
www.sailorjack.com

Type of Lodging: Motel

Room Rates: $40–$90. AAA, AARP and **5% Pets Welcome™** discounts.

Pet Charges & Deposits: $6 per stay.

Pet Policy: Designated rooms only. Manager's prior approval required. Pets must not be left unattended.

Amenities: Cable TV, refrigerators, microwaves, sauna, spas.

Pet Amenities: List of nearby veterinarians maintained. Dog runs. Exercise area. Lincoln City Wayside Park is located at Highway 101 and First Street SE.

Rated: 2 Paws — 37 rooms and 3 suites.

Sailor Jack's Oceanfront Motel is absolutely, positively, directly on the beach. There are numerous amenities and accommodations in the three-story buildings, but the main draw here is location. Besides being on the beach, Sailor Jack's is only one mile from the Chinook Winds Casino—non-stop casino action, live entertainment and one of the coast's biggest buffets. It's also one mile from the Lincoln City Factory Outlet Center for those disposed to shopping.

The Studio & The Lighthouse

24 Idaho Street
P.O. Box 761
Manzanita, OR 97130
503-368-4248
www.the-studio-lighthouse.com

Type of Lodging: Vacation Rentals
Room Rates: $125.
Pet Charges & Deposits: $5 per day.
Pet Policy: Sorry, no cats. Manager's prior approval required.
Amenities: None.
Pet Amenities: Beachfront property. List of nearby veterinarians maintained. Nehalem Bay State Park nearby.
Rated: 2 Paws — 2 units.

The two units comprising The Studio & The Lighthouse are unique sanctuaries for rest and renewal, both with breathtaking views of the Pacific Ocean. The two-story Studio, designed by an artist, is just above the pines on the Manzanita oceanfront. The Manzanita area has outstanding restaurants, hiking, kayaking, massage, astrological readings, art galleries, crabbing, surfing, bird watching and whale watching. In other words, it's a place to leave the rush and crush of the modern world behind while you indulge your spiritual and physical well-being.

Windmill Inn

1950 Biddle Road
Medford, OR 97504
800-547-4747 • 541-779-0050
www.windmillinns.com

Type of Lodging: Hotel
Room Rates: $59–$89, including continental breakfast delivered to rooms. AAA, AARP and *10% Pets Welcome*™ discounts.
Pet Charges & Deposits: None.
Pet Policy: None. All Pets Welcome.
Amenities: Cable TV, refrigerators, microwaves, pool, whirlpool, hot tubs, sauna, bicycles, guest laundry, irons and ironing boards, hairdryers.
Pet Amenities: Hawthorne Park and Bear Creek Pathway nearby
Rated: 4 Paws — 121 rooms and 2 suites.

The moment you arrive at the Windmill Inn, you can relax because the details will be taken care of by the hotel's gracious staff. The Inn's rooms are inviting and guaranteed to provide you a wonderful stay, particularly when you borrow a book from the motel's "Best Seller" lending library (perhaps they might even have a "dog eared" copy of *Pets Welcome*™). The city of Medford is known nationwide for its pears and is also headquarters for Rogue River National Forest (fishing and rafting). Harry & David's Country Village lets you explore the world of the famed gift baskets and packing plant. The History Center contains memorabilia of southern Oregon housed in a remodeled 1940s J.C. Penney department store.

Hallmark Resort Newport

744 Southwest Elizabeth
Newport, OR 97365
888-448-4449 • 541-265-2600
www.hallmarkinns.com

Type of Lodging: Hotel

Room Rates: $119–$229. AAA and AARP discounts.

Pet Charges & Deposits: $5 per day.

Pet Policy: Sorry, no cats. Designated rooms only.

Amenities: Cable TV, refrigerators, microwaves, pool, Jacuzzi, spas, restaurant, lounge.

Pet Amenities: Pet blankets and treat bags available. Exercise area. South Beach State Park and Cape Perpetua Park nearby.

Rated: 3 Paws — 154 rooms and 4 suites.

Hallmark Resort Newport is an enticing hotel with many of its decidedly upscale rooms having ocean views with balcony and fireplace. You'll find yourself spending time in the large, attractive lobby, which has its own ocean view area. Newport, located on a peninsula between the Pacific Ocean and Yaquina Bay, has been a resort community for more than a century. Clamming, crabbing and fishing are popular recreational activities. Devil's Punch Bowl has a bowl shaped rock formation; when the tide is high, water roars in and fills it. The Oregon Coast Aquarium houses a 40,000-square-foot aquarium on six acres. Yaquina Bay Lighthouse, built in 1871, is furnished in the same style as when it was built.

Inn at Cape Kiwanda

33105 Cape Kiwanda Drive
Pacific City, OR 97135
888-965-7001 • 503-965-7001
www.innatcapekiwanda.com
innkeeper@oregoncoast.com

Type of Lodging: Inn

Room Rates: $109–$219. AAA, AARP and *10% Pets Welcome*™ discounts.

Pet Charges & Deposits: $10 per day.

Pet Policy: Designated rooms only.

Amenities: Cable TV, refrigerators, honor bar, fitness center, guest laundry, fireplaces, balconies, ocean views.

Pet Amenities: Welcome letter for pets. Pet blanket and dog biscuits provided on arrival, water and food bowls available. List of nearby veterinarians maintained. Exercise area. Cape Kiwanda State Park is across the street from the Inn. Warm water wash down station for removing sand and salt water available. A 12-year-old Golden Retriever, Ginger, is the Inn's mascot.

Rated: 5 Paws — 35 rooms.

The Inn at Cape Kiwanda is both pet-friendly and human-friendly. All of the rooms come with a gas-fired fireplace and five of the rooms have whirlpools. There's a gift shop on the premises, and all rooms are housed in three-story structures with exterior corridors. Cape Kiwanda and Pacific City, like so much of Pacific Coastal Oregon, is a land of wondrous beach walks, dramatic rocks rising out of the water, quirky beach towns with names you've never heard of, but once you've been there, will never forget. In short, it's a perfect vacation destination.

Holiday Inn Express

600 Southeast Nye
Pendleton, OR 97801
800-HOLIDAY • 541-966-6520

Type of Lodging: Hotel

Room Rates: $69–$109 including enhanced continental breakfast. AAA, AARP and *10% Pets Welcome™* discounts.

Pet Charges & Deposits: $10 per stay.

Pet Policy: Designated rooms only.

Amenities: Cable TV, refrigerators, microwaves, safes, pool, Jacuzzi, hot tubs, irons and ironing boards, hairdryers.

Pet Amenities: List of nearby veterinarians maintained. Exercise area. Eight city parks nearby.

Rated: 3 Paws — 64 rooms and 3 suites.

Holiday Inn Express, a first-class lodging, affords all king- or queen-sized beds, free newspaper, free locals calls and large accommodations. Kids stay free in their parents' rooms. You can't visit Pendleton without visiting the famous Pendleton Woolen Mills, which offers guided tours of the manufacturing facility. The Tamastslikt Cultural Institute houses exhibits displaying the history and traditions of the Cayuse, Umatilla and Walla Walla Native American tribes.

Red Lion Hotel Pendleton

304 Southeast Nye Avenue
Pendleton, OR 97801
800 RED LION • 541-276-6111
www.redlion.com

Type of Lodging: Hotel

Room Rates: $49–$74. AAA, AARP and Entertainment discounts.

Pet Charges & Deposits: $20 refundable deposit.

Pet Policy: Designated rooms only.

Amenities: Cable TV, pool, hot tubs, irons and ironing boards, coffeemakers, restaurant, lounge.

Pet Amenities: Exercise area. Several city parks nearby.

Rated: 3 Paws — 170 rooms and 4 suites.

Expect a royal welcome at the Red Lion Hotel at bargain rates. Restaurants, a lounge and world-class amenities complete the picture of a wonderful place to stay while you're in Pendleton. The Pendleton Round-Up, one of the West's premier rodeos, has been playing to packed houses since 1910. The Round-Up Hall of Fame, underneath the south grandstand, exhibits memorabilia of the rodeo, as well as Western and Native American artifacts. The Umatilla County Historical Society displays historical items in a refurbished 1909 railway depot.

Travelodge

411 Southwest Dorion Avenue
Pendleton, OR 97801
800-578-7878 • 541-276-7531
a1h@ucinet.com

Type of Lodging: Motel
Room Rates: $55–$99, including continental breakfast. AAA, AARP and *10% Pets Welcome™* discounts.
Pet Charges & Deposits: $10 per day
Pet Policy: Small pets only. Designated rooms only. Manager's prior approval required.
Amenities: Cable TV, refrigerators, microwaves.
Pet Amenities: List of nearby veterinarians maintained. Exercise area. City park across from the property.
Rated: 2 Paws — 36 rooms.

Travelodge is a comfortable, newly remodeled property directly across the street from Pendleton City Hall. Free breakfast and free local phone calls are thoughtful amenities. Pendleton has many attractions to entice you. Pendleton Underground Tours take you on a trip back to the city's wild past, through tunnels where Chinese laborers lived and business thrived. At Wildhorse Casino Resort, you'll experience the thrill of winning with over 330 video slot machines, blackjack, live keno, high stakes bingo, off-track betting or poker.

Benson Hotel

309 Southwest Broadway
Portland, OR 97205
888-523-6766 • 503-228-2000
www.bensonhotel.com
sales@bensonhotel.com

Type of Lodging: Hotel
Room Rates: $220–$375. AAA and *10% Pets Welcome™* discounts.
Pet Charges & Deposits: $50 nonrefundable deposit.
Pet Policy: Designated rooms only.
Amenities: Cable TV, complimentary wine tasting, honor bar, safes.
Pet Amenities: Pet bed and turndown treat available. List of nearby veterinarians maintained. Park nearby.
Rated: 4 Paws — 287 rooms and 9 suites.

Whether you're lucky enough to live in Portland or are just passing through, you'll quickly appreciate the charm of this wonderful Pacific Northwest city. The Benson qualifies as one of the grand American hotels, a Grand Dame even today. Completed in 1912, the Hotel was opulent and luxurious with Austrian crystal chandeliers, Circassian walnut walls, and Italian marble floors—and that's just the lobby. Portland combines mountain vistas, a deep-water harbor, the confluence of two major rivers, the Columbia and the Willamette, historic brick buildings and modern glass and steel structures.

Howard Johnson Portland Airport Hotel

7101 Northeast 82nd Avenue
Portland, OR 97220
800-345-3896 • 503-255-6722
www.nw.motorlodges.com

Type of Lodging: Hotel

Room Rates: $54–$59, including coffee and fruit. AAA, AARP, AKC, ABA and *30% Pets Welcome*™ discount.

Pet Charges & Deposits: $10 per stay.

Pet Policy: None. All Pets Welcome.

Amenities: Cable TV, pool, Jacuzzi, restaurant, lounge.

Pet Amenities: List of nearby veterinarians maintained. Large vacant field directly north of the property provides a great exercise area. Madison High School Park is located at 82nd and Sysque.

Rated: 4 Paws — 134 rooms. Three-time Gold Medal Award Winner.

Located in picturesque Portland, guests of the Howard Johnson Portland Airport Hotel enjoy the convenience of Portland International Airport, and complimentary shuttle service. Amenities include an outdoor pool, sauna, whirlpool, restaurant, queen- and king-sized smoking and non-smoking rooms—and all within minutes of downtown and local attractions.

Quality Inn Portland Airport

8247 Northeast Sandy Boulevard
Portland, OR 97220
800-246-4649 • 503-256-4111
www.choicehotels.com

Type of Lodging: Hotel

Room Rates: $67–$84, including continental breakfast. AAA, AARP, AKC, ABA and *10% Pets Welcome*™ discounts.

Pet Charges & Deposits: $15 per stay.

Pet Policy: None. All Pets Welcome.

Amenities: Cable TV, pool, refrigerators, microwaves, whirlpools, fireplaces, coffeemakers, irons & ironing boards, dataports.

Pet Amenities: List of nearby veterinarians maintained. Exercise area. Gov. Tom McCall Waterfront Park is located 15 minutes from the hotel.

Rated: 3 Paws — 113 rooms and 6 suites.

Spend some "Quality Inn" time in Oregon. Quality Inn affords first-class accommodations in an upscale atmosphere at great rates. You're only 20 minutes away from Multnomah Falls, Oregon's major year-round tourist attraction. The Columbia River Gorge, an incredibly scenic meeting of land and water, is close by. Standout Portland museums include the Oregon History Center, Portland Art Museum and the Oregon Museum of Science & Industry. Of course, it's your own fault if you miss Washington Park, particularly the International Rose Test Garden and the extensive Japanese Gardens.

Anchor Bay Inn

1821 Highway 101
Reedsport, OR 97467
800-767-1821 • 541-271-2149
www.ohwy.com/or/a/anchobin.htm
anchorbay@presys.com

Type of Lodging: Motel
Room Rates: $37–$64, including continental breakfast. AAA and AARP discounts.

Pet Charges & Deposits: $5 per day.

Pet Policy: Designated rooms only. Manager's prior approval required. Pets must not be left unattended.

Amenities: Cable TV, refrigerators, microwaves, pool.

Pet Amenities: List of nearby veterinarians maintained. City park is 2 blocks away on Highway 101.

Rated: 2 Paws — 20 rooms and 1 suite.

Anchor down for the night at the Anchor Bay Inn, an affordable, clean and comfortable motel, located on Highway 101 on the scenic Oregon coast. In its early days, Reedsport suffered so many floods that the buildings and sidewalks were elevated three to eight feet above ground. Finally, after a flood in 1964 devastated the city, a dike was built to protect the lower town. Nearby Umpqua Lighthouse State Park, next to Oregon Dunes National Recreation Area, was built in 1892 and has a red beam that is visible for more than 20 miles.

Best Western Oceanview Resort

414 North Prom
Seaside, OR 97138
800-234-8439 • 503-738-3334
www.oceanviewresort.com

Type of Lodging: Hotel
Room Rates: $65–$300. AAA and AARP discounts.

Pet Charges & Deposits: $15 per day.

Pet Policy: Designated rooms only. Manager's prior approval required. Pets must not be left unattended.

Amenities: Cable TV, refrigerators, microwaves, pool, whirlpool, spa, restaurant, lounge.

Pet Amenities: List of nearby veterinarians maintained. Beach is located in front of the hotel.

Rated: 3 Paws — 104 rooms and 21 suites.

The tastefully decorated guestrooms offer spectacular views of either the Pacific Ocean or lush green mountains. Some rooms have the added amenities of a spacious living room, gas fireplace, oversized whirlpool tubs or kitchenettes. When it comes to recreation activities, you'll find plenty to do here. The hotel's heated indoor swimming pool and spa are inviting. Be sure to explore the shops and historical attractions that the charming town of Seaside has to offer.

Comfort Inn at Sisters/Mountain Shadow RV Park

P.O. Box 938
Sisters, OR 97759
541-549-7829

Type of Lodging: Motel

Room Rates: $69–$95, including continental breakfast. AAA, AARP and *10% Pets Welcome*™ discounts.

Pet Charges & Deposits: None.

Pet Policy: Designated rooms only. Manager's prior approval required.

Amenities: Cable TV, pool, whirlpool.

Pet Amenities: List of nearby veterinarians maintained. Dog runs. Exercise area. Tumallo State Park nearby.

Rated: 2 Paws — 50 rooms and 100 RV spaces.

The Comfort Inn at Sisters is a unique, fun place to stay. The facility is built in an 1800s Western theme and is nestled in pine trees off the highway. The rooms, however, are very spacious and decidedly contemporary. Sisters is named for the snowcapped Three Sisters mountain peaks. On the edge of the high desert, Sisters is said to have the largest concentration of commercially raised llamas in the United States. The McKenzie Pass Scenic Highway offers panoramic views of the Cascades and nearby lava fields. Skiers will find outstanding facilities at the Hoodoo Ski Area, 22 miles to the west of town.

Doubletree Hotel Eugene/Springfield

3280 Gateway Road
Springfield, OR 97477
800-222-TREE • 541-726-8181
www.doubletreeeugene.com

Type of Lodging: Hotel

Room Rates: $69–$139. AAA, AARP, AKC and *30% Pets Welcome*™ discounts.

Pet Charges & Deposits: $10 per day.

Pet Policy: None. All Pets Welcome.

Amenities: Cable TV, safes, pool, hot tubs, coffeemakers, irons and ironing boards.

Pet Amenities: All-natural heart shape doggie treats at check-in. List of nearby veterinarians maintained. Exercise area. Allen Baker Park is located at Coburg and Centennial.

Rated: 4 Paws — 234 rooms and 7 suites.

The Doubletree Hotel is known for its high quality and attention to every detail, and the Eugene / Springfield member of the chain is no exception. Guests benefit from numerous amenities and services including free parking and complimentary airport courtesy transportation. There's also more than 12,000 square feet of flexible function space, two restaurants and nightly entertainment at the Doubletree Lounge. Springfield, separated from its sister city Eugene by the Willamette River, has a diversified economy, including forest products, technology and medical services. The giant Weyerhauser Company conducts guided tours of its pulp and paper manufacturing facilities.

Tolovana Inn

3400 South Hemlock
Tolovana Park, OR 97145
800-333-8890 • 503-436-2211
www.tolovanainn.com

Type of Lodging: Inn
Room Rates: $61–$262. AAA, AARP
and *10% Pets Welcome™* discounts.
Pet Charges & Deposits: $10 per day.
Pet Policy: Designated rooms only.
Pets must not be left unattended.
Amenities: Cable TV, refrigerators,
microwaves, safes, pool, whirlpool, hot
tubs, spas, fitness center, game room.
Pet Amenities: List of nearby veterinarians maintained. Exercise area. Park
and beach nearby.
Rated: 3 Paws — 175 rooms.

Experience the power of a winter storm with crashing waves and the wind racing along the shore. Wade among the tide pools. At twilight, watch the sun disappear into the sea. Tolovana Inn features standard hotel rooms, studio-, one- and two-bedroom suites with kitchens, fireplaces and private balconies. Tolovana Inn is Cannon Beach's premier oceanfront condominium resort overlooking Haystack Rock. Located in the stunning northwest corner of Oregon, this is one of the most stunning Pacific vistas you'll ever experience.

Phoenix Inn Suites

477 Northwest Phoenix Drive
Troutdale, OR 97060
800-824-6824 • 503-669-6500
www.phoenixinn.com
phoen901@ipinc.net

Type of Lodging: Inn
Suite Rates: $55–$120, including
extended complimentary breakfast
buffet. AAA, AARP, Senior and Business
Travelers discounts
Pet Charges & Deposits: $10 per day.
Pet Policy: Designated rooms only.
Manager's prior approval required.
Amenities: Refrigerators, microwaves,
pool, Jacuzzi, hairdryers, coffeemakers,
irons and ironing boards.
Pet Amenities: List of nearby veterinarians maintained. Exercise area. Lewis &
Clark State Park, Glenn Otto City Park,
Dabney State Park and Oxbow Street
Park nearby.
Rated: 3 Paws — 73 suites.

At the Phoenix Inn, you'll enjoy spacious mini-suites, each with a loveseat, worktable, microwave, refrigerator and coffeemaker. Accommodations are first-class, local phone calls and a daily newspaper are free and kids stay free in their parents' room. Phoenix Inn is convenient to downtown Portland (20 minutes), Mount Hood (less than an hour) and Multnomah Falls (20 minutes). Troutdale is the western gateway to the Columbia River Gorge. Downtown looks like it did when it was built in the 1920s.

Wayfarer Resort

46725 Goodpasture Road
Vida, OR 97488
800-627-3613 • 541-896-3613
www.wayfarerresort.com
wayfarer1@juno.com

Type of Lodging: Cottages
Cottage Rates: $65–$220.
Pet Charges & Deposits: $10 per day.
Pet Policy: Designated rooms only.
Amenities: Cable TV, refrigerators, microwaves.
Pet Amenities: List of nearby veterinarians maintained. Exercise area. Willamette National Forest nearby.
Rated: 3 Paws — 13 cottages.

When you pass between Eugene and Springfield on the Interstate 5, get off at Exit 194A. Go east 25½ miles on Highway 126 until you come to the Covered Bridge. Cross the bridge and go four more miles. Then you come to a place that's far enough from the beaten track for utmost privacy, yet close enough for visiting, shopping, or a night on the town in Eugene-Springfield. Wayfarer Resort consists of completely furnished cabins perched on the banks of the McKenzie River and tumbling Marten Creek. The forested Cascades rise all around you. Paradise found— and it's pet-friendly, too.

Old Welches Inn Bed & Breakfast

26401 East Welches Road
Welches, OR 97067
503-622-3754
www.lodging-mthood.com
innmthood@cs.com

Type of Lodging: B&B
Room Rates: $96–$163, including stocked pantry in cottage. **20% (on two or more nights) Pets Welcome™** discount.
Pet Charges & Deposits: None.
Pet Policy: Sorry, no cats. Designated rooms only. Manager's prior approval required.
Amenities: Satellite TV, microwaves.
Pet Amenities: Welcome cookies, cedar beds and basket of toys available. List of nearby veterinarians maintained. Exercise area. Wildwood Park is located at Highway 26 and Park Entrance. Mount Hood Wilderness and National Forest nearby.
Rated: 4 Paws — 4 rooms and 1 cottage.

You'll find the following verse on the walls of Old Welches Inn Bed & Breakfast: "We never had a dog that stole our towels or whatever, played the TV too loud, or had noisy fights with its traveling companion. We never had a dog that got drunk and broke up the furniture or got sick. SO—if your dog can and will vouch for you, you're welcome too!" One hour away from Portland, but like so much of Oregon, a world away from the city. That's what you'll find in this circa 1890 B&B in the foothills of Mount Hood. It's hard to say enough about this place, which was the first hotel and summer resort established in the Mount Hood area. Go and see for yourself what the word charming really means.

Best Western Woodburn

2887 Newberg Highway
Woodburn, OR 97071
800-766-6433 • 503-982-6515
www.bestwestern.com
haliday@webster.com

Type of Lodging: Hotel
Room Rates: $49–$99, including continental breakfast. AAA and AARP discounts.
Pet Charges & Deposits: $10 per stay.
Pet Policy: Pets must not be left unattended.
Amenities: Cable TV, refrigerators, microwaves, pool, Jacuzzi, hot tubs.
Pet Amenities: List of nearby veterinarians maintained. Exercise area. Legion Park and Champoeg Park nearby.
Rated: 3 Paws — 81 rooms and 6 suites.

Best Western Woodburn features large rooms, meeting rooms for up to 70 people, a business center, convenience shop, outdoor pool and hot tub. There's a dataport in every room. Woodburn is located in the Willamette Valley, in the heart of Oregon's wine country. It's halfway between Salem, Oregon's scenic capital city, and Portland, the state's great metropolis. Spirit Mountain Casino, Oregon's largest and newest gaming facility, is just 45 minutes away, as is the breathtaking Columbia River Gorge and Oregon's largest waterfall, Multnomah Falls.

Morning Star, A Bed & Breakfast

95668 Highway 101 South
Yachats, OR 97498
541-547-4412
www.morningstarbandb.com

Type of Lodging: B&B
Room Rates: $100–$200, including full breakfast.
Pet Charges & Deposits: None.
Pet Policy: Designated rooms only. Manager's prior approval required.
Amenities: Refrigerators, honor bar, Jacuzzi, oceanfront property.
Pet Amenities: German Shepherd is official tour guide. List of nearby veterinarians maintained. Exercise area. Ocean and Forest nearby.
Rated: 3 Paws — 3 rooms and 1 cottage.

The Morning Star Bed & Breakfast is a quiet, family establishment perched on a spectacular oceanfront bluff, with wide vistas of headlands, horizons, and coastal breakers. The front door opens onto a beautiful slate entry where you will be greeted by J.J., a German Shepherd who will provide free beach tours any time. Take walks along the shore, searching for storm-tossed treasures, or star gaze from the Morning Star's open-air Jacuzzi. You need not go into town. You need not wander up and down the coastal road from one small place to another, each more picturesque than the last. But then again, maybe that's exactly what you'll want to do.

See Vue Motel

95590 Highway 101 South
Yachats, OR 97498
541-547-3227
www.seevue.com

Type of Lodging: Motel
Room Rates: $42–$75.
Pet Charges & Deposits: $5 per day.
Pet Policy: Designated rooms only.
Amenities: Fully equipped kitchens, ocean views, fireplaces.
Pet Amenities: Doggie bag with poop scoop baggies, biscuits and rawhides available upon request. Towels and sheets for pet use available. List of nearby veterinarians maintained. Exercise area. Stone Field Beach, Bob's Creek, Cape Perpetua and National Forests nearby.
Rated: 3 Paws — 10 rooms.

Every room at See Vue Motel is guaranteed to give you an ocean view. All units are set on a bluff where the mountains meet the sea. Each is uniquely decorated with plants, antiques and rustic charm. Yachats is one of the most scenic spots on the central Oregon coast. Just south of town is Cape Perpetua, the highest point on the Oregon coast. From an 800-foot high headland, the view is stunning. Yachats is also popular with fishermen who come here between April and October to catch hundreds of tiny smelt who come to the beach to spawn, or who take salmon and steelhead from the nearby Yachats River. At the Sea Vue Motel, they may forget your name, but they always remember your pet. Past guests include parrots, ferrets, pigs, turtles and a paraplegic chipmunk.

PENNSYLVANIA

Nickname: Keystone State
Population: 11,994,016
Area: 46,058 square miles
Climate: Continental with wide fluctuations in seasonal temperatures.
Capital: Harrisburg
Entered Union: Dec.12,1787
Motto: Virtue, liberty and independence.
Song: Pennsylvania
Flower: Mountain Laurel

Tree: Hemlock
Bird: Ruffed Grouse
Famous Pennsylvanians: Marian Anderson, Maxwell Anderson, James Buchanan, Andrew Carnegie, Perry Como, Stephen Foster, Benjamin Franklin, Robert Fulton, Milton Hershey, Gene Kelly, Grace Kelly (Princess Grace of Monaco), Margaret Mead, Joe Montana, Arnold Palmer, Robert E. Peary, Betsy Ross, Will Smith, James Stewart, Jim Thorpe, Andy Warhol.

History: Several Native American tribes were living in peace at the time the Swedes established the first settlement in 1643. In 1655, the Dutch seized the settlement, but lost it to the British in 1664. King Charles gave the region to William Penn in 1681. Philadelphia was the capital of the colonies during most of the Revolution. Both the Declaration of Independence (1776) and the Constitution (1787) were signed in Philadelphia, home of the renowned Benjamin Franklin. The Civil War Battle of Gettysburg, July 1-3, 1863, marked a turning point in the war.

Janey Lynn Motel

3567 Business Route 220
Bedford, PA 15522
814-623-9515
www.bedford.net/janeylynn
janeylynn@bedford.net

Type of Lodging: Motel
Room Rates: $25–$55, including continental breakfast. AAA and *10% Pets Welcome™* discounts.
Pet Charges & Deposits: $5 per day.
Pet Policy: Small pets only. Designated rooms only. Manager's prior approval required.
Amenities: Cable TV, refrigerators, microwaves.
Pets Amenities: Dog runs.
Rated: 2 Paws — 21 rooms and 1 suite.

In two words, the Janey Lynn Motel can be described as pleasant and peaceful. It also has among the most reasonable rates we've seen. Janey Lynn Motel is situated in the rolling hills of south central Pennsylvania in the foothills of the Allegheny Mountains. Old Bedford Village is a 40-building reproduction of an 18th century Pennsylvania village, complete with local residents demonstrating crafts of a bygone era. The Motel is close to Blue Knob State Park and the Covered Bridges of Historic Bedford.

Blue Berry Mountain Inn

HC1, Box 1102 - Thomas Road
Blakeslee, PA 18610
570-646-7144
www.blueberrymountaininn.com

Type of Lodging: B&B
Room Rates: $90–$135, including full breakfast. AAA and *10% Pets Welcome™* discounts.
Pet Charges & Deposits: $20 per stay. $50 refundable deposit.
Pet Policy: Designated rooms only. Manager's prior approval required. Pets must not be left unattended.
Amenities: Cable TV, refrigerators, microwaves, pool, whirlpool, billiard room.
Pets Amenities: List of nearby veterinarians maintained. Exercise area. Hickory Run State Park is located off Route 940.
Rated: 3 Paws — 5 rooms and 1 suite.

Blue Berry Mountain Inn affords hospitality, charm and grace in the Pocono Mountains of Northeastern Pennsylvania, two hours from New York City, two hours from Philadelphia and a world away from either of them. The Inn is nestled among mountains, streams, lakes and ponds, on hundreds of acres. You're within 30 minutes of downhill and cross-country skiing, golf, horseback riding, mountain biking, whitewater rafting, fine dining and even outlet shopping.

Inn at Turkey Hill

991 Central Road
Bloomsburg, PA 17815
570-387-1500
www.innatturkeyhill.com
info@innatturkeyhill.com

Type of Lodging: Inn
Room Rates: $98–$190, including continental breakfast.
Pet Charges & Deposits: $15 per stay.
Pet Policy: Designated rooms only.
Amenities: Cable TV, refrigerators, Jacuzzi.
Pets Amenities: Dog treats available. List of nearby veterinarians maintained. Exercise area. Bloomsburg Park nearby.
Rated: 3 Paws — 23 rooms

Comfortable rooms, beautiful surroundings, and a gracious, accommodating staff make The Inn at Turkey Hill a special place to visit any time of the year. The 1839 farmhouse had been lovingly restored and its peaceful charm is magnificent. Bloomsburg is located in the middle of Pennsylvania's rolling hills and rich farmlands, and is convenient to State College, Williamsport and Wilkes-Barre. But there's a hidden secret right on the premises, the Restaurant at The Inn at Turkey Hill—actually three distinct dining rooms each with their own personality, each heralded by "locals" throughout the state.

Glendorn – A Lodge in the Country

1032 West Corydon Street
Bradford, PA 16701
800-843-8568 • 814-362-6511
www.glendorn.com
glendorn@glendorn.com

Type of Lodging: Inn
Room Rates: $375–$2,100, including full meal plan.
Pet Charges & Deposits: $75 per day.
Pet Policy: Designated rooms only.
Amenities: Cable TV, refrigerators, microwaves, pool, hot tubs.
Pets Amenities: List of nearby veterinarians maintained. Exercise area. Allegheny National Park nearby.
Rated: 3 Paws — 9 cabins and 4 suites.

The urge to snoop through drawers and closets at Glendorn, a 1,280-acre estate in northwest Pennsylvania, just south of the New York border, is irresistible. You'll find old photos, inscribed trophies, even a menagerie of glass animals. Glendorn is as much a baronial log cabin as it is a fairy tale cottage. Its great hall encompasses the heart and spirit of a Grand Lodge. It's like being back at summer camp, albeit an incredibly luxurious summer camp, this time as an adult. It's way up in north central Pennsylvania, practically on the New York border and it really is unique.

Ramada Inn Breezewood

Route 30
P.O. Box 307
Breezewood, PA 15533
800-535-4025 • 814-735-4005
www.bedford.net/ramada

Type of Lodging: Hotel

Room Rates: $49–$89, including apple cider. AAA and AARP discounts.

Pet Charges & Deposits: None

Pet Policy: None. All Pets Welcome.

Amenities: Satellite TV, sauna, restaurant.

Pets Amenities: List of nearby veterinarians maintained. Exercise area. Buchanan State Park and Shawnee State Park nearby.

Rated: 3 Paws – 123 rooms

Ramada Inn provides fine accommodations and amenities, including a top notch three-meal-a-day restaurant in tiny Breezewood, 12 miles north of the Maryland state line in south central Pennsylvania. Here, you're in the foothills of the Alleghenies, quietly far away from the hubbub of the big cities. This is cross-country skiing country, a land of rolling hills and fertile fields—a land in which to relax and enjoy life.

Lodge at Chalk Hill

Box 240
Chalk Hill, PA 15421
800-833-4283 • 724-438-8880
www.thelodgeatchalkhill.com
thelodge@dc1.net

Type of Lodging: Hotel

Room Rates: $49–$180, including continental breakfast. AAA, AARP and *5% Pets Welcome*™ discounts.

Pet Charges & Deposits: $10 per day.

Pet Policy: Designated rooms only.

Amenities: Cable TV.

Pets Amenities: Dog runs. Exercise area. Walking path around Lake Lenore on the lodging premises. Ohiopyle State Park nearby.

Rated: 2 Paws – 61 rooms and 7 suites

Escape to the mountains and enjoy the natural beauty and serenity of the Lodge at Chalk Hill and yet still be close to West Virginia, close to Maryland, in southwestern Pennsylvania. You're close to the Laurel Caverns and Fort Necessity National Battlefield, and you'll find superlative white water rafting nearby. Kentucky Knob is one of the later creations of Frank Lloyd Wright. Built in 1953 of tidewater red cypress and native fieldstone, it's laid out on a hexagonal grid with an open floor plan and so much glass that it's sometimes hard to tell if you are indoors or out. The "of the mountains" motif is completed by a sculpture park and woodland trail on the property's grounds.

Budget Motel

Interstate 80, Exit 51
East Stroudburg, PA 18301
800-233-8144 • 570-424-5451
www.budmotel.com
reservations@ptd.net

Type of Lodging: Motor Lodge
Room Rates: $50–$90, including coffee. AAA discount.
Pet Charges & Deposits: $25 refundable deposit.
Pet Policy: Designated rooms only. Manager's prior approval required. Pets must not be left unattended.
Amenities: Cable TV, refrigerators, microwaves, restaurant.
Pets Amenities: List of nearby veterinarians maintained. Exercise area. Dansbury Park nearby.
Rated: 3 Paws — 115 rooms.

Once in a while you find a motel that's out of the ordinary, a place that's filled with small, extra touches that give it a special personality. Budget Motel of the Poconos is such a place. It's a place to unwind and relax. The Poconos have been a summering place for New Yorkers and Pennsylvanians since the 19th century. There are 13 developed ski areas, more than 30 golf courses and the third largest lake in Pennsylvania. Delaware Water Gap National Recreation Area encompasses some 70,000 acres. Over 200 miles of scenic roads traverse the valleys and rivers of this spectacular park.

Golden Pheasant Inn

River Road, Route 32
Erwinna, PA 18920
800-830-4GPI • 610-294-9595
www.goldenpheasant.com

Type of Lodging: B&B
Room Rates: $75–$155, including continental breakfast.
Pet Charges & Deposits: $15 per day.
Pet Policy: No pets over 40 lbs. Designated rooms only. Manager's prior approval required.
Amenities: Refrigerators, microwaves, Jacuzzi, fireplaces.
Pet Amenities: List of nearby veterinarians maintained. Exercise area. Tinicum Park and Delaware Canal State Park nearby.
Rated: 3 Paws — 6 rooms and 1 suite.

This magical country inn and restaurant is nestled between the Delaware River and the Pennsylvania Canal in Bucks County. Perfect for a weekend getaway or an exquisite country meal, the Golden Pheasant Inn is just over an hour from New York City or Philadelphia and only 20 minutes north of New Hope, Pennsylvania. Celebrating its tenth anniversary this year, this Inn remains a Bucks County gem. Sleep soundly in one of the romantic guestrooms or the cottage suite, featuring four-poster queen-sized canopy beds, private baths and a generous continental breakfast. All rooms have river and canal views and are furnished in French, English and American antiques. The cottage suite has a peaceful porch overlooking the Delaware Canal and comes equipped with a kitchenette and sitting room.

Baymont Inn Harrisburg / Hershey

200 North Mountain Road
Harrisburg, PA 17112
877-BAYMONT • 717-540-9339
www.baymontinns.com

Type of Lodging: Inn

Room Rates: $65–$95, including continental breakfast. AAA, AARP, Military and Government discounts.

Pet Charges & Deposits: None

Pet Policy: None. All Pets Welcome.

Amenities: Cable TV, refrigerators, microwaves, hairdryers, irons and ironing boards, voicemail, free newspaper.

Pets Amenities: Exercise area. Bright's Park, River Front and Wildwood Natural Area nearby.

Rated: 3 Paws — 58 rooms and 8 suites.

Baymont Inn invariably delivers a great room loaded with amenities, and this Harrisburg property is ideally located between Pennsylvania's state capital and the Chocolate Capital of the World. In Harrisburg, make sure you visit the State Museum of Pennsylvania, which chronicles Pennsylvania's history from the Earth's beginning to the present. The State Capitol is a magnificent building in a 13-acre park (more than 600 rooms). You're also very, very close to the Gettysburg Battlefield National Monument and to Hershey, Pennsylvania, where the aroma of chocolate perpetually wafts through the city.

Comfort Inn – Harrisburg East

4021 Union Deposit Road
Harrisburg, PA 17109
800-253-1409 • 717-561-8100
www.harrisburgpacomfortinn.com

Type of Lodging: Hotel

Room Rates: $79–$109, including continental breakfast. AAA and AARP discounts.

Pet Charges & Deposits: None.

Pet Policy: None. All Pets Welcome.

Amenities: Cable TV, pool, free local calls, coffeemakers, hairdryers, irons & ironing boards.

Pets Amenities: List of nearby veterinarians maintained. Park nearby.

Rated: 4 Paws — 115 rooms.

Housed in a solid five-story structure, Comfort Inn offers excellent value in Pennsylvania's state capital. Riverfront Park on the Capital Area Greenbelt, contains war memorials and a sunken flower garden by the Susquehanna River. Two impressive mansions, both on Front Street, are the Fort Hunter Mansion and Park (built in 1787, enlarged in 1814) and the John Harris/Simon Cameron Mansion (built in 1766, enlarged in 1863). The Pride of the Susquehanna offers a cruise on an authentic paddlewheeler.

Best Western Genetti Lodge

Route 309, RR2, Box 37
Hazleton, PA 18201
570-454-2494

Type of Lodging: Motor Lodge
Room Rates: $55–$99, including continental breakfast. AAA and AARP discounts.
Pet Charges & Deposits: $5 per stay.
Pet Policy: No pets over 100 lbs. Designated rooms only.
Amenities: Cable TV, pool, whirlpool.
Pets Amenities: List of nearby veterinarians maintained. Exercise area.
Rated: 2 Paws — 90 rooms and 7 suites.

Tasteful appointments, a value-conscious price and numerous amenities make the Best Western Genetti Inn a fine choice if you're stopping in Hazleton, located halfway between New York City and Philadelphia, on the southern edge of the Pocono Mountains. The Greater Hazleton Historical Society Museum contains exhibits relating to Native Americans of the Pocono area, the mining and railroad industries, sports, the military, and the life of Hazleton native and world-renowned actor Jack Palance.

Hampton Inn & Suites

747 East Chocolate Avenue
Hershey, PA 17033
800-HAMPTON • 717-533-8400
his_016@yahoo.com

Type of Lodging: Hotel
Room Rates: $89–$159, including continental breakfast. AAA, AARP and **10% Pets Welcome™** discounts.
Pet Charges & Deposits: $15 per stay.
Pet Policy: None. All Pets Welcome.
Amenities: Cable TV, refrigerators, microwaves, pool, workout room.
Pets Amenities: List of nearby veterinarians maintained. Close proximity to a pet exercise facility.
Rated: 3 Paws — 77 rooms and 33 suites

More than just another Chocolate Avenue hostelry, Hampton Inn provides a restful, invigorating experience with amenities galore. Milton Hershey founded his namesake town in 1903 to provide an attractive industrial community. Today, the town is aromatic with the smell of chocolate and filled with such destination activities as Hershey Park (over 60 rides, including eight roller coasters and six water rides), the Hershey Museum, Hershey's Chocolate World (the official visitor center for the Hershey area) and Hershey Gardens, a 23-acre botanical garden.

Motel 6 - Downtown

430 Napoleon Place
Johnstown, PA 15901
800-466-8356 • 814-536-1114
www.motel6johnstown.com
motel6@surfshop.net

Type of Lodging: Motel

Room Rates: $41–$75. AAA and AARP discounts.

Pet Charges & Deposits: None.

Pet Policy: Pets must not be left unattended.

Amenities: Cable TV, free local calls.

Pets Amenities: List of nearby veterinarians maintained. Exercise area. Babcock State Park is located off Route 56. Central Park is located at Main and Franklin Streets.

Rated: 3 Paws — 47 rooms. Motel 6 Star Property. One of Top 10 Motel 6's in nation.

"We'll leave the light on for you," is more than just an advertising phrase at this brand new, "Star Property" Motel 6—surprisingly upscale property, rated in the Top 10 of all Motel 6's. Disastrous floods have all but destroyed Johnstown on four occasions. The Inclined Plane, with a grade of 71% is one of the steepest inclined passenger planes in the country. The Johnstown Flood Museum is a "must see" for those interested in the devastating flood of 1889.

Days Inn - Lebanon/Lickdale

3 Everest Lane
Jonestown, PA 17038
800 DAYS INN • 717-865-4064

Type of Lodging: Inn

Room Rates: $58–$125, including continental breakfast. AAA, AARP, AKC, ABA and *10% Pets Welcome™* discounts.

Pet Charges & Deposits: $10 per stay.

Pet Policy: Pets must not be left unattended.

Amenities: Cable TV, refrigerators, microwaves, Jacuzzi, workout room, guest laundry.

Pets Amenities: List of nearby veterinarians maintained. Memorial Park is located 10 miles from the Inn, at Routes 443 and 72.

Rated: 2 Paws — 51 rooms and 19 suites.

You'll find Days Inn at the intersection of Interstates 81 and 78, between Hershey, Lebanon and Harrisburg at a whistle stop called Jonestown. But its location is as welcome as its fine amenities. It's six miles to the Penn National Horse Races, 15 miles to Hershey Park and Chocolate World, 20 miles to the State Capitol at Harrisburg and only 30 miles to the Amish Country, a world removed from the 21st century.

Super 8

2129 Lincoln Highway East
Lancaster, PA 17602
800-800-8000 • 717-393-8888
www.super8.com

Type of Lodging: Motel

Room Rates: $40–$82, including morning coffee. AAA, AARP and *10% Pets Welcome™* discounts.

Pet Charges & Deposits: $10 per day.

Pet Policy: Manager's prior approval required. Pets must not be left unattended.

Amenities: Cable TV, safes.

Pets Amenities: List of nearby veterinarians maintained. Exercise area.

Rated: 2 Paws — 99 rooms and 2 suites.

Super 8 is clean, comfortable, affordable and well worth a stay. Having said all of that, there are three more words that say even more: Pennsylvania Dutch Country. Lancaster is right in the middle of it all—the Amish and Mennonite communities, the immense outlet center, the table-groaning buffets, the Village of Intercourse, Bird In Hand and an unforgettable day or two in some of the richest and most productive (as well as beautiful) land in the United States.

Lady of the Lake

157 Route 30 East
Ligonier, PA 15658
724-238-6955
www.ladyofthelakebandb.com

Type of Lodging: B&B

Room Rates: $95–$125, including full breakfast. AAA and *5% Pets Welcome™* discounts.

Pet Charges & Deposits: $10 per day. $25 refundable deposit.

Pet Policy: No pets over 20 lbs. Designated rooms only. Manager's prior approval required. Pets must not be left unattended. Horses welcome.

Amenities: Cable TV, refrigerators, microwaves, pool, whirlpool, sauna, tennis, 30-acre lake with fishing.

Pets Amenities: List of nearby veterinarians maintained. Dog runs. Lynn Run Park nearby.

Rated: 3 Paws — 8 rooms and 1 suite on 60 acres.

Lady of the Lake is a quaint 60-acre retreat in the heart of the Ligonier Valley. Ligonier itself is a small, romantic town with unique shops and an abundance of fine dining. Fort Ligonier is a reconstruction of an English fort built in 1758. Idlewild Park has seven theme areas with amusement rides, waterslides, live entertainment and picnicking. Mister Rogers' Neighborhood of Make Believe, one of the theme areas, takes youngsters on a trolley ride to see life-size characters from the TV show.

Comfort Inn

300 Gateway Drive
Mansfield, PA 16933
800-822-5470 • 570-662-3000
www.comfortmansfield.com
manscomf@ptd.net

Type of Lodging: Hotel
Room Rates: $60–$104, including continental breakfast buffet. AAA, AARP and *10% Pets Welcome™* discounts.
Pet Charges & Deposits: $10 per stay.
Pet Policy: No pets over 50 lbs. Designated rooms only. Pets must not be left unattended.
Amenities: Cable TV.
Pets Amenities: None
Rated: 3 Paws — 100 rooms.

Comfort Inn provides just that—a great deal of comfort in spacious rooms with wonderful amenities—in Pennsylvania's rugged-yet-genteel northern lake and canyon country. You are 25 miles from Pennsylvania's own Grand Canyon, one mile from Mansfield University and 40 miles from the Corning Glass Museum, over the border in New York. There's plenty of boating and fishing. Watkins Glen Raceway is nearby. It's a beautiful vacationland getaway from the big cities of the Middle Atlantic seaboard.

Howard Johnson Inn

835 Perry Highway
Mercer, PA 16137
800-542-7674 • 724-748-3030

Type of Lodging: Inn
Room Rates: $74–$81, including full breakfast. AAA and AARP discounts.
Pet Charges & Deposits: None.
Pet Policy: None. All Pets Welcome.
Amenities: Cable TV, pool, Jacuzzi, hot tubs.
Pets Amenities: List of nearby veterinarians maintained. Exercise area.
Rated: 3 Paws — 102 rooms.

Howard Johnson Inn is a wonderfully appointed Three-Paw property as far west as you can go in Pennsylvania, just 15 minutes from Ohio and four minutes from Interstate 79, right in the middle of Western Pennsylvania's Amish Dutch country and historical Mercer County. Mercer County Courthouse, built in 1909, is two miles away. Neshannock Woods preserves the area's furniture-making heritage with Traditional Restoration handcrafted furniture. Main Street in Volant, eight miles south, is a real, old-fashioned "Main Street USA" with over 50 small shops offering Amish, Country and Victorian gifts.

Red Roof Inn

2729 Mosside Boulevard
Monroeville, PA 15146
800-RED ROOF • 412-856-4738
www.redroof.com

Type of Lodging: Motel
Room Rates: $47–$67.
Pet Charges & Deposits: None.
Pet Policy: None. All Pets Welcome.
Amenities: Cable TV, guest laundry.
Pets Amenities: Exercise area. Boyce Park is located on Old Frankstown Road.
Rated: 3 Paws — 117 rooms.

Red Roof Inn offers pleasant accommodations in the Pittsburgh area. Once an eyesore, the country's largest inland port, at the point where the Allegheny and Monongahela Rivers join to form the Ohio River, has literally reinvented itself into a major metropolis. Pittsburgh's numerous museums include the Carnegie Museum of Natural History, the Carnegie Science Center, the Car & Carriage Museum, the Pittsburgh Children's Museum and the Fort Pitt Museum. Monroeville's Sri Venkateswara Temple, one of ten Hindu temples in the United States, is modeled after a temple in southern India.

1870 Wedgwood Inn

111 West Bridge Street
New Hope, Pennsylvania 18938
215-862-2570
www.1870wedgewoodinn.com

Type of Lodging: Inn
Room Rates: $90–$225, including continental breakfast and "Tea and Tidbits."
Pet Charges & Deposits: $20 per day.
Pet Policy: Sorry, no cats Designated rooms only. Manager's prior approval required.
Amenities: Cable TV, refrigerators, microwaves, pool, whirlpool, private porches, gazebos.
Pet Amenities: List of nearby veterinarians maintained. Exercise area includes 2 acres. Delaware Canal State Park is a block away. Washington Crossing State Park is an hour away.
Rated: 3 Paws — 12 rooms and 6 suites on two acres.

The 1870 Wedgwood Inn offers bed and breakfast lodgings year-round in a gracious 1870 Victorian as well as a historic Classic Revival stone manor house, circa 1833. Surrounded by two acres of beautifully manicured grounds, the Inn is only steps from the heart of New Hope's historic district. Hardwood floors, lofty windows and antique furnishings recreate a warm, comfortable 19th century feeling among Wedgwood pottery, original art, hand-made quilts and fresh flowers. Fresh fruit salad, hot croissants and homebaked goods are served each morning on the sunporch, in the gazebo or in your private bedroom.

❀ ❀ ❀ ❀ ❀

Loews Philadelphia Hotel

1200 Market Street
Philadelphia, PA 19107
800-235-6397 • 215-627-1200
www.loewshotels.com

Type of Lodging: Hotel

Room Rates: $145–$365. AAA and *5% Pets Welcome*™ discounts.

Pet Charges & Deposits: None.

Pet Policy: Small pets only. Designated rooms only.

Amenities: Cable TV, refrigerators, safes, Jacuzzi, spas.

Pets Amenities: Pet bowls, treats and leashes available. List of nearby veterinarians maintained. Rittenhouse Square Park is located at 18th and Walnut Streets.

Rated: 5 Paws — 583 rooms and 36 suites.

The Loews Philadelphia Hotel, a beloved architectural icon in the City of Brotherly Love, completed in 1932 as headquarters for the Philadelphia Saving Fund Society, the first banking institution in the United States, has just gone through a $115 million complete gutting and restoration to come out very much a Five-Paw 21st century superstar. The amenities are far too numerous to mention—it would be like trying to describe everything you should see in Philadelphia, from the Liberty Bell to Ben Franklin's first hospital built in the United States, from the Franklin Institute Science Museum to the Mummers Museum, and from the Philadelphia Museum of Art to...well, just about anything. If you're going to see Philadelphia, you can see most of what there is to see on foot, and you should surely wander through all the "neighborhoods" you can. It truly is one of the world's most fascinating cities.

Pantall Hotel

135 East Mahoning Street
Punxsutawney, PA 15767
800-872-6825 • 814-938-6600
www.pantallhotel.com

Type of Lodging: Hotel

Room Rates: $49–$105.

Pet Charges & Deposits: Call for deposit information.

Pet Policy: No pets over 50 lbs. Designated rooms only.

Amenities: Cable TV.

Pets Amenities: List of nearby veterinarians maintained. Barclay Square Park nearby

Rated: 2 Paws — 75 rooms and 2 suites.

OK, everyone, what happens on February 2 each year that puts Punxsutawney on the Today show, CNN and all the big networks? Hint: it deals with a fellow named "Punxsutawney Phil." Each year since 1887, hundreds of folk have gone down to Gobbler's Knob in Sportsman's Park at dawn to urge the most famous of groundhogs from his den. The German immigrants who settled in the area brought the legend that the groundhog's seeing his shadow on February 2 predicts six more weeks of winter to this country. It might be hard to find accommodations at the Pantall Hotel the night of February 1.

Best Western Dutch Country Inn & Suites

4635 Perkiomen Avenue
Reading, PA 19606
800-828-2830 • 610-779-2345

Type of Lodging: Inn

Room Rates: $94–$129. AAA, AARP and *10% Pets Welcome*™ discounts.

Pet Charges & Deposits: $10 per day

Pet Policy: Small pets only. Designated rooms only.

Amenities: Cable TV, VCRs, refrigerators, microwaves, pool, hot tubs, coffeemakers, fitness center.

Pets Amenities: List of nearby veterinarians maintained. Dog runs.

Rated: 3 Paws — 57 rooms and 12 suites.

Best Western Dutch Country Inn is a solid, first-class lodging in the large, well-situated city of Reading, which, for some reason, is pronounced "Red-ding." It's minutes from the outlets and antique complexes. The Mid-Atlantic Car Museum and the Mid-Atlantic Air Museum are entertaining and educational. Among the inhabitants of the Air Museum are a Martin 4-0-4 airliner, a Capitol Airlines Viscount, the first night fighter ever built, a Douglas DC-3 and a North American B-25 Mitchell Bomber.

Nittany Budget Motel

2070 Cato Avenue
State College, PA 16801
814-238-0015

Type of Lodging: Motel
Room Rates: $40–$150, including continental breakfast. AAA, AARP and *10% Pets Welcome™* discounts.
Pet Charges & Deposits: $7–$10 per day.
Pet Policy: Designated rooms only.
Amenities: Cable TV, refrigerators, microwaves.
Pets Amenities: Exercise area.
Rated: 2 Paws – 23 rooms.

Yes, State College really is the name of the city, and Budget Motel is just that, a fine budget choice of lodging. Both Penn State University and its namesake town are located in the fertile Nittany Valley of central Pennsylvania. Penn State is the Commonwealth's largest university, with 75,000 students at 23 locations statewide, 40,000 of them at the State College campus.

Holiday Inn

700 West Main Street
Uniontown, PA 15401
800-258-7238 • 724-437-2816
www.uniontownpaholidayinn.com
uniontowns2@crownam.com

Type of Lodging: Hotel
Room Rates: $89. AAA and AARP discounts.
Pet Charges & Deposits: None.
Pet Policy: Sorry, no cats.
Amenities: Cable TV, pool, whirlpool, Holidome.
Pets Amenities: Exercise area. Fallingwaters, Kentucky Knob, Fort Necessity and Ohiopyle Parks nearby.
Rated: 3 Paws – 178 rooms and 4 suites.

When you stay at a Holiday Inn, you know you'll be staying in a first-class lodging where you'll be treated with friendly respect and enjoy the finest amenities. Uniontown is in the Laurel Highlands of Western Pennsylvania, an area packed with historic sites and recreation venues. General George C. Marshall was born here and Revolutionary War General Edward Braddock is buried southeast of town, near Fort Necessity National Battlefield. The Laurel Caverns, five miles east of town, have been popular both for exploration and for tourism since the 1700s.

Radisson Hotel Sharon

Route 18 and Interstate 80, Exit 1 North
West Middlesex, PA 16159
800-358-7261 • 724-528-2501
www.radisson.com
rhi_wmid@radisson.com

Type of Lodging: Hotel

Room Rates: $78–$98. AAA, AARP and *10% Pets Welcome™* discounts.

Pet Charges & Deposits: None.

Pet Policy: Small pets only. No pets over 25 lbs.

Amenities: Cable TV, refrigerators, microwaves, pool, whirlpool, spa, hot tubs.

Pets Amenities: Buhl Park nearby.

Rated: 3 Paws — 148 rooms and 5 suites.

Prepare to be rewarded with the utmost hospitality and personal comfort in the Radisson Hotel Sharon. You're in the midst of northern Pennsylvania's industrial belt. Youngstown is 15 miles away, and Akron, Ohio is 40 miles distant. The Hotel is almost exactly halfway between Cleveland (65 miles) and Pittsburgh (60 miles). Another industrial city, Erie, is 90 miles away.

Inn at Reading

1040 Park Road
Wyomissing, PA 19610
610-372-7811
www.innatreading.com
innatreading@msn.com

Type of Lodging: Hotel

Room Rates: $89–$149. AAA, AARP and Quest discounts.

Pet Charges & Deposits: None.

Pet Policy: Designated rooms only.

Amenities: Cable TV, safes.

Pets Amenities: List of nearby veterinarians maintained. Exercise area. Gringo Mill Park nearby. Small city park behind the hotel.

Rated: 3 Paws — 228 rooms and 18 suites.

The Inn at Reading affords large rooms with colonial décor in a series of two-story buildings. Amenities are first rate and you'll find a fine night's lodging here. The Berks County Heritage Center in Reading focuses on the rich agricultural heritage and the history of transportation in rural Pennsylvania. Wertz's Covered Bridge is the longest single-span covered bridge in the state. The Gruber Wagon Works started in 1882 as a one-man trade shop and grew to a mass-production wagon manufacturing company. Alas, its business declined precipitously with the arrival of the horseless carriage a few years later. Today, it's part of the Berks County Heritage Center displays.

York Super 8

40 Arsenal Road
York, PA 17404
800-800-8000 • 717-852-8686

Type of Lodging: Motel
Room Rates: $42–$68, including coffee and tea. AAA, AARP, AKC, ABA and *10%* *Pets Welcome*™ discounts.
Pet Charges & Deposits: $5 per day.
Pet Policy: Designated rooms only.
Amenities: Cable TV, safes.
Pets Amenities: Exercise area.
Rated: 2 Paws — 94 rooms.

"Life's great at Super 8" is not just a meaningless statement. York was our nation's capital from September 30, 1777 to June 27, 1778, while the British occupied Philadelphia. Like practically every town or hamlet in Pennsylvania, it is steeped in history. Recent history can be experienced at the Harley Davidson Motorcycle Final Assembly Plant and Museum. You can visit history at the Historical Society of York County or at the Golden Plough Tavern, General Horatio Gates House & Bobb Log House. For a real off-the-wall, uplifting experience, visit the York Barbell Museum and USA Weightlifting Hall of Fame.

RHODE ISLAND

Nicknames: Little Rhody; Ocean State
Population: 900,819
Area: 1,231 square miles
Climate: Invigorating and changeable.
Capital: Providence
Entered Union: May 29, 1790
Motto: Hope.
Song: Rhode Island
Flower: Violet
Tree: Red Maple

Bird: Rhode Island Red
Famous Rhode Islanders: George M. Cohan, Nelson Eddy, Nathaniel Greene, Matthew Perry, Oliver Perry, Gilbert Stuart.

 History: When the Europeans arrived, Narragansett, Niantic, Nipomuc and Wampanoag peoples lived in the region. Verrazano visited the area in 1524. Roger Williams founded the first permanent settlement in Providence in 1636 after he was exiled from the Massachusetts Bay colony. Quaker and Jewish immigrants seeking freedom of religion began arriving in the 1650s. Rhode Island was the first colony to renounce its allegiance to King George III on May 4, 1776. Initially opposed to joining the Union, Rhode Island was the last of the original colonies to ratify the Constitution in 1790.

Bay Willows Inn

1225 Aquidneck Avenue
Middletown, RI 02842
401-847-8400
www.baywillowsinn.com

Type of Lodging: Motor Lodge

Room Rates: $39–$169, including coffee. AAA and AARP discounts.

Pet Charges & Deposits: $10 per day.

Pet Policy: Designated rooms only. Manager's prior approval required.

Amenities: Cable TV, refrigerators, microwaves.

Pet Amenities: List of nearby veterinarians maintained. Dog runs. Exercise area. Beaches nearby.

Rated: 2 Paws — 14 rooms and 7 suites.

The Bay Willows Inn offers relaxing rooms at reasonable rates. Guestrooms have air conditioning, private baths and cable television. This newly renovated, pet-friendly motor lodge is located only minutes from downtown, mansions and beaches.

The Kings' Rose

1747 Mooresfield Road
South Kingston, RI 02879
888-230 ROSE • 401-783-5222
kingsrose@efortress.com

Type of Lodging: B&B

Room Rates: $90–$150, including full breakfast.

Pet Charges & Deposits: None.

Pet Policy: Sorry, no cats. Manager's prior approval required. Pets may not be left alone in rooms.

Amenities: Cable TV, honor bar.

Pet Amenities: List of nearby veterinarians maintained. Exercise area. Trustom Wildlife Preserves is located on Matunuck Schoolhouse Road.

Rated: 3 Paws — 6 rooms and 1 suite. Listed on the National Register of Historic Places.

Built in 1933, the Kings' Rose is listed on the National Historic Register. This Neo-Colonial residence has English gardens, perennial terrace and fish pool, rose arbor and tennis courts nestled among the oaks, pine, hornbeam, magnolia, dogwood, azalea and sourwood trees, including the largest sourwood tree in Rhode Island. The public rooms include a large parlor, library with television and sunroom/bar. The Rose is minutes from several state and town beaches, Trustom National Wildlife Preserve, University of Rhode Island and the Block Island Ferry. There are local activities to enjoy including boating, fishing, golfing, antiquing and many more.

Larchwood Inn

521 Main Street
Wakefield, RI 02879
800-275-5450 • 401-783-5454

Type of Lodging: Country Inn
Room Rates: $40–$140.
Pet Charges & Deposits: $5 per day.
Pet Policy: Manager's prior approval required. Pets are not allowed in public areas of the inn.
Amenities: None.
Pet Amenities: List of nearby veterinarians maintained. Exercise area.
Rated: 3 Paws — 18 rooms.

Located in the quiet village of Wakefield, Larchwood Inn has survived the necessities of modernization while preserving the charm of its past. Century-old trees dot the grounds of this 160-year-old country inn. This three-story manor is surrounded by a wide expanse of landscaped grounds and by South County beaches. Each guestroom has been individually decorated and all are furnished with carefully selected period pieces. Local attractions include beautiful surf and sheltered beaches, making Larchwood Inn a perfect base for swimming, fishing, biking or bird watching.

SOUTH CAROLINA

Nickname: Palmetto State
Population: 3,885,736
Area: 31,189 square miles
Climate: humid subtropical.
Capital: Columbia
Entered Union: May 23, 1788
Motto: *Dum Spiro, Spero* (While I breathe, I hope).
Song: Carolina
Flower: Yellow Jessamine

Tree: Palmetto
Bird: Carolina Wren
Famous South Carolinians: John C. Calhoun, DuBose Heyward, Ernest F. Hollings, Andrew Jackson, Jesse Jackson, Ronald McNair, Thomas Sumter, Strom Thurmond.

History: Cherokee, Catawba and Muskogean peoples lived on the land at the time English colonists settled near the Ashley River in 1670, then moved to the site of Charleston ten years later. The colonists seized the government in 1775 and the royal governor fled. The British took Charleston in 1780, but were defeated at Kings Mountain the same year. In the 1830s, South Carolinians adopted the Nullification Doctrine, which held that a state could void an Act of Congress. The state was the first to secede from the Union, 1860, and Confederate troops forced the surrender of Fort Sumter in Charleston Harbor, launching the Civil War. South Carolina was readmitted in 1868.

Comfort Inn & Suites

3608 Richland Avenue
Aiken, SC 29801
800-228-5150 • 803-641-1100

Type of Lodging: Motel

Room Rates: $55–$75, including continental breakfast. AAA, AARP, AKC and *10% Pets Welcome™* discounts.

Pet Charges & Deposits: $10 per day. $10 refundable deposit.

Pet Policy: None. All Pets Welcome.

Amenities: Cable TV, VCRs, refrigerators, microwaves, hairdryers, honor bars, pool, indoor spa, guest laundry, fitness room.

Pet Amenities: Park nearby.

Rated: 2 Paws — 48 rooms and 20 suites.

Comfort Inn is an excellent choice in Aiken. Free local phone calls are a nice extra. Aiken is in the sand hills region of the state, and its mild climate makes it wonderful equestrian country. There are three training racetracks. Carriage roads and bridle paths wind through Hitchcock Woods preserve. Aiken County Historical Museum, housed in a 1830 estate, depicts late 18th and 19th century life in Aiken County. Hopelands Gardens & Thoroughbred Racing Hall of Fame contains racing silks, trophies, photographs and horse racing memorabilia.

Howard Johnson Express Inn

3651 Trask Parkway
Beaufort, SC 29906
800-446-4656 • 843-524-6020

Type of Lodging: Motel

Room Rates: $65–$80, including continental breakfast. AAA and AARP discounts.

Pet Charges & Deposits: $25 per stay.

Pet Policy: No pets over 25 lbs.

Amenities: Cable TV, refrigerators, microwaves, pool, coffeemakers.

Pet Amenities: Hunting Island State Park nearby.

Rated: 3 Paws — 63 rooms. Howard Johnson Inn of the Year 2000, Gold Medal and President's Award Winner.

Not only is this HoJo a Gold Medal Award winner and a President's Award winner, but also it was selected as the Howard Johnson Express Inn of the Year for 2000. It's a wonderful property, situated in a picturesque old port town. Beaufort has many pre-Revolutionary and antebellum houses, surrounded by lovely gardens along narrow, oak-canopied streets. Most notable is the 1717 Thomas Hepworth House. The Beaufort Museum is housed in a 1798 arsenal. Parris Island Marine Corps RD is five miles from the lodging and the Marine Corps Air Station is only two miles distant.

Radisson Hotel Charleston

170 Lockwood Boulevard
Charleston, SC 29403
800-968-3569 • 843-723-3000
www.radisson.com
rhi-chsc@radisson.com

Type of Lodging: Hotel

Room Rates: $99–$189. AAA and AARP discounts.

Pet Charges & Deposits: $50 refundable deposit.

Pet Policy: Sorry, no cats. No pets over 20 lbs. Designated rooms only. Manager's prior approval required.

Amenities: Cable TV, pool, fitness center.

Pet Amenities: List of nearby veterinarians maintained. Brittlebank Park is across the street from the Hotel.

Rated: 3 Paws — 333 rooms and 4 suites.

The Radisson is a full service hotel, centrally located in one of America's most charming cities. Cultured and refined, this quintessentially Southern "Queen City" is a beautifully preserved historical treasure. Numerous cobblestone streets are lined with 18th and 19th century architectural gems. Middleton Place, overlooking the Ashley River, is a wondrous estate known for its elegant gardens designed to resemble those of 18th century Europe. Drayton Hall, a 1738 Ashley River mansion, is so genuine that to this day it does not have electricity or plumbing.

Town & Country Inn & Conference Center

2008 Savannah Highway
Charleston, SC 29407
800-334-6660 • 843-571-1000
www.thetownandcountryinn.com
reservations@thetownandcountryinn.com

Type of Lodging: Hotel

Room Rates: $69–$139. AAA, AARP and *10% Pets Welcome™* discounts.

Pet Charges & Deposits: $50 refundable deposit.

Pet Policy: Manager's prior approval required.

Amenities: Cable TV, refrigerators, microwaves, pools, whirlpool, Jacuzzi, fitness center, restaurant, lounge.

Pet Amenities: List of nearby veterinarians maintained. Charleston has several city parks and beaches.

Rated: 3 Paws — 124 rooms and 12 suites.

Personalized hospitality and fine, upscale accommodations are a hallmark of the lovely Town & Country Inn. The Inn, a full service hotel, is the closest accommodations to world famous gardens and plantations. It's only three miles from historic downtown Charleston. Calhoun Mansion, a Victorian mansion built about 1876, is one of the most elaborate showplaces in the Old South. Beth Elohim Synagogue, organized in 1749, is the nation's oldest synagogue in continuous use and marked the beginning of Reform Judaism in the United States. The Dock Street Theater, America's first building designed for theatrical performances, opened its doors in 1736. Magnolia Plantation and the Audubon Swamp Garden are not to be missed.

Holiday Inn – Coliseum

630 Assembly Street
Columbia, SC 29201
803-799-7800

Type of Lodging: Hotel
Room Rates: $99–$109. AAA, AARP
and **15% Pets Welcome™** discounts.
Pet Charges & Deposits: None.
Pet Policy: None. All Pets Welcome.
Amenities: Cable TV, fitness room.
Pet Amenities: Finlay Park is located
on Assembly Street at Taylor.
Rated: 4 Paws – 168 rooms and 7
suites.

Holiday Inn – Coliseum is a splendid, first-class high-rise hotel located in the heart of South Carolina's capital. Columbia was designated South Carolina's capital in 1786. A convention met there in December 1860 to draft the Ordinance of Secession, but because of a smallpox epidemic, the meeting moved to Charleston, where the ordinance was signed. The Hampton-Preston Mansion and Garden, an 1818 mansion house, displays life as it was before the War Between the States. The South Carolina State Museum, one of the first totally electric textile mills in the world, has four floors of displays of the state's history, hands-on exhibits, and the Lipscomb Art Gallery, which has changing exhibits.

Comfort Inn at Carowinds

3725 Avenue of the Carolinas
Fort Mill, SC 29715
803-548-5200
ftmill-gm@rfsmgmt.com

Type of Lodging: Hotel
Room Rates: $59–$89, including
continental breakfast. AAA and AARP
discounts.
Pet Charges & Deposits: $25 per stay.
Pet Policy: None. All Pets Welcome.
Amenities: Cable TV, refrigerators,
microwaves, hot tubs, seasonal pool.
Pet Amenities: Large parking lot adjacent to the property.
Rated: 3 Paws – 143 rooms and 10
suites.

Comfort Inn, though in South Carolina, straddles the North Carolina border and might even be considered part of greater Charlotte. It's a fine lodging, replete with fine amenities and a pet-friendly staff. Major attractions include Paramount's Carowinds Theme Park: ten theme areas depict different facets of the Carolinas' past and present and there's fun for every member of the family. It's only seven miles to Ericsson Stadium, home of the NFL's Carolina Panthers and ten miles to Charlotte Coliseum where the NBA's Charlotte Hornets hold court. All Nations Church is three miles distant. Cherry Park Softball Facility in Rock Hill, South Carolina is 12 minutes' drive. There's much to do indeed in this corner of the state.

Mansfield Plantation
Bed & Breakfast Country Inn

1776 Mansfield Road
Georgetown, SC 29440
800-355-3223 • 843-546-6961
www.bbonline.com/sc/mansfield/
Mansfield_plantation@prodigy.net

Type of Lodging: B&B

Room Rates: $95–$135, including full breakfast and bedtime chocolates.

Pet Charges & Deposits: None.

Pet Policy: None. All Pets Welcome.

Amenities: Color TV, VCRs, refrigerators, bicycles, boat access to the Black River.

Pet Amenities: List of nearby veterinarians maintained. Dog runs. Exercise area. Mansfield Plantation is located on 900 private acres where pets can run, exercise and play games with their owners. Pets love it here! Mansfield is located near a pet-friendly beach, Huntington Beach State Park.

Rated: 5 Paws — 8 rooms in 3 guesthouses. Listed on National Register of Historic Places.

Situated at the southern end of South Carolina's Grand Strand, Mansfield Plantation Bed & Breakfast Country Inn is its own holiday destination. Set on 900 acres in the heart of South Carolina's Tidelands, Mansfield Plantation is an authentic antebellum rice plantation listed on the National Register of Historic Places. An avenue of noble live oak trees draped in Spanish moss leads you to this wonderful piece of the aristocratic Old South. Three charming guesthouses feature private entrances, handsome furnishings, floral chintz fabrics, fireplaces with beautifully carved mantelpieces and woodwork and full private baths. Walk or bike in the woods, explore the old rice fields, go boating on the river or picnic on the lawn. Enjoy hammocks and swings. The serene environment and elegant atmosphere blend beautifully to make your visit a lasting memory.

Microtel Inn – Airport/Pelham

20 Interstate Court
Greenville, SC 29615
888-297-7866 • 864-297-7866
www.microtelinn.com

Type of Lodging: Hotel
Room Rates: $39–$59, including continental breakfast. *10% Pets Welcome™* discount.
Pet Charges & Deposits: $25 nonrefundable deposit.
Pet Policy: None. All Pets Welcome.
Amenities: Cable TV.
Pet Amenities: Park nearby.
Rated: 3 Paws — 122 rooms.

There's room for everyone at Microtel. Rooms are compact, neat and the price is certainly within budget considerations. Greenville became known as the textile center of the world after the Civil War, when many mills located from the Northeast. Today, the city has more than 60 city parks. Bob Jones University's Art Gallery and Biblical Museum contains more than 400 religious paintings by European artists from the 13th through 19th century, while the Greenville County Museum of Art houses American art from the colonial period to the present, with emphasis on Southern art.

Barefoot Properties of Hilton Head
Lagoon Villas & Waterford Villas

100 The Courtyard Building
Hilton Head Island, SC 29928
800-232-8421 • 843-842-5555
www.barefootproperties.net
barefootproperties@info.net

Type of Lodging: Vacation rentals
Suite Rates: $750–$1,400 per week. AAA, AARP, AKC and ABA discounts.
Pet Charges & Deposits: None.
Pet Policy: Designated properties only.
Amenities: Cable TV, refrigerators, microwaves, pool, whirlpool, Jacuzzi, hot tubs.
Pet Amenities: List of nearby veterinarians maintained. Exercise area. Sea Pines Nature Preserve is located on Pinckney Island.
Rated: 3 Paws — 64 suites.

Lagoon Villas is situated on Sea Pines Plantation, the first (and largest) community on Hilton Head Island (5,000 acres). Waterford Villas is located on Shipyard Plantation, a nationally recognized tennis and golf resort. The pet-friendly three-bedroom villas at Lagoon Villas all have lagoon or pool views. Two-bedroom villas at Waterford, located right next to Shipyard Golf Course, are the perfect home for the golfer. Hilton Head Island, off the southern coast of South Carolina, is the largest island between New Jersey and Florida, 12 miles long and up to five miles wide. Recreational facilities include 25 golf courses, 300 tennis courts, riding stables, bicycle trails and marinas. Wildlife and waterfowl habitats include the Sea Pines Forest Preserve, Audubon Newhall Preserve, and the Pinckney Island National Wildlife Refuge.

The Red Horse Inn

310 North Campbell Road
Landrum, SC 29356
864-895-4968
www.theredhorseinn.com
theredhorseinn@aol.com

Type of Lodging: B&B in Cottages

Room Rates: $125–$155, including continental breakfast. AAA and AARP discounts.

Pet Charges & Deposits: $20 per stay. $50 refundable deposit.

Pet Policy: No pets over 60 lbs. Designated rooms only. Manager's prior approval required.

Amenities: Cable TV, refrigerators, microwaves, whirlpool.

Pet Amenities: Treats available. Exercise area. There are 9 state parks off Route 11 close by. Miles of trails on the property's 190 acres.

Rated: 3 Paws — 5 cottages.

The Red Horse Inn is a fine, traditional bed and breakfast housed in luxurious cottages with mountain views. Each of the charming, Victorian-style cottages has been lovingly decorated and furnished with modern amenities. In addition to the bedroom, there's a cozy sleeping loft that makes this a romantic hideaway. Landrum is close to Jones Gap State Park on scenic Highway 11. But the real attraction here is the location, a hilltop with views of surrounding mountains and countryside.

El Dorado Motel

2800 South Ocean Boulevard
Myrtle Beach, SC 29577
800-537-8349 • 843-626-3559

Type of Lodging: Motel

Room Rates: $29–$72. AAA and AARP discounts.

Pet Charges & Deposits: $5–$10 per day.

Pet Policy: Sorry, no cats. No pets over 20 lbs. Designated rooms only. Manager's prior approval required.

Amenities: Cable TV, refrigerators, microwaves, pool, whirlpool, sauna, guest laundry, BBQs.

Pet Amenities: List of nearby veterinarians maintained. Exercise area. Myrtle Beach State Park and Huntington State Park nearby. Pets can be walked on the beach.

Rated: 2 Paws — 41 rooms.

El Dorado Motel is a beautiful family motel located on the quiet south end of Myrtle Beach. It boasts direct beach access, is only three miles from Broadway at the Beach and seven miles from Murrell's Inlet, South Carolina's seafood capital. Myrtle Beach is at the center of The Grand Strand, which runs 60 miles from near the North Carolina border south to the banks of the Santee River. It's made up of several communities, from small fishing villages to glitzy Miami Beach-style highrises, and is a premier summer beach destination.

Mariner

7003 North Ocean Boulevard
Myrtle Beach, SC 29572
843-449-5281
www.myrtlebeachmariner.com
the-mariner@altavista.net

Type of Lodging: Hotel
Room Rates: $39–$169, including continental breakfast and Tuesday night BBQ. AAA, AARP, AKC and *10% Pets Welcome*™ discounts.
Pet Charges & Deposits: $9 per day. $100 refundable deposit.
Pet Policy: Sorry, no cats.
Amenities: Cable TV, refrigerators, pools, wading pool, public beach across the street.
Pet Amenities: Pet social on Thursdays. List of nearby veterinarians maintained. Exercise area. Myrtle Beach State Park is located on Business 17 South. Pets are allowed on the beach anytime from September 15 through May 15, and after 5:00 p.m. the rest of the year.
Rated: 3 Paws — 7 rooms and 26 suites.

Chart your course to a great Myrtle Beach vacation at Mariner, which offers guests a choice of rooms, fully equipped efficiencies and two-bedroom suites. There's absolutely no smoking anywhere on the premises—a relaxing tropical atmosphere due to lush landscaping and a plethora of hummingbirds everywhere on the property. In addition to everything else you can experience on the Grand Strand, visit the Medieval Times Dinner and Tournament, which lets visitors dine in a European castle while watching an 11th century royal tournament and Ripley's Aquarium, where guests walk through an underwater tunnel to view sharks, moray eels, lionfish and giant octopus.

Best Western Newberry Inn

11701 S.C. Highway 34
Newberry, SC 29108
803-276-5850

Type of Lodging: Motel
Room Rates: $38–$55, including deluxe continental breakfast. AAA, AARP, AKC, ABA and *15% Pets Welcome*™ discounts.
Pet Charges & Deposits: $5 per day.
Pet Policy: No pets over 25 lbs.
Amenities: Cable TV, refrigerators, microwaves, pool.
Pet Amenities: List of nearby veterinarians maintained. Exercise area. Newberry County Park nearby.
Rated: 3 Paws — 113 rooms and 3 suites.

Best Western Newberry Inn gives you luxury accommodations at a very affordable price. It's a premier lodging in the region. Newberry is located 30 miles northwest of Columbia on Interstate 26. The Newberry Opera House, Newberry College and the Japanese Gardens are should-see attractions.

Red Roof Inn – Charleston North

7480 Northwoods Boulevard
North Charleston, SC 29406
800 RED ROOF • 843-572-9100
www.redroof.com
i0142@redroof.com

Type of Lodging: Motel
Room Rates: $40–$81. AAA and Sam's Club discounts.
Pet Charges & Deposits: None.
Pet Policy: Pets must not be left unattended.
Amenities: Cable TV.
Pet Amenities: None.
Rated: 3 Paws — 109 rooms.

Red Roof Inn – Charleston North features affordable rooms in one of America's premier tourist destinations. When in Charleston, be sure to take a trip to Fort Sumter National Monument in Charleston Harbor. This brick fortification, built between 1829 and 1860 on a manmade island, was where Confederate troops directed the opening shots of the Civil War. After a two-day bombardment, the small Union fort surrendered. The Confederacy continued to occupy the fort until February 1865.

Stayover Lodge

2070 McMillan Avenue
North Charleston, SC 29406
843-554-1600

Type of Lodging: Inn
Room Rates: $50–$55, including toast and coffee. *10% Pets Welcome™* discount.
Pet Charges & Deposits: $50 refundable deposit.
Pet Policy: Designated rooms only.
Amenities: Pool, kitchenettes.
Pet Amenities: List of nearby veterinarians maintained. Exercise area. Nearby city parks.
Rated: 2 Paws — 97 rooms.

When price *is* an object, but you want a nice room for the night, you'd do well to consider Stayover Lodge near Charleston Airport. One of the best ways to see and savor Charleston is by walking. The "Battery Tour" takes in the Charleston County Courthouse, St. Michael's Episcopal Church, City Hall, the Heyward-Washington House, Cabbage Row, the Nathaniel Russell House, the Edmonstron-Alston House, The Battery and Calhoun Mansion. Meanwhile, the "Cabbage Row" walking tour will take you to the Old Powder Magazine, Huguenot Church, Dock Street Theater, Old Exchange and Provost Junction and numerous other historic houses and museums.

Retreat Myrtle Beach

500 Main Street
North Myrtle Beach, SC 29582
800-645-3618 • 843-280-3015
www.retreatmyrtlebeach.com
rtreatmc@sccoast.net

Type of Lodging: Cottages & Condos

Room Rates: $400–$3,500 per week. AAA and *5% Pets Welcome™* discounts.

Pet Charges & Deposits: $50–$100 per stay.

Pet Policy: Designated units only.

Amenities: Refrigerators, microwaves, pool, oceanfront on first block off beach area.

Pet Amenities: List of nearby veterinarians maintained. McLean Park is located off Main Street. Pets are allowed on nearby beach at all hours after September 4, with leash. From March 1 to September 4, pets are allowed on beach only after 5:00 p.m.

Rated: 3 Paws — 75 units.

Retreat is a wonderful concept, successfully carried out. The company manages a series of cottages and condominiums, each different, each unique. Prices very widely depending on the location and amenities of each unit, and you should send for the company's catalogue to help you select what's best for you. The Grand Strand vacation mecca includes both inland and beach destinations. There's truly something for everyone. Kaminski House Museum (Georgetown), built in the 1760s, contains American and European furnishings from the 17th through 20th centuries, while Brookgreen Gardens (Murrell's Inlet) contains more than 500 sculptures by 19th century and contemporary American artists.

Southwood Manor Bed & Breakfast

100 East Main Street
P.O. Box 434
Ridge Spring, SC 29129
800-931-1786 • 803-685-5100
sothent@pbtcomm.net

Type of Lodging: B&B

Room Rates: $65–$75, including full breakfast. AARP discount.

Pet Charges & Deposits: None.

Pet Policy: Manager's prior approval required. Horses welcome.

Amenities: Refrigerators, microwaves, tennis, pool, 2000-feet grass airstrip.

Pet Amenities: List of nearby veterinarians maintained. Exercise area.

Rated: 3 Paws — 3 rooms and 1 suite.

Southwood Manor is a Georgian Colonial Plantation located in a sleepy country town. It's antebellum from start to finish, surrounded by cotton fields and pecan groves, with a working cotton gin across the street. This is the true flavor of the South. Hens range free on the gracious grounds, while a horse or two nibble beyond the paddock. Sip lemonade while you lounge by the oversized pool or drink iced tea after tennis. Golf courses are nearby, as is the lovely town of Aiken, the horse training capital of the South. You can enjoy polo at the winter playing fields, race horses at the training track or you can tour the Montmorenci Vineyards.

Quality Hotel & Conference Center

7136 Asheville Highway
Spartanburg, SC 29303
864-503-0780

Type of Lodging: Hotel
Room Rates: $59–$99, including full breakfast. AAA, AARP and *10% Pets Welcome™* discounts.
Pet Charges & Deposits: None.
Pet Policy: No pets over 20 lbs. Designated rooms only.
Amenities: Cable TV, pool, restaurant.
Pet Amenities: List of nearby veterinarians maintained.
Rated: 3 Paws — 141 rooms and 6 suites.

Quality Hotel & Conference Center is an impressive six-story high rise with comfy rooms, a restaurant and numerous amenities. It's a perfect home away from home in Spartanburg, one of the South's leading textile manufacturing cities as well as one of the world's largest peach shipping centers. Nearby Walnut Grove Plantation is an 18th century plantation furnished with pre-1830 antiques. The kitchen displays 18th century wood, wrought iron, tin and earthenware utensils. Other buildings on the plantation include a doctor's office, drover's house, a school, a smithy and numerous barns.

Magnolia House Bed & Breakfast

230 Church Street
Sumter, SC 29150
888-666-0296 • 803-775-6694
www.bbonline.com/sc/magnolia
magnoliahouse@sumter.net

Type of Lodging: B&B
Room Rates: $75–$145, including full breakfast. Business and Military discounts.
Pet Charges & Deposits: None.
Pet Policy: Manager's prior approval required.
Amenities: Cable TV, private phone lines, French spoken.
Pet Amenities: Owner's pets on premises. List of nearby veterinarians maintained. Fenced exercise area. Hampton Park is within walking distance of the B&B.
Rated: 3 Paws — 4 rooms and 1 suite.

Magnolia House is a stately Greek Revival home, which was built in 1907. The soothing fountains, cool lawns and flowering gardens, along with front and rear wraparound porches, create a relaxing atmosphere. In the winter months, a cozy fire invites you to sip a cup of hot tea and get lost in your favorite book. Founded in 1785, Sumter was named for a Revolutionary War hero. Today, it's one of South Carolina's leading lumber and agricultural areas. The nearby Sumter National Forest contains 360,000 acres that encompass the southern Appalachians, the rolling terrain of the Piedmont and the upper reaches of the Savannah River.

SOUTH DAKOTA

Nicknames: Coyote State; Mount Rushmore State

Population: 733,133

Area: 77,121 square miles

Climate: extremes of temperature, persistent winds, low precipitation and humidity.

Capital: Pierre

Entered Union: Nov. 2, 1889

Motto: Under God, the people rule.

Song: Hail, South Dakota

Flower: Pasqueflower

Tree: Black Hills Spruce

Bird: Chinese Ring-Necked Pheasant

Famous South Dakotans: Sparky Anderson, Tom Brokaw, Crazy Horse, Thomas Daschle, Myron Floren, Cheryl Ladd, George McGovern, Billy Mills, Pat O'Brien, Sitting Bull.

 History: The French explored the region in 1742. The U.S. acquired the area in 1803 as part of the Louisiana Purchase. A trading post was opened at Fort Pierre in 1817. Gold was discovered in the Black Hills in 1874, leading to the Great Dakota Boom of 1879. In 1889, conflicts with Native Americans led to the Great Sioux Agreement, which established reservations and opened up more land for white settlement. The massacre of Native American families at Wounded Knee in 1890 essentially marked the end of the Native American way of life in the United States. Mount Rushmore, one of the most famous landmarks in the United States appears on the cover of this book.

BROOKINGS, SOUTH DAKOTA (Pop. 16,300)

Staurolite Inn & Suites

2515 East Sixth Street
Brookings, SD 57000
800-362-1516 • 605-692-9421

Type of Lodging: Motel

Room Rates: $45–$110, including continental breakfast. AAA, AARP, AKC, ABA and *10% Pets Welcome™* discounts.

Pet Charges and Deposits: None.

Pet Policies: None. All Pets Welcome.

Amenities: Cable TV, refrigerators, microwaves, pool, whirlpool, restaurant.

Pet Amenities: Exercise area.

Rated: 3 Paws — 102 rooms and 5 suites.

Brookings' premier lodging choice for families and individuals in need of a home away from home has spacious and beautifully decorated rooms. Guests can enjoy fine dining at Arthur B's Steakhouse and Lounge. Area attractions include South Dakota State University, McCrory Gardens, State Agricultural Heritage Museum, Royal River Casino, Terry Redlin Art Center and many fishing and state parks.

Chief Motel

120 Mount Rushmore Road
Custer, SD 57730
605-673-2318
www.custer-sd.com

Type of Lodging: Motel

Room Rates: $29 and up.

Pet Charges & Deposits: $5 per day.

Pet Policies: Designated rooms only.

Amenities: Cable TV, refrigerators, microwaves, pool, hot tub.

Pet Amenities: List of nearby veterinarians maintained. Exercise area. Two city parks in town. Custer State Park is only 5 miles away.

Rated: 2 Paws — 33 rooms.

The Chief Motel is a small but centrally located motel. All guestrooms are on the ground floor with parking in front of each room. Often called the "Black Hills Vacation Headquarters," Mount Rushmore National Monument, Crazy Horse Mountain Carving, Cathedral Spires, Custer State Park, Jewel Cave National Monument and Wind Cave National Park are all within a 20-mile radius.

Lodge at Palmer Gulch

P.O. Box 295
Hill City, SD 57745
605-574-2525
palmergulch@aol.com

Type of Lodging: Hotel

Room Rates: $105–$165, including coffee & newspaper. AAA and AARP discounts.

Pet Charges & Deposits: None.

Pet Policies: Designated rooms only.

Amenities: Satellite TV, refrigerators, microwaves, sauna.

Pet Amenities: Dog runs.

Rated: 3 Paws — 56 rooms and 6 suites.

At the foot of Harney Peak, the highest point in the United States East of the Rockies, Palmer Gulch adjoins the Black Elk Wilderness Area, the Norbeck Wildlife Preserves and the Black Hills National Forest. Your family can experience this special environment on your own terms. Well-mannered saddle horses are ready to take you exploring. Nature walks, hiking trails, mountain bike paths and rock climbing start from the resort. Take the kids fishing at the pond, then gather 'round the campfire in the cool evening to watch the stars.

Super 8 Motel

800 Mammoth Street
Hot Springs, SD 57747
604-745-3888

Type of Lodging: Motel

Room Rates: $45–$110, including continental breakfast. AAA and AARP discounts.

Pet Charges & Deposits: $25 refundable deposit.

Pet Policy: None. All Pets Welcome.

Amenities: None.

Pet Amenities: Butler Park is 3 blocks from the motel.

Rated: 3 Paws — 48 rooms.

The Super 8 Motel in Hot Springs is a clean, well-run establishment located right next door to the Mammoth Site, which has one of the largest concentrations of mammoth bones found to date. It is the only "as it was" site for mammoth bones in North America. The Black Hills Wild Horse Sanctuary is a private wilderness area where horses roam free. Hot Springs is noted for its mineral springs and is a year-round recreation area.

First Lady Inn

P.O. Box 677
Keystone, SD 57751
800-252-2119 • 605-666-4990

Type of Lodging: Hotel

Room Rates: $84–$135, including continental breakfast. AARP discount.

Pet Charges & Deposits: $7 per day.

Pet Policy: Designated rooms only. Manager's prior approval required.

Amenities: Cable TV, pool, hot tub, guest laundry, game room.

Pet Amenities: List of nearby veterinarians maintained. Exercise area.

Rated: 2 Paws — 39 rooms and 2 suites.

The First Lady Inn is the closest accommodation to Mount Rushmore. It has luxury rooms with king- and queen-sized beds, new swimming pool, hot tub, cable television, air conditioning and phones. Located on Highway 16A just past the Rushmore Aerial Tramway, the First Lady Inn is within walking distance of shopping, dining and entertainment.

Fort Randall Inn

Highways 18 and 281
Pickstown, SD 57367
800-340-7801 • 605-487-7801

Type of Lodging: Motel

Room Rates: $36–$60. AAA and AARP discounts.

Pet Charges & Deposits: None.

Pet Policy: Manager's prior approval required.

Amenities: Cable TV.

Pet Amenities: List of nearby veterinarians maintained. Exercise area.

Rated: 3 Paws — 17 rooms and 1 suite.

Only a quarter-mile from the water, the Fort Randall Inn offers large rooms with queen-sized beds and cable television at affordable rates. There is excellent year-round fishing in Lake Francis Case and fast-water fishing below the Fort Randall Dam. Boating and water-skiing are popular summer sports here. Both sail and motorboats are common sights in the summertime. A beautiful nine-hole golf course and a clubhouse complete with dining room and bar are open from April 15 through October 15. The motel is located only three miles from the Fort Randall Casino.

Ramada Inn

1721 La Crosse Street
Rapid City, SD 57701
800-272-6232 • 605-342-1300

Type of Lodging: Hotel

Room Rates: $69–$299. AAA, AARP and *10% Pets Welcome™* discounts.

Pet Charges & Deposits: $25 per stay.

Pet Policy: Designated rooms only.

Amenities: Cable TV, refrigerators, pool, whirlpool, fitness center, restaurant, lounge, casino.

Pet Amenities: List of nearby veterinarians maintained. Exercise area. City park is located at Anamosa off of La Crosse Street.

Rated: 3 Paws — 139 rooms.

Lying at the base of the Black Hills in western South Dakota, only 30 minutes from Mount Rushmore, is the Ramada Inn. Even though it is one of the city's newest convention centers, the style is definitely old world, with a rich, refined Victorian Queen Anne mood throughout, highlighted by elegant touches such as concierge services.

Super 8 Motel

2124 La Crosse Street
Rapid City, SD 57701
800-800-8000 • 605-348-8070
www.super8.com

Type of Lodging: Motel

Room Rates: $38–$140, including continental breakfast. AAA discount.

Pet Charges & Deposits: $5 per day.

Pet Policy: Designated rooms only. Manager's prior approval required.

Amenities: Cable TV, refrigerators, microwaves, safes.

Pet Amenities: List of nearby veterinarians maintained. Exercise area. Custer State Park nearby.

Rated: 3 Paws — 118 rooms. Pride of Super 8 and Manager of the Year.

The Super 8 Motel has comfortable and spacious rooms offering two double beds that are perfect for traveling families. Mount Rushmore is 25 miles away. Bear Country U.S.A. is a drive-through wildlife park featuring elk, wolves, Rocky Mountain goats, bighorn sheep and buffalo, all roaming free in their native habitat. Black Hills Gold provides a close-up view of artisans making gold jewelry. In the mood for a chuckwagon dinner and western music show? Both the Circle B Ranch and the Flying T Chuckwagon Supper and Show will fill your needs. Ellsworth Air Force Base features the South Dakota Air and Space Museum.

Exel Inn

1300 West Russell Street
Sioux Falls, SD 57104
800-367-3935 • 605-331-5800
www.exelinns.com

Type of Lodging: Hotel

Room Rates: $32–$59, including continental breakfast. AARP discount.

Pet Charges & Deposits: $100–$200 refundable deposit on extended stays.

Pet Policy: No pets over 25 lbs. Designated rooms only. Manager's prior approval required. Limit two pets per room.

Amenities: Hairdryers, coffeemakers, irons.

Pet Amenities: List of nearby veterinarians maintained. Terrace Park is located at Madison and West Avenue.

Rated: 3 Paws — 104 rooms.

The Exel Inn is conveniently located near Howard Wood Field, Joe Foss Airport, Empire Mall and downtown Sioux Falls. The hotel provides long-term airport parking. The Great Plains Zoo houses approximately 400 animals. Many displays resemble the animals' natural habitats. Siouxland Heritage Museum exhibits the history of Sioux Falls and Minehaha County.

Kelly Inn

3101 West Russell
Sioux Falls, SD 57107
800-635-3559 • 605-338-6242

Type of Lodging: Motel

Room Rates: $59–$79, including continental breakfast. AAA and AARP discounts.

Pet Charges & Deposits: None.

Pet Policy: None. All Pets Welcome.

Amenities: Cable TV, refrigerators, microwaves, safes, whirlpool.

Pet Amenities: Elmwood Park is 2 blocks away from the motel.

Rated: 3 Paws — 40 rooms and 3 suites.

Kelly Inn offers business class guestrooms with a microwave, refrigerator and dataport. The suites have a fireplace, wet bar and whirlpool. It is located near Sioux Falls Arena and Convention Center, Great Plains Zoo and Museum and Elmwood Golf Course. The settlement of Sioux Falls resulted from the proximity of stone quarries and the Big Sioux River. From a five-story-high observation tower in Falls Park, visitors can watch the river as it flows over the falls. The Center for Western Studies has a permanent exhibit on the history and culture of the Great Plains.

Ramada Limited

407 South Lyons Avenue
Sioux Falls, SD 57106
605-330-0000

Type of Lodging: Hotel

Room Rates: $45–$149, including continental breakfast. AAA, AARP and *10% Pets Welcome™* discounts.

Pet Charges & Deposits: $15 deposit, refundable on smoking rooms and nonrefundable on non-smoking rooms.

Pet Policy: Designated rooms only.

Amenities: Cable TV, refrigerators, microwaves, safes, pool, whirlpool, room, guest laundry, business center, casino.

Pets Amenities: List of nearby veterinarians maintained. Dog runs. Exercise area. Park is located on Kiwanis Avenue.

Rated: 3 Paws — 64 rooms and 4 suites.

The Ramada Limited of Sioux Falls is located off Interstate Highway 29 and West 12th Street (Exit 79). It is one of Sioux Falls newest properties. All guestrooms feature refrigerators, microwaves and clock radios, most rooms have a sofa. Guests have use of the indoor swimming pool, whirlpool, fitness room, guest laundry facilities, minimart, executive business center and casino.

Kelly Inn

540 East Jackson
Spearfish, SD 57783
800-635-3559

Type of Lodging: Motel

Room Rates: $45–$99, including continental breakfast. AAA and AARP discounts.

Pet Charges & Deposits: None.

Pet Policy: Pets can be left alone in rooms for short periods of time.

Amenities: Cable TV, pool, hot tub.

Pet Amenities: List of nearby veterinarians maintained. Exercise area behind motel. City park is located 7 blocks from the motel.

Rated: 3 Paws — 50 rooms.

The Kelly Inn in Spearfish has a brand new outdoor pool and whirlpool. It is conveniently located near Deadwood and Spearfish Canyon. The Black Hills Passion Play, situated in an amphitheater west of town, has presented the last seven days in the life of Christ, in 22 scenes, since 1939. The Thoen Stone Monument commemorates the ill-fated journey of Ezra Kind's party, only to be killed by Native Americans before they could return home. Before his death, Kind etched their story in stone, which was discovered in 1932.

TENNESSEE

Nickname: Volunteer State

Population: 5,483,535

Area: 42,146 square miles

Climate: Humid continental to the north; humid subtropical to the south.

Capital: Nashville

Entered Union: June 1, 1796

Motto: Agriculture and commerce.

Song: Tennessee Waltz

Flower: Iris

Tree: Tulip Poplar

Bird: Mockingbird

Famous Tennesseans: Roy Acuff, Davy Crockett, Ernie Ford, Aretha Franklin, Morgan Freeman, Al Gore, Jr., Alex Haley, W.C. Handy, Sam Houston, Dolly Parton, Minnie Pearl, Dinah Shore, Bessie Smith, Alvin York.

History: Creek and Yuchi peoples populated the area when Spanish explorers first visited the area in 1541. Cherokee moved into the area in the early 18th century. English traders crossed the Great Smoky Mountains from the east, while France's Marquette and Joliet sailed down the Mississippi on the west in 1673. The first permanent settlement was by Virginians in 1769. The state seceded from the Union in 1861, but 30,000 Tennessee Volunteers fought for the Union. Tennessee was readmitted in 1866 and was the only former Confederate state not to have a postwar military government. Nashville," Music City USA," is emblematic of American music.

Bolivar Inn

658 West Market Street
Bolivar, TN 38008
901-668-3372

Type of Lodging: Motel

Room Rates: $25–$45. AAA discount.

Pet Charges & Deposits: $1–$5 per stay.

Pet Policy: None. All Pets Welcome.

Amenities: Cable TV, refrigerators, microwaves.

Pet Amenities: Chickasaw State Park is located 12 miles from the motel.

Rated: 3 Paws — 39 rooms.

The pet-friendly Bolivar Inn has a spacious lot for you and your pet to enjoy. There are many restaurants nearby and the Chickasaw State Park is only 12 miles from the motel.

Cedar Hill Resort

2371 Cedar Hill Road
Celina, TN 38551
800-872-8393 • 931-243-3201
www.cedarhillresort.com

Type of Lodging: Resort

Room Rates: $52–$225.

Pet Charges & Deposits: $15 per day.

Pet Policy: Manager's prior approval required.

Amenities: Cable TV, refrigerators, microwaves, pool.

Pet Amenities: List of nearby veterinarians maintained.

Rated: 3 Paws — 37 rooms on Dale Hollow Lake.

Once you visit Cedar Hill Resort, you and your pet will want to come back for many years to come. Located on Dale Hollow Lake, Cedar Hill Resort is nestled in the Cumberland Mountains. There's some great fishing, water skiing, house boating and scuba diving. You and your pet will enjoy the crystal-clear water and a pristine environment. This complete resort offers modern, well-equipped cabins, boats and houseboats, motel rooms, swimming pool, restaurant and dock facilities. No mosquitoes will be found here! Calm water with an average summer water temperature of 82° makes for a great vacation.

Days Inn Lookout Mountain West / Tiftonia

3801 Cummings Highway
Chattanooga, TN 37419
800-329-7466 • 423-821-6044
www.daysinn.com

Type of Lodging: Motel

Room Rates: $53–$83, including continental breakfast. AAA and AARP discounts.

Pet Charges & Deposits: $10 per day.

Pet Policy: Designated rooms only.

Amenities: Cable TV, refrigerators, microwaves, pool.

Pet Amenities: Exercise area.

Rated: 3 Paws — 82 rooms.

Located at the foot of historic Lookout Mountain, Days Inn Lookout Mountain West specializes in tours, convention groups, families and tourists. This motel is a cost-conscious and delightfully pet-friendly establishment, only minutes from all major attractions. Centrally located, this is a great base for those traveling to the surrounding cities such as Knoxville, Atlanta, Nashville and Birmingham.

Hachland Hill Inn

1601 Madison Street
Clarksville, TN 37043
931-647-4084

Type of Lodging: Inn

Room Rates: $95–$175.

Pet Charges & Deposits: None.

Pet Policy: Designated rooms only. Manager's prior approval required.

Amenities: Fireplaces, private entrances, famous dining.

Pet Amenities: List of nearby veterinarians maintained. Exercise area.

Rated: 3 Paws — 10 rooms.

The Colonial-style Hachland Hill Inn offers guests more than just charming guestrooms and suites furnished with antiques. There's also plenty of gracious Southern hospitality. This enchanting Inn offers guests unexpected pleasures. Guests will no doubt be tempted to take pooches for a stroll around the lovely grounds adorned with fields of wildflowers and even a bird sanctuary. Renowned author, gourmet chef and Inn owner Phila Hach prides herself on making the Hachland Hill Inn one of the South's favorite destinations for charming accommodations and fine dining.

Ramada Limited

3100 Wilma Rudolph Boulevard
Clarksville, TN 37040
931-552-0098

Type of Lodging: Motel

Room Rates: $60–$80, including continental breakfast. AAA, AARP and *15% Pets Welcome*™ discount.

Pet Charges & Deposits: Call for refundable deposit information.

Pet Policy: Small pets only. Designated rooms only.

Amenities: Cable TV, safe, pool.

Pet Amenities: Dog runs.

Rated: 3 Paws — 41 rooms.

The Ramada Limited is located at Exit 4 off Interstate 24 next to the Cracker Barrel Restaurant. Nashville, the Country Music Capital of the World, is approximately 40 miles east of Clarksville and the Fort Campbell Army Post is approximately 15 minutes away. All guestrooms are equipped with king-sized beds, remote control cable television and message phones. Relax by the swimming pool, sauna and whirlpool. Within walking distance of fine dining and shopping and minutes away from Beachaven Winery and golfing.

Econo Lodge

1100 South Jefferson Avenue
Cookeville, TN 38506
800-446-6900 • 931-528-1040

Type of Lodging: Motel

Room Rates: $50–$90, including continental breakfast. AAA, AARP and *10% Pets Welcome*™ discounts.

Pet Charges & Deposits: $5 per day.

Pet Policy: None. All Pets Welcome.

Amenities: Cable TV, refrigerators, microwaves, pool.

Pet Amenities: Exercise area. Creek Park nearby.

Rated: 3 Paws — 70 rooms. Econo Lodge Chain Gold Award Winner.

Econo Lodge is a fine budget chain and the Cookeville unit is no exception. The modern town of Cookeville offers many fine attractions including Burgess Falls State Park, Country Club, Cookeville Mall, Falls Creek Falls, Standing Stone State Park, Vanity Fair Outlets, Ironwood Golf Course and Hidden Hollow Amusement Park.

Mountain Harbor Inn

1199 Highway 139
Dandridge, TN 37725
865-397-3345
www.mountainharborinn.com

Type of Lodging: B&B

Room Rates: $65–$125, including full breakfast.

Pet Charges & Deposits: $10 per day. Credit card imprint required as deposit.

Pet Policy: Pets may not be left unattended.

Amenities: Cable TV, refrigerators, microwaves.

Pet Amenities: List of nearby veterinarians maintained. Exercise area. Douglas Dam Overlook is located on Douglas Dam Road.

Rated: 3 Paws — 4 rooms and 8 suites.

The Mountain Harbor Inn strives for a balance between luxury, comfort and beauty. Ensconced in a scenic mountain setting on Douglas Lake, the Inn's charming guestrooms are decorated with antiques and quilts. Pillared porches beckon guests to relax and enjoy the serenity of the surrounding mountains and lake. The Inn is ideal for a weekend getaway or an extended vacation. No matter what season you choose to visit, each has its own beauty and special events to offer. Spend the day exploring the area with your dog or head to town and buy one of the locally crafted rockers for your own. Boat launching and docking areas are available for those who wish to spend the day on the lake fishing for bass. There are even charter services available to take anglers to the best fishing spots.

Garden Plaza Hotel

211 Mockingbird Lane
Johnson City, TN 37604
800-3-GARDEN • 423-929-2000

Type of Lodging: Hotel

Room Rates: $79–$120. AAA, AARP, AKC and ABA discounts.

Pet Charges & Deposits: None.

Pet Policy: Manager's approval required.

Amenities: Cable TV, pool, whirlpool, health club privileges, valet laundry, airport transportation, restaurant, lounge.

Pet Amenities: None.

Rated: 3 Paws — 181 rooms and 5 suites.

If you are looking for a full service hotel with Southern hospitality, then experience what the Garden Plaza Hotel has to offer. From the distinctive rooms and affordable rates to the in-house dining, the home-grown attention to detail is unsurpassed. Centrally located near many historic areas, business communities, scenic parks, unique shops and challenging golf courses, the Garden Plaza Hotel is a perfect choice for those traveling on a short business trip or an extended vacation. Spend your day relaxing by the pool with a good book, exploring the wonders of area attractions or romping with your dog at one of the local parks.

Holiday Inn

101 West Springbrook Drive
Johnson City, TN 37604
800 HOLIDAY • 423-282-4611
hi101@preferred.com

Type of Lodging: Hotel

Room Rates: $91 and up. AAA and AARP discounts.

Pet Charges & Deposits: Credit card imprint required as deposit.

Pet Policy: Designated rooms only. Manager's prior approval required.

Amenities: Cable TV, safe, pool.

Pet Amenities: List of nearby veterinarians maintained. Exercise area. Kiwanis Park is located 3 miles from the hotel on West Market Street.

Rated: 3 Paws — 205 rooms and 4 suites.

The Holiday Inn encompasses all that a hotel should be and more. The staff strives to exceed your expectations, attending to your every need and provide you with the very best in warm, hospitable surroundings. The unique architectural design captures the refreshing atmosphere and offers striking views of East Tennessee. Guests will find shopping and theaters within a short walking distance.

Microtel Inn

309 North Peters Road
Knoxville, TN 37922
800-579-1683 • 865-531-8041
www.microtelinn.com

Type of Lodging: Hotel

Room Rates: $40–$70.

Pet Charges & Deposits: None.

Pet Policy: Designated rooms only.

Amenities: Cable TV, safes.

Pet Amenities: Smoky Mountain National Park nearby.

Rated: 3 Paws — 105 rooms.

Microtel Inn is a great place to stay when visiting Knoxville. Guests will find many local attractions nearby including Knoxville Zoo, Market Place, Windsor Square, Knoxville Airport, Smoky Mountains, West Town Mall, Pigeon Forge, University of Tennessee and downtown Knoxville.

Super 8 Downtown West

6200 Papermill
Knoxville, TN 37923
800-800-8000 • 865-584-8511

Type of Lodging: Motel

Room Rates: $40–$60. AAA, AARP and *10% Pets Welcome*™ discounts.

Pet Charges & Deposits: $25 refundable deposit.

Pet Policy: None. All Pets Welcome.

Amenities: Cable TV, refrigerators, microwaves, safes, pool.

Pet Amenities: List of nearby veterinarians maintained. Exercise area. Park is located on Lyson Cumberland Avenue.

Rated: 3 Paws — 138 rooms and 2 suites.

Located in the heart of the Smoky Mountains, you and your pet will not be disappointed when you stay at the Super 8 Downtown West. Guest amenities include in-room coffeemaker, express checkout, fitness center, free local phone calls, 24-hour front desk, laundry services, meeting facilities, modem lines, free newspaper, free parking, outdoor pool and cable television. The motel is located minutes from the University of Tennessee, Convention Center, West Town Mall and Dollywood.

Comfort Inn - Airport/Graceland

1581 East Brooks Road
Memphis, TN 38116
800-228-5150 • 901-345-3344
www.comfortinn.com/hotel/tn090

Type of Lodging: Motel

Room Rates: $59–$79, including continental breakfast. AAA, AARP and *10% Pets Welcome*™ discounts.

Pet Charges & Deposits: $10 per day.

Pet Policy: None. All Pets Welcome.

Amenities: Cable TV, pool, hot tubs, refrigerators, alarm clock radios.

Pet Amenities: None.

Rated: 3 Paws — 60 rooms.

Comfort Inn Airport encourages you and your pet to come stay with them at their newly constructed motel near Graceland. Each guestroom has a hairdryer, cable television and alarm clock radio. The motel is minutes from the airport and downtown Memphis.

Howard Johnson Express Inn

2424 South Church Street
Murfreesboro, TN 37127
800-446-4656 • 615-896-5522

Type of Lodging: Motel

Room Rates: $35–$79, including continental breakfast. AAA, AARP, AKC and ABA discounts.

Pet Charges & Deposits: $5 per day.

Pet Policy: Small pets only.

Amenities: Cable TV, refrigerators, microwaves, pool, Jacuzzis.

Pet Amenities: List of nearby veterinarians maintained. Old Fort Parkway nearby.

Rated: 2 Paws — 80 rooms and 15 suites.

Howard Johnson Express Inn affords you and your pet clean, comfortable rooms at a very affordable price. Nearby attractions include Murfreesboro, Nashville, Music City, Opryland Hotel, Middle Tennessee State University and the Nissan plant.

Loews Vanderbilt Plaza Hotel

2100 West End Avenue
Nashville, TN 37203
615-320-1700
www.loewsvanderbilt.com
loewsvanderbilt@loewshotels.com

Type of Lodging: Hotel

Room Rates: Call for room rates. AAA discount.

Pet Charges & Deposits: None.

Pet Policy: No pets over 50 lbs.

Amenities: Cable TV, honor bars, safes, spa, two restaurants, lounge.

Pet Amenities: Pet menu from room service. Treats, mats and bowl available. List of nearby veterinarians maintained. Exercise area. Centennial Park is located on West End Avenue.

Rated: 5 Paws — 340 rooms and 13 suites.

Loews Vanderbilt Plaza Hotel is at the center of Nashville's educational, medical and business district, just steps from renowned Vanderbilt University. Each guestroom features a refreshment center, coffeemaker, fax machine, hairdryer, iron and ironing board, dual-line phone with voice-mail, dataport and well-lighted work desk. Guests are within walking distance of many shops, restaurants and major city attractions and only minutes from Opryland USA and Nashville International Airport.

Mountain Mist Rentals & Realty

2225 Parkway Suite 1
P.O. Box 1324
Pigeon Forge, TN 37868
800-634-5814 • 865-428-5427
www.mountainmistrentals.com
cabins@vic.com

Type of Lodging: Chalets

Chalet Rates: $100–$450. *$10 off (per stay) Pets Welcome™* discount.

Pet Charges & Deposits: $50–$100 nonrefundable deposit.

Pet Policy: Designated chalets only.

Amenities: Cable TV, VCRs, refrigerators, microwaves, pool, whirlpool, hot tubs, BBQ grills, fireplaces, guest laundry.

Pet Amenities: List of nearby veterinarians maintained. Great Smoky Mountain National Park nearby.

Rated: 4 Paws — 84 chalets and log cabins.

Come and enjoy your "home away from home" at Mountain Mist Rentals and Realty. Let the natural beauty of the Smoky Mountains be the backdrop for your vacation. Just a short drive from Pigeon Forge and the Great Smoky Mountain National Park, these chalets and log cabins offer you the opportunity to commune with nature, the kids to Dollywood, shop at the outlet malls and round out the day with an evening of fine entertainment at one of the local music theaters. The avid sportsman can enjoy a day of hiking and fishing, or opt for one of the nearby golf courses. Ski at Ober Gatlinburg, go horseback riding on a mountain tour or while away the day relaxing in the hot tub on the deck of your mountain cabin.

Mountain Laurel Cabins

146 Black Marsh Hollow Road
Townsend, TN 37882
865-448-9657
http://wwikle.home.mindspring.com
wwikle@mindspring.com

Type of Lodging: Cabins

Cabin Rates: $95. *5% Pets Welcome™* discount.

Pet Charges & Deposits: Call for charges information. Call for deposit information.

Pet Policy: None. All Pets Welcome.

Amenities: Cable TV, VCRs, refrigerators, microwaves, whirlpool.

Pet Amenities: Great Smoky Mountain National Park nearby.

Rated: 3 Paws — 2 hand-hewn log cabins.

Just off Black Marsh Hollow Road in Townsend in the peaceful Smoky Mountains are the Mountain Laurel Cabins. Here you will find three hand-hewn log cabins with rustic appeal and modern amenities. The cabins are located near Gatlinburg, Pigeon Forge, Cades Cove and the Great Smoky Mountain National Park, so there are plenty of sights to see and places for you and your pet to explore.

Pearl's of the Mountains Cabin Rentals

7717 East Lamar Alexander Parkway
Townsend, TN 37882
800-324-8415 • 865-448-8801

Type of Lodging: Cabin & Chalet Rental
Cabin Rates: Call for rates.
Pet Charges & Deposits: $10 per day.
Pet Policy: Manager's prior approval required.
Amenities: Cable TV, refrigerators, microwaves, pool, Jacuzzi, guest laundry, fireplaces.
Pet Amenities: List of nearby veterinarians maintained. Exercise area. Great Smoky Mountain National Park nearby.
Rated: 4 Paws — 3 cabins.

Located near the Great Smoky Mountains National Park are Pearl's of the Mountains Cabin Rentals. Here you will have the best views of the Smokies from your own private cabin. All cabins come fully equipped with towels, linens, soaps, firewood for the fireplace, cable television, VCRs, telephones, guest laundry facilities, individual climate controls, as well as kitchens with microwaves and dishwashers, making them an excellent choice for a private getaway. Stroll down to the river with the dog and wet your fishing line, have a picnic or go for a swim in the river.

❖ ❖ ❖ ❖ ❖

Twin Valley Ranch
Bed and Breakfast Horse Ranch

2848 Old Chihowee Road
Walland, TN 37886-2144
800-872-2235 • 865-984-0980
www.bbonline.com/tn/twinvalley

Type of Lodging: Cabins

Room Rates: $75–$95.

Pet Charges & Deposits: None.

Pet Policy: Designated rooms only. Manager's prior approval required. Horses welcome.

Amenities: Refrigerators, microwaves, hiking trails, horseback riding, outdoor grill, petting zoo.

Pet Amenities: List of nearby veterinarians maintained. Exercise area. Great Smoky Mountain National Park nearby.

Rated: 5 Paws — 2 rooms and 1 cabin on a 260-acre horse ranch.

Wake up to the mountain's morning mist and breathtaking views at Twin Valley Ranch Bed and Breakfast Horse Ranch. Surrounded by tranquility and simple country living, guests may choose to share the unique log home with its rustic log interior, two-story mountain stone fireplace and individually decorated rooms featuring special homey touches, or stay in the private log cabin nestled in the hills. The fully equipped cabin sleeps up to six people, offers a kitchenette, full bath and a sunny deck to enjoy the mountain views.

This mountain resort is a perfect place to bring your horse. The Ranch has a grassy corral, complete with its own stream and shelter; or use one of the paddocks, with a shelter and running water. There are many trails throughout the scenic hills and valleys of this 260-acre ranch. You may arrange for a guided tour or head out on your own. For those who would rather "rough it" on the trail, there is a one-room primitive shelter, where you can stop and relax in the hammock for two. When the stars come out, build a roaring campfire and breathe in the peace and quiet of nature.

TEXAS

Nickname: Lone Star State
Population: 20,044,141
Area: 267,277 square miles
Climate: Extremely varied; driest region is in the west (Trans-Pecos); the wettest region is in the northeast.
Capital: Austin
Entered Union: Dec. 29,1845
Motto: Friendship.
Song: Texas, Our Texas

Flower: Bluebonnet
Tree: Pecan
Bird: Mockingbird
Famous Texans: Stephen Austin, James Bowie, Carol Burnett, George Bush, George W. Bush, Joan Crawford, Dwight Eisenhower, Farrah Fawcett, Sam Houston, Howard Hughes, Lyndon B. Johnson, Tommy Lee Jones, Janis Joplin, Sandra Day O'Connor, Ross Perot, Dan Rather, Sam Rayburn, Sissy Spacek, George Strait.

 History: More than 100 Native American tribes lived in the area at the time of European contact. Americans moved into Texas in the early 19th century. Mexico won independence from Spain in 1821. Santa Anna became dictator of an area that included Texas in 1835. Texans rebelled. Santa Anna wiped out the rebellion at the Alamo in 1836, but Sam Houston's Texans defeated the Mexican troops at San Jacinto. Independence was proclaimed the same year. The Republic of Texas was a nation until 1845, when it was admitted to the Union.

AUSTIN, TEXAS (Pop. 465,600)

Exel Inn of Austin

2711 Interstate 35 South
Austin, TX 78741
800-367-3935 • 512-462-9201
www.exelinns.com

Type of Lodging: Hotel
Room Rates: $46–$79, including continental breakfast. AARP discount.
Pet Charges & Deposits: $100–$200 refundable deposit on extended stays.
Pet Policy: No pets over 25 lbs. Designated rooms only. Manager's prior approval required. Limit two pets per room.
Amenities: Irons, coffeemaker, full-length mirror, hairdryers.
Pet Amenities: Zilker Park is located on the corner of Martin Creek and South LaMar.
Rated: 2 Paws — 89 rooms.

Exel Inn is a good choice for travelers who wish to have access to St. Edwards University, State Capitol, Convention Center, Palmer Auditorium/City Coliseum, University of Texas, LBJ Library and downtown Austin. All Exel Inns offer alarm clock radios, micro-fridges, modem jacks, free local phone calls and wake-up service.

La Quinta Inn & Suites Hotel

11901 North Mopac Expressway
Austin, TX 78759
800-531-5900 • 512-832-2121
www.laquinta.com
lq0937gm@laquinta.com

Type of Lodging: Hotel

Room Rates: $85–$145, including continental breakfast. AAA and AARP discounts.

Pet Charges & Deposits: None.

Pet Policy: No pets over 25 lbs.

Amenities: Cable TV, refrigerators, pool, hot tub, hairdryers, irons and ironing boards.

Pet Amenities: Balcores Park is located at Duval and Amherst.

Rated: 3 Paws — 141 rooms and 8 suites.

The La Quinta Inn & Suites is a new, conveniently located hotel with many features designed to create a relaxing, residential feeling: a sun-drenched lobby, beautiful courtyard, spa, heated pool, fitness center, laundry facilities and free breakfast. The inviting rooms offer rich wood furniture, crown molding, spacious tile bathrooms, big televisions, oversized desks, coffeemakers, hairdryers, irons and ironing boards, two dataport phones, free local calls and voicemail.

Ramada Inn

1502 Texas Avenue
College Station, TX 77840
800-228-2828 • 979-693-9891
ramada@cox-internet.com

Type of Lodging: Inn

Room Rates: $56–$125. AAA, AARP and AKC discounts.

Pet Charges & Deposits: $10 per stay.

Pet Policy: None. All Pets Welcome.

Amenities: Cable TV, honor bar, safes, pool, Jacuzzi, hairdryers, irons and ironing boards, restaurant.

Pet Amenities: List of nearby veterinarians maintained.

Rated: 3 Paws — 164 rooms and 4 suites.

Whether you and your pet are visiting, passing through or on business, the Ramada Limited will be the place you will want for your stay. Guest amenities include free local telephone calls, 24-hour front desk, laundry services, meeting facilities, free parking, RV or truck parking, outdoor pool, restaurant, safe-deposit box and cable television. The Hotel is only minutes from Reed Arena and tour-friendly George Bush Library and Forsythe Gallery. Other area attractions include Texas A&M University, Texas World Speedway, Messina Hof Winery and many area sports and recreation facilities.

Best Western Corpus Christi Inn

2838 South Padre Island Drive
Corpus Christi, TX 78415
800-445-9463 • 361-854-0005

Type of Lodging: Inn

Room Rates: $49–$99, including continental breakfast. AAA, AARP, AKC and ABA discounts.

Pet Charges & Deposits: $25 deposit of which $10 is refundable.

Pet Policy: Designated rooms only.

Amenities: Cable TV, pool, whirlpool, hot tubs, free local calls.

Pet Amenities: List of nearby veterinarians maintained.

Rated: 3 Paws — 141 rooms and 1 suite.

Best Western Corpus Christi Inn is conveniently located in the business district of Corpus Christi. A friendly staff will attend to you and your pet. The guestrooms have king-sized beds, work desk and remote control cable television. You are just minutes away from the U.S.S. Lexington, Texas State Aquarium and Convention Center. The beautiful beaches of Padre Island National Seashore and Malaquite Beach are only 20 minutes away. It's only a short drive to other attractions such as the famous King Ranch of Kingsville, the Aransas Wildlife Refuge (winter home of the whooping crane) and Homeport, Naval Station Ingleside.

Ramada Limited

5501 Interstate 37
Corpus Christi, TX 78408
361-289-5861
ramadasl@caller.infi.net

Type of Lodging: Hotel

Room Rates: $69–$99, including continental breakfast. AAA, AARP, AKC and *10% Pets Welcome™* discounts.

Pet Charges & Deposits: $25 per stay.

Pet Policy: None. All Pets Welcome.

Amenities: Cable TV, safes, pool, whirlpool, fitness room, putting green.

Pet Amenities: List of nearby veterinarians maintained.

Rated: 3 Paws — 155 rooms and 2 suites.

If you and your pet's travel plans take you to Corpus Christi, you are certain to find Ramada Limited the place to stay that will make your trip a memorable one. It is the value choice for the mid-market travelers seeking great service from a pet-friendly staff. The hotel is a short drive to many major attractions, businesses and shopping areas in the area including the U.S.S. Lexington, Texas State Aquarium, Botanical Gardens and Port Aransas.

Days Inn – North Dallas

13313 Stemmons Freeway
Dallas, TX 75234
800 DAYS INN • 922-488-0800
www.daysinn.com

Type of Lodging: Inn

Room Rates: $49–$59, including continental breakfast. AAA, AARP, AKC, ABA and *3% Pets Welcome*™ discounts.

Pet Charges & Deposits: $10 refundable deposit.

Pet Policy: None. All Pets Welcome.

Amenities: Cable TV, refrigerators, safes, pool, whirlpool, Jacuzzi, hairdryers, irons and ironing boards.

Pet Amenities: List of nearby veterinarians maintained. Park nearby.

Rated: 4 Paws — 70 rooms and 4 suites.

Days Inn provides pleasant, comfortable accommodations. Free local calls, guest laundry, remote control cable television and modem lines are convenient amenities. Area attractions that must not be missed include the Galleria Mall with ice skating, Vista Ridge (one of the world's largest malls), Texas Stadium (where you can see the Rangers), Six Flags, the Ballpark in Arlington, Lone Start Park and Wet-N-Wild Water Park. Dallas/Forth Worth International Airport, Addison and Love Field Airports are all minutes away.

Exel Inn of Denton

4211 Interstate 35 East North
Denton, TX 76207
800-367-3935 • 940-383-1471
www.exelinns.com

Type of Lodging: Hotel

Room Rates: $41–$60, including continental breakfast. AARP discount.

Pet Charges & Deposits: $100–$200 refundable deposit on extended stays.

Pet Policy: No pets over 25 lbs. Designated rooms only. Manager's prior approval required. Limit two pets per room.

Amenities: Irons, coffeemakers, full-length mirrors.

Pet Amenities: None.

Rated: 2 Paws — 112 rooms.

Exel Inn is a good choice for travelers who wish to have easy access to Mills Outlet Mall, University of North Texas, Texas Woman's University, Denton Municipal Airport, Golden Triangle Mall, Dallas/Fort Worth International Airport and downtown Denton.

Howard Johnson Inn

8887 Gateway West
El Paso, TX 79925
800-446-4656 • 915-591-9471

Type of Lodging: Inn

Room Rates: $52–$74. AAA, AARP and *10% Pets Welcome™* discounts.

Pet Charges & Deposits: None.

Pet Policy: None. All Pets Welcome.

Amenities: Cable TV, refrigerators, safes, pool, restaurant, free local calls.

Pet Amenities: List of nearby veterinarians maintained. Eastside Corral is located at 8929 Viscount Street.

Rated: 4 Paws — 140 rooms.

The moment you and your pet arrive, the staff at the Howard Johnson will make you feel at home. From the smiles of the hospitality staff to the surprisingly affordable accommodations, your comfort is at the forefront. Guest accommodations include large inviting rooms with the comforts of home such as cable television, recliners, desks, pool, restaurant, guest laundry and a fitness room. When visiting El Paso, you'll find plenty of sunshine, scenic mountains and trolley tours available to Old Mexico. El Paso is also the gateway to Carlsbad Caverns, White Sands National Monument, New Mexico's wine valley, camping, hiking and skiing in the Ruidoso Mountains.

Homestead Village Guest Studios

1601 River Run
Fort Worth, TX 76107
800 STAYHSD • 817-338-4808
www.stayhsd.com
mgrftw@stayhsd.com

Type of Lodging: Hotel

Studio Rates: $56–$76. *20% Pets Welcome™* discount.

Pet Charges & Deposits: $50 nonrefundable deposit.

Pet Policy: None. All Pets Welcome.

Amenities: Cable TV, fully equipped kitchens, safes, voicemail, irons and ironing boards.

Pet Amenities: List of nearby veterinarians maintained. Exercise area. Trinity Park is located at Riverwalk.

Rated: 4 Paws — 97 studios.

Designed especially for extended stay travelers, Homestead Village Guest Studios has attractive studio rooms featuring a fully equipped kitchen. Plus, there's a comfortable workspace. So whether you are traveling on business for a few days or a few weeks, or perhaps relocating to a new area, Homestead offers just what you'll need to settle in comfortably. Nearby attractions include Casa Mañana Theater, Fort Worth Zoo, Kimbell Art Museum, Modern Art Museum and Will Rogers Memorial Center.

La Quinta Inn & Suites

4700 North Freeway
Fort Worth, TX 76137
800-531-5000 • 817-222-2888

Type of Lodging: Inn

Room Rates: $69–$109, including continental breakfast. AAA and AARP discounts.

Pet Charges & Deposits: None.

Pet Policy: None. All Pets Welcome.

Amenities: Cable TV, refrigerators, microwaves, pool, whirlpool, hot tubs.

Pet Amenities: List of nearby veterinarians maintained. Exercise area.

Rated: 4 Paws – 127 rooms and 6 suites.

Fort Worth's La Quinta Inn and Suites is housed in a new design of the La Quinta brand that is definitely worth checking into. Guestrooms feature a fresh décor, floor-length draperies, built-in closet, enhanced bathrooms with ceramic tile floors, designer vanities, cable television, coffeemakers and alarm clock radios. Area attractions include Kimball Art Museum, Six Flags, Texas Motor Speedway, Ballpark in Arlington, Fossil Creek Golf Course, Will Rogers Coliseum, Tarrant County Convention Center and Coors Distributing.

Residence Inn by Marriott

5801 Sandshell Drive
Fort Worth, TX 76131
800-331-3131 • 817-439-1300
www.residenceinn.com/dfwri

Type of Lodging: Hotel

Suite Rates: Call for rates. AAA and AARP discounts.

Pet Charges & Deposits: $75–$100 nonrefundable deposit.

Pet Policy: Manager's prior approval required.

Amenities: Refrigerators, microwaves, pool, Jacuzzi.

Pet Amenities: Pet area.

Rated: 3 Paws – 114 suites.

At Residence Inn by Marriott, combining all the comforts of home with a passion for making every guest feel welcome, has perfected the extended-stay experience. The spacious suites offer separate living and sleeping areas, plenty of space for relaxing, entertaining or meeting with colleagues and a fully equipped kitchen. Start your day with complimentary breakfast in the Gatehouse and join the weekly barbecue—a Residence Inn tradition. There's lots to do and see nearby, including tennis, squash, golfing at Colonial Golf Course or Fossil Creek Golf Course, Fort Worth Zoo, Tarrant County Convention Center, Texas Motor Speedway and Will Rogers Coliseum.

Days Inn of Granbury

1339 North Plaza Drive
Granbury, TX 76048
800-858-8607 • 817-573-2691
www.daysinn.com

Type of Lodging: motel

Room Rates: $59–$89, including continental breakfast. AAA, AARP and *10% Pets Welcome*™ discounts.

Pet Charges & Deposits: $20 per stay.

Pet Policy: Manager's prior approval required.

Amenities: Cable TV, refrigerators, microwaves, pool.

Pet Amenities: None.

Rated: 3 Paws — 60 rooms and 17 suites.

Days Inn's staff is dedicated to ensuring a comfortable, enjoyable stay for each of their guests. Each guestroom offers individual climate controls, remote control cable television, alarm clock radio and telephones. This is a great nearby retreat for a day, a weekend or longer—located only 35 miles southwest of Fort Worth.

Comfort Suites

6221 Richmond Avenue
Houston, TX 77057
719-787-0004

Type of Lodging: Hotel

Suite Rates: $98–$185, including continental breakfast. AAA, AARP and *10% Pets Welcome*™ discounts.

Pet Charges & Deposits: $25 per stay.

Pet Policy: No pets over 30 lbs. Designated rooms only.

Amenities: Cable TV, refrigerators, microwaves, pool, hot tubs.

Pet Amenities: Briar Grove Park is located on Richmond Avenue.

Rated: 3 Paws — 62 suites.

Located in Houston's premier shopping, entertainment and business district, the Comfort Suites caters to all your creature comforts. Suites have coffeemakers, refrigerators, microwaves, modem lines, large desk, three phones, sitting area, cable television, alarm clock radio and spacious bathrooms with a phone and hairdryer. A business center, fitness center, outdoor pool and Jacuzzi, guest laundry and deluxe continental breakfast make you and your pet's stay an overall great experience. The Galleria, Sharpstown Mall, NASA Space Center, Astro World and Astro Dome are all within 25 miles.

La Quinta Inn & Suites – Houston Galleria

1625 West Loop South
Houston, TX 77027
800 NU ROOMS • 713-355-3440
www.laquinta.com
lq0963dos1@laquinta.com

Type of Lodging: Inn & Suites
Room Rates: $99–$135, including continental breakfast. AAA discount.
Pet Charges & Deposits: None.
Pet Policy: No pets over 20 lbs.
Amenities: Cable TV, refrigerators, microwaves, safes, pool, Jacuzzi, coffeemakers, hairdryers, irons and ironing boards.
Pet Amenities: List of nearby veterinarians maintained. Exercise area. Memorial Park nearby.
Rated: 4 Paws — 156 rooms and 17 suites.

The all-new La Quinta Inn & Suites is definitely a great place for you and your pet to stay. It features distinctively quiet guestrooms with rich wood furniture, enhanced lighting, dataport phones and spacious bathrooms. All rooms have cable television plus an in-room entertainment system featuring first-run movies and video games. The deluxe two-room suites include separate sitting and sleeping areas with double vanities, a sleeper sofa, two closets, ergonomic work space, swivel tilt chair, oversized desk, speaker phone and more. You are minutes away from Astroworld, Arboretum and Nature Center, Bayou City Place and Memorial Park, as well as many museums, theatres and universities.

Residence Inn by Marriott

525 Bay Area Boulevard
Houston, TX 77058
800-331-3131 • 281-486-2424
www.residenceinn.com/houcl

Type of Lodging: Hotel
Suite Rates: $119–$145, including continental breakfast and social hour. AAA and AARP discounts.
Pet Charges & Deposits: $6 per day. $50 nonrefundable deposit.
Pet Policy: None. All Pets Welcome.
Amenities: Cable TV, refrigerators, microwaves, pool, Jacuzzi, SportCourt®, fitness room.
Pet Amenities: List of nearby veterinarians maintained. Dog runs. Exercise area. Challenger Memorial Park and Watter Hall County Park nearby.
Rated: 4 Paws — 110 suites.

The Residence Inn by Marriott is an all-suite hotel, featuring studio and two-bedroom suites, living rooms and fully equipped kitchens. Complimentary breakfast is served daily and there is a social hour every weeknight. There is a heated pool, hot tub, SportCourt® and fitness room. Local attractions and landmarks include Armand Bayou Nature Center, Astrodome, Astroworld, Baybrook Mall, San Jacinto Monument, Space Center, Texas Ice Stadium and Gulf Greyhound Park.

Residence Inn by Marriott – Astrodome

7710 Main Street
Houston, TX 77030
800-331-3131 • 713-660-7993
www.residenceinnhouston.com
dosresidence@pchmanagement.com

Type of Lodging: Hotel

Suite Rates: Call for rates.
Complimentary weekday happy hour.
AAA and AARP discounts.

Pet Charges & Deposits: $5 per day.
$50 nonrefundable deposit.

Pet Policy: No pets over 35 lbs.

Amenities: Cable TV, fully equipped
kitchens, pool, Jacuzzi.

Pet Amenities: Dog runs. Exercise area.
Park nearby.

Rated: 3 Paws – 285 suites.

Whether you and your pet are visiting Houston on business or vacation, Residence Inn Astrodome is a splendid hotel choice for you. The large accommodations include fully equipped kitchens with full-sized appliances. Most suites even have fireplaces. Centrally located, Residence Inn by Marriott Houston is just minutes from Texas Medical Center, Astroworld, Astrodome and downtown Houston.

Comfort Inn DFW Airport

8205 Esters Boulevard
Irving, TX 75063
972-929-0066
comfdfw@texas.net

Type of Lodging: Hotel

Room Rates: $60–$80, including
continental breakfast. AAA, AARP and
10% Pets Welcome™ discounts.

Pet Charges & Deposits: $10 per day.
$25 nonrefundable deposit.

Pet Policy: No pets over 20 lbs.

Amenities: Cable TV, refrigerators,
microwaves, safes, pool, whirlpool, hot
tubs, spa.

Pet Amenities: Exercise area.
Grapevine Park nearby.

Rated: 3 Paws – 146 rooms.

Slick, comfortable, spotless and moderately priced, Irving's Comfort Inn is a wonderful choice when you're in the area. There are many attractions within a 30-mile radius, including Galleria Mall, JFK Memorial Plaza, Ranger Stadium, Hurricane Harbor, Six Flags, Baylor Medical Center, and many business headquarters including Mary Kay Cosmetics and Xerox.

Super 8 Motel

401 West Interstate 30, Exit 146
Mount Vernon, TX 75457
903-588-2882

Type of Lodging: Motel
Room Rates: $44–$54, including continental breakfast. AAA, AARP and *10% Pets Welcome*™ discounts.
Pet Charges & Deposits: $5 per stay.
Pet Policy: None. All Pets Welcome.
Amenities: Cable TV, refrigerators, microwaves.
Pet Amenities: Dog runs. Exercise area.
Rated: 3 Paws — 44 rooms.

The Mount Vernon Super 8 Motel was built in 1996 and still maintains its sparkle. The guestrooms have telephones with modem jacks, cable television, recliners and desks. Nearby you will find Lake Cypress, Lake Monticello, Lake Bob Sandlin and Lake Fork. It is a great base for those traveling to Bogata, Como, Deport, Omaha, Rocky Mound, Talco, Winfield, Winnsboro, Sulpiler Springs and Mount Pleasant

Days Inn

3075 East Highway 80
Odessa, TX 79761
800-325-2525 • 915-335-8000

Type of Lodging: Hotel
Room Rates: $46–$54, including continental breakfast. AAA, AARP and *10% Pets Welcome*™ discounts.
Pet Charges & Deposits: None.
Pet Policy: None. All Pets Welcome.
Amenities: Cable TV, refrigerators, microwaves, pool, hairdryers, irons and ironing boards, lounge.
Pet Amenities: None.
Rated: 3 Paws — 95 rooms and 1 suite.

For today's traveler, the Odessa Days Inn is a rare find. With rates well below comparable hotels, it offers more extras, more value and more to write home about. The guestrooms offer attractive baths with thick towels, cable television, free local calls and continental breakfast. Days Inn features a covered entrance, clean lobby, an outdoor swimming pool and sun deck. Just minutes away from fine dining, shopping, golfing, museums, theaters, a symphony orchestra and plenty of sunshine to enjoy them all. Odessa is an oil town, conference and distribution center, as well as home of Odessa College and a University of Texas campus.

Southwind Inn

600 Davis Street
Port Isabel, TX 78578
956-943-3392
southwindinn@prodigy.net

Type of Lodging: Motel

Room Rates: $30–$120.

Pet Charges & Deposits: $5 per stay.

Pet Policy: Sorry, no cats. Small pets only. Designated rooms only. Manager's prior approval required.

Amenities: Cable TV, refrigerators, pool.

Pet Amenities: List of nearby veterinarians maintained. Exercise area.

Rated: 2 Paws — 17 rooms.

The Southwind Inn is located in scenic Port Isabel, two miles from the Gulf of Mexico and one block from Laguna Madre. You and your pet are within walking distance of restaurants and a fishing pier. The rooms are furnished with cable television, telephones, individual climate controls, refrigerators and coffeemakers. The motel offers beautiful views of Laguna Madre, South Padre Island, the Queen Isabella Causeway and the Port Isabel Lighthouse.

Residence Inn by Marriott

1040 Waterwood
Richardson, TX 75082
800-331-3131 • 972-669-5888
www.residenceinn.com/dalrh
ri.dalrh.dos@Marriott.com

Type of Lodging: Hotel

Suite Rates: $69–$139, including full breakfast.

Pet Charges & Deposits: $8 per day.

Pet Policy: None. All Pets Welcome.

Amenities: Cable TV, fully equipped kitchens, safes, pool, whirlpool.

Pet Amenities: List of nearby veterinarians maintained. Exercise area. Park is located at Plano Road and Lookout Drive.

Rated: 3 Paws — 120 suites.

Residence Inn by Marriott combines all the comforts of home with a passion for making every guest feel welcome. It's a perfect extended-stay experience. The suites offer separate living and sleeping areas, plenty of space for relaxing, entertaining or meeting with colleagues, and a fully equipped kitchen with refrigerator, microwave and coffeemaker. Start your day with complimentary breakfast in the Gatehouse and join the weekly barbecue—a Residence Inn tradition. There's lots to do and see nearby, including Collin Creek Mall, Galleria, Northpark Mall, Owens Farm, Southfork, University of Texas campus, as well as tennis and golfing.

Laguna Reef Hotel

1021 Water Street
Rockport, TX 78382
800-248-1057 • 361-729-1742
www.lagunareef.com
laguna@dbstech.com

Type of Lodging: Hotel

Room Rates: $70–$250, including continental breakfast. AAA, AARP, Corporate, Military and *10% Pets Welcome*™ discounts.

Pet Charges & Deposits: $5 per day. $40 refundable deposit.

Pet Policy: No pets over 20 lbs.

Amenities: Pool, picnic area.

Pet Amenities: List of nearby veterinarians maintained.

Rated: 3 Paws — 21 rooms and 50 suites.

Whether you stay for a weekend of fishing or a winter of content, Laguna Reef Hotel offers the beauty of the coast and the comforts of home with a flexibility of accommodations. Located on the major migration path traveled by hundreds of species of birds, Rockport is visited by hummingbirds, herons, cardinals and cranes. First-class fishing starts right outside your door with trout, redfish, flounder and deep-sea tournament action. You can see whooping cranes, native javelina, deer and alligators north of Rockport at the Aransas Wildlife Refuge.

Purple Sage Motel

1501 East Coliseum Drive
Snyder, TX 79549
800-545-5792 • 915-573-5491
www.placestostay.com
psmotel@snydertex.com

Type of Lodging: Motel

Room Rates: $43–$63, including breakfast buffet. AAA, AARP and *10% Pets Welcome*™ discounts.

Pet Charges & Deposits: Credit card imprint required as deposit.

Pet Policy: None. All Pets Welcome.

Amenities: Cable TV, refrigerators, microwaves, pool, coffeemakers.

Pet Amenities: List of nearby veterinarians maintained.

Rated: 3 Paws — 45 rooms.

The Purple Sage Motel is a one-story motel with two wings, one either side of the outdoor pool. A large Mulberry shade tree and glider separate the front area from the three wings of rooms in the back section. The guestrooms offer individual climate controls, direct dial phone, hairdryer, microwave, television and refrigerator.

Devil's River Days Inn

1312 North Service Road
Sonora, TX 76950
800-329-7466 • 915-387-3516

Type of Lodging: Motel

Room Rates: $40–$65, including continental breakfast. AAA, AARP and *10% Pets Welcome*™ discounts.

Pet Charges & Deposits: $2 per day.

Pet Policy: None. All Pets Welcome.

Amenities: Cable TV, refrigerators, microwaves, pool.

Pet Amenities: List of nearby veterinarians maintained.

Rated: 3 Paws — 99 rooms.

Days Inn provides pleasant accommodations. Free local calls, guest laundry, cable television and continental breakfast are convenient amenities. Sonora is perched on the western slope of the Edwards Plateau, in an area once occupied only by Apache Indians. The town that touts itself as "The Real West" began as a trading post and stagecoach stopover between San Antonio and El Paso. Nearby activities include golfing and tennis.

La Piedra Inn

309 Interstate 20 East
Terrell, TX 75160
800-289-3323 • 972-563-2676

Type of Lodging: Motel

Room Rates: $40–$55, including continental breakfast. AAA, AARP, AKC, ABA and *10% Pets Welcome*™ discounts.

Pet Charges & Deposits: $5 per stay.

Pet Policy: No pets over 25 lbs.

Amenities: Cable TV, refrigerators, microwaves, pool.

Pet Amenities: List of nearby veterinarians maintained. Exercise area. Tawkiki National Park nearby.

Rated: 3 Paws — 60 rooms.

Nestled in the country, between the edge of East Texas and Dallas, you will find the La Piedra Inn able to meet your needs, whether you're a business or pleasure traveler. Local attractions include Terrell Carnegie Library Museum, Silent Wings Museum and Southwestern Christian College.

Best Western Inn of Van Horn

1705 West Broadway
P.O. Box 309
Van Horn, TX 79855
www.bestwestern.com

Type of Lodging: Motel

Room Rates: $45–$65, including continental breakfast. AAA, AARP, AKC, ABA, Government and *10% Pets Welcome™* discounts.

Pet Charges & Deposits: None.

Pet Policy: None. All Pets Welcome.

Amenities: Cable TV, refrigerators, microwaves, pool, coffeemakers.

Pet Amenities: Dog runs. Exercise area. Park is located across the street from the motel.

Rated: 4 Paws — 60 rooms.

Just a few hours from Carlsbad Caverns, the Guadeloupe Mountains, Big Bend National Park and Fort Davis Historical Park, you'll find the Best Western Inn of Van Horn. The ground-level rooms feature king- and queen-sized beds, cable television and a free continental breakfast. They are West Texas proud and West Texas friendly!

Best Western Village Inn

1618 Expressway
Vernon, TX 76384
800-600-5417 • 940-552-5417
www.bestwestern.com/villageinnvernon

Type of Lodging: Inn

Room Rates: $54–$59. AAA, AARP and *10% Pets Welcome™* discounts.

Pet Charges & Deposits: $5 per day.

Pet Policy: No pets over 10 lbs.

Amenities: Cable TV, pool, restaurant, lounge.

Pet Amenities: List of nearby veterinarians maintained. Exercise area.

Rated: 3 Paws — 46 rooms.

The Best Western Village Inn is located a short drive from Vernon State Hospital, Texas A&M Research Station, Doan's Crossing, Waggoner Ranch and Lake Kemp.

Best Western Palm Aire

415 South International Boulevard
Weslaco, Texas 78596
800-248-6511 • 956-969-2411

Type of Lodging: Hotel

Room Rates: $51–$109. AAA, AARP and *10% Pets Welcome*™ discounts.

Pet Charges & Deposits: None.

Pet Policy: No pets over 30 lbs.

Amenities: Cable TV, refrigerators, microwaves, pool, whirlpool, Jacuzzi, hot tubs, spas, indoor racquetball courts, tennis, fitness room, restaurant, lounge.

Pet Amenities: List of nearby veterinarians maintained. Exercise area. Harlon Block Park is located at 1200 East Sixth Street. Weslaco City Park is located at 300 North Airport Road. Gibson Park is located at 301 South Border.

Rated: 3 Paws — 193 rooms and 60 suites.

Located in the heart of the semi-tropical Rio Grande Valley, Best Western Palm Aire is just minutes away from all major Valley cities and three convenient airports, including the 5,000-feet airstrip in Weslaco. The warm accommodations and facilities include restaurant, lounge, health club and meeting facilities. Guests are ten minutes from both shopping in Mexico and a natural wildlife bird sanctuary. South Padre Island Beach is within a 45-minute drive.

Toenail Moon Retreat

3200 F.M. 3237
Wimberley, TX 78676
877-327-9138 • 512-328-6887
www.toenailmoon.homestead.com

Type of Lodging: B&B/Guest Ranch

Room Rates: $75–$200, including Hill Country casual breakfast.

Pet Charges & Deposits: $15 per day.

Pet Policy: Manager's prior approval required. Horses welcome.

Amenities: Satellite TV, fully equipped kitchen, private swimming hole, paddleboats, fishing dock, petting zoo.

Pet Amenities: List of nearby veterinarians maintained. Exercise area including 10 fenced acres.

Rated: 4 Paws — 3 suites.

Located in the gorgeous Hill Country of Texas, three miles from shopping in the Village square, you'll find the Toenail Moon Retreat. This ranch-style cedar home with a stone porch is very romantic. You are pretty much on your own once you get there—complete privacy. There are tons of activities, including horseback riding, numerous rivers and creeks to explore, wineries to sample and all this only 35 minutes from Austin and 70 minutes from San Antonio. If a relaxed, laid-back vacation is what you crave, Toenail Moon Retreat is your destination.

Best Western Inn by the Lake

Star Route 1, Box 252
Zapata, TX 78076
800-399-1558 • 956-765-8403

Type of Lodging: Motel

Room Rates: $50–$70, including continental breakfast. AAA, AARP and *10% Pets Welcome™* discounts.

Pet Charges & Deposits: $20 refundable deposit.

Pet Policy: Designated rooms only.

Amenities: Cable TV, refrigerators, microwaves, pool, picnic area, guest laundry facilities.

Pet Amenities: List of nearby veterinarians maintained. Exercise area. Romeo Flores Park nearby.

Rated: 3 Paws — 57 rooms.

The Best Western Inn by the Lake is located adjacent to Falcon Lake on the Rio Grande River and is only 45 minutes from the bridge to Mexico. Offering many activities, including fishing and bird watching, this is a great base for those wishing to visit San Ygnacio. Laredo International Airport is 50 miles away.

UTAH

Nickname: Beehive State

Population: 2,129,836

Area: 84,904 square miles

Climate: arid, ranging from warm desert in the southwest to alpine in the northeast.

Capital: Salt Lake City

Entered Union: Jan. 4, 1896

Motto: Industry.

Song: Utah, We Love Thee

Flower: Sego Lily

Tree: Blue Spruce

Bird: Seagull

Famous Utahans: Maude Adams, Ezra Taft Benson, J. Willard Marriott, Merlin Olsen, the Osmond family, Ivy Baker Priest, George Romney, Brigham Young, Loretta Young.

History: Ute, Gosiute, Southern Paiute and Navajo peoples occupied the area at the time of European contact. Mormons arrived and settled the land in 1847, creating a prosperous economy and, to this day, they strongly predominate in the state. The State of Deseret was organized in 1849 and requested admission to the Union in 1850. Congress established the region as a Territory and Brigham Young was appointed governor. The Union Pacific and Central Pacific Railroads met near Promontory Point on May 10, 1869, creating the first transcontinental railroad. Statehood was not achieved until 1896, after the Mormon Church discontinued its practice of polygamy.

Best Western Butch Cassidy Inn

161 South Main
Beaver, UT 84713
800 WESTERN • 435-438-2438
www.bestwestern.com/butchcassidyinn

Type of Lodging: Motel

Room Rates: $39–$89. AAA and AARP discounts.

Pet Charges & Deposits: None.

Pet Policy: Small pets only. Manager's prior approval required. Pets must not be left unattended.

Amenities: Cable TV, Jacuzzi, spas.

Pet Amenities: List of nearby veterinarians maintained. Exercise area. Park nearby.

Rated: 3 Paws — 21 rooms and 3 suites.

Enjoy beautiful rooms with an at-home feeling when you visit the Best Western Butch Cassidy Inn, conveniently located off Interstate 15. Just minutes away from Elk Meadows Ski Area, golfing and fishing, you can fill your day with outdoor activities. Or, if you like to spend the day enjoying the scenery, drive to Bryce Canyon National Park or the Cove Fort Museum. At the Best Western Butch Cassidy Inn, attractive rooms and pet-friendly, professional service will help you and your pet feel at home.

Aquarius Inn

290 West Main Street
P.O. Box 304
Bicknell, UT 84715
800-833-5379 • 435-425-3835
www.aquariusinn.com

Type of Lodging: Motel

Room Rates: $30–$45.

Pet Charges & Deposits: $5 per day. $25 refundable deposit.

Pet Policy: None. All Pets Welcome.

Amenities: Cable TV.

Pet Amenities: List of nearby veterinarians maintained. Exercise area. Capital Reef National Park is located 13 miles from the motel.

Rated: 3 Paws — 26 rooms.

Aquarius Inn boasts large rooms at an affordable price—a luxurious setting without a high price. The on-premises family recreational facilities include basketball, volleyball, horseshoe pits and playground. Nature buffs will enjoy Capital Reef National Park, located just 13 miles away. It is not uncommon to see nature at its best, with antelope, deer, elk, moose, wild turkeys, bald and golden eagles and buffalo from the last free roaming herd. Learn about the Indians who left the petroglyphs (ancient Indian writings) and how Butch Cassidy and the Wild Bunch were able to elude the lawmen in this magnificent country.

Kokopelli Inn

Highway 91
P.O. Box 27
Bluff, UT 84512
800-541-8854 • 435-672-2322
www.kokoinn.com

Type of Lodging: Motel

Room Rates: $50–$60, including free coffee, tea and hot chocolate. AAA and AARP discounts.

Pet Charges & Deposits: $10 per day.

Pet Policy: None. All Pets Welcome.

Amenities: Cable TV.

Pet Amenities: Exercise area. Hovenweep National Park is 35 miles from the motel. Canyonlands National Park is located 84 miles from the motel.

Rated: 3 Paws – 26 rooms.

The community of Bluff is tiny but full of life. Located 50 miles north of Monument Valley, in the heart of Utah's Canyon Country, the Kokopelli Inn makes an ideal home base for visiting Mesa Verde, Canyonlands National Park, Valley of the Gods, Monument Valley and Lake Powell. The Inn is situated in a complex that includes a convenience store (K&C Trading Post) and a small RV park. At K&C, you will find gas, groceries, a deli, general merchandise and a fine selection of handmade Indian arts and crafts. Modestly priced, the Kokopelli Inn is located off the beaten track, in the middle of nowhere, where the proprietors are known for their warmth and hospitality.

Boulder Mountain Lodge

20 North Highway 12
Boulder, UT 84716
800-556-3446 • 435-335-7460
www.boulder-utah.com
bmlut@color-country.net

Type of Lodging: Motor Lodge

Room Rates: $59–$149.

Pet Charges & Deposits: $9 per day.

Pet Policy: Designated rooms only. Pets are not allowed upstairs.

Amenities: Cable TV, refrigerators, microwaves.

Pet Amenities: List of nearby veterinarians maintained. Exercise area. Park nearby.

Rated: 3 Paws – 18 rooms and 2 suites.

Boulder Mountain Lodge is an oasis of calm luxury in the middle of Utah's widest, most remote sandstone canyon country. The tiny town of Boulder was the last community in America to receive its mail by mule train, and today still feels remote and undiscovered. Above the Lodge, Boulder Mountain and the Aquarius Plateau rise like an alpine island of lakes, aspens and evergreens over a sea of sandstone canyons. This intimate complex of detached buildings is grouped around an 11-acre lake, the Lodge's own bird sanctuary. The architecture is Western eclectic at its best: reddish stucco, rose sandstone blocks, massive timbers and pitched, rusted metal roofs. The rooms and suites are furnished with understated elegance, traditional quilts and craftsman-quality wooden furniture, against a restful backdrop of white plaster and exposed beams.

Rainbow Country Bed and Breakfast

586 East 300 South
P.O. Box 333
Escalante, UT 84726
800-252 UTAH • 435-826-4567
www.color-country.net/~rainbow/
rainbow@color-country.net

Type of Lodging: B&B

Room Rates: $55–$65, including full breakfast. AAA discount.

Pet Charges & Deposits: None.

Pet Policy: None. All Pets Welcome.

Amenities: Cable TV, microwaves, hot tub, pool table.

Pet Amenities: Exercise area. Several National Parks nearby.

Rated: 4 Paws — 4 rooms and 2 suites.

A visit to Escalante will offer you an opportunity to experience the stunning beauty of its narrow canyons, slick rock hills and towering sandstone formations. Here you can explore ancient petrified forests and marvel at prehistoric Indian rock art. Dixie National Forest is a stunning area; it has numerous lakes with great fishing. While at Escalante's first bed and breakfast, you can combine touring and relaxing in the Grand Staircase-Escalante National Monument. You will enjoy hearty food, a hot tub and the wrap-around sun deck, with sweeping vistas of the surrounding mountains and desert.

Big Horn Lodge

550 South Main
Moab, UT 84532
800-325-6171 • 435-259-6171
www.moabbighorn.com
office@moabbighorn.com

Type of Lodging: Motel

Room Rates: $40–$80. AAA, AARP and *10% Pets Welcome*™ discounts.

Pet Charges & Deposits: $5 per day.

Pet Policy: Designated rooms only.

Amenities: Cable TV, refrigerators, pool, coffeemakers, guest laundry, restaurant.

Pet Amenities: List of nearby veterinarians maintained. Arches National Park, Dead Horse Point State Park and Canyonlands National Park nearby.

Rated: 3 Paws — 58 rooms.

Located in the heart of Canyonlands and just five miles from Arches National Park is one of Moab's finest lodging accommodations, the Big Horn Lodge. Dead Horse State Park and Canyonlands National Park, with its "Island in the Sky" viewpoints, are minutes away. Moab is home to the famous Slickrock Bike Trail, and the Big Horn Lodge allows you to keep your mountain bikes in your room. The inn specializes in package deals, including whitewater rafting on the Colorado River, four-wheel drive jeeping on Poison Spider Mesa or the Moab Rim Trail, or exploring hundreds of other trails throughout Utah. Whether horseback riding, rock climbing, hiking, mountain biking, 4×4 jeeping, four wheeling, rafting, swimming or sightseeing, Moab is the place to play.

Entrada Ranch

P.O. Box 567
Moab, UT 84532
435-257-5796
www.entrada-ranch.com
entrada@lasal.net

Type of Lodging: Guest Ranch & Wilderness Lodge

House Rates: $65–$145.

Pet Charges & Deposits: $20 per stay.

Pet Policy: None. All Pets Welcome. Horses welcome.

Amenities: Refrigerators, microwaves, BBQ, horseshoe pits.

Pet Amenities: List of nearby veterinarians maintained. Exercise area. Pet sitters available with notice. Arches National Park is 40 miles from the ranch. Canyonlands National Park is 50 miles from the ranch.

Rated: 5 Paws — 3 houses and 2 cabins on 400 acres.

This 400-acre ranch is set along the picturesque Dolores River, in a wild, remote, slickrock location with three miles of private river beaches, a world-class swimming hole and private redrock canyons. But Entrada is not for everyone. This is a wilderness guest ranch, not a dude ranch—40 miles from town, way back in the canyons on a pretty rough nine-mile dirt road. Your pet will love it here—dogs have lots of room to run and a river to jump in, making it the perfect dog vacation. Guest accommodations range from the Deck House, with its four-poster bed, fireplace, wood stove and washer and dryer, to El Shack Cabin, with its outdoor hot shower and "historic" outhouse. The Kokopelli Trail, a world-renowned mountain bike trail that runs from Grand Junction, Colorado, to Moab, Utah, passes within three miles of Entrada Ranch. It is among the dozens of great mountain-bike trails located within a short distance of the ranch.

Red Stone Inn

535 South Main
Moab, UT 84532
800-772-1972 • 435-259-3500
www.moabredstone.com
office@moabredstone.com

Type of Lodging: Motel
Room Rates: $60–$70, including coffee. AAA, AARP, AKC, ABA and *Pets Welcome*™ discounts.
Pet Charges & Deposits: $5 per day.
Pet Policy: Designated rooms only.
Amenities: Cable TV, kitchenettes, guest laundry, BBQ area.
Pet Amenities: List of nearby veterinarians maintained. Arches National Park and Canyonlands National Park nearby.
Rated: 3 Paws — 52 rooms.

Red Stone Inn provides guestrooms with kitchenettes and cable television. There is an area behind the building to walk and exercise your pet. Moab is home to the famous Slickrock Bike Trail and the Red Stone Inn allows you to keep your mountain bikes in your room. Explore world-famous Arches National Park, only three miles from Moab, as well as nearby Canyonlands National Park, Fisher Towers rock formation, the scenic Colorado River canyon along Highway 128, and so much more. Moab is the hub for endless opportunities for hiking, mountain biking, four-wheeling, rafting, swimming or sightseeing in redrock country.

Ben Lomond Historic Suite Hotel

2510 Washington Boulevard
Ogden, UT 84401
888-627-8897 • 801-627-1900
www.benlomondhotel.com

Type of Lodging: Hotel
Suite Rates: $119–$229, including full breakfast and full breakfast buffet. AAA, AARP and *25% Pets Welcome*™ discounts.
Pet Charges & Deposits: $50 refundable deposit.
Pet Policy: None. All Pets Welcome.
Amenities: Cable TV, refrigerators, microwaves.
Pet Amenities: Treats available. List of nearby veterinarians maintained. Ogden Municipal Gardens is directly across the street from the hotel.
Rated: 4 Paws — 122 suites. Listed on both the State and National Register of Historic Places.

Built in the year 1927 and a legacy from the gracious age of Grand Hotels, the Ben Lomond Historic Suite Hotel, with its "exuberant and voluptuously eclectic interiors," features charm, nostalgia, comfort and beauty. Every newly furnished suite has a separate living room and sleeping room with a king- or queen-sized bed. For added comfort, all suites come equipped with a wet bar/refrigerator, coffeemaker, hairdryer, iron and ironing board, two cable televisions, large desk, two phones with dataports, alarm clock radio and exquisite views of Ogden's scenery.

Radisson Resort Park City

2121 Park Avenue
P.O. Box 1778
Park City, UT 84060
435-649-5000
www.radissoninn-parkcity.com

Type of Lodging: B&B

Room Rates: $89–$209. AAA and AARP discounts.

Pet Charges & Deposits: $15 per day.

Pet Policy: None. All Pets Welcome.

Amenities: Cable TV, pool, hot tub.

Pet Amenities: Exercise area.

Rated: 3 Paws — 131 rooms and 6 suites.

Radisson Resort Park City offers a spectacular Rocky Mountain setting within minutes of year-round outdoor activities. It is within three miles of three world-class Ski Resorts and 1½ miles from Park City's historic Main Street. Enjoy skiing, snowmobiling, sleigh rides, mountain biking, hiking, hot air balloon rides, horseback riding and golfing. The complimentary Park City Shuttle stops at the front door and takes you to the ski resorts as well as historic Main Street. After an invigorating day in the mountains, relax in one of Radisson Resort Park City's guestrooms. Each room comes with a hairdryer, coffeemaker, iron and ironing board, mini bar, dataport telephone, work desk, individual climate controls and cable television.

Homestead Village Guest Studios

975 East 6600 South
Salt Lake City, UT 84121
800 STAY HSD • 801-685-2102
www.stayhsd.com

Type of Lodging: Extended Stay Hotel

Studio Rates: $50–$70.

Pet Charges & Deposits: $15 per day or $150 deposit for extended stays of which $75 is refundable.

Pet Policy: None. All Pets Welcome.

Amenities: Cable TV, fully equipped kitchens.

Pet Amenities: Wheeler Historic Farm is located at 900 East 6500 South.

Rated: 3 Paws — 129 studios.

The Homestead Village Guest Studios are designed specifically for extended stay travelers. Each studio features a fully equipped kitchen, a workspace with computer dataport, free local phone calls and personalized voicemail—all at surprisingly affordable rates. Nearby attractions include Cottonwood Mall, Delta Center/Salt Palace, Fashion Place Mall, Hogie Zoo, Mormon (LDS) Temple and many ski areas.

Hotel Monaco

15 West 200 South
Salt Lake City, UT 84101
877-294-9710 • 801-595-0000
www.monaco-saltlakecity.com
slcmonaco1@aol.com

Type of Lodging: Hotel

Room Rates: $79–$199. AAA, AARP, AKC, ABA and *Pets Welcome*™ discounts.

Pet Charges & Deposits: None.

Pet Policy: None. All Pets Welcome.

Amenities: Cable TV, refrigerators, honor bar, CD stereos, fax machines, hairdryers, robes, ironing centers, fitness room.

Pet Amenities: Live goldfish upon request. Toys, treats, food & water bowls available. List of nearby veterinarians maintained. Pioneer Park is located at 3rd West 4th South.

Rated: 5 Paws — 225 rooms and 32 suites.

With its early Deco, French-inspired architecture and sensually rich décor, the Hotel Monaco is very clear in its intentions towards you and your pet: "come in and welcome." But in case you can't bring your pet, this extremely pet-friendly property offers travelers a temporary pet—a complimentary goldfish. A companion goldfish may be requested when making a reservation or at check-in and is delivered to the guests' room for their stay. The trained hotel staff administers goldfish care and feeding. Located in the heart of downtown Salt Lake, Hotel Monaco is within easy walking distance to Salt Palace Convention Center, Capitol Theatre, Abravanel Hall, Salt Lake Art Center, Delta Center and Temple Square.

Quality Inn City Center

154 West 600 South
Salt Lake City, UT 84101
800-521-9997 • 801-521-2930
qicc@utah.com

Type of Lodging: Hotel
Room Rates: $49–$79. AAA and *15% Pets Welcome™* discounts.
Pet Charges & Deposits: None.
Pet Policy: Designated rooms only.
Amenities: Cable TV, refrigerators, safe, pool, Jacuzzi, hot tub, restaurant, lounge.
Pet Amenities: List of nearby veterinarians maintained. Exercise area. Pioneer Park is located at 3rd West 4th South.
Rated: 3 Paws — 311 rooms and 22 suites on 6 acres.

The Quality Inn City Center is ideally located in the heart of downtown Salt Lake City. Within walking distance are the Delta Center, Salt Palace Convention Center, Symphony Hall and historic Temple Square. Two major shopping malls, dozens of restaurants and clubs and numerous other attractions are also close by. The Quality Inn City Center offers many benefits inside its lovely six-acre garden complex, surrounding its guestrooms and suites. Guests may choose to dine in at The Pines restaurant or relax in the Cantina Lounge.

Quality Inn Midvalley

4465 South Century Drive
Salt Lake City, UT 84123
800-268-5801 • 801-268-2533
www.sunbursthospitality.com

Type of Lodging: Hotel
Room Rates: $70–$100, including continental breakfast. AAA, AARP and *20% Pets Welcome™* discounts.
Pet Charges & Deposits: $5 per day. $25 nonrefundable deposit.
Pet Policy: Designated rooms only.
Amenities: Cable TV, pool, guest laundry, irons and ironing boards, coffeemakers.
Pet Amenities: List of nearby veterinarians maintained. Exercise area. Murray Park is located on State Street 5150 South.
Rated: 3 Paws — 131 rooms and 9 suites.

Quality Inn Midvalley offers a complete menu of amenities and features at rates you and your pet will find surprisingly affordable. Whether business, pleasure or both, guests have immediate freeway access to downtown Salt Lake City and historic Temple Square, area ski resorts and all points along the metropolitan Wasatch Front from Ogden to Provo. Quality Inn serves as a hub for excursions to Utah's all-year recreation spots including Snowbird and Park City, world-famous national parks, the Great Salt Lake, high mountain fishing and backpacking adventures throughout the state.

Green Valley Spa

1871 West Canyon View Drive
St. George, UT 84770
800-237-1068 • 435-628-8060
www.greenvalleyspa.com

Type of Lodging: Resort
Room Rates: $2,800–$3,700 per week, including breakfast, lunch and dinner. Call for daily rates.
Pet Charges & Deposits: $25 per day. $500 refundable deposit.
Pet Policy: No pets over 25 lbs.
Amenities: Cable TV, refrigerators, microwaves, safe, pool, whirlpool, hot tubs, full service spa.
Pet Amenities: List of nearby veterinarians maintained. Zion National Park and Snow Canyon State Park nearby.
Rated: 3 Paws — 35 rooms and 10 suites.

The Green Valley Spa is located in the painted scenery of St. George in southern Utah, just minutes from Snow Canyon, Zion National Park and Mesquite, Nevada. Everything is included in the weekly rates, including a deluxe room, eight body treatments, all taxes and gratuities, breakfast, lunch, dinner, golf instruction, tennis instruction, guided hikes, aerobic classes and use of all resort amenities. Southern Utah offers some of the most diverse activities in the southwest. Guests may enjoy great hiking, mountain biking, golfing, rock climbing, boating, horseback riding, water and snow skiing, several national parks, dinosaur reserves, fine dining, shopping and gambling.

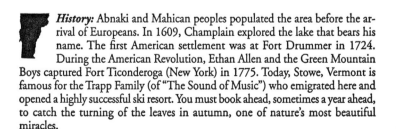

VERMONT

Nickname: Green Mountain State
Population: 593,740
Area: 9,615 square miles
Climate: Temperate, with considerable temperature extremes, heavy snowfall in mountains.
Capital: Montpelier
Entered Union: March 4, 1791
Motto: Freedom and Unity.
Song: These Green Mountains

Flower: Red Clover
Tree: Sugar Maple
Bird: Hermit Thrush
Famous Vermonters: Ethan Allen, Chester A. Arthur, Calvin Coolidge, George Dewey, John Dewey, Stephen A. Douglas, Dorothy Canfield Fisher, James Fisk.

History: Abnaki and Mahican peoples populated the area before the arrival of Europeans. In 1609, Champlain explored the lake that bears his name. The first American settlement was at Fort Drummer in 1724. During the American Revolution, Ethan Allen and the Green Mountain Boys captured Fort Ticonderoga (New York) in 1775. Today, Stowe, Vermont is famous for the Trapp Family (of "The Sound of Music") who emigrated here and opened a highly successful ski resort. You must book ahead, sometimes a year ahead, to catch the turning of the leaves in autumn, one of nature's most beautiful miracles.

Inn at Highview

753 East Hill Road
Andover, VT 05143
802-875-2724
www.innathighview.com
hiview@aol.com

Type of Lodging: Inn
Room Rates: $115–$165, including full breakfast.
Pet Charges & Deposits: None.
Pet Policy: Designated suites only. Manager's prior approval required.
Amenities: Microwaves, pool.
Pet Amenities: Exercise area. Green Mountain National Forest nearby.
Rated: 3 Paws — 6 rooms and 2 suites.

A rambling farmhouse, the Inn at Highview sits high on East Hill. From its handsome wide porch and lush, planted grounds, you are treated to a dazzling view of the mountains. Guestrooms are beautifully appointed, with antique furnishings and canopy beds with country quilts and goose-down comforters. Skiing is just minutes away. Okemo Mountain is a mere 10 to 15 minutes away, or take a little more time and head for Bromley, Stratton or Killington, in 45 minutes or less.

Hollow Inn and Motel

278 South Main Street
Barre, VT 05641
800-998-9444 • 802-479-9313
www.hollowinn.com

Type of Lodging: Motel
Room Rates: $59–$109, including continental breakfast. AAA and AARP discounts.
Pet Charges & Deposits: $10 per day.
Pet Policy: Designated rooms only.
Amenities: Cable TV, pool, whirlpool, Jacuzzi, hot tubs.
Pet Amenities: Exercise area. Grotin City Park nearby.
Rated: 3 Paws — 41 rooms.

Located in the heart of Barre off Interstate 89, the Hollow Inn's guestrooms offer contemporary comfort, cable television and VCRs. Efficiency rooms and kitchenettes are available upon request. Local area attractions include the Vermont State Capitol Building located eight miles from the hotel. Morse Farm's Sugar Shack offers maple sugar tours and the Rock of Ages features a scenic visit to a 100-year-old quarry. Local cultural activities include the Barre Opera House, Billing's Farm and Museum, the Pavilion and the T.W. Wood Art Gallery.

Bennington Motor Inn

*143 West Main Street
(Vermont Route 9)
Bennington, VT 05201
800-359-9900 • 802-442-5479
www.coolcruisers.net/
  benningtonmotorinn.htm
zink@together.net*

Type of Lodging: Motel

Room Rates: $58–$88.

Pet Charges & Deposits: $15–$20 per day.

Pet Policy: Designated rooms only. Manager's prior approval required.

Amenities: Cable TV, refrigerators.

Pet Amenities: Exercise area. Woodford State Park is located 8 miles from the motel.

Rated: 2 Paws — 15 rooms and 1 suite.

The Bennington Motor Inn is family-owned and operated. It offers newly decorated, cozy colonial charm and all modern conveniences, including private shower baths, individual climate controls, and most importantly, a comfortable night's rest. Just up the road is the Bennington Museum, where you can walk back through history and view Revolutionary artifacts, including the original 1776 Bennington Battle flag, as well as the Grandma Moses Schoolhouse Museum Collection of fine originals. Just around the bend is the beautiful Old First Church with its historic cemetery, including the gravesite of the poet, Robert Frost and his beloved wife. Monument Avenue, with its stately old colonials, will lead you to the Bennington Battle Monument.

Colonial Motel & Spa

*889 Putney Road
Brattleboro, VT 05301
800-239-0032 • 802-257-7733
www.colonialmotel.com
colonial@together.net*

Type of Lodging: Motel

Room Rates: $49–$80, including continental breakfast. AAA and AARP discounts.

Pet Charges & Deposits: $10 per day.

Pet Policy: None. All Pets Welcome.

Amenities: Cable TV, pool, spa, whirlpool.

Pet Amenities: List of nearby veterinarians maintained. Dog runs. Exercise area. Big open lawns.

Rated: 3 Paws — 73 rooms and 5 suites.

The Colonial Motel and Spa is set far back from the main road, providing a quiet atmosphere with attractive views of the hills surrounding Brattleboro. The rooms range from economy to executive suites and offer a wide range of extras, including patios to enjoy the lovely views, free local calls, air conditioning, access to the picnic area and the modern Spa and fitness room with a wooden sauna, an outdoor hot tub and two pools. Brattleboro has a rich and varied history along with a vibrant arts community. Visit the many galleries, shops and theaters. The motel is located close to shopping centers and a movie theater along Putney Road. There are opportunities to go hiking, biking, swimming and canoeing.

Bel-Aire Motel

111 Shelburne Road
Burlington, VT 05401
877-887-5337 • 802-863-3116

Type of Lodging: Motel

Room Rates: $36–$85, including continental breakfast. AAA, AARP, AKC, ABA, any animal charity member and *10% Pets Welcome™* discounts.

Pet Charges & Deposits: $5 per stay.

Pet Policy: Manager's prior approval required.

Amenities: Cable TV, refrigerators, microwaves, free local calls.

Pet Amenities: Continental breakfast treats for dogs, cats and hamsters. List of nearby veterinarians maintained. Exercise area.

Rated: 3 Paws — 12 rooms and 1 suite.

The Bel-Aire Motel sits in a huge park. Your pet will love to run around during the summer. While in Burlington, try to visit the Shelburne Museum, Shelburne Farms, Lake Champlain, Vermont Teddy Bear Factory and go shopping at Church Street Market Place.

Inn on the Common

1162 North Craftsbury Road
P.O. Box 75
Craftsbury Common, VT 05827
800-521-2233 • 802-586-9619
www.innonthecommon.com

Type of Lodging: Inn

Room Rates: $250–$300, including full breakfast and dinner.

Pet Charges & Deposits: $15 per stay. Manager's prior approval required.

Pet Policy: Manager's prior approval required.

Amenities: Pool, tennis court.

Pet Amenities: A play date with the Inn dog, Tyler, who plays nicely with any size and breed dog, in the 5-acre meadow behind the Inn. List of nearby veterinarians maintained.

Rated: 4 Paws — 16 rooms on 15 acres.

The Inn is situated on a panoramic hilltop surrounded by beautifully landscaped acres of land. It is located in Craftsbury Common, a village of white clapboard homes in Vermont's pristine Northeast Kingdom, where the roads run along ridges and brilliantly green farmland falls away to the distant mountains. Guests are invited to enjoy the pool or clay tennis courts or simply to explore the back roads throughout this scenic area. During winter, the Craftsbury Nordic Center trails crisscross the kind of red-barn-spotted farmscape that speaks Vermont. After a day on the trails, enjoy The Wellness Barn, a state-of-the-art fitness center featuring spas and saunas that is located ten minutes away.

Silver Maple Lodge & Cottages

520 U.S. Route 5 South
Fairlee, VT 05045
800-666-1946 • 802-333-4326
www.silvermaplelodge.com

Type of Lodging: B&B

Room Rates: $59–$89, including continental breakfast. AARP and *10% Pets Welcome™* discounts.

Pet Charges & Deposits: None.

Pet Policy: Designated rooms only. Manager's prior approval required.

Amenities: None.

Pet Amenities: Exercise area. List of nearby veterinarians maintained.

Rated: 3 Paws — 15 rooms.

The Silver Maple is one of Vermont's oldest continuously operating country inns. The centerpiece of this historic property is an antique farmhouse dating back to the late 1700s, which was expanded in the Victorian-style in the mid 1800s. The inn, which first opened its doors to travelers in the 1920s, has been restored and refurbished. The lodge is filled with many of the inn's original antique furnishings and exposed 200-year-old hand-hewn beams remain. Nearby attractions include the Quechee Gorge, Maple Grove Maple Museum, Ben & Jerry's Ice Cream Factory, the Cabot Farmer's Cooperative Creamery, Billings Farm & Museum, the Calvin Coolidge homestead and the Saint-Gaudens National Historic Site.

Cascades Lodge & Restaurant

58 Old Mill Road
Killington, VT 05751
800-345-0113 • 802-442-3731
www.cascadeslodge.com
info@cascadeslodge.com

Type of Lodging: Hotel

Room Rates: $69–$269, including full breakfast; AAA, AARP, AKC, ABA and *10% Pets Welcome™* discounts.

Pet Charges & Deposits: $10 per day, with a $25 minimum charge.

Pet Policy: Designated rooms only. Pets are allowed in summer and fall only.

Amenities: Cable TV, pool, hot tub, small nautilus area, masseuse, pub.

Pet Amenities: Each pet room has a sliding glass door to an outdoor patio.

Rated: 3 Paws — 40 rooms and 6 suites. Award-winning dining.

Enjoy Vermont from the Cascades, a classic lodge where winter comes alive. The New England landscape offers alpine or cross-country skiing, snowmobiling, snowshoeing or ice-skating. Area notables include the Quechee Gorge, Maple Grove Maple Museum, Norman Rockwell Museum, Ben & Jerry's Ice Cream Factory, the Cabot Farmer's Cooperative Creamery, Billings Farm & Museum and the Plymouth Cheese Factory.

Cortina Inn and Resort

103 U.S. Route 4
Killington, VT 05751
800-451-6108 • 802-773-3333
www.cortinainn.com
cortina1@aol.com

Type of Lodging: Guest Ranch

Room Rates: $124–$224, including full breakfast. AAA and *10% Pets Welcome*™ discounts.

Pet Charges & Deposits: $5 per day.

Pet Policy: Designated rooms only.

Amenities: Cable TV, refrigerators, microwaves, safes, pool, Jacuzzi, spas.

Pet Amenities: Treats available. List of nearby veterinarians maintained. Exercise area. Gifford Woods State Park nearby.

Rated: 4 Paws — 91 rooms and 6 suites.

The Cortina Inn, located amidst Vermont's scenic beauty, blends hospitality and cozy charm with the luxury of a fine resort. Each room is decorated individually, offering fresh flowers, brass beds and handmade quilts. Choose from several challenging golf courses nearby or play tennis on one of Cortina's eight courts. Seasonal activities include snowmobiling, sleigh rides, ice skating and snowshoeing in winter and mountain biking, hiking and fly-fishing in summer.

Val Roc Motel

Route 4
Killington, VT 05751
800-238-8762 • 802-422-3881
www.valroc.com
valrock@vermontel.com

Type of Lodging: Motel

Room Rates: $60–$110, including continental breakfast. AAA, AARP, AKC, ABA and *10% Pets Welcome*™ discounts.

Pet Charges & Deposits: Call for charges.

Pet Policy: Manager's prior approval required.

Amenities: Cable TV, refrigerators, microwaves, pool, hot tub, game room, tennis, basketball, playground.

Pet Amenities: List of nearby veterinarians maintained. Exercise area. Echo Lake State Park, Appalachian Trail and Long Trail nearby.

Rated: 3 Paws — 24 rooms.

Val Roc Motel is located in ski country, just a quarter mile from the Killington Skyeship Gondola and Northeast Passage. All rooms feature private bath, cable television, refrigerator, phone and coffeemaker. In the summer, enjoy golfing, hiking, biking and tennis. Val Roc Motel is convenient to Echo Lake State Park, Appalachian Trail and Long Trail.

Econo Lodge

51 Route 4 East
Mendon, VT 05701
800-992-9067 • 802-773-6644
econokillington@aol.com

Type of Lodging: Hotel

Room Rates: $42–$95, including continental breakfast. AAA, AARP and *Pets Welcome*™ discounts.

Pet Charges & Deposits: Credit card imprint required as deposit.

Pet Policy: Designated rooms only. Manager's prior approval required.

Amenities: Cable TV, pool, whirlpool, free local calls.

Pet Amenities: List of nearby veterinarians maintained. Gifford Woods State Park nearby.

Rated: 3 Paws — 27 rooms and 3 suites.

The Econo Lodge is ideally located for statewide touring as well as skiing at Killington Ski Area. This charming retreat combines warm, intimate qualities with luxuries of a large hotel. Guestrooms feature private baths, direct dial phones, cable television and air conditioning. It is only three miles from Killington's Pico Ski Area. If skiing is not on your to-do list, other local attractions include Norman Rockwell Museum, Queechee Gorge and Woodstock Village.

Red Clover Inn

7 Woodward Road
Mendon, VT 05701
800-752-0571 • 802-775-2290
www.redcloverinn.com
redclovr@vermontel.com

Type of Lodging: Inn

Room Rates: $185–$450, including full breakfast and gourmet dinner.

Pet Charges & Deposits: $10 per day.

Pet Policy: Sorry, no cats. Designated rooms only. Manager's prior approval required.

Amenities: Cable TV, pool, whirlpools, restaurant and pub.

Pet Amenities: List of nearby veterinarians maintained. Exercise area. Lots of trails nearby.

Rated: 4 Paws — 12 rooms and 2 suites on 13 picturesque acres. Award-winning dining.

General John Woodward built the Red Clover Inn as a private retreat in 1840. Once inside, the Inn feels like a large, cozy home with exposed wood beams and a roaring fire in the fieldstone fireplace. Guestrooms are beautifully appointed with private baths. Many rooms boast fireplaces, whirlpools and picturesque mountain views. The Red Clover Inn is convenient to Killington and the Pico Mountains. Try cross-country skiing on well-groomed trails during winter. During the warmer months, swim in the knoll-top pool, hike, bike or horseback ride the Appalachian or Long Trail. Enjoy Music on the Mountain concerts or Summer Stock Theater. The Inn is a perfect place to view the changing seasons during autumn, pick apples or browse for antiques.

Inn at the Hill

1724 East Main Street
Newport, VT 05855
800-258-6748 • 802-334-6748
www.innatthehill.com

Type of Lodging: Inn

Room Rates: $56–$75, including continental breakfast. AAA discount.

Pet Charges & Deposits: $5 per day.

Pet Policy: Sorry, no cats. Designated rooms only.

Amenities: Cable TV.

Pet Amenities: Dog runs. Exercise area. Gardner Park is only 3 minutes from the Inn.

Rated: 3 Paws — 15 rooms and 1 suite on beautiful manicured grounds.

This romantic inn is only six miles from the Canadian border, duty-free shops and casino gambling. Guestrooms feature cable television, individual climate controls, elegant private baths and direct dial phones. The Inn at the Hill is an ideal spot to watch the changing of the seasons. You'll find a diverse group of activities to enjoy, including swimming, boating, hiking, biking, snowmobiling and, of course, skiing.

Fairbanks Inn

401 Western Avenue
St. Johnsbury, VT 05319
802-748-5666

Type of Lodging: Inn

Room Rates: $65–$125, including continental breakfast. AAA, AARP, AKC, ABA, CAA and *10% Pets Welcome™* discounts.

Pet Charges & Deposits: $5 per day.

Pet Policy: Designated rooms only.

Amenities: Cable TV, pool.

Pet Amenities: A very large area and brook behind the Inn provide an exercise area. List of nearby veterinarians maintained. Arnold Park is located on Main Street.

Rated: 3 Paws — 41 rooms and 2 suites.

The Fairbanks Inn is centrally located in the beautiful Northeast Kingdom town of St. Johnsbury. The view from your private courtyard balcony offers over two acres of lovely landscaped scenery including the heated swimming pool, putting green and nature's own babbling brook. If your interests lie in seasonal activities like skiing, snowmobiling, hiking, skating, bicycling, golfing, boating or swimming, the Fairbanks Inn provides easy access to these and more. A visit to Maple Grove Farms and Museum, the Fairbanks Museum and Planetarium are not to be missed.

Best Western Windjammer Inn & Conference Center

1076 Williston Road
South Burlington, VT 05403
800-371-1125 • 802-863-1125
www.bestwestern.com/windjammerinn

Type of Lodging: Hotel
Room Rates: $59–$159, including continental breakfast. AAA and AARP discounts.
Pet Charges & Deposits: $5 per day.
Pet Policy: Designated rooms only.
Amenities: Cable TV, refrigerators, microwaves, pool, whirlpool, restaurant, pub.
Pet Amenities: Exercise area.
Rated: 3 Paws — 169 rooms and 4 suites on 52 acres.

Located on 52 acres of land, the Best Western Windjammer Inn & Conference Center is only two miles from the heart of Burlington. It has a beautiful outdoor pool, an indoor pool and health spa with Jacuzzi, sauna and exercise equipment. Guests can experience the charm of the Church Street Marketplace, the Flynn Theater, Lake Champlain and an array of shops, restaurants, clubs and more. Outside Burlington, enjoy some of the best skiing in the East or sample some of Vermont's finest products at the Ben & Jerry's Factory, Cabot Creamery, the Cider Mill or the Lake Champlain Chocolate Company.

Stowe Inn at Little River

123 Mountain Road
Stowe, VT 05672
800-227-1108 • 802-253-4836
www.stoweinn.com
info@stoweinn.com

Type of Lodging: Inn
Room Rates: $70–$120, including continental breakfast. *10% Pets Welcome™* discount.
Pet Charges & Deposits: $10 per stay.
Pet Policy: Designated rooms only.
Amenities: Cable TV, pool, Jacuzzis, fireplaces.
Pet Amenities: List of nearby veterinarians maintained. Exercise area. Mount Mansfield State Park nearby.
Rated: 3 Paws — 42 rooms.

The Inn is a restored circa-1825 manor located in the heart of Stowe Village. Casual elegance describes the guestrooms, which feature quilts, coverlets, antiques and country furnishings that add to the charm and decor. Lovely gardens and grounds and an outdoor hot tub and pool add to the Inn's amenities. Long appreciated for its spectacular mountain scenery, Stowe offers a wide palette of activities to choose from, whatever the season. From world-renowned skiing and art galleries, to fresh vegetable stands and antique automobile rallies, Stowe welcomes active participation by its many visitors.

Topnotch at Stowe Resort and Spa

4000 Mountain Road
Stowe, VT 05602
800-451-8686
www.topnotch-resort.com
topnotch@sover.net

Type of Lodging: Resort

Room Rates: $180–$310. AAA discount.

Pet Charges & Deposits: None.

Pet Policy: None. All Pets Welcome.

Amenities: Cable TV, refrigerators, safes, pool, spas, tennis courts.

Pet Amenities: List of nearby veterinarians maintained. Exercise area. Park nearby.

Rated: 5 Paws — 90 rooms and 24 suites on 120 acres.

Located on 120 acres of Vermont countryside at the foot of Mount Mansfield, Topnotch at Stowe is Stowe's only AAA Four-Diamond resort. To complement the meeting and spa facilities, the resort offers diverse accommodations from unusually spacious guestrooms and suites to two- and three-bedroom luxury town homes. Finely detailed wood and stone interiors echo the natural surroundings. Glass walls open onto views of Vermont's Green Mountains, and at night the resort nestles into the woods.

Topnotch at Stowe is two miles from Mount Mansfield and five miles from the village of Stowe. Take the trolley to the "Ski Capital of the East" for downhill skiing or stay at the resort to cross-country ski on the 25 kilometers of touring trails.

Ye Olde England Inne

433 Mountain Road
Stowe, VT 05672
800-477-3771 • 802-253-7558
www.englandinn.com
englandinn@aol.com

Type of Lodging: Inn
Room Rates: $125–$375, including full breakfast.
Pet Charges & Deposits: Call for refundable deposit.
Pet Policy: Designated rooms only.
Amenities: Cable TV, refrigerators, pool, Jacuzzi, hot tubs, spas, restaurants.
Pet Amenities: List of nearby veterinarians maintained. Exercise area. Green Mountain National Park and Mount Mansfield nearby.
Rated: 3 Paws — 13 rooms and 13 suites.

Set on a tree-covered bluff with incredible views of Stowe Village, Mt. Mansfield and the Green Mountains, the Ye Olde England Inne offers guests a sense of relaxation and peace they have not felt since childhood. The Inne has garnered many awards for hospitality and its distinctive cuisine, and your innkeepers were recently honored as Vermont Innkeepers of the Year. Guests can spend their days at the nearby Spa, enjoying a sleigh ride or having a secret waterfall picnic.

Powderhound Inn

P.O. Box 369
Warren, VT 05674
800-548-4022 • 802-496-5100
www.powderhoundinn.com
phound@madriver.com

Type of Lodging: Condos
Suite Rates: $80–$150. AAA and *10% Pets Welcome™* discounts.
Pet Charges or Deposits: $5 per day.
Pet Policy: None. All Pets Welcome.
Amenities: Swimming pool, hot tubs, volleyball, croquet, tennis courts, refrigerators, full bar in winter, restaurant.
Pet Amenities: List of nearby veterinarians maintained. Exercise area.
Rated: 3 Paws — 44 suites.

The Powderhound is located in the heart of central Vermont, in the scenic Mad River Valley. The century-old converted farmhouse overlooks a peaceful, rustic setting at the entrance to the Sugarbush resort area. Each of the suites features a living room area with cable television, kitchenette, separate bedroom and private bath, offering comfort and privacy for up to four guests. The Mad River Valley offers an assortment of year-round activities, from hiking to biking, horseback riding, canoeing and fishing, as well as lots of sightseeing. Sugarbush and Mad River Glen offer some of the best skiing in the East and provide a challenge for every level. The valley also offers a wide variety of winter adventures with cross-country skiing, snowshoeing, sleigh rides and winter fun.

Snow Goose Inn

Route 100, Box 366
West Dover, VT 05356
888-604-7964 • 802-464-3984
www.snowgooseinn.com
gooseinn@aol.com

Type of Lodging: B&B

Room Rates: $85–$350, including full breakfast and hor d'eouvres & wine in the evening. AAA discount.

Pet Charges & Deposits: $20 per day. $100 refundable deposit.

Pet Policy: Designated rooms only.

Amenities: Cable TV, hot tubs, fireplaces, private decks.

Pet Amenities: List of nearby veterinarians maintained. Exercise area. Buzzy Town Park nearby.

Rated: 3 Paws — 11 rooms and 2 suites.

Conveniently located in West Dover, just a little over a mile south of Mount Snow, Snow Goose Inn is set back away from Route 100, among three acres of pine, birch, maple and beech trees. Each luxurious room is appointed with period antique furniture, private bath, cable TV and plush featherbeds. Many of the rooms also have wood-burning fireplaces, two-person Jacuzzi tubs and private decks. The Snow Goose Inn is just a short walk or drive to many restaurants, hiking trails, mountain biking, golfing, downhill and cross-country skiing, snowmobiling, antiquing and a multitude of other activities.

Inn at Quail Run

106 Smith Road
Wilmington, VT 05363
800-34 ESCAPE • 802-464-3362
www.theinnatquailrun.com
quailrunvt@aol.com

Type of Lodging: Inn

Room Rates: $89–$220, including award-winning full breakfast. *5% Pets Welcome™* discount.

Pet Charges & Deposits: $15 per day.

Pet Policy: Designated rooms only.

Amenities: Cable TV, honor bar, pool, Jacuzzi, Saturday night dinners and bonfires.

Pet Amenities: Play date with Inn's two resident dogs may be arranged. List of nearby veterinarians maintained. Exercise area. Lake Whitingham, Morly Stark State Park and Jamaica State Park nearby.

Rated: 4 Paws — 12 rooms and 1 suite on 15 wooded acres.

Off the beaten track and nestled in the woods, yet only 3½ miles from Mount Snow, The Inn at Quail Run offers spectacular views of the Deerfield Valley and Haystack Mountain. Guestrooms have a private bath, cable television, with antique or brass beds that provide gracious and romantic accommodations. Play ping-pong or watch television in the first-floor rooms. Aspen, the Inn's seven-year-old mutt and Leo, the two-year-old Newfoundland "puppy" are very friendly and a play date can be arranged. The Inn is located on private wooded acres. You and your pet will enjoy many hiking trails that abut the Green Mountain National Forest.

VIRGINIA

Nickname: The Old Dominion
Population: 6,872,912
Area: 42,326 square miles
Climate: mild and equable.
Capital: Richmond
Entered Union: June 25, 1788
Motto: *Sic Semper Tyrannis* (Thus always to tyrants).
Song Emeritus: Carry Me Back to Old Virginny

Flower: Dogwood
Tree: Dogwood
Bird: Cardinal
Famous Virginians: Richard E. Byrd, Henry Clay, Jerry Falwell, William Henry Harrison, Patrick Henry, Thomas Jefferson, Robert E. Lee, Meriwether Lewis & William Clark, James Madison, John Marshall, Pocahontas, Edgar Allen Poe, Zachary Taylor, John Tyler, Booker T. Washington, George Washington, Woodrow Wilson.

 History: English settlers founded Jamestown in 1607. Virginians forced the Royal Governor to flee in 1775. During the American Revolution, Benedict Arnold burned Richmond and Petersburg for the British in 1781, but that same year Britain's General Cornwallis was trapped at Yorktown and surrendered, effectively ending the Revolution. Virginia seceded from the Union in 1861. Richmond became the capital of the Confederacy. Hampton Roads, site of the battle of the Monitor and the Merrimac, is one of the largest naval ports in the United States.

ALEXANDRIA, VIRGINIA (Greater D.C. Area) (Pop. 111,200)

Executive Club Suites

610 Bashford Lane
Alexandria, VA 22314
800-535-2582 • 703-739-2582
www.dcexeclub.com

Type of Lodging: Hotel
Suite Rates: $100–$190, including continental breakfast. AAA, Military, Government and *30% Pets Welcome™* discounts.
Pet Charges & Deposits: $50 per month. $250 refundable deposit.
Pet Policy: Designated rooms only.
Amenities: Cable TV, refrigerators, microwaves, safes, seasonal pool.
Pet Amenities: Pet beds for dogs. Park nearby.
Rated: 3 Paws — 78 suites.

Executive Club Suites gives you incredible luxury and incredible value, particularly considering how close you are to our nation's capital. It is a lovely three-level, garden-style apartment hotel with every amenity you can think of and a wonderfully pet-friendly management. The Suites are only 1½ miles from Ronald Reagan Washington National Airport, four miles from downtown Washington, D.C., with its multitude of attractions, three miles from the Pentagon, and minutes from charming Old Town Alexandria, with its shopping, dining and historic sites.

Executive Club Suites

108 South Courthouse Road
Arlington, VA 22204
800-535-2582 • 703-522-2582
www.dcexeclub.com

Type of Lodging: Hotel

Suite Rates: $100–$190, including continental breakfast. AAA, Military, Government and *30% Pets Welcome*™ discounts.

Pet Charges & Deposits: $50 per month. $250 refundable deposit.

Pet Policy: Designated rooms only.

Amenities: Cable TV, refrigerators, microwaves, safes, seasonal pool.

Pet Amenities: Pet beds for dogs. Park nearby.

Rated: 3 Paws — 78 suites.

Executive Club Suites provides the same marvelous luxury and an unbelievable price as its sister lodging in Alexandria. Whichever one you choose, you are assured of the most comfortable stay in the D.C. area. Located in the heart of Arlington, Executive Club Suites is central to all major government, business, and tourist destinations in the Washington D.C. metropolitan area. It's two miles from the Pentagon, four miles from Capital Hill and three miles from Reagan Washington National Airport.

Comfort Inn

203 Interstate Drive
Covington, VA 24426
800-228-5160 • 540-962-2141

Type of Lodging: Motel

Room Rates: $71–$99, including full breakfast. AAA, AARP and *10% Pets Welcome*™ discounts.

Pet Charges & Deposits: $10 per stay.

Pet Policy: Pets must not be left unattended.

Amenities: Cable TV, refrigerators, pool, whirlpool.

Pet Amenities: Douthat State Park is 20 miles from the motel.

Rated: 3 Paws — 45 rooms and 25 suites.

Comfort Inn is a strikingly attractive low-rise lodging with wonderful, upscale rooms and suites, situated in the Allegheny Mountain region of the Appalachians. It's 20 miles from fishing, swimming, and water skiing at Douthat State Park or Lake Moomaw, 30 miles to skiing at Homestead Resort. Nearby, the Painted Elephant Restaurant serves up hickory smoked ribs and other American favorites.

Best Western Coachman Inn

437 Roanoke Road
Daleville, VA 24083
800-628-1958 • 540-992-1234
www.guests-inc.com
bwco@rbnet.com

Type of Lodging: Motel
Room Rates: $52–$72, including continental breakfast. AAA, AARP, Hikers and *10% Pets Welcome™* discounts.
Pet Charges & Deposits: $10 per stay.
Pet Policy: Designated rooms only.
Amenities: Cable TV, refrigerators, microwaves, pool, coffeemakers, irons and ironing boards.
Pet Amenities: List of nearby veterinarians maintained. Exercise area. The Appalachian Trail runs through the property. The motel is minutes from the National Forest.
Rated: 3 Paws — 98 rooms on 10 acres.

Best Western Coachman Inn is conveniently located in the southern Shenandoah Valley, with dramatic views of the Blue Ridge Mountains and the Appalachian Trail. It features guestrooms with king-sized or double beds on a nicely landscaped 10-acre property minutes away from downtown Roanoke, the commercial and medical center of southwest Virginia. Roanoke proudly displays its history in the Center in the Square, a restored 1914 warehouse adjacent to the historic farmer's market. Three levels of exhibits include a science museum, planetarium, local history museum, free art museum and the Mills Mountain Theater, the city's major performing arts venue. Virginia's Explore Park is an 1,100-acre living history and recreation area, featuring a 1671 Native American village.

Days Inn

921 West Atlantic Street
Emporia, VA 23847
800-329-7466 • 804-634-9481
www.daysinn.com

Type of Lodging: Motel
Room Rates: $42–$66, including full breakfast. AAA and AARP discounts.
Pet Charges & Deposits: Call for charges information.
Amenities: Cable TV, refrigerators, microwaves, pool.
Pet Amenities: List of nearby veterinarians maintained. Veterans Park is located on Main Street.
Rated: 2 Paws — 121 rooms.

Days Inn – Emporia delivers high standards of service that are always warm, friendly and attentive. The rooms are spacious and spotless, kids stay free with their parents and the Inn provides exceptional value. Emporia is 16 miles from the North Carolina state line. The Pork Festival in June and the Peanut Festival in September afford a glimpse of the major industries in the city. Richmond is little more than an hour away and Colonial Williamsburg is an easy 90-mile drive from the motel.

Doe Run at Groundhog Mountain

Mile Post 189, Blue Ridge Parkway
P.O. Box 280
Fancy Gap, VA 24328
800-325-6189 • 540-398-2212
www.doerunlodge.com
doerun@tcia.net

Type of Lodging: Inn & Resort

Suite Rates: $99–$225. AAA and AARP discounts.

Pet Charges & Deposits: $25 per stay—*waived if you show Pets Welcome™.*

Pet Policy: Designated rooms only.

Amenities: Refrigerators, microwaves, safes, pool, whirlpool, Jacuzzi, hot tubs, fishing pond, tennis courts, bar, restaurant.

Pet Amenities: List of nearby veterinarians maintained. Exercise area. Blue Ridge Parkway nearby. Many woods, fields and hiking trails nearby.

Rated: 4 Paws — 46 suites.

During the year 2000, the Doe Run hosted a wedding on the grounds for members of the "Greyhound Friends." The attendants were all greyhounds! The luxurious Doe Run is in middle of the Blue Ridge Mountains, somewhere between Roanoke and Fancy Gap, at a place called Groundhog Mountain. You can set your own pace with sports, hiking, fishing, sightseeing, tennis, or outright relaxation. Situated practically on the North Carolina border, the Doe Run is on the Blue Ridge Parkway. You can take a relaxed drive north to the majesty of Shenandoah National Park and the Luray Caverns or south to Asheville's spectacular Biltmore House & Gardens.

Dunning Mills Inn

2305 C. Jefferson Davis Highway
Fredericksburg, VA 22401
540-373-1252
www.dunningmills.com

Type of Lodging: Hotel

Suite Rates: $59–$95, including coffee & donuts. AAA, AARP and *Pets Welcome™* discounts.

Pet Charges & Deposits: $5 per day. $200 refundable deposit.

Pet Policy: Designated rooms only. Pet agreement needs to be signed at time of deposit.

Amenities: Cable TV, fully equipped kitchens, pool, Jacuzzi.

Pet Amenities: List of nearby veterinarians maintained. Exercise area. Park nearby.

Rated: 3 Paws — 54 suites.

Dunning Mills Inn offers luxury suites with every convenience and amenity, yet its rates are below that of comparable hotel rooms. It's a people- and pet-friendly inn, with park benches and barbecue grills interspersed throughout the complex, and a widely used lending library in the lobby. You can obtain a combination ticket that enables you to see a plethora of historic attractions: the Rising Sun Tavern, the Mary Washington House, the James Monroe Museum and the Hugh Mercer Apothecary Shop.

Quality Inn

543 Warrenton Road
Fredericksburg, VA 22406
800-633-6443 • 540-373-0000
www.qualityinn.com-Fredericksburg.va

Type of Lodging: Hotel

Room Rates: $43 and up, including coffee. AAA, AARP and *10% Pets Welcome*™ discounts.

Pet Charges & Deposits: $8 per day.

Pet Policy: Designated rooms only.

Amenities: Cable TV, pool, hairdryers, irons and ironing boards.

Pet Amenities: List of nearby veterinarians maintained. Exercise area.

Rated: 3 Paws — 80 rooms.

Quality Inn is a decidedly upscale lodging that features newly decorated rooms. Kids stay free with their parents. The entire city of Fredericksburg is a living history museum. The Rising Sun Tavern, built in 1760 for George Washington's brother Charles, was a place where it can truly be said that "George Washington frequently slept here." George Washington bought the Mary Washington House for his mother, who lived there until her death in 1789. The Hugh Mercer Apothecary Shop displays 18th century medicinal and surgical supplies: leeches, lancets, purges and herbs.

Comfort Inn

1440 East Market Street
Harrisonburg, VA 22801
540-433-6066

Type of Lodging: Hotel

Room Rates: $70–$120, including continental breakfast. AAA, AARP and *10% Pets Welcome*™ discounts.

Pet Charges & Deposits: None.

Pet Policy: Pet contract to be signed by any guest staying with a pet.

Amenities: Cable TV, refrigerators, microwaves, pool.

Pet Amenities: Exercise area. Purcell Park, Hillandale Park and Kiwanis Park are located within 2 miles of the hotel. George Washington National Forest and Skyline Drive are located within 20 miles of the hotel.

Rated: 3 Paws — 94 rooms and 8 suites. Comfort Inn of the Year 1989-1990 and five-time Gold Award Winner.

Comfort Inn is a great base from which to explore Harrisonburg and its surrounding mountains. James Madison University's Convention Center is a mile away. The Shenandoah Caverns are 15 miles away. A little known fact is that Gary Jennings, the world-renowned historical novelist *(Aztec, The Journeyer, Spangle, Raptor)* lived in the nearby Massanutten mountain village for three years while he worked on *Aztec Autumn*.

The Village Inn

4979 South Valley Pike
Harrisonburg, VA 22801
800-736-7355 • 540-434-7355
www.shenandoah.org/villageinn
thevillageinn@aol.com

Type of Lodging: Motel
Room Rates: $57–$67, including continental breakfast on Sunday. AAA discount.
Pet Charges & Deposits: $5 per day.
Pet Policy: None. All Pets Welcome.
Amenities: Cable TV, pool, whirlpool.
Pet Amenities: List of nearby veterinarians maintained. Exercise area. Purcell Park is located at Monument and Main Street.
Rated: 3 Paws — 36 rooms and 1 suite.

The Village Inn is conveniently located on Highway 11, just off Interstate 81 in the picturesque Shenandoah Valley. It has rooms with all the modern amenities. Harrisonburg is less than an hour from Lexington, home of Virginia Military Institute, Washington & Lee University, and the Stonewall Jackson House. Novelist Gary Jennings was born near Lexington. It was through him that we learned to ask the locals to direct us to "Stonewall's Balls."

Garden & Sea Inn

4188 Nelson Road
New Church, VA 23415
800-824-0672 • 757-824-0672
www.gardenandseainn.com
innkeeper@gardenandseainn.com

Type of Lodging: B&B
Room Rates: $75–$185, including full breakfast. AAA, AARP, AKC, ABA and *Pets Welcome*™ discounts.
Pet Charges & Deposits: None.
Pet Policy: None. All Pets Welcome.
Amenities: Cable TV, refrigerators, whirlpool, Jacuzzi, restaurant.
Pet Amenities: List of nearby veterinarians maintained. Exercise area. Assateague State Beach in Maryland is 45 minutes away—it's a good beach for dogs. Lodging is located near Chincoteague Island—dogs are allowed on Chincoteague, but not on the Virginia end of Assateague.
Rated: 3 Paws — 7 rooms and 1 suite.

The Garden & Sea Inn, built circa 1802, is an historic bed & breakfast that offers fine dining and romantic lodging nestled in the quiet, rural setting of New Church, minutes from the islands of Chincoteague and Assateague, home of the famous wild ponies (as in *Misty of Chincoteague*). Although local legends have it that these ponies survived the shipwreck of a 16th century Spanish galleon, most historians believe that they were brought over by the first English colonists, who turned the herds loose in the late 1600s when the horses began to damage their crops.

Comfort Inn

12330 Jefferson Avenue
Newport News, VA 23602
800-368-2477 • 757-249-0200
www.newportc.com

Type of Lodging: Inn

Room Rates: $79–$99, including continental breakfast. AAA and *10% Pets Welcome*™ discounts.

Pet Charges & Deposits: None.

Pet policy: Must bring pet vaccination card.

Amenities: Cable TV, refrigerators, microwaves, pool.

Pet Amenities: Deer Park is located at 11523 Renger Avenue.

Rated: 3 Paws — 124 rooms.

Comfort Inn affords you all the modern amenities with colonial ambiance in three-story buildings with secure interior corridors. The Hampton Roads Area, made up of Newport News, Norfolk and Virginia Beach, has drawn maritime adventurers since the 1607 arrival of the English colonists. Today it is home to one of the largest concentrations of naval ships in the country, as well as Langley Air Force Base. There are incomparable maritime museums in the area, as well as the General Douglas MacArthur Memorial, the outstanding Chrysler Museum of Art and the Norfolk Botanical Garden.

Ramada Inn

501 East Washington Street
Petersburg, VA 23803
800-272-6232 • 804-733-0700

Type of Lodging: Hotel

Room Rates: $59–$64. AAA, AARP and *10% Pets Welcome*™ discounts.

Pet Charges & Deposits: None.

Pet Policy: Sorry, no cats. No pets over 25 lbs. Designated rooms only.

Amenities: Cable TV, microwaves, safes, pool, restaurant, lounge.

Pet Amenities: Battlefield Park nearby.

Rated: 3 Paws — 165 rooms and 2 suites.

The Ramada Inn affords outstanding value for the money, with beautifully appointed rooms, a large outdoor pool, recreation area, exercise and laundry rooms. Petersburg originated in 1645 as Fort Henry, and by the time it was incorporated as a city in 1850, it had become a thriving industrial and commercial center. Petersburg National Battlefield is a 2,700-acre preserve that commemorates ten months of grim trench warfare that sapped the strength of General Robert E. Lee's Confederate army and led to the fall of Richmond.

AmeriSuites – Richmond/Arboretum

201 Arboretum Place
Richmond, VA 23236
800-833-1516 • 804-560-1566
www.amerisuites.com
locra@primehospitality.com

Type of Lodging: Hotel

Suite Rates: $69–$149, including continental breakfast. AAA and AARP discounts.

Pet Charges & Deposits: $10 per day.

Pet Policy: No pets over 10 lbs.

Amenities: Cable TV, refrigerators, microwaves, pool, hairdryers, irons and ironing boards, fitness center.

Pet Amenities: Iron Bridge Park nearby.

Rated: 3 Paws — 128 suites

AmeriSuites is affordably priced and provides you with amenities such as guest laundry, free newspaper, hairdryer, iron and ironing board and fitness center. The tiny outpost of Richmond, founded in 1637, became Virginia's capital in 1779. It was named the Confederate capital during the Civil War, but was evacuated in April 1865 when fires destroyed much of the old city. There is much to see in today's Richmond: Agecroft Hall, initially built in England in the late 15th century and shipped to the United States in the 1920s; Beth Ahavah, Virginia's museum of Jewish history and culture; the Museum of the Confederacy, one of the nation's largest collections of Conderate artifacts, paintings and documents; and the White House of the Confederacy.

Days Inn West Broad

2100 Dickens Road
Richmond, VA 23230
800-329-7466 • 804-282-3300

Type of Lodging: Hotel

Room Rates: $58–$98, including continental breakfast. AAA and AARP discounts.

Pet Charges & Deposits: $6 per stay.

Pet Policy: Designated rooms only.

Amenities: Cable TV, refrigerators, microwaves, safes, pool, hairdryers.

Pet Amenities: List of nearby veterinarians maintained. Exercise area. Brookfield Office Park is located on the 6600 block of West Broad Street and offers many walking trails.

Rated: 3 Paws — 180 rooms.

Days Inn, on Dickens Road near the West Broad Street Exit, is a well laid-out lodging with excellent amenities. Its location, seven miles from downtown Richmond, affords one an ample opportunity to visit important sights. Visit the Virginia Historical Society Center for Virginia History, the Valentine Museum of the Life & History of Richmond and the Virginia Museum of Fine Arts. The latter houses, among other things, a large collection of Fabergé jeweled objects, including five Russian Imperial Easter eggs and a life-sized marble statue of the Roman emperor Caligula dating from the first century.

Executive Club Suites

1730 Arlington Boulevard
Rosslyn, VA 22209
800-535-2582 • 703-525-2582
www.dcexeclub.com

Type of Lodging: Hotel

Suite Rates: $100–$190, including continental breakfast. AAA, Military, Government and **30% Pets Welcome™** discounts.

Pet Charges & Deposits: $50 per month. $250 refundable deposit.

Pet Policy: Designated rooms only.

Amenities: Cable TV, refrigerators, microwaves, safes, seasonal pool.

Pet Amenities: Dogs beds available. Park nearby.

Rated: 3 Paws — 78 suites.

Like the Executive Club Suites in Alexandria and Arlington, this Executive Club Suites is one of the most exceptionally well priced lodgings we've found. It offers a pet-friendly discount off rack rates to readers of this book! The hotel is just blocks from the heart of Rosslyn and the Rosslyn Metro, one mile from lively Georgetown and the center of Washington, D.C. and four miles from the State Department. Arlington National Cemetery is a very short distance away. The value of an Executive Suite stay is unmatched.

Baymont Inn Roanoke/Salem

140 Sheraton Drive
Salem, VA 24153
877-229-6668 • 540-562-2717
www.baymontinns.com

Type of Lodging: Motel

Room Rates: $50–$105, including continental breakfast. AAA, AARP and **10% Pets Welcome™** discounts.

Pet Charges & Deposits: No charge if guest uses pet-designated rooms; $5 per day if guest uses another room.

Pet Policy: Pets must not be left unattended.

Amenities: Cable TV, refrigerators, microwaves, pool, whirlpool, Jacuzzi, irons and ironing boards, hairdryers, coffeemakers.

Pet Amenities: List of nearby veterinarians maintained. Exercise area. Longwood Park nearby.

Rated: 3 Paws — 61 rooms and 6 suites.

The Baymont Inn was newly built in January 1998. It affords a breathtaking view of the Blue Ridge Mountains, and it is surely one of the most accommodating and comfortable lodgings in southwestern Virginia. Amenities are almost too numerous to mention and the pet-friendly staff is dedicated to making your stay a wonderful experience. Salem's Dixie Caverns offers 45-minute guided tours of the still-growing caverns. The Salem Museum, housed in an 1845 store, traces Salem's development from its earliest days and is certainly worth a visit.

Ashton Country House B&B

1205 Middlebrook Avenue
Staunton, VA 24401
800-296-7819 • 540-885-7819
www.bbhost.com/ashtonbnb
ashtonhouse@aol.com

Type of Lodging: B&B

Room Rates: $70–$150, including full breakfast. AAA, AARP and *10% Pets Welcome*™ discounts.

Pet Charges & Deposits: $10 per day.

Pet Policy: Please bring pet bedding. Designated rooms only. Manager's prior approval required.

Amenities: Cable TV, refrigerators, microwaves.

Pet Amenities: List of nearby veterinarians maintained. Exercise area. Property has 25 acres of pasture for pets to walk and run with owner. Gypsy Hill Park **is** located at Churchville and Thornrose Avenues. Shenandoah Nat'l Park and George Washington Nat'l Forest nearby.

Rated: 3 Paws — 5 rooms and 1 suite on 25 acres.

As more than one visitor has said, the Ashton Country House B&B rekindles your spirit and renews the energy of all your senses. It was built in 1860 in the grand style of the Victorian mindset, and was occupied by Confederate troops during the Civil War. Ashton's guestrooms are designed for the comfort and enjoyment of travelers. Staunton is one of the oldest cities west of the Blue Ridge Mountains, having been settled in 1732. Surprisingly unscathed during the Civil War, Staunton has one of Virginia's finest collections of 19th century architecture. The Frontier Culture Museum is a living history museum with reconstructed working farms of the 17th, 18th and 19th centuries.

Best Inn of Staunton

96 Baker Lane
Staunton, VA 24401
800-BEST INN • 540-248-5111
www.bestinnofstaunton.com

Type of Lodging: Motor Lodge

Room Rates: $45–$75, including continental breakfast. AAA, AARP, Military, Government and *10% Pets Welcome*™ discounts.

Pet Charges & Deposits: $6 per day.

Pet Policy: Designated rooms only. Manager's prior approval required.

Amenities: Cable TV, safes, pool.

Pet Amenities: Exercise area. Gypsy Hill Park nearby.

Rated: 3 Paws — 100 rooms.

Best Inn of Staunton represents fine value for the money: clean, comfortable, affordable and pet-friendly. Staunton was the early home of Woodrow Wilson, the most recent of the eight Virginia-born presidents. The Woodrow Wilson Birthplace and Museum is restored to depict Wilson's family life in the Shenandoah Valley before the Civil War. "Touch baskets" allow visitors to handle many of the period pieces in the house. The museum, adjacent to the birthplace, features seven galleries showing Wilson's life as a scholar, university president, politician, statesman and President of the United States. There's an extensive Victorian garden on the premises.

Days Inn

372 White Hill Road
Staunton, VA 24401
540-337-3031
www.daysinn.com
daysinn_Staunton@yahoo.com

Type of Lodging: Hotel

Room Rates: $44–$139, including continental breakfast. AAA and AARP discounts.

Pet Charges & Deposits: $6 per day.

Pet Policy: None.

Amenities: Cable TV, refrigerators, pool.

Pet Amenities: Exercise area. Gypsy Hill Park is located off Exit 220 in downtown Staunton.

Rated: 2 Paws — 118 rooms

Days Inn is a fine budget choice when you're in the middle of the beautiful and historic Shenandoah Valley. Nearby attractions include the Horse Center, University of Virginia, James Madison University, Virginia Military Institute in nearby Lexington, and Skyline Drive, which affords outstanding views of the Blue Ridge and the Valley. Trinity Episcopal Church was built in 1855 on the site of the building in which the Virginia Assembly took refuge from the British in 1781.

Hessian's EconoLodge

3554 Lee Jackson Highway
Staunton, VA 24401
800-214-6540 • 540-337-1231

Type of Lodging: Motel

Room Rates: $40–$75, including continental breakfast. AAA, AARP and *Pets Welcome*™ discounts.

Pet Charges & Deposits: $6 per day.

Pet Policy: Designated rooms only. Manager's prior approval required.

Amenities: Cable TV, refrigerator, pool, playground.

Pet Amenities: Exercise area. Walnut Hills Campground nearby.

Rated: 2 Paws — 32 rooms. 1999 Choice Hotels International's Ruby Award Winner.

Hessian's EconoLodge offers excellent value for a very low price, and is a cost-conscious choice when you're in the area. Staunton is a wonderful place to stroll—history surrounds you and the Shenandoah Valley, justifiably lauded in song, is truly one of nature's most gracious lands. Just south of nearby Lexington is one of the natural wonders of the world, Natural Bridge. A limestone cave collapsed to expose this 23-story high natural arch. Over 300 feet below ground, the Natural Bridge Caverns displays stalagmites, stalactites, hanging gardens, underground streams and waterfalls.

Travelodge

2619 Lee Highway
Troutville, VA 24175
800-578-7878 • 540-992-6700
www.travelodge.com

Type of Lodging: Motel

Room Rates: $45–$75, including continental breakfast. AAA, AARP and *10% Pets Welcome*™ discounts.

Pet Charges & Deposits: $6 per day.

Pet Policy: Designated rooms only.

Amenities: Cable TV, coffeemakers, free local calls.

Pet Amenities: List of nearby veterinarians maintained. Exercise area. Walrond Park nearby.

Rated: 2 Paws — 108 rooms.

Travelodge provides affordable, comfortable accommodations in southwestern Virginia. Troutville is a northern suburb of Roanoke, the "big city" in this part of Virginia. Two museums of unusual interest in Roanoke are the Harrison Museum of African American Culture, housed in Harrison School, the first public high school for African American children in the city, and the To The Rescue Museum, which affords a look into national emergency services performed by medical technicians and paramedics. Also worth seeing is the Virginia Museum of Transportation, a historic freight station, which contains vintage steam, electric and diesel locomotives.

Ramada Limited

70 Lodge Lane
Verona, VA 24482
800-2 RAMADA • 540-248-8981
www.ramada.com

Type of Lodging: Motel

Room Rates: $45–$95, including continental breakfast. AAA, AARP and *10% Pets Welcome*™ discounts.

Pet Charges & Deposits: $5 per day.

Pet Policy: Designated rooms only. Pets must not be left unattended.

Amenities: Cable TV, safes, pool.

Pet Amenities: List of nearby veterinarians maintained. Dog runs. Exercise area. Gypsy Hill Park nearby.

Rated: 3 Paws — 100 rooms.

Ramada Limited was newly renovated in 1998 and is spotlessly maintained. Verona is located in the heart of the Shenandoah Valley with easy access to Interstate 81. In nearby Waynesboro, the P. Buckley Moss Museum features the work of the local artist, situated in a 19th century building. Shenandoah Valley scenery and the local Amish and Mennonite people of the area are featured in Moss's artwork. The museum also reflects the artist's devotion to helping those with learning disabilities. New Market Battlefield State Historical Park commemorates the Civil War battle where 257 cadets from the Virginia Military Institute aided veteran Confederate troops in victory over the Union forces on May 15, 1864, less than a year before Appomattox.

Heritage Inn

1324 Richmond Road
Williamsburg, VA 23185
800-782-3800 • 757-229-6220
www.heritageinnwmsb.com
heritageinn@widomaker.com

Type of Lodging: Motel
Room Rates: $40–$90, including continental breakfast. AAA and AARP discounts.
Pet Charges & Deposits: None.
Pet Policy: Designated rooms only.
Amenities: Cable TV, pool.
Pet Amenities: List of nearby veterinarians maintained. Exercise area. Mid-County Park is located at 3793 Ironbound Road.
Rated: 3 Paws — 54 rooms.

Heritage Inn is a perfect choice when you're in one of America's penultimate historic areas. It's in the heart of Williamsburg, and who hasn't heard of—and dreamt of visiting—Colonial Williamsburg, perhaps the most famous pre-Revolutionary site in the United States. Williamsburg is only one of three important small cities in what's become known as "Virginia's Historic Triangle." The others are Jamestown and Yorktown. Visiting these three places is like taking a life-illustrated course in U.S. History 101. Places and faces here step right out of the pages of every American History textbook you've ever read.

Quality Inn Woodbridge

1109 Horner Road
Woodbridge, VA 22191
800-228-5151 • 703-494-0300
cdavenport@apluslodging.com

Type of Lodging: Hotel
Room Rates: $60–$170, including deluxe continental breakfast. AAA, AARP, ABA, CAA and *10% Pets Welcome™* discounts.
Pet Charges & Deposits: $10 per day.
Pet Policy: No pets over 50 lbs. Designated rooms only.
Amenities: Cable TV, pool, coffeemakers, dataports, irons & ironing boards, hairdryers.
Pet Amenities: List of nearby veterinarians maintained. Exercise area. Prince William Forest Park nearby.
Rated: 3 Paws — 92 rooms and 2 suites.

Quality Inn promises a 100% satisfaction guarantee, and it's obvious from the moment you step in the door that you will enjoy your stay here. It's located in an area where you might get confused by some of the names. Although it's technically in Woodbridge, the Inn is actually situated in Potomac Mills, a suburb of our nation's capital. It's within easy access to the sights of Washington, D.C., George Washington's famed plantation at Mount Vernon, unique shopping in the quaint village of Occoquan and the lively factory outlets of Potomac Mills.

Econo Lodge

1160 East Main Street
Wytheville, VA 24382
800-553-2666 • 540-228-5517
www.apluslodging.com
va229@apluslodging.com

Type of Lodging: Hotel

Room Rates: $29–$99, including continental breakfast. AAA, AARP and *12% Pets Welcome™* discounts.

Pet Charges & Deposits: $10 per day.

Pet Policy: No pets over 200 lbs.

Amenities: Cable TV, refrigerators, microwaves, coffeemakers.

Pet Amenities: List of nearby veterinarians maintained. Wytheville Recreation Park is located at North Fourth and Main Streets.

Rated: 2 Paws — 72 rooms

Econo Lodge is a great cost-conscious stopover for traveling while you're headed north or south on Interstate 81. Wytheville, a transportation and vacation center in the Blue Ridge Highlands, almost on the North Carolina border, is an historically important community that dates back to the Revolutionary and Civil Wars. The Shot Tower, built in 1807, resembles a fortress and was once used to manufacture lead shot. Here, you'll find the derivation of the term, "a round of ammunition." Foster Falls, two miles from the tower, is headquarters for New River Trail State Park, a 57-mile greenway along a former railroad right of way.

WASHINGTON

Nickname: Evergreen State

Population: 5,756,361

Area: 70,637 square miles

Climate: Mild, dominated by the Pacific Ocean and protected by the Cascade mountains, wet throughout the year.

Capital: Olympia

Entered Union: Nov.11,1889

Motto: *Ali* (By and By).

Song: Washington, My Home

Flower: Western Rhododendron

Tree: Western Hemlock

Bird: Willow Goldfinch

Famous Washingtonians: Bing Crosby, William O. Douglas, Bill Gates, Henry M. Jackson, Gary Larson, Mary McCarthy, Edward R. Murrow, Minoru Yamasaki.

History: A plethora of peaceful Native American peoples inhabited the area at the time Spain's Bruno Hezeta sailed the coast in 1775. In 1792, British naval officer George Vancouver mapped the Puget Sound area. That same year, American Captain Robert Gray sailed up the Columbia River. John Jacob Astor established a post at Fort Okanogan in 1811. The final agreement on the border of Washington and Canada was made with Britain in 1846, and Washington became part of the Oregon Territory. Gold was discovered in 1855, but today's Washington "gold" consists of Microsoft, Costco, and Boeing.

Fidalgo Country Inn

7645 State Route 20
Anacortes, WA 98221
800-244-4179 • 360-293-3494
www.nwcountryinns.com/fidalgo

Type of Lodging: Hotel

Room Rates: $69–$169, including continental breakfast. AAA and AARP discounts.

Pet Charges & Deposits: $20 per day.

Pet Policy: Designated rooms only.

Amenities: Cable TV, refrigerators, microwaves, pool, whirlpool, Jacuzzi, hot tubs.

Pet Amenities: Exercise area. Deception Pass State Park nearby.

Rated: 3 Paws — 46 rooms and 4 suites.

Less than two hours drive from Seattle or Vancouver, B.C., you come to the first of the San Juan Islands—Fidalgo. Anacortes, at the tip of Fidalgo Island, is connected to the mainland by bridges and by daily toll ferry service. Fidalgo Country Inn is located just minutes from the Anacortes ferry terminal and Deception Pass on Whidbey Island. It features deluxe guestrooms, luxury suites, a lobby fireplace and a wonderful ambience. Mount Erie is five miles south of Anacortes via a fine paved road. At 1,270 feet, it's the highest point on the island and from there you can see Mount Baker, Mount Rainier, the Olympic Mountains, the Cascade Range and the San Juan Islands.

Old Brook Inn

7270 Old Brook Lane
Anacortes, WA 98221
800-503-4768 • 360-293-4768
www.oldbrookinn.com

Type of Lodging: B&B

Room Rates: $80–$90, including continental breakfast.

Pet Charges & Deposits: None.

Pet Policy: None. All Pets Welcome.

Amenities: Cable TV, microwaves, safes.

Pet Amenities: List of nearby veterinarians maintained. Exercise area. B&B has 10 acres on which pets can roam to their hearts' content.

Rated: 4 Paws — 2 rooms.

Old Brook Inn gives its guests, both two- and four-legged, a great deal of tender loving care. It's a cheerful, highly recommended lodging. The Anacortes Museum contains maritime and local history exhibits, as well as a research library. The W.T. Preston, the last snag boat to operate on Puget Sound, is now a maritime museum that features the vessel's original furnishings. Gaming can be found at nearby Swinomish Casino & Bingo, three miles east of town.

Val-U-Inn

805 Lakeway Drive
Bellingham, WA 98226
800-443-7777 • 360-671-9600
valu-inn-res@quest.com

Type of Lodging: Motel

Room Rates: $55–$85, including
continental breakfast. AAA and AARP
discounts.

Pet Charges & Deposits: $5 per day.

Pet Policy: Sorry, no cats. No pets over
50 lbs. Designated rooms only. Pets
must not be left unattended.

Amenities: Cable TV, spa.

Pet Amenities: None.

Rated: 2 Paws — 79 rooms and 3
suites.

Tidy and immaculately clean, Val-U-Inn represents excellent value for your money when you're in Bellingham. Amenities include an indoor spa, free newspaper, free airport and cruise terminal shuttles. Bellingham is the southern terminal of the Alaska Marine Highway, as well as the gateway to White Rock, in nearby British Columbia. As such, it is home to Squalicum Harbor, one of the largest marinas on Puget Sound, numerous cruises to the San Juan Islands and points north and a plethora of fine maritime museums.

Timberland Inn & Suites

1271 Mount Saint Helens Way
Castle Rock, WA 98611
360-274-6002
timber@kalama.com

Type of Lodging: Motel

Room Rates: $45–$120. AAA discount

Pet Charges & Deposits: $5 per day.

Pet Policy: None. All Pets Welcome.

Amenities: Cable TV, refrigerators,
microwaves, Jacuzzi, free local calls.

Pet Amenities: Seaquest State Park is
located 5 miles from the motel.

Rated: 3 Paws — 40 rooms and 10
suites.

Timberland Inn & Suites affords you all the comforts of home at an affordable price in tasteful two-story structures. King- or queen-sized beds, direct dial phones in every room and other amenities make Timberland Inn a fine choice of lodging. Although the 150-foot-high rock after which the town was named is impressive, the big attraction in these parts is Mount Saint Helens. The Mount Saint Helens Cinedome Theater depicts the 1980 eruption and its aftermath. The Mount Saint Helens National Volcanic Monument Visitor Center is five miles east of town on the Spirit Lake Highway.

Nordlig Motel

West 101 Grant Street
Chewelah, WA 99019
509-935-6704
www.nordlig.com
star@nordlig.com

Type of Lodging: Motel

Room Rates: $42–$48, including continental breakfast. AAA and AARP discounts.

Pet Charges & Deposits: $3 per stay.

Pet Policy: None. All Pets Welcome.

Amenities: Cable TV, refrigerators, microwaves, Jacuzzi.

Pet Amenities: List of nearby veterinarians maintained. Chewelah City Park is located a block from the motel.

Rated: 3 Paws — 14 rooms.

From handmade quilts to fluffy absorbent towels, from refrigerators and hot pots in each room to the seven-person hot tub in the communal area, Nordlig Motel in Chewelah welcomes you with a homey atmosphere. Chewelah is ten miles to alpine and nordic skiing, 3½ miles to Las Vegas-style gambling, and sits amid the heart of great fishing, mountain biking, snowmobiling and all sorts of outdoor activities.

Stewart Lodge

805 West First Street
Cle Elum, WA 98922
877-233-5358 • 509-674-4548

Type of Lodging: Motel

Room Rates: $43–$65, including continental breakfast. AAA discount.

Pet Charges & Deposits: $5 per day.

Pet Policy: Designated rooms only. Manager's prior approval required.

Amenities: Cable TV, refrigerators, microwaves, pool, Jacuzzi.

Pet Amenities: Dog runs. Exercise area. Cle Elum City Park nearby.

Rated: 2 Paws — 36 rooms.

Stewart Lodge is a very affordable place decorated in a country motif. It sports unique pine furnishings and allows you free local telephone calls. Cle Elum, "swift water" in the Native American Kittitas tongue, is at the entrance to the Wenatchee and Mount Baker-Snoqualmie National Forests. You can enjoy nearly every conceivable outdoor activity in these vast forests. Iron Horse State Park offers a scenic hiking and horse trail that extends 113 miles along the Yakima River. The John Wayne Pioneer Trail takes you through a particularly impressive stand of forest.

Victorian Bed & Breakfast

P.O. Box 761
Coupeville, WA 98239
360-678-5305
www.whidbeyvictorianbandb.com

Type of Lodging: B&B

Room Rates: $70–$100, including full breakfast. AAA discount.

Pet Charges & Deposits: $10 per stay. $100 refundable deposit.

Pet Policy: Designated rooms only. Manager's prior approval required.

Amenities: Refrigerators.

Pet Amenities: List of nearby veterinarians maintained. Exercise area. Park nearby.

Rated: 3 Paws — 2 rooms and 1 suite. Listed on the National Register of Historic Places.

In 1889, Washington pioneer Jacob Jenne built an Italianate Victorian home in the town of Coupeville on beautiful Whidbey Island. More than a century later, the Victorian Bed & Breakfast, proudly provides gracious accommodations throughout the year to Whidbey Island visitors. Coupeville's colorful heritage is alive and well. Called the City of Sea Captains for its many seafaring settlers, the town blends its early Native American lore with a unique maritime history and a vigorous pioneer spirit. All around, you'll find stately Victorian homes, quaint wharf and waterfront shops and the distinctive character of surrounding Ebey's Landing National Historic Reserve.

Edmonds Harbor Inn

130 West Dayton
Edmonds, WA 98020
800-441-8033 • 425-771-5021
www.nwcountryinns.com
nwcinns@seanet.com

Type of Lodging: Inn

Room Rates: $69–$169, including continental breakfast. AAA, AARP and *10% Pets Welcome™* discounts.

Pet Charges & Deposits: $10 per day.

Pet Policy: No pets over 25 lbs. Designated rooms only.

Amenities: Cable TV, refrigerators, microwaves, irons and ironing boards, coffeemakers, hairdryers, dataports.

Pet Amenities: List of nearby veterinarians maintained. Exercise area. Marina Beach Park, Olympic Beach Park and Edmonds City Park are all within walking distance.

Rated: 3 Paws — 77 rooms and 14 suites.

Located 25 minutes from both Seattle and Everett, the Harbor Inn is situated 1½ blocks from the waterfront in the heart of Edmonds. Despite its proximity to two urban centers, Edmonds is as picturesque a small town as you'll find in Washington. There are breathtaking views of the Olympic Mountains and snow-capped Mount Baker. Then there's the Edmonds waterfront with its lovely beaches. Watch the ferryboats plying Puget Sound or go fish for salmon from the public pier. Specialty shops, art galleries and fine waterfront restaurants: they're all here, just outside your door.

Nites Inn Motel

1200 South Ruby
Ellensburg, WA 98926
509-962-9600
www.televar.com/~nites
nites@televar.com

Type of Lodging: Motel

Room Rates: $46–$56, including continental breakfast. AAA, AARP, Seniors, Commercial, Long-Haul Trucks and *10% Pets Welcome*™ discounts.

Pet Charges & Deposits: $7 per day.

Pet Policy: Pets must be on leash.

Amenities: Cable TV, refrigerators, microwaves, coffeemakers, guest laundry.

Pet Amenities: List of nearby veterinarians maintained. Exercise area. Park nearby.

Rated: 3 Paws — 32 rooms.

Nites Inn provides fine value in the heart of the Kittitas Valley where the Wenatchee, Nez Perce and Yakima Indians, usually hostile to one another, once hunted and fished together in peace. Kittitas County Historical Society Museum displays Native American artifacts and pioneer articles, while the Clymer Museum exhibits the works of Western artist John Ford Clymer.

Miller Tree Inn

654 East Division Street
P.O. Box 1565
Forks, WA 98331
800-943-6563 • 360-374-6806
www.millertreeinn.com
millertreeinn@centurytel.net

Type of Lodging: B&B

Room Rates: $105–$150, including full breakfast. *Seasonal Pets Welcome*™ discount.

Pet Charges & Deposits: $10 per day.

Pet Policy: Designated rooms only.

Amenities: Cable TV, refrigerators, microwaves, hot tubs.

Pet Amenities: List of nearby veterinarians maintained. Exercise area. Olympic National Park and Bogachiel State Park nearby

Rated: 2 Paws — 6 rooms and 1 suite.

Miller Tree Inn mimics the style of genuine European bed and breakfasts. It offers simple rooms and a welcoming family atmosphere. Forks is an important Olympic Peninsula logging community which draws its name from the forks of three nearby rivers. There are spectacular runs of steelhead trout during summer and winter. The Forks Timber Museum displays items from the 1870s to the 1950s, including a pioneer kitchen, logging equipment and a fire lookout tower.

Harbour Inn

1606 East Main Street
P.O. Box 1350
Freeland, WA 98249
360-331-6900
harbrinn@whidney.com

Type of Lodging: Motel
Room Rates: $69–$90, including continental breakfast.
Pet Charges & Deposits: $6 per day.
Pet Policy: Designated rooms only. Manager's prior approval required.
Amenities: Cable TV, microwaves.
Pet Amenities: List of nearby veterinarians maintained. Exercise area. Double Bluff Beach (off-leash dog area) nearby.
Rated: 3 Paws — 20 rooms.

The Harbour Inn has very well-kept rooms, varying in size from compact to spacious. There's a large lawn with picnic tables and horseshoes. The preserved buildings, farms, parks, scenic drives and military fortifications demonstrate a historical record of the area's exploration and settlement. Whidbey Island has several notable, quaint, scenic towns. Go from one to the other and you'll discover new vistas around every corner.

Blair House Bed & Breakfast

345 Blair Avenue
Friday Harbor, WA 98250
800-899-3030 • 360-378-5907
www.fridayharborlodging.com

Type of Lodging: B&B
Room Rates: $150–$185, including full breakfast.
Pet Charges & Deposits: None.
Pet Policy: Designated rooms only.
Amenities: Cable TV, refrigerators, pool, hot tubs.
Pet Amenities: List of nearby veterinarians maintained. Exercise area.
Rated: 2 Paws — 4 rooms and 1 cottage.

Blair House is located on San Juan Island, just five short blocks from the ferry landing. The Cottage, 800 square feet of private living where you, your children and your pets are welcome, offers all the amenities of home, including a queen-sized bed in the bedroom, a queen hide-a-bed and a rollaway bed. San Juan Island, the westernmost of the major islands, consists of rolling hills, small farms and patches of forest. As you proceed west, you come to more rugged terrain. Friday Harbor, the island's largest town, is a bustling port of call.

Best Western Wesley Inn

6575 Kimball
Gig Harbor, WA 98335
888-462-0002 • 253-858-9690
www.wesleyinn.com

Type of Lodging: Hotel

Room Rates: $90–$169, including continental breakfast. AAA, AARP and *10% Pets Welcome*™ discounts

Pet Charges & Deposits: $10 per day.

Pet Policy: None. All Pets Welcome.

Amenities: Cable TV, refrigerators, microwaves, pool, Jacuzzi, spa, coffeemakers.

Pet Amenities: Treats available. List of nearby veterinarians maintained. Exercise area. Gig Harbor Park is located on the corner of Vernhandson and Crescent Valley Drive Northwest.

Rated: 4 Paws — 53 rooms.

Best Western Wesley Inn is a New England-style country inn that combines Pacific Northwest-style and casual elegance with charm, hospitality and personalized service. The small bay on which Gig Harbor is located was discovered by accident, when the Wilkes expedition was seeking refuge from a storm. Five miles northwest of Tacoma, the harbor is a major marina for pleasure craft and commercial fishing boats. Besides being convenient to the Tacoma area, Gig Harbor has an individual, Scandinavian personality. Finholm's Market Place, at the north end of the harbor, has more than a dozen intriguing shops.

Kennewick Super 8 Motel

626 North Columbia Center Boulevard
Kennewick, WA 99336
800-800-8000 • 509-736-6888
www.super8motels.com

Type of Lodging: Motel

Room Rates: $47–$72, including coffee in lobby. AAA, AARP, AKC and *10% Pets Welcome*™ discounts.

Pet Charges & Deposits: $25 refundable deposit.

Pet Policy: None. All Pets Welcome.

Amenities: Cable TV, refrigerators, pool, spas, guest laundry, 24-hour front desk.

Pet Amenities: List of nearby veterinarians maintained. Columbia Park is located about 7 blocks from the motel.

Rated: 3 Paws — 92 rooms and 3 suites. Pride of Super 8 Award Winner.

Kennewick's Super 8 is a very attractive lodging with cozy rooms and many amenities. Kennewick, which means "winter paradise" in the Yakima Native American language, is the best grape producing area in the state. Huge hydroelectric dams and irrigation projects have shaped this area near the confluence of the Columbia, Snake and Yakima Rivers into one of the country's major alfalfa, corn and bean producing areas. The Oasis Waterworks is a nine-acre amusement park with waterslides, a river ride and numerous game arcades.

Island Tyme Bed & Breakfast

4940 South Bayview Road
Langley, WA 98260
800-898-8963 • 360-221-5078
www.islandtymebb.com
islandty@whidbey.com

Type of Lodging: B&B

Room Rates: $95–$140, including full breakfast.

Pet Charges & Deposits: None.

Pet Policy: Designated rooms only. Pets must not be left unattended.

Amenities: Cable TV, Jacuzzi.

Pet Amenities: List of nearby veterinarians maintained. Exercise area. Double Bluff Park is located at Double Bluff Road and Shore Avenue. South Whidbey Recreation Area and Lone Lake nearby.

Rated: 3 Paws — 4 rooms and 1 suite.

Island Tyme is a wonderful, old "painted lady," a three-story Victorian done up in cottage white, rose grenadine and forest green, replete with turned spindles, ruffled shingles, gingerbread gables, turret and a covered porch. Langley is on the south end of Whidbey Island, 8½ miles from the Clinton/Mukilteo Ferry. It's perched on a bluff overlooking the Saratoga Passage with spectacular views of Camano Island, Mount Baker and the Cascades. Visit the gift shops, historic museums, local winery and Double Bluff beach. Life can be wonderful when you take advantage of everything to see and do here.

Der Ritterhof

190 U.S. Highway 2
P.O. Box 307
Leavenworth, WA 98826
800-255-5845 • 509-548-5845
www.deritterhof.com
imjinfo@crownet.com

Type of Lodging: Motel

Room Rates: $74–$180, including continental breakfast. AAA discount.

Pet Charges & Deposits: $10 per stay.

Pet Policy: Domestic pets only. Pets must not be left unattended.

Amenities: Cable TV, refrigerators, microwaves, pool, hot tubs.

Pet Amenities: There are 7 dogs and 1 cat who share managing duties. List of nearby veterinarians maintained. Exercise area. The motel sits on 4 acres in a park-like area.

Rated: 4 Paws — 51 rooms including 3 suites.

Leavenworth, Washington's world famous Bavarian village, is a year-round tourist magnet, and wonderfully friendly, cozy, homey Der Ritterhof is certainly one of the reasons why. Fred and Sue McClaskey claim to be the owners, but truth to tell, the real managers are seven adorable dogs and one very independent cat. In addition to the wonderful village atmosphere, there's also the Wenatchee River, one of Washington's premier rafting streams. Visit Tumwater Canyon as it blazes with color every fall.

Evergreen Inn

1117 Front Street
Leavenworth, WA 98826
800-327-7212 • 509-548-5515
www.evergreeninn.com
info@evergreeninn.com

Type of Lodging: Motel

Room Rates: $65–$135, including continental breakfast. AAA, AARP, AKC, ABA and *10% weekday Pets Welcome™* discounts.

Pet Charges & Deposits: $10 per day.

Pet Policy: No pets over 35 lbs. Designated rooms only.

Amenities: Cable TV, refrigerators, microwaves, Jacuzzi, hot tubs.

Pet Amenities: List of nearby veterinarians maintained. Exercise area. Property has its own park.

Rated: 3 Paws — 30 rooms and 10 suites.

The compact, charming Evergreen Inn with Bavarian décor in a quiet setting, gives you a choice of several types of accommodations, from single rooms to two-bedroom units with fireplace or whirlpool. Red-Tail Canyon Farm provides sleigh rides in the winter and hayrides in the summer on a 120-acre working draft horse ranch. Dozens of specialty shops can be found on Front Street in downtown Leavenworth.

Obertal Motor Inn

922 Commercial Street
Leavenworth, WA 98826
800-537-9382 • 509-548-5201
www.obertal.com
obertal@rightathome.com

Type of Lodging: Motel

Room Rates: $65–$139, including continental breakfast. AAA, AARP and *10% Pets Welcome™* discounts.

Pet Charges & Deposits: $10 per day

Pet Policy: Designated rooms only.

Amenities: Cable TV, refrigerators, microwaves, hot tubs.

Pet Amenities: List of nearby veterinarians maintained. Blackbird Island Park and Enchantment Park are both on Commercial Street.

Rated: 3 Paws — 27 rooms and 6 suites.

Obertal Motor Inn, located on Commercial Street in the very middle of the charming Bavarian village of Leavenworth, is a perfect center for the exploration of this storybook town. There are at least five major white water rafting excursion companies located on the Wenatchee River. The Leavenworth National Fish Hatchery is part of the Grand Coulee Dam project. Nearly two million Chinook salmon are raised at the hatchery each year.

Anchorage Cottages

2209 Boulevard North
Long Beach, WA 98631
800-646-2351 • 360-642-2351
www.theanchoragecottages.com
info@theanchoragecottages.com

Type of Lodging: Cottages

Cottage Rates: $59–$113. AAA, ABA and Seniors discounts.

Pet Charges & Deposits: $6 per stay.

Pet Policy: Designated cottages only. Pets must not be left unattended.

Amenities: Cable TV, fully equipped cottages, fireplaces, clam and fish cleaning rooms.

Pet Amenities: Exercise area. Private path to the beach.

Rated: 2 Paws — 10 cottages.

Your cottage at Anchorage Cottages will be spic 'n' span and cozy. Kitchens and fireplaces are ready to go. Decks and patio areas are attractively landscaped. Long Beach is where Lewis and Clark found the Pacific Ocean. The Peninsula is located in the southwest corner of Washington, where the mighty Columbia River meets the Pacific Ocean. The area has 28 miles of hard sand beach. The World Kite Museum and Hall of Fame displays hundreds of kites from around the world and from many periods in history. The Pacific Coast Cranberry Research Center details the process used in planting and harvesting cranberries.

Hudson Manor Inn

1616 Hudson Street
Longview, WA 98632
360-425-1100

Type of Lodging: Inn

Room Rates: $41–$55, including continental breakfast. AAA and *10% Pets Welcome™* discounts.

Pet Charges & Deposits: $2 per day.

Pet Policy: Designated rooms only. Limit three pets per room.

Amenities: Cable TV, refrigerators, microwaves, pool.

Pet Amenities: List of nearby veterinarians maintained. Dog runs. Sacajawea and Longview City Parks two blocks from the inn.

Rated: 3 Paws — 28 rooms and 2 suites.

Hudson Manor Inn is a compact, two-story inn with exterior corridors and budget-priced rooms. It's right in the center of Longview, one of the largest planned cities in the United States. It was in the Longview area that settlers met in 1852 to petition for the creation of a separate territory north of the Columbia River. Congress divided the areas into the Oregon and Washington Territories a year later. The city itself was not incorporated until 1923. The Nutty Narrows Bridge is a 60-feet sky bridge designed to provide squirrels a safe passage over Olympia Bay near the Civic Center. The Port of Longview affords 45-minute tours of the port facilities.

FenWold Cottage & Gardens

80 Port Stanley Road
Lopez Island, WA 98261
360-468-3062
www.fenwoldcottage.com
fenwold@rockisland.com

Type of Lodging: B&B
Suite Rates: $98–$86, including full breakfast.
Pet Charges & Deposits: None.
Pet Policy: None. All Pets Welcome.
Amenities: Refrigerators, hot tubs.
Pet Amenities: List of nearby veterinarians maintained. Exercise area. Odlin County Park is located across from Ferry Road which intersects with Port Stanley Road.
Rated: 3 Paws — 1 suite.

FenWold Cottage & Gardens, a Northwest-style cottage built in 1983, combines the rustic elements of wood paneling, wrought iron and natural fabrics, softened by the surrounding gardens that provide color and texture year-round. It's located one mile from the ferry landing, across from Odlin County Park, on Lopez Island, the third largest of the San Juan Islands. It 's a place where the pace is leisurely. Activities include kayaking, bicycling, hiking, beachcombing, wildlife viewing and scuba diving.

Lynnwood Landmark Inn

4300 Alderwood Mall Boulevard
Lynnwood, WA 98036
800-275-0805 • 425-775-7447

Type of Lodging: Hotel
Room Rates: $79–$92, including deluxe breakfast. AAA, AARP and *15% Pets Welcome™* discounts.
Pet Charges & Deposits: $25 nonrefundable deposit.
Pet Policy: None. All Pets Welcome.
Amenities: Pool, whirlpool, weight room.
Pet Amenities: Welcome package available. List of nearby veterinarians maintained. Exercise area. Edmonds Dog Beach and Green Lake Dog Park are within 20 minutes from the hotel.
Rated: 4 Paws — 99 rooms and 1 suite.

Lynnwood Landmark Inn provides moderate-priced accommodations convenient to both Seattle and Everett. Nearby Everett has had an intriguing industrial history. Selected as a major industrial center-to-be in 1890, the Panic of 1893 killed Everett's first industrial chapter. In 1900, Frederick Weyerhaeuser established a sawmill on the town's waterfront, which quickly grew into one of the world's largest lumber mills. But the current chapter of Everett's history began in the mid-1960s, when Boeing converted an abandoned Air Force base south of the city into a place to build its 747 aircraft. Visit the Boeing Production Facility, which offers one-hour tours of what may well be the most fascinating manufacturing plant in the world.

Ocean Crest Resort

4652 State Route 109
P.O. Box 07
Moclips, WA 98562
360-276-4465
ocncrest@techline.com

Type of Lodging: Resort

Room Rates: $55–$140. AAA, AARP and *10% Pets Welcome*™ discounts.

Pet Charges & Deposits: $12 per day

Pet Policy: Designated rooms only.

Amenities: Cable TV, refrigerators, microwaves, pool, spa, restaurant, lounge, weight room, sauna, whirlpool, masseuse, gift shop.

Pet Amenities: List of nearby veterinarians maintained. Exercise area. State Park is located a mile from the resort. Olympic National Park is located 25 miles from the resort. Private beach access and wooded walkways.

Rated: 3 Paws — 21 rooms and 24 suites.

The Ocean Crest Resort truly lets you get away from it all, in a unique setting where the forest meets the sea. Descend through its wooded ravine and stroll along the beach. Work out your stress in the Resort's recreation center or soak it away in the Resort's pool and spa. The Qumalt Casino is 15 miles away. The Qumalt Native American Museum is only ten miles from the Resort.

Acorn Motor Inn

31530 State Route 20
Oak Harbor, WA 98277
800-280-6646 • 360-675-6646

Type of Lodging: Motel

Room Rates: $48–$78, including continental breakfast. AAA, AARP, AKC and *10% Pets Welcome*™ discounts.

Pet Charges & Deposits: $10 per day for first 7 days.

Pet Policy: Designated rooms only. Pets must not be left unattended.

Amenities: Cable TV, refrigerators.

Pet Amenities: List of nearby veterinarians maintained. City park is only a block away.

Rated: 2 Paws — 26 rooms and 2 suites

Acorn Motor Inn is a neat, compact property, housed in a two-story structure with exterior corridors. Oak Harbor is the largest town on Whidbey Island. Many of the first settlers were Dutch and their heritage is reflected throughout the city. Deception Pass State Park contains 4,124 acres of freshwater lakes, forest, marshland, sand dunes and offshore islands. The Deception Pass Bridge affords a panorama of the channel.

Sunset View Resort

25517 Park Avenue
P.O. Box 399
Ocean Park, WA 98640
800-272-9199 • 360-665-4494
www.washingtoncoast.com
sunsetview@willapabay.org

Type of Lodging: Motel

Room Rates: $67–$187. AAA, AARP, AKC, ABA and *seasonal Pets Welcome*™ discounts.

Pet Charges & Deposits: $10 per stay.

Pet Policy: Designated rooms only.

Amenities: Cable TV, refrigerators, hot tubs, spas.

Pet Amenities: List of nearby veterinarians maintained. Dog runs. Exercise area. Close to city and state parks. There is a dog path to beach and it is only 400 feet from the ocean.

Rated: 3 Paws — 52 rooms.

At Sunset View Resort, fifteen minutes north of Long Beach on the Long Beach Peninsula, you'll experience wonderful family accommodations among pristine forests and seemingly endless beaches. Relax, retreat, revitalize as you enter a different, somehow more relaxed world. Guestrooms offer great views of the ocean. Go clamming or surf fishing, watch the ocean waves, fly a kite and indulge yourself. Situated in Washington's southwest, the noisiest thing you'll hear here is the crashing Pacific surf.

Ponderosa Motor Lodge

1034 South Second Avenue
Okanogan, WA 98840
800-732-6702 • 509-422-0400
http://wsb.datapro.net/ponderosa

Type of Lodging: Motel

Room Rates: $41–$48. AAA, AARP and *5% Pets Welcome*™ discounts.

Pet Charges & Deposits: None.

Pet Policy: None. All Pets Welcome.

Amenities: Cable TV, refrigerators, microwaves, pool.

Pet Amenities: List of nearby veterinarians maintained. Exercise area. Okanogan Legion Park and North Cascades National Park nearby

Rated: 2 Paws — 24 rooms and 1 suite.

Ponderosa Motor Lodge is a family-owned and operated establishment that guarantees your satisfaction. The rooms are spotless, you get free local calls, and kids and pets stay free. Okanogan started out its life as Alma in 1888, was renamed Pogue in 1905 and was finally re-renamed Okanogan in 1907. Okanogan Bingo & Casino is located near the lodging, as is the Okanogan County Historical Museum, which exhibits objects pertaining to local history, including a reproduction of a 19th century Main Street.

Puget View Guesthouse

7924 61st Northeast
Olympia, WA 98516
360-413-9474
www.bbonline.com/wa/pugetview

Type of Lodging: B&B

Cottage Rates: $99–$129, including continental breakfast.

Pet Charges & Deposits: $10 per day.

Pet Policy: No pets over 25 lbs. Manager's prior approval required.

Amenities: Refrigerator, microwave.

Pet Amenities: List of nearby veterinarians maintained. Exercise area. Property is next door to Tolmie State Park.

Rated: 3 Paws — 1 cottage.

Puget View Guesthouse may well be the smallest establishment in this book, but that doesn't stop it from being one of the most charming. It's a secluded 1930s log cottage on the shore of Puget Sound with stunning marine and mountain views. People have come to appreciate its peaceful beauty and comfortable hospitality since 1984. Olympia's State Capital Museum is housed in a 32-room California mission-style mansion. It displays photographs and historic documents pertaining to Northwest Native Americans, pioneer settlements, and Washington Territorial and State government. The Capitol Campus is an impressive government park. The 287-feet diameter dome of the Capitol is one of the largest in the world.

GuestHouse Inn

220 Bravo Terrace
Port Orchard, WA 98366
360-895-7818
www.orchardhospitality.com

Type of Lodging: Inn

Room Rates: $54–$125, including continental breakfast. AAA and AARP discounts.

Pet Charges & Deposits: $10 per day

Pet Policy: No pets over 25 lbs.

Amenities: Cable TV, refrigerators, microwaves, safes, pool, whirlpool.

Pet Amenities: None.

Rated: 3 Paws — 55 rooms and 3 suites.

You'll find a pet-friendly greeting at the GuestHouse Inn. In addition to great accommodations, you'll find great amenities including an indoor pool, spa, fitness room and meeting room. Magnificent views of mountains and lush forests give way to a golfer's paradise. There are unique shops in the harborside downtown area and your exactly four miles from the Bremerton-Seattle ferry.

Palace Hotel

1004 Water Street
Port Townsend, WA 98368
800-962-0741 • 360-385-0773
www.olympus.net/palace
palace@olympus.net

Type of Lodging: Hotel

Room Rates: $59–$189, including continental breakfast. AAA, AARP, AKC, ABA and *10% Pets Welcome*™ discounts.

Pet Charges & Deposits: $10 per day

Pet Policy: No pets over 150 lbs.

Amenities: Cable TV, refrigerators, microwaves, Jacuzzi.

Pet Amenities: Pet treats with continental breakfast delivered to room door. List of nearby veterinarians maintained. Exercise area. There are miles of public beaches located within a block of the hotel.

Rated: 4 Paws — 12 rooms and **5** suites.

Have you ever wanted to know what it would have been like to live in Victorian times? You need go no farther than the Palace Hotel, which, in the European tradition, occupies the two upper floors of the Captain Tibbals Building, a classic, three-story brick building built in 1889 at a cost of $28,000. From 1925 to 1933, it was known as "The Palace of Sweets," since it housed a hotel that also served as a brothel. The Madam, Marie, and her "girls," left town after an early morning raid by the sheriff in the mid-1930s. Every room is uniquely decorated in a Victorian theme and you truly may never want to leave the hotel to see the sights of Port Townsend.

Poulsbo Inn

18680 Highway 305
Poulsbo, WA 98370
800-597-5151 • 360-779-3921
www.poulsboinn.com
salesmgr@poulsboinn.com

Type of Lodging: Hotel

Room Rates: $79–$115, including continental breakfast. AAA and AARP discounts.

Pet Charges & Deposits: $10 per day.

Pet Policy: Designated rooms only. Limit two pets per room.

Amenities: Cable TV, refrigerators, safes, pool, Jacuzzi, fitness room.

Pet Amenities: Exercise area. Raab Park is located on Hostmark Street. Pet walking area with pet waste disposal site.

Rated: 3 Paws — 72 rooms.

The Poulsbo Inn is in the heart of the Scandinavian city of Poulsbo. All units are very homey. Some rooms have a breathtaking panorama of the Olympic Mountains and Liberty Bay. Poulsbo ("Paul's Place" in Norwegian) was settled by Norwegians in 1882 and developed into a fishing and farming community. The Marine Science Center has educational exhibits and live marine specimens.

Holiday Inn Express Hotel & Suites

Southeast 1190 Bishop Boulevard
Pullman, WA 99163
800-HOLIDAY • 509-334-4437
www.hiexpress.com/pullmanwa

Type of Lodging: Hotel

Room Rates: $79–$99, including continental breakfast. AAA, AARP, AKC, ABA and *20% Pets Welcome*™ discounts.

Pet Charges & Deposits: None.

Pet Policy: Designated rooms only.

Amenities: Cable TV, refrigerators, microwaves, pool, Jacuzzi.

Pet Amenities: List of nearby veterinarians maintained. Exercise area. Bill Chipman Trail, Pullman City Playfields and Reaney Park nearby. Washington State University Veterinary Hospital is less than a mile from the hotel.

Rated: 3 Paws — 95 rooms and 30 suites.

Holiday Inn Express affords numerous upscale amenities at a very affordable price. Pullman is home to Washington State University, which was founded in 1890. This major educational institution is justifiably proud of its museums, which house special collections focusing on anthropology, modern art, veterinary medicine and zoology.

Best Western Tower Inn

1515 George Washington Way
Richland, WA 98352
800-635-3980 • 509-946-4121
www.towerinn.net
towersales@nwinpo.net

Type of Lodging: Hotel

Room Rates: $59–$99, including continental breakfast. AAA and AARP discounts.

Pet Charges & Deposits: $25 per stay.

Pet Policy: None. All Pets Welcome.

Amenities: Cable TV, refrigerators, large indoor pool, Jacuzzi, free local calls.

Pet Amenities: List of nearby veterinarians maintained. Exercise area. Jefferson Park across the street. Bike path along the river.

Rated: 3 Paws — 195 rooms and 5 suites.

Best Western Tower Inn is housed in a six-story high-rise building with interior corridors and numerous splendid amenities. It's a first-class choice, 2½ miles north of the city center. In 1944, Richland joined Oak Ridge (Tennessee), Los Alamos (New Mexico) and Argonne Laboratory (Chicago) as a development site for the atomic bomb. Today, in addition to its major centers of technological industries, Richland is the center for the area's vineyards, fields and orchards. The Plant Two Visitors Center describes the workings of a commercial nuclear power plant. Three Rivers Children's Museum has a wonderful assortment of hands-on adventures for children.

Colwell Best Value Inn

501 West First Avenue
Ritzville, WA 99169
800-341-8000 • 509-659-1620
www.colwellmotorinn.com

Type of Lodging: Motel

Room Rates: $40–$65, including coffee, tea, hot cocoa and cookies. AAA, AARP, Seniors and *10% Pets Welcome*™ discounts.

Pet Charges & Deposits: $4 per day. $25 refundable deposit.

Pet Policy: No pets over 50 lbs. Designated rooms only. Manager's prior approval required.

Amenities: Cable TV, refrigerators, microwaves, summer pool, Jacuzzi, sauna, guest laundry, BBQ, picnic area.

Pet Amenities: List of nearby veterinarians maintained. Dog runs. Exercise area. Ritzville City Park is located at Division and 8th.

Rated: 2 Paws — 22 rooms and 3 suites.

Colwell Best Value Inn gives you large, spacious rooms at a small, affordable price. All units have at-the-door parking, winter plug-ins and you get free local telephone calls. Ritzville is centrally located in Washington's Inland Empire. The motel is close to the Burroughs Historical Museum, the Downtown Historic District and Palouse Falls. You might be fortunate to arrive during the annual Antique Car Show.

Alexis Hotel

1007 First Avenue
Seattle, WA 98104
800-426-7033 • 206-624-4844
www.alexishotel.com

Type of Lodging: Hotel
Room Rates: $230–$725. AAA discount.
Pet Charges & Deposits: None.
Pet Policy: None. All Pets Welcome.
Amenities: Cable TV, refrigerators, honor bar, safe.
Pet Amenities: Special doggie dining menu and biscuits on request at the front desk. Staff will walk your dog on request. Myrtle Edwards Park is located at the end of Pier 70, just minutes from the Hotel.
Rated: 5 Paws — 70 rooms and 39 suites. Listed on the National Register of Historic Places.

Seattle is one of the great cities of the United States, and the historic Alexis Hotel is surely a world-class hotel. The Alexis has presided elegantly in the heart of downtown since the turn of the 20th century. The Hotel has welcomed royalty, luminaries, and leaders from around the world. Travel & Leisure magazine said, "Rarely has so much quality been congregated under one roof." Pike Place Market, a Seattle tradition, is a "must see," and the Space Needle, Seattle's signature symbol to the world, is a "must experience" when you're in the Emerald City.

Holiday Inn Sea-Tac

17338 International Boulevard
Seattle, WA 98188
877-5 SEATAC • 206-248-1000
revmgr_5114@firstworld.net

Type of Lodging: Hotel

Room Rates: $129–$159. AAA and AARP discounts.

Pet Charges & Deposits: $20 per day

Pet Policy: No pets over 20 lbs. Designated rooms only.

Amenities: Cable TV, pool, whirlpool, fitness room, lounge, revolving restaurant.

Pet Amenities: Angle Lake Park is located at 195th and International Boulevard.

Rated: 3 Paws — 260 rooms.

A prime location, exceptional facilities and a commitment to personalized service make the Holiday Inn Sea-Tac the ideal choice when visiting Western Washington. The hotel is located directly across from Seattle-Tacoma International Airport, fifteen minutes from Seattle, Tacoma and Bellevue. The Seattle Art Museum has a superb collection of Asian, African and Northwest Coast Native American art, while the Nordic Heritage Museum focuses on Scandinavian cultural contributions to life in the Pacific Northwest, from the 18th century to the present. Another museum, the Museum of Flight, features the history of aviation technology from the 13th century through the late 1930s and includes exhibits of everything from a DC-3 to a supersonic M/D-21 Blackbird.

La Quinta Inn – Sea Tac Airport

2824 South 188th Street
Seattle, WA 98188
800-531-5900 • 206-241-5211
www.laquinta.com

Type of Lodging: Hotel

Room Rates: $79–$99, including continental breakfast. AAA and AARP discounts.

Pet Charges & Deposits: None.

Pet Policy: None. All Pets Welcome.

Amenities: Cable TV, safes, pool, hot tubs.

Pet Amenities: Exercise area. Park nearby.

Rated: 3 Paws — 143 rooms.

Combining typical La Quinta first-class quality, a six-story building with interior corridors, quiet rooms adjacent to the airport and a superb central location, La Quinta Inn is a great home away from home in the Seattle area. A unique Seattle adventure is Bill Speidel's Underground Tour, which departs from Pioneer Place Park. It explores the five-block area around Pioneer Square with its turn-of-the-20th century storefronts, subterranean sidewalks and businesses created when street levels were raised between eight and 35 feet following a fire in 1889. Woodland Park Zoo houses more than 300 species of animals representative of the worldwide ecosystem, focusing primarily on the Tropical Rain Forest and the Temperate Forest.

Cimarron Motor Inn

9734 Northwest Silverdale Way
Silverdale, WA 98383
800-213-5076 • 360-692-7177
www.oxfordsuites.com

Type of Lodging: Motel

Room Rates: $65–$75, including continental breakfast. AAA, AARP, AKC, ABA and *10% Pets Welcome*™ discounts.

Pet Charges & Deposits: $10 per stay.

Pet Policy: No pets over 20 lbs.

Amenities: Cable TV, refrigerators, safes, microwave.

Pet Amenities: Waterfront Park is located at Byron Street and Bayshore.

Rated: 2 Paws — 54 rooms and 9 suites.

Cimarron Motor Inn is a clean, comfortable, well-priced lodging in downtown Silverdale. The small town is located on Dyes Inlet and is a center for fishing, kayaking, boating and marine outdoor sports.

Russell House Bed & Breakfast

902 East Water Street
P.O. Box F
South Bend, WA 98586
888-484-6907 • 360-875-6487
www.willapabay.org/~jrowan

Type of Lodging: B&B

Room Rates: $75–$100, including full breakfast. AAA, AARP, AKC, ABA and *5% Pets Welcome*™ discounts.

Pet Charges & Deposits: $10 per day.

Pet Policy: Manager's prior approval required.

Amenities: Cable TV, refrigerators, microwaves, honor bar.

Pet Amenities: List of nearby veterinarians maintained. Exercise area. South Bend Park is located on Robert Bush Drive.

Rated: 3 Paws — 3 rooms and 1 suite.

The beautiful Victorian mansion that houses Russell House Bed & Breakfast was built on Alta Vista Hill in 1891, as a 25th anniversary gift from John Russell to his wife, Annie. It affords a panoramic 360-degree view of the town of South Bend and the Willapa River, and the open fields and wooded slopes of the Willapa Hills. Once described as a gilded palace of extravagance, the 1911 Pacific County Courthouse is an example of Second Renaissance Revival architecture. Chinook Native American crafts and artwork, as well as exhibits pertaining to the lumber, oyster and fishing industries, can be found at the Pacific County Historical Society Museum.

Best Inn & Suites

6309 East Broadway
Spokane, WA 99212
800-BEST INN • 509-535-7185
www.hotels-west.com

Type of Lodging: Motel

Room Rates: $39–$99, including continental breakfast. AAA, AARP, AKC, ABA and *10% Pets Welcome*™ discounts.

Pet Charges & Deposits: None.

Pet Policy: None. All Pets Welcome.

Amenities: Cable TV, refrigerators, microwaves, pool, hot tubs, spas.

Pet Amenities: List of nearby veterinarians maintained. Dog runs. Exercise area. Park nearby.

Rated: 4 Paws — 69 rooms and 3 suites.

With easy access off Interstate 90 (Exit 236) and just minutes from the Spokane County Fair & Expo Center, Best Inn & Suites is a sparkling, attractive lodging on well-landscaped grounds. Take in a ball game at nearby Spokane Indians Baseball Stadium, stay for Bloomsday, the Lilac Festival or Pig Out in the Park. Spokane Falls, at their best during spring and early summer, can best be seen from the Monroe Street Bridge. There are also six local wineries offering tours and wine tastings.

Best Western Pheasant Hill

12415 East Mission Avenue
Spokane, WA 99216
509-926-7432
www.bestwesternspokane.com
bwphgm@earthlink.net

Type of Lodging: Motel

Room Rates: $69–$189, including continental breakfast. AAA and AARP discounts.

Pet Charges & Deposits: None.

Pet Policy: Designated rooms only.

Amenities: Cable TV, refrigerators, microwaves, safes, pool, Jacuzzi, spas, irons and ironing boards, coffeemakers, hairdryers.

Pet Amenities: List of nearby veterinarians maintained. Exercise area. Mirabeau Point Park is located at Indiana and Mirabeau Parkway.

Rated: 3 Paws — 105 rooms and 4 suites.

Housed in a four-story earth tone structure, ten minutes east of downtown Spokane, Best Western Pheasant Hill features well-decorated guestrooms and a plethora of first-class amenities. Bing Crosby attended Gonzaga University, one of 28 Jesuit colleges in the country, and was awarded an honorary doctorate from that institution in 1937. Today, the Bing Crosby Collection contains a substantial collection of memorabilia that belonged to the crooner. The Cheney Cowles Memorial Museum has a major display about the historic development of the Inland Empire, including displays focusing on mining, timber and farming.

Shilo Inn Hotel & Restaurant

East 923 Third Avenue
Spokane, WA 99202
800-222-2244 • 509-535-9000
www.shiloinns.com
spokane@shiloinns.com

Type of Lodging: Hotel

Room Rates: $69–$99. AAA, AARP and *10% Pets Welcome*™ discounts.

Pet Charges & Deposits: $10 per day

Pet Policy: Designated rooms only.

Amenities: Cable TV, refrigerators, microwaves, safes, pool, whirlpool, Jacuzzi, hot tubs, spas, sauna, steam room, exercise center, free shuttle, rooftop restaurant and lounge with 270° city view.

Pet Amenities: Dog runs. Exercise area. Liberty Park is located 2 blocks east of the hotel.

Rated: 3 Paws — 105 rooms and suites.

Shilo Inn is a first-class hotel that provides "affordable excellence" in the heart of the city. In addition to exemplary rooms, you should dine at the Hotel's rooftop restaurant, which gives an unparalleled view of the city. The Hotel has always been a pet-friendly facility and has even hosted functions for police dog training. Manito Park in Spokane features a conservatory, Japanese garden, a perennial garden, rose garden, lilac garden and a formal garden. This is one of the Pacific Northwest's premier garden parks.

Sheraton Tacoma Hotel

1320 Broadway Plaza
Tacoma, WA 98402
800-845-9466 • 253-572-3200
www.sheratontacoma.com
sales@sheratontacoma.com

Type of Lodging: Hotel

Room Rates: $87–$450. AAA, AARP and *25% Pets Welcome*™ discounts.

Pet Charges & Deposits: $250 refundable deposit.

Pet Policy: No pets over 30 lbs. Manager's prior approval required. Pets must not be left unattended.

Amenities: Cable TV, valet service, gift shop, honor bars, safe, restaurant.

Pet Amenities: Fireman's Park is located at "A" Street and 9th Avenue.

Rated: 3 Paws — 319 rooms and 8 suites.

The Sheraton Tacoma Hotel, a 26-story skyscraper, not only gives you deluxe comfort, but also affords you panoramic views of Mount Rainier and Puget Sound. Although almost gobbled up by nearby Seattle, Tacoma very much retains its own independent flavor. Point Defiance Park has several miles of woodland trails, scenic views of mountain and waterfront, a major Japanese Garden and an entire day's worth of natural entertainment. The Zoo & Aquarium features Asian elephants, beluga whales, a Pacific walrus, polar bears, sea otters, sharks and snow leopards.

Guesthouse Inn & Suites

*1600 74th Avenue Southwest
Tumwater, WA 98501
877-847-7152 • 360-943-5040*

Type of Lodging: Hotel

Suite Rates: $79–$150, including continental breakfast. AAA, AARP, AKC and *10% Pets Welcome™* discounts.

Pet Charges & Deposits: $10 per day. $10 nonrefundable deposit.

Pet Policy: Designated rooms only.

Amenities: Cable TV, refrigerators, microwaves, safes, pool, hot tubs, irons and ironing boards.

Pet Amenities: List of nearby veterinarians maintained. Exercise area.

Rated: 3 Paws — 59 suites.

Although the immaculately clean, spacious and comfortable, Guesthouse Inn & Suites facility is located in the smaller city of Tumwater (yes, the home of Olympia beer!), it's actually only three miles away from Washington's state capital at Olympia. You can visit the lovely state capitol grounds or visit the Olympia Miller Brewing Company for tastings and a video tour. Of course, you might also choose to marvel at the great outdoors in this wonderful, woodsy place.

Best Western Cascade Inn

*960 Highway 20
P.O. Box 813
Winthrop, WA 98862
800-468-6754 • 509-996-3100
www.winthropwa.com
cascade@methow.com*

Type of Lodging: Hotel

Room Rates: $55–$73, including continental breakfast. AAA, AARP and *10% Pets Welcome™* discounts.

Pet Charges & Deposits: $10 per day.

Pet Policy: Sorry, no cats. No pets over 40 lbs. Designated rooms only.

Amenities: Cable TV, pool, hot tubs.

Pet Amenities: List of nearby veterinarians maintained. Dog runs. Exercise area. Pearygin Lake nearby. Many hiking and walking trails nearby. The property extends to the Methow River, approximately 200 feet from the hotel.

Rated: 3 Paws — 63 rooms.

What makes tiny Winthrop such a tourist draw? Lots of things. Most important, when you enter the town, you're right back in an old-time western movie—but for real. There's a colorful main street with rows of false-fronted buildings, wooden boardwalks and old-fashioned streetlights. The White Buck Museum has more than 10,000 antiques and collectibles, some dating back to the 18th century. The entire town seems more like a living museum of the Old West than something that belongs in the 21st century—but that's what makes it so much fun. Of course, if you're into horseback riding, river rafting, hiking, fishing, cross-country skiing and the like, you've come to the right place.

The Virginian Resort

808 North Cascade Highway
P.O. Box 237
Winthrop, WA 98862
800-854-2834 • 509-996-2535
www.methow.com/lodging
Virginian@methow.com

Type of Lodging: Motel
Room Rates: $50–$95. AAA and AARP discounts.
Pet Charges & Deposits: $5 per day.
Pet Policy: None. All Pets Welcome.
Amenities: None.
Pet Amenities: Treats available. List of nearby veterinarians maintained. Large grass field next to the motel. Pearygin Lake and Okonoga National Forest nearby. Trail to Methow River next to motel.
Rated: 3 Paws — 37 rooms.

Why would anyone name a motel in fabulous, old-time Winthrop "The Virginian?"—because it fits so naturally with the town. Poet and author Owen Wister lived in Winthrop, a mining boomtown, in the early 1900s. He described Winthrop's sites and citizens in his most famous novel, *The Virginian*. It's easy to become so mesmerized by the sights, sounds, smells and tastes of this wonderful pioneer town that you forget to look around you and notice you're in the middle of the glorious Cascade Mountains. With all this to lure you, the town is only four hours' drive from Seattle. The motel is located near a trail system with lots of opportunity for hiking, as trails start within walking distance of the property.

The Winthrop Inn

P.O. Box 265
Winthrop, WA 98862
800-444-1972 • 509-996-2217
www.winthrop-inn.com
wininn@methow.com

Type of Lodging: Motel
Room Rates: $55–$95, including continental breakfast. AAA, AARP, AKC, ABA and *$5 Pets Welcome*™ discounts.
Pet Charges & Deposits: $7 per day
Pet Policy: Sorry, no cats.
Amenities: Refrigerators, microwaves, pool, hot tubs.
Pet Amenities: List of nearby veterinarians maintained. Dog runs. Exercise area. Pearrigan State Park is located on East Chewuck Road.
Rated: 2 Paws — 30 rooms.

The Winthrop Inn is a characteristic two-story mountain structure near the Methow River. Winthrop's Shafer Museum includes several pioneer structures. There's a log cabin built by Guy Waring, the town founder, in 1897, a general store, a print shop, a post office and a millinery shop. It's well worth the ride to get to Winthop.

Holiday Inn Express

1001 East "A" Street
Yakima, WA 98901
800 HOLIDAY • 509-249-1000

Type of Lodging: Hotel

Room Rates: $66–$85, including continental breakfast. AAA and AARP discounts.

Pet Charges & Deposits: $6 per day.

Pet Policy: No pets over 70 lbs. Designated rooms only.

Amenities: Cable TV, refrigerators, microwaves, pool, Jacuzzi.

Pet Amenities: Sarge Hubbard Park is located a mile from the hotel.

Rated: 3 Paws — 87 rooms and 3 suites.

Quiet and comfortable—exactly what you're looking for when you travel far from home, and Holiday Inn Express won't let you down. Year-round attractions in Yakima include Native American petroglyphs, scattered along an old trail leading to the Wenas Mountains. Yakima Canyon, a popular rockhound haunt, also affords fine fishing in the Yakima River. You can see Mount Rainier and Mount Adams in the distance.

Oxford Suites

1701 Terrace Heights Drive
Yakima, WA 98901
800-404-7848 • 509-457-9000
www.oxfordsuites.com
eves@oxfordsuites.com

Type of Lodging: Hotel

Suite Rates: $75–$159, including evening Manager's reception. AAA and AARP discounts.

Pet Charges & Deposits: $15 per stay.

Pet Policy: No pets over 20 lbs.

Amenities: Cable TV, refrigerators, microwaves, pool, Jacuzzi, river views.

Pet Amenities: Exercise area. Property is located adjacent to a nature path. Sarge Hubbard Park is less than a mile from the hotel.

Rated: 3 Paws — 107 suites.

You can always depend on Oxford Suites for upscale, downright roomy accommodations and the Yakima unit is no exception. Yakima is the gateway to the Yakima Valley wine country, which has more than 20 wineries. The Yakima Greenway extends for ten miles along the Yakima River, from Selah Gap to Union Gap, and features a nine-mile paved walking and bike path—ideal for pets. Want to have an evening of old-time entertainment? Try the Capitol Theater, a restored vaudeville house.

Sun Country Inn

1700 North First Street
Yakima, WA 98901
800-559-3675 • 509-248-5650

Type of Lodging: Inn

Room Rates: $52–$66, including continental breakfast. AAA, AARP, Government, Corporate and *10% Pets Welcome*™ discounts.

Pet Charges & Deposits: $5 per day.

Pet Policy: Pets must not be left unattended.

Amenities: Cable TV, refrigerators, microwaves, pool.

Pet Amenities: List of nearby veterinarians maintained. Yakima Greenway Path is just 2 blocks from the Inn.

Rated: 2 Paws — 70 rooms and 1 suite.

Formerly the Comfort Inn, the newly renovated Sun County Inn is a wonderfully accommodating inn ideally situated near Yakima's city center. The Yakima Valley Museum in Franklin Park has a large collection of carriages, coaches and wagons, Yakima Native American artifacts, a re-created blacksmith shop, a working soda fountain and a hands-on children's center. The Yakima Electric Railway Museum offers rides on vintage trolleys and the 46-acre arboretum of noted for its flowering tree collection.

WEST VIRGINIA

Nickname: Mountain State

Population: 1,806,928

Area: 24,231 square miles

Climate: Humid continental climate except for marine modification in the lower panhandle.

Capital: Charleston

Entered Union: June 20, 1863

Motto: *Montani Semper Liberi* (Mountaineers are always free).

Songs: The West Virginia Hills; This Is My West Virginia; West Virginia, My Home Sweet Home

Flower: Big Rhododendron

Tree: Sugar Maple

Bird: Cardinal

Famous West Virginians: Pearl Buck, Thomas "Stonewall" Jackson, Don Knotts, Michael Owens, Walter Reuther, Cyrus Vance, Charles "Chuck" Yeager.

History: Sparsely inhabited at the time of European contact, the area was primarily Native American hunting grounds. British explorers reached the New River in 1671. George Washington explored the area in 1753 and Daniel Boone traversed it in 1774. The area was part of Virginia, but resented being ruled from the east. When Virginia seceded from the Union in 1861, the Wheeling Convention repudiated secession and created a new state, Kanawha, which was renamed West Virginia. It was admitted to the Union in 1863.

Super 8 Motel

2208 Pleasant Valley Road
Fairmont, WV 26554
800-800-8000 • 304-363-1488
www.super8.com

Type of Lodging: Motel

Room Rates: $50–$91, including continental breakfast. AAA, AARP and **10% Pets Welcome™** discounts.

Pet Charges & Deposits: None.

Pet Policy: None. All Pets Welcome.

Amenities: Cable TV, refrigerators, Jacuzzi, free local calls.

Pet Amenities: Morn's Park is located on Pleasant Valley Road.

Rated: 3 Paws — 54 rooms and 8 suites. Pride of Super 8 Award Winner.

Fairmont is in covered bridge country, between Morgantown and Clarksburg. Originally two towns, Palatine and Middletown, Fairmont occupies steep hills surrounding the Monongahela River. Today, high-tech development of software competes with coal mining as a source of income for the populace. Pricketts Fort State Park contains a reconstructed log fort similar to the one built on the site in 1774.

Hampton Inn

975 Foxcroft Avenue
Martinsburg, WV 25401
304-267-2900
www.hamptoninn.com
mbgwv01@hi-hotel.com

Type of Lodging: Hotel

Room Rates: $75–$89, including continental breakfast. AAA and AARP discounts.

Pet Charges & Deposits: None.

Pet Policy: None. All Pets Welcome.

Amenities: Cable TV, coffeemakers, irons and ironing boards, hairdryers, free local phone calls.

Pet Amenities: Exercise area. City and county parks nearby.

Rated: 3 Paws — 99 rooms.

Hampton Inn is a great place to stay when in the extreme northeastern part of the state, a stone's throw from the Pennsylvania border. Founded in the 18th century, Martinsburg was an important shipping center by the 1850s. Today, it's a growing and distribution point for apples and peaches. Nearby Harpers Ferry, at the confluence of the Potomac and Shenandoah Rivers, separates Maryland, Virginia and West Virginia. The federal arsenal and armory built in 1796 was the target of abolitionist John Brown's raid. During the Civil War, the Union command regarded Harpers Ferry as the key to Washington, DC. Today, Harpers Ferry National Historical Park contains six paths through history: Industry, John Brown, Civil War, African American History, Environmental History, and Transportation.

Sleep Inn

1015 Oakvale Road
P.O. Box 5625
Princeton, WV 24740
888-259-8543 • 304-431-2800
www.sleepinn.com/hotel/wv414
sleepinnprince@sleepinn.com

Type of Lodging: Motel

Room Rates: $50–$95, including continental breakfast. AAA, AARP and *10%* Pets Welcome™ discounts.

Pet Charges & Deposits: None.

Pet Policy: No pets over 35 lbs. Pets must not be left unattended.

Amenities: Cable TV, microfridges.

Pet Amenities: Lit of nearby veterinarians maintained. Princeton City Park nearby.

Rated: 2 Paws – 81 rooms. 1997-98 & 1999-2000 Choice Hotels International Gold Hospitality Award Winner.

Sleep Inn – Princeton has been awarded the Choice Hotels International Gold Hospitality Award for 1997-98 and 1999-2000, and with good reason. It's a sparkling lodging with heated indoor pool and spa, modem outlets in rooms and a meeting room for corporate business. Princeton is close to Winterplace Ski Resort, an Exhibition Coal Mine, Wolf Creek Native American Village and the Crab Orchard Historical Museum.

Best Western Summersville Lake Motor Lodge

1203 South Broad Street
Summersville, WV 26651
800-214-9551 • 304-872-6900

Type of Lodging: Motor Lodge

Room Rates: $44–$72, including continental breakfast. AAA discount.

Pet Charges & Deposits: $5 per day.

Pet Policy: Pets must not be left unattended.

Amenities: Cable TV, refrigerators, microwaves.

Pet Amenities: None.

Rated: 2 Paws – 58 rooms.

Best Western Summersville Lake Motor Lodge offers upscale accommodations at very reasonable rates. Summersville is located on U.S. Highway 19, between Sutton and Beckley. Summersville Lake is one of the state's premier outdoor recreation area. The Gauley River nearby is known for its rapids, whitewater rafting and fishing opportunities. Carnifex Ferry Battlefield State Park commemorates a civil war battle fought here in 1861. The park museum contains Civil War relics.

WISCONSIN

Nickname: Badger State
Population: 5,250,446
Area: 65,499 square miles
Climate: Long, cold winters and short, warm summers, tempered by the Great Lakes.
Capital: Madison
Entered Union: May 28, 1848
Motto: Forward.
Song: On, Wisconsin!
Flower: Wood Violet

Tree: Sugar Maple
Bird: Robin
Famous Badgers: Edna Ferber, King Camp Gillette, Harry Houdini, Robert LaFollette, Alfred Lunt, Georgia O'Keeffe, William Rehnquist, John Ringling, Donald K. "Deke" Slayton, Spencer Tracy, Thorsten Veblen, Orson Welles, Laura Ingalls Wilder, Frank Lloyd Wright.

History: Ojibwa, Menominee, Winnebago, Kickapoo, Sauk Fox and Potawotami peoples inhabited the region when Jean Nicolet sailed into Green Bay in 1634. The British took over in 1763. Even though the U.S. won the land after the American Revolution, the British were not ousted until after the war of 1812. Farmers followed lead miners, and a fort was established at Prairie du Chien in 1816. After the Black Hawk War of 1832, all tribal land in Wisconsin was transferred to the U.S. government. Some 96,000 soldiers from Wisconsin served on the Union side during the Civil War.

ALGOMA, WISCONSIN (Pop. 3,300)

Algoma Beach Motel

1500 Lake Street, Highway 42
Algoma, WI 54201
888-254-6621 • 920-487-2844
www.harborwalk.com
algoma1@aol.com

Type of Lodging: Motel
Room Rates: $50–$75, including continental breakfast. AAA, AARP and **5%** *Pets Welcome*™ discounts.
Pet Charges & Deposits: $10 per day.
Pet Policy: Designated rooms only.
Amenities: Cable TV, refrigerators, microwaves.
Pet Amenities: List of nearby veterinarians maintained. Exercise area. City beach dog walk area and Peterson Park nearby.
Rated: 3 Paws — 28 rooms.

Algoma's only lakefront motel offers a private sand beach and scenic Lake Michigan views. Your pet will love walking on the private sandy beach, frolicking in the water and going for a swim. Enjoy a leisurely stroll along the famous Algoma Boardwalk and see exciting fishing activities in the harbor on Lake Michigan where sport fishing began. Hike or bike on the National Ice Age Trail, or enjoy golf or tennis. In the winter, guests may enjoy snowmobiling, cross-country skiing or ice fishing. Algoma is the "gateway" to scenic Door County, which is just a 30 minute drive where you can find state parks, Ridges Sanctuary, the Door County Trout Boil, many arts and crafts shops and Washington Island.

Scenic Shore Inn

2221 Lake Street
Algoma, WI 54201
920-487-3214
www.scenicshoreinn.com
scenicshoreinn@itol.com

Type of Lodging: Motel
Room Rates: $40–$55, including complimentary coffee.
Pet Charges: None.
Pet Policy: Cats are only allowed if declawed. No pets over 20 lbs. Manager's prior approval required.
Amenities: Cable TV, refrigerators, microwaves.
Pet Amenities: List of nearby veterinarians maintained. Exercise area is 2½ acres.
Rated: 3 Paws — 13 rooms.

Scenic Shores Inn offers an unsurpassed scenic setting with all the rooms overlooking beautiful Lake Michigan. All rooms are over-sized and luxurious with queen-sized beds, cable television and air conditioning. Snow-mobile enthusiasts can snowmobile to and from the front door. Enjoy friendly small-town hospitality while exploring all Algoma has to offer, including excellent restaurants, winery tours, antique shops, golf courses, sport fishing, beaches and the Ahnapee State Trail.

Best Western Midway Hotel

3033 West College Avenue
Appleton, WI 54914
800-528-1234 • 920-731-4141
www.midwayhotels.com
bwmsales@execpc.com

Type of Lodging: Hotel
Room Rates: $89–$149, including continental or full breakfast. AAA and AARP discounts.
Pet Charges & Deposits: $10 per day.
Pet Policy: Designated rooms only. Pets are not allowed in pool area.
Amenities: Cable TV, refrigerators, microwaves, pool, whirlpool, sauna, fitness room, airport shuttle service.
Pet Amenities: Outagamie County Dog Park nearby.
Rated: 3 Paws — 103 rooms.

Located in the heart of the Fox River Valley, Best Western Midway Hotel is directly off Highway 41, only half a mile from Fox River Mall and two miles from downtown Appleton. The accommodations feature a number of extra amenities such as coffeemakers, refrigerators or microwaves, cable televisions, two telephones with modem connection, voicemail, hairdryers, irons and ironing boards, full-length mirrors and state-of-the-art electronic door locks. Nearby you'll find "all-season" recreation including boating, swimming, snowmobiling and fishing.

Comfort Suites Comfort Dome

3809 West Wisconsin Avenue
Appleton, WI 54914
920-730-3800
www.wiscohotels.com
appro101@aol.com

Type of Lodging: Hotel

Suite Rates: $89–$179, including continental breakfast and free beverages in the lounge. AAA, AARP and *10% Pets Welcome*™ discounts.

Pet Charges & Deposits: None.

Pet Policy: None. All Pets Welcome.

Amenities: Cable TV, refrigerators, microwaves, pool, whirlpool, hot tubs.

Pet Amenities: List of nearby veterinarians maintained. Exercise area.

Rated: 4 Paws — 130 suites.

The Comfort Suites Comfort Dome is the first of its kind in the world, featuring a breathtaking indoor recreation center. Indulge yourself in the pool, sauna, whirlpool and game room. Experience a workout in the fitness center or take a short trip to the new Gold's Gym free of charge for guests. Guests will feel refreshed and revitalized as the journey continues to the suite, complete with refrigerator, microwaves and coffeemaker. Some suites even have whirlpools.

Exel Inn of Appleton

210 Westhill Boulevard
Appleton, WI 54914
800-367-3935 • 920-733-5551
www.exelinns.com

Type of Lodging: Hotel

Room Rates: $36–$66, including continental breakfast. AARP discount.

Pet Charges & Deposits: $100–$200 refundable deposit on extended stays.

Pet Policy: No pets over 25 lbs. Designated rooms only. Manager's prior approval required. Limit two pets per room.

Amenities: Irons, coffeemakers, full-length mirrors.

Pet Amenities: Tullah Park is located on the corner of College Avenue and Tullah.

Rated: 2 Paws — 104 rooms.

Exel Inn is a good choice for travelers who wish to have access to Fox River Mall, Fox Cities Stadium, Children's Museum, Outagamie County Airport, Lawrence University, Wisconsin International Raceway and downtown Appleton. All Exel Inns offer alarm clock radios, microfridges, modem jacks, free local phone calls and wake-up service.

Woodfield Suites

3730 West College Avenue
Appleton, WI 54914
800-338-0008 • 920-734-7777
www.woodfieldsuites.com

Type of Lodging: Hotel

Suite Rates: $100–$175, including continental breakfast and complimentary cocktails. AAA and AARP discounts.

Pet Charges & Deposits: $10 per day up to $50 limit.

Pet Policy: Designated rooms only. Small pets only. Manager's prior approval required.

Amenities: Cable TV, refrigerators, microwaves, pool, safes, fitness center, steam room, hot tubs, sauna, play area.

Pet Amenities: List of nearby veterinarians maintained. Outagamie County Pet Exercise Area, Newbery Trail and CE Recreation Trail nearby.

Rated: 3 Paws — 98 suites.

The Woodfield Suites includes microwaves, refrigerators, wet bars, hairdryers and televisions. An indoor pool, whirlpool, steam room, sauna, fitness center, play land, video games, Ping Pong tables and pool table are available for all guests. Guest laundry and valet dry-cleaning are available. There are many points of interest including the Fox River Mall, Children's Museum, Barlow Planetarium and Fox Cities Stadium. Sports fans—the Green Bay Packers are 25 miles away.

Bakers Sunset Motel & Cottages

8404 Highway 57
P.O. Box 126
Baileys Harbor, WI 54202
920-839-2218
www.bakersunsetmandc.com
bakersunsetmotel&cottages@dcwis.com

Type of Lodging: Motel and Cottages

Room Rates: $48–$115.

Pet Charges & Deposits: $6 per day.

Pet Policy: Manager's prior approval required. Pet must not be left unattended. Cats must be declawed. Limit two pets per room.

Amenities: Refrigerators, microwaves, play area.

Pet Amenities: List of nearby veterinarians maintained. Exercise area. Property sits on 7½ acres with walking trails. Peninsula State Park is located at 9262 Shore Road. Newport State Park is located in Ellison Bay.

Rated: 3 Paws — 7 rooms and 4 cottages on 7 acres.

Bakers Sunset Motel & Cottages are on the quiet side of Door County, on Highway 57 just north of Baileys Harbor. With over seven acres of park-like setting, there is plenty of room for you and your pet to play. There are campfire pits, Weber grills and picnic tables for all to enjoy. The cottages are housekeeping units and have everything you would need except food. Baileys Harbor has been called the "Brown Trout Capital" of the area. Along with brown trout, Door County offers some of the finest fishing, including small mouth bass, walleye, northern, perch, rainbow, lake trout and Chinook salmon.

Days Inn

919 Highway 54 East
Black River Falls, WI 54615
800-329-7466 • 715-284-4333
www.daysinn.com
brfdaysinn@discover-net.net

Type of Lodging: Hotel
Room Rates: $55–$130, including continental breakfast. AAA, AARP and *Pets Welcome™* discounts.
Pet Charges & Deposits: None.
Pet Policy: No pets over 25 lbs. Designated rooms only.
Amenities: Cable TV, pool, whirlpool, sauna.
Pet Amenities: List of nearby veterinarians maintained. Exercise area. State forests nearby.
Rated: 3 Paws – 84 rooms.

The Days Inn is centrally located for the traveler who wishes to visit Black River Falls, Lacrosse, Eau Claire, Torah, Sprat and Majestic Pines Casino areas. The Black River Falls area and surrounding Jackson County offer unsurpassed beauty and an abundance of recreational activities. The most popular involve canoeing, fishing, snowmobiling, ATVing, scuba diving and golf. The natural scenic beauty of the Jackson County Forest and Black River State Forest accounts for 185,000 acres.

Viking Motel

201 South First Street
Cameron, WI 54822
715-458-2111
theviking@marcus-online.net

Type of Lodging: Motel
Room Rates: $50–$80. AAA discount.
Pet Charges & Deposits: None.
Pet Policy: Small pets only. Manager's prior approval required.
Amenities: Cable TV.
Pet Amenities: Exercise area.
Rated: 3 Paws – 20 rooms.

The Viking Motel is a lovely small motel in northern Wisconsin. Guests may park directly in front of their room. Each room contains a remote control television, two lovely rocking chairs, a desk and chair and coffeemaker. The bathrooms are all ceramic tile, very spacious with lovely large tubs and showers. Within a 45 minute drive from the Viking Motel, guests may enjoy boating, fishing, golfing, hiking, horseback riding, skiing, tennis and a variety of winter sports.

Best Western Quiet House & Suites

1130 North Johns Street
Dodgeville, WI 53533
800-528-1234 • 608-935-7739
www.quiethouse.com

Type of Lodging: Motel

Room Rates: $93–$150, including continental breakfast on weekdays. AAA and AARP discount.

Pet Charges & Deposits: $15 per day.

Pet Policy: Designated rooms only. Manager's prior approval required. Pets must not be left unattended.

Amenities: Cable TV, refrigerators, microwaves, pool, whirlpool, hot tubs.

Pet Amenities: List of nearby veterinarians maintained. Governor Dodge State Park and Military Ridge State Trail nearby.

Rated: 3 Paws – 36 rooms and 3 suites.

In the late 1800s Julius Vogt established the original Quiet House in Milwaukee, featuring comfort and hospitality. Four generations later, they continue this tradition, blending 100 years of hospitality with 21st century service and amenities. The specialty suites include Oriental, Art Deco, Pyramid, Vintage Cabin, Roman Bath, Hi-Tech Contemporary and others make your stay at Quiet House & Suites unique. Historic Dodgeville, headquarters of Land's End, is the hub of south central Wisconsin—with scenic beauty and close to many attractions. Items not to be missed include the House on the Rock, Governor Dodge State Park, Frank Lloyd Wright's Taliesin, American Players' theatre and historic Mineral Point.

Days Inn

844 Railroad Street North
P.O. Box 995
Eagle River, WI 54521
800 DAYS INN • 715-479-5151
www.daysinn.com
eadays@newnorth.net

Type of Lodging: Motel

Room Rates: $49–$99, including continental breakfast. AAA and AARP discounts.

Pet Charges & Deposits: None.

Pet Policy: Designated rooms only.

Amenities: Cable TV, refrigerators, microwaves, safes, pool, whirlpool, hot tubs, hairdryers, irons and ironing boards.

Pet Amenities: List of nearby veterinarians maintained.

Rated: 3 Paws – 93 rooms.

Days Inn invites you and your pet to celebrate the glory of every season in Eagle River. With world-class fishing, water sports, golf, hiking, biking, sightseeing, touring fascinating historic sites, wildlife viewing, birding, wetlands, pure glacial lakes and wilderness rivers—great times are there for the making. Area attractions include World Championship Snowmobile Derby Track, Ice Castle, Hockey Hall of Fame, Lac Vieux Desert Casino and Nicolet National Forest.

Edgewater Inn and Resort

5054 Highway 70 West
Eagle River, WI 54521
888-334-3987 • 715-479-4011
www.edgeinn.com
edgewater@edgeinn.com

Type of Lodging: Resort

Room Rates: $40–$90, including continental breakfast. Call for cottage rates. AAA, AARP and *10% Pets Welcome*™ discounts.

Pet Charges & Deposits: $10 per stay.

Pet Policy: Manager's prior approval required.

Amenities: Cable TV, fully equipped kitchens, waterfront views, enclosed porches.

Pet Amenities: List of nearby veterinarians maintained. Exercise area. Nicolet National Forest nearby.

Rated: 4 Paws — 13 rooms and 6 cottages on 5 acres.

The Edgewater Inn is located half a mile west of downtown Eagle River. You are only minutes away from the Nicolet National Forest and thousands of lakes, not to mention fine restaurants, golf courses, tennis, canoeing, riding stables and historical boat rides. The area is noted for hundreds of miles of hiking and biking trails. The fun doesn't end in the summer—winter offers snowshoeing, cross-country skiing and world-famous snowmobile trails. The Edgewater sits on more than five acres, with a professional volleyball court, basketball court, waterfront beach and kids' play area.

Exel Inn of Eau Claire

2305 Craig Road
Eau Claire, WI 54701
800-367-3935 • 715-834-3193
www.exelinns.com

Type of Lodging: Hotel

Room Rates: $38–$65, including continental breakfast. AARP discount.

Pet Charges & Deposits: $100–$200 refundable deposit on extended stays.

Pet Policy: No pets over 25 lbs. Designated rooms only. Manager's prior approval required. Limit two pets per room.

Amenities: Irons, hairdryers, coffeemakers, full-length mirrors.

Pet Amenities: Carson Park is located at Clairmont and Menominee Streets.

Rated: 2 Paws — 100 rooms.

Exel Inn of Eau Claire is another fine budget choice in a well-run budget chain. This comfortable, well-maintained property has clean, unpretentious rooms, with ample truck parking and a whirlpool room. It is located near the University of Wisconsin campus, Fanny Hill Dinner Theater, Oakwood Mall, Eau Claire Municipal Airport and downtown Eau Claire.

Fenmore Hills Motel

5814 Highway 18 West
Fennimore, WI 53809
608-822-3281

Type of Lodging: Motel

Room Rates: $60–$125, including coffee and tea. AAA and AARP discounts.

Pet Charges & Deposits: None.

Pet Policy: Pets must not be left unattended.

Amenities: Cable TV, refrigerators, microwaves, whirlpool.

Pet Amenities: List of nearby veterinarians maintained. Exercise area.

Rated: 3 Paws — 17 rooms and 7 suites.

Fennimore Hills Motel is the ideal vacation hideaway that will help make your stay in southwest Wisconsin memorable. This two-story contemporary complex is situated at the highest point in Grant County, overlooking many miles of rolling hills, wooded roads and fertile farms. Southwest Wisconsin is an ideal recreation area with activities that include boating, fishing, golfing, hiking, snowmobiling and cross-country skiing. There are many tourist attractions including The House on the Rock, Wisconsin's #1 attraction, where you will find one-of-a-kind exhibits such as the World's Largest Carousel. Another must-try activity is river boating on the Mississippi River.

Harbor House Inn

12666 Highway 42
Gills Rock, WI 54210
920-854-8796
www.door-county-inn.com

Type of Lodging: B&B

Room Rates: $65–$175, including continental plus breakfast.

Pet Charges or Deposits: $15 per day.

Pet Policy: Pets must not be left unattended. Manager's prior approval required.

Amenities: Refrigerators, microwaves, whirlpool, hot tub.

Pet Amenities: List of nearby veterinarians maintained. Exercise area. Newport State Park and many others nearby.

Rated: 3 Paws — 12 rooms, 1 suite and 2 cottages.

In the quaint fishing village of Gills Rock, you and your pet will find Harbor House. This is a great place to kick back on the private beach and enjoy the colorful sunsets over the harbor and bluffs of the Green Bay waters. With more than 90 years of history, the Inn is thoughtfully restored, with guestrooms tastefully done in period furniture. All rooms offer private baths and most have refrigerators and microwaves. During the day, take time to relax on the private beach or walk to the ferry, shopping and dining. Later, enjoy an authentic Norwegian sauna cabin and spa. Bike rentals are available to ride on country roads or off-road trails.

Exel Inn of Milwaukee Northeast

5485 North Port Washington Road
Glendale, WI 53217
800-367-3935 • 414-961-7272
www.exelinns.com

Type of Lodging: Hotel

Room Rates: $52–$80, including continental breakfast. AARP discount.

Pet Charges & Deposits: $100–$200 refundable deposit on extended stays.

Pet Policy: No pets over 25 lbs. Designated rooms only. Manager's prior approval required. Limit two pets per room.

Amenities: Irons, coffeemakers, full-length mirrors.

Pet Amenities: Lincoln Park is located at Hampton and Interstate 43.

Rated: 2 Paws — 124 rooms.

Exel Inn is a good choice for travelers who wish to have easy access to Bay Shore Mall, Lake Michigan, Summerset Grounds, Mecca/Bradley Center, University of Milwaukee, Milwaukee County Stadium, State Fairgrounds, Milwaukee County Zoo and Mitchell International Airport. While in Milwaukee, don't miss the Couty Museum. Particularly noteworthy is their spectacular 19th century town display on the top floor.

Baymont Inn

2840 South Oneida Street
Green Bay, WI 54313
877-229-6668 • 920-494-7887
www.baymontinns.com/greenbay/
baymontgb@aol.com

Type of Lodging: Motel

Room Rate: $62–$74, including continental breakfast. AAA and AARP discounts.

Pet Charges & Deposits: $50 refundable deposit.

Pet Policy: No pets over 50 lbs. Pet must not be left unattended.

Amenities: None.

Pet Amenities: Cable TV.

Rated: 3 Paws — 78 rooms.

Baymont Inn delivers you and your pet a clean, comfortable room that welcomes you with a bed, cable television, coffeemaker and complimentary coffee. The Bay Beach Wildlife Sanctuary, Green Bay Botanical Gardens, Green Bay Packers Hall of Fame, Joannes Aquatic Center, Lambeau Field and Stadium Tours, National Railroad Museum and Oneida Bingo and Casino are all within 15 miles of Baymont Inn.

Exel Inn of Green Bay

2870 Ramada Way
Green Bay, WI 54304
800-367-3935 • 920-499-3599
www.exelinns.com

Type of Lodging: Hotel

Room Rates: $43–$62, including continental breakfast. AARP discount.

Pet Charges & Deposits: $100 -$200 refundable deposit on extended stays.

Pet Policy: No pets over 25 lbs. Designated rooms only. Manager's prior approval required. Limit two pets per room.

Amenities: None.

Pet Amenities: None.

Rated: 2 Paws — 104 rooms.

Exel Inn of Eau Claire is another fine budget choice in a well-run budget chain. It is located near the University of Wisconsin campus, Club Fit Health Club, Bay Park Square Mall, Lambeau Field and Packers Hall of Fame, Brown County Arena and Expo Hall, Oneida Bingo Hall and Casino, Austin Straubel Airport, National Railroad Museum, Weidner Center and downtown Green Bay.

Best Western Northern Pine Inn

9966 North Highway 27
Hayward, WI 54843
800-777-7996 • 715-634-4959
www.haywardlakes.com/npii.htm

Type of Lodging: Motel

Room Rates: $59–$79, including continental breakfast. AAA and AARP discounts.

Pet Charges & Deposits: $5 per day.

Pet Policy: Pet must not be left unattended.

Amenities: Cable TV, refrigerators, microwaves, indoor pool, whirlpool, Jacuzzi.

Pet Amenities: List of nearby veterinarians maintained. Exercise area.

Rated: 4 Paws — 39 rooms and 3 suites.

Stay at the Best Western Northern Pine Inn and discover a vibrant spot of pet-friendly people, inviting places and endless activities, any time of year. Nestled in the resort area of Hayward, enjoy nature with its sandy lakes, fishing, horseback riding, golfing and skiing. Hayward is known as the home of the Lumberjack World Championships, American Birkebeiner and National Fresh Water Fishing Hall of Fame.

Hazelhurst Inn Bed & Breakfast

6941 Highway 51
Hazelhurst, WI 54531
715-356-6571
hzhrstbb@mewnorth.net

Type of Lodging: B&B
Room Rates: $50–$60, including full breakfast.
Pet Charges & Deposits: $10 per day.
Pet Policy: Manager's prior approval required.
Amenities: Cable TV, refrigerators.
Pet Amenities: List of nearby veterinarians maintained. Dog runs. Exercise area. Property is located on hiking and biking trails.
Rated: 4 Paws — 4 rooms.

Hazelhurst Inn is a "Come On In and Make You And Your Pet At Home," bed and breakfast establishment. Relax near the fireplace or savor the view from the sitting room. This country-style home is nestled in Wisconsin's Northwoods. Located on 18 acres of woodlands adjacent to the Bearksin State Trail, you and your pet are invited to enjoy the beauty and serenity of the area. Other area activities to enjoy are antiquing, shopping, biking, boating, canoeing, fishing, golfing, hiking, cross-country skiing, swimming and snowmobiling.

Days Inn

850 Tenth Avenue North
Hurley, WI 54534
715-561-3500
days-inn@portup.com

Type of Lodging: Hotel
Room Rates: Call for room rates. AAA, AARP and *10% Pets Welcome™* discounts.
Pet Charges & Deposits: None.
Pet Policy: Designated rooms only.
Amenities: Cable TV, refrigerators, microwaves, pool, whirlpool.
Pet Amenities: List of nearby veterinarians maintained. Richelli Park nearby.
Rated: 3 Paws — 70 guestrooms. Days Inn Five-Sunburst Award Winner.

Conveniently located on Highway 51, near the junction of Highways 2 and 51, the Days Inn offers cozy rooms. Hurley is located in an area known as "Big Snow Country." This area offers over 350 kilometers of cross-country skiing, hiking, bicycling, ATVing and snowmobiling. Visitors may also enjoy downhill skiing on three mountain ranges with 60 miles of slopes within a 15-minute drive of the hotel. The Hurley/Iron Country area has the most spectacular waterfalls in Wisconsin both in height and scenery. Other local attractions include the Iron Country Museum, which houses the area's most extensive collection of Penokee Iron Range artifacts and the Eagle Bluff Golf Club.

Exel Inn of La Crosse

2150 Rose Street
La Crosse, Wisconsin 54603
800-367-3935 • 608-781-0400
www.exelinns.com

Type of Lodging: Hotel

Room Rates: $40–$75, including continental breakfast. AARP discount.

Pet Charges & Deposits: $100–$200 refundable deposit on extended stays.

Pet Policy: No pets over 25 lbs. Designated rooms only. Manager's prior approval required. Limit two pets per room.

Amenities: Irons, coffeemakers, full-length mirrors.

Pet Amenities: None.

Rated: 2 Paws — 101 rooms.

Exel Inn is a good choice for travelers who wish to have easy access to Bridgeview Shopping Center, Valley View Mall, La Crosse Municipal Airport, University of Wisconsin, Convention Center and downtown La Crosse. All Exel Inns offer alarm clock radios, microfridges, modem jacks, free local phone calls and wake-up service.

T.C. Smith Historic Inn Bed & Breakfast

865 Main Street
Lake Geneva, WI 53147
800-423-0233 • 262-248-1097
www.tcsmithinn.com

Type of Lodging: B&B

Room Rates: $125–$365, including full breakfast buffet.

Pet Charges & Deposits: None.

Pet Policy: Sorry, no cats. Designated rooms only. Manager's prior approval required.

Amenities: Cable TV, refrigerators, microwaves, whirlpool, Jacuzzi.

Pet Amenities: Your pet will receive their own towels upon arrival. List of nearby veterinarians maintained. Exercise area. Public beach and Library Park are located across the street from the B&B.

Rated: 4 Paws — 6 rooms and 2 suites.

The T.C. Smith mansion, built in 1845 as a private home, is today an elegant bed and breakfast inn located in the heart of downtown Lake Geneva. Its proprietors graciously opened the massive carved wood doors to all who seek to experience the luxurious warmth and ambiance of the Grand Victorian era. Be sure to explore the courtyard, where you will be treated to brilliant floral Victorian period gardens replete with neo-classic statuettes, a goldfish pond, water garden and quiet benches. The Inn is a genuine oasis in the center of downtown Lake Geneva.

Sunrise Lodge

5894 West Shore
Land O' Lakes, WI 54540
800-221-9689 • 715-547-3684
www.sunriselodge.com
sunlodge@newnorth.net

Type of Lodging: Cottages & Executive Units

Room Rates: $68–$184. Call for rate plans. *10% Pets Welcome*™ discount.

Pet Charges & Deposits: None.

Pet Policy: None.

Amenities: Cable TV, refrigerators, microwaves.

Pet Amenities: List of nearby veterinarians maintained. Ottawa National Park and Nicolet National Forest nearby.

Rated: 4 Paws — 15 cottages and 7 Executive Units.

Easily one of the best places for a family vacation in northern Wisconsin, this four-season recreational resort is located in the Nicolet National Forest in Wisconsin. Sunrise Lodge is perched on 750 feet of lakeshore property, offering a wide assortment of activities for the entire family. The newly irrigated Land O'Lakes golf fairways make a popular nine-hole course. Horseback riding is a pleasure on the Eagle River and Conover. Bike, jog or walk the Sunrise Nature Fitness Trail and explore the Nicolet Forest. Antique Shops, unique gift stores and craft shows are all close by. In the winter, there are snowmobiles, skiing and ice fishing.

Best Western West Towne Suites

650 Grand Canyon Drive
Madison, WI 53719
608-833-4200

Type of Lodging: Motel

Room Rates: $54–$104, including full breakfast. AAA, AARP, AKC, ABA and *10% Pets Welcome*™ discounts.

Pet Charges & Deposits: $25 refundable deposit.

Pet Policy: No pets over 12 lbs. Designated rooms only. Manager's prior approval required.

Amenities: Cable TV, refrigerators, safes, coffeemakers.

Pet Amenities: List of nearby veterinarians maintained. Exercise area. Elver City Park nearby.

Rated: 3 Paws — 101 rooms and 25 suites.

You and your pet will enjoy the highest degree of hospitality and service at the Best Western West Towne Suites. All rooms include refrigerators, wet bars and cable television. If shopping is on the agenda, you will find it easily—only one block from the hotel. For a little adventure, take a trip to the Cave of the Mounds or Wisconsin Dells and House on the Rock. Whatever you and your pets needs are, the staff will be sure to meet and surpass them at the Best Western West Towne Suites.

Collins House Bed & Breakfast

704 East Gorham Street
Madison, WI 53703
608-255-4230
www.collinshouse.com
inncollins@aol.com

Type of Lodging: B&B

Room Rates: $95–$160, including full breakfast. AAA discount.

Pet Charges & Deposits: None.

Pet Policy: Pets must not be left unattended. Must be leashed in common areas. Manager's prior approval required.

Amenities: Refrigerators, microwaves, Jacuzzi.

Pet Amenities: Park nearby.

Rated: 3 Paws — 5 rooms. Listed on the National Register of Historic Places.

When you and your pet enter the Collins House Bed & Breakfast, you will be drawn through the oak library to the breakfast and sitting rooms, where, through the windows, you may see the University crew team rowing past on shimmering Lake Mendota, Madison's largest lake. Collins House is listed on the National Register of Historic Places as an example of Prairie School architecture. It is located only six blocks from the Capitol, eight blocks from downtown and State Street and one mile from the University of Wisconsin campus.

East Towne Suites

4801 Annamark Drive
Madison, WI 53704
800-950-1919 • 608-244-2020
www.globaldialog.com/~easttown
easttown@globaldialog.com

Type of Lodging: Hotel

Suite Rates: $66–$89, including full breakfast and appetizer in the evening. AAA and AARP discounts.

Pet Charges & Deposits: $20 refundable deposit.

Pet Policy: None. All Pets Welcome.

Amenities: Cable TV, refrigerators, microwaves, pool, whirlpool, hot tubs.

Pet Amenities: Exercise area.

Rated: 3 Paws — 123 suites.

Whether you and your pet are traveling on business, vacation or just want to get away from it all, East Towne Suites is the hotel for you. Their affordable rates, exemplary service and fantastic café will make your stay a pleasure. They provide free airport transportation, refrigerators in all suites and free appetizers each evening. Located only five miles from the airport, East Towne Suites is only minutes from the Capitol, University of Wisconsin and shopping.

Exel Inn of Madison

4202 East Towne Boulevard
Madison, WI 53704
800-367-3935 • 608-241-3861
www.exelinns.com

Type of Lodging: Hotel
Room Rates: $45–$76, including continental breakfast. AARP discount.
Pet Charges & Deposits: $100–$200 refundable deposit on extended stays.
Pet Policy: No pets over 25 lbs. Designated rooms only. Manager's prior approval required. Limit two pets per room.
Amenities: Hairdryers, irons, coffeemakers, full-length mirrors.
Pet Amenities: Reindahl Park is located on the corner of Portage and East Washington.
Rated: 3 Paws — 100 rooms.

Exel Inn is a convenient place to stay when traveling to Madison. It is located near East Towne Mall, Princeton Health Club, Dane County Regional Airport, the Capitol, Monona Terrace Convention Center, University of Wisconsin, Dane County Expo Center and downtown Madison. Guest amenities include a state-of-the-art fitness center, microfridges, free local phone calls and modem jacks.

Holiday Inn Express of Madison

722 John Nolen Drive
Madison, WI 53713
800-465-4329 • 608-255-7400
www.exelinns.com

Type of Lodging: Hotel
Room Rates: $75–$99, including continental breakfast. AARP discount.
Pet Charges & Deposits: $100–$200 refundable deposit on extended stays.
Pet Policy: No pets over 25 lbs. Designated rooms only. Manager's prior approval required. Limit two pets per room.
Amenities: Irons, coffeemakers, freshly baked cookies.
Pet Amenities: Olin Park is located on John Nolen Drive.
Rated: 3 Paws — 92 rooms.

Holiday Inn Express is a good choice for travelers who wish to have easy access to the Alliant Energy Center, Monona Terrace Convention Center and downtown Madison. Guest amenities include fitness room, alarm clock radios, microfridges, modem jacks, free local phone calls and wake-up service.

Microtel Inn & Suites

2139 East Springs Drive
Madison, WI 53704
888-258-1283 • 608-242-9000
www.microtelinn.com
microtel.madisonwi@worldnet.att.net

Type of Lodging: Hotel

Room Rates: $43–$130. AAA and AARP discounts.

Pet Charges & Deposits: $10 per stay.

Pet Policy: None. All Pets Welcome.

Amenities: Cable TV, free morning paper.

Pet Amenities: List of nearby veterinarians maintained. Park nearby.

Rated: 3 Paws — 100 rooms and 10 suites.

When you and your pet stay at the Microtel Inn & Suites, there will be no cause for complaint. Located within five miles of the F.L. Wright Convention Center, Dane County Airport, East Towne Mall, MATC Campus, University of Wisconsin and the State Capitol, it provides you and your pet with a pleasant room.

Inn on Maritime Bay

101 Maritime Drive
Manitowoc, WI 54220
800-654-5353 • 920-682-7000
www.innonmaritimebay.com

Type of Lodging: Hotel

Room Rates: $79–$150. AAA, AARP and *10% Pets Welcome™* discounts.

Pet Charges & Deposits: $25 per stay.

Pet Policy: Designated rooms only. Pets must not be left unattended.

Amenities: Cable TV, safes, pool, whirlpool.

Pet Amenities: List of nearby veterinarians maintained. Exercise area. Point Beach State Forest is 10 miles from the hotel.

Rated: 3 Paws — 100 rooms and 7 suites.

You and your pet will find the Inn on Maritime Bay something really special! Located on the shore of Lake Michigan, surrounded by a colorful marina and scenery to write home about. Enjoy all of the Inn's conveniences plus the areas great attractions! Visit the next-door neighbor—the Wisconsin Maritime Museum, or the adjacent Manitowoc Maritime Harbor and Marina. Other nearby attractions include the Capital Civic Center, Zunker's Antique Car Museum, Rahrwest Art Museum and Pinecrest Historical Village.

Best Western Quiet House & Suites

10330 North Port Washington Road
Mequon, WI 53092
800-528-1234 • 262-241-3677
www.quiethouse.com

Type of Lodging: Motel

Room Rates: $111–$200, including continental breakfast and free newspaper. AAA and AARP discounts.

Pet Charges & Deposits: $15 per day.

Pet Policy: Manager's prior approval required.

Amenities: Cable TV, refrigerators, microwaves, pool, whirlpool, Jacuzzi.

Pet Amenities: List of nearby veterinarians maintained.

Rated: 3 Paws — 43 rooms and 12 suites.

One of the oldest German settlements, Mequon is a suburb of Milwaukee along Lake Michigan. Visit historic sites in nearby Cedarburg and don't miss all the festivals Milwaukee has to offer. Nearby, you will find plenty of golfing, fishing and shopping.

Super 8 Motel of Minocqua

Highway 51 & Highway 70 West
P.O. Box 325
Minocqua, WI 54548
800-800-8000 • 715-356-9541

Type of Lodging: Motel

Room Rates: $59–$100, including continental breakfast. AAA and AARP discounts.

Pet Charges & Deposits: None.

Pet Policy: Designated rooms only. Pets must not be left unattended.

Amenities: Cable TV, refrigerators, microwaves, whirlpool, hot tubs.

Pet Amenities: List of nearby veterinarians maintained. Exercise area. Torpy Park nearby.

Rated: 3 Paws — 33 rooms and 1 suite.

You and your pet will enjoy your stay at the Super 8 Motel of Minocqua. Located near the Jim Pecks Game Farm, Circle M Family Amusement Park, Northern Lights Playhouse, lakes, snowmobile trails and dozens of restaurants, it is a good place to stay whether you are traveling for business or pleasure.

Exel Inn of Milwaukee South

1201 West College Avenue
Oak Creek, WI 53154
800-367-3935 • 414-764-1776
www.exelinns.com

Type of Lodging: Hotel

Room Rates: $49–$74, including continental breakfast. AARP discount.

Pet Charges & Deposits: $100–$200 refundable deposit on extended stays.

Pet Policy: No pets over 25 lbs. Designated rooms only. Manager's prior approval required. Limit two pets per room.

Amenities: Irons, coffeemakers, full-length mirrors.

Pet Amenities: List of nearby veterinarians maintained. Mudd Lake Park is located at 6380 South 35th Street.

Rated: 2 Paws — 109 rooms.

Exel Inn is a good choice for travelers who wish to have access to Mitchell International Airport, Southridge Mall, Summerfest Grounds, Mecca/Bradley Center, Milwaukee County Stadium, State Fairgrounds, Milwaukee County Zoo and downtown Milwaukee. All Exel Inns offer alarm clock radios, microfridges, modem jacks, free local phone calls and wake-up service.

Knights Inn

9420 South 20th Street
Oak Creek, WI 53154
414-761-3807

Type of Lodging: Motel

Room Rates: $50–$80. AAA, AARP and *10% Pets Welcome*™ discounts.

Pet Charges: $10 for the first night. $15 refundable deposit.

Pet Policy: None. All Pets Welcome.

Amenities: Cable TV, refrigerators, microwaves, guest laundry.

Pet Amenities: None.

Rated: 4 Paws — 115 rooms.

People choose to stay at the Knights Inn because it is centrally located near major tourist attractions, shopping districts, manufacturing centers and is on a stopover point to Chicago, Madison, Wisconsin Dells and Green Bay. Within 20 minutes, guests will find Mitchell International Airport, State Fair Grounds, Milwaukee County Stadium, MECCA Convention Center, Marcus Amphitheater, Discovery World, Milwaukee Repertory Theater, Performing Art Center, Milwaukee County Zoo, Mitchell Park Horticultural Conservatory and several malls.

Park Plaza Hotel & Convention Center

One North Main Street
Oshkosh, WI 54901
800-365-4458 • 920-231-5000
www.parkplazaoshkosh.com
mail@parkplazaoshkosh.com

Type of Lodging: Hotel

Room Rates: $75–$125, including full breakfast. AAA and AARP discounts.

Pet Charges & Deposits: None.

Pet Policy: Small pets only. Designated rooms only. Manager's prior approval required.

Amenities: Cable TV, refrigerators, safes, pool, whirlpool.

Pet Amenities: Riverside Park is located across the street from the Hotel.

Rated: 3 Paws — 179 rooms and 3 suites.

The heart of a great hotel resides in the personal care and dedication of its staff. At the Oshkosh Park Plaza Hotel & Convention Center, you'll find trained, experienced professionals who are eager to make your next visit a memorable event. Each guestroom and suite has a spectacular view of either the Fox River or Lake Winnebago. The Plaza Club on the seventh floor offers complimentary cocktails and hors d'oeuvres. The local area is full of entertaining things to do. There are many recreational sports like bowling, boat cruises, swimming, snowmobiling, horseback riding, tennis, golfing and hiking.

Exel Grand Hotel of Waukesha

2840 North Grandview Boulevard
Pewaukee, WI 53072
262-524-9300
www.exelinns.com

Type of Lodging: Hotel

Room Rates: $69–$85, including continental breakfast. AARP discount.

Pet Charges & Deposits: $100–$200 refundable deposit on extended stays.

Pet Policy: No pets over 25 lbs. Designated rooms only. Manager's prior approval required. Limit two pets per room.

Amenities: Irons, hairdryers, coffeemakers, freshly baked cookies.

Pet Amenities: None.

Rated: 2 Paws — 97 rooms.

Exel Inn is a convenient place to stay when traveling to Milwaukee. Guest amenities include a state-of-the-art fitness center, microfridges, free local phone calls, guest laundry, business center, indoor pool and freshly baked cookies every evening.

Best Western Quiet House & Suites

Highway 18 and Highway 35 South
Prairie du Chien, WI 53821
800-528-1234 • 608-326-4777
www.quiethouse.com

Type of Lodging: Hotel

Room Rates: $83–$150, including weekday continental breakfast. AAA and AARP discounts.

Pet Charges & Deposits: $15 per day.

Pet Policy: Small pets only. Pets may not be left unattended.

Amenities: Cable TV, coffeemakers, refrigerators, microwaves, pool, whirlpool, hot tubs.

Pet Amenities: None.

Rated: 2 Paws — 40 rooms and 2 suites.

In the late 1800s Julius Vogt established the original Quiet House in Milwaukee, featuring comfort and hospitality. Four generations later, they continue this tradition, blending 100 years of hospitality with 21st century service and amenities. The specialty suites include Oriental, Art Deco, Pyramid, Vintage Cabin, Roman Bath, Hi-Tech Contemporary and others that make your stay at Quiet House & Suites unique. Prairie du Chien is the second oldest city in Wisconsin located at the foot of the Mississippi River bluffs. Historic sites include the Fort Crawford Medical Museum, Effigy Mounds National Monument, Wyalusing State Park and the Villa Louis Victorian Mansion. Treat yourself to antique shopping, golfing, fishing, sightseeing or riverboat gambling.

Knights Inn

1149 Oakes Road
Racine, WI 53406
800-843-5644 • 262-886-6667
www.knightsinn.com

Type of Lodging: Hotel

Room Rates: $36–$59, including continental breakfast. AAA and AARP discounts.

Pet Charges & Deposits: None.

Pet Policy: None. All Pets Welcome.

Amenities: Cable TV, Jacuzzi, coffeemakers, guest laundry.

Pet Amenities: Exercise area. Pritchard Park is located at Hwyll and Ohio Streets.

Rated: 3 Paws — 106 rooms.

The Knights Inn provides outstanding value through a pet-friendly staff; well-maintained accommodations; and inviting, up-to-date surroundings—all at a great price! All guestrooms are at ground level. Other facilities and amenities include coffeemakers, 24-hour front desk, free parking, free local telephone calls, meeting and banquet facilities, RV or truck parking, cable television and laundry services. Nearby you and your pet will find a beach, tennis, fishing, golfing, restaurants and shopping.

Currier's Lakeview Lodge

2010 East Sawyer Street
Rice Lake, WI 54868
800-433-5253 • 715-234-7474
www.chamber.rice-
lake.wi.us/members/curriers
lakeview@charter.net

Type of Lodging: Motel

Room Rates: $49–$140, including continental breakfast. AAA and AARP discounts.

Pet Charges & Deposits: None.

Pet Policy: Sorry, no cats. Manager's prior approval required. Pets must not be left unattended.

Amenities: Cable TV, kitchenettes, refrigerators, beaches, boat rentals.

Pet Amenities: List of nearby veterinarians maintained. Exercise area.

Rated: 3 Paws — 18 rooms and 1 suite.

Currier's Lakeview Resort Motel is Rice Lakes' only all-season resort motel. Located on the east shore of Rice Lake, it sits on a four-acre peninsula with a bay on either side and the lake right outside your door. Partially wooded grounds contain an array of wildflowers and wildlife for you and your pet to enjoy. Surprisingly, all this is only a short distance from downtown, shopping and fine restaurants. All guestrooms face the lake and feature large windows to enjoy the views. The decor is reminiscent of a charming family place on the lake. Recreational activities include swimming, boating, paddle boating, canoeing, barbecuing and rowing.

Baymont Inn

2932 Kohler Memorial Drive
Sheboygan, WI 53081
800-301-0200 • 920-457-2321
www.baymontinns.com

Type of Lodging: Hotel

Room Rates: $69–$99, including continental breakfast. AAA, AARP and *10% Pets Welcome™* discounts.

Pet Charges & Deposits: $25 refundable deposit.

Pet Policy: No pets over 50 lbs. Designated rooms only.

Amenities: Cable TV, coffeemakers, hairdryers, irons, dataports.

Pet Amenities: List of nearby veterinarians maintained. Old Plank Trail nearby.

Rated: 3 Paws — 95 rooms and 1 suite.

At Baymont Inn, you and your pet will always find a bright, spacious room filled with comfort. The extra-long beds, in-room coffeemakers, free local calls, and cable television are just the beginning. Local points of interest include Memorial Mall, Kohler, Elkhart Lake's Road America and downtown Sheboygan.

Best Value Inn Parkway

3900 Motel Road
Sheboygan, WI 53081
800-341-8000 • 920-458-8338

Type of Lodging: Motel

Room Rates: $42–$52, including AAA, AARP, AKC, ABA and *10% Pets Welcome™* discounts.

Pet Charges & Deposits: $5–$8.50 per day.

Pet Policy: Designated rooms only.

Amenities: Satellite TV, refrigerators, microwaves.

Pet Amenities: List of nearby veterinarians maintained. Exercise area is over 2½ acres of meadows for your pet to enjoy. Kohler-Terry Andrae State Park nearby.

Rated: 3 Paws – 32 rooms located on 11 acres.

The Best Value Inn is a quiet, pleasantly decorated motel in Sheboygan. It offers you and your pet many amenities, including king-sized beds, direct dial phones, individual climate controls, picnic and grilling areas, refrigerator, and lots of nearby activities. It is located near Kohler-Terry Andrae State Park where you will find 2½ miles of beautiful sandy beaches, a boardwalk, Sanderling Nature Center, children's playground, numerous hiking trails and a park for all ages. Also nearby is the Black River Hiking Trail, Indian Mound Park, Sheboygan County Historical Center, River Front Boardwalk, Fish Shanty Village and Kohler Art Center.

Super 8 Motel

3402 Wilgus Road
Sheboygan, WI 53081
800-800-8000 • 920-458-8080
www.innworks.com

Type of Lodging: Motel

Room Rates: $45–$65, including continental breakfast. AAA and AARP discounts.

Pet Charges & Deposits: $10 per stay.

Pet Policy: Sorry, no cats.

Amenities: Cable TV, one free 8-minute long distance call each night.

Pet Amenities: Exercise area.

Rated: 3 Paws – 60 rooms.

Located off Highway 23, Super 8 Motel in Sheboygan provides you and your pet with an immaculate and spotless room at a budget-conscious price. It is located near St. Nicholas Hospital and downtown Sheboygan.

Justin Trails Bed & Breakfast Resort

7452 Kathryn Avenue
Sparta, WI 54656
800-488-4521 • 608-269-4522
www.justintrails.com

Type of Lodging: B&B
Room Rates: $95–$250, including full breakfast.
Pet Charges & Deposits: $10 per day.
Pet Policy: Designated rooms only.
Amenities: Refrigerators, microwaves, whirlpool.
Pet Amenities: List of nearby veterinarians maintained. Exercise areas including 8 miles of walking and running trails for you and your pet to enjoy.
Rated: 4 Paws – 3 rooms, 1 suite and 3 cabins on 200 acres.

Justin Trails Bed & Breakfast Resort is a third-generation dairy farm that has been in the Justin family since 1914. The diversification into the farm vacation business began with the opening of the Nordic Ski Center, set amidst the scenic, wooded hills and valleys of southwestern Wisconsin. Three private luxury cabins, with all the comforts of a fine bed and breakfast, supplement the quaint 1920s farmhouse. Guestrooms feature fluffy pillows, Laura Ashley linens, hand-crafted country decor and daily maid service. Private log cabins offer queen-sized, hand-crafted beds, double whirlpool tubs, gas fireplaces and a porch or deck.

Holiday Inn

1501 North Point Drive
Stevens Point, WI 54481
800-922-7880 • 715-341-1340
www.holidayinnsp.com
hidesk@coredcs.com

Type of Lodging: Hotel
Room Rates: $99–$129. AAA and AARP discounts.
Pet Charges & Deposits: $25 per day.
Pet Policy: No pets over 25 lbs. Designated rooms only.
Amenities: Cable TV, pool, whirlpool, restaurant, lounge.
Pet Amenities: List of nearby veterinarians maintained. Green Circle Park is located a block from the hotel.
Rated: 3 Paws – 285 rooms and 10 suites.

Unquestionably the area's most complete hotel, the newly renovated Holiday Inn Stevens Point puts you and your pet in the center of everything. Thoughtful amenities and stylish interiors evoke the comforts of home in each guestroom and suite. Dine in the popular Mesquite Grill, where they put an extra measure of flair on a variety of American and continental classics or spend an exhilarating evening at Mortimer's, a lively place for entertainment and libations. Try the new Holidome that features an indoor pool. Sentry World Golf Course is just across the way.

Super 8 Motel

247 North Division Street
Stevens Point, WI 54481
800-800-8000 • 715-341-8888
www.innworks.com

Type of Lodging: Motel

Room Rates: $45–$65, including continental breakfast. AAA and AARP discounts.

Pet Charges & Deposits: $10 per stay.

Pet Policy: Sorry, no cats. Manager's prior approval required.

Amenities: Cable TV, safes, one free 8-minute long distance call each night.

Pet Amenities: Exercise area.

Rated: 3 Paws — 60 rooms.

Super 8 Motel is a good choice for travelers who wish to have access to Stevens Point, Wisconsin Rapids, Wausau, Iola, Oshkosh, Wisconsin Dells, University of Wisconsin, Almond, Amherst, Amherst Junction, Arpin, Auburndale, Biron, Evergreen and Hancock. Guests have microwave, fax machine, copy machine, meeting room, dataport phones and extra-long phone cords available upon request.

Holiday Inn Express of Racine

13339 Hospitality Court
Sturtevant, WI 53177
800-465-4329 • 414-884-0200
www.exelinns.com

Type of Lodging: Hotel

Room Rates: $69–$94, including continental breakfast. AARP discount.

Pet Charges & Deposits: $100–$200 refundable deposit on extended stays.

Pet Policy: No pets over 25 lbs. Designated rooms only. Manager's prior approval required. Limit two pets per room.

Amenities: Irons, coffeemakers, guest laundry, freshly baked cookies.

Pet Amenities: Union Grove County Park nearby.

Rated: 2 Paws — 107 rooms.

Holiday Inn Express of Racine is another fine budget choice in a well-run budget chain. This well-maintained property has clean, unpretentious rooms, with a business center, meeting room, guest laundry facilities and a whirlpool room. It is located near the Dairyland Greyhound Racetrack, Mitchell International Airport, Great Lakes Dragway, Great America, Gurnee Mills Outlet Mall and downtown Racine.

Lark Inn

229 North Superior Avenue
Tomah, WI 54660
800-447 LARK • 608-372-5981
www.larkinn.com

Type of Lodging: Motel

Room Rates: $55–$80, including continental breakfast. AAA, AARP, AKC, ABA, Government, Military and Family discounts.

Pet Charges & Deposits: $6 per day.

Pet Policy: Limit two pets per room.

Amenities: Cable TV, refrigerators, microwaves, voicemail, dataports, VCRs, wet bars, kitchenettes, guest laundry, General Store & Grill.

Pet Amenities: List of nearby veterinarians maintained. Exercise area. Winnebago Park and Lark Park are located ½ mile from the motel. Mill Bluff State Park is located 8 miles from the motel.

Rated: 3 Paws — 19 rooms and 6 suites.

Impressive with its gambrel roofs, dormer windows and country porches, the Lark Inn has sheltered travelers since the turn of the century, when it consisted of several log cabins. Nestled in the heart of Tomah, the Inn is an easy stroll from antique shops, museums, craft shops and fine dining. Explore the surrounding Amish community, the Mississippi River Valley near La Crosse or the scenic Wisconsin Dells area while based here.

Exel Inn of Wausau

116 South 17th Street
Wausau, WI 54401
800-367-3935 • 715-842-0641
www.exelinns.com

Type of Lodging: Hotel

Room Rates: $42–$59, including continental breakfast. AARP discount.

Pet Charges & Deposits: $100–$200 refundable deposit on extended stays.

Pet Policy: No pets over 25 lbs. Designated rooms only. Manager's prior approval required. Limit two pets per room.

Amenities: Irons, hairdryers, coffeemakers, full-length mirrors.

Pet Amenities: Marathon Park is located at Highway 52 and 17th Avenue.

Rated: 2 Paws — 122 rooms.

Exel Inn is a good choice for travelers who wish to have easy access to Wausau Insurance Companies, Westwood Conference Center, Wausau Shopping Mall, Grand Theatre, Rib Mountain Ski Area, Leigh Yawkey Woodson Art Museum, Cedar Creek Mall, Central Wisconsin Airport and downtown Wausau. All Exel Inns offer alarm clock radios, microfridges, modem jacks, free local phone calls and wake-up service.

Park Inn International

2101 North Mountain Road
Wausau, WI 54401
800-928-7281 • 715-842-0711
www.parkinnwausau.com
mail@parkinnwausau.com

Type of Lodging: Hotel

Room Rates: $66–$74, including full breakfast. AAA, AARP and *10% Pets Welcome*™ discounts.

Pet Charges & Deposits: None.

Pet Policy: None. All Pets Welcome.

Amenities: Cable TV, pool, whirlpool, restaurant, lounge.

Pet Amenities: List of nearby veterinarians maintained. Exercise area. Rib Mountain State Park nearby.

Rated: 4 Paws — 116 rooms and 3 suites.

Whether you and your pet visit the Rib Mountain area for business or pleasure, you will find the Park Inn International dedicated to making your stay a successful experience. With such amenities as whirlpool suites, indoor pool, game room, fitness room, valet service, conference center, restaurant and lounge, you and your pet are sure to enjoy your stay. Centrally located in Wisconsin, it is easily accessible to major cities by car or by air. Downtown Wausau is only four miles east of Park Inn.

Exel Inn of Milwaukee West

115 West Mayfair Road
Wauwatosa, WI 53226
800-367-3935 • 414-257-0140
www.exelinns.com

Type of Lodging: Hotel

Room Rates: $50–$75, including continental breakfast. AARP discount.

Pet Charges & Deposits: $100–$200 refundable deposit on extended stays.

Pet Policy: No pets over 25 lbs. Designated rooms only. Manager's prior approval required. Limit two pets per room.

Amenities: Irons, coffeemakers, full-length mirrors.

Pet Amenities: None.

Rated: 2 Paws — 122 rooms.

Exel Inn of Milwaukee West is another fine budget choice in a well-run budget chain. This comfortable property has unpretentious rooms. It is located near the Mayfair Mall, Milwaukee County Zoo, State Fairgrounds, Pettit National Ice Center, Milwaukee County Stadium, Summerfest Grounds, Mitchell International Airport and downtown Milwaukee.

Delton Oaks Resort

730 East Hiawatha Drive
Wisconsin Dells, WI 53965
888-374-6257 • 608-253-40992
www.deltonoaks.com
deltonoaks@jvlnet.com

Type of Lodging: Resort
Room Rates: $80–$165.
Pet Charges & Deposits: $10 per day. $100 refundable deposit.
Pet Policy: Sorry, no pit bulls or rottweilers. Manager's prior approval required.
Amenities: Cable TV, refrigerators, microwaves, pool, whirlpool, campfires, playground, BBQ area, beach.
Pet Amenities: List of nearby veterinarians maintained. Exercise area. Mirror Lake State Park and Rocky Arbor State Park are both within 3 miles of the resort. Pets may swim in lake.
Rated: 3 Paws — 10 rooms and 19 suites.

Delton Oaks Resort is a small, family-oriented and family-run Lake Delton resort. All guest units have electric heat, air conditioning and cable television. To preserve the vacation atmosphere, the rooms do not have phones. All kitchens are equipped with stove, refrigerator, toaster, coffeemaker, dishes, linens and towels. Guests may enjoy, the large, safe beach, heated pool, playground, picnic area, volleyball, bonfire, rowboats, paddle boats, free docking facilities, two large piers and plenty of fishing. The Resort is located directly behind Noah's Ark, the biggest waterpark in the world.

Lakeview Retreat

40 Bayer Lane
Wisconsin Dells, WI 53965
888-374-6257
www.lakeviewretreat.com

Type of Lodging: Private Home
Room Rates: $140 per night. Call for group and weekly rates.
Pet Charges & Deposits: $10 per day. $100 refundable deposit.
Pet Policy: Sorry, no pit bulls or rottweilers. Manager's prior approval required.
Amenities: Cable TV, fully equipped kitchen, whirlpool, laundry room.
Pet Amenities: List of nearby veterinarians maintained. Exercise area. Mirror Lake State Park and Rocky Arbor State Park are both within 3 miles of the house. Pets may swim in lake.
Rated: 3 Paws — A large, private home that sleeps up to ten people located right next door to Delton Oaks Resort.

The same folks who operate Lakeview Retreat run the Delton Oaks Resort. This private home offers the privacy and beauty of a lakefront home. This two-bedroom, two-bath home is cozy for two or sleeps ten people comfortably. It offers three sofa sleepers, a beautiful sandy beach, boat dock, bonfire pit and use of the Delton Oaks Resort pool.

Super 8 Motel

3410 Eighth Street South
Wisconsin Rapids, WI 54494
800-800-8000 • 715-423-8080
www.innworks.com

Type of Lodging: Motel

Room Rates: $45–$65, including continental breakfast. AAA and AARP discounts.

Pet Charges & Deposits: $10 per stay.

Pet Policy: Sorry, no cats. Manager's prior approval required.

Amenities: Cable TV, safes, one free long distance call each night.

Pet Amenities: Exercise area.

Rated: 3 Paws — 48 rooms.

Super 8 Motel is a good choice for travelers who wish to have access to Wisconsin Rapids, Wisconsin Dells, Wausau, Stevens Point, Iola, Oshkosh, Nekoosa, Port Edwards, Almond, Arpin, Auburndale, Biron, Friendship, Junction City and Lake Wazeecha. Amenities include microwave, fax machine, copy machine, meeting room, dataports and extralong phone cords.

WYOMING

Nicknames: Equality State; Cowboy State

Population: 479,602

Area: 97,818 square miles

Climate: Semi-desert conditions throughout; true desert in the Big Horn and Great Divide basins.

Capital: Cheyenne

Entered Union: July 10, 1890

Motto: Equal Rights.

Song: Wyoming

Flower: Indian Paintbrush

Tree: Plains Cottonwood

Bird: Western Meadowlark

Famous Wyomingites: James Bridger, William F. "Buffalo Bill" Cody, Nellie Tayloe Ross.

History: Shoshone, Crow, Cheyenne, Oglala Sioux and Arapaho tribes lived in the area before the coming of the white man. John Colter was the first to see the Yellowstone area, 1807-8. Trappers and fur traders came in the 1820s. Fort Laramie and Fort Bridger became important stops in the pioneer trails to the West Coast. Population grew with the coming of the Union Pacific Railroad in 1868. Wyoming was the first state in the Union to grant women the vote in 1869. Disputes between large landowners and small cattle ranchers resulted in the Johnson County Cattle War in 1892. Federal troops were called in to restore order.

Royal Resort

P.O. Box 3250
Alpine, WY 83128
800-343-6755 • 307-654-7545
www.royal-resort.com
royalresorts@silverstar.com

Type of Lodging: Hotel

Room Rates: $65–$105, including continental breakfast. AAA and AARP discounts.

Pet Charges & Deposits: $5 per day

Pet Policy: Sorry, no cats. No pets over 25 lbs. Designated rooms only.

Amenities: Cable TV, hot tubs.

Pet Amenities: List of nearby veterinarians maintained. Exercise area. Bridger National Forest nearby.

Rated: 2 Paws — 44 rooms and 1 suite.

Royal Resort is a lovely European-style inn. Some of the guestrooms are quite large. The hotel is housed in two three-story structures with interior corridors. The Resort offers horse rentals, whitewater trips and guided fishing in summer; snow machine rentals, guided and unguided cross-country skiing and ice fishing in winter. It's 36 miles to Jackson Hole, 43 miles to Teton National Park and a two-hour drive to Yellowstone.

Days Inn Casper

301 East "E" Street
Casper, WY 82601
800 DAYS INN • 307-234-1159
www.the.daysinn.com/casper10269
10269@hotel.cendant.com

Type of Lodging: Motel

Room Rates: $52–$72, including continental breakfast. AAA and AARP discounts.

Pet Charges & Deposits: None.

Pet Policy: None. All Pets Welcome.

Amenities: Cable TV, refrigerators, microwaves, safes, pool.

Pet Amenities: List of nearby veterinarians maintained. Exercise area. City park is located on Center at 8th Street.

Rated: 3 Paws — 121 rooms

Days Inn is a bright, cheery place that offers well-furnished rooms, in-room coffee, outside cold weather plug-ins, dataport phones and a 24-hour desk staff. Casper began as a ferry site on the Oregon Trail in 1847, when Mormon settlers found out they could make money by ferrying westbound pioneers across the North Platte River. The big money did not come until 1889, however, when oil was discovered in the area. Days Inn is close to the Casper Planetarium, Historic Downtown Casper and the Wyoming Science and Discovery Center.

Parkway Plaza Hotel

123 West "E" Street
Casper, WY 82601
800-270 STAY • 307-235-1777
www.parkway_plaza.net
info@parkway_plaza.net

Type of Lodging: Hotel

Room Rates: $55–$225. AAA, AARP and *10% Pets Welcome™* discounts.

Pet Charges & Deposits: $25 refundable deposit.

Pet Policy: None. All Pets Welcome.

Amenities: Cable TV, refrigerators, microwaves, pool, whirlpool, café, steakhouse, lounge.

Pet Amenities: List of nearby veterinarians maintained. Exercise area. The hotel is located on the North Platte River with jogging path and blue ribbon trout stream.

Rated: 3 Paws — 280 rooms and 15 suites.

Parkway Plaza Hotel has rooms ranging from modest to quite spacious and luxurious. Housekeeping is excellent and the staff is very friendly. Free local calls and a free morning newspaper are added amenities. Casper's Tate Geological Museum displays fossils, minerals, meteorites, and jade, as well as dinosaur, fish, bird, mammal and reptile bones. Fort Caspar Museum has a reconstruction of the fort and exhibits of Native American and pioneer artifacts.

Nagle Warren Mansion B&B

222 East 17th Street
Cheyenne, WY 82001
800-811-2610 • 307-637-3333
www.naglewarrenmansion.com

Type of Lodging: B&B

Room Rates: $98–$150, including full breakfast.

Pet Charges & Deposits: $10 per day.

Pet Policy: Designated rooms only. Manager's prior approval required.

Amenities: Cable TV, whirlpool, workout room, garden.

Pet Amenities: List of nearby veterinarians maintained. Halliday Park is located at 17th and Morrie.

Rated: 4 Paws — 11 rooms and 1 suite. Listed on the National Register of Historical Buildings.

The Nagle Warren Mansion, located in downtown Cheyenne and on the National Register of Historic Buildings, features the best of the old and the new West. The circa 1888 mansion is elegant, with contemporary comfort in each of its rooms. This is surely the most elegant B&B in Wyoming. Former Governor and U.S. Senator Francis E. Warren called it home. The State Capitol is a neoclassic sandstone building, with a 50-foot diameter golden dome. The Cheyenne Street Railway Trolley takes you on a two-hour sightseeing tour of the city. Cheyenne was the first major city encountered by westbound travelers after they left Nebraska.

Hunter Peak Ranch

Painter Route
P.O. Box 1731
Cody, WY 82414
307-587-3711
www.nezperce.com/ranchhp.html
hpr@wtp.net

Type of Lodging: Inn

Room Rates: $90–$240. Call for weekly rates.

Pet Charges & Deposits: $10 per day or $25 per week.

Pet Policy: No pets over 50 lbs. Designated rooms only. Manager's prior approval required.

Amenities: Fully equipped kitchens.

Pet Amenities: List of nearby veterinarians maintained. Exercise area. Yellowstone National Park nearby.

Rated: 3 Paws — 3 cabins and 6 suites.

Located on the Upper Clark's Fork River at an elevation of 6,700 feet, the Hunter Peak Ranch lies adjacent to the North Absaroka and Beartooth Wilderness areas. This is some of the most magnificent country you will ever see. The Ranch was homesteaded in 1909 and started taking guests in 1912. The original structure is built out of hand-hewn logs, with a beautiful river rock fireplace, and now houses the lodge room and dining room of this family-owned business. The modern housekeeping cabins and suites feature fully equipped kitchens and comfortable furnishings. Ranch activities include pack trips, horseback riding, fishing, hiking, swimming, ice skating and snowmobiling.

Pinnacle Buttes Lodge & Campground

3577 U.S. Highway 26
Dubois, WY 82513
800-934-3569 • 307-455-2506
www.pinnaclebuttes.com

Type of Lodging: Cabins

Cabin Rates: $70–$160. AARP discount.

Pet Charges & Deposits: $50 refundable deposit.

Pet Policy: Sorry, no cats.

Amenities: Pool, hot tubs, café, bar, gift shop, gas station.

Pet Amenities: List of nearby veterinarians maintained. Exercise area. Located in Shoshone National Forest.

Rated: 3 Paws — 10 cabins.

You'll be treated like family at Pinnacle Buttes, a totally friendly, family-run operation on Togwotee Pass, known as one of the best places in the United States for snowmobiling and sledding. Dubois, at nearly 7,000 feet elevation, is near Union Pass, the only place in the United States from which three rivers flow in different directions. Fish Creek is the source of the Columbia River, Jakey's Fork flows to the Mississippi and Roaring Fork flows to the Colorado River. There are 44 active glaciers in the nearby Fitzpatrick Wilderness.

Mad Dog Ranch Cabins

P.O. Box 7737
Jackson, WY 83002
307-733-3729
www.maddogranch.com
info@maddogranch.com

Type of Lodging: Guest Ranch
Cabin Rates: $149–$189.
Pet Charges & Deposits: None.
Pet Policy: Designated rooms only. Manager's prior approval required. Pets must not be left unattended.
Amenities: Cable TV, fully equipped kitchens, hot tubs, fireplace, phones.
Pet Amenities: Exercise area. Grand Teton Park nearby.
Rated: 3 Paws — 9 cabins on 5 acres.

The newly remodeled cabins on Mad Dog Ranch have two bedrooms, a sleeping loft, a full bath and kitchen, wood burning stove, cable television and accommodate up to six persons. Since the cabins sit on a five-acre ranch, there's plenty of privacy. Jackson Hole Ski Resort at Teton Village is five miles from the ranch. Access to the Snake River is only half a mile away. Jackson is a vacationer's paradise. The Bar J Chuckwagon presents a traditional Western meal followed by an evening of family entertainment. Teton Wagon Train & Horse Adventure offers a four-day, three-night guided wagon train trip along back roads between Grand Teton and Yellowstone National Parks. There's whitewater rafting on the Snake River, wonderful restaurants, world-class shopping and a holiday full of memorable fun.

Window on the Winds B&B

P.O. Box 996
Pinedale, WY 82941
888-367-1345 • 307-367-2600
www.windowonthewinds.com

Type of Lodging: B&B
Room Rates: $45–$125, including full breakfast.
Pet Charges & Deposits: None.
Pet Policy: None. All Pets Welcome.
Amenities: Cable TV, refrigerators, hot tubs.
Pet Amenities: List of nearby veterinarians maintained. Exercise area. Park nearby.
Rated: 4 Paws — 4 rooms and 1 suite.

Decorated in a striking Western and Plains Native American décor, Window On The Winds is a perfect base for your adventures in the Wind River Mountains. Comfy bedrooms with lodgepole queen beds, adorned with hand-made European-style down duvets, and plenty of pillows, a hot tub set among flowers, ivy and culinary herbs in the Sun Room, and an upstairs living room with relaxing furnishings, books, games and balcony, all combine with Leanne McClain's kitchen wizardry to make your stay truly memorable. The Wind River Range contains some of the highest mountain peaks in Wyoming, the seven largest glaciers in the continental U.S., and hundreds of glacial lakes filled with native trout.

Sleep Inn

1400 Higley Boulevard
Rawlins, WY 82301
307-328-1732

Type of Lodging: Motel
Room Rates: $55–$80, including continental breakfast. AAA, AARP and *10% Pets Welcome™* discounts.
Pet Charges & Deposits: None.
Pet Policy: Designated rooms only.
Amenities: Cable TV, sauna, guest laundry.
Pet Amenities: List of nearby veterinarians maintained. Exercise area. Bolton Park is located at Washington and Davis Streets.
Rated: 3 Paws — 81 rooms.

Sleep Inn features modern, very well maintained rooms in a two-story structure with interior corridors. There's a game room, a family restaurant, and a convenience store and gift shop next door. Rawlins was a departure point for the Union Pacific Railroad. The ruins of Fort Fred Steele, built in 1868 to protect early railroads and settlers, are 15 miles east of the town. Throughout the 1870s, Rawlins was a true Wild West town with more than its share of outlaw activity. When "Big Nose" George Parrot was lynched by a vigilante mob in 1879, the remaining 24 known outlaws left town the next morning. Among the notable sights in this wool and hay producing center are the Carbon County Museum (Western artifacts) and the Wyoming Frontier Prison.

Best Western Inn at Sundance

2719 East Cleveland Street
P.O. Box 927
Sundance, WY 82729
800-238-0965 • 307-283-2800
www.blackhillslodging.com
info@blackhillslodging.com

Type of Lodging: Inn
Room Rates: $44–$109, including continental breakfast. AAA, AARP, Seniors, Corporate and *10% Pets Welcome™* discounts.
Pet Charges & Deposits: $25 refundable deposit.
Pet Policy: No pets over 40 lbs.
Amenities: Cable TV, safes, pool, whirlpool, guest laundry, irons and ironing boards, hairdryers.
Pet Amenities: List of nearby veterinarians maintained. Exercise area. Sundance City Park is located at East Cleveland and 9th Streets.
Rated: 3 Paws — 44 rooms.

Best Western Inn at Sundance has beautiful oversized guestrooms with great Black Hills views—these rooms are quiet and built for a good night's rest. Numerous amenities make this a fine lodging choice indeed. Sundance is situated in the northeast corner of Wyoming, just over the state line from South Dakota's Black Hills and Mount Rushmore. It's known as the "Whitetail Deer Capital of the World." The name of the city is derived from the fact that it lies at the foot of Sundance Mountain, so named because the Sioux Native Americans held councils and religious ceremonies here.

Sundance Mountain Inn

26 Highway 585
P.O. Box 947
Sundance, WY 82729
888-347-2794 • 307-283-3737
www.sundancewyoming.com/
  sundancemountaininn
info@blackhillslodging.com

Type of Lodging: Inn

Room Rates: $39–$99, including continental breakfast. AAA, AARP, Seniors, Corporate and *10% Pets Welcome™* discounts.

Pet Charges & Deposits: $25 refundable deposit.

Pet Policy: No pets over 40 lbs.

Amenities: Cable TV, indoor pool, whirlpool, guest laundry, gift shop.

Pet Amenities: List of nearby veterinarians maintained. Exercise area. Sundance Creek Walking Path on property.

Rated: 2 Paws — 40 rooms and 2 suites.

Sundance Mountain Inn affords bright, modern rooms in a wonderfully traditional motel setting. Free local calls, alarm clock radios and a pet-friendly atmosphere make this a worthwhile place to stay when you're in the Black Hills area. Harry Longabaugh assumed his nickname, "the Sundance Kid," during his 18-month incarceration in Crook County jail for horse stealing. The history of "the Kid" is commemorated at the Crook County Museum and Art Gallery. It's twenty-eight miles from the Inn to Devil's Tower National Monument, a huge monolith resembling a mammoth tree stump, which rises 867 feet from its base and is the dominant sight in northeastern Wyoming. A huge prairie dog colony in the immediate vicinity provides unusual entertainment.

Elephant Head Lodge

1170 Yellowstone Highway
Wapiti, WY 82450
307-587-3980
www.elephantheadlodge.com
vacation@elephantheadlodge.com

Type of Lodging: Inn

Cabin Rates: $100–$170.

Pet Charges & Deposits: None.

Pet Policy: Designated rooms only.

Amenities: Restaurant.

Pet Amenities: List of nearby veterinarians maintained. Exercise area. The Inn is located 11 miles east of Yellowstone National Park in the heart of the Shoshone National Forest, the oldest forest in America.

Rated: 3 Paws — 12 cabins.

Phil, Joan, Bernice, Gretchen and Nicole Lamb run a fabulous country operation—twelve cozy sleeping cabins arranged like a horseshoe around the Main Lodge and Log Cabin Restaurant. The historic cabins have been modernized without destroying their character. Most guests stay three to five days to do some horseback riding and use the Lodge as a base for touring Yellowstone and visiting Cody, Wyoming. Returning guests often choose the lodging's "Package Plan," and use the Lodge as a no frills Dude Ranch, complete with everything but the mandatory square dance.

Index

About the Authors

Nadine Guarrera, at the ripe old age of 26, has led many lives. Born in Sicily of mixed Sicilian-Romanian parentage, this beautiful sprite has visited over 100 countries, speaks five languages fluently, and has served as editor and editorial assistant for many books in the popular Cooking Secrets series, including *Cooking With the Masters of Food & Wine,* and *California Wine Country Cooking Secrets,* as well as *Pets Welcome™: National First Edition, Pets Welcome™: California Second Edition,* and *Pets Welcome™: Mid-Atlantic & Chesapeake Edition.* She is presently working on her bachelor's degree at California State University, Monterey Bay, and has lived on California's Monterey Peninsula since she immigrated from Sicily at the age of 13.

Hugo N. Gerstl is a nationally famous trial lawyer and author (*How To Cut Your Legal Bills In Half; How To Survive & Profit from Your Son's Bar Mitzvah*) whose passion is world travel. He has traveled to 47 states, virtually all of Europe except the Scandinavian and Baltic countries, the Middle East, and South Africa, and has lived in Turkey for two years. Although he is still recovering from the loss of Harry, his 15-year-old Old English Sheepdog, he is somewhat consoled by a pesky and frisky cat, Her Royal Highness, the Princess Victoria ("that darned cat," for short), who still manages his home. He counts as his greatest blessing his marriage to Lorraine. Between them, they have raised five adult children.

Colleen M. Olis co-authored *California Wine Country Cooking Secrets.* She was born and raised on California's fabled Monterey Peninsula and has enjoyed successful careers in banking, the legal field (she is a quali-

fied paralegal), and book publishing, where she has served in virtually every capacity. She and her husband Alvin reside in Monterey. She served as final concept/language editor for *Pets Welcome™: National Second Edition.*

Herb Chelner, a true rocket scientist, was an instrumental part of the team that developed the landing system for the Boeing 747 aircraft as well as the lunar landing module. In 1981, he rescued a struggling company, and has turned it into a substantial and highly respected force in government and commercial measurement instrumentation. He is currently working on the biography of a man whom he calls "the real Indiana Jones." Herb still mourns the passing of his beloved "best friend," Elliott. However, Sharon, his wife of many, many years, and his two adult children serve to somewhat soften the blow.

Lorraine Gerstl, author of the popular *Jewish Cooking Secrets From Here & Far* and co-author of *California Wine Country Cooking Secrets,* grew up in Johannesburg, South Africa. After graduating from the University of South Africa, she taught deaf children in all grades before starting her own family. For the past thirteen years, she has taught third grade full time at Santa Catalina School in Monterey, developed national curriculum for the Monterey Bat Aquarium, and served as adjunct editor-reviewer for Allyn & Bacon Educational Publishers. She and her husband, Hugo, reside in Carmel, California. They have five grown children.

River Gurtin moved from his native New Jersey to California in 1970, where he attended Monterey Peninsula College and studied business and theater. In 1976, he opened the first bagel bakery on California's central coast. Under his guidance, the business grew and developed into a seven-store regional chain. Meanwhile, he became a nationwide consultant in opening and establishing bagel bakeries. River retired from The Bagel Bakery in 2000. He currently spends his time providing small business consulting, studying photography, and hiking with his wife, Diana, a practicing psychologist.

Elaine Eakin Macdonald was born in China Lake, California and grew up, among other places, in the San Francisco Bay area. She graduated Law School from Santa Clara University School of Law, then served four years as a Judge Advocate in the United States Navy. Elaine is licensed to practice in both California and Florida. It was while serving as a Public Defender in Florida that she met her husband, Erle. Now claiming that she is "retired" from law (at an age when most lawyers are just starting to hit their stride), this extraordinarily talented interior decorator spends the lion's share of her waking hours as mommy to two beautiful daughters.

Erle T. Macdonald was born in Fairfax, Virginia and grew up in Jacksonville, Florida. On his nineteenth birthday, he joined the Jacksonville Police Force. A few years later, he walked into a used computer store and presented the owner with a bold proposal: teach me all you know about computers and I'll work for free. The rest is a true Horatio Alger story: bought the computer owner out, turned the business into gold, sold it, started another computer business, turned it into gold, etc. An entrepreneur of worldwide proportions, Erle, who now owns several businesses, resides in Carmel, California with his wife Elaine and their two daughters.

Howard Morton grew up in the western part of Los Angeles, California. He served as a U.S. Naval Officer for over twenty years. With one successful career behind him, but too young to let his engineering and mechanical talents be put out to pasture, Howard became a Registered Patent Agent and today is President of Morton & Associates in Monterey. A dedicated Mason, he and his wife Michele, fourth grade teacher at Santa Catalina School in Monterey, reside in Carmel Valley, California, where they pamper their cat, Nurdle.

Kristi Padley is a Texan, born and bred, who now resides with her husband David (a career Coast Guardsman) and her first son, Cameron, in Nashua, New Hampshire. Kristi is a proud graduate of Texas A&M University (Communications, Business). She served as National Sales Director for Four Paws Press's predecessor before moving to the East Coast, where she served in Regional Sales for FOS Sales & Service of New York. She is presently National Sales Director for Four Paws Press.

Brad Smith is one of the founding partners and is now the President of Smith-Bowen Communications, Inc., a nationally renowned and award-winning public relations, advertising, and graphic design firm. He has over 20 years of consumer and retail advertising and marketing experience, as well as 10 years of commodity board marketing experience. He is an avid traveler and outdoorsman, a fervent mountain biker, and a rabid San Francisco 49er football fan. He lives in the countryside near the Monterey Peninsula with his wife, Susan, an art teacher at Monterey's Santa Catalina School, and their daughter Tara, a highly accomplished artist.

Reader's Response Card

Please return to:
Four Paws Press
2600 Garden Road, Suite 224
Monterey, CA 93940
info@fourpawspress.com
Fax 831-649-8007

Please assist us in updating our next edition. If you have discovered an interesting or charming lodging that allows pets, or any special neighborhood parks that allow pets, with or without a leash, please let us hear from you and include the following information:

Type of Lodging:
☐ Hotel   ☐ Motel   ☐ Suites   ☐ Resort   ☐ B&B   ☐ Condo or Apartment
☐ Motor Inn/Motor Lodge   ☐ Cottage or Cabin   ☐ Guest Ranch   ☐ RV Park

Lodging Name: _____

Lodging Address: _____

City: _____ State: _____ ZIP: _____

Phone: _____

Comments: _____

_____

_____

Park Name: _____

Address or Cross Streets: _____

_____

City: _____ State: _____

Phone (if known): _____ Leashes required? ☐ Yes ☐ No

Comments: _____

_____

_____

We appreciate your assistance. It's wonderful to discover new and interesting places to take your pets.

Order Form

Four Paws Press, LLC
2600 Garden Road, Suite 224
Monterey, CA 93940
831-375 PAWS (7297)
831-649-8007 FAX
www.fourpawspress.com

Send _____ copies of *Pets Welcome*™ *America's South* at $15.95 each.

Send _____ copies of *Pets Welcome*™ *California* at $15.95 each.

Send _____ copies of *Pets Welcome*™ *New England and New York* at $15.95 each.

Send _____ copies of *Pets Welcome*™ *Pacific Northwest* at $15.95 each.

Send _____ copies of *Pets Welcome*™ *Southwest* at $15.95 each.

Send _____ copies of *Pets Welcome*™ *National Edition* at $19.95 each.

Add $4.50 postage and handling for the first book ordered and $1.50 for each additional book. Please add 7.25% sales tax per book, for those books shipped to California addresses.

Please charge my ☐ VISA ☐ MasterCard

Card number: _____

Expiration date: _____ Signature: _____

Enclosed is my check for $ _____

Name: _____

Address: _____

City: _____ State: _____ ZIP:_____

☐ This is a gift. Please send books directly to:

Name: _____

Address: _____

City: _____ State: _____ ZIP:_____

☐ Autographed by the author

Autographed to: _____